SpringBoard®
English
Language Arts

TEACHER EDITION   ENGLISH IV

About The College Board

The College Board is a mission-driven not-for-profit organization that connects students to college success and opportunity. Founded in 1900, the College Board was created to expand access to higher education. Today, the membership association is made up of over 6,000 of the world's leading educational institutions and is dedicated to promoting excellence and equity in education. Each year, the College Board helps more than seven million students prepare for a successful transition to college through programs and services in college readiness and college success—including the SAT® and the Advanced Placement Program®. The organization also serves the education community through research and advocacy on behalf of students, educators, and schools. For further information, visit collegeboard.org.

ISBN: 978-1-4573-1291-5

1 2 3 4 5 6 7 8   20 21 22 23 24 25 26

Printed in the United States of America

Acknowledgements

The College Board gratefully acknowledges the outstanding work of the classroom teachers who have been integral to the development of this program. The end product is testimony to their expertise, understanding of student learning needs, and dedication to rigorous and accessible English Language Arts instruction.

Lance Balla
Everett School District Everett, Washington

Robert J. Caughey
San Dieguito Union High School District San Diego, California

Paul De Maret
Poudre School District Fort Collins, Colorado

Nancy Gray
Brevard County Schools Viera, Florida

Nimat Jones
ICEF Public Schools, Los Angeles, California

Susie Lowry
Volusia County School District Deland, Florida

Glenn Morgan
San Diego Unified School District San Diego, California

Julie Pennabaker
Quakertown Community School District Quakertown, Pennsylvania

Kimberlyn Slagle
Lafayette Parish School System Lafayette, Louisiana

Maria Torres-Crosby
Hillsborough County Public Schools Tampa, Florida

Carisa Barnes
San Diego Unified School District San Diego, California

Susie Challancin
Bellevue School District 405 Bellevue, Washington

Sylvia Ellison
Hillsborough County Public Schools Hillsborough, Florida

Charise Hallberg
Bellevue School District 405 Bellevue, Washington

Karen Kampschmidt
Fort Thomas Independent School District Fort Thomas, Kentucky

Michelle Lewis
Spokane Public School Spokane, Washington

John Murray
Garland Independent School District Sachse, Texas

Bryan Sandala
School District of Palm Beach County West Palm Beach, Florida

Sarah Smith Arceneaux
Lafayette Parish School System Lafayette, Louisiana

Susan Van Doren
South Lake Tahoe, California

Leia Bell
Hillsborough County Public Schools Tampa, Florida

Doug Cole
Cherry Creek School District Greenwood Village, Colorado

Karen Fullam
Hillsborough County Public Schools Tampa, Florida

T.J. Hanify
Bellevue School District 405 Bellevue, Washington

Karen Kennedy
Peninsula School District Peninsula, Washington

John Marshall
Mead School District Mead, Washington

Kristen J. Ohaver
Charlotte-Mecklenburg Schools Charlotte, North Carolina

Angela Seiler
Rio Rancho Public School District Rio Rancho, New Mexico

Holly Talley
Hillsborough County Public Schools Ruskin, Florida

JoEllen Victoreen
San Jose Unified School District San Jose, California

Alysa Broussard
Lafayette Parish School System Lafayette, Louisiana

Cari Davis
Rio Rancho Public School District Rio Rancho, New Mexico

Michael Gragert
Plano Independent School District Plano, Texas

Jessi Hupper
Peninsula School District Gig Harbor, Washington

LeAnn Klepzig
Bradley County Schools Cleveland, Tennessee

Cassandra Mattison
Hillsborough County Public Schools Tampa, Florida

Amanda Olinger
Harrisburg School District Harrisburg, South Dakota

Amanda Shackelford
Lafayette Parish School System Lafayette, Louisiana

Derek Thomas
Hillsborough County Public Schools Tampa, Florida

Rebecca Wenrich
Peninsula School District Gig Harbor, Washington

Research and Planning Advisors

We also wish to thank the members of our SpringBoard Advisory Council and the many educators who gave generously of their time and their ideas as we conducted research for both the print and online programs. Your suggestions and reactions to ideas helped immeasurably as we created this edition. We gratefully acknowledge the teachers and administrators in the following districts.

ABC Unified School District
Cerritos, California

Allen Independent School District
Allen, Texas

Bellevue, School District 405
Bellevue, Washington

Burnet Consolidated Independent School District
Burnet, Texas

Community Unit School District 308
Oswego, Illinois

Fresno Unified School District
Fresno, California

Frisco Independent School District
Frisco, Texas

Garland Independent School District
Garland, Texas

Grapevine-Colleyville Independent School District
Grapevine, Texas

Hamilton County Schools
Chattanooga, Tennessee

Hesperia Unified School District
Hesperia, California

Hillsborough County Public Schools
Tampa, Florida

ICEF Public Schools
Los Angeles, California
IDEA Public Schools
Weslaco, Texas

Irving Independent School District
Irving, Texas

Keller Independent School District
Keller, Texas

KIPP Houston
Houston, Texas

Lafayette Parish Schools
Lafayette Parish, Louisiana

Los Angeles Unified School District
Los Angeles, California

Lubbock Independent School District
Lubbock, Texas

Mansfield Independent School District
Mansfield, Texas

Midland Independent School District
Midland, Texas

Milwaukee Public Schools
Milwaukee, Wisconsin

New Haven School District
New Haven, Connecticut

Ogden School District
Ogden, Utah

Rio Rancho Public Schools
Rio Rancho, New Mexico

San José Unified School District
San José, California

Scottsdale Unified School District
Scottsdale, Arizona

Spokane Public Schools
Spokane, Washington

Tacoma Public Schools
Tacoma, Washington

SpringBoard English Language Arts

Lori O'Dea
Executive Director
Content Development

Natasha Vasavada
Executive Director,
Pre-AP & SpringBoard

Doug Waugh
VP, SpringBoard & Pre-AP
Programs

Sarah Balistreri
Senior Director
ELA Content Development

Florencia Duran Wald
Senior Director
ELA Content Development

Julie Manley
Senior Director
Professional Learning

Joely Negedly
Senior Director
Pre-AP Humanities

Jessica Brockman
Product Manager
English Language Arts

Suzie Doss
Director
SpringBoard Implementation

Jennifer Duva
Director
English Language Arts

Spencer Gonçalves
Director
Digital Content Development

Rebecca Grudzina
Senior Editor
English Language Arts

Georgia Scurletis
Senior Instructional Writer
Pre-AP English Language Arts

Abigail Johnson
Editor
English Language Arts

Casseia Lewis
Assistant Editor
English Language Arts

Natalie Hansford
Editorial Assistant
English Language Arts

Table of Contents

CONTENTS

CONTENTS

CONTENTS

ACTIVITY **Unit 4: Creating Perspectives**

CONTENTS

Resources

Texts not included in these materials.

Introduction to
SpringBoard English Language Arts

About SpringBoard ELA

SpringBoard is a different kind of instructional program for grades 6–12. Developed by teachers for teachers, SpringBoard offers core instructional materials in print and digital form that are aligned to College and Career Readiness Standards, Advanced Placement (AP) coursework, and the SAT Suite of Assessments. The program features student materials, teacher resources, and formative and summative assessments, as well as professional learning for teachers and administrators. SpringBoard was built around a simple belief: if you give teachers the best materials, engaging methods, and ongoing professional support, then student success will surely follow.

Instructional Materials

SpringBoard English Language Arts supplies a Student Edition and Teacher Edition, in print and digital form, for each grade level. You can customize the basic curriculum with materials including Language Workshop, Close Reading Workshop, and Writing Workshop.

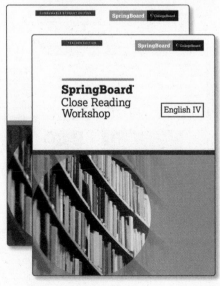

Design that Begins with the End in Mind

- Based on the Understanding by Design model, SpringBoard teaches students the skills and knowledge that matter most to meet AP and college and career readiness standards.

- Teachers and students start each unit by unpacking the assessment so that students know where they're heading and why the skills they're developing matter.

- Teachers and students receive clear, standards-aligned learning targets when they begin each activity.

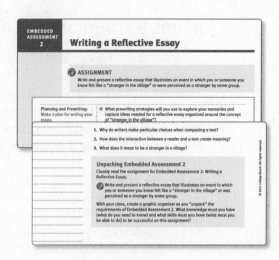

The Practice of Reading Closely

- SpringBoard puts a special focus on close reading, giving students strategies and structure for developing this key skill.

- Students encounter compelling texts—fiction, nonfiction, poetry, drama, visuals, and film.

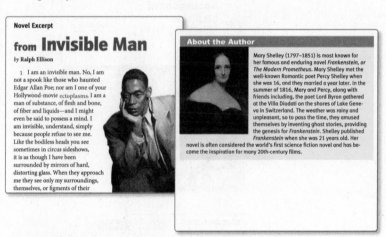

A Living System of Learning

- SpringBoard puts students in charge of how they learn to create a more dynamic classroom experience.

- With a flexible design and rich library of tools and resources, SpringBoard helps educators personalize instruction to meet student needs.

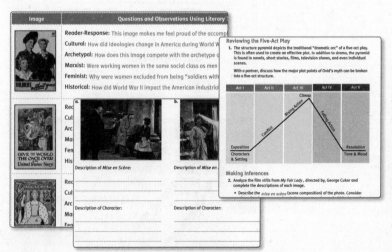

Bringing the Classroom to Life

SpringBoard has a simple mission: to give teachers and districts the exact kind of support they want to bring more life to the classroom—and greater success to students.

When you enter a SpringBoard classroom you don't hear a teacher talking in the front of the room. You hear a buzz of excitement, with students working together and taking charge of how they learn. That's what the teachers who designed SpringBoard wanted for their classrooms, so they created a curriculum and materials that are focused on real classroom needs, encouraging teacher and student involvement.

SpringBoard helps teachers translate the expectations of state standards into engaging daily lessons. We believe that reading, writing, speaking, and listening should all be learned together. You'll see examples of our integrated approach throughout our materials. And we put a special focus on close reading, giving students strategies and structure for developing this key skill.

Our Approach to Reading

In SpringBoard ELA, we move right into compelling texts—fiction, nonfiction, poetry, drama, visuals, and film—and give teachers the tools, supports, and pedagogical approaches that will help students engage with the content.

The Practice of Reading Closely

Texts take center stage in the SpringBoard ELA classroom, where students will prepare for close, critical reading of a wide range of materials. With teacher guidance, high school students develop the habits of close reading that will serve them for a lifetime.

- **As You Read:** Students prepare for the first reading of a text with guidance about which elements to notice and annotate, questions to ask before and during reading, and genre characteristics to pay attention to.

- **First Reading:** Students read and annotate. They begin to comprehend the text and uncover meaning as they read individually, in pairs, in groups, or together as a class.

- **Making Observations:** Students pause during or right after the first reading to observe the small details within a text in order to arrive at a deeper understanding of the whole.

- **Returning to the Text:** Students continue to deepen their understanding of the text by responding to a series of text-dependent questions. They use text evidence, speak with new vocabulary words, reflect on their classmates' ideas, and make connections among texts, ideas, and experiences.

- **Working from the Text:** Students use the text as a source as they move from reading and analysis to productive work, including academic discussion and writing.

Reading Independently

SpringBoard students practice good reading habits in class so that they can read challenging texts in other classes and on their own. Independent reading is an integral part of every SpringBoard English Language Arts unit. At the beginning of each grade, students learn how to make a plan for independent reading. **Independent Reading Lists** in each unit give students a jump-start on selecting texts by offering a list of suggested titles, including a number of Spanish-language titles, that connect to the themes, genres, and concepts of the SpringBoard unit.

While students work their way through each unit, they respond to **Independent Reading Links** that prompt them to make connections between the reading they're doing on their own and the skills and knowledge they're developing in class. Twice per unit, **Independent Reading Checkpoints** give students a chance to reflect on and synthesize their independent reading in an informal writing assignment or discussion.

Reading to Build Knowledge

SpringBoard units are designed thematically so that students can delve deeply into the overarching topics, themes and ideas. Each unit begins with essential questions that relate to the ideas and texts within the unit. Students return to these questions throughout the unit, each time refining their responses as their understanding increases and they are able to cite new evidence that supports their points of view. Students also have the opportunity to conduct both on-the-spot and extended research, asking and answering questions, evaluating multiple sources, and synthesizing information.

Twice a unit, students engage in a **Knowledge Quest**, which involves reading a collection of texts curated around a topic, theme, or idea, and completing some text-dependent tasks. On these quests, students build their knowledge of the topics as well as related vocabulary. Each Knowledge Quest begins with a Knowledge Question and supporting questions that focus student learning. After students read the final text in a set, they have the opportunity to return to the Knowledge Question and demonstrate their growing understanding of the topic by responding to a writing-to-sources prompt or engaging in an academic discussion.

At the end of a Knowledge Quest, students are encouraged to continue building their knowledge of the topic by going to **Zinc Reading Labs** and searching for and reading related texts. Zinc Reading Labs offers a variety of informational and literary texts that you can assign and that students can self-select. Vocabulary sets for each text provide additional practice opportunities that can be assigned for classwork or homework.

Students' independent reading can also enhance their understanding of the topics being covered in class if they are interested. SpringBoard's **Independent Reading Lists** include suggested books that relate to the topics and themes from each unit. By choosing those books students can see a different side of the topic, learn new words, and discover other topics they might want to explore more deeply.

Through engagement with a wide range of content-rich informational and literary texts, and work on an array of tasks that let them demonstrate their increasing understanding, SpringBoard supports students to build knowledge of topics, themes, and ideas.

Reading to Gain Perspectives

Gaining Perspectives features use a text as a jumping off point for examining an issue or concern relevant to students. Students are asked to consider the perspectives of others and to empathize with others who have different points of view. They are asked think about social and ethical norms and to recognize the family, school, and community resources available to them. When relevant, Gaining Perspectives features include standards-aligned tasks that require students to make social studies and/or health education connections. Each Gaining Perspectives feature concludes with a writing task, in which students summarize the classroom discussion in their Reader/Writer Notebooks.

Understanding Text Complexity

Understanding text complexity is a key part of advancing students' knowledge and skills through reading. Students should read texts that are appropriately challenging—not so challenging that students get frustrated and give up, but not so easy that students get bored and stagnate. For each prose text in SpringBoard English Language Arts, teachers will see text complexity guidance:

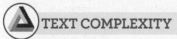 TEXT COMPLEXITY

Overall: Complex
Lexile: 1000L
Qualitative: Moderate Difficulty
Task: Challenging (Evaluate)

Discerning the complexity of a text involves examining the text in a few different ways:

- A **Lexile** score indicates the complexity as measured by an algorithm that analyzes text characteristics including sentence length and word frequency.
- Expert teachers assigned a **qualitative rating** of High, Moderate, or Low Difficulty by considering qualities including the text's implicit and explicit meanings, the author's use of language to achieve a purpose, the organizational patterns and structure of the text, the sophistication of vocabulary, and cognitive and knowledge demands of each text.
- **Task** requirements are designated as High, Moderate, or Low based on the cognitive demands of the task associated with the text. Anderson and Krathwohl's taxonomy was used for this analysis, and verbs such as evaluate, analyze, and understand are included as descriptors. (Reader variables such as motivation and background must be determined at the classroom level.)
- After analyzing each text based on these factors, teachers assigned an **overall rating** of Accessible, Complex, or Very Complex, with Complex representing on-grade-level texts.

Our Approach to Writing

SpringBoard English Language Arts provides a scaffolded approach to writing in all the major modes, emphasizing argumentative, informational, and narrative. Students write often, and they learn to become critical reviewers of their own and their peers' work through frequent opportunities for revision and editing. They learn to plan with purpose, audience, topic, and context in mind; develop drafts with engaging ideas, examples, facts and commentary; revise for clarity, development, organization, style, and diction; and edit using the conventions of the English language.

The Craft of Writing

As students read texts by skilled authors, they observe the many choices those authors make. They tune in to the ways authors purposefully use words, sentences, and structures to convey meaning. After analyzing and critiquing others' work, students learn to apply their understanding of author's craft to their own written products. A few SpringBoard features help them do just that:

- **Writing prompts** scaffold to the Embedded Assessments and give students practice with writing texts in multiple genres, including personal narratives, argumentative essays, editorials, letters, myths, research papers, and more. Writing to Sources writing prompts drive students back to texts they have read or viewed to mine for evidence.
- **Focus on the Sentence** tasks help students process content while also practicing the craft of writing powerful sentences.
- **Grammar & Usage** features highlight interesting grammar or usage concepts that appear in a text, both to improve students' reading comprehension and to help them attend to these concepts as they craft their own texts.
- **Language & Writer's Craft** features address topics in writing such as style, word choice, and sentence construction.
- **Language Checkpoints** offer in-depth practice with standard English conventions and usage and guide students to revise sample sentences as well as their own work.

Modes of Writing

SpringBoard provides multiple opportunities for authentic, task-based writing and writing to sources. Direct instruction in writing in different modes—narrative, argumentative, and informational—is a primary focus of each unit of instruction, and students learn to consider task, audience, and purpose in structuring and organizing their writing.

- Guided writing instruction focuses on analysis and argument, but also allows students opportunities to develop creative writing skills.

- Instruction emphasizes the writing process with modeling the incorporation of details, reasons, and textual evidence to support ideas.

- Structured opportunities require short and extended student research in order to practice evaluating sources, gathering relevant evidence, and citing and reporting findings accurately.

- A wide range of research-based strategies are embedded within the instructional activities that take students through the writing process and encourage best practices.

- Mode-specific writing workshops, formative writing prompts, and performance-based Embedded Assessments with Scoring Guides provide regular practice.

Writing with a Focus on the Sentence

SpringBoard English Language Arts leverages sentence writing strategies that were developed by The Writing Revolution. These evidence-based strategies are part of the Hochman Method, the Writing Revolution's system for teaching writing across all content areas and grades that builds from the foundation of sentences to help students master techniques for writing powerful paragraphs and full-length compositions. The Writing Revolution emphasizes the importance of embedding writing and grammar instruction into content. That's why SpringBoard's **Focus on the Sentence** tasks integrate sentence-level writing into the curriculum. These tasks not only help students learn and practice important grammar concepts and sentence forms, but they also provide a chance for students to process and demonstrate understanding of texts, images, class discussions, and other content.

Our Approach to Vocabulary

Vocabulary is threaded throughout each unit and developed over the course of the SpringBoard English Language Arts year. Students are given ample opportunities to read and hear new words, explore their meanings, origins, and connotations, and use them in written and oral responses.

- Important academic and literary terms that students need to actively participate in the ELA classroom are called out in the student book.

- Challenging vocabulary terms found in reading passages are glossed at the point of use.

- Periodic Word Connections boxes guide students through the process of exploring a word with multiple meanings and nuances, an interesting etymology, a telling root or affix, a helpful Spanish cognate, a relationship to another word, or a connection to another content area.

Zinc Reading Labs

Zinc Reading Labs combines the best features of a typical vocabulary program with those of a typical reading program and makes reading and learning new words a game. Zinc offers a variety of nonfiction and fiction texts that teachers can assign (and students can choose from) based on individual needs and interest. Each article has a corresponding vocabulary set that pre-teaches challenging words through spaced repetition, ensuring students genuinely learn and internalize the vocabulary. Additional vocabulary games focus on SAT/ACT power words and foundational words for English language learners. All of the tests are auto-graded and teachers can use the detailed reports to plan for differentiation.

SpringBoard and Pre-AP

Shared Instructional Vision

SpringBoard and Pre-AP's shared instructional vision and principles are evident in every SpringBoard activity. We place a deliberate focus on learning that sets students on a pathway to AP and college readiness, enabling students to slow down and spend time tackling excellent texts and meaningful tasks. The following principles are central to SpringBoard and are shared across every Pre-AP course, resulting in a powerful multiplier effect for students' skills across disciplines.

Close Observation and Analysis
... to notice and consider

When reading, SpringBoard students are guided to pause to make observations and notice details in the text before being asked to analyze or explain. Only after they have noticed and enjoyed elements of the text do they then return to the text for deeper analysis and inferential thinking. This close reading sequence supports students in interacting and engaging with the text in increasingly meaningful ways.

Evidence-Based Writing
... with a focus on the sentence

SpringBoard offers varied and frequent writing opportunities, with specific attention to developing complex and precise sentences as the building block to sophisticated paragraph and essay length writing. Instead of being isolated from reading, sentence-level grammar and writing exercises are integrated into the curriculum to enhance students' comprehension and ability to compose a variety of texts.

Higher-Order Questioning
... to spark productive lingering

Each unit opens with essential questions that relate to the topics, themes, and texts within that unit. Students return to these questions throughout the unit and refine their answers as new evidence emerges. SpringBoard also encourages students to craft their own questions, and to dig deeply into the texts they read. After each passage, students evaluate the meaning of the text and examine the choices that the author made when writing it.

Academic Conversations
... to support peer-to-peer dialogue

SpringBoard classrooms are places where students engage in collaborative learning. Students participate in discussion groups, writing groups, debates, Socratic seminars and literature circles. These activities create an environment where students develop the ability to share, compare, critique, debate, and build on others' ideas to advance their learning.

Pre-AP Course Connections

SpringBoard's English I and English II courses have been designed with their counterpart official Pre-AP courses in mind. Students using the SpringBoard program in English I and II will be strategically prepared for the Pre-AP system of formative assessments, thereby setting them on a natural pathway toward AP success.

SpringBoard and PSAT/SAT

We want students to be rewarded for the hard work they do in their English Language Arts courses, including when they sit down to take important assessments. Therefore, SpringBoard English Language Arts focuses on the same essential knowledge and skills that are the center of the Evidence-Based Reading and Writing sections of the SAT Suite of Assessments. To make our alignment transparent, we conducted a research study, the results of which showed strong to exemplary alignment between SpringBoard ELA and the corresponding SAT Suite tests. This means that SpringBoard ELA students are getting ready for the SAT, PSAT/NMSQT, PSAT™ 10, and PSAT™ 8/9 in the classroom every day. SAT Connections are called out in the teacher edition to show targeted opportunities for students to practice skills that will serve them well on the SAT.

Teacher Edition Features

Planning the Unit

We believe that purposeful planning leads to powerful learning experiences. That's why each unit starts with support for lesson planning, guidance on differentiation, and information about unit resources. The Planning the Unit provides the following information:

- Descriptions of the context and instructional sequence of the unit to help teachers see how each activity scaffolds toward the Embedded Assessments

- A list of notable AP and SAT connections in the unit

- A cognate directory that provides the Spanish cognates for unit vocabulary terms

- Unit Resources at a Glance chart outlining resources like assessments, English language development supports, foundational language skills supports, and more

- Resources to support independent reading, including a list of suggested texts

- Detailed Instructional Pathways to help teachers thoughtfully plan the best way to approach the unit in response to students' learning needs

Instructional Pathways

SpringBoard is designed to allow teachers to personalize instruction to meet student needs. Teachers can find information in the Planning the Unit to help them build a customized pathway through each unit that delivers the support and practice students need most.

- **English Language Arts Pathway:** student-centered activities that gradually develop the skills and knowledge needed for the Embedded Assessments and are aligned to grade-level standards

- **Language Development Pathway:** linguistically accommodated activities that advance students' English language proficiency through vocabulary support, leveled texts that build background knowledge, guided close reading, sentence frames for academic discussions, and foundational language skills support

- **Flexible Pathways:** flexible activities from SpringBoard's Close Reading Workshop, Writing Workshop, or Flexible Novel Units that enable teachers to extend, support, or customize instruction

Instructional Guidance

Plan-Teach-Assess-Adapt

In the teacher edition, every activity is organized into four phases: Plan, Teach, Assess, and Adapt. Plan contains information about pacing and materials. Teach guides the class through the main steps of the activity with thoughtful suggestions for how to conduct close readings, how to group students, and when to check for understanding. Assess calls out opportunities to measure student progress. Adapt suggests ways to adjust an activity in response to students' needs.

Teacher to Teacher

Additional suggestions are sprinkled through activities in Teacher to Teacher features. These boxes give practical classroom tips, recommend additional resources to enhance and support the activity, and suggest ways to differentiate and extend instruction.

Differentiation

A rich library of tools, resources, and supports lets teachers adapt their instruction for all students, including those who need extra support, those who are still learning English, and those who are ready to go further.

Leveled Differentiated Instruction

Throughout the activities in the SpringBoard program, teachers will find Leveled Differentiated Instruction features that offer suggestions for scaffolding the challenging tasks of the activity. The suggestions provide the tools that learners at various levels of language proficiency need to successfully participate in class. Teachers will discover that the scaffolding suggestions model techniques that they can adapt to other tasks in other activities.

The differentiation spans six levels. The first four levels map to the proficiency level descriptors defined by WIDA:

Beginning Beginning represents the initial stage of language acquisition.

Developing Developing represents the intermediate stage of proficiency, where students understand simple, high-frequency spoken English used routinely.

Expanding Expanding represents the advanced stage of proficiency, where students understand grade-appropriate English with support.

Bridging Bridging represents the advanced high stage of proficiency, where students need little support to understand grade-appropriate English.

Support Support scaffolds learning for students who may not be English language learners but still need support with reading and producing grade-level academic language.

Extend Extend suggests ways to stretch students who are ready for a challenge.

As students become more proficient in English, teachers can select flexibly from the leveled scaffolding options provided to find the one that will enable the student to complete the task successfully while remaining appropriately challenged. The ultimate goal is to build students' capacity so they can perform tasks with increasing independence.

Instructional Supports for Differentiation

Among the resources available to SpringBoard teachers is a collection of graphic organizers and English language development strategies that can help scaffold instruction in boundless and creative ways. One effective way to support English language learners and students who are struggling with a task is to give them a graphic organizer that helps spark ideas, activate metacognition, organize thoughts, or frame academic discussion. The resources section of this book includes dozens of graphic organizers designed to do just that. In addition, the final part of the SpringBoard Learning Strategies section includes strategies and techniques teachers can use to boost students' ability and confidence with using academic language. Like all other strategies, they can be used flexibly, and teachers can experiment to see which strategies work best with a given set of students, and then weave them throughout instruction.

Language Workshop

Research supports the notion that all students, including those who are still developing English language skills, should have the opportunity to read complex and engaging texts appropriate for their grade level. That's why SpringBoard offers Language Workshops alongside each English Language Arts course. Language Workshops map directly to each ELA unit and include robust differentiation options that can be used flexibly depending on learners' needs. Supports include vocabulary previews and practice, accessible texts that help students build background knowledge, scaffolded close reading and discussion of an anchor text that's shared with ELA, and more. Because Language Workshops are so closely integrated with ELA, they build a bridge to help English language learners and other students progress smoothly toward proficiency with grade level skills.

Assessment for Learning

With SpringBoard English Language Arts, teachers have frequent opportunities to monitor student progress over the course of the year. Assessment for learning is the philosophical basis of assessment opportunities in SpringBoard, and we make assessment and evaluation transparent and explicit so students and teachers can focus on the key skills and knowledge to be learned.

Integrated Assessments

Each unit of SpringBoard English Language Arts is built from **Embedded Assessments** that drive the instructional pathway and give students and teachers a clear destination so they can "begin with the end in mind." These come with scoring support for teachers including scoring guides and student examples. Along the way, there are many opportunities built into daily lessons for teachers to make sure their students are on track:

- **Making Observations** questions help teachers quickly gauge students' initial understanding of key details in a text.

- **Returning to the Text** includes text-dependent questions aligned to College and Career Readiness Standards that guide students to develop and demonstrate their comprehension and analysis of a text.

- **Check Your Understanding** tasks occur at key moments in the instructional sequence when it is appropriate for students to demonstrate learning before moving on to subsequent work.

- **Focus on the Sentence** provides a quick but worthwhile opportunity for teachers to assess students' understanding of key concepts or comprehension of texts, films, discussions, or visuals.

- **Graphic organizers** throughout the student edition prompt students to map out ideas, evidence, and analysis based on the materials they're studying.

- **Writing prompts** provide useful evidence of how students are progressing toward the Embedded Assessment task. Sometimes, the responses to writing prompts can be used as early drafts that students later develop and revise for the Embedded Assessment.

- **Reflection** questions follow each Embedded Assessment and provide opportunities for students to take ownership of their learning by identifying strategies that worked for them.

Activity Quizzes on SpringBoard Digital

Activity Quizzes are quick, multiple choice assessments that assess students' learning of the knowledge and skills practiced in SpringBoard activities. Teachers can select which quizzes to assign over the span of a unit to monitor student understanding and make instructional adjustments based on results. These assessments are available on SpringBoard Digital.

Unit Assessments on SpringBoard Digital

Unit Assessments are aligned to the standards in each half unit of SpringBoard English Language Arts. Each assessment includes multiple choice and open-response questions, modeled on the types of questions students will encounter on assessments including the SAT. These assessments are available on SpringBoard Digital.

Workshops

Language Workshop

SpringBoard Language Workshop is a part of the SpringBoard program that is dedicated to building academic language proficiency in all students, including English language learners. The Language Workshop delivers grade-level English Language Arts content and tasks through the lens of developing students' academic language skills. Every activity in every workshop gives students an opportunity to listen, speak, read, and write at a level that can grow with them as they become more proficient in English.

- Each Language Workshop corresponds to one half of an ELA unit.

- Language Workshops have the same Embedded Assessments as ELA, only they are modified to be collaborative.

- Every Language Workshop activity has explicit guidance about where it is most appropriate in the sequence of ELA instruction.

- Familiar teacher edition features streamline the planning process.

- Spanish language translations of two complete activities per workshop allow Spanish-speaking students to build on their primary language literacy by reading and discussing complex, grade-appropriate texts.

Close Reading Workshop

SpringBoard English Language Arts addresses the skill of reading with deliberate attention to purpose, audience, language, and tone with activities in every unit that guide students through the steps of close reading. We also offer Close Reading Workshops, which can be used with the SpringBoard program as extra support or on their own.

The workshops offer a variety of high-quality texts, including fiction, nonfiction, and visual texts. The selected passages are appropriate for multiple close readings, and they increase in complexity from grade to grade.

Each workshop includes three texts that students read multiple times. After every reading, students use various close reading strategies, such as marking the text or SOAPSTone, to understand the content. These strategies include individual and collaborative approaches, and they support different student abilities and learning styles.

The workshops end with an assessment, which teachers can assign as an individual, small-group, or whole-class activity. The assessments always require synthesis of the three texts from the workshop, but responses may take the form of an essay, a debate, a discussion, or a multimedia presentation.

Writing Workshop

Beyond the writing instruction included in every English Language Arts unit, SpringBoard also offers stand-alone workshops—10 per grade level—for a deep dive into this skill. The Writing Workshop provides students with direct instruction of the writing process and practice writing in modes including narrative, argumentative, and informational, as well as creative modes like poetry and script writing. Each workshop includes four activities structured to gradually move students from class writing exercises to writing independently.

During the workshop, students are guided through planning, drafting, revising and editing, researching (if applicable), and other steps. All writing workshops are accompanied by a Scoring Guide that outlines the performance expectations for each writing mode and provides an evaluation tool for the learning targets identified at each grade level.

Additional ELA Tools and Supports

SpringBoard Digital

SpringBoard puts students in charge of what they learn and gives teachers the flexibility and support they need. SpringBoard Digital is an interactive program that provides always-available online content that's accessible from any device—desktop computer, laptop, tablet, or interactive whiteboard. The student edition allows users to interact with the text, respond to prompts, take assessments, and engage with a suite of tools, all in the digital space. Teachers get access to a correlations viewer that embeds correlations at point of use, a lesson planner, progress reports, grading, messaging, and more.

Zinc Reading Labs

All SpringBoard users have access to Zinc Reading Labs, where teachers and students can find a huge library of reading material chosen specifically to align with the SpringBoard curriculum.

Zinc offers students:

- Fresh and engaging nonfiction and fiction content for independent reading.
- Interactive games, quizzes, and tasks that build skills and confidence.
- Freedom of choice: Zinc's massive and ever-growing library means that all students should find texts they want to read.

Zinc offers teachers:

- Alignment to SpringBoard unit themes: Teachers browse by unit to find companion articles to the texts they're using in class and can even select vocabulary sets that are aligned to unit texts.
- Standards alignment: Quiz questions are aligned with standards so teachers can easily target specific skills.
- Detailed reporting based on results of Zinc's auto-graded quizzes.

Turnitin Revision Assistant

When students develop drafts of an available Embedded Assessment through SpringBoard Digital, they can use a tool called Turnitin Revision Assistant. This online tool gives instant feedback to students as they write so they can polish their drafts and practice their revision skills. The feedback model Revision Assistant uses is based on scoring by SpringBoard teachers, and it's trained to assess the same rubric areas that they assess.

Revision Assistant offers students:

- A template to help them create an outline.
- Actionable, instant feedback in specific areas such as structure, use of language, and ideas.
- Identification of strengths and weakness in their writing.

Teachers can access students' improved drafts and see the feedback, which lets them:

- Gain insight to student progress over time.
- Use feedback in student writing conferences.
- Identify trends in student writing to inform instruction.

SpringBoard Works

Research-based

SpringBoard is a research-based, classroom-tested curriculum created by teachers for teachers. As classroom practitioners, SpringBoard's creators understand the central role that research plays in designing effective English Language Arts instruction. They also have the hands-on experience to know what works in the classroom. Incorporating research from the field with practical experience, SpringBoard makes learning goals clear and scaffolds instruction so students master those goals.

SpringBoard uses the widely respected Wiggins and McTighe "Understanding by Design" model. The program "back maps" from a defined set of essential skills and knowledge that is shown to propel students on their path to college and career. Each SpringBoard unit begins by unpacking the Embedded Assessment, and there are multiple formative assessments throughout each unit to measure progress toward that goal. This instructional design allows students and teachers to see the connections between the work they're doing in everyday activities and the larger instructional goals of the unit and the school year.

SpringBoard's lesson design also takes into account the work of the American Institutes for Research in its focus on students moving through multiple levels of cognitive engagement: progressing fluidly from comprehension and understanding, to analysis, and ultimately to synthesis and the creation of new content. Each lesson is designed to allow for the type of facilitation and flexibility referenced by Charlotte Danielson in her work on teacher instruction. We have also integrated the research of Marzano and Pickering by building students' background knowledge in the area of academic vocabulary development. Finally, SpringBoard is directly informed by Robyn Jackson's work on rigorous instruction. As Jackson suggests, our content requires students to be "active, not passive," and our units feature activities that stress "implicit meaning, ambiguity, layers, and complexity."

Making an Impact

Statewide and nationwide studies demonstrate that SpringBoard is generating positive results. One measure of that success: SpringBoard has been shown to improve both engagement in the classroom and readiness for college. One nationwide study, comparing SpringBoard and non-SpringBoard schools, showed a considerable increase in the number of students enrolled in AP Exams and courses, as well as increased SAT performance.

SpringBoard helps more students succeed:

- High schools using SpringBoard showed a 48% increase in students taking AP Exams in English—and an even greater increase among black and Hispanic students.

- SpringBoard schools saw a 4–8% increase in AP and PSAT/NMSQT performance and saw SAT scores rise 26 points on average.

- High schools using SpringBoard for three to five years had substantially more students taking AP courses.

- SpringBoard has been shown to improve AP scores, particularly among black and Hispanic students.

A Letter to the Teacher

Dear Teacher,

We at SpringBoard are always learning from teachers like you, asking for your ideas and mining your best practices to create a program that puts students at the center of instruction. As a result, the SpringBoard classroom is one in which students can practice reading closely, writing effectively, thinking critically, working collaboratively, and speaking confidently with a teacher who is prepared to guide, support, and challenge them.

We know that the dedicated teachers who use this program come to it with a variety of experiences that they can—and should—bring to the classroom. We celebrate the amazing work that is being done in high schools around the country, and hope that all teachers who use SpringBoard can make it their own. To that end, let us share some thoughts with you.

We believe in starting each unit by showing students the Embedded Assessment assignment. By asking students to identify the skills and knowledge they will need for the task, we give them ownership of their learning. Students should be able to see how every class period develops these important skills and builds their knowledge.

We believe that learning how to learn is as important as learning the content of an English Language Arts and Reading course. A solid foundation in close reading and writing will serve students in every content area in every grade—and in every future career. SpringBoard includes a range of reading and writing strategies, and you are encouraged to choose those that work well with your students.

We believe that instruction needs to be differentiated, but common assessments are a necessary tool to drive that differentiation. The results of a common assessment will let you plan instruction based on what you see in your students' work, and might foster rich discussions in your professional learning communities and district meetings.

Finally, we hope you will take the time to become part of the larger SpringBoard community of teachers, all of whom are focused on preparing all students for college and career success. Let yourself be inspired and challenged during professional development, find support through our online community, and share your ideas with us. The SpringBoard family welcomes you.

Sincerely,
The SpringBoard Team

Context

In this unit, students are introduced to the concept of *perspective* and are asked to consider how one's perception determines his or her interpretation of the world. A corollary of this fact is the idea that one's perception of reality is often filtered through various values, prejudices, and attitudes. In this unit, students will learn about and apply multiple literary theories as filters in order to have deeper and richer ways to think about, interpret, and critique literature and life. Literary theory is presented to introduce the idea that the world is full of ideologies, theories, and biases through which students construct an understanding of their own as well as others' experiences. Studying theory is a means to make students aware of competing visions of truth that they will examine and define from multiple perspectives.

Suggested Texts and Materials

You will need to prepare and/or acquire materials for the following activities:

- Activity 1.4: projector or computers for viewing image (optional)
- Activity 1.20: DVD of *Edward Scissorhands* or clip from some other film that illustrates the *stranger in the village* concept (optional)

Instructional Sequence

The sequence of instruction begins by introducing students to six literary theories that they will use to interpret literature: Reader-Response Criticism, Cultural Criticism, Archetypal Criticism, Marxist Criticism, Feminist Criticism, and Historical Criticism. They will have opportunities to apply these theories to a variety of written and visual texts. Students will also examine models of argumentation and explore how authors build an argument, building towards Embedded Assessment 1, where students write a rhetorical analysis.

In the second half of the unit, students will engage in several activities that ask them to examine the function and use of stylistic elements in a variety of texts and the impact these elements have on the reader. Students read James Baldwin's essay "Stranger in the Village," and explore the concept of being a "stranger in a village" throughout the second half of the unit. Students will then transfer their knowledge of these specific elements (point of view, imagery, diction, detail, syntax, and theme) to the creation of their own reflective essay for Embedded Assessment 2.

AP® CONNECTIONS

In this unit, students will focus on refining these important skills and knowledge areas for AP/College Readiness:

- Identifying and describing the components of the rhetorical situation (Activities 1.8, 1.9)
- Explaining the function of choices writers make for specific contexts and to accomplish a purpose (Activities 1.3, 1.4, 1.5, 1.6, 1.7, 1.10)
- Explaining how a line of reasoning relates to a claim, how the organization of a text creates coherence and reflects a line of reasoning, and how a transitional element contributes to the reasoning of an argument. (Activities 1.8, 1.9, 1.10)
- Focusing deliberate attention on the craft of sentence-level writing (Activities 1.2, 1.5, 1.9, 1.18)

SAT® CONNECTIONS

In this unit, students will practice many important skills that will help them succeed on the SAT and other college readiness exams, including:

- Explaining how an author builds an argument to persuade an audience (Activity 1.10 and Embedded Assessment 1)
- Recognizing and correcting problems in modifier placement (LC 1.15)

Unpacked Embedded Assessments

Embedded Assessment 1: Writing a Rhetorical Analysis Essay	Embedded Assessment 2: Writing an Reflective Essay
Skills and Knowledge:	**Skills and Knowledge:**
• Analyze and evaluate an argumentative text's central ideas and key details.	• Develop an informational text to incorporate the thematic concept of *the stranger in the village*.
• Use text evidence to support a claim.	• Apply the organizational structure of a reflective essay.
• Represent an argumentative text accurately, without misrepresenting or interpreting the text.	• Draft a reflective text with clear controlling ideas and illustrative details.
• Develop ideas and support a claim using a logical structure.	• Make stylistically appropriate choices (e.g., with tone, diction, detail, syntax).
• Incorporate transitions in writing to connect ideas within and between paragraphs.	• Use transitions to connect ideas.
• Use precise language and a variety of sentence structures.	• Use a variety of strategies to revise and refine writing to present technically sound texts.

Cognate Directory

Encouraging students to notice the connections between their primary language and English can help them develop academic vocabulary more quickly. If your class includes Spanish speakers, consider adding the following cognates to the classroom Word Wall. For English Language Learners whose primary language is not Spanish, consider using an online translator or dictionary to support comprehension of vocabulary terms.

Unit 1 Vocabulary Terms with Spanish Cognates

Academic Vocabulary	
English	**Spanish**
imperialism	imperialismo
marginalize	marginar
perception	percepción
rhetorical devices	dispositivos retóricos

Literary Terms	
English	**Spanish**
Cultural Criticism	crítica cultural
diction	dicción
literary criticism	crítica literaria
literary theories	teorías literarias
prologue	prólogo

Activity Features at a Glance

The activities in every ELA unit reflect the interconnected nature of reading, writing, listening, speaking, and thinking. The Activity Features at a Glance chart highlights the types of tasks or supports that students and teachers will encounter in each activity.

 Writing and Revision

 Grammar and Language

 Listening, Speaking, and Discussion

 Independent Reading

 Vocabulary Development

 ELL Support

 Knowledge Quest

 Gaining Perspectives

ELA Activity	Activity Features
1.1	Listening, Independent Reading, ELL
1.2	Writing, Grammar, Listening, Vocabulary, ELL
1.3	Listening, Independent Reading, Vocabulary, ELL
1.4	Listening, ELL
1.5	Writing, Grammar, Listening, Independent Reading, Vocabulary
1.6	Writing, Listening, Vocabulary, ELL
1.7	Writing, Grammar, Listening, Independent Reading, Vocabulary, ELL
1.8	Writing, Listening, Independent Reading, Vocabulary, ELL, Gaining Perspectives
1.9	Writing, Grammar, Listening, ELL, Knowledge Quest
1.10	Writing, Independent Reading

ELA Activity	Activity Features
1.11	Writing, Listening, Independent Reading
1.12	Listening, Independent Reading
1.13	Writing, Listening, Vocabulary, ELL
1.14	Listening, Writing, Vocabulary, ELL
1.15	Grammar, Listening, ELL
LC 1.15	Writing, Grammar, Listening
1.16	Writing, Grammar, Listening, Independent Reading, ELL
1.17	Writing, Grammar, Listening, ELL, Knowledge Quest
1.18	Writing, Grammar, Listening, Independent Reading, Vocabulary, ELL, Knowledge Quest

Unit Resources at a Glance

Formative Assessment Opportunities	Digital Assessments	Family Connections
Text-dependent questions Writing prompts Check Your Understanding tasks Focus on the Sentence tasks Language Checkpoint exercises Language & Writer's Craft practice	Activity Quizzes 1.2–1.18 Unit Assessment Part 1 Unit Assessment Part 2 SBD	Suggestions for Independent Reading Family Letters (English and Spanish) Student Reports SBD
English Language Development	**Foundational Skills**	**Independent Reading**
Leveled Differentiated Instruction Graphic Organizers ELD Strategies Language Workshop 1A Language Workshop 1B	Foundational Skills Screening Assessment Observational Look-fors Foundational Skills Workshop	My Independent Reading List Independent Reading Links Independent Reading Checkpoints Independent Reading Log Reader/Writer Notebook Suggestions for Independent Reading

⊕ Suggestions for Independent Reading

This list, divided into the categories of **Literature** and **Nonfiction/Informational Text**, comprises titles related to the themes and content of the unit. For their independent reading, students can select from this wide array of titles, which have been chosen based on complexity and interest. Spanish-language titles are included for those students who can read with greater independence or at a higher grade level in Spanish than in English, since building on their first language literacy can bolster their acquisition of English. Titles on this list have been suggested by teachers and school librarians, but you should be sure to preview texts to assess their appropriateness for your specific students and setting. You can also encourage students to do their own research and select titles that intrigue them.

Unit 1: Perception Is Everything

Literature		
Author	**Title**	**Lexile**
Bray, Libba	*Going Bovine*	680L
Conrad, Joseph	*Heart of Darkness*	1050L
Cunningham, Michael	*The Hours*	960L
Defoe, Daniel	*Robinson Crusoe*	920L
Far, Sui Sin	*Mrs. Spring Fragrance: A Collection of Chinese-American Short Stories*	N/A
Golden, Arthur	*Memoirs of a Geisha*	1000L
Greene, Graham	*Brighton Rock*	680L
Huxley, Aldous	*Brave New World*	870L
Jordan, Hillary	*Mudbound*	N/A

Kingsolver, Barbara	*The Poisonwood Bible*	960L
Kitamura, Katie	*A Separation*	N/A
Lahiri, Jhumpa	*The Namesake*	1140L
McEwan, Ian	*Atonement*	N/A
Orwell, George	*Down and Out in Paris and London*	1020L
Orwell, George	*Rebelión en la granja*	1030L
Paton, Alan	*Cry, the Beloved Country*	860L
Plath, Sylvia	*The Bell Jar*	1140L
Salinger, J.D.	*Nine Stories*	N/A
Shihab Nye, Naomi	*19 Varieties of Gazelle: Poems of the Middle East*	N/A
Stevenson, Robert Louis	*The Strange Case of Dr. Jekyll and Mr. Hyde*	1060L

Nonfiction/Informational Text

Author	Title	Lexile
Baldwin, James	*The Fire Next Time*	1300L
Bartolettii, Susan Campbell	*Growing Up In Coal Country*	1110L
Cofer, Judith Ortiz	*The Latin Deli: Telling the Lives of Barrio Women*	N/A
Culler, Jonathan	*Literary Theory: A Very Short Introduction*	1370L
Friedan, Betty	*The Feminine Mystique*	N/A
Galbraith, John	*The Affluent Society*	N/A
Goleman, Daniel	*Emotional Intelligence: Why It Can Matter More Than IQ*	N/A
Hershey, John	*Hiroshima*	1190L
James, Henry	*Varieties of Religious Experience*	1360L
Lewis, Michael	*Moneyball*	N/A
McCourt, Frank	*Angela's Ashes: A Memoir*	1110L
Mukherjee, Siddhartha	*The Emperor of All Maladies: A Biography of Cancer*	N/A
Paravisini-Gebert, Lizabeth	*Jamaica Kincaid: A Critical Companion*	1530L
Riis, Jacob	*How the Other Half Lives*	N/A
Vonnegut, Kurt	*A Man Without a Country*	N/A
Wallace, David Foster	*A Supposedly Fun Thing I'll Never Do Again*	N/A
Watson, James	*The Double Helix: A Personal Account of the Discovery of the Structure of DNA*	1201L
Wright, Richard	*Black Boy*	950L

Instructional Pathways

Teachers can build customized pathways through this unit by making purposeful choices about which resources to use based on students' learning needs. The charts below outline a few possible pathways to show how teachers might integrate digital assessments, Language Workshops, Close Reading Workshops, and Writing Workshops into instruction. Additional planning resources—including detailed standards correlations—are available on SpringBoard Digital.

English Language Arts Unit 1: Perception Is Everything			
Activity	**SBD Digital Assessments**	**Pacing**	
Activity 1.1: Previewing the Unit	N/A	1	
Activity 1.2: Perception Is Everything	Activity Quiz 1.2	1	
Activity 1.3: Introducing Reader-Response Criticism	Activity Quiz 1.3	3	
Activity 1.4: Applying Reader-Response Criticism	Activity Quiz 1.4	1	
Activity 1.5: Creating Meaning	Activity Quiz 1.5	1	
Activity 1.6: Exploring Poetic Form	Activity Quiz 1.6	1	
Activity 1.7: Another Perspective on the World	Activity Quiz 1.7	2	
Activity 1.8: Exploring Rhetoric	Activity Quiz 1.8	1	
Activity 1.9: Critiquing and Evaluating an Argument	Activity Quiz 1.9	3	
Activity 1.10: Explain How an Author Builds an Argument	Activity Quiz 1.10	1	
Activity 1.11: Evaluating a Peer's Essay	Activity Quiz 1.11	1	
Embedded Assessment 1: Writing a Rhetorical Analysis Essay	**Unit Assessment Part 1**	2	1
Activity 1.12: Unpacking Embedded Assessment 2	Activity Quiz 1.12	1	
Activity 1.13: What Is Cultural Criticism?	Activity Quiz 1.13	1	
Activity 1.14: Applying Cultural Criticism	Activity Quiz 1.14	2	
Activity 1.15: Digging Deeper for Meaning	Activity Quiz 1.15	2	
LC1.15: Language Checkpoint: Placing Modifiers (optional)	Activity Quiz LC 1.15	1	
Activity 1.16: Reflecting on an Event	Activity Quiz 1.16	2	
Activity 1.17: Being a Stranger	Activity Quiz 1.17	2	
Activity 1.18: Understanding the Stranger's Perception of the Village	Activity Quiz 1.18	2	
Embedded Assessment 2: Writing a Reflective Essay	**Unit Assessment Part 2**	2	1

Total 50-minute Class Periods: 32–35

Language Development Pathway

Consider using some or all of the Language Workshop and Foundational Skills Workshop activities with English Language Learners or with any student who would benefit from extra support with academic English. More detailed guidance about the timing of Language Workshop and Foundational Skills Workshop activities in relation to the ELA unit and about the purpose of each activity can be found in the Language Workshop teacher edition.

Language Workshop 1A and 1B

Activity or Workshop			Pacing	
Language Workshop 1A.1: Genre Focus			1	
Activity 1.1: Previewing the Unit			1	
Activity 1.2: Perception Is Everything			1	
Activity 1.3: Introducing Reader-Response Criticism			3	
Activity 1.4: Applying Reader-Response Criticism			1	
Activity 1.5: Creating Meaning			1	
Activity 1.6: Exploring Poetic Form			1	
Activity 1.7: Another Perspective on the World			2	
Activity 1.8: Exploring Rhetoric			1	
Language Workshop 1A.7: Language Checkpoint			1	
Language Workshop 1A.2: Building Knowledge			1	
Language Workshop 1A.3: Academic Vocabulary			1	
Language Workshop 1A.4: Vocabulary Preview and Practice			1	
Activity 1.9: Critiquing and Evaluating an Argument	OR	**Language Workshop 1A.5:** Close Reading of an Anchor Text*	3	1
		Language Workshop 1A.6: Academic Collaboration*		1
Activity 1.10: Explain How an Author Builds an Argument			1	
Activity 1.11: Evaluating a Peer's Essay			1	
Embedded Assessment 1: Writing a Rhetorical Analysis Essay	OR	**Collaborative Embedded Assessment: Writing a Rhetorical Analysis Essay**	2	4

Activity or Workshop		Pacing	
Activity 1.12: Unpacking Embedded Assessment 2		1	
Activity 1.13: What Is Cultural Criticism?		1	
Activity 1.14: Applying Cultural Criticism		2	
Language Workshop 1B.1: Genre Focus		1	
Language Workshop 1B.2: Building Knowledge		1	
Language Workshop 1B.3: Academic Vocabulary		1	
Language Workshop 1B.4: Vocabulary Preview and Practice		1	
Activity 1.15: Digging Deeper for Meaning	**Language Workshop 1B.5:** Close Reading of an Anchor Text*	2	1
	Language Workshop 1B.6: Academic Collaboration*		1
LC 1.15: Language Checkpoint: Placing Modifiers (optional)		1	
Activity 1.16: Reflecting on an Event		2	
Activity 1.17: Being a Stranger		2	
Language Workshop 1B.7: Language Checkpoint		1	
Activity 1.18: Understanding the Stranger's Perception of the Village		2	
Embedded Assessment 2: Writing a Reflective Essay	**Collaborative Embedded Assessment:** Writing a Reflective Essay	2	4

Total 50-minute Class Periods: 32–47

* These activities are available in Spanish.

Foundational Skills Workshop

The Foundational Skills Workshop offers instructional and practice materials for providing small-group instruction to students who are still developing foundational reading skills.

Activity	Pacing
Activity 1: Practicing Letter-Sound Relationships	15 min.
Activity 2: Recognizing Words by Sight	10 min.
Activity 3: Words with Inconsistent but Common Spellings	
Activity 4: Irregularly Spelled Words	
Activity 5: Common Prefixes	
Activity 6: Common Suffixes	35–40 min. per activity
Activity 7: Using Roots and Affixes to Read Multisyllabic Words	
Activity 8: Reading Multisyllabic Words	
Activity 9: Reading Informational Text with Purpose and Understanding	
Activity 10: Reading Poetry with Fluency	

Flexible Pathways

Teachers may build a flexible pathway that focuses on developing students' close reading and writing skills with the Close Reading and Writing Workshops. Each workshop addresses a specific set of standards and includes multiple assessment opportunities to allow students to demonstrate the knowledge and skills that are the focus of that workshop.

Close Reading Workshops

Workshop	Genre Focus	Assessment Opportunities	Pacing
Close Reading Workshop 1: Informational/Literary Nonfiction Texts	Essays Visual Text	Writing Prompt Debate/Discussion Multimedia Presentation	8
Close Reading Workshop 3: Poetry	Poetry Visual Text	Writing Prompt Debate/Discussion Multimedia Presentation	8

Writing Workshops

Workshop	Genre Focus	Assessment Opportunities	Pacing
Writing Workshop 1: The Writing Process	n/a	Writing as a Class Independent Writing	5
Writing Workshop 2: Argumentative Response	Argument	Writing as a Class Writing with a Peer Independent Writing	7
Writing Workshop 7: Narrative Nonfiction: Reflective Essay	Reflective Essay	Writing as a Class Writing with a Peer Independent Writing	6
Writing Workshop 8: Poetry	Poetry	Writing as a Class Writing with a Peer Independent Writing	6

UNIT 1

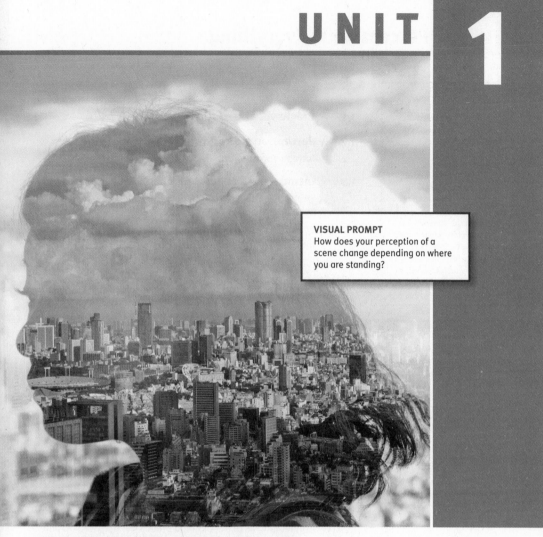

VISUAL PROMPT
How does your perception of a scene change depending on where you are standing?

PERCEPTION IS EVERYTHING

That invisibility to which I refer occurs because of a peculiar disposition of the eyes of those with whom I come in contact. A matter of the construction of their inner eyes, those eyes with which they look through their physical eyes upon reality.

—from *Invisible Man* by Ralph Ellison

Leveled Differentiated Instruction Directory

For guidance on differentiating tasks for English language learners at various levels of language proficiency, refer to the Leveled Differentiated Instruction suggestions in these activities:

1.1: Allow students to choose independent reading in their home language.

1.2: Have students work in groups on their **OPTIC** graphic organizers.

1.3: Use a cognate bridge or analysis of a simple poem to aid understanding of the TP-CASTT strategy.

1.4: Provide extra practice applying critical lenses.

1.6: Challenge students to write new poems using extended metaphors or poetic forms.

UNIT 1

Read aloud the unit title, "Perception Is Everything," and the quotation. Discuss with students what they think the author means by "inner eyes." Allow a brief time for reflection and writing on the question: Can you think of a time when your feelings or beliefs about something affected your external perception of it? Share responses in partner, small-group, or whole-class discussion.

Have students look at the photo and respond to the visual prompt. You may want to have students **think-pair-share** to write a short response or discuss their responses as a class.

 TEACHER TO TEACHER

To have students begin to think about the concept of perception and how our perspectives, values, prejudices, and attitudes shape how we view reality, you may want to ask them to think about situations in which they and others witnessed or participated in the same event and came away with vastly different perspectives on what happened. Was it disorienting to realize that their perspectives could differ so much from others' perspectives? Students will explore Essential Questions about perspective several times throughout the unit.

CONTENTS

Have the students **skim/scan** the activities and texts in this unit. Have them note any texts they have heard about but never read and any activities that sound particularly interesting.

GOALS

Have students read the goals for the unit and mark any words that are unfamiliar to them. Have students add these words to the classroom Word Wall, along with definitions.

You may also want to post these goals in a visible place in the classroom for the duration of this unit, allowing you and students to revisit the goals easily and gauge progress throughout the unit.

VOCABULARY DEVELOPMENT

Adding to vocabulary knowledge is essential for reading fluency. Students will encounter new vocabulary in this unit in multiple ways:

- Academic Vocabulary
- Literary Terms
- Vocabulary in Context (terms glossed in text selections)
- Word Connections
- Oral discussions

Encourage students to use new vocabulary expressively in class discussions and in writing. Have them keep a **Reader/Writer Notebook** in which they record new words, their meanings, and their pronunciations.

See the Resources section for examples of graphic organizers suitable for word study. Having students use word-study graphic organizers will greatly enhance their understanding of new words and their connection to unit concepts and to the broader use of advanced and discipline-based terms.

Have students review the list of academic and literary terms and sort them in a QHT Chart. Revisit the chart periodically to see how students' understanding progresses throughout the unit.

LANGUAGE DEVELOPMENT

Several recurring SpringBoard features focus on building students' knowledge of grammar and usage concepts. Language and Writer's Craft features guide students to examine a writer's use of a language concept in context before incorporating the concept into their own writing. Grammar & Usage features briefly highlight and explain an interesting grammar or usage concept that appears in a text, both to improve students' reading comprehension and to increase their understanding of the concept. Periodic Language Checkpoints offer in-depth practice with standard English conventions and usage and guide students to revise sample sentences as well as their own work.

UNIT 1

Perception Is Everything

GOALS

- To apply Reader-Response and Cultural Criticism in determining an author's purpose, audience, and message
- To evaluate the effectiveness of an author's organizational and stylistic choices in texts across genres
- To strategically use text evidence to support commentary and critiques of an author's work
- To write texts that use a logical structure, precise language, and effective genre characteristics

VOCABULARY

ACADEMIC
imperialism
marginalize
paradox
perception
rhetorical devices

LITERARY
Cultural Criticism
diction
literary criticism
literary theories
prologue
Reader-Response Criticism

Leveled Differentiated Instruction Directory (continued)

1.7: Give students the **Idea Connector** graphic organizer to assist them in forming compound and complex sentences.

1.8: Support students in using the SOAPSTone strategy by allowing them to work in groups.

1.9: Give students extra practice identifying the elements of an argument.

1.13: Offer support for understanding the cultural context of a poem by making connections.

1.14: Use audio to support students in understanding the tone and voice of a poem. Provide the **Venn Diagram for Writing a Comparison** graphic organizer to assist students in preparing for a Socratic Seminar comparing poems.

CONTENTS

My Independent Reading List

Leveled Differentiated Instruction Directory (continued)

1.15: Allow students to try choral reading to improve fluency and increase confidence.

1.16: Have students use the **Narrative Analysis and Writing** graphic organizer as a prewriting activity for a reflective essay.

1.18: Model how to use metacognitive markers and paraphrase the text.

UNIT 1

INDEPENDENT READING

In this unit, students will explore the concept of multiple perspectives as they read a variety of genres. Their independent reading selections should complement the unit's focus. The Planning the Unit section of the Teacher's Edition and the Resources section of the Student Edition contain reading lists to help you and your students find the right books.

Independent Reading Links in the unit periodically prompt students to reflect on the reading they are doing outside of class and to make connections to the texts, themes, and ideas addressed in the unit.

KNOWLEDGE QUEST

Within the unit, students will engage in two Knowledge Quests. They will read collections of texts about social advocacy issues and being a stranger in a new place, building their understanding of the topics and related vocabulary. Each Knowledge Quest begins with a knowledge question and supporting questions that focus student learning. After students read the final text in a set, they will have the opportunity to return to the Knowledge Question and express their growing understanding of the topic by responding to a writing-to-sources prompt or engaging in an academic discussion.

 TEACHER TO TEACHER

The SpringBoard program is designed so that students interact with texts in meaningful ways, such as notetaking and annotating, to facilitate comprehension and analysis. Have students use Reader/Writer Notebooks actively for vocabulary study, answers to text-dependent questions, predictions and questions about texts, reflections, responses to Independent Reading Links, and so on. The Reader/Writer Notebooks are not listed as part of the materials for each activity, but the expectation is that students will access them frequently.

ACTIVITY
1.1 Previewing the Unit

PLAN

Materials: web graphic organizer to unpack Embedded Assessment 1
Suggested Pacing: 1 50-minute class period

TEACH

1 Ask for a volunteer to read aloud the Learning Targets.

2 Give students a few moments to read the About the Unit silently to themselves so that they can **skim and scan** the information. Lead a brief class discussion on the word *criticism*, by first asking students for an on-the-spot definition and then guiding them to a broader understanding of what it means in the current context. Invite students to consider what Reader-Response Criticism and Cultural Criticism might be about.

3 Ask students to think-pair-share responses to the Essential Questions. Students will revisit these questions throughout the unit to develop a more mature understanding of these ideas.

4 Ask students to find the Embedded Assessment 1 assignment and Scoring Guide. Lead students through a close reading of the assignment, steps, and Scoring Guide criteria. Instruct students to mark the text by underlining or highlighting the places in the text that mention a skill or knowledge necessary to succeed on the assessment.

5 Instruct students to summarize or paraphrase the skills and knowledge they have underlined or highlighted with a partner or small group. As you conduct a large-group discussion, create a web graphic organizer that lists the knowledge and skills.

6 Have students use the questions in the Planning Independent Reading section to help them choose a book to bring to the discussion group. After they've completed student step 1 in their Reader/Writer Notebooks, invite volunteers to share with the class the book they chose and their reasons for choosing it.

Learning Strategies

Graphic Organizer
Marking the Text
Paraphrasing
Think-Pair-Share

My Notes

Learning Targets

- Preview the big ideas of the unit.
- Create a plan for reading independently.
- Identify and analyze the knowledge and skills needed to complete Embedded Assessment 1.

Preview

In this activity, you will explore the big ideas and tasks of the unit and make plans for your independent reading.

About the Unit

In this unit, you will examine the choices authors make to inform and shape the perception of readers. You will begin by deeply evaluating and critiquing poetry and then apply these skills to more complex literary and argumentative texts. This unit also introduces literary theories, which you will use to interpret texts and the world. Studying literary theory is a means to make you aware that the world is full of ideologies, theories, and biases through which we construct an understanding of our individual experiences and the world around us. You will apply Reader-Response Criticism in the first half of this unit and Cultural Criticism in the latter half.

Essential Questions

Based on your current knowledge, how would you answer these questions?

1. Why do writers make particular choices when composing a text?

2. How does the interaction between a reader and a text create meaning?

3. What does it mean to be a stranger in a village?

Unpacking Embedded Assessment 1

Closely read the assignment for Embedded Assessment 1: Writing a Rhetorical Analysis Essay.

Write an essay in which you critique and evaluate how the author of "Tipping System Exacerbates Unfair Pay at Restaurants" builds an argument to convince her audience that restaurant workers deserve fair wages from their employers instead of tips. In your essay, explain and evaluate how Kathleen Kingsbury uses one or more of the features in the directions that precede the passage (or features of your own choosing) to develop her argument. Be sure that your critique focuses on the most relevant features of the passage. Your essay should not explain whether you agree with Kingsbury's claims, but rather it should explain and evaluate how Kingsbury builds an argument to persuade the audience. Paraphrase the assignment in your own words. What do you need to know to be able to complete this assessment successfully? What skills must you have to complete the task successfully?

College and Career Readiness Standards

Focus Standards:

RL.11–12.1 Cite strong and thorough textual evidence to support analysis of what the text says explicitly as well as inferences drawn from the text, including determining where the text leaves matters uncertain

RL.11–12.7 Analyze multiple interpretations of a story, drama, or poem (e.g., recorded or live production of a play or recorded novel or poetry), evaluating how each version interprets the source text. (Include at least one play by Shakespeare and one play by an American dramatist.)

Planning Independent Reading

To enhance this unit's focus, look for literature or nonfiction that includes multiple perspectives. Each of the literary theories you will study in this course can help you analyze and understand your independent reading texts in new and enlightening ways. Consider how these readings connect to what you read in the unit and to your own perspectives. Choose exceptional readings to recommend to and discuss with your peers. To help you choose the right book, use the following questions as a guide.

- What have you enjoyed reading in the past? What is your favorite book or favorite type of book? Who is your favorite author?
- When you select a potential book, preview it. What do the front and back covers show you? What type of visual is shown? What types of fonts and colors are used? Are there awards or brags that tell you about the book?
- Read the first few pages. Are they interesting? How does the author try to hook you to keep reading? What can you tell about the characters and setting so far? Does this seem too hard, too easy, or just right?
- How do you think literary theory might change your perspective of the texts you are reading independently?

Reading Discussion Groups

Follow your teacher's oral guidance through a book pass. Practice previewing each book by looking at the covers and reading the first few pages.

4. In your Reader/Writer Notebook, record each book's title and author, something from your previewing that stands out to you, and your rating of the book.

5. After previewing each book and thinking about the goals of this unit, do you want to continue reading the book you brought to the group or choose something else?

   Create an Independent Reading Plan to help you set personal reading goals. Keep this plan in your Reader/Writer Notebook.

   I have chosen to read _____

   _____.

   by (author) _____.

   because (reason from previewing) _____

   _____.

   I will set aside time to read at (time, place) _____

   _____.

   I should finish this text by (date) _____.

6. Record your daily reading pace in your Independent Reading Log. Write a brief daily report in your log responding to what you have read. Include in your report questions or predictions about what you have read.

7. Respond to the Independent Reading Links you encounter throughout the unit.

College and Career Readiness Standards

RL.11–12.10 By the end of grade 12, read and comprehend literature, including stories, dramas, and poems, at the high end of the grades 11-CCR text complexity band independently and proficiently.

L.11–12.5 Demonstrate understanding of figurative language, word relationships, and nuances in word meanings.

Additional Standards Addressed:

RL.11–12.2, SL.11–12.1c, W.11–12.10

ACTIVITY 1.1 continued

7 Guide students to make a final choice and create their Independent Reading Plan.

➤ TEACHER TO TEACHER

Consider setting up a class spreadsheet or online document where students can add their chosen independent reading titles along with short descriptions and reviews. This can help students locate new texts to read independently, as well as provide them with practice tracking sources for shared writing assignments.

LEVELED DIFFERENTIATED INSTRUCTION

In this activity, students may need support planning their independent reading.

Beginning As students develop their independent reading plans, consider giving students at an early stage in their English language development the option of reading a text in their home language. These students can build on native language literacy as they begin to develop academic English.

ASSESS

Monitor students as they unpack the Embedded Assessment to evaluate their understanding of how to identify skills and knowledge needed. Make sure students are marking the text and identifying correctly the necessary skills. Look for notes that ensure students understand the criteria involved.

ADAPT

Throughout the unit, revisit the web graphic organizer to reinforce the purpose of each activity. Discuss with students how each activity allows them to practice the skills and knowledge needed for success on the Embedded Assessment. This process will be repeated for the second half of the unit in preparation for Embedded Assessment 2.

PLAN

Materials: highlighters

Suggested Pacing: 1 50-minute class period

TEACH

1 Read through the Learning Targets and Preview with students.

2 Vocabulary Development: Review the Academic and Literary Vocabulary with students. Ask them to work with a partner to brainstorm words to define the concepts of *perception*, *literary criticism*, and *literary theories*.

3 After students have read the information about Literary Criticism, have them meet in small groups to discuss the information and their understanding of it. Consider grouping students with developing English skills with those at a more advanced level. Guide the discussion by having students discuss what cultural factors might affect how someone perceives a text or an image.

4 As students complete the Focus on the Sentence activity, circle through the room to offer help as needed. If students are having difficulty paraphrasing the definition of Literary Criticism, have them go back to the description and highlight or mark the most significant words and ideas.

LEVELED DIFFERENTIATED INSTRUCTION

Students at an advanced level may benefit from additional time spent on the activity.

Extend If students complete the Focus on the Sentence task quickly, ask them to write a third sentence—this time an exclamation—that expresses what the student thinks about literary criticism so far.

Learning Strategies

Marking the Text
OPTIC

VOCABULARY

ACADEMIC
A **perception** is one person's interpretation of sensory or conceptual information.

LITERARY
Literary criticism is the formal practice of interpreting, evaluating, and explaining the meaning and significance of literary works. Scholars often use specific **literary theories**—systematic, conceptual methods of analyzing texts—when they engage in literary criticism.

My Notes

Learning Targets

- Understand the fundamentals of literary criticism and six literary theories.
- Apply literary theories to analyze, question, and interpret images.
- Summarize your observations and understanding of the impact of literary theories.

Preview

In this activity, you will be introduced to six literary theories and their definitions. You will use the key assumptions of a critical perspective to analyze and question illustrations.

Literary Criticism

Our experiences, relationships, and interactions shape how we perceive the world around us. How one person perceives an event unfolding in front of them can be dramatically different than how another perceives the same event. These varied perceptions are at the heart of literary criticism.

Literary criticism does not always involve being negative or critical about a piece of writing. Instead, it is a formal practice that scholars of literature use to interpret, evaluate, and explain the meaning and significance of literary works. Because we all bring different perceptions to the classroom, *how* we analyze, interpret, and evaluate literature varies greatly. But literary criticism doesn't require scholars to agree. In fact, it encourages scholars to engage in ongoing discourse about the meaning of literary works and their significance to the broader human experience.

Becoming skilled at literary criticism has benefits beyond the study of literature, too. Learning to read a text from various critical perspectives can help readers become agile and skillful thinkers who are capable of exploring the world outside the boundaries of one's own limited perceptions.

☑ Focus on the Sentence

Write two complete sentences in response to what you have learned so far about literary criticism. The first should be a statement that paraphrases the definition of literary criticism in your own words. The second should be a question you have about literary criticism.

Statement: Literary criticism is a formal way of studying and interpreting literature that often uses literary theories.

Question: How is literary criticism different from how we've been studying texts all through high school?

College and Career Readiness Standards

Focus Standards:

RL.11–12.1 Cite strong and thorough textual evidence to support analysis of what the text says explicitly as well as inferences drawn from the text, including determining where the text leaves matters uncertain.

RL.11–12.2 Determine two or more themes or central ideas of a text and analyze their development over the course of the text, including how they interact and build on one another to produce a complex account; provide an objective summary of the text.

1.2

Literary Theory

Scholars use a number of different literary theories, sometimes called critical theories or lenses, to uncover meaning in literary works. Each theory is made up of a set of assumptions or concepts that a reader applies to the text in order to understand it in new ways.

Studying literary theories can help a reader to become aware of competing perceptions of truth and to learn that a text can be understood through a filter of ideologies, values, and perspectives. Being able to apply different theories to a text expands a reader's worldview and adds dimensions to understanding a text.

The following six literary theories will give you the tools to understand texts in novel and challenging ways over the course of this school year. These are not the only literary theories that exist, but they are among the most commonly used theories for exploring literature. Imagine each theory as a lens, like a pair of tinted glasses, that adds color to the interpretation of a text. No single lens or theory provides the clearest view of the world. Instead, each one allows a reader to make meaning from a piece of literature in a different way.

As you read each definition, underline words and phrases that strike you as most essential to understanding the theory.

Literary Theory	Key Assumptions
Reader-Response Criticism Reader Response Criticism focuses on a reader's active engagement with a text. The reader's response to any text is shaded by the reader's own experiences, ethics, moral values, and general views of the world. For example, the response to *To Kill a Mockingbird* may depend on the reader's sense of outrage on behalf of someone unjustly accused of a crime.	• When encountering a text, the reader creates meaning from a personal interaction with the text. • A discussion of a text should take into account the reader as well as the reading situation. • Different readers formulate different acceptable interpretations because a text allows for a range of acceptable interpretations for which textual support is available.
Cultural Criticism Cultural Criticism asserts that differing religious beliefs, ethnicities, class identifications, political beliefs, and individual viewpoints affect how texts are created and interpreted. What it means to be a part of—or excluded from—a specific cultural group contributes to an understanding of texts in relation to culture.	• Ethnicity, religious beliefs, social class, and other cultural features are crucial components in formulating plausible interpretations of a text. • It is essential to examine the relationship between dominant cultures and those with less power or authority.
Archetypal Criticism Archetypes are universal symbols—images, characters, motifs, or patterns that recur in the myths, dreams, oral traditions, songs, literature, and other texts of peoples widely separated by time and place. Archetypal Criticism deals with the similarities of these patterns in the literature of widely diverse cultures. For example, most cultures have stories that present a version of the Hero's Journey.	• Certain images recur in texts from diverse cultures that share a common interpretation—water, sun, colors, trees, and settings such as gardens and deserts. • Certain characters recur—the hero, the trickster, the great mother, the wise old man, the prodigal son. • Certain motifs and patterns recur—creation stories, the quest, voyage to the underworld, journey, and initiation.

College and Career Readiness Standards

L.11–12.5 Demonstrate understanding of figurative language, word relationships, and nuances in word meanings.

SL.11–1.2 Integrate multiple sources of information presented in diverse formats and media (e.g., visually, quantitatively, orally)

in order to make informed decisions and solve problems, evaluating the credibility and accuracy of each source and noting any discrepancies among the data.

Additional Standards Addressed:
L.11–12.6

ACTIVITY 1.2 continued

TEACHER TO TEACHER

To get a firmer grasp on literary criticism, students may find it helpful to read a contemporary book review. You may wish to bring in an excerpt from the *Los Angeles Review of Books*, *The New York Review of Books*, or a similar source.

5 Have students work with a partner to read about Literary Theory. Then, before reading through the table describing the different theories, have them engage in a quick conversation exploring their ideas about how ideologies and values shape perception of a text. Have student volunteers share their ideas with the class.

6 As students read through the descriptions of the various theories in the table, circle the room to make sure they are highlighting and marking key ideas of each definition.

Literary Theory	Key Assumptions
Marxist Criticism Marxist Criticism asserts that economics provides the foundation for all social, political, and ideological reality. Economic inequalities between classes create conflict and a power structure that influences all other aspects of life. For example, status in the community in *Their Eyes Were Watching God* can be examined from an economic point of view.	• All aspects of humanity are based on the struggle for economic power. • The basic struggle in human society is between the haves and the have-nots. • The struggle between social classes is inevitable but also drives social transformation.
Feminist Criticism Feminist interpretation focuses on relationships between genders. It examines the patterns of thought, behavior, values, enfranchisement, and power in relations between and within the sexes. A Feminist reading of *Their Eyes Were Watching God*, for example, may examine the novel as an example of a heroine's journey.	• Issues of gender and sexuality are central to artistic expression. • A patriarchal society conveys the notion of male dominance through the images of women in its texts. • Fictional portrayals of female characters often reflect and create stereotypical social and political attitudes about women. • Many classic literary texts lack complex female figures and treat the female reader as an outsider. • Texts authored by women may have different viewpoints than texts authored by men.
Historical Criticism While acknowledging the importance of the literary text, the Historical approach recognizes the significance of historical information in interpreting literature. This perspective assumes that texts both influence and are influenced by the times in which they are created. For example, an interpretation of *Things Fall Apart* by Chinua Achebe may be enhanced by an understanding of the effects of colonialism in present-day African life.	• A text cannot be separated from its historical context, which is a web of social, cultural, economic, personal, and political factors. • An understanding of a text is enhanced by the study of beliefs and artifacts (such as diaries, films, paintings, and letters) in existence when the text was created.

Introducing the Strategy: OPTIC

OPTIC is an acronym for **o**verview, **p**arts, **t**itle, **i**nterrelationships, and **c**onclusion. This strategy is useful for close analysis of visual texts, including paintings, photographs, advertisements, maps, charts, or graphs. By viewing the details of an image in this order, readers develop an interpretation of the image's meaning or theme.

Viewing through the Lenses

In small groups, use the **OPTIC** strategy to closely examine each of the following images. Then return to each image for a second look, this time through the lens of the literary theories.

1. Record your observations about the image you are viewing. Follow the steps of the OPTIC strategy outlined here.

   Overview: Write notes on what the image appears to be about.

   Parts: Zoom in on the different parts of the image. Describe any details that seem important.

   Title: Highlight the words of the title if there is one.

   Interrelationships: How are the elements of the image related?

   Conclusion: Draw a conclusion about the image as a whole. What does the visual mean?

7 Go over the **OPTIC** strategy with students. Make sure students understand each step of the strategy and how they are to use it when looking at an image. Answer any questions they have about implementing the steps.

8 After students have recorded their observations about the images have them respond to student step 2. Circle the room and check to make sure they give concise summaries and are engaged with listening and offering additional ideas.

9 Review the instructions for student step 3 and clarify as necessary. Have them look back over the annotations they made about the descriptions of each theory, consulting their Reader/Writer Notebooks as needed.

10 Lead students in a class discussion about the ideas they added to their graphic organizer. Throughout the discussion, make sure students are drawing from their knowledge of key assumptions for each literary theory.

2. Briefly share your observations with your group in a clear and concise summary. Listen as your group members share their observations, and respond by offering additional ideas or asking questions.

3. Assign one of the literary theories to each member of your group. Revisit the images, this time imagining that you are viewing the image through the lens of your assigned theory. What questions do you have or observations can you make about the images when you are viewing from the perspective of a critical theory? Record your ideas in the graphic organizer.

Image	Questions and Observations Using Literary Theories
	**Reader-Response:** This image makes me feel proud of the accomplishments of women. **Cultural:** How did ideologies change in America during World War II? **Archetypal:** How does this image compete with the archetype of the 1940s housewife? **Marxist:** Were working women in the same social class as men serving in the military? **Feminist:** Why were women excluded from being "soldiers with guns"? **Historical:** How did World War II impact the American industrial labor force?
	Reader-Response: This image is distinctly different from the recruitment ads I have seen. **Cultural:** Are the representations of different cultures in this image accurate? **Archetypal:** The sailors on the elephant look like adventurers. **Marxist:** What does the position of the men in the image above everyone else say about class? **Feminist:** Are women part of the intended audience of this recruitment ad? **Historical:** What was happening in the United States at the time this ad was created?
	**Reader-Response:** While the image is interesting, it would not compel me to buy shoes. **Cultural:** What country are the three figures in the image from? **Archetypal:** How does this image fit or depart from typical depictions of royalty? **Marxist:** This ad seems to be targeting rich people or people who want to appear rich. **Feminist:** What is this ad saying about what makes a woman "of quality"? **Historical:** Was $2.50 worth a lot at the time this image was created?
	**Reader-Response:** How do my ideas of charity connect to this image's message? **Cultural:** How were "the needy" marginalized at this time? **Archetypal:** How has milk been used symbolically in this image? **Marxist:** Was the milk fund a sincere effort to help "the needy" or was it used to appease them? **Feminist:** How are women included or excluded from this message? **Historical:** What economic conditions at the time led to the need for a "milk fund"?

4. **Discussion:** Share your most relevant or interesting questions and observations in a class discussion. Listen as your classmates share their discoveries and follow up by asking questions and purposefully offering ideas and judgments.

☑ **Check Your Understanding**

Based on the information in your the graphic organizer, did your understanding of each image change after applying literary theories? How does a viewer's perspective create meaning in a given text?

11 Have students respond to the Check Your Understanding in a quickwrite.

LEVELED DIFFERENTIATED INSTRUCTION

In this activity, students may need support identifying image details or key assumptions for a literary theory.

Beginning For the OPTIC activity, support students who are at an early stage in their English language development by having them work in a group and encouraging them to use words and phrases in their primary languages as they view the images. Have each member of the group work with a partner on one step of the OPTIC strategy. Then have them **think-pair-share** their answers with the other group members

Developing Support students by providing them with copies of the **OPTIC** graphic organizer from the resources section. Have students work in pairs or small groups to take notes in the graphic organizer.

ASSESS

Discuss students' responses to the Check Your Understanding task. Their responses should show that they have an understanding of the literary theories and can articulate how theories helped them interpret the images. Make sure their answers refer to key elements of the theories and specific aspects of the images.

ADAPT

If students need additional help understanding a literary theory, have them work with partners to show how the theory focuses on different aspects of a text, image, or medium. Then have them apply that theory to a critique of a popular game, TV show, or website of their choice.

PLAN

Materials: computers with access to the Internet or print copies of dictionaries and encyclopedias

Suggested Pacing: 3 50-minute class periods

TEACH

1 Read the Learning Targets and Preview sections with your students.

2 Have students read and briefly discuss the definition of Reader-Response Criticism in the Literary Vocabulary box. Tell students they will learn more about Reader-Response Criticism after their initial reading of the poem.

3 Read aloud the Introducing the Strategy: Metacognitive Markers box and answer any questions students may have.

4 Review the As You Read tasks students will complete while reading the poem.

5 Ask a student volunteer to read the About the Author. Check students' comprehension by asking them to determine what aspect of her life may have influenced Wheatley's poetry.

TEACHER TO TEACHER

To reinforce the concept of Reader-Response Criticism, ask students if they have ever had to move to a new place that they did not choose. Invite a few students to share their experiences. Explain that these are examples of personal experiences that can impact a reader's engagement with a text.

Learning Strategies

Think-Pair-Share
TP-CASTT
Summarizing
Activating Prior Knowledge

My Notes

Learning Targets

- Analyze how two poems from different periods treat the same theme.
- Apply the Reader-Response Criticism to an analysis of a poem.

Preview

In this activity, you will read and analyze two poems. Then, you will learn about Reader-Response Criticism and revisit your analysis of the poems through this lens.

Introducing the Strategy: Metacognitive Markers

Metacognition refers to the thinking you do about your own learning. Using metacognitive markers involves marking the text with symbols to reflect the thinking you are doing as you read. After reading, you can scan the text and use your metacognitive markers to quickly find evidence when you are talking or writing about a text. Here are the markers:

- ? Use a question mark for questions you have about the text.
- ! Use an exclamation point for a reaction to what you are reading.
- * Use an asterisk for a comment about the text.

As You Read

- Use metacognitive markers to interact with the text.
- Circle unknown words and phrases. Try to determine the meaning of the words by using context clues, word parts, or a dictionary.

About the Author

Phillis Wheatley (c. 1753–1784) was age 13 when she wrote her first published poem. Born in West Africa, Wheatley was kidnapped at the age of eight and brought to Boston on a slave ship. Her life was unusual for a slave, as her owners encouraged Wheatley to read and provided her with lessons in multiple subjects. In 1773, she published *Poems on Various Subjects, Religious and Moral* and became the first African American and the third American woman to publish a book of poems. Wheatley wrote several poems to honor George Washington and visited him at his invitation in 1776. Though she was freed from slavery, Wheatley was never able to find support for her second volume of poetry.

College and Career Readiness Standards

Focus Standards:

RL.11–12.1 Cite strong and thorough textual evidence to support analysis of what the text says explicitly as well as inferences drawn from the text, including determining where the text leaves matters uncertain.

RL.11–12.5 Analyze how an author's choices concerning how to structure specific parts of a text (e.g., the choice of where to begin or end a story, the choice to provide a comedic or tragic resolution) contribute to its overall structure and meaning as well as its aesthetic impact.

L.11–12.5a Interpret figures of speech (e.g., hyperbole, paradox) in context and analyze their role in the text.

Additional Standards Addressed:

L.11–12.4c, L.11–12.4d

Poetry

On Being Brought from Africa to America

by **Phillis Wheatley**

T'was mercy brought me from my Pagan land,

Taught my **benighted** soul to understand

That there's a God, that there's a Saviour too:

Once I redemption neither sought nor knew.

5 Some view our **sable** race with scornful eye,

"Their colour is a diabolic die."

Remember, Christians, Negros, black as Cain,

May be refin'd, and join th' angelic train.

Making Observations
- What's your first impression about the theme of the poem?
- What emotions do you feel after reading the poem?

---

benighted: unenlightened

sable: black

---

6 FIRST READ: Before students read the poem, ask them to make an inference about the subject of the poem based on its title. Request a student volunteer to read the poem. As students follow along, monitor their comprehension by ensuring they are completing the As You Read tasks.

7 After reading the poem, check student comprehension by asking them to paraphrase and summarize the events of the poem and to share what they marked during their first reading. Students can refer to their summaries and mark-up to help them answer the Making Observations questions.

Scaffolding the Text-Dependent Questions

1. **The first stanza of "On Being Brought from Africa," introduces a paradox. Using evidence from the poem, describe the paradox.** What is the "Pagan Land?" How did life change when she left? L.11–12.5a, W.11–12.5

2. **What can you infer about the meaning of the word diabolic from its use in the poem? Write a definition in your own words. Verify your** definition by checking a dictionary. Are there word roots or context clues? RL.11–12.1

3. **How would you describe the tone of "On Being Brought from Africa," and does it shift? Cite specific words and phrases to support your answer.** What is the mood of the poem at the beginning? At the end? RL.11–12.5, W.11–12.5

1.3

8 Have students read the About the Author section. Ask them to explain how knowing Lazarus's background and the circumstances under which she wrote "The New Colossus" may affect how they connect with and react to the poem.

9 **FIRST READ:** Before students read the poem, have them look at the title and activate their prior knowledge about the word colossus. Have students share their ideas based on the title and what they know about the word. Request a student volunteer to read the poem. As students follow along, monitor their comprehension by ensuring they are completing the As You Read tasks.

My Notes

About the Author

Emma Lazarus (1849–1887) was born in New York City, the daughter of Jewish immigrants who came to the United States from Portugal during the time of the American Revolution. Lazarus received an extensive education at home and demonstrated the ability to analyze and write poetry at a young age. She wrote "The New Colossus" as a contribution to a fundraiser to generate money for the construction of a pedestal for the Statue of Liberty. Lazarus initially refused, but another writer convinced her to use the opportunity to express the plight of refugee immigrants. After Lazarus's death, a friend helped renew public interest in the poem. In 1903, it was inscribed on a plaque that remains on display inside the pedestal.

Poetry

The New Colossus[1]

by **Emma Lazarus**

Not like the brazen giant of Greek fame,
With conquering limbs astride from land to land;
Here at our sea-washed, sunset gates shall stand
A mighty woman with a torch, whose flame
5   Is the imprisoned lightning, and her name
Mother of Exiles. From her beacon-hand
Glows world-wide welcome; her mild eyes command
The air-bridged harbor that twice cities frame.
"Keep, ancient lands, your storied pomp" cries she
10   With silent lips. "Give me your tired, your poor,
Your huddled masses yearning to breathe free,
The wretched refuse of your teeming shore.
Send these, the homeless, tempest-tossed to me:
I lift my lamp beside the golden door!"

---

[1] **Colossus:** refers to the Colossus of Rhodes, one of the seven wonders of the ancient world.

Scaffolding the Text-Dependent Questions

4. Consider the title "The New Colossus." Consult with a dictionary and other reference materials to explain the importance of the title to the poem. How does the new Colossus compare to the original? How is the new Colossus personified? How do these qualities of the new Colossus relate to the theme of the poem? L.11–12.4c, L.11–12.4d, W.11–12.5

5. What type of verse is "The New Colossus," and how does its structure contribute to the overall effect of the poem? Read the poem aloud to better understand its structure. At which point do you notice a shift in topics? How does this shift contribute to the poem's ability to appeal to the reader's emotions? RL.11–12.5, W.11–12.5

1.3

Making Observations
- What details or images stand out to you the most?
- What questions about the theme will you ask yourself as you reread the poem?

Returning to the Text
- Reread the poems to answer these text-dependent questions.
- Write any additional questions you have about the text in your Reader/Writer Notebook.

1. The first stanza of "On Being Brought from Africa," introduces a paradox. Using evidence from the poem, describe the paradox.

   In the first stanza, Wheatley expresses gratitude for God's mercy in granting her redemption and delivering her from her "pagan land." A paradox is introduced because her enslavement in America leads to her "benighted" soul being set free in a spiritual sense.

2. What can you infer about the meaning of the word *diabolic* from its use in the poem? Write a definition in your own words. Verify your definition by checking a dictionary.

   The word *diabolic* means "evil" or "like a devil." In context, the meaning is implied by the use of the word *scornful,* the comparison to the Biblical figure of Cain, who killed his brother Abel, and the contrast with "th' angelic train."

3. How would you describe the tone of "On Being Brought from Africa," and does it shift? Cite specific words and phrases to support your answer.

   The tone of the first stanza could be interpreted as condoning slavery as a means of receiving redemption. Before coming to America, Wheatley describes her soul as "benighted" and credits "mercy" with removing her ignorance. The next stanza takes a turn, as it confronts the reader with assumptions made about the black race.

VOCABULARY

ACADEMIC
A paradox is a statement that appears to contain two contradictory or incompatible points, but upon closer examination it can reveal a hidden truth to the reader or viewer.

10 After reading the poem, check student comprehension by asking them to summarize the theme of the poem and to share what they marked during their first reading. Students can refer to their summaries and mark-up to help them answer the Making Observations questions.

11 **RETURNING TO THE TEXT:** Have students answer the text-dependent questions individually. If they have difficulty, scaffold the questions by rephrasing them or breaking them down into smaller parts. See the Scaffolding the Text-Dependent Questions boxes for suggestions.

12 Call attention to the Academic Vocabulary box. Help students understand the concept of paradox by providing clear examples, such as Hamlet's "I must be cruel, only to be kind." Other examples include Oscar Wilde's "I can resist anything but temptation" and the marketing slogan "The more you spend, the more you save." Prompt students to think of additional examples from popular culture.

13 After students have responded to the text-dependent questions, allow them to freewrite an initial interpretation of each of the poems. Ask them to mark the text to signal words or phrases that support their interpretation.

14 Read through Introducing the Strategy: **TP-CASTT**, reviewing each step to make sure students understand the meaning of the topics in the acronym and how to use them.

15 Have students **think-pair-share** to analyze each of the poems using the TP-CASTT strategy and filling in the graphic organizer. If needed, explain that diffusing is a strategy for close reading of text. Using this strategy, the reader reads a passage to identify unfamiliar words. The reader uses context clues, dictionaries, and/or thesauruses to discover the meaning of unfamiliar words. Writing notes about meaning or substituting synonyms for unfamiliar words helps the reader increase comprehension of the text.

LEVELED DIFFERENTIATED INSTRUCTION

Use the following supports to help students internalize the TP-CASTT strategy.

Beginning Support students who are at an early stage in their English language development by using a cognate bridge strategy. Add cognates that correspond to the steps in TP-CASTT to the class word wall: *título, paráfrasis, connotación, actitud, turnos, título, tema.*

Developing Have students complete a TP-CASTT analysis of a simple, well-known poem, such as "The Owl and the Pussycat" (Lear), "If" (Kipling), or "The Road Not Taken" (Frost). You may want to have copies on hand to pass out.

1.3

4. Consider the title "The New Colossus." Consult a dictionary and other reference materials to explain the connection and importance of the title to the poem.

Colossus means "a statue that is much bigger than life size," which describes the Statue of Liberty. Lazarus contrasts this modern statue with the ancient Colossus of Rhodes, built to celebrate victory in war. "The New Colossus" serves to replace the old and, in contrast to the original, she welcomes newcomers.

5. What type of verse is "The New Colossus," and how does its structure contribute to the overall effect of the poem?

The poem is a sonnet in which the first eight lines establish a contrast between the old Colossus and the new. The final six lines create an abrupt change in the poem as the Statue of Liberty becomes the narrator, welcoming the "huddled masses."

Introducing the Strategy: TP-CASTT

This reading strategy is used to analyze a poetic text by identifying and discussing each topic in the acronym: **T**itle, **P**araphrase, **C**onnotation, **A**ttitude, **S**hift, **T**itle again, and **T**heme. The strategy is a guide designed to lead you in an analysis of a literary text. It is a good idea to begin at the top and work your way down the elements. However, you will find that as you study one element, you will naturally begin to explore others. For example, a study of connotation often leads to a discussion of tone and shifts. Revisiting the title often leads to a discussion of the theme, or author's message.

Working from the Text

6. Use the **TP-CASTT** strategy to analyze the poems. Record your responses in the graphic organizer that follows. Read each poem several times, each time discussing aspects of the TP-CASTT strategy and recording your responses.

Strategy	Response
Title: Look at the title without looking at the rest of the poem. What do you think the poem will be about?	Student responses will vary.
Paraphrase: After diffusing the text, translate the most challenging lines of the poem into your own words (you may need to reread the text several times). Then briefly summarize the poem in such a way that the meaning is maintained.	Wheatley: Lines 5–6 imply that black people are seen as animals and as evil. The poem declares being brought to America a spiritual blessing and then introduces the idea that prejudice towards black people is anti-Christian. Lazarus: Lines 9–10 speak against people from other countries who have exiled their poor in favor of wealth. The poem portrays the Statue of Liberty as a strong woman who is welcoming all of those who need shelter and a home.
Connotation: Mark the text by highlighting the diction (words and phrases) used for positive effect (color 1) and/or negative effect (color 2). Then study the diction to determine a pattern and record your analysis.	Wheatley: pleasant thoughts about spiritual freedom in America: *mercy, God, Saviour, redemption* as opposed to the unpleasant reality of racism in America: *sable, scornful, diabolic, die, black as Cain*. Lazarus: positive description of the Statue of Liberty: *mighty woman, Mother of Exiles, world-wide welcome, mild eyes* in contrast to the condition of the refugees: *tired, poor, huddled masses, yearning, wretched refuse*.
Attitude (Tone): Consider the speaker's attitude in the poem. How does her attitude change from the start of the poem to its end?	Wheatley: The speaker's words first show a calm gratitude and then become forceful in speaking out against racism. Lazarus: The speaker's words move from a descriptive comparison to a personal narrative. The speaker then asserts an authoritative welcome to all who seek refuge.

ACTIVITY 1.3 continued

16 Have students share some of their responses from the chart. Ask them how easy it was to use this strategy and whether it helped them discover anything new in their analysis of the poems.

17 Pause at this point in the activity for the Check Your Understanding task. Ask students to share the line they chose in each poem and why they chose it.

1.3

Strategy	Response
Shift: Look for shifts, or changes in the poem. These shifts are meant to draw your attention, and might take the form of punctuation, transition words, stanza length, or structural changes. Identify a shift in the poem.	Wheatley: The shift of focus from the speaker's experience with religion to a claim she makes about racism happens in line 5. Lazarus: The shift of focus from a description that compares two statues to a monologue spoken by the Statue of Liberty happens in line 9.
Title: Look at the title again. How is your interpretation of it different now that you've analyzed the poem more deeply? Can you confirm or correct your initial hypotheses?	Wheatley: The title seems less simplistic than it initially did as the blending of religious freedom with enslavement creates an unexpected complexity. Lazarus: The title seems more fitting now that the comparison of "The New Colossus" to the old is clear.
Theme: Determine the author's message conveyed in the poem. Identify a theme in the poem (such as family or the human condition). Then, write a statement about the underlying theme of the poem.	Wheatley: One major theme is spiritual freedom through redemption. The underlying theme is that the same God who redeemed the speaker welcomes all people, regardless of color. Lazarus: One major theme is opportunity: overcoming adversity to find a new life. The underlying theme seems to be that such an opportunity can only transpire through the extension of sympathy and welcome.

☑ Check Your Understanding

Choose a line from each poem that illustrates a related theme found in both poems. In a few sentences, analyze the two poems' treatment of a related theme.

Reader-Response Criticism

Your personal attitudes, beliefs, and experiences influence how you derive meaning from text. Examining the way in which you understand a text involves using critical lenses. A critical lens is a way of judging or analyzing a work of literature.

Reader-Response Criticism suggests that readers' perspectives often determine their perceptions. The critical lens of Reader-Response Criticism asks you to be aware of your personal attitudes, beliefs, and experiences as you read. It focuses on the relationships among the reader, the reader's situation, and the text. The theory suggests that the process of making meaning relies not only on the text itself, but also on the qualities and motivations of the individual who is interacting with the text.

The diagram illustrates this idea:

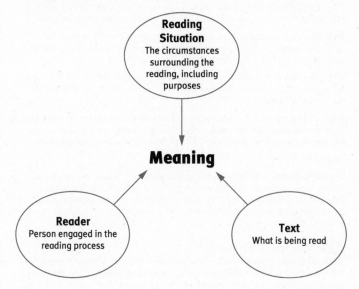

My Notes

LITERARY

Reader-Response Criticism focuses on a reader's active engagement with a piece of print or nonprint text. The reader's response to any text is shaped by the reader's own experiences, social ethics, moral values, and general views of the world.

VOCABULARY

---

18 Begin your introduction of Reader-Response Criticism by asking students to discuss what they normally read, where they read most often, and why they read. Ask whether and how their personal responses to a text are affected by where and why they read.

19 **Vocabulary Development:** Review the Literary Vocabulary with students. Ask them to work with a partner to brainstorm words to define the concept of *Reader-Response Criticism*.

20 Instruct students to read the information on Reader-Response Criticism and to mark the text to identify key ideas. Invite them to take notes on the diagram to offer another way to think about Reader-Response Criticism.

21 Next, engage students in a group discussion about the ways in which the reader, the reading situation, and the text can affect the process of making meaning.

 TEACHER TO TEACHER

If you find that your students need additional help with understanding the elements of Reader-Response Criticism, model interpreting the first two stanzas of one of the poems (or the entire poem), using the read aloud strategy, before asking volunteers to share their interpretations.

22 Ask students to read the explanations in The Elements of Reader-Response Criticism section. Suggest that they mark the text or annotate it as needed to make sure they understand each explanation.

23 Have students complete the Check Your Understanding task, either in discussion or in writing.

ASSESS

Review students' responses to the second Check Your Understanding task. Make sure they discuss the three elements of Reader-Response Criticism and demonstrate an understanding of the ways these elements may contribute to a reader's interpretation of a text. Students should be able to summarize and explain Reader-Response Criticism to a partner, for example.

ADAPT

If students need additional help writing their responses to the second Check Your Understanding task, have them work with a partner to compare and contrast their analyses of the poem. Then have them use their discussion of the text to draft individual analyses using the elements of Reader-Response Criticism.

1.3

My Notes

INDEPENDENT READING LINK

Read and Respond

Think about your independent reading text. In what ways does your personal response to the text depend on where and why you are reading the text? Consider how your own experiences and background affect your reading of the text and how someone with a different background might view it differently. Then, write a short reflection on your response in your Reader/Writer Notebook.

The Elements of Reader-Response Criticism

The Reader

Reader-Response critical theory examines the person doing the reading. In Reader-Response criticism, the reader is seen not as a passive recipient of the meaning in the text, but as an active co-creator of meaning. Any text presents gaps which the reader, through imaginative engagement with the text, completes. Over time, the responses of readers form a range of meanings ascribed to a text. Because of the centrality of the reader in the construction of meaning, reader-response criticism does not view texts as having single, fixed meanings. Instead, reader-response theorists believe a range of defensible interpretations can be produced. To apply this theory, you must examine how your own opinions, attitudes, beliefs, and background knowledge factor into your perspective.

The Reading Situation

The reading situation includes *why* you are engaged in reading, *when* you are reading, and *where* you are reading. All of these factors affect your perception.

Why: What is your purpose for reading? You may be reading a text because the subject matter interests you, your teacher assigned it, or you need to learn something in order to complete a task.

When: Perhaps a story was written hundreds of years ago, but you are reading it in the 21st century. Your perspective will differ from that of the writer and of the text's original readers.

Where: If you are reading a text written by someone from a community like yours, you may understand the text more readily or relate to the author in certain ways that you don't if you are reading a text by someone from a very different locale.

The Text

The text is defined as whatever is being read, viewed, or heard, and may include videos, audio, and websites. Textual features vary, depending on the source. For example, a textbook presents text differently from the way a magazine or a pamphlet does. Numerous other factors, from level of difficulty to the font, influence the text.

☑ Check Your Understanding

Think about your initial analysis of "On Being Brought from Africa to America" and "The New Colossus." Describe the Reader, the Reading Situation, and the Text. How did the interaction of these three elements influence your understanding and analysis of the poem? In particular, examine the way your Metacognitive Markers demonstrate your responses as a reader and illuminate the ways you constructed meaning in the text.

Applying Reader-Response Criticism

Learning Targets
- Identify poetic devices and evaluate how they contribute to the mood and meaning of a poem.
- Evaluate a poem, paying special attention to the interaction of form, sound, and wordplay.
- Evaluate how three poems from the same period treat similar themes.

Preview
In this activity, you will analyze how a poet uses sound, form, figurative language, and structure to convey meaning. After analyzing a poem in one small group, you will join another group who studied a different poem to share your analyses in a collaborative discussion.

Introducing the Strategy: QHT

QHT is a strategy for thinking about your own understanding of vocabulary words. The letters stand for **Q**uestions, **H**eard, and **T**each:

Q: words you may have seen but you are not sure about their meaning

H: words you have heard before but may not know them well

T: words you know so well you could teach them to someone else

To use QHT, think about how well you know each term and label each term with a letter.

Tools for Poets: Reviewing Poetic Devices

Poetic devices are literary techniques that authors use to strengthen and enhance their work. These devices are often used in poetry, but writers often employ these literary techniques in all types of writing. Before reading your assigned poem, review the different poetic devices listed in the following chart. Developing an understanding of these devices will help you to identify and discuss the strategic choices that a writer makes.

1. Expand your background knowledge about these poetic devices by marking each word with Q, H, or T.

Poetic Device	Q/H/T	Your Definition
alliteration		the repetition of initial consonant sounds in words that are close together
assonance		the repetition of similar vowel sounds in accented syllables, followed by different consonant sounds, in words that are close together
consonance		the repetition of final consonant sounds in stressed syllables with different vowel sounds
hyperbole		exaggeration used to suggest strong emotion or create a comic effect

Learning Strategies
Discussion Groups
Marking the Text
QHT
Think-Pair-Share

My Notes

College and Career Readiness Standards

Focus Standards:

RL.11–12.4 Determine the meaning of words and phrases as they are used in the text, including figurative and connotative meanings; analyze the impact of specific word choices on meaning and tone, including words with multiple meanings or language that is particularly fresh, engaging, or beautiful. (Include Shakespeare as well as other authors).

RL.11–12.9 Demonstrate knowledge of eighteenth-, nineteenth- and early-twentieth-century foundational works of American literature, including how two or more texts from the same period treat similar themes or topics.

ACTIVITY 1.4

PLAN

Suggested Pacing: 1 50-minute class period

TEACH

1 Read the Learning Targets and Preview sections with your students. Lead an informal discussion about the poetic devices students remember from "On Being Brought From Africa to America" or "The New Colossus" and how they affected the overall mood or feeling of the poem. Then, divide them into small discussion groups and assign one of the three poems to each group.

2 Read through the Introducing the Strategy: QHT section with students and answer any questions. Have students practice using the QHT method by writing the following poetic terms on the board for them: *onomatopoeia, rhyme, haiku, meter.* Remind students that they can use various reading strategies to help them. Have volunteers name strategies, such as using context or consulting reference materials.

3 Have students complete the Poetic Devices chart using the QHT strategy. Afterwards, by show of hands, ascertain which terms students were most and least familiar with and write them on the board. Have volunteers who labeled one or more words with a "T" practice explaining them to the class.

4 Review metaphor and personification by having a brief discussion of the definitions in the Academic Vocabulary box.

TEACHER TO TEACHER

Provide students with a list of nouns/sentence starters and have them brainstorm their own metaphors or similes for each. They might also try using personification. Afterwards, have them share their responses with the class. Possibilities include: *The sunset was…, the mountains were…, the dilapidated house was like…*

5 Preview the As You Read tasks. Suggest that students refer to the chart frequently while reading through and underlining the poem's poetic devices. If they encounter a word or line they think is using a poetic device but are unsure which device it is, have them make a note to go back to the word or phrase later.

6 Remind students to read the About the Author box for their assigned poem before reading. Have students consider how the author's background might have shaped his or her writing and perspective. Also ask students to discuss how, if at all, their response to the poem is already being formed—perhaps by the author's photograph, the bio, or the shape or length of the poem.

1.4

Poetic Device	Q/H/T	Your Definition
imagery		the verbal expression of sensory experience; descriptive language used to create word pictures
meter		a pattern of stressed and unstressed syllables in poetry
extended metaphor		a sustained comparison between two unlike things in which one thing is spoken of as if it were another
personification		a figure of speech that gives human qualities to an animal, object, or idea
rhyme scheme		a consistent pattern of rhyme throughout a poem

My Notes

2. Work with a partner to record definitions for each term. For terms you know well or have heard before, write your own definition. Then use the glossary to validate your understanding. Use a glossary to look up the terms that you have labled "T." Record a paraphrased definition for each term in the chart.

As You Read

- Underline any poetic devices that you notice in the poem.
- Circle unknown words and phrases. Try to determine the meaning of the words by using context clues, word parts, or a dictionary.

About the Author

E. E. Cummings (1894–1962) was an experimental poet whose work continues to enjoy widespread popularity. During his career, Cummings examined traditional themes such as love and childhood, but he explored these themes with innovative methods, such as incorporating typography into the poem's meaning, or using words such as *if* and *because* as nouns. Cummings's work was not at first successful, but he began to receive greater recognition in 1945 when his work was discovered and championed by a new generation of rebellious young poets who saw him as a kindred spirit. In 1950, he was awarded a fellowship by the American Academy of Poets, and later (1958) the Bollingen Prize in Poetry. By the time of his death in 1962, Cummings had published almost one thousand poems.

College and Career Readiness Standards

L.11–12.5 Demonstrate understanding of figurative language, word relationships, and nuances in word meanings.

L.11–12.5a Interpret figures of speech (e.g., hyperbole, paradox) in context and analyze their role in the text.

Additional Standards Addressed:
RL.11–12.1, RL.11–12.2, RL.11–12.5, W.11–12.9a, L.11–12.4, L.11–12.4a, SL.11–12.1

Poetry

My Notes

in just –

by **E. E. Cummings**

    in just-

    spring   when the world is mud-

    luscious the little

    lame balloonman

5 whistles   far   and wee

    and eddieandbill come

    running from marbles and

    piracies and it's

    spring

10 when the world is puddle-wonderful

    the queer

    old balloonman whistles

    far   and   wee

    and bettyandisabel come dancing=

15 from hop-scotch and jump-rope and

    it's

    spring

    and

       the

20   goat-footed

    balloonMan   whistles

    far

    and

    wee

Making Observations

- What imagery catches your attention?
- Which of the poet's structural or stylistic choices stand out to you?

7 **FIRST READ:** Have students read their assigned poem in small groups or **Think-Pair-Share.** As students are reading, move about the classroom to monitor their progress. Be sure they are engaged with the texts, underlining poetic devices, and circling difficult words. Remind students to check the glossed words in the sidebars.

Scaffolding the Text-Dependent Questions

3. What happens when the "balloonman whistles far and wee"? Paraphrase what happens in lines 6–9. Explain the meaning in your own words. RL.11–12.4

4. What can you infer from details in the poem about how the author feels about springtime? Use specific evidence from the poem to support your answer. What descriptive words does the author use in lines 10–19? What can you infer from those words? RL.11–12.1, RL.11–12.5

5. What effect do the short line lengths (lines 16–19 and 22–24) have on the sound of the poem? Imagine how the poem might read with longer lines. Would the pace be faster or slower? Would it feel smoother or more choppy? RL.11–12.5

8 When students have finished, have them work together to answer the Making Observations questions for their poem.

1.4

My Notes

_____
_____
_____
_____
_____
_____
_____
_____
_____
_____
_____
_____
_____
_____
_____
_____
_____
_____
_____
_____
_____
_____
_____
_____

About the Author

Sylvia Plath (1932–1963) captured the intensity of her turbulent life in an autobiographical novel and personal, revealing poetry. An accomplished scholar and writer, Plath won many awards as a young woman, including a scholarship to Smith College and a Fulbright fellowship to Newnham College in Cambridge University. In 1956, she married poet Ted Hughes.

As their marriage dissolved, Plath produced poems of striking pain and power. These poems were published in the collection *Ariel* (1965), which appeared after her suicide in 1963.

Poetry

Mushrooms

by **Sylvia Plath**

Overnight, very

Whitely, discreetly,

Very quietly

Our toes, our noses

5   Take hold on the loam,

Acquire the air.

Nobody sees us,

Stops us, betrays us;

The small grains make room.

10 Soft fists insist on

Heaving the needles,

The leafy bedding,

Even the paving.

Our hammers, our rams,

15 Earless and eyeless,

Perfectly voiceless,

Widen the crannies,

Shoulder through holes. We

Diet on water,

discreetly: without attracting attention
loam: soil that plants thrive in
crannies: cracks

Scaffolding the Text-Dependent Questions

6. How does Cummings's use of line breaks and spacing contribute to the playful mood of the poem? Can you identify conscious patterns? How did you feel when you first glanced at the poem? Did the arrangement of the words cause you to "hear" the poem differently in your head? How did you feel about the pattern of the lines after several readings? RL.11–12.2, RL.11–12.5

7. What human characteristics does Plath attribute to the mushrooms? What effect does her use of personification have on the reader's understanding of the mushrooms? Does the personification suggest that the mushrooms are a metaphor for something else? RL.11–12.5

20 On crumbs of shadow,

Bland-mannered, asking

Little or nothing.

So many of us!

So many of us!

25 We are shelves, we are

Tables, we are meek,

We are edible.

Nudgers and shovers

In spite of ourselves.

30 Our kind multiplies:

We shall by morning

Inherit the earth.

Our foot's in the door.

My Notes

Making Observations
- What imagery catches your attention?
- Which of the poet's structural or stylistic choices stand out to you?

Scaffolding the Text-Dependent Questions

8. How does the word "whitely" in line 2 add to the description of the mushrooms' growing? Consider the word's literal meaning. What nonliteral meanings could it have? RL.11–12.2, RL.11–12.5

9. Identify the central metaphor in the poem. What idea is the metaphor conveying? Use evidence to support your interpretation. What features of the mushrooms does Plath focus on? How does personification add to the feeling she's trying to convey? RL.11–12.2, RL.11–12.5

10. Which poetic devices does Plath employ and how do they affect your understanding of the poem? Which poetic devices can you identify in the poem? RL.11–12.2, RL.11–12.5

11. What is Plath's key idea in this poem? What language does she use to convey this to her audience? What phrase or image seems most essential and why? RL.11–12.2, RL.11–12.5

My Notes

Anne Sexton (1928–1974) pursued poetry in her adult life as a means of coping with depression. Sexton's work reflects the emotional turmoil that filled her life, and she often wrote about controversial and difficult subjects. Her writing was known for its brilliant imagery. A very popular poet in her lifetime, Sexton won numerous honors and awards. Despite launching a successful writing career and winning the Pulitzer Prize for Poetry in 1967, Sexton eventually lost her battle with mental illness and committed suicide.

Poetry

Water

by **Anne Sexton**

We are fishermen in a flat scene.

All day long we are in love with water.

The fish are naked.

The fish are always awake.

5 They are the color of old spoons

and caramels.

The sun reaches down

but the floor is not in sight.

Only the rocks are white and green.

10 Who knows what goes on in the halls below?

Making Observations
- What imagery catches your attention?
- Which of the poet's structural or stylistic choices stand out to you?

Scaffolding the Text-Dependent Questions

12. Based on the details from the poem, what do you think the water represents? How does Sexton refer to water in the first and second lines? In what way is water alluded to in the last line? Think about how these direct or implied descriptions of water are connected. RL.11–12.2, W.11–12.5

13. Analyze the use of personification in the poem, paying special attention to line 7. What effect does the poet create through the use of this figurative language? Personification lends human characteristics to objects. What object does Sexton personify? What human action does this object take? How does this action impact the tone of the poem? RL.11–12.5, W.11–12.5

Returning to the Text

- Reread your assigned poem to answer these text-dependent questions.
- Write any additional questions you have about the poem in your Reader/Writer Notebook.

"in just—"

3. What happens when the "balloonman whistles far and wee"?

   The children stop playing their games and come to see him.

4. What can you infer about how the speaker feels about springtime? Use specific evidence from the poem to support your answer.

   Cummings uses original words such as "mud-luscious" (lines 2 and 3) and "puddle-wonderful" (line 10) to suggest a child's sense of delight at being outdoors on a spring day. The details of the children playing marbles and hopscotch help create a tone of playful delight.

5. What effect do the short line lengths (lines 16–19 and 22–24) have on the sound of the poem?

   They make the end of the poem sound choppy. The lines reflect the action of jumping rope or playing hopscotch. Each line is a small jump to the next, which gives the poem a playful rhythm.

6. How does Cummings's use of line breaks and spacing contribute to the mood of the poem? Can you identify conscious patterns?

   Cummings uses line breaks and arrangement of words in a very deliberate way. The use of line breaks and spacing conveys certain ideas—for example, writing "bettyandisabel" as one word suggests that the two girls are inseparable, and the line breaks create playful patterns that echo the pattern of children skipping and jumping.

Scaffolding the Text-Dependent Questions

14. Consider the lines, "They are the color of old spoons/and caramels." Why do you think Sexton used these words to describe the fish? What effect does it have on you as a reader? Do the words "old spoons" and "caramels" strike you as an unusual way to describe fish? What imagery do these words create? What do you associate with each of the words?
RL.11–12.4, L.11–12.5, W.11–12.5

15. What is the significance of the line "All day long we are in love with water" within the context of the rest of the poem? Use text evidence to support your interpretation. What is the central theme of the poem? Using the theme as context, why is the line important? What other line in the poem also supports the theme?
RL.11–12.1, RL.11–12.4, W.11–12.5

ACTIVITY 1.4 continued

9 **RETURNING TO THE TEXT:** Have students answer the text-dependent questions in their small groups. Remind them to use text evidence in their responses.

10 Move from group to group and listen in as students answer the text-dependent questions. If they have difficulty, scaffold the questions by rephrasing them or breaking them down into smaller parts. See the Scaffolding the Text-Dependent Questions boxes for suggestions.

"Mushrooms"

7. What human characteristics does Plath attribute to the mushrooms? What effect does her use of personification have on the reader's understanding of the mushrooms?

   The mushrooms in the poem have human physical features, such as toes, noses, fists, and feet. They take human actions when they heave the needles, "diet on water," ask for "little or nothing," and plan to "inherit the earth." This personification causes readers to imagine the mushrooms as an army that is poised to quietly take over the world.

8. How does the word "whitely" in line 2 add to the description of the mushrooms' growing?

   It creates an off rhyme with "overnight" and "quietly," and it adds a literal description of the mushrooms' appearance. It may also suggest that the mushrooms have a ghostlike quality.

9. Identify the central metaphor in the poem. What idea is the metaphor conveying? Use evidence to support your interpretation

   The mushrooms themselves are the central metaphor, representing the idea of the collective power of women. The words "discreetly," and "bland-mannered," point to stereotypical views of women as well-mannered and docile, but the poem shows how they have both unstoppable determination and power in numbers.

10. Which poetic devices does Plath employ and how do they affect your understanding of the poem? Use text evidence to support your response.

    Plath uses repetition, assonance, consonance, and alliteration throughout the poem; for example, Plath uses assonance in "soft fists insist," and "our toes, our noses" and repetition of the "-ly" sound in the first stanza ("whitely," "very quietly"). The poem "feels" like it rhymes even though it doesn't. The slow rhythm suggests a collective voice.

11. What is Plath's key idea in this poem? What languge does she use to convey this to her audience?

    Plath uses specific language to suggest the meek will prevail; for example, "discreetly/very quietly," "nobody sees us," and "voiceless." The "takeover" is gradual; the mushrooms slowly increase in strength and numbers. "Soft fists," become "hammers and rams," and finally "our foot's in the door."

"Water"

12. Based on details from the poem, what do you think the water represents?

The water represents what we do not know and perhaps do not want to know. Sexton opens

the poem saying "We are fishermen in a flat scene," which creates an image of people sitting

on the surface of life. This implies that people go through life unaware of what they do not

know and unaware of what could be happening beyond the obvious.

13. Analyze the use of personification in the poem, paying attention to line 7. What effect does the poet create through the use of this figurative language?

Sexton uses personification when describing how the sun "reaches down." There is a sense of

the sun attempting to reach down and rescue someone but not quite being able to reach them

as shown in the words, "but the floor is not in sight." This creates a tone of hopelessness.

14. Consider the lines, "They are the color of old spoons/ and caramels." Why do you think Sexton used these words to describe the fish? What effect does it have on you as a reader?

These lines create surprising and arresting imagery. Sexton compares the fish to two objects

that we would not normally use to describe fish. "Old spoons" and "caramels" create a

nostalgic, almost bittersweet feeling of the past. The caramels suggest a sweetness that does

not last.

15. What is the significance of the line "All day long we are in love with water" within the context of the rest of the poem? Use text evidence to support your interpretation.

This line captures the central theme of the poem: people live their lives "in love" with what

they think they know. The phrase "fishermen in a flat scene" supports this. People are

content to go through life only seeing the surface, not going deeper. This interpretation is also

supported by the last line, "Who knows what goes on in the halls below?"

ACTIVITY 1.4 continued

LEVELED DIFFERENTIATED INSTRUCTION

Many students will benefit from additional activities to support and extend their understanding of critical frameworks.

Expanding Have students choose one of the other critical lenses covered earlier in the unit and apply it as a lens to one of the three poems. Ask them to write a short interpretation of the poem using this theory.

Extend Have students conduct research into one of the three poets and choose another poem of theirs that they like. Then ask them to use Reader-Response Criticism to analyze the poem and write a short summary of their analysis.

TEACHER TO TEACHER

This introduction to Reader-Response Criticism uses poetry because, in many cases, students have preconceived ideas of when, how, and why to read poetry. As students continue through the unit, consider starting discussions with a question that reminds students of the aspects of Reader-Response that affect their perceptions and interpretive efforts. What do they bring to the experience of reading the text?

11 Discuss the Auden quote in student step 16. Use ideas discovered in the quote to establish the notion that there can be more than one way to read a poem.

12 In preparation for their group discussion, have students consider their poem from the perspective of Reader-Response Criticism.

13 Have the small groups discuss the poem and try to come to a consensus about its meaning, comparing their responses to those of their peers. If there are conflicting interpretations, encourage them to look back at the poem to see if one interpretation is better supported by the text.

14 Use a jigsaw strategy to reconfigure the groups so that each of the poems is represented in all the groups. Ask students to share the poem from their earlier group and present an interpretation of it through the lens of Reader-Response Criticism.

15 Have students compare the use of poetic devices in all three poems.

16 Have students complete the Check Your Understanding independently and then discuss their responses in these new groups.

ASSESS

Review students' responses to the Check Your Understanding task. Students should be able to articulate their initial response to the poem as well as their new interpretation. They should use at least one piece of text evidence from the poem to support their response.

ADAPT

If students need additional help, provide them with sentence frames, such as: *I originally thought the poem was about _____, because _____. In our discussion, [classmate] mentioned that _____. This made me change my mind, because _____, and now I think that _____.*

My Notes

Working from the Text

16. Reflect on this statement by W. H. Auden, and then discuss it with a partner. How does it apply to Reader-Response Criticism?

   "What a poem means is the outcome of a dialogue between the words on the page and the person who happens to be reading it; that is to say, its meaning varies from person to person."

17. In preparation for a group discussion, revisit the poem you worked with closely and analyze it from the perspective of Reader-Response Criticism. Write a short, interpretive response.

   • How do your experiences, attitudes, and values as the reader contribute to your understanding of the text?

   • What elements of the text itself affect your perception of the poem's meaning?

   • How did the reading situation affect your interpretation?

18. Now that you have used Reader-Response Criticism, share your interpretation of the poem with your group. To what extent do you and your peers agree on an interpretation of the poem?

19. How does the poet use poetic devices and precise language to achieve a specific effect? Compare the poetic style of Cummings and Plath to Sexton. Discuss the choices that the poet made to convey a specific message to his or her audience. Refer to the list of poetic devices at the beginning of the activity as needed.

20. Compare and contrast how all three poets treat nature as a theme in the poems you have studied.

☑ Check Your Understanding

How did your interpretation of the poem change after considering the poet's deliberate word choice?

Creating Meaning

Learning Targets
- Analyze the way a poet uses imagery and diction to create particular effects.
- Evaluate and critique how an author uses language to convey a sensory experience to readers.

Preview
In this activity, you will read a poem before evaluating and critiquing the poet's use of imagery, sensory details, and diction. Then you will write a literary analysis explaining how the poet's language choices contribute to the poem's effect.

As You Read
- Underline any memories the author describes that prompt you to create mental images.
- Circle unknown words and phrases. Try to determine the meaning of words by using context clues, word parts, or a dictionary.

Poetry

I Remember

by **Edward Montez**

from **Calafia: The California Poetry Project**
Ishmael Reed, Project Director

I remember the scent of acorn soup cooking and deer meat frying in quiet evenings of summer.

And shivering under thin blankets in winter and watching the wall paper dance to the force of the winter winds outside.

5   I remember the cry of an owl in the night and I knew it was an ominous warning, a cry of death.

I remember running in the dust behind the medicine truck when it came to the reservation, lifesavers was a free treat.
And grandpa sitting in his favorite resting chair under his favorite
10 shade tree with his dog "Oly" by his side.

I remember running naked and screaming with my aunt in hot pursuit, a stick in her hand, she always caught me.

And every summer we would swim in the river and let the sun bake us until we were a shade less than purple, basking on the riverbank,
15 undisturbed, at peace.

Learning Strategies
Brainstorming
Discussion
Rereading
Think-Pair-Share

INDEPENDENT READING LINK
Read and Connect

Select a passage from your independent reading that contains strong imagery or particularly effective diction. Which words or phrases stand out? Why do you think the author chose to use those specific words or phrases to convey his or her message? Write a paragraph in which you evaluate the author's language choices.

My Notes

PLAN

Suggested Pacing: 1 50-minute class period

TEACH

1 Read the Learning Targets and Preview with your students. If needed, help students define the terms *imagery*, *sensory language*, *and diction*. Then **discuss** their purpose and function in writing.

➤ TEACHER TO TEACHER

To provide further support for understanding imagery and sensory language, have students review their assigned poem from Activity 1.4. Give them time to underline or highlight any lines of the poem that use imagery or sensory language.

2 Preview the As You Read tasks. Engage students in a discussion of mental images. Lead them to see that they constantly create mental images when reading. Ask them how they can pay more attention to these images, and then prompt them to write down details of their mental images as they read the poem.

3 FIRST READ: Ask a student to read the poem aloud while the others read along silently. As students are reading, monitor their progress. Be sure they are engaged with the text. In addition to the As You Read tasks, you might have students mark any imagery or sensory language they notice in the poem.

College and Career Readiness Standards

Focus Standards:

RL.11–12.1 Cite strong and thorough textual evidence to support analysis of what the text says explicitly as well as inferences drawn from the text, including determining where the text leaves matters uncertain.

RL.11–12.3 Analyze the impact of the author's choices regarding how to develop and relate elements of a story or drama (e.g., where a

story is set, how the action is ordered, how the characters are introduced and developed).

RL.11–12.5 Analyze how an author's choices concerning how to structure specific parts of a text (e.g., the choice of where to begin or end a story, the choice to provide a comedic or tragic resolution) contribute to its overall structure and meaning as well as its aesthetic impact.

4 After students are finished reading, assess their comprehension by posing the Making Observations questions. Encourage students to look at the notes they made on their mental images to guide their responses. If their comprehension falters and if time allows, consider choosing another volunteer to read the poem aloud a second time.

1.5

My Notes

And I remember grandma toiling in the bean fields while I played with my army truck on the fender of a "49" Plymouth.

I remember going to the movies in town on Saturday nights with fifty cents in my pocket, thirty-five cents for the ticket and the rest
20 was mine.

Eating popcorn and drinking water from a discarded coke cup and rooting for the Indians to win, and they never did, but that was yesterday.

Making Observations
• What sights, smells, or sounds do you notice in this poem?
• How would you describe the speaker's childhood?

College and Career Readiness Standards

L.11–12.4 Determine or clarify the meaning of unknown and multiple-meaning words and phrases based on grades 11–12 reading and content, choosing flexibly from a range of strategies.

W.11–12.3d Use precise words and phrases, telling details, and sensory language to convey a vivid picture of the experiences, events, setting, and/or characters.

W.11–12.5 Develop and strengthen writing as needed by planning, revising, editing, rewriting, or trying a new approach, focusing on addressing what is most significant for a specific purpose and audience.

Additional Standards Addressed:
RL.11–12.2, L.11–12.2, W.11–12.2b

Returning to the Text

- Reread the poem to answer these text-dependent questions.
- Write any additional questions you have about the text in your Reader/Writer Notebook.

1. **What phrase repeats at the beginning of most stanzas? Why do you think the poet chooses to repeat this phrase?**

   The poet repeats the phrase "I remember" at the beginning of most stanzas to make a connection to the title and to emphasize that each detail is a distinct memory from childhood. In doing so, he immerses the reader in a montage of childhood memories.

2. **How does the poet include the reader in his memory?**

   Montez uses very precise language and specific wording to evoke the world of his childhood as vividly as possible. Montez also uses sensory language, referring to smells, sounds, sights, and tactile experiences He does this in order to immerse readers in the world of his childhood, as if they were there.

3. **How does the poet's diction affect your understanding of the memories described?**

   The personal voice of the poem and straightforward diction feel authentic; the language avoids drawing attention to itself, allowing the reader to relate more easily to the people and places depicted in the poem.

4. **How does the poem end? What details from earlier in the poem help the reader make meaning from the final stanza?**

   The poem ends with a bittersweet memory. The reference to "the Indians" in the final stanza connects to "acorn soup" (line 1) and "the reservation" (line 8). These details suggest the speaker's childhood experiences took place on a reservation, where life may have been joyful and challenging.

Working from the Text

5. Writers often use precise details and diction to appeal to the reader. Use your annotations to evaluate the details Montez includes in his poem. As you complete the graphic organizer, focus on how the poet uses specific imagery, details, and diction to retell a childhood memory.

My Notes

> **LITERARY**
> **VOCABULARY**
>
> Diction is the writer's choice of words. Writers make stylistic choices about which words to use to convey a particular voice and tone.

ACTIVITY 1.5 continued

5 Vocabulary Development: Review the Literary Vocabulary with students. Ask them to work with a partner to brainstorm words to define the term *diction*.

6 RETURNING TO THE TEXT: Have students answer the text-dependent questions individually. If they have difficulty, scaffold the questions by rephrasing them or breaking them down into smaller parts. See the Scaffolding the Text-Dependent Questions box for suggestions.

7 Direct students to the Working from the Text section and model for them how to fill in the first row of the graphic organizer. Then, have them complete the rest of the chart on their own. Invite students to **think-pair-share** responses.

Scaffolding the Text-Dependent Questions

1. What phrase repeats at the beginning of most stanzas? Why do you think the poet chooses to repeat this phrase? What effect does this phrase have on you as a reader? RL.11–12.5

2. How does the poet include the reader in his memory? Name two or three memories the author describes. How does he make them come alive for you? What makes them easy for you to imagine? RL.11–12.1, RL.11–12.5

3. How does the poet's diction affect your understanding of the memories described? What methods does the author use to convey a sense of authenticity? How does the language engage the reader? What kind of text evidence can you find to support this idea? RL.11–12.4

8 Revisit the concepts of *detail* and *diction* as they contribute to imagery. Use students' responses on the graphic organizer to conduct an analysis of Montez's use of detail and diction to convey his perception of childhood. Model this process initially, and then direct students to work in small groups. Afterward, lead students in a discussion about how language conveys meaning and advances ideas in texts.

9 Read aloud the questions posed in student step 6. If necessary, reread the poem for students. Allow students time to answer the questions with a partner. Then engage in a class discussion to examine how Montez's use of imagery, detail, and diction contributes to voice and point of view. Use these questions to prompt students' thinking:

- How does point of view, the lens through which the narrator is presenting the information, affect the reader's interpretation of the events?
- What is the writer's tone? How is it influenced by diction, imagery, detail, and point of view?

	Example from the Text (Underline key words and phrases.)	What is the effect of word choice in this line?	Replace one or more of the key words/phrases. How does the line's meaning or effect change?
Visual Imagery (sight)	"And I remember grandma toiling in the bean fields while I played with my army truck on the fender of a '49' Plymouth" (lines 16–17)	The description helps the reader picture an older woman hard at work on a farm while a child amuses himself with toys. The year and make of the truck convey that the memory is from a long time ago	"And I remember grandma basking in the bean fields while I played with my army truck on the fender of a pickup." Basking does not carry the same sense of challenge that *toiling* does. The word *pickup* is less precise than *"49" Plymouth*.
Auditory Imagery (sound)	"I remember the cry of an owl in the night..." (line 5)	The word *cry* conveys a sense of urgency or fear.	"I remember the hoot of an owl in the night..." The word *hoot* sounds similar to the actual sound an owl makes, but it carries a more neutral connotation than the word *cry*.
Tactile Imagery (touch)	"And shivering under thin blankets in winter and watching the wall paper dance to the force of the winter winds outside." (lines 3–4)	These words describe the experience of being very cold when trying to sleep. Readers may be able to empathize with the speaker's discomfort.	"And snuggling under heavy blankets in winter and watching the wall paper dance to the force of the winter breeze outside." This version conveys a cozy, comfortable experience rather than the cold and uncomfortable experience in the original line.
Olfactory / Gustatory Imagery (smell/taste)	"I remember the scent of acorn soup cooking and deer meat frying..." (line 1)	The foods the poet chooses to include are specific to a particular place and may not be familiar to many readers. The word *scent* has a positive connotation, implying that these smells were good.	"I remember the stench of chicken soup cooking and pancakes frying." *Stench* has a negative connotation, implying a bad smell. Chicken soup and pancakes are typical to many households, and therefore do not help tie the experience to a specific location.

Scaffolding the Text-Dependent Questions

4. How does the poem end? What details from earlier in the poem help the reader make meaning from the final stanza? What parallels or contrasts stand out in comparing the early part of the poem with the ending? RL.11–12.1, RL.11–12.4

Evaluating and Critiquing Author's Craft

6. Now that you have evaluated some of the key elements of the poem, evaluate the poet's use of language. Use the following questions to guide your discussion with a partner.

   • Which lines might evoke an emotional response in readers?

   • Which lines illuminate a theme found in the poem?

   • How effective is the poet's diction in helping the reader understand the speaker's memories?

7. **Quickwrite:** Do you think Montez's use of imagery, specific details and diction is effective? Use specific evidence from the text to support your commentary.

☑ Check Your Understanding

Think about Edward Montez's poem "I Remember" and write a new response to the unit Essential Question: Why do writers make particular choices when composing a text?

Writing Prompt: Informational

Revisit any of the poems you have read so far in this unit. Write a paragraph explaining how the poet purposefully uses language in the poem to convey meaning or to create a specific effect on the reader. Be sure to:

• Describe key genre characteristics such as precise language, structural elements, and the use of poetic devices.

• Incorporate examples from a poem read in this unit.

• Use academic vocabulary and standard English capitalization, punctuation, and spelling.

My Notes

ACTIVITY 1.5 continued

10 As students complete the quickwrite, circulate through the room to make sure they understand imagery and diction. If they are having trouble answering the question, point out an example of diction and ask the student to rewrite the line so it has a more formal tone.

11 Have students **think-pair-share** responses to the Check Your Understanding task.

12 For the writing prompt, instruct students to revisit one poem and focus on how it uses language to show meaning and create effects.

ASSESS

Students' paragraphs for the writing prompt should show that they understand how characteristics of poetry, such as sensory language, careful use of diction, and structure, are used in the poem to create meaning and effect. Look for examples and explanations of how specific poetic devices are used. Paragraphs should use academic vocabulary and conform to standard English conventions for capitalization, punctuation, and spelling.

ADAPT

If students need additional help making connections between the poetic elements and their effects on meaning and tone, consider rereading the Montez poem, this time removing or muting one or two specific techniques. Then ask students to comment on the difference that the images, diction, and details make in the effect of the lines on the reader.

✍ WRITING PROMPT: INFORMATIONAL

The following standards are addressed in the writing prompt:

• RL.11–12.6
• W.11–12.2
• W.11–12.4
• L.11–12.2

PLAN

Suggested Pacing: 1 50-minute class period

TEACH

1 Read through the Learning Targets and Preview with students, and go over definitions of the terms *figurative language*, *literary devices*, and *poetic form*. Using the poems in previous activities, engage students in a brief discussion of examples of each term.

2 **Vocabulary Development:** Direct students to the Vocabulary entry in the sidebar. Discuss the meaning of *allegory* and ask students what they think an "extended metaphor" is. Elicit responses and discussion, and then invite students to offer examples of allegories from literature and film.

3 Have students read the About the Author and make notes on what they think are the most significant aspects of Blake's bio to consider when reading his poetry.

➤ TEACHER TO TEACHER

Use the Word Connections features throughout the student book to help students identify and internalize patterns in the formation of English words. Model correct pronunciations, or have students listen to recorded pronunciations online. Have students listen to and practice saying the words, and encourage them to use newly acquired words in their spoken discussions and in written products to reinforce meaning and vocabulary attainment. Add words frequently to the class Word Wall to provide a visual reminder.

4 Have students skim the As You Read section. Ask students to restate each bullet in their own words to ensure comprehension.

Learning Strategies

Brainstorming
Discussion Groups

WORD CONNECTIONS

Etymology

The word allegory comes from the Greek *allegoria*, which literally means "a speaking about something else." In literature, allegory describes a type of extended metaphor in which authors represent complex or abstract ideas about the real world through characters, events, or other elements. George Orwell's 1945 novel *Animal Farm* is among the most well-known examples of allegory in literature. The story, which focuses on a group of animals who overthrow their human farm owners, serves as a sharp commentary on the rise of communism under Josef Stalin.

My Notes

Learning Targets

• Analyze and evaluate the effects of literary devices and form in an allegorical poem.
• Write an original poem that includes figurative language, literary devices, and a distinct poetic form to achieve a desired effect.

Preview

In this activity, you will move from analyzing how an author crafts a poem to writing your own poem. After reading a poem and analyzing the author's use of figurative language, structure, and punctuation, you will research and discuss poetic forms with a partner. Then you will strategically incorporate various literary elements to achieve a desired effect in your own writing.

As You Read

• Highlight descriptive language the author uses.
• Circle unknown words and phrases. Try to determine the meaning of the words by using context clues, word parts, or a dictionary.

About the Author

William Blake (1757–1827) was among the earliest Romantic poets in mid 18th-century England. Blake and the other Romantics wrote with an emphasis on human feelings and emotions, as well as with a deeply felt concern about the effects of technology and industrialization on the human spirit and human interactions. Blake incorporates into his poems his own visions of God and the supernatural realm, but they often return to common Romantic themes: the plight of the innocent in danger and despair and the inherent alienation of the human condition. These themes are especially present in his *Songs of Experience* (1794), which includes the poem "A Poison Tree." That volume was later combined with its predecessor, *Songs of Innocence* (1789), and given the subtitle *Shewing the Two Contrary States of the Human Soul*.

College and Career Readiness Standards

Focus Standards:

RL.11–12.6 Analyze a case in which grasping a point of view requires distinguishing what is directly stated in a text from what is really meant.

L.11–12.5. Demonstrate understanding of figurative language, word relationships, and nuances in word meanings.

W.11–12.3d Use precise words and phrases, telling details, and sensory language to convey a vivid picture of the experiences, events, setting, and/or characters.

Poetry

A Poison Tree

by **William Blake**

I was angry with my friend;
I told my wrath, my wrath did end.
I was angry with my foe:
I told it not, my wrath did grow.

5 And I waterd it in fears,
Night & morning with my tears:
And I sunned it with smiles,
And with soft deceitful wiles.

And it grew both day and night.
10 Till it bore an apple bright.
And my foe beheld it shine,
And he knew that it was mine.

And into my garden stole,
When the night had veild the pole;
15 In the morning glad I see;
My foe outstretched beneath the tree.

Making Observations
• What happens to the speaker's foe?
• What imagery stands out to you in this poem?

wiles: tricks or lies

5 **FIRST READ:** As they read "A Poison Tree" individually, circulate to make sure students are engaging with the poem and annotating it as they go.

6 Engage students in a discussion using the Making Observations bullet points as a guide. Have them write down at least one image, an emotion, and a significant word or two that stayed with them. Have students share their observations with a partner.

College and Career Readiness Standards

W.11–12.10 Write routinely over extended time frames (time for research, reflection, and revision) and shorter time frames (a single sitting or a day or two) for a range of tasks, purposes, and audiences.

Additional Standards Addressed:

RL.11–12.2, RL.11–12.5, L.11–12.6

7 **RETURNING TO THE TEXT:** Have students answer the text-dependent questions in pairs. If they have difficulty, scaffold the questions by rephrasing them or breaking them down into smaller parts. See the Scaffolding the Text-Dependent Questions boxes for suggestions.

8 Have students work in pairs to fill in the Working from the Text graphic organizer.

TEACHER TO TEACHER

Read aloud or print and distribute copies of several short fables, such as "The Tortoise and the Hare," "The Grasshopper and the Ant," "The Fox and the Grapes," etc. Have students work in small groups to think-pair-share reactions to the fables and engage them in a discussion of what the animals in the stories symbolize. How are the tales allegories?

9 Have students work in pairs or in small groups to respond to the On the Spot Research questions. You may want to assign one or two poetic forms to each group or pair. Before they begin, have some suggestions on hand for websites where they can find appropriate information. Circulate the room and help students as needed.

10 Once they've completed their research, have each group or pair share their information with the class. Have one student from each group read a short excerpt (perhaps one verse, or 4–5 lines) of the poem they found to demonstrate the rhyme scheme or meter.

11 Engage the class in a discussion of the forms. Ask which one they like best and which one they like least. Which one do they think would be easiest to try their hand at writing? Which one do they think would be the most difficult?

12 Before they respond to student step 7 and the writing prompt, have students spend a few minutes **brainstorming** a childhood memory. Ask them to freewrite for five minutes, then read over their writing and highlight the most interesting or unusual images, words, or phrases.

1.6

Returning to the Text
- Reread the poem to answer these text-dependent questions.
- Write any additional questions you have about the text in your Reader/Writer Notebook.

1. What message is Blake trying to convey to the reader?

The author's message seems to be that holding in anger will fester, becoming, over time, literally toxic. Blake uses the extended metaphor about plant life to convey this message. This is most evident in the third stanza, where his wrath "grew both day and night./ Till it bore an apple bright."

2. What causes the speaker's wrath to grow? Cite specific details from the text to support your response.

In the first stanza the speaker reveals "I was angry with my foe:/ I told it not, my wrath did grow." Eventually the speaker is consumed "Night & morning" with his emotions and his anger continuing to fester and grow.

3. How does the rhyme scheme affect the meaning of the poem?

The rhyme scheme consists of simple couplets that give the poem an upbeat rhythm similar to a nursery-rhyme. Blake might have used simplistic, rhythmic language to underscore that anger is a basic human emotion.

4. How does the author develop a moral lesson in this poem?

He uses allusions to develop an allegorical poem. The garden in the fourth stanza refers to the biblical Garden of Eden. As the speaker presents a shining poison apple to a foe, he represents the deceitful serpent that tempts Adam and Eve. These allusions and the extended metaphor of a toxic plant teach the reader the negative effects of suppressed anger.

Scaffolding the Text-Dependent Questions

1. What message is Blake trying to convey to the reader? Is there a message that is implied rather than stated directly? Is the poet's message clear or vague? RL.11–12.2, RL.11–12.6

2. What causes the speaker's wrath to grow? Cite specific details from the text to support your response. How does the word choice help convey the message? How might you paraphrase these lines in modern language? RL.11–12.1

3. How does the rhyme scheme affect the meaning of the poem? What one word would you use to describe the feeling the poem gives you? Do you think the speaker is a good person? Do you think he feels regret? RL.11–12.2, RL.11–12.6

4. How does the author develop a moral lesson in this poem? Do you think the poet thinks anger is positive or negative? RL.11–12.5, L.11–12.5

1.6

Working from the Text

5. Analyze the effect of various elements in the poem using the chart that follows:

Element	Quotation	Effect
rhyme		
word choice		
repetition		
punctuation		

On the Spot Research

6. With your group, use the following questions to conduct research on one of the following poetic forms: *villanelle, sonnet, ode, haiku, pantoum, concrete poem, prose poem, ballad, limerick.* Jot down notes about the form you have selected.

   • What do you notice about the form?
   • What is the rhyme scheme? For example: *aabb, abcabc, abad.*
   • Which syllables are stressed and unstressed?
   • What mood or feeling does the form typically create?
   • What is a well-known example of a poem that uses this form?
   • What poets are most associated with the form?

7. With a partner, discuss how you would use your respective poetic forms to write about a childhood memory. Spend a few minutes brainstorming ideas for an original poem using either of the forms. As you brainstorm ideas, consider the purpose of your poem:

   • Will it tell a story, teach a lesson, or focus on a single image, such as a scene from nature?
   • Will the tone be playful, melancholy, or reflective?

   After brainstorming, write down any interesting words or images you may want to incorporate into your poem.

☑ Check Your Understanding

What choices does a writer consider when composing a poem? How can diction, punctuation, and rhythm have a specific effect on the reader?

📝 Writing Prompt: Literary

Select one of the poetic forms you researched and discussed. Write an original poem using elements from this form. Be sure to:

• Consider the effect you wish your poem to have on the reader and its overall message.
• Use inventive diction, original language.
• Make appropriate use of tone and voice.
• Use sound, structure, and rhythm to enhance meaning.

 WRITING PROMPT: LITERARY

The following standards are addressed in the writing prompt:
• W.11–12.4   • L.11–12.3
• W.11–12.9   • L.11–12.6

ACTIVITY 1.6 continued

13 Pair students (if you haven't done so already) and have them respond to student step 7.

14 While students are writing their poems, have them refer frequently to the checklist in the writing prompt box.

LEVELED DIFFERENTIATED INSTRUCTION

Consider differentiating instruction to support or challenge students as they write poems in this activity.

Developing Have students use the **Web Organizer** to record ideas while brainstorming. Encourage them to jot down symbols or quick drawings when brainstorming, and then to turn to a dictionary or online translator to help them find precise English vocabulary to use as imagery in their poems.

Extend Have students who are ready for a bigger challenge write a second poem, this time using one of the other poetic forms researched and discussed during On the Spot Research.

ASSESS

Check that students are sufficiently engaged with the writing prompt. You should see evidence of brainstorming and understanding of the poetic form they've chosen (for example, rhyme scheme, meter, lines per stanza, and so on). Make sure students are attempting to follow the correct form.

ADAPT

If students are struggling to come up with an idea for their poem or to model it on the poetic form they've chosen, have them first write the "story" of their poem as prose. Encourage them to use a thesaurus to come up with interesting language choices (you may want to direct them to an online rhyming dictionary if appropriate for their form). Then, have them work on "rearranging" the lines of their prose piece into a poetic form.

ACTIVITY 1.7

PLAN

Materials: highlighters in two colors

Suggested Pacing: 2 50-minute class periods

TEACH

1 Read the Learning Targets and Preview with your students. Introduce the idea of a prologue. Explain that students should highlight lines in the prologue where Ellison conveys what the narrator is and what he is not.

2 Preview the As You Read tasks, ensuring students understand the instructions. Have students use two different highlighters to mark up the text—one color for statements that define what the narrator is and one for statements that define what he is not.

3 Direct students to read the About the Author, and then engage them in a discussion of what elements of the author's bio they think will be most significant in understanding his writing. Ask them to consider the context of the time period in which he was writing (the United States in the 1950s).

Learning Strategies

Graphic Organizer
Quickwrite
Sketching
Visualizing

My Notes

Learning Targets
- Evaluate the effectiveness of an author's diction and syntax.
- Analyze how an author's purpose and audience contribute to language and stylistic choices.
- Compare how two different authors use language, diction, and syntax to connect with their audience.

Preview
In this activity, you will read the prologue and analyze an author's use of diction and syntax. Then you will consider how an author's purpose and intended audience affect language and stylistic choices. Finally, you will compare the ways the two writers have made language choices to achieve particular effects on their reader.

As You Read
- Highlight statements where the narrator defines what he is and what he is not.
- Circle unknown words and phrases. Try to determine the meaning of the words by using context clues, word parts, or a dictionary.

About the Author

Although Ralph Ellison's novelistic output is small, its influence is huge. Ellison (1914–1994) is best known for his novel *Invisible Man* (1952). In his masterpiece, an unnamed narrator struggles against racism and urban alienation to find an identity. Ellison employs an all-embracing style—combining elements of African American folklore, Native American mythology, and classical allusions—which he likens to a jazz musician's improvisation on traditional themes. Ellison is also known for his short stories and for nonfiction writing on literature, music, and African American issues. Though Ellison detested being labeled a black writer, he accepted the label *minority writer*, because, as he put it, "the individual is a minority."

College and Career Readiness Standards

Focus Standards:

RL.11–12.1 Cite strong and thorough textual evidence to support analysis of what the text says explicitly as well as inferences drawn from the text, including determining where the text leaves matters uncertain.

RL.11–12.2 Determine two or more themes or central ideas of a text and analyze their development over the course of the text, including how they interact and build on one another to produce a complex account; provide an objective summary of the text.

Novel Excerpt

from **Invisible Man**

by **Ralph Ellison**

1   I am an invisible man. No, I am not a spook like those who haunted Edgar Allan Poe; nor am I one of your Hollywood-movie ectoplasms. I am a man of substance, of flesh and bone, of fiber and liquids—and I might even be said to possess a mind. I am invisible, understand, simply because people refuse to see me. Like the bodiless heads you see sometimes in circus sideshows, it is as though I have been surrounded by mirrors of hard, distorting glass. When they approach me they see only my surroundings, themselves, or figments of their imagination—indeed, everything and anything except me.

2   Nor is my invisibility exactly a matter of a biochemical accident to my epidermis. That invisibility to which I refer occurs because of a peculiar disposition of the eyes of those with whom I come in contact. A matter of the construction of their inner eyes, those eyes with which they look through their physical eyes upon reality. I am not complaining, nor am I protesting either. It is sometimes advantageous to be unseen, although it is most often rather wearing on the nerves. Then too, you're constantly being bumped against by those of poor vision. Or again, you often doubt if you really exist. You wonder whether you aren't simply a phantom in other people's minds. Say, a figure in a nightmare which the sleeper tries with all his strength to destroy. It's when you feel like this that, out of resentment, you begin to bump people back.

3   And, let me confess, you feel that way most of the time. You ache with the need to convince yourself that you do exist in the real world, that you're a part of all the sound and the anguish, and you strike out with your fists, you curse and you swear to make them recognize you. And, alas, it's seldom successful.

> **Making Observations**
> • How does the narrator define himself?
> • What are your initial thoughts about the narrator's perspective?

GRAMMAR & USAGE

Sentence Variety
Effective writers vary sentence length for effect. Too many long, complex sentences can lose the reader, yet too many short sentences can sound choppy or unsophisticated. Short sentences can also sometimes lack clarity by not including transitions to show relationships between ideas. However, short sentences can be used for effect, making an important idea stand out.

Notice the difference in length between the last two sentences in the prologue. Consider the way Ellison conveys relationships among the ideas within the long, next-to-last sentence. How does this add to the impact of the final short sentence?

ectoplasms: ghosts
epidermis: skin

 4   FIRST READ: Conduct a shared reading of the novel excerpt. As students take turns reading, circulate the room to make sure they are engaged with the text and making annotations.

 TEXT COMPLEXITY

Overall: Complex
Lexile: 870L
Qualitative: Moderate Difficulty
Task: Moderate (Analyze)

TEACHER TO TEACHER

After the first read, it may be useful to play the audio recording of the text, so students can appreciate Ellison's tone and hear the underlying argument that he is presenting to his audience.

5 Following their first reading, have students skim the Making Observations questions and make notes on what they found most interesting or arresting in the text. Then have students work in groups to think-pair-share their observations.

College and Career Readiness Standards

RL.11–12.3 Analyze the impact of the author's choices regarding how to develop and relate elements of a story or drama (e.g., where a story is set, how the action is ordered, how the characters are introduced and developed.)

L.11–12.3a Vary syntax for effect, consulting references (e.g., Tufte's Artful Sentences) for guidance as needed; apply an understanding of syntax to the study of complex texts when reading.

Additional Standards Addressed:
RL.11–12.4, RL.11–12.5, RL.11–12.6, RL.11–12.10, W.11–12.3d, W.11–12.10

6 RETURNING TO THE TEXT: Have students answer the text-dependent questions in the same small groups. If they have difficulty, scaffold the questions by rephrasing them or breaking them down into smaller parts. See the Scaffolding the Text-Dependent Questions boxes for suggestions.

7 Vocabulary Development: Review the meaning of the literary term *prologue*. Have students work in pairs to define the term in their own words and think of both examples and non-examples.

8 Shift the focus of study from comprehension to deeper analysis by directing students' attention to the Grammar & Usage box. Ask them to identify several types of sentences, from short to longer and more complex, in Ellison's writing. In group discussion, consider whether and how the sentence variety makes the text more engaging to read.

1.7

VOCABULARY

LITERARY
A prologue occurs at the beginning of a literary work and takes place within the narrative action.

My Notes

Returning to the Text

- Reread the prologue to answer these text-dependent questions.
- Write any additional questions you have about the text in your Reader/Writer Notebook.

1. According to the text, what does the narrator view as the reason for his invisibility?

   In paragraph 1, the narrator explains that he is invisible "simply because people refuse to see me." Although he is "a man of substance, of flesh and bone, of fiber and liquids," and therefore is not literally invisible, he experiences a sense of being invisible because of others' perceptions of him.

2. How would you describe the narrator's diction and syntax in the first two paragraphs of the prologue? What effect does this have on the tone of the passage? Use text evidence to support your answer.

   The narrator's elevated diction and syntax clearly mark him as an intelligent person. He uses vocabulary to create a mock-scientific tone ("a matter of biochemical accident to my epidermis"). Furthermore, the narrator's formal diction presents an ironic contrast with his palpable anger over the way he is treated by others. The overall tone is one of irony and repressed resentment.

3. What details explain what causes the narrator to begin to "bump people back"? How do these details contribute to texts overall message?

   The narrator feels unseen and "surrounded by mirrors of hard, distorting glass." He questions if he's "a phantom in other people's minds," which "wear[s] on his nerves." "Bumping people back," is a means of asserting his existence not only to others but to himself as well.

4. What is the effect of the author's use of semicolons and dashes in the first paragraph?

   The author uses dashes to create dramatic pauses and to emphasize important ideas about his experience. He uses a semicolon in the second sentence to balance and dismiss two obvious interpretations of the phrase "invisible man."

Scaffolding the Text-Dependent Questions

1. According to the text, what does the narrator view as the reason for his invisibility? Look for the clue word "because" in paragraph 1. RL.11–12.1, RL.11–12.2, RL.11–12.6

2. How would you describe the narrator's diction and syntax in the first two paragraphs of the prologue? **What effect does this have on the tone of the passage? Use text evidence to support your answer.** How would you describe the sentences? Are they long or short? Flowing or choppy? Try rewriting one or two and then reading the passage again. RL.11–12.4

Working from the Text

5. In the prologue from *Invisible Man*, the narrator contrasts how he believes himself to be in reality with how others perceive him. Working with a partner, create two quick illustrations in in your Reader/Writer Notebook that demonstrate the narrator's contrasting perceptions of self. Use words or phrases from the text to write a short caption for each of your illustrations.

How the Narrator Sees Himself	How Others See the Narrator
Caption:	**Caption:**
The narrator is an intelligent man of "flesh and bone" who often feels weary, resentful, and angry that people do refuse to see him for who he really is.	The narrator appears distorted and fragmented as a result of people looking at him through "their inner eyes."

6. If the prologue from *Invisible Man* had been written as an argument instead of a work of fiction, what would the central claim be? Use your own words to state the text's central message in the form of a claim.

Even though I am invisible, my invisibility isn't due to any physical deformity or problem within myself. Rather, it is the result of others' incorrect perceptions of me, owing to the faulty construction of their inner eyes.

7. When making an argument, authors often try to appeal to their audience's emotions, intellect, or sense of morality and justice. How does Ellison's use of language—including word choice and sentence structure—support the claim you wrote in the previous step? Which type of appeal appears most evident in this text?

Ellison's mock-scientific tone, along with his formal syntax and diction, indicates that his appeal is primarily one of *logos*, or logic. He primarily offers evidence that appeals to the reader's *reason* to back up his central claim.

8. How might the effect of this piece be different if the author had chosen to write a nonfiction argumentative text instead of a novel? Why do you think Ellison chose to communicate his message through fiction rather than nonfiction?

Fiction allows Ellison to explore the concept of invisibility in ways that are metaphorical and allegorical. Furthermore, fiction allows him to bypass the defenses that most people automatically put up when reading a nonfiction argument, allowing the reader to be more open to his ideas.

9 Have students work with a partner to complete the **graphic organizer** in Working from the Text. Afterward, have them work individually to visualize the prologue, creating a self-representation based partly on Ellison's description. Begin this process by asking students to **visualize** the prologue and **sketch** images on their own paper to reflect the ideas that describe the narrator's multiple and conflicting images of self. The narrator spends time saying both what he is and what he is not. Discuss both the significance and effect of these images and ideas.

10 Direct students' attention to the Language & Writer's Craft: Syntax section. Read the introductory paragraph and continue by asking students what they notice about the syntax, or sentence structure, of the piece. Work with students to complete the chart and to examine Ellison's sentence patterns. Discuss how his use of language works to advance his ideas.

11 Instruct students to complete student steps 6, 7, and 8 individually and then move into a think-pair-share to consult on their responses.

12 Explain to students that a writer's control and manipulation of sentences is a strong determiner of voice. After you and the students have discussed their work on the chart in the Language & Writer's Craft, ask them to number all of the sentences in the prologue (you may want to narrow their focus to the first paragraph only) and then identify each sentence by type and explain its impact on the piece as a whole.

Scaffolding the Text-Dependent Questions

3. What details explain what causes the narrator to begin to "bump people back"? How do these details contribute to the text's overall message? Find that phrase (at the end of paragraph 2). What does the speaker say before that? What leads him to feel that way? RL.11–12.2, RL.11–12.3

4. What is the effect of the narrator's use of semicolons and dashes in the first paragraph? Read the passage aloud, emphasizing the pauses created by the semicolons and dashes. Now read the passage again, ignoring them. How does the tone or feeling of the paragraph change? RL.11–12.4

13 As students complete the Language & Writer's Craft practice, circulate the room and offer help as needed. If students are having trouble, suggest they first highlight or circle the different types of sentences—complex sentences, fragments, and parallel structure. Ask them to consider, as well, sentence length. Suggest they try breaking a long sentence into smaller ones, or combining two or more sentences.

LEVELED DIFFERENTIATED INSTRUCTION

In this activity, students may need support revising their writing for syntactical variety.

Beginning Allow students to work in pairs to create complex sentences using the **Idea Connector** graphic organizer. Have them revise their own sentences using words such as *and* or *because*.

Developing Allow students to work in pairs using the **Idea Connector** graphic organizer. When revising their own sentences, ask students to focus on creating complex sentences using phrases such as *in order to* or *even though*.

Expanding Arrange students in groups of three and assign them one type of syntax listed on the chart (fragments, complex sentences, or parallel structure) to focus on when revising their writing. Then have students share their examples with their peers. Finally, students can work collaboratively to revise their remaining **quickwrite** sentences.

Support Have students return to the text to highlight examples of fragments, complex sentences, and parallel structure, each in its own color. This will provide students with a bank of examples to select from when revising their own writing.

Extend Challenge students to select another text from the unit and to describe their perception of themselves in the style of that author.

1.7

LANGUAGE & WRITER'S CRAFT: Syntax

Syntax is the way words are arranged to form phrases, clauses, and sentences. Authors choose different kinds of sentence structures depending on the sentence's function and the intended effect on the reader. Read the descriptions and the examples provided. Then revisit the prologue from *Invisible Man* to find additional examples, and explain how each is used to advance the tone or theme of the text. Record your ideas in the chart that follows.

Analyzing Elements of Syntax in *Invisible Man*	Additional Examples from the Text
A **fragment** is a word group that is not a complete sentence. It may be lacking a subject, a verb, or both. Although you should usually avoid using fragments, they are sometimes used for effect. **Example:** *Nor is my invisibility exactly a matter of a biochemical accident to my epidermis.*	**Additional Example:** *Say, a figure in a nightmare which the sleeper tries with all his strength to destroy.* **Function:** Ellison uses this fragment to set apart a particularly striking image from the sentence to which it relates.
A **complex sentence** contains one independent clause and one or more dependent, or subordinate, clauses. **Example:** *Like the bodiless heads you see sometimes in circus sideshows, it is as though I have been surrounded by mirrors of hard, distorting glass.*	**Additional Example:** *I am invisible, understand, simply because people refuse to see me.* **Function:** Ellison uses a complex sentence to express a causal relationship. The main idea is that he is invisible. The subordinate clause ("simply because people refuse to see me") explains the cause of his invisibility.
Parallel structure is the use of the same pattern of words to show that two or more ideas are related and have the same level of importance. **Example:** *You ache with the need to convince yourself that you do exist in the real world, that you're a part of all the sound and the anguish, and you strike out with your fists, you curse and you swear to make them recognize you.*	**Additional Example:** *I am a man of substance, of flesh and bone, of fiber and of liquids—and I might even be said to possess a mind.* **Function:** Ellison uses parallelism—several prepositional phrases in a row—to catalog the elements of his being.

PRACTICE Choose two or three sentences from the passage and rewrite them using different syntax, diction, and vocabulary for effect (use a thesaurus for the vocabulary as needed). Then write new sentences that build off the sentences you've rewritten. Include a fragment, a complex sentence, and one using parallel structure.

14 Have students work with a partner to respond to the Check Your Understanding.

15 Have students respond to the writing prompt. Suggest that students use a simple comparison chart to organize their ideas before they start writing. The chart can help them construct their thesis statement.

16 For the Independent Reading Link, pair students whose authors' styles contrast so that they can note the differences in how the authors use their style to communicate a perspective.

☑ Check Your Understanding

With a partner discuss why writers make particular choices when composing a text. How might the intended purpose or audience contribute to an author's decisions?

① INDEPENDENT READING LINK

Read and Discuss

Select a passage from your independent reading that showcases the author's writing style. Analyze the way the author's style helps communicate a perspective. Share your analysis with a partner and discuss how the styles of your authors compare.

✏ Writing Prompt: Literary Analysis

Write a short essay in which you analyze and compare the use of language, including diction and syntax, in the prologue to *Invisible Man* to the use of language in one of the poems you have read so far in the unit. Compare the ways the two writers have made language choices to achieve particular effects on their reader. Be sure to:

- Begin with a clear comparative thesis statement.
- Explain the effectiveness of each author's word choice.
- Incorporate text evidence to support your analysis.
- Organize information in a logical structure.

ASSESS

Make sure students' written responses to the Writing Prompt articulate a clearly defined thesis statement and offer text evidence that shows an understanding of syntax and diction. Students should demonstrate an understanding of how the use of language creates certain effects in each piece, explain the effectiveness of language in each piece, and include text evidence to support their statements. Look for students to vary the syntax in their own sentences—they should, for instance, use a variety of sentence structures and use punctuation for effect.

ADAPT

If students need additional help analyzing the use of language, suggest that they start first with the effects and then look to their annotations and notes from the activity to see how specific word choices and structures created each effect.

WRITING PROMPT: LITERARY ANALYSIS

The following standards are addressed in the writing prompt:

- RL.11–12.1
- RL.11–12.4
- W.11–12.2d
- W.11–12.5

PLAN

Suggested Pacing: 1 50-minute class period

TEACH

1 Go over the Learning Targets with students and read through the Preview.

2 **Vocabulary Development:** Define the term *rhetoric*, and then introduce the idea of a rhetorical question. Pose a rhetorical question, and then have students come up with a few of their own. Ask students what they think is the purpose of a rhetorical question. Then ask students to work with a partner to brainstorm words to clarify their understanding of the term.

3 Read through each step of the **SOAPSTone** strategy. Then have students use it to answer questions about the prologue to *Invisible Man*. Have them spend a few minutes identifying the speaker, occasion, audience, purpose, subject, and tone of the selected text.

4 Ask students to use the SOAPSTone strategy for a quick analysis of their independent reading. Then have volunteers share their responses with the class.

★ TEACHER TO TEACHER

Help students internalize the SOAPSTone strategy by showing them how they can use it to analyze not only text but other forms of media as well. Show a short YouTube video—this could be a short documentary, an instructional film, or a humorous sketch—and engage the class in a casual discussion of the film using SOAPSTone steps.

5 Direct students to read the About the Author section. Then have them complete the Opening Writing Prompt by writing one or two short statements making inferences about the author's purpose and subject.

Exploring Rhetoric

Learning Strategies

Questioning the Text
SOAPSTone

VOCABULARY

ACADEMIC
Rhetorical devices are specific techniques that are used in writing to create a literary effect or enhance the effectiveness of an author's message. For example, in argumentative texts authors often try to appeal to the reader's emotions and sense of logic in order to persuade the reader.

My Notes

Learning Targets

- Evaluate an author's purpose and determine the target audience in an argumentative text.
- Identify and analyze how an author uses rhetorical devices to build an effective argument.

Preview

In earlier activities, you looked closely at the choices authors make in poetry and literary texts to connect with their audience. Now you will apply what you've learned about the effectiveness of diction, text structure, and figurative language to the study of arguments. In this activity, you will analyze an argumentative text and how the author uses rhetorical devices to persuade her audience.

Introducing the Strategy: SOAPSTone

SOAPSTone stands for **S**peaker, **O**ccasion, **A**udience, **P**urpose, **S**ubject, and **T**one. It is a reading and writing tool for analyzing the relationship among a writer, his or her purpose, and the target audience of the text. SOAPSTone guides you in asking questions to analyze a text or to plan for writing a composition.

- **Speaker:** The speaker could be the author or a character or narrator the author invents.
- **Occasion:** The occasion is the time and place of the text; it is the context that prompted the writing.
- **Audience:** The audience is the person or persons to whom the piece is directed.
- **Purpose:** The purpose is the reason behind the text or what the writer wants the audience to think as a result of reading or hearing the text.
- **Subject:** The subject is the focus of the text.
- **Tone:** Tone is the speaker's attitude toward the subject.

📝 Opening Writing Prompt

Read the About the Author for Aruna Kashyap and the title of the argument and answer the following question.

- Based on the title and the details in the author's biography, what do you think the author's purpose and subject will be?

College and Career Readiness Standards

Focus Standards:

RI.11–12.1 Cite strong and thorough textual evidence to support analysis of what the text says explicitly as well as inferences drawn from the text, including determining where the text leaves matters uncertain.

RI.11–12.2 Determine two or more central ideas of a text and analyze their development over the course of the text, including how they interact and build on one another to provide a complex analysis; provide an objective summary of the text.

RI.11–12.5 Analyze and evaluate the effectiveness of the structure an author uses in his or her exposition or argument, including whether the structure makes points clear, convincing, and engaging.

1.8

As You Read

- Look for details about the speaker, occasion, audience, purpose, subject, and tone (SOAPSTone elements). Note these details in a two-column SOAPSTone chart in your Reader/Writer Notebook.
- Circle unknown words and phrases. Try to determine the meaning of the words by using context clues, word parts, or a dictionary.

My Notes

About the Author

Aruna Kashyap is senior counsel for the women's rights division of Human Rights Watch, an international nonprofit organization that advocates for human rights worldwide. With a background in litigation, Kashyap spent the early years of her career working as a lawyer for the India Center for Human Rights and Law. Her work now focuses on women's labor and economic rights and violence against women.

Argumentative Text

Clothing Brands Need to Step Up and Keep Women Safe in Their Factories

by **Aruna Kashyap**

1   In a recent survey of experts, countries were ranked according to how safe they are for women. India came out as the most dangerous, followed by Afghanistan and Syria. Leaving aside the survey's obvious challenges – including its attempt to use six measures to compare 10 very different countries – it paints a dire picture for women's safety in the world. One area in which women everywhere face discrimination, inequality, harassment or violence in their everyday lives is in their workplace. Governments and corporations must contend with how to keep women safe when they are working.

2   Globally, [women's rights] movements have forced many companies to revisit their gender pay gap and anti-harassment policies. The momentum has spurred discussions for a new international labor standard that squarely addresses violence and harassment in the workplace.

3   As in the apparel industry, for example, where women make up much of the global workforce. Apparel companies should do more to create work spaces free of violence and harassment... This is not just for the benefit of their own employees, but also for the customers and clients walking into their stores; the models who are the face of their clothes; and the workers producing their clothes and shoes in factories around the world.

College and Career Readiness Standards

RI.11–12.6 Determine an author's point of view or purpose in a text in which the rhetoric is particularly effective, analyzing how style and content contribute to the power, persuasiveness or beauty of the text.

W.11–12.10 Write routinely over extended time frames (time for research, reflection, and revision) and shorter time frames (a single sitting or a day or two) for a range of tasks, purposes, and audiences.

L.11–12.4c Consult general and specialized reference materials (e.g., dictionaries, glossaries, thesauruses), both print and digital, to find the pronunciation of a word or determine or clarify its precise meaning, its part of speech, its etymology, or its standard usage.

Additional Standards Addressed:
SL.11–12.1, L.11–12.6, L.11–12.2a

---

6 Preview the As You Read tasks. Before they begin reading, encourage students to make a two-column SOAPSTone chart that they can fill in as they read.

7 FIRST READ: Conduct a shared read of the passage. Have one student read the first five paragraphs, another the next five, and so on. Circulate the room to make sure students are engaging with the text, circling words, and filling in their charts.

TEXT COMPLEXITY

Overall: Complex
Lexile: 1100L
Qualitative: Moderate Difficulty
Task: Moderate (Analyze)

8 Pause after paragraph 5 to check comprehension and direct students to the glossed vocabulary. To check comprehension, have students respond to the following questions in writing or orally:

- Where are the most unsafe workplaces for women in the world?
- Why does the essay focus in particular on apparel factories?
- What call to action is stated in the first few paragraphs?

1.8

My Notes

Worker sews garments inside a factory in Gazipur, Bangladesh. Bangladesh is the world's second largest apparel exporter after China.

4   In May, when I was speaking to garment workers about the conditions in factories, I met Roja R., a married woman in her thirties who worked in a factory in the Indian city of Mysore making clothing for international brands. She told me the cutting section supervisor had been stalking her. She said he misused his access to her cell number, calling her after work hours to harass her. He promised that if she submitted to his demands, he would give her a more manageable workload and assured her that he would quickly approve requests for time off work.

5   Roja resisted. She complained to the factory administration. But the person she spoke with laughed and told her: "This is normal practice and you need to adjust." Nobody in the factory's management took the steps that Indian law requires to stop harassment. That includes setting up an internal complaints committee and disseminating and publicly displaying the names and contact information of committee members. Companies are also supposed to develop a policy against harassment and widely publicize it through harassment-prevention training programs.

6   The harassment went on for months, Roja said. She was losing sleep. Coming from a conservative family, she worried that her husband would find out, blame her and stop her from going to work. By the time I met her, the problems still hadn't been resolved. Another of her co-workers also told me she was harassed in a different part of the same factory.

7   Even in their desperation for some respite from the harassment, they had one plea: They wanted the clothing brands they work for to help fix the problem, but not by cutting ties with the factory. If the factory lost business,

disseminating: sharing publicly

Scaffolding the Text-Dependent Questions

1. What are three actions that Kashyap argues brands should take to improve conditions for their workers? Where does Kashyap suggest concrete actions for brands to take? What context can you look for? What specific words does she use? RI.11–12.2, RI.11–12.5

2. What is the most likely reason that Kashyap included the story of Roja R.? How does this example affect her argument? How did you feel after reading the story of Roja R.? What sort

of appeal is Kashyak using here? What effect does it have on her argument? RI.11–12.5, RI.11–12.6

3. How does Kashyap's language affect your perception of her argument? Is her use of language appropriate for her topic and audience? Is her language formal or informal? Does she sound knowledgeable? Is her language appropriate for an argument? RI.11–12.4, RI.11–12.6

these women could lose their jobs. They feared not just for their own livelihoods, but also for those of their colleagues.

8 The factory's management exploited this fear. The women say supervisors had threatened them, telling them that any mention of harassment or other complaints to the monitors who inspect factories for labor compliance would cause problems. The women were told: "You will take away food from many mouths. Do you want everyone to eat mud?"

9 Brands need to be held accountable for monitoring and remediating labor conditions in factories they source from, rather than being allowed to conveniently distance themselves from labor abuses.

10 No doubt a brand should be able to cut ties with a factory that is a repeat offender, one that shows zero willingness to put in place legal protections and to abide by international human rights standards. But before taking that step, companies need to find ways to help factories improve and ensure that workers can safely raise their issues.

11 Investing in the underlying infrastructure that translates paper codes of conduct into actual practice is key to any meaningful effort. Brands should take steps toward this goal.

12 First, they should publish information about the factories that supply their products, which makes it easier for workers to find out which brands buy from that factory and whom to contact when problems occur. Many apparel companies have been leaders on transparency, but many others have yet to follow good industry practices for making details about their business easily available.

13 Second, brands should recognize the limits of social and labor compliance checks (known as "social audits" in industry parlance), in which it may not be possible to address issues like harassment effectively. Monitors are expected to document "evidence" or sufficiently corroborate complaints they get from workers before they can report it. Studies by CARE and other organizations show how often workers themselves under-report and sometimes do not even recognize harassment.

14 Third, merely having monitors check periodically whether or not a workplace has a complaint system is not good enough. The absence of well-trained, independent and gender-sensitive committees to look into complaints, coupled with a lack of strong anti-retaliation procedures, risk stripping these systems of any credibility. In numerous cases from South Asia, I have found that women workers who dared to speak up … had experienced retaliation.

15 That included factory management not allowing the complainant to work, suddenly finding fault with her productivity and quality of work, or warning that she was a troublemaker.

INDEPENDENT READING LINK

Read and Connect

Think about your independent reading text, and the issues the characters are concerned with. What is an argument one of the characters makes, or might make, in response to their concerns? Analyze how you think the character would present their argument. Would they use appeals to reason, to logic, or to ethics? Would they employ logical fallacies? Now choose another character from your text and consider how they would react to the argument. Would they agree or disagree? What counterargument might they make?

My Notes

infrastructure: system

parlance: language

complainant: person or group filing a legal complaint

9 Pause after paragraph 10. Continue comprehension check by asking a volunteer to summarize Roja R.'s story.

10 Pause after paragraph 15 to check comprehension and direct students to the glossed vocabulary. Have students respond to the following questions to check comprehension: Why is it difficult for workers to file complaints about harassment? What steps does the author suggest brands should take to improve workers' safety?

Scaffolding the Text-Dependent Questions

4. In paragraph 10, what is the counterclaim that Kashyap addresses and how does she respond to it? Why do you think she advises against this solution? Why does Kashyap cite facts when responding to the counterclaim? Do you think acknowledging it was a good thing? Do you agree with her? RI.11–12.5

5. What is the structure of this text? What purpose does this structure achieve? Create a brief outline of the text. What does she do in the introduction? Where is her thesis statement? Does she give context first or go straight to her argument? RI.11–12.5, RI.11–12.6

11 Following the reading, have partners think-pair-share to discuss their Making Observations notes. Listen in on group discussions to gauge comprehension.

1.8

My Notes

16 Another problem is that often brands do their own training and monitoring. In fact, it may be more effective for multiple brands buying garments from the same factory to pool their resources to create a single, comprehensive and effective system for that factory.

17 They could ensure that there are effective and accessible grievance-redress systems for workers if their problems are not resolved at the factory level. Instead of requiring workers to find and use a different complaints procedure for each brand, which is time-consuming and difficult for workers, there should be a simple and effective process for them to lodge complaints. And the process should result in clear outcomes when problems are found. Without effective grievance redress that leads to binding outcomes, brands should know that their talk of protecting workers' rights is pure rhetoric.

18 In late May and early June, governments, employers' and workers' organizations concluded the first round of negotiations for a binding International Labor Organization (ILO) standard to address violence and harassment in the workplace supplemented by a non-binding recommendation. Another round of discussions will follow next year.

19 Apparel and footwear companies should call on employers' organizations and governments to unequivocally support a binding standard in next year's negotiations. That would be a major step toward helping make the world a safer place for women.

Making Observations
- After reading the argument for the first time, what did you learn about the author's purpose?
- Which ideas from the argument stand out to you the most?

redress: resolution
unequivocally: clearly and strongly

12 **RETURNING TO THE TEXT:** Have students answer the text-dependent questions in the same pairs. If they have difficulty, scaffold the questions by rephrasing them or breaking them down into smaller parts. See the Scaffolding the Text-Dependent Questions boxes for suggestions.

Returning to the Text

• Reread the argument to answer these text-dependent questions.

• Write any additional questions you have about the argument in your Reader/Writer Notebook.

1. What are three actions that Kashyap argues brands should take to improve conditions for their workers?

   They should publish information about the factories that supply their products; they should

   recognize the limits of social and labor compliance checks; they should recognize (and

   work towards remedying) the absence of well-trained, independent, and gender-sensitive

   committees to look into complaints.

2. What is the most likely reason that Kashyap included story of Roja R.? How does this example affect her argument?

   She likely included the story to engage the reader's sympathy, making it more likely readers

   will be spurred to action. Roja R.'s story allows the reader to connect with a real person and

   witness the human toll of harassment and abuse, rather than simply seeing factory workers

   as statistics or abstractions.

3. How does Kashyap's language affect your perception of her argument? Is her use of language appropriate for her topic and audience?

   Kashyap uses formal language and a neutral tone, which, along with the evidence she

   presents, helps establish her as a rational and informed authority. This makes her argument

   stronger because the reader trusts her.

4. In paragraph 10, what is the counterclaim that Kashyap addresses and how does she respond to it? Why do you think she advises against this solution?

   She acknowledges the counterclaim that companies should cut ties with factories that have

   demonstrated widespread abuses. She indicates that this is a viable choice when all other

   solutions have been tried, but that companies should first try and improve conditions. She

   states that cutting ties will not end abusive conditions in the long term.

13 In new pairs, instruct students to complete a SOAPSTone analysis in Working from the Text.

14 Ask students to discuss with their partners which elements were easiest to identify and which were more difficult.

15 Have students complete student step 7 with their partners.

16 Once students have discussed the rhetorical appeals used in the text, write on the board: Pathos (Emotional), Logos (Rational), and Ethos (Ethical), leaving space under each. Explain that ethos also includes features that suggest the speaker is trustworthy, fair, and knowledgeable. Have students share the examples they found from the text and write them under the appropriate heading. Discuss Kashyap's use of appeals.

LEVELED DIFFERENTIATED INSTRUCTION

In this activity, students may need support identifying the audience, purpose, subject, and tone of the text.

Beginning Support students who are at an early stage in their English language development by having them work in groups to complete the SOAPSTone activity. Have them use the conferencing strategy to fill in gaps in each others' knowledge.

Developing Remind students that the notes they took during reading should help them identify the audience, purpose, subject, and tone. Encourage students to go back over their notes and then share their notes with others in the group to complete the SOAPSTone chart.

Bridging After groups have completed the SOAPSTone chart, encourage them to share ideas about how the audience and the purpose drive the tone of the piece.

1.8

5. How is the text structured? What purpose does this structure achieve?

The author first establishes some general facts and background about the discrimination and harassment women face worldwide. She then discusses the conditions in India specifically, before moving on to a personal story about Roja R., a factory worker in India. Kashyap gives the reader context and organizes information in a simple, logical way.

Working from the Text

6. With a partner, use the SOAPSTone strategy to analyze how Aruna Kashyap builds her argument. Use your notes from the first reading of the text to help support your answers.

Element	Who/What?
Speaker	
Occasion	
Audience	
Purpose	
Subject	
Tone	

7. Continue working with a partner to trace the author's use of rhetorical appeals in the text. Name specific examples from the text.

- Appeals to readers' emotions:
- Appeals to readers' sense of logic:
- Appeals to ethics and other features that show the writer's credibility/trustworhiness:

8. Use Reader-Response Criticism to think about how the reading situation, the text, and you as a reader interact to make meaning from this text. How do your own beliefs, experiences, and values influence your likeliness to be persuaded by the author's argument?

 Gaining Perspectives

You read about how working conditions in some countries are not safe and improvements need to be made. The author of the text gives some ideas on what could be done to improve conditions. Choose a manufacturer such the maker of your favorite clothing or backpack. Conduct On the Spot research to learn about where and how the product is manufactured. How can you ensure that the people who created this item for you are fairly treated? What options are available for you, as a consumer, to influence working conditions? Consider traditional methods as well as social media platforms. Present your ideas to the class and choose which option would be most beneficial to create social change.

LANGUAGE & WRITER'S CRAFT: Hyphenation

Hyphens have many uses and can change the meaning of a sentence. Hyphens are used to join two or more words that function as a single adjective before a noun.

Example: *Globally, [women's rights] movements have forced many companies to revisit their gender pay gap and <u>anti-harassment</u> policies.*

PRACTICE Look over "Clothing Brands Need to Step Up and Keep Women Safe in Their Factories" again. List the five other examples of hyphenation from the text. If the hyphenated word functions as an adjective, write the noun it modifies.

☑ **Check Your Understanding**

What one language selection or rhetorical choice did the author make that added to the persuasiveness of this argumentative text? If you were the author, what might you have done differently to make the piece more persuasive?

ACTIVITY 1.8 continued

Extend After their initial reading of Kashyap's argument, have students pretend they are a representative from a clothing brand and write a response. The response could take the form of a rebuttal, a "letter to the editor," or a company memo.

17 Draw students' attention to the Gaining Perspectives feature. Have pairs discuss how citizens in a community can impact a cause. As they brainstorm ways to help workers achieve better working conditions, ask them to think about why some options are more effective than others. After pairs present their ideas, have the class vote on which option would be the most beneficial to create social change, and ask students to explain the reasons for their votes.

18 As students complete the Language & Writer's Craft practice, remind them that if a hyphen is used to create a single adjective, it must also modify a noun, preceding the noun it modifies. Consider pointing out the dashes in the first paragraph of the text and using this opportunity to clarify the difference between hyphens and dashes. After reviewing students' work as a class, ask volunteers to create their own sentences with hyphenated words.

19 Have students respond to the Check Your Understanding in a brief paragraph.

20 Direct students to respond to the Independent Reading Link.

ASSESS

Student responses to Check Your Understanding should demonstrate strong comprehension of why the author made certain rhetorical choices to achieve her purpose. Look for clear explanations of how the author's rhetoric made the speech more persuasive.

ADAPT

If students need support in identifying rhetorical choices and their purpose, pose questions about the text, such as: What is the author trying to accomplish? Was she writing to a specific group of people?

ACTIVITY
1.9

Critiquing and Evaluating an Argument

PLAN

Suggested Pacing: 3 50-minute class periods

TEACH

1 Read the Learning Targets and Preview sections with your students. Review the terms *appeals* and *counterarguments* if necessary.

2 Go over the elements in the Reviewing the Structure of an Argument section, defining terms and giving examples as needed. Be sure students understand the purpose and function of these elements. If students need support or scaffolding, refer to Writing Workshop 2: Argumentative Writing.

3 Give students a thesis statement for an argument, such as "Later school start times improve student performance." Divide students into five groups and assign each group an element of argument. Have groups work to come up with the elements in response to the proposed thesis. Afterward, have each group share their work and engage the class in discussion about how well they used the element.

Learning Strategies

Activating Prior Knowledge
Marking the Text

My Notes

Learning Targets

- Explain and evaluate the reasoning in a significant U.S. text as well as its effectiveness in the area of public advocacy.
- Analyze how two or more texts address similar themes or topics, including the purpose and rhetorical approach of each.
- Critique and evaluate the effectiveness of a speech's structure, appeals, evidence, and treatment of counterarguments.
- Integrate ideas from multiple texts to build knowledge and vocabulary about advocacy on social issues.

Preview

In this activity, you will review the characteristics and structural elements of an argument before reading and critiquing a speech and a piece of legislation.

Reviewing the Structure of an Argument

Before reading the arguments in this part of the unit, review the following structural elements of an argument.

The Hook
- Grabs readers' attention and catches their interest
- May establish a connection between reader and writer and provide background information
- Might be an anecdote, image, definition, or quotation

The Claim
- Usually comes in the opening section of a text
- States the author's main point
- Can be straightforward and direct (for instance, "I believe that ...")

Concessions and Rebuttals
- Recognize arguments made by the other side
- Build credibility by showing ability to discuss each side with apparent objectivity
- Grant that the other side has some validity
- Argue against the opposing viewpoint by showing that the author's side has more validity

Support
- Sets out the reasoning behind an argument
- Provides evidence of the claim (data, quotations, anecdotes, and the like)
- May include appeals to logic, emotions, or ethics

College and Career Readiness Standards

Focus Standards:

RI.11–12.8 Delineate and evaluate the reasoning in seminal U.S. texts, including the application of constitutional principles and use of legal reasoning (e.g., in U.S. Supreme Court majority opinions and dissents) and the premises, purposes, and arguments in works of public advocacy (e.g., The Federalist, presidential addresses).

RI.11–12.9 Analyze seventeenth-, eighteenth-, and nineteenth-century foundational U.S. documents of historical and literary significance (including The Declaration of Independence, the Preamble to the Constitution, the Bill of Rights, and Lincoln's Second Inaugural Address) for their themes, purposes, and rhetorical features.

W.11–12.8 Gather relevant information from multiple authoritative print and digital sources, using advanced searches effectively; assess the

My Notes

Call to Action

- Draws the argument to a close and restates the claim
- May make a final, new appeal to values
- May voice a final plea
- Sums up the argument and asks the reader to do something or take action

📝 Opening Writing Prompt

Read Florence Kelley's biography and the first two paragraphs of her speech and then respond to the following question.

- Consider this introduction through the lens of Reader-Response. How does the reader (you or Kelley's intended audience, the National American Woman Suffrage Association) and the situation (her delivery of the speech in 1905 or reading it in present day) affect the meaning and impact of the introduction? Are Kelley's words affected by the shift in audience?

As You Read

- Mark the text where you notice the elements of a good argument: hook, claim, concessions and refutations, support, and call to action. (You can even abbreviate them as H, C, C&R, S, and C2A.)
- Circle unknown words and phrases. Try to determine the meaning of the words by using context clues, word parts, or a dictionary.

About the Author

Florence Kelley (1859–1932) was an American social worker and reformer. Starting in 1892 in Chicago, Kelley did extensive investigative work delving into slum and sweatshop conditions. Her findings and articles sparked legislators to limit women's working hours, prohibit child labor, and regulate sweatshops. She was also instrumental in groundbreaking legislation for minimum wages. She delivered the following speech before the convention of the National American Woman Suffrage Association in Philadelphia on July 22, 1905. This association fought to allow women the right to vote in elections, which was achieved on a national level in 1920.

ACTIVITY 1.9 continued

4 Have students complete the Opening Writing Prompt in their Reader/Writer notebooks.

5 Preview the As You Read tasks, noting the abbreviations for each element.

6 Direct students to read the About the Author. Have them highlight what they think are the most significant aspects of Florence Kelley's biography.

College and Career Readiness Standards

strengths and limitations of each source in terms of the task, purpose, and audience; integrate information into the text selectively to maintain the flow of ideas, avoiding plagiarism and overreliance on any one source and following a standard format for citation.

W.11–12.9.b Apply grades 11–12 Reading standards to literary nonfiction (e.g., "Delineate and evaluate the reasoning in seminal U.S.

texts, including the application of constitutional principles and use of legal reasoning [e.g., in U.S. Supreme Court Case majority opinions and dissents] and the premises, purposes, and arguments in works of public advocacy [e.g., The Federalist, presidential addresses]").

Additional Standards Addressed:

RI.11–12.1, RI.11–12.4, RI.11–12.5, RI.11–12.6, SL.11–12.1b, L.11–12.5

7 Direct students to the Knowledge Question. Ask volunteers to explain what *advocacy* means. Have pairs discuss responses to the question.

8 FIRST READ: Choose one or two student volunteers and have them read the passage as a persuasive speech, while others read along silently. Interrupt the readers occasionally to review glossed vocabulary. As students are reading, monitor their progress. Be sure they are engaged with the text and marking the elements of a good argument.

TEXT COMPLEXITY

Overall: Complex
Lexile: 1300L
Qualitative: Moderate Difficulty
Task: Moderate (Analyze)

TEACHER TO TEACHER

The Library of Congress (www.loc.gov) digital collections contain thousands of photographs documenting many topics connected to the readings in this course, including child labor. Searching for the work of photographer Lewis Hine may yield particularly worthwhile results.

1.9

KNOWLEDGE QUEST

Knowledge Question:
How can you make a convincing case about a problem that inspires people to take action?
In Activity 1.9, you will read a speech and a text that examine the topic of advocacy. While you read and build knowledge about the topic, think about your answer to the Knowledge Question.

My Notes

textile: woven fabric
repealed: overturned
enfranchised: allowed to vote

Speech

to the National American Woman Suffrage Association

by Florence Kelley

1 We have, in this country, two million children under the age of sixteen years who are earning their bread. They vary in age from six and seven years (in the cotton mills of Georgia) and eight, nine and ten years (in the coal-breakers of Pennsylvania), to fourteen, fifteen and sixteen years in more enlightened states.

2 Tonight while we sleep, several thousand little girls will be working in textile mills, all the night through, in the deafening noise of the spindles and the looms spinning and weaving cotton and wool, silks and ribbons for us to buy.

3 In Alabama the law provides that a child under sixteen years of age shall not work in a cotton mill at night longer than eight hours, and Alabama does better in this respect than any other southern state. North and South Carolina and Georgia place no restriction upon the work of children at night; and while we sleep little white girls will be working tonight in the mills in those states, working eleven hours at night.

4 In Georgia there is no restriction whatever! A girl of six or seven years, just tall enough to reach the bobbins, may work eleven hours by day or by night. And they will do so tonight, while we sleep.

5 Nor is it only in the South that these things occur. Alabama does better than New Jersey. For Alabama limits the children's work at night to eight hours, while New Jersey permits it all night long. Last year New Jersey took a long backward step. A good law was repealed which had required women and [children] to stop work at six in the evening and at noon on Friday. Now, therefore, in New Jersey, boys and girls, after their 14th birthday, enjoy the pitiful privilege of working all night long.

6 In Pennsylvania, until last May it was lawful for children, 13 years of age, to work twelve hours at night. A little girl, on her thirteenth birthday, could start away from her home at half past five in the afternoon, carrying her pail of midnight luncheon as happier people carry their midday luncheon, and could work in the mill from six at night until six in the morning, without violating any law of the Commonwealth.

7 If the mothers and the teachers in Georgia could vote, would the Georgia Legislature have refused at every session for the last three years to stop the work in the mills of children under twelve years of age?

8 Would the New Jersey Legislature have passed that shameful repeal bill enabling girls of fourteen years to work all night, if the mothers in New Jersey were enfranchised? Until the mothers in the great industrial states

---

Scaffolding the Text-Dependent Questions

1. What factual information does Kelley present about child labor? How is she making appeals to her audience's logic, emotions, or sense of ethics with this information? Scan the article for lines where Kelley cites statistics or specifics about laws. What commentary does she provide? How might these facts and commentary affect a reader? RI.11–12.2, RI.11–12.5, RI.11–12.8

2. Where does Kelley state her claim? How is it effective in its placement and rhetorical style? Look for a place in the essay where Kelley stops presenting evidence. What does she say then? What is her point? Does she present this point as a statement or a question? RI.11–12.8, RI.11–12.9

ACTIVITY 1.9 continued

9 Have students pair up to think-pair-share answers to the Knowledge Quest questions. Move about the room to monitor student responses and gauge comprehension.

are enfranchised, we shall none of us be able to free our consciences from participation in this great evil. No one in this room tonight can feel free from such participation. The children make our shoes in the shoe factories; they knit our stockings, our knitted underwear in the knitting factories. They spin and weave our cotton underwear in the cotton mills. Children braid straw for our hats, they spin and weave the silk and velvet wherewith we trim our hats. They stamp buckles and metal ornaments of all kinds, as well as pins and hat-pins. Under the sweating system, tiny children make artificial flowers and neckwear for us to buy. They carry bundles of garments from the factories to the tenements, little beasts of burden, robbed of school life that they may work for us.

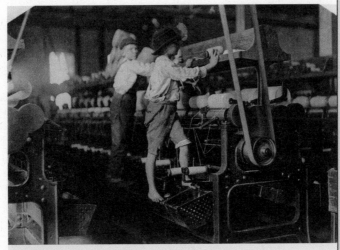

Textile workers were often so young that they had to stand on the spinning frames to replace empty bobbins.

9   We do not wish this. We prefer to have our work done by men and women. But we are almost powerless. Not wholly powerless, however, are citizens who enjoy the right of petition. For myself, I shall use this power in every possible way until the right to the ballot is granted, and then I shall continue to use both.

10   What can we do to free our consciences? There is one line of action by which we can do much.

11   We can enlist the workingmen on behalf of our enfranchisement just in proportion as we strive with them to free the children. No labor organization in this country ever fails to respond to an appeal for help in the freeing of the children.

12   For the sake of the children, for the Republic in which these children will vote after we are dead, and for the sake of our cause, we should enlist the workingmen voters, with us, in this task of freeing the children from toil!

My Notes

⌀ Knowledge Quest
- What strikes you about Kelley's speech?
- Who and what is Kelley advocating for?
- What part of Kelley's speech inspires you to want to act?

tenements: overcrowded apartment buildings
wholly: completely
petition: making a formal written request for change

Scaffolding the Text-Dependent Questions

3. How does the phrase "little beasts of burden" affect the tone and effectiveness of Kelley's speech to inspire people to take action? Reread paragraph 8. Think about what "beasts of burden" are in a literal sense. Who is Kelley comparing to beasts of burden in a figurative sense? What does this tell you about her tone? What effect might her choice of words have on readers? RI.11–12.5

4. What is Kelley's call to action, and how does it relate to her claim about the need for women's suffrage? What does Kelley say women have the power to do? How does that contrast with the right to vote? RI.11–12.5, RI.11–12.8, RI.11–12.9

10 Preview the As You Read tasks, noting the abbreviations for each. To ensure understanding, ask volunteers to explain what U.S. Constitutional principles are. Briefly discuss how to recognize text alignment with these principles.

11 Direct students to read the About the Document and engage them in a discussion about Kelley's work as an advocate. Ask them to consider the state of child labor practices in the early 1900s as the impetus for change and government involvement at the federal level.

12 Review the Knowledge Question with students. Remind them to think about their answer to the Knowledge Question as they read and build knowledge about the topic.

13 FIRST READ: Conduct a shared reading. As students take turns reading, circulate the room to make sure they are engaged with the text and making annotations.

1.9

KNOWLEDGE QUEST

Knowledge Question:
How can you make a convincing case about a problem that inspires people to take action?

My Notes

bureau: a government agency
mortality: death rate

As You Read

- Mark the text where you notice what type of text it is, its purpose, and any evidence that the text is consistent with U.S. constitutional principles. (Abbreviate your markings as T, P, and E.)
- Circle unknown words and phrases. Try to determine the meaning of words by using context clues, word parts, or a dictionary.

About the Document

In addition to advocating for significant changes in child labor laws, Florence Kelley was also instrumental in the founding of the U.S. Children's Bureau. Kelley and her friend Lillian D. Wald conceived the idea in 1903. Their goal was to establish a federal agency to promote child health and welfare. A friend of Wald's informed President Theodore Roosevelt of the idea, and he immediately invited Kelley and Wald to the White House to discuss it. For years, individuals and groups campaigned to have the idea signed into law. After 11 bills, the act to create the Children's Bureau was finally passed by Congress in 1912. President William Howard Taft signed the bill on April 9, 1912.

Informational Text

Children's Bureau Act

An Act To establish in the Department of Commerce and Labor a bureau to be known as the Children's Bureau.

1 *Be it enacted by the Senate and House of Representatives of the United States of America in Congress assembled,* That there shall be established in the Department of Commerce and Labor a bureau to be known as the Children's Bureau.

2 That the said bureau shall be under the direction of a chief, to be appointed by the President, by and with the advice and consent of the Senate, and who shall receive an annual compensation of five thousand dollars. The said bureau shall investigate and report to said department upon all matters pertaining to the welfare of children and child life among all classes of our people, and shall especially investigate the questions of infant mortality, the birth-rate, orphanage, juvenile courts, desertion, dangerous occupations, accidents and diseases of children, employment, legislation affecting children in the several states and territories. But no official, or agent, or representative of said bureau shall, over the objection of the head of the family, enter any house used exclusively as a family residence. The chief of said bureau may from time to time publish the results of these investigations in such manner and to such extent as may be prescribed by the Secretary of Commerce and Labor.

3 That there shall be in said bureau, until otherwise provided for by law, an assistant chief, to be appointed by the Secretary of Commerce and Labor, who shall receive an annual compensation of two thousand four hundred dollars;

Scaffolding the Text-Dependent Questions

5. What argument does Kelley make over the course of her speech? Who is her intended audience? What change does Kelley hope to see happen? How does she envision this change occurring? How would you explain these ideas in one sentence? Do you think Kelley's audience is mostly sympathetic to or mostly hostile to her ideas? RI.11–12.2, RI.11–12.5, RI.11–12.8

6. What do the first five lines of the Act establish? Why is this structure important to the effectiveness of the text? What entity is being founded in the first line? Who is formalizing its existence? What source empowers this group? RI.11–12.8, RI.11–12.9

14 Have students pair up to think-pair-share answers to the Knowledge Quest questions. Move about the room to monitor student responses and gauge comprehension.

one private secretary to the chief of the bureau, who shall receive an annual compensation of one thousand five hundred dollars; one statistical expert, at two thousand dollars; two clerks of class four; two clerks of class three; one clerk of class two; one clerk of class one; one clerk, at one thousand dollars; one copyist, at nine hundred dollars; one special agent, at one thousand four hundred dollars, one special agent, at one thousand two hundred dollars, and one messenger at eight hundred and forty dollars

4   That the Secretary of Commerce and Labor is hereby directed to furnish sufficient quarters for the work of this bureau at an annual rental not to exceed two thousand dollars..

5   That this Act shall take effect and be in force from and after its passage.

Approved, April 9, 1912.

⌀ Knowledge Quest

- What do you notice about the structure of this text?
- What questions does this text raise for you?
- How is advocacy represented in the text?

My Notes

Scaffolding the Text-Dependent Questions

7. According to Section 2, who directs the bureau and what rights does it have? How are these rights effective in their placement within the text? Who does the bureau ultimately report to? What is the bureau commissioned to do? Whose rights are more extensive: the bureau's or the family's? RI.11–12.8, RI.11–12.9

8. A premise is an idea on which an action is based. Upon what premise do you think the Act is based? What evidence from the text supports your ideas? What action was taken according to the Act? Why was this action taken? What specific child-based issues are to be investigated and reported on? RI.11–12.4, RI.11–12.8

15 **RETURNING TO THE TEXT:** Have students answer the text-dependent questions in pairs. If they have difficulty, scaffold the questions by rephrasing them or breaking them down into smaller parts. See the Scaffolding the Text-Dependent Questions boxes for suggestions.

1.9

Returning to the Text

- Reread the speech to answer these text-dependent questions.
- Write any additional questions you have about the speech in your Reader/ Writer Notebook.

"*to the* National American Woman Suffrage Association"

1. What factual information does Kelley present about child labor? How is she making appeals to her audience's logic, emotions, or sense of ethics with this information?

   Kelley shares facts about the ages and specific hours that children are legally allowed to work in various states. These facts appeal to the sympathies of the audience as women and mothers and also to the ethical concerns of protecting vulnerable people, such as children. The details of the laws in various states lends credibility to the truth that child laborers exist.

2. Where does Kelley state her claim? How is it effective in its placement and rhetorical style?

   Kelley makes her claim in paragraph 7. Her rhetorical question sets up the relationship between child labor and women's suffrage. Its placement after the list of disturbing facts about the legal support for child labor is an important part of her argument that if women could vote, this kind of abuse would not happen.

3. **KQ** How does the phrase "little beasts of burden" affect the tone and effectiveness of Kelley's speech to inspire people to take action?

   It suggests a tone of deep anger intended to appeal to the emotions of her audience. Kelley uses vivid language to compare working children to farm animals. She uses the phrase to compel her listeners to take action.

4. **KQ** What is Kelley's call to action, and how does it relate to her claim about the need for women's suffrage?

   Kelley's call to action is to urge women, until they get the vote, to petition and enlist the workingmen of the United States to stop the scourge of laws that allow child labor abuse. Without the power to vote, women cannot make their voices directly heard by policy-makers and must do so indirectly.

5. What argument does Kelley make over the course of her speech? Who is her intended audience?

   She wants to end child labor, and she argues that the only way to do this is by giving women the right to vote because ethically "enfranchised" women (and men) will vote to "free our consciences from participation in this great evil."

Scaffolding the Text-Dependent Questions

9. Summarize the purpose of Sections 3, 4, and 5. Why do you think these sections were placed at the end of the text? What are the main ideas in Sections 3–5? How do these sections compare in importance to Sections 1–2? RI.11–12.2, RI.11–12.6, W.11–12.5

10. How are the Children's Bureau Act and the speech to the National American Woman Suffrage Association similar in their approach to advocacy? Do the texts appeal to logic? To emotion? What solutions do the texts propose? RI.11–12.8

Children's Bureau Act

6. What do the first five lines of the Act establish? Why is this structure important to the effectiveness of the text?

   The first five lines of the Act establish the legal existence of the Children's Bureau. The

   opening lines clearly state the Bureau was created lawfully and in alignment with the U.S.

   Constitution. Structuring the argument to present this information at the outset establishes

   the Bureau's credibility.

7. According to Section 2, who directs the bureau and what rights does it have? How are these rights effective in their placement?

   Section 2 states that the chief who directs the bureau reports to the President. It provides

   sweeping authority to the bureau, extending to all classes of people and including investigations

   across a wide range of issues. The bureau's rights are listed first and the family's rights are listed

   second. This structure emphasizes the bureau's considerable authority.

8. **KQ** A *premise* is an idea on which an action is based. Upon what premise do you think the Act is based? What evidence from the text supports your ideas?

   The Act is based on the premise that there is a need for a federally governed entity whose

   primary responsibility is to address the well-being of children in the United States. The details

   in the Act, "infant mortality, the birth-rate, orphanage, juvenile courts, desertion...," indicate

   that these specific issues are areas that require investigation and reporting.

9. Summarize the purpose of Sections 3, 4, and 5. Why do you think these sections were placed at the end of the text?

   The purpose of Section 3 is administrative and reviews how the bureau will be structured and

   funded. Sections 4 and 5 state clarify where the bureau will work and how long it will be in

   effect. These sections are placed last because they are of lesser importance than establishing

   the power of the bureau and explaining its role.

10. **KQ** How are the Children's Bureau Act and the speech to the National American Woman Suffrage Association similar in their approach to advocacy?

    Both texts appeal to a sense of justice and fairness, laying out ways in which the government

    can promote the common good.

16 Keep students in pairs to complete the Analysis chart in the Working from the Text section. When they have completed the chart, have students move into small groups to complete step 12. Point out to students that they will be comparing Kelley's speech and the text of the Children's Bureau Act in this step.

17 Direct students to complete the Focus on the Sentence section. Once they've finished, have volunteers read their sentences aloud for critique, or pair students to edit and revise each other's sentences. Consider pairing students who are at a more advanced level with those with beginning or developing writing skills.

1.9

Working from the Text
"*to the* National American Woman Suffrage Association"

11. Use the graphic organizer that follows to analyze Kelley's use of the elements of argument.

Element of Argument	Analysis
The Hook: Does the speaker grab readers' attention from the opening sentence? If so, how is this accomplished?	
The Claim: Does Kelley state her claim in a direct, straightforward way?	
Concessions and Rebuttals: Does Kelley discuss the merits of the counterargument to establish her credibility and objectivity? Does she rebut the opposing argument?	
Support: Does Kelley offer compelling evidence to support her claim? If so, how is this evidence presented?	
Call to Action: Does Kelley present a clear call to action? If so, what actions does the author want the readers to take?	

12. In a small group compare the effectiveness and the various elements of Kelley's speech and the Children's Bureau Act. Use the following questions to guide your discussion:

- What is the purpose of each text? How is structure used to convey the purpose of each?
- What types of evidence does Kelley use in her speech? Is evidence used in the Act? Why or why not?
- What topic is presented in each of the documents? How are rhetoric and structure used to emphasize the topic in each?
- What is the historical significance of each document? Do both texts shape the future? How?

☑ Focus on the Sentence

Use the following subordinating conjunctions to write three sentences evaluating or critiquing the rhetorical choices in both texts.

Because Kelley repeats the phrase "while we sleep," she effectively appeals to her audience's feelings of pity or guilt to make them agree with her argument.

Although the details about child labor laws are compelling, the sudden shift to a discussion about women's right to vote muddles the overall clarity and credibility of Kelley's argument.

In order to effectively establish credibility as a newly established government entity, the bureau first aligns itself with the Constitution as lawful and empowered.

1.9

 Knowledge Quest

Think about how Kelley advocated for the rights of children. Write an informative text that tells people how they can make a convincing case about a problem that inspires people to take action. Be sure to:

- Clearly introduce the topic and logically organize your ideas.
- Cite evidence from the text that represents the most significant and relevant details.
- Use precise language and topic-specific vocabulary.

 INDEPENDENT READING LINK

You can continue to build your knowledge about advocacy by reading other articles at ZINC Reading Labs. Search for keywords such as *social issues* or *advocacy*.

ZINC

ACTIVITY 1.9 continued

18 Return to the Knowledge Question. Have pairs discuss Kelley's effectiveness as an advocate. Encourage students to take notes to help them with the writing task. Review writing expectations with students using the "be sure to" points.

19 Encourage students to continue building knowledge on this topic as suggested in the Independent Reading Link.

LEVELED DIFFERENTIATED INSTRUCTION

In this activity, students may need support identifying and analyzing the elements of an argument.

Beginning Support students who are at an early stage in their English language development by having them work in groups to complete the Working from the Text activity. Have them use the **conferencing** strategy to fill in gaps in each other's knowledge.

Extend Have individual students or partners conduct quick research about the history of women's suffrage and other social issues of the period. How did the issue of women's suffrage overlap with other issues? When did women win the right to vote in various countries around the world? Ask students to share their findings with the class.

ADAPT

If students need additional help completing the Focus on the Sentence task, review the uses of *because*, *although*, and *in order to* and what relationships these conjunctions set up between the dependent clause and independent clause.

ASSESS

Check students' responses to the Focus on the Sentence task. Their responses should make complete sentences and demonstrate understanding of Kelley's rhetorical choices.

PLAN

Suggested Pacing: 1 50-minute class period

TEACH

1 With your students, read the Learning Targets and Preview.

SAT® CONNECTIONS

This activity enables students to practice the type of writing they will perform on the SAT Essay test: explaining how an author builds an argument to persuade an audience. Allowing students to respond to this prompt in a timed setting will help them practice using their time efficiently.

2 Read the Introduction aloud. Briefly review how *analyze* applies in this context, referencing examples from previous activities. Spend some time answering questions and clarifying any areas students feel they need help with.

3 Read the writing prompt aloud. Pause after the three bullets to emphasize that students are not merely asked to *find* evidence, reasoning, and stylistic and persuasive devices, but to *explain how* the authors use these rhetorical elements to achieve their purpose.

 TEACHER TO TEACHER

If you anticipate that students will need assistance with time management, write a checklist on the board that outlines the steps they will need to take while writing their essays (some may be optional) and a reasonable time allotment for each. For example, you might write on the board "Step 1: Skim text and annotate significant ideas or word choices: 10 minutes."

Explain How an Author Builds an Argument

Learning Strategies

Brainstorming
Drafting
Rereading

My Notes

Learning Targets
- Analyze the structure of an argument.
- Write a timed rhetorical analysis essay that includes an introduction and conclusion, uses relevant and accurate textual evidence, and adheres to standard English conventions.

Preview

In this activity, you will read and analyze an argumentative text and then write a rhetorical analysis of the text in a timed setting.

Introduction

This activity is designed to help you practice writing a rhetorical analysis essay similar to the one you will write for the Embedded Assessment. In this activity, however, you will practice writing in a timed setting. You will have 50 minutes to read, analyze, and write about the text, so be sure to use your time wisely. Read the prompt carefully, annotate the text, and leave yourself time to quickly review what you have written at the end. Your essay will be evaluated in the areas of reading, analysis, and writing.

Prompt

As you read the passage, consider how the authors, Riskin and Farrell, use

- evidence, such as facts or examples, to support claims,
- reasoning to develop ideas and to connect claims and evidence,
- stylistic or persuasive elements, such as word choice or appeals to emotion, to add power to the ideas expressed.

Write an essay in which you explain how Riskin and Farrell build an argument to persuade their audience that child labor in the U.S. agricultural sector is a disgrace and needs to be changed. In your essay, analyze how Riskin and Farrell use one or more of the features listed previously (or features of your own choice) to strengthen the logic and persuasiveness of their argument. Be sure that your analysis focuses on the most relevant features of the passage. Your essay should not explain whether you agree with Riskin and Farrell's claims but rather explain how the authors build an argument to persuade their audience. Conclude your essay by restating the main ideas in your analysis, including your evaluation of the authors' use of rhetorical elements.

College and Career Readiness Standards

Focus Standards:

RI.11–12.6 Determine an author's point of view or purpose in a text in which the rhetoric is particularly effective, analyzing how style and content contribute to the power, persuasiveness or beauty of the text.

W.11–12.2b Develop the topic thoroughly by selecting the most significant and relevant facts, extended definitions, concrete details,

quotations, or other information and examples appropriate to the audience's knowledge of the topic.

W.11–12.2c Use appropriate and varied transitions and syntax to link the major sections of the text, create cohesion, and clarify the relationships among complex ideas and concepts.

Argumentative Text

Profiting on the Backs of Child Laborers

October 12, 2000

by **Victoria Riskin and Mike Farrell, co-chairs of the California committee (south) of Human Rights Watch**

1 Damaris was 13 years old when she began working in the broccoli and lettuce fields of Arizona. During peak season, she would often work 14 hours a day in 100-degree temperatures. For months on end she suffered frequent nosebleeds and nearly passed out on several occasions. Despite illness from exposure to dangerous pesticides, she kept on working. "It was very difficult," she told Human Rights Watch. "I just endured it."

2 Between 300,000 and 800,000 children like Damaris are working as hired laborers in commercial U.S. agriculture today. These farmworker children weed cotton fields, pick lettuce and cantaloupe, and climb rickety ladders in cherry and apple orchards. They often work 12 or more hours a day, sometimes beginning at 3 or 4 in the morning. They risk serious illness, including cancer and brain damage, from exposure to pesticides, and suffer high rates of injury from working with sharp tools and heavy machinery.

3 Despite long and grueling days, some child farmers are paid only $2 an hour. Many of them drop out of school, too exhausted to study. Nearly half of them never graduate from high school. Lacking other options, many are relegated to a lifetime of low-wage field labor that perpetuates the cycle of farmworker poverty through generations.

4 Agriculture is the most dangerous occupation open to minors in the United States. Work-related fatalities among child farm workers are five times higher than for children working in nonagricultural jobs, and an estimated 100,000 children suffer agriculture-related injuries annually in the United States.

5 The long-term effects of pesticide exposure are not yet completely known, but have been linked to cancer, brain tumors, brain damage and birth defects. Child farm workers interviewed by Human Rights Watch for a recent study described working in fields still wet with poison and being exposed to pesticide drift from spraying in nearby fields. One 16-year-old boy told us that he mixed and sprayed pesticides several times a week, but wore no mask or protective clothing because his employer told him he had nothing to worry about.

6 Despite the hazards of agricultural work, current U.S. labor law allows children working in agriculture to work at younger ages and for longer

My Notes

TEXT COMPLEXITY

Overall: Complex
Lexile: 1200L
Qualitative: Moderate Difficulty
Task: Moderate (Analyze)

4 Tell students to do their best and let them know that they will spend the next class period revising their essays and addressing any difficulties they may have. Circulate as students read the prompt silently, read the essay, and respond to the prompt. Do not offer assistance. Call time after 50 minutes and collect the essays.

College and Career Readiness Standards

W.11–12.2d Use precise language, domain-specific vocabulary, and techniques such as metaphor, simile, and analogy to manage the complexity of the topic.

W.11–12.2e Establish and maintain a formal style and objective tone while attending to the norms and conventions of the discipline in which they are writing.

W.11–12.2f Provide a concluding statement or section that follows from and supports the information or explanation presented (e.g., articulating implications or the significance of the topic).

Additional Standards Addressed:

RI.11–12.1, RI.11–12.2, W.11–12.8

5 Ask students to write a one-paragraph reflection on their essay for homework. Tell students to think about how they went about accomplishing the assignment. Have them address what they thought they did well during their timed writing and what they might change in the future to help them better analyze an argument.

6 Remind students to complete the Independent Reading Link.

ASSESS

When looking at students' timed essays, make sure they have an understanding of the prompt—they should be systematically describing how the authors build their argument. Students should clearly note the types of appeals being used and whether the tone and language choices are effective. Be sure they specify evidence that lends credibility to the argument.

ADAPT

If students are struggling to break down how the authors build their argument, have them start by writing down or noting the most important word, figure, or sentence in each paragraph.

1.10

INDEPENDENT READING LINK

Read and Discuss

Select a passage from your independent reading in which one character presents an argument, or attempts to persuade another character. Analyze what the stakes are for each character, how their argument reflects their personality, and how the author uses diction and syntax to communicate the character's perspective to the reader. Share your analysis with a partner and discuss how the characters in your respective texts compare in terms of their points of view.

My Notes

hours than minors in other jobs. Surprisingly, the 14-hour days worked by a 13-year-old are not prohibited by law. Children as young as 12 can legally work unlimited hours in agriculture. In contrast, kids cannot work in the fast-food industry before age 14 and are limited to no more than three hours of work on a school day until age 16. This legal double standard amounts to de facto race-based discrimination, since the vast majority of farmworker children are Latino and other racial minorities.

7 This shameful tolerance for abusive child labor in American fields stands in stark contrast to U.S. leadership in combating child labor overseas. The U.S. devotes $30 million a year to international programs to end abusive child labor—a tenfold increase from just two years ago. Last year, the U.S. became one of the first countries to ratify a new international convention to eliminate the worst forms of child labor, including such practices as child slavery, debt bondage, sexual exploitation, and forced labor. Congress recently acted to deny trade preferences to countries that fail to meet their legal obligations to end such abusive child labor.

8 This commitment to abolish inappropriate child labor abroad must be matched by a commitment to protect children from abusive labor here in the United States. Labor laws that exempt agriculture from basic child labor restrictions date back to 1938, a time when nearly a quarter of Americans still lived on farms, and Congress was understandably reluctant to regulate the ability of children to work their parents' land. The reality today is vastly different. The overwhelming number of child farm workers are not working their families' farms, but are hired laborers in large-scale commercial agriculture…

9 Child labor in U.S. agriculture is America's shameful secret. Our laudable efforts to protect children from exploitative labor overseas appear deeply hypocritical unless matched by efforts … to protect children here at home.

Evaluating a Peer's Essay

Learning Targets
- Collaborate with a peer in giving and receiving constructive feedback.
- Formulate critical responses that are clearly articulated and explained.

Preview

In this activity, you will work collaboratively with classmates to read and evaluate each other's essays using the Embedded Assessment 1 Scoring Guide. You will then revise and edit your essay based on feedback you receive.

Learning Strategies
Close Reading
Marking the Text
Peer Editing
Sharing and Responding

My Notes

The Writing Process

The previous activity gave you practice writing in a timed setting, which you have likely experienced when taking exams. More often, writers engage in an ongoing process where they plan, draft, revise, and edit a piece of writing before eventually publishing it. Engaging in this process will strengthen your ability as a writer.

1. **Quickwrite:** Take a couple of minutes to jot down your thoughts about how the steps of the writing process can help you strengthen your skills as a writer. Then share your thoughts with a partner.

Reviewing the Scoring Guide

Use the following steps to help you as you review the Embedded Assessment Scoring Guide.

2. Review the Scoring Guide and read the descriptions for each element, left to right, before moving on to the next one. Make sure you understand how each is scored—if not, ask a partner or your teacher for clarification.

3. As you read, think about which elements you will need the most help with. Make notes to revisit these areas of your paper first.

4. Now read through your paper again, and look at each category of the Scoring Guide—Ideas/Comprehension, Structure, and Language.

5. Identify which of the three categories you made the most notes in.

6. Now write down ideas for concrete steps you can take to improve these areas in your paper—for instance, you might write "review sentence structure."

Giving and Receiving Feedback

7. Exchange drafts with a partner. Skim through your partner's paper and look for obvious errors. Are there typos, misspellings, confusing grammar, or sentences that are poorly written? Consult print or digital resources such as *Merriam-Webster's Dictionary, Merriam-Webster's Dictionary of Usage*, or *Garner's Modern American Usage* to help you resolve spelling and more complex usage questions.

College and Career Readiness Standards

Focus Standards:

RI.11–12.1 Cite strong and thorough textual evidence to support analysis of what the text says explicitly as well as inferences drawn from the text, including determining where the text leaves matters uncertain.

SL.11–12.1b Work with peers to promote civil, democratic discussions and decision-making, set clear goals and deadlines, and establish individual roles as needed.

W.11–12.2b Develop the topic thoroughly by selecting the most significant and relevant facts, extended definitions, concrete details, quotations, or other information and examples appropriate to the audience's knowledge of the topic.

Additional Standards Addressed:

W.11–12.4, W.11–12.5

ACTIVITY 1.11

PLAN

Suggested Pacing: 1 50-minute class period

TEACH

1 Read through the Learning Targets and Preview with students. Then engage students in a discussion of what constitutes appropriate critical feedback. Emphasize the importance of specificity. In small groups, have students **think-pair-share** both helpful and unhelpful critical responses to a piece of writing.

2 Have students read through The Writing Process individually. Briefly discuss the importance of writing in multiple stages. Ask students to name some methods they can use to help them in the writing process. Elicit responses such as *outlining*, *freewriting/brainstorming, mind-mapping*, and *research*. Then have students complete the quickwrite.

3 After students have read through the Reviewing the Scoring Guide section and identified which areas they need the most help with, take an informal survey of the class to categorize students by these areas. Then have them work in small groups to brainstorm concrete steps for improving their work in these areas.

4 Review the steps in the Giving and Receiving Feedback section. Be sure students understand the evaluation process.

5 As students work with a partner to complete student steps 7–12, circulate through the room and check on their work. Make sure they are consulting the Scoring Guide, working neatly, and leaving specific, appropriate feedback on their partner's paper.

⭐ TEACHER TO TEACHER

Consider reviewing basic proofreading marks and abbreviations with students. You could pass out copies of a chart or, if your classroom has the capability, project one.

6 Have students take a few minutes to respond to the Check Your Understanding prompt. Ask volunteers to share their responses. Elicit explanations of how partner feedback helped students develop their selected concrete actions.

7 Direct students to the Independent Reading Checkpoint. They may find it helpful to create a brief checklist, or you may want to prepare a questionnaire to hand out before the activity. Questions for works of fiction could include: *What's the setting? Who is the main character? What is the central conflict?* Questions for nonfiction pieces could include *What is the author's purpose? What rhetorical devices are used?* and so on. Once they've written their short overview, have volunteers share their presentations with the class.

ASSESS

While student pairs are evaluating each other's drafts, make sure they are giving specific, helpful feedback. Monitor discussions to ensure that students are communicating respectfully and asking questions to clarify any feedback they don't understand. Make sure that the actions students list in their Check Your Understanding responses are concrete, actionable steps.

ADAPT

If students are having difficulty articulating concrete steps in the Check Your Understanding prompt, work with them to identify steps they can take. For example, the action *review sentence structures* offers a good start but is a little broad. Instead, you could recommend students add *check to make sure I'm using a variety of sentence structures* to their list of concrete actions.

1.11

My Notes

8. Read the paper again carefully. Use a pencil or pen to mark corrections. Circle or underline words or phrases that could use editing, and write an explanation in the margin. You might write "spelling," "lowercase," "insert comma," or notes like "This sentence feels off to me" or "not sure about this word choice."

9. Consult the Scoring Guide descriptions. Consider each element of the essay and make a check or other indication in the appropriate column. Note: sometimes you'll find an element that falls between two categories. Use your best judgment.

10. Write a brief summary for the author. Be sure and point out the things the essay does well, and be as detailed as possible about the areas that need improvement.

11. When you receive your own draft back, carefully look through each note and correction your partner made. Do you agree? Make note of any patterns that you see. For instance, you may realize that you have one grammatical issue that occurs repeatedly.

12. Have a conversation with your partner. This will give both of you the opportunity to ask detailed questions and discuss the issues in a deeper way.

☑ Check Your Understanding

List three concrete actions you will take in response to your classmate's feedback that will help you produce a strong essay for the Embedded Assessment. Put a star next to the action you will take first.

🔒 Independent Reading Checkpoint

Think about the ideas and perspectives from your independent reading from this half of the unit, and look back over previous Independent Reading Links in this unit. Then create a short presentation about your reading to give to the class. The organization, content, and style of your speech should be appropriate for a formal classroom presentation.

As you prepare your presentation, use text evidence to support your ideas. Communicate your perspective clearly and distinctly. Organize your ideas so each topic in the presentation is clearly defined and listeners can follow your presentation easily. You should give a brief overview of the story and characters, discuss the central conflict of the story, and talk about the author's purpose, use of language, and poetic (if fiction) or rhetorical (if nonfiction) devices. Finally, discuss how you feel the reading was relevant to or enhanced your understanding of other readings in this unit.

Writing a Rhetorical Analysis Essay

 ASSIGNMENT

Write an essay in which you critique and evaluate how the author of "Tipping System Exacerbates Unfair Pay at Restaurants" builds an argument to convince her audience that restaurant workers deserve fair wages from their employers instead of tips. In your essay, explain and evaluate how Kathleen Kingsbury uses one or more of the features in the directions that precede the passage (or features of your own choosing) to develop her argument. Be sure that your critique focuses on the most relevant features of the passage. Your essay should not explain whether you agree with Kingsbury's claims. Instead it should explain and evaluate how Kingsbury builds an argument to persuade the audience.

Planning and Prewriting: Take time to plan for writing your essay.	■ What prewriting strategies will you use, such as reading and annotating the source text, to prepare for writing? ■ What features of argumentative texts will you keep in mind as you read the source text? ■ How will you consider audience and purpose when planning your writing? ■ How can you use your knowledge of the genre characteristics of rhetorical analysis as you plan your writing?
Drafting: Determine how you will include the elements of a rhetorical analysis that will assure a successful draft.	■ How will you use genre characteristics and craft to produce a focused, structured, and coherent essay? ■ How will you use an organizational structure appropriate to your purpose, audience, topic, and context? ■ How can you develop your draft with details, examples, and commentary that support your analysis? ■ How will you review your draft to ensure that your essay follows your plan?
Evaluating and Revising: Review and revise to make your work the best it can be.	■ How can you revise your draft to improve clarity, development, organization, style, diction, and sentence fluency, both within and between sentences? ■ How can you use feedback from your peers and criteria from the Scoring Guide to inform your revision?
Checking and Editing: Confirm that your final draft is ready for publication.	■ What resources, such as a style guide, will you use to make sure your final draft demonstrates a command of standard English conventions? ■ How will you make sure to publish the final draft in a way that is appropriate for your audience?

Reflection

After completing this Embedded Assessment, think about how you went about accomplishing this assignment and respond to the following question:

- Consider this assignment from the perspective of Reader-Response Criticism. How was your critique influenced by the reader (you) and the reading situation (an assessment)? How might your essay be different if you read the text at a different time and for a different purpose?

College and Career Readiness Standards

Focus Standards:

RI.11–12.1 Cite strong and thorough textual evidence to support analysis of what the text says explicitly as well as inferences drawn from the text, including determining where the text leaves matters uncertain.

RI.11–12.5 Analyze and evaluate the effectiveness of the structure an author uses

in his or her exposition or argument, including whether the structure makes points clear, convincing, and engaging.

RI.11–12.6 Determine an author's point of view or purpose in a text in which the rhetoric is particularly effective, analyzing how style and content contribute to the power, persuasiveness or beauty of the text.

EMBEDDED ASSESSMENT 1

Materials: sticky notes
Suggested Pacing: 2 50-minute class periods

 TEACHER TO TEACHER

If you choose to modify this Embedded Assessment by changing the assignment for some or all of your students, be sure that you have properly scaffolded the necessary skills and knowledge. Also consider selecting a Pulitzer Prize-winning editorial that has a clear claim and use of appeals.

1 Review the assignment with the class and have students mark the text to identify all the requirements. Gauge comprehension by calling on various students to state the requirements.

2 **Planning and Prewriting:** Read the first section of the table with your students. Then take a few minutes to discuss each of the bulleted questions with students. For example, ask students what additional strategies they could use in addition to reading and annotating and elicit responses. Encourage students to list concrete, specific ideas or actions in response to the remaining questions. Suggest they choose one or two to focus on in their essay.

3 **Drafting:** Encourage students to come up with a rough organizational structure and then fill in details to create their draft. Remind students that showing the connections among ideas will help lend coherence to their draft. Instruct students to write a clear, compelling conclusion that supports the information in their essays and reiterates the significance of their explanations.

4 If needed, conduct writing conferences to ensure appropriate responses. Consider mini-lessons on using appropriately neutral language, crafting a response using facts, and identifying logical fallacies.

5 **Evaluating and Revising:** Remind students to use the Scoring Guide criteria to ensure they have met the expectations for this assessment.

6 **Checking and Editing:** Direct students to revisit the Word Wall to examine newly acquired vocabulary. Have them incorporate those words into their drafts. Encourage students to review their drafts to ensure that they are using and spelling basic vocabulary words correctly.

7 **Reflection:** Have students respond to the reflection question and hand in the response with their essays.

8 **Portfolio:** Collect all notes for and drafts of the essay and present them together to show the process students completed in successfully accomplishing the task.

SCORING GUIDE

When you score this Embedded Assessment, you may wish to download and print copies of the Scoring Guide from SpringBoard Digital. In this way, you can have a copy to mark for each student's work.

SAT® CONNECTIONS

This Embedded Assessment provides practice with the following important SAT skill: explaining how an author builds an argument to persuade an audience.

SCORING GUIDE

Scoring Criteria	Exemplary	Proficient	Emerging	Incomplete
Ideas	The essay demonstrates: • an in-depth understanding of the text's central idea(s) and key details • skillful use of textual evidence and support for claims • freedom from factual errors or interpretations of the text • a well-considered evaluation of the structure, features, and/or stylistic techniques used by the author	The essay demonstrates: • an effective understanding of the text's central idea(s) and key details • appropriate use of textual evidence and support for claims • freedom from significant factual errors or interpretations of the text • an adequate evaluation of the structure, features, and/or stylistic techniques used by the author	The essay demonstrates: • a very basic understanding of the text's central idea(s) and key details • limited use of textual evidence and/or weak support for claims • possible errors of fact or interpretation of the text • a limited evaluation of the structure, features, and/or stylistic techniques used by the author	The essay demonstrates: • little to no understanding of the text's central idea(s) and key details • little to no use of textual evidence and/or relevant support for claims • numerous errors of fact and/or interpretation of the text • little to no evaluation of the structure, features, and/or stylistic techniques used by the author
Structure	The essay includes: • a logical structure with an insightful claim and effective order • cohesive, well-developed paragraphs that develop specific ideas and support the essay • clear transitions that connect ideas smoothly within and between paragraphs	The essay includes: • a logical structure with a plausible claim and effective order • cohesive paragraphs that develop ideas and support the essay • transitions that connect ideas within and between paragraphs	The essay includes: • an inadequate structure with an unclear claim • paragraphs with little to no cohesion, under-developed ideas, and/or limited support for the essay • minimal transitions within and/or between paragraphs	The essay includes: • a missing or inadequate structure with no identifiable claim • paragraphs with a complete lack of cohesion, unclear ideas, and/or no support for the essay • few if any transitions within and/or between paragraphs
Use of Language	The essay demonstrates: • a effective command of language, with advanced vocabulary and precise word choice • a wide variety of sentence structures that strategically emphasize key points • few or no errors in a standard English conventions.	The essay demonstrates: • an adequate command of language, with appropriate vocabulary and precise word choice • a variety of sentence structures that support key points • slight errors in standard English conventions.	The essay demonstrates: • little command of language, with simplistic vocabulary and/or vague word choice • repetitive or incomplete sentence structures • several errors in standard English conventions.	The essay demonstrates: • no command of language, with incorrect vocabulary and/or confusing word choice • a number of incomplete sentences • many errors in standard English conventions.

College and Career Readiness Standards

L.11–12.6 Acquire and use accurately general academic and domain-specific words and phrases, sufficient for reading, writing, speaking, and listening at the college and career readiness level; demonstrate independence in gathering vocabulary knowledge when considering a word or phrase important to comprehension or expression.

SL.11–12.6 Adapt speech to a variety of contexts and tasks, demonstrating a command of formal English when indicated or appropriate.

W.11–12.2b Develop the topic thoroughly by selecting the most significant and relevant facts, extended definitions, concrete details, quotations, or other information and examples appropriate to the audience's knowledge of the topic.

About the Author

Kathleen Kingsbury joined the *New York Times* as deputy editorial page editor in 2017. Prior to that, Kingsbury served on the editorial board of the *Boston Globe* where, in 2015, she won a Pulitzer Prize for a series of editorials called "Service Not Included." The series, including the editorial "Tipping System Exacerbates Unfair Pay at Restaurants," gave readers insight into the high rates of poverty experienced by workers in the restaurant and food services industry.

Prompt

As you read the passage, consider how Kathleen Kingsbury uses

- evidence, such as facts or examples, to support claims,
- reasoning to develop ideas and to connect claims and evidence,
- stylistic or persuasive elements, such as word choice or appeals to emotion, to add power to the ideas expressed.

Editorial

Tipping System Exacerbates Unfair Pay at Restaurants

by **Kathleen Kingsbury**

1   Tipping is said to have started in the Roman Empire as a means to reward servants and slaves. Americans adopted the custom only after the Civil War, but it stuck: Diners doled out some $40 billion in gratuities in 2012, according to industry experts. Yet the entrenchment of tipping has given restaurant owners a pretext to avoid paying their workers a proper wage. The tip system should be uprooted—or at least returned to its roots as a purely voluntary reward for excellent service.

2   Other than restaurants, few other industries let bosses rely mainly on customers' generosity to set employee wages. Owners are happy to save on labor costs. Back when tips still came mainly in cash (and therefore could conveniently be left off income tax forms), this arrangement probably made sense to workers, too.

3   That's changed in the era of credit card payments. Only the wait staff at the priciest establishments can count on big tips leading to livable incomes. Wage theft—the nonpayment of owed wages or tips—is now commonplace at restaurants. Overall, the vast majority of servers and other front-of-the-house employees have been left with little control over how much income they make each week.

My Notes

College and Career Readiness Standards

W.11–12.2c Use appropriate and varied transitions and syntax to link the major sections of the text, create cohesion, and clarify the relationships among complex ideas and concepts.

W.11–12.2d Use precise language, domain-specific vocabulary, and techniques such as metaphor, simile, and analogy to manage the complexity of the topic.

W.11–12.2e Establish and maintain a formal style and objective tone while attending to the norms and conventions of the discipline in which they are writing.

W.11–12.2f Provide a concluding statement or section that follows from and supports the information or explanation presented (e.g., articulating implications or the significance of the topic).

My Notes

4 A busy Friday evening shift can mean good money, only to be followed by a slow Sunday afternoon where tips total $20 for a whole shift. If a diner doesn't like his meal, his dissatisfaction with the kitchen could reduce the take-home pay of his server, the busser who cleared his table, and even the host who seated him. Work performed outside regular shifts typically goes unpaid, and bad weather or illness may lead to no pay at all.

5 Rakel Papke earned good tips as a waitress at Braza Bar and Grill, a popular Everett restaurant. Yet in nine months of working there, she received only six paychecks—and, she says, those checks arrived only after she asked. "They basically only paid me to keep me quiet," Papke adds. So she recently filed a formal complaint with Attorney General Martha Coakley's office, asking her former employer for the more than $4,000 she is owed in back pay.

6 Some of the volatility that Papke and others like her experience would be eased if restaurant-goers routinely left higher tips. But while most people are accustomed to adding a 15 to 20 percent gratuity regardless of the quality of service, others set their own tipping standards, which may include a host of factors beyond a server's control. Still others—angry customers, foreigners who don't understand the custom—leave nothing at all. American restaurants could emulate most of the rest of the developed world, where service charges are automatically tacked on to dinner tabs. Some eateries in New York and California have made headlines for simply including the cost of labor in their menu prices and banning tips altogether.

7 More realistic, however, would be systemic change through stronger wage laws and better enforcement of those regulations. The Massachusetts Legislature is currently debating whether to raise the minimum wage, and the state Senate last November voted to raise the minimum for tipped workers, pegging it to 50 percent of the minimum for other workers.

...

8 Even better, however, would be to pass a law that would prohibit a separate tipped minimum wage, as seven other states have done. Workers would be guaranteed $8, or whatever the current full minimum wage is. Then, any tips they received would be what most customers already see them as—bonuses.

9 The nation's largest state, California, for decades has not allowed tipped workers' base pay to fall below the regular minimum wage. From fusion bistros in Los Angeles to sushi bars in San Francisco where the fish is flown in daily, the industry is booming and expected to expand by 9.1 percent over the next decade. In fact, in California and the six other states without a separate tipped wage—Alaska, Nevada, Montana, Minnesota, Oregon, and Washington state—job growth in the industry is expected to exceed Massachusetts' over the next 10 years, in some cases by more than double. The poverty rate for tipped workers in these states was 12.1 percent, compared with 16.1 percent in states with the lowest tipped minimum, according to a 2011 analysis by the Economic Policy Institute.

...

My Notes

10 Women, who make up about 73 percent of tipped workers, are disproportionately harmed. Waitresses in some gritty bars and grills say they feel compelled to flirt with customers and laugh at offensive jokes just to preserve their income. Even then, they earn an average of $0.50 less per hour than male tipped workers, government statistics show. Doing away with the tipped minimum and giving these women a steadier paycheck would be the quickest way to restore their dignity.

11 Under the current system, restaurants must pay wait staff $2.63 an hour. A server's wages plus her tips for every two-week pay period must also average out to at least $8 an hour, the regular state minimum wage. If not, then her employer is legally required to make up the difference.

12 Reality is messier. The government agencies that enforce wage laws largely depend on violations being reported, and some restaurant owners have found they can underpay workers without consequence. Nationwide, an Aspen Institute study suggests that nearly 40 percent of restaurant workers earn at or below the federal minimum wage of $7.25, even with tips factored in.

13 A 2009 study of 4,400 workers in New York, Los Angeles, and Chicago found that more than one-quarter of tipped workers were not even paid the lower tipped minimum wage, and 12 percent had seen their tips stolen by an employer or supervisor, which is illegal…

14 Ending the tipped minimum wage would be the first step to preventing this kind of abuse. Frequenting and encouraging eateries that include a service charge in the price of a meal is another.

15 Until then, tip well.

PLAN

Materials: poster paper or display for unpacking Embedded Assessment 2

Suggested Pacing: 1 50-minute class period

TEACH

1 Go over the Learning Targets with students and then have them read Making Connections. Ask what other aspects of culture might come into play when using the Cultural Criticism lens.

2 Ask students to think-pair-share responses to the three Essential Questions, considering how their answers have changed since the beginning of the unit.

3 Ask students to find the Embedded Assessment 2 assignment and Scoring Guide. Lead students through a **close reading** of the assignment, steps, and Scoring Guide criteria. Instruct students to **mark the text** by underlining or highlighting the skills or knowledge necessary to succeed on the assessment.

4 Review the criteria on the Presenting Scoring Guide, located in the Resources section of the student edition. Clarify any expectations specific to the presenting portion of this Embedded Assessment.

5 Instruct students to summarize/paraphrase with a partner or small group the skills and knowledge they have underlined or highlighted. As you conduct a large-group discussion, create a web **graphic organizer** that lists the knowledge and skills.

 TEACHER TO TEACHER

Revisit the web graphic organizer throughout the unit. Pointing students back to the web reinforces the purpose of each activity they are doing and how each activity allows them to practice the skills and knowledge needed for success on the Embedded Assessment.

Learning Strategies

Graphic Organizer
Marking the Text
Close Reading

My Notes

Learning Targets

- Reflect on big ideas for the second half of the unit.
- Create a plan for reading independently.
- Identify and analyze the knowledge and skills needed to complete Embedded Assessment 2 successfully.

Preview

In this activity, you will explore the big ideas and tasks of the second half of the unit and make a plan for your independent reading.

Making Connections

In the first part of this unit, you looked closely at the choices authors make to shape the perception of readers. You used Reader-Response Criticism to examine a variety of texts to understand how your own perspective and experiences can affect how you interpret a text. In this part of the unit, you will continue to build reading, writing, and collaborative skills as you apply another literary theory—Cultural Criticism—to your reading. Using the lens of Cultural Criticism, you will interpret texts by analyzing elements of culture, such as religious beliefs, class identification, or political beliefs. By the end of the unit, you will have gained a deeper understanding of the texts you are reading and be prepared to write and present a reflective essay for Embedded Assessment 2.

Essential Questions

Reflect on your responses to the Essential Questions at the beginning of the unit. Would you change your responses now, and, if so, how?

1. Why do writers make particular choices when composing a text?

2. How does the interaction between a reader and a text create meaning?

3. What does it mean to be a stranger in a village?

Unpacking Embedded Assessment 2

Closely read the assignment for Embedded Assessment 2: Writing a Reflective Essay.

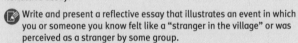 Write and present a reflective essay that illustrates an event in which you or someone you know felt like a "stranger in the village" or was perceived as a stranger by some group.

With your class, create a graphic organizer as you "unpack" the requirements of Embedded Assessment 2. What knowledge must you have (what do you need to know) and what skills must you have (what must you be able to do) to be successful on this assignment?

College and Career Readiness Standards

Focus Standards:

RI.11–12.3 Analyze a complex set of ideas or sequence of events and explain how specific individuals, ideas, or events interact and develop over the course of the text.

RI.11–12.10 By the end of grade 12, read and comprehend literary nonfiction at the high end of the grades 11–CCR text complexity band independently and proficiently.

W.11–12.5 Develop and strengthen writing as needed by planning, revising, editing, rewriting, or trying a new approach, focusing on addressing what is most significant for a specific purpose and audience.

Additional Standards Addressed:

RI.11–12.4, RI.11–12.5, W.11–12.5, L.11–12.4c

1.12

🕮 Planning Independent Reading

In the second half of the unit, continue your study of different perspectives by selecting an independent reading text that explores an aspect of culture. You might look at a reading in which the author examines his or her place in one's own or another's culture. Write a brief reflection in your Reader/Writer Notebook considering the text you have chosen from the perspective of Reader-Response Criticism.

My Notes

ACTIVITY 1.12 continued

6 Have students conduct preliminary research to find texts that might be appropriate for independent reading. Once they have made a list of possible texts, remind them to focus on aspects that are relevant to the cultural background of the author and the cultural context of the text.

7 After students have chosen a text, ask each student to come up with two questions about the text before they start reading. Remind students to keep in mind their two questions as they read and decide whether each question has been answered.

8 Have students complete the reflection prompt in the Planning Independent Reading box.

ASSESS

Check the graphic organizer students created as they unpacked Embedded Assessment 2 to make sure they have identified key skills and areas of knowledge that apply to writing and presenting a reflective essay. Look for notes that ensure students understand the criteria involved.

ADAPT

If students need additional help unpacking the Embedded Assessment, have them conduct a close read of the criteria in the Exemplary column of the Scoring Guide. Ask them to put some of the requirements in their own words to show that they understand what will be asked of them.

 TEACHER TO TEACHER

Throughout the rest of the unit, students will explore what it means to be a stranger in the village. Ask them to note anything they come across in their experiences outside the classroom that seems to touch upon this theme. Students can also interview people who may have had the experience of being a stranger in the village. Ask them what they might ask this person and help them prepare a list of questions.

PLAN

Suggested Pacing: 1 50-minute class period

TEACH

1 Read the Learning Targets and Preview with students.

2 **Vocabulary Development:** Review the Literary and Academic Vocabulary with students. Have them define *culture* (the shared beliefs, customs, practices, and social behavior of a group of people) and identify elements of culture (religion, class, politics, family, gender, foods, music, nationality, ethnicity). Then ask students to define *marginalize* in their own words, providing examples and non-examples. Introduce Cultural Criticism by asking students to predict what the theory is about based on their understanding of the word culture and their prior knowledge of critical theory.

3 Break students into four small **discussion groups** and have them each discuss one of the four common ideas about Cultural Criticism. Then have them present summaries of their discussion to the class. Ensure that the class discussion clarifies any misunderstandings.

4 To prepare students to read the Luis Rodriguez poem and consider its cultural framework, focus students' attention on the culture of their school. Ask them to consider which school rules they would change and why they would change them if they were able to do so. After a few responses, ask students why the school rules would look different if they, rather than the current administration, were in charge. Point out that those in power make rules and that power can have its own culture.

 TEACHER TO TEACHER

If students need additional help understanding Cultural Criticism, you may wish to have students role-play a scenario exploring an obvious context in which a member of a marginalized culture must negotiate an action with a member of a dominant culture.

What Is Cultural Criticism?

Learning Strategies

Discussion Groups
Levels of Questions
Marking the Text
Rereading

VOCABULARY

LITERARY
Cultural Criticism focuses on the elements of culture and how they affect one's perceptions and understanding of texts.

ACADEMIC
To **marginalize** someone is to limit their participation in mainstream social, cultural, or economic activities.

My Notes

_____
_____
_____
_____
_____
_____
_____
_____
_____
_____
_____
_____
_____
_____
_____

Learning Targets
- Use cultural context to understand a poem's language and meaning.
- Make connections between the ideas in a poem and society.
- Identify specific literary devices in a poem that serve the author's connection to the reader.

Preview
In this activity, you will read, analyze, and discuss a poem through the Cultural Criticism lens. You will then use this understanding to write an analytical paragraph about a stanza of the poem.

Cultural Criticism
Earlier in this unit you learned about literary theories and how to use Reader-Response criticism to analyze a text. In this half of the unit, you will apply Cultural Criticism to a series of texts.

Cultural Criticism is another critical lens through which a text can be viewed. This literary theory often explores works that are traditionally marginalized by mainstream society. This approach examines the effects of race, class, and gender perspectives in the analysis of texts. Cultural criticism evaluates whether these perspectives are dominant, mainstream, or marginalized. The following statements reflect four common ideas about the use of Cultural Criticism as a lens for understanding literature:

- Ethnicity, religious beliefs, sexual identity, and so on are crucial components in formulating interpretations of texts.
- While the emphasis is on diversity of approach and subject matter, Cultural Criticism is not the only means of exploring meaning in texts.
- An examination of the relationship between dominant cultures and marginalized cultures is essential.
- When looking at a text through the perspective of marginalized people, new understandings emerge.

Cultural Criticism often examines texts from the position of those individuals who are in some way marginalized or not part of the dominant culture.

As You Read
- Underline words and phrases that convey the writer's culture and the relationships between the people in the poem.
- Circle unknown words and phrases. Try to determine the meaning of the words by using context clues, word parts, or a dictionary.

College and Career Readiness Standards

Focus Standards:

RL.11–12.4 Determine the meaning of words and phrases as they are used in the text, including figurative and connotative meanings; analyze the impact of specific word choices on meaning and tone, including words with multiple meanings or language that is particularly fresh, engaging, or beautiful. (Include Shakespeare as well as other authors.)

L.11–12.5 Demonstrate understanding of figurative language, word relationships, and nuances in word meanings.

Additional Standards Addressed:
RL.11–12.1, RL.11–12.2, W.11–12.10, W.11–12.4, W.11–12.5, L.11–12.4c

5 Go over the As You Read with students. Use the first stanza of the poem to model creating a mental image. Ask the students how this stanza makes them picture Watts and the stores the author talks about. Help them understand what to annotate by providing an example or two from the first stanza.

6 Have students read the About the Author box. Then discuss Rodriguez's life and career. Have students consider how his background might have shaped his writing and perspective.

7 FIRST READ: Because this poem is fairly short, have the students read it out loud to each other in small groups. Each student should take at least one stanza.

8 Ask students to pause after each stanza and note any images that come to mind. Tell them to share what that stanza might make them see, hear, feel, or even smell.

9 As students read, remind them to think about who the speaker is. Ask them to note the place in the poem they became aware of the speaker's identity.

10 Be sure they are engaged with the text and annotating words and phrases that convey elements of culture and relationships between people in the poem. Evaluate whether the selected reading mode is effective.

About the Author

Luis J. Rodriguez (b. 1954) is recognized as a major figure in contemporary Chicano literature and has received numerous awards for his work as a poet and journalist. Rodriguez was born in El Paso, Texas but grew up in the Watts neighborhood of Los Angeles. As a teenager, he joined a gang, but he later found belonging in the Chicano movement. Works like *Always Running: La Vida Loca, Gang Days in L.A.*, and poetry collections like *The Concrete River* deal with the struggle to survive in a chaotic urban setting.

Poetry

Speaking with Hands

by **Luis J. Rodriguez**

There were no markets in Watts.
There were these small corner stores
we called *marketas*
who charged more money
5   for cheaper goods than what existed
in other parts of town.

The owners were often thieves in white coats
who talked to you like animals,
who knew you had no options;
10 who knew Watts was the preferred landfill
of the city.

One time, Mama started an argument
at the cash register.
In her broken English,

My Notes

Scaffolding the Text-Dependent Questions

1. What idea does the author convey to the reader by using the phrase "preferred landfill of the city" to describe his neighborhood? What is a synonym for the word *landfill*? What do people normally do at a landfill or dump? What does a landfill look like? What can you infer from the author's choice to use this comparison? RL.11–12.4

2. In stanza 3, why does the speaker's mother start "an argument at the cash register"? Use details from the text to make inferences about what she wants. Reread the first and third stanzas. Which lines tell you about the goods found in the *marketas*? Whom does Mama fight with and what line tells you what she is fighting about? RL.11–12.1

LEVELED DIFFERENTIATED INSTRUCTION

In this activity, students may need help understanding the context of "Speaking with Hands."

Beginning For students who are at an early stage of English language development, consider using images or other visuals to support comprehension of the text. Help them to develop background understanding of overpriced neighborhood stores by sharing images of urban corner stores and asking them to say or write statements about what they observe. Ask them how they can connect these images to the poem.

Developing Ask students to talk about whether they have ever shopped for food. Where do they go and why? What choices do they have in their communities? Why do they think food might be more expensive in poorer communities even though people may have less money to pay for it? How do they think that affects the people in those communities? How can they connect this to the poem?

Expanding Ask students to think about other texts they have read that remind them of the poem. Ask them to discuss why they are making a connection between the texts. Remind them to think of theme, voice, setting, and how those elements reflect cultural background.

Extend Ask students to write a short piece about buying something, either when they were alone or with a parent or friend. Ask them to think about what was most important to them, how the transaction proceeded, and what roles people played. How do they think the various people felt about their respective roles? What role do they think cultural background played in their experience? Have them share their pieces with each other. Consider asking them to turn the piece into a short dramatic sketch with dialogue.

1.13

My Notes

15 speaking with her hands,

she had us children stand around her

as she fought with her grocer

on prices & quality & dignity.

Mama became a woman swept

20 by a sobering madness;

she must have been what Moses saw

in the burning bush,

a pillar of fire

consuming the still air

25 that reeked of overripe fruit

and bad meat from the frozen food

section.

She refused to leave

until the owner called the police.

30 The police came and argued too,

but Mama wouldn't stop.

They pulled her into the parking lot,

called her crazy …

and then Mama showed them crazy!

35 They didn't know what to do

but let her go, and Mama took us children

back toward home, tired of being tired.

Making Observations
- What is Mama's experience in the corner store?
- What details from the poem can you visualize?

Scaffolding the Text-Dependent Questions

3. How does the author use imagery to tell more about his mother in lines 19–24? How does this imagery help us understand what he feels about her? Reread lines 19–24. What biblical reference does the speaker include in the text? What might this reference mean? How does it help the reader understand the speaker's feelings toward Mama? RL.11–12.4

4. Why do you think the author inserted an ellipsis (…) in line 33? What impact does it create for the reader? Remember, an ellipsis indicates a long pause. Think about what was happening just before the ellipsis. How does a pause at this point in the text affect the reader? RL.11–12.5

Returning to the Text

- Reread the poem to answer these text-dependent questions.
- Write any additional questions you have about the poem in your Reader/Writer Notebook.

1. What idea does the author convey to the reader by using the phrase "preferred landfill of the city" to describe his neighborhood?

The author's choice of words suggests that Watts is a poor and powerless neighborhood that

people from other areas of the city regard as a dump. It suggests a lack of respect.

2. In stanza 3, why does the speaker's mother start "an argument at the cash register"? Use details from the text to make inferences about what she wants.

Based on details in the first two stanzas and in line 18, the mother is likely arguing about

having to pay high prices for poor quality food and objecting to the grocer's taking advantage

of poor people who have nowhere else to shop for food.

3. How does the author use imagery to tell us more about his mother in lines 19–24? How does this imagery help us understand what he feels about her?

The author compares his mother to Moses' "burning bush" and a "pillar of fire" to convey that

she is someone filled by an almost holy anger. He refers to her "sobering madness," which

suggests that he thinks her anger is righteous, not out of control.

4. Why do you think the author inserted an ellipsis (…) in line 33? What effect does it create for the reader?

The ellipsis builds suspense at a key point in the poem. After the police pull Mama into the

parking lot and call her "crazy," the ellipsis indicates a pause in which the reader does not

know what will happen next. Then, Mama "showed them crazy!" Readers can only imagine

what that was like, given Mama's fury at the grocer.

ACTIVITY 1.13 continued

11 Within their groups, have students answer the Making Observations questions. When they're finished, gauge general comprehension by having a representative from each group share with the class. If it becomes clear their comprehension is lacking, reread key points of the poem, or the whole thing.

12 RETURNING TO THE TEXT: Have students continue to work in their small groups to answer the text-dependent questions. Ask them to discuss the questions among themselves. Remind them that everyone in the group should contribute. If they have difficulty, scaffold the questions by rephrasing them or breaking them down into smaller parts. See the Scaffolding the Text-Dependent Questions boxes for suggestions.

13 After students have responded to the text-dependent questions, ask them to reread the poem silently, marking the text and preparing Levels of Questions (literal, interpretive, and universal) for a discussion of the poem through the lens of Cultural Criticism.

14 In small discussion groups, students should use the Levels of Questions in Working from the Text to engage in discussion and deepen their analysis.

 TEACHER TO TEACHER

The following are sample questions that you might share with students:

Literal
- What is the name of the narrator's neighborhood?
- What is the main incident that happens in the poem?

Interpretive
- Why did Mama make her children stand around as she argued with the store owner?
- Why does the author compare Mama's "madness" to "the burning bush" from the Bible?

Universal
- Why is going crazy an expression of "tired of being tired"?
- Does speaking broken English marginalize people?

15 Based on their discussions, ask students to prepare an oral reading that conveys their interpretation of the poem through the perspective of Cultural Criticism. Students should share their oral interpretations in their small groups.

16 In a class discussion, lead students to think about this question: "Is there a definitive reading of a poem, or are there multiple interpretations?"

17 After the discussion, have students work independently to respond to the Check Your Understanding task.

18 Direct students' attention to the writing prompt. Remind them to draw upon their own analysis and their group discussions when responding to the prompt.

ASSESS

Check writing prompt responses to make sure students have analyzed the poem through a lens of Cultural Criticism. Be sure they used evidence related to the cultural issues, such as class, addressed in the poem. Their responses should have a clear topic sentence, relevant examples, and a concluding statement.

ADAPT

If students are challenged by the concepts of cultural criticism, read the poem aloud once more, asking students to note the different words and phrases that help them understand the author's cultural and economic background. Have them work with a selection from their independent reading, noting things that reveal cultural context. If they have been freewriting in their journals or notebooks, ask them if they can find words and phrases that might indicate their own cultural background to a reader who does not know them personally. Point out to students that the signifiers of cultural context and social class can take many forms and remind them to be alert to these forms as they read and write.

1.13

My Notes

Working from the Text

5. Using the lens of Cultural Criticism, write Levels of Questions (three for each level)—literal, interpretative, and universal—to explore the preceding text. Discuss with your group the meaning of this poem when read through that lens.

- **Literal:** Why weren't there markets in Watts?
- **Interpretive:** Why is the speaker's mother frustrated by the corner store owner?
- **Universal:** In what ways are people in impoverished areas impacted by a lack of access to quality goods and services?

Literal: _____

Interpretative: _____

Universal: _____

☑ Check Your Understanding
How do you think different cultural backgrounds can influence how a reader understands Rodriguez's poem?

> **✍ Writing Prompt: Literary Analysis**
> Write a paragraph analyzing one stanza of the poem "Speaking with Hands" through the lens of Cultural Criticism. Does the author's work speak to larger cultural and societal issues? Be sure to:
> - Include a clear topic sentence that responds to the prompt.
> - Choose words that keep the author's meaning when you paraphrase or summarize lines in the stanza .
> - Use evidence from the text, including direct quotations if appropriate, to support your ideas.
> - Organize your ideas clearly and provide a concluding statement.
> - Place modifiers correctly.

✍ WRITING PROMPT: LITERARY ANALYSIS

The following standards are addressed in the writing prompt:
- RL.11–12.1
- RL.11–12.2
- W.11–12.2d
- W.11–12.4
- W.11–12.5

Applying Cultural Criticism

PLAN

Materials: projector or computers for viewing image (optional)
Suggested Pacing: 2 50-minute class periods

TEACH

1 Introduce this activity by reviewing the Learning Targets and Preview and explaining to students that they are going to be applying the concept of Cultural Criticism to two texts, both dealing with the subject of imperialism. Direct students' attention to the definition of *imperialism* in the Academic Vocabulary box.

2 Read together Applying Cultural Criticism to the Concept of Imperialism. Have students **activate prior knowledge** by filling out the **KWHL Chart** in pairs or small groups. If necessary, be sure they have reread and reviewed the characteristics of Cultural Criticism from the previous activity.

Learning Targets

- Compare and contrast two different poets' perspectives in a Socratic Seminar.
- Use Cultural Criticism to analyze the concept of imperialism in written and visual texts.

Preview

In this activity, you will use Cultural Criticism to examine two poems that have contrasting views of imperialism. You will then participate in a Socratic Seminar to discuss and analyze the poems further. Finally, you will apply your knowledge of imperialism and of Cultural Criticism to a written analysis of a visual text.

Learning Strategies

Activating Prior Knowledge
KWHL Chart
Socratic Seminar
Questioning the Text

ACADEMIC

Imperialism is the policy of extending the rule or influence of one country over other countries or colonies. The word also refers to the political, military, or economic domination of one country by another.

VOCABULARY

Applying Cultural Criticism to the Concept of Imperialism

In the last activity, you learned that Cultural Criticism suggests that being a part of—or excluded from—a specific group or culture contributes to and affects our understanding of texts. In the next series of activities, you will apply the concept of Cultural Criticism to the concept of imperialism.

Use the KWHL chart that follows to begin exploring the concept of imperialism. Fill in what you already know about imperialism, what you want to know, and how you will learn what you want to know. After reading and discussing the texts in this activity, return to the chart to fill in the last column with reflections on what you have learned.

Imperialism

Know	Want to Know	How Will I Learn It?	What Have I Learned?

College and Career Readiness Standards

Focus Standards:

RL.11–12.5 Analyze how an author's choices concerning how to structure specific parts of a text (e.g., the choice of where to begin or end a story, the choice to provide a comedic or tragic resolution) contribute to its overall structure and meaning as well as its aesthetic impact.

RL.11–12.6 Analyze a case in which grasping a point of view requires distinguishing what is directly stated in a text from what is really meant (e.g., satire, sarcasm, irony, or understatement).

3 Direct students to the Opening Writing Prompt. Divide students into groups of four, and assign each group a number. Assign Kipling's "The White Man's Burden" to the odd-numbered groups and McNeill's "The Poor Man's Burden" to the even-numbered groups. Ask students write down their inferences about the subject of the poem. Have each group share their work with the class.

4 Explain that authors sometimes respond directly to one another through their texts. Tell them McNeill's "The Poor Man's Burden" was written in response to Kipling's "The White Man's Burden" and that each text presents a distinct point of view or perspective on imperialism and colonialism. Point out that looking at the poems through the lens of Cultural Criticism helps readers clearly understand those perspectives.

5 Review the As You Read directions with your students. Help them understand what to annotate by modeling with an example from each poem.

6 Have students read the About the Author box for their assigned poem and briefly discuss how each author's background might have shaped his writing and perspective. For example, Kipling was a British man living in India when that nation was a British colony. McNeill was an activist who worked to protect the rights of laborers. How might these positions have affected each author's view of the world?

1.14

My Notes

sullen: resentful

🖊 Opening Writing Prompt

Read the titles of the two poems that you will encounter in this activity and respond to the following question.

- Based on the titles what inference can you make about the subject of the poem? What connection might there be between the two poems?

As You Read

- Underline words and phrases that reveal the speaker's perspective on imperialism.
- Circle unknown words and phrases. Try to determine the meaning of the words by using context clues, word parts, or a dictionary.

About the Author

Rudyard Kipling (1865 –1936) was a British author known for his support of British colonialism and imperialism. Born to British parents in Bombay (now Mumbai), India, in 1865, Kipling was educated in England. He returned to India, where he worked for seven years as a journalist. Kipling was awarded the Nobel Prize for Literature in 1907. His children's books, including *Just So Stories* (1902), *Kim* (1901), and *The Jungle Books* (1894, 1895), are considered classics. "The White Man's Burden" was published in 1899.

Poetry

The White Man's Burden

by **Rudyard Kipling**

> Take up the White Man's burden—
> Send forth the best ye breed—
> Go bind your sons to exile
> To serve your captives' need;
> 5 To wait, in heavy harness,
> On fluttered folk and wild—
> Your new-caught sullen peoples,
> Half devil and half child.
> Take up the White Man's burden—

College and Career Readiness Standards

RL.11–12.9 Demonstrate knowledge of eighteenth-, nineteenth- and early-twentieth-century foundational works of American literature, including how two or more texts from the same period treat similar themes or topics.

SL.11–12.1a Come to discussions prepared, having read and researched material under study; explicitly draw on that preparation by referring to evidence from texts and other research on the topic or issue to stimulate a thoughtful, well-reasoned exchange of ideas.

SL.11–12.2 Integrate multiple sources of information presented in diverse formats and media (e.g., visually, quantitatively, orally) in order to make informed decisions and solve problems, evaluating the credibility and accuracy of each source and noting any discrepancies among the data.

Additional Standards Addressed:

RL.11–12.1, RL.11–12.2, RL.11–12.3, RL.11–12.4, RL.11–12.10, W.11–12.10, L.11–12.5, L.11–12.6

My Notes

10 In patience to abide,

To veil the threat of terror

And check the show of pride;

By open speech and simple,

An hundred times made plain,

15 To seek another's profit,

And work another's gain.

Take up the White Man's burden—

The savage wars of peace—

Fill full the mouth of Famine,

20 And bid the sickness cease;

And when your goal is nearest

(The end for others sought)

Watch sloth and heathen folly

Bring all your hope to naught.

25 Take up the White Man's burden—

No tawdry rule of kings,

But toil of serf and sweeper—

The tale of common things.

The ports ye shall not enter,

30 The roads ye shall not tread,

Go mark them with your living

And mark them with your dead.

Take up the White Man's burden—

And reap his old reward:

35 The blame of those ye better

The hate of those ye guard—

The cry of hosts ye humour

(Ah, slowly!) toward the light:—

"Why brought ye us from bondage,

40 Our loved Egyptian night?"

---

abide: continue to tolerate

sloth: laziness

heathen: uncivilized

tawdry: showy yet insubstantial

---

7 **FIRST READ:** Because the McNeill poem is a response to the Kipling poem, have students pair off: one student from the "Kipling group" and the other student from the "McNeill group." Have each student read "their" poem out loud to the other. Ask the listeners to make notes on what they felt as they listened to the poem.

Scaffolding the Text-Dependent Questions

1. How does the author use repetition in the structure of this poem to convey his message? What phrase is repeated in each stanza? What is different about this phrase in the final stanza? How would the poem sound without the repeated first line of each stanza? How would you summarize the contents of each stanza? How does the minor change in the first line of the final stanza affect your understanding?
RL.11–12.5

2. The author used the image of a white man taking up a burden. Based on the context of the poem, who is the "White Man" and what is his "burden"? Do you think the "White Man" is one person or a type of person? Is the "burden" one task or many? Which words and details from the poem help you understand these concepts?
L.11–12.5

1.14

My Notes

Take up the White Man's burden—
Ye dare not stoop to less—
Nor call too loud on Freedom
To cloak your weariness;
45 By all ye will or whisper,
By all ye leave or do,
The silent sullen peoples
Shall weigh your God and you.
Take up the White Man's burden!
50 Have done with childish days—
The lightly proffered laurel,
The easy ungrudged praise:
Comes now, to search your manhood
Through all the thankless years,
55 Cold, edged with dear-bought wisdom,
The judgment of your peers.

proffered: offered

Scaffolding the Text-Dependent Questions

3. What kind of figurative language does the speaker used to describe colonized people in stanzas 3? Why does this express this attitude towards them? What impression does Kipling give of colonized people and their culture in this stanza? What words give convey that impression? RL.11–12.6

4. How do the "silent sullen peoples" feel about the "White Man" who calls them "captives" but also serves their "need"? **What do the words "silent" and "sullen" suggest about the speaker's attitude toward them?** Based on the language, what can you infer about the perspective of the people who are under the "White Man's" rule? How do they contribute to the "burden"? How might they feel and act if the speaker labels them as "silent" and "sullen"? RL.11–12.4

8 As students are reading, monitor their progress. Be sure they are engaged with the text and annotating words and phrases that convey a perspective on imperialism. Remind them to generate questions about the poem and record them in the margin as they read.

9 **Vocabulary Development:** Discuss the Word Connections with students. Ask students to think of other words that share the root *servus*. As an extension, have students complete the **Roots and Affixes Brainstorm** graphic organizer.

About the Author

Born in Massachusetts, George McNeill (1836–1906) grew up in an era when workers put in long hours and had few protections from poor or even dangerous working conditions. McNeill became a labor leader and activist who worked for improved working conditions (such as the eight-hour work day) and social reform. McNeill, a critic of imperialism, responded to Kipling with this satirical offering in 1899, a few months after Kipling's poem was published.

Poetry

The Poor Man's Burden

by **George McNeill**

Pile on the Poor Man's Burden—
Drive out the beastly breed;
Go bind his sons in exile
To serve your pride and greed;
5   To wait in heavy harness,
Upon your rich and grand;
The common working peoples,
The serfs of every land.
Pile on the Poor Man's Burden—
10 His patience will abide;
He'll veil the threat of terror
And check the show of pride.
By pious cant and humbug
You'll show his pathway plain,
15 To work for another's profit
And suffer on in pain.
Pile on the Poor Man's Burden—
Your savage wars increase,
Give him his full of Famine,
20 Nor bid his sickness cease.
And when your goal is nearest
Your glory's dearly bought,
For the Poor Man in his fury,
May bring your pride to naught.

My Notes

WORD CONNECTIONS

Etymology
The word serf refers to the lowest class in medieval feudal society: the peasants who worked the land under a lord. *Serf* is an Old French word derived from the Latin word *servus*, meaning "servant" or "slave." Serfs were completely bound to the land owned by their lords, so they were, in a sense, slaves.

serfs: servant or slave
cant: insincere or hypocritical words

Scaffolding the Text-Dependent Questions

5. What is the speaker's attitude toward imperialism and colonialism in the poem? Which lines from the poem indicate this attitude? Scan the final three stanzas in the poem for words and details that reveal how the speaker feels about his role within an imperial system. Is it a positive or negative experience? Why does the speaker (and other white men) continue to take up the "burden"? RL.11–12.2, RL.11–12.6

6. Scan the first three stanzas of Kipling's poem. What language has McNeill borrowed from Kipling? How does he use irony as a literary device in this poem? Look at nearby words and phrases in McNeill's poem that can help you determine how McNeill's attitude contrasts with that of Kipling. How does use Kipling's language to emphasize that contrast? RL.11–12.6

10 After the pairs have read both poems, prompt them to answer the Making Observations questions together.

11 Have the students compare notes and discuss their emotional responses to each poem.

LEVELED DIFFERENTIATED INSTRUCTION

Some students may need support reading and comprehending the poem in this activity.

Beginning To support students who are at an early stage of English language development, consider using the passage audio for "The White Man's Burden," available on SpringBoard Digital. Reading along as they listen to the audio can boost students' comprehension. Additionally, the audio performance provides a clear model for pronunciation and intonation. Have students practice sounding out words and phrases that may be challenging to them. Ask them to think about how the sound of the words contributes to the poem.

Developing Enable students to practice reading the poem aloud by first doing so chorally, with you leading. Then have them read the poem a second time, this time out loud with a partner.

Support Following reading, have students work in groups to discuss and analyze an assigned stanza. Have groups summarize what they think the stanza means. Encourage them to emphasize what the stanza expresses about imperialism.

Extend Have individual students or partners conduct quick research about the political and social issues present at the time the poem was written. Have students analyze how these issues impacted and formed McNeill's views on imperialism. Ask students to cite the poem in their analysis.

1.14

My Notes

25 Pile on the Poor Man's Burden—
Your Monopolistic rings
Shall crush the serf and sweeper
Like iron rule of kings.
Your joys he shall not enter,
30 Nor pleasant roads shall tread;
He'll make them with his living,
And mar them with his dead.
Pile on the Poor Man's Burden—
The day of reckoning's near—

35 He will call aloud on Freedom,
And Freedom's God shall hear.
He will try you in the balance;
He will deal out justice true:
For the Poor Man with his burden
40 Weighs more with God than you.
Lift off the Poor Man's Burden—
My Country, grand and great—
The Orient has no treasures
To buy a Christian state,

45 Our souls brook not oppression;
Our needs—if read aright—
Call not for wide possession.
But Freedom's sacred light.

Making Observations
- How would you describe your intial reaction to each poem?
- What did you think each poem was about when you read the title? Did the poem confirm your hypothesis?

Scaffolding the Text-Dependent Questions

7. Who is the intended audience for McNeill's poem? What words or details tell you? Skim the first few stanzas of the poem for clues about whom the speaker addresses in the poem. To whom do the words "you" and "your" refer? What kind of person is the speaker addressing? How do you know? RL.11–12.2, RL.11–12.4

8. Who does "He" refer to in lines 37–38? According to the speaker, what will he do? How does this compare to Kipling's presentation of a similar issue? Reread the seventh and eighth stanzas for the antecedent to the pronoun "he." What actions does the speaker predict "He" will take? How is "He" different in his actions from the "you" addressed in the poem? Reread stanza 10 of the Kipling poem. Whose belief's does Kipling deem important? RL.11–12.5

1.14

Returning to the Text

- Reread your assigned poem to answer these text-dependent questions.
- Write any additional questions you have about the poem in your Reader/Writer Notebook.

"The White Man's Burden"

1. How does the author use repetition to convey his message? What phrase is repeated in each stanza? What is different about this phrase in the final stanza?

   The author repeats the line "Take up the White Man's burden," at the beginning of each stanza

   to emphasize that he is making a plea to his fellow "white man." Each stanza explores an

   aspect of what the "White Man's Burden" entails. The first line of the final stanza is the only

   one to end in an exclamation point instead of a dash, emphasizing the command.

2. The author used the image of a white man taking up a burden. Based on the context of the poem, who is the "White Man" and what is his "burden"?

   The "White Man" is a European or American colonialist. His perceived "burden" is to extend

   security, order, and a Eurocentric version of civilization to his colonized people—whether they

   want them or not.

3. What kind of figurative language does the speaker use to describe colonized people in stanza 3? Why does he express this attitude towards them?

   The speaker refers to colonized peoples as "fluttered folk" and "wild," implying that they are

   unreliable and have no real civilization compared to the "White Man." He calls them "half-

   devil" and "half-child" implying that they are not fully human or not capable of acting like

   adults. This is used to justify colonization.

4. How do the "silent sullen peoples" feel about the White Man who calls them "captives" but also serves their "need"? What do the words "silent" and "sullen" suggest about the speaker's attitude toward them?

   They do not appreciate and may even resent the efforts of the White Man (probably because

   the efforts are being imposed through the force of colonization). According to the speaker,

   they judge or "weigh" the White Man's faith and intentions. The words "silent" and "sullen"

   suggest that the speaker sees them as lacking gratitude.

ACTIVITY 1.14 continued

12 RETURNING TO THE TEXT:
Have students remain in their pairs to answer the text-dependent questions. Have each student in the pair answer the questions related to "their" poem. Then have them switch poems. After that, ask them to compare their answers. If they have difficulty, scaffold the questions by rephrasing them or breaking them down into smaller parts. See the Scaffolding the Text-Dependent Questions boxes for suggestions. Note that questions 1–5 relate to Kipling's poem and questions 6–9 relate to McNeill's poem.

TEACHER TO TEACHER

The goal is for these new groups to be large enough for students to extend and deepen their analyses of the assigned poem, but at the same time small enough to be effective.

Scaffolding the Text-Dependent Questions

9. How does McNeill's tone shift at the end of the poem? How does he address the reader and how can this affect readers' response to the poem? Reread lines 41–48 and look for words that signal a shift in the speaker's attitude and focus. How would you describe the speaker's attitude at the beginning of the poem? How does it compare or contrast to his tone at the end? Who is the "you" at the end of the poem? What does McNeill want this "you" to do? RL.11–12.4

LEVELED DIFFERENTIATED INSTRUCTION

Students may need support preparing for a Socratic Seminar and discussing the poems with peers.

Beginning Before students attempt to answer the pre-seminar questions, have them work in pairs to note similarities and differences between the two poems using the **Venn Diagram for Writing a Comparison** graphic organizer.

Developing Allow students to work in pairs to answer the pre-seminar questions. Have them take turns entering notes in the **Venn Diagram for Writing a Comparison** graphic organizer in response to each question. Encourage students to use these notes during the Socratic Seminar.

Expanding As students answer the pre-seminar questions, have them use **the Venn Diagram for Writing a Comparison** graphic organizer to record the key contrasts between the poems' perspectives. When responding to the pre-seminar questions, encourage students to use academic language such as *The poet's attitude toward imperialism suggests that ...* and *This line from the text creates the impression that ...*

Support Ask students to mark the line or stanza in the poems where textual evidence can be found for each pre-seminar question. Students can then easily reference the texts during the Socratic Seminar.

Extend Have students read "A Black Man's Burden" by H. T. Johnson and compare it, using the pre-seminar questions, to the other two poems.

---

5. What is the speaker's attitude toward imperialism and colonialism in the poem? Which lines from the poem indicate this attitude?

The speaker believes that imperialism and colonialism are righteous causes that help promote peace, health, and order (stanza 3). He describes the task of aiding less fortunate nations as difficult and thankless work that yields only "blame of those ye better/The hate of those ye guard" but that he nonetheless regards as a responsibility of "manhood" (line 53).

"The Poor Man's Burden"

6. Scan the first three stanzas of Kipling's poem. What language has McNeill borrowed from Kipling? How does he use irony as a literary device in this poem?

McNeill uses irony to present a perspective that is the opposite of Kipling's. McNeill borrows key words and phrases such as "breed" and "bind in exile." In McNeill's poem these words and phrases are ironic. He is commenting on the plight of the working poor, not sympathizing with colonialists like Kipling does.

7. Who is the intended audience for McNeill's poem? What words or details tell you?

McNeill's poem addresses wealthy capitalists who require the poor to serve them. He refers to "your pride and greed," "your savage wars," and "Your Monopolistic rings."

8. Who does "He" refer to lines 37–38? According to the speaker, what will he do? How does this compare to Kipling's presentation of a similar issue?

"He" refers to "Freedom's God," who will judge the wealthy for their abuse and exploitation of the working poor because the "Poor Man with his burden/ Weighs more with God than" the wealthy capitalist. Kipling uses the phrase "your God" (line 48) to imply that God is the deity of white imperialists.

9. How does McNeill's tone shift at the end of the poem? How does he address the reader and how can this affect readers' response to the poem?

With the line "Lift off the Poor Man's Burden," the tone shifts from ironic to sincere. He exhorts his audience to allow everyone to experience "Freedom's sacred light." He also changes the poem's focus from "you" (the wealthy) to "our souls" and "our needs." This invites readers to be part of the struggle for justice.

Working from the Text

Introducing the Strategy: Socratic Seminar

A **Socratic Seminar** is a focused discussion that is tied to an essential question, topic, or selected text. You participate by asking questions to initiate a conversation that continues with a series of responses and additional questions. In a Socratic Seminar, you must support your opinions and responses using specific textual evidence.

10. Reread the poems to compare their perspectives and to prepare for a Socratic Seminar. Respond to the pre-seminar questions and two to three of the questions generated from your reading. For each question, use details from each text to support your response. Pre-seminar questions:

   - What is each poet's attitude toward imperialism?
   - What is the difference between the "white man's burden" and the "poor man's burden"?
   - To what extent do these poems reflect different cultural perspectives?
   - How does the language and imagery used by these poets reflect the culture of their historical time period?

Participating in the Socratic Seminar

11. A successful seminar depends on the participants and their willingness to engage in the conversation. Be mindful of the following:

   - Focus on being part of a collaborative effort by making sure everybody has a chance to ask questions and offer insights. Acknowledge that not all participants will agree on every point.
   - Use evidence from the text to support your own ideas. Cite evidence from the text when you are responding to the ideas of others.
   - Make sure you speak respectfully to other participants. Summarize points of agreement or disagreement before justifying your own perspective.
   - Begin the seminar by asking one of the pre-seminar questions. From there, ask additional questions to explore one another's interpretation of the poems.

Post-Seminar Reflection

12. Review your responses to the pre-seminar questions and reflect on what you learned in the seminar. Add key learnings to the KWHL Chart at the beginning of this activity.

   - How has your understanding of imperialism improved?
   - How has your understanding of the lens of Cultural Criticism improved?
   - How would you rate your participation in the seminar?
   - What will you do differently in your next seminar?

13 Read and briefly discuss Introducing the Strategy: Socratic Seminar.

14 Next combine students from odd and even groups to form larger groups of 8 to 12 students to compare perspectives and prepare for the Socratic Seminar. Each new group should include an equal or almost equal number of students who have discussed each of the poems. Remind students to reread the poems as necessary and refer to specific lines and details to support their thinking as they respond to the bulleted pre-seminar questions in the Working from the Text section.

15 With students still in their new, combined groups, review the bulleted list in the Participating in a Socratic Seminar section. Answer any questions students may have. Then, conduct a Socratic Seminar using the pre-seminar questions and any additional questions the students have generated.

16 As students participate in the Socratic Seminar, check for a well-rounded understanding of Cultural Criticism, incorporating concepts of nationality, ethnicity, and social class.

17 To conclude the Socratic Seminar and to check understanding, have students respond to the Post-Seminar Reflection questions individually.

TEACHER TO TEACHER

Advertising is a powerful medium for conveying cultural values. Ask students to note any advertisements they have seen recently in print or on screen. Ask them to discuss the intended audience for the advertisement and how that advertisement reflects certain cultural values. Ask them how they would respond as a writer, expressing thoughts in prose or poetry that support the ideas in the advertisement or contradict them.

18 Have students work in pairs to analyze the advertisement and respond to the questions. You may wish to recommend students use the OPTIC strategy. Remind students of the five parts of the strategy:

- Overview
- Parts
- Title/Text
- Interrelationships
- Conclusions

My Notes

Analyzing an Advertisement

13. Choose an effective strategy, such as OPTIC, to analyze this advertisement from 1899.

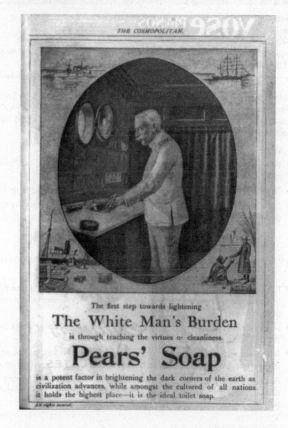

14. Who is the target audience of this advertisement? What details support your answer?
    The target audience is colonialists and imperialists—white men of the dominant culture.

15. What literary reference do you find in this advertisement? How does the advertisement use this reference to send a message? What effect does this create? Use details to support your answer.

The advertisement refers to Kipling's poem, "The White Man's Burden." The poem praises imperialism as virtuous and good. The advertisement associates the soap with that view of imperialism and implies that those who use this soap are rejecting "dirtiness" and aligning with purity by taking part in imperialism. Details that support this message include imagery of the distinguished white male navy officer, the imperial ships, the missionary; the diction of the text: "teaching the virtues of cleanliness," "brightening the dark corners of the earth," "civilization advances," and "cultured."

☑ **Check Your Understanding**

In what ways is the perspective of imperialism portrayed in the advertisement similar to or different from the perspective of imperialism conveyed by the two poems you read in this activity?

> 📝 **Writing Prompt: Literary Analysis**
>
> Think about the text, illustration, and layout of the Pears' Soap advertisement from an 1890s magazine. Write an interpretation of this advertisement using the lens of Cultural Criticism. Be sure to:
>
> - Summarize the message of this advertisement.
> - Include evidence from the advertisement to support your ideas.
> - Use ideas and specific vocabulary terms from the Cultural Criticism lens in your interpretation of this advertisement.

My Notes

WRITING PROMPT: LITERARY ANALYSIS

The following standards are addressed in the writing prompt:

- RL.11–12.1
- W.11–12.4
- L.11–12.6

ACTIVITY 1.14 continued

19 Ask students to respond to the Check Your Understanding question in a short written response.

20 To wrap up the activity, have students respond to the writing prompt. Remind them to deconstruct the prompt before answering it. To provide practice with timed writing assignments, consider providing students a total of 25 minutes to respond.

ASSESS

Review students' responses to the Check Your Understanding question. Responses should make clear connections between the attitudes about imperialism conveyed in the poems and the attitude conveyed by the advertisement.

The writing prompt will provide a chance to assess students' understanding of the elements of Cultural Criticism. Make sure students have explicitly stated their interpretation of the advertisement, provided specific details from the advertisement to support their ideas, and demonstrated a clear application of Cultural Criticism.

ADAPT

If students need additional help applying a Cultural Criticism lens to the poems and the advertisement in preparation for writing their interpretations, consider having small groups participate in a purposeful dialogue in response to the Check Your Understanding question and the writing prompt. As students grow through the year, they are expected to master this kind of academic discourse. You may need to sit in as a participant at first, modeling respectful cooperation, open-ended questioning, responses that build on others' ideas, and respectful challenges to their peers' interpretations.

PLAN

Materials: sticky notes
Suggested Pacing: 2 50-minute class periods

TEACH

1 Read the Learning Targets and Preview with your students. Ask them to name examples of British literature and locate on a map the two regions of British imperialism being considered in this and the previous activities.

2 Read As You Read with your students. If necessary, remind students of what rhetorical strategies are and have volunteers name some common rhetorical devices.

3 Ask students to read the About the Author box. Ask them if they can define the words *precocious* and *voracious* or determine the meaning of the words from context. Use a dictionary if necessary to verify the meanings. Ask them what impression they have of Kincaid from the short biography.

Learning Strategies

Discussion Groups
Graphic Organizer
Marking the Text
Sketching

My Notes

Learning Targets

- Analyze a reflective essay by closely reading the text.
- Analyze British literature from different time periods paying close attention to how each author develops a perspective on the effects of imperialism.
- Analyze how an author uses rhetorical devices to convey point of view and tone.

Preview

In this activity, you will read an essay and analyze the author's attitude toward her subject. Then you will compare the author's views of imperialism to the views reflected in Rudyard Kipling and George McNeill's poems.

As You Read

- Highlight any rhetorical strategies you observe in the text.
- Circle unknown words and phrases. Try to determine the meaning of the words by using context clues, word parts, or a dictionary.

About the Author

Jamaica Kincaid (b. 1949) was born Elaine Potter Richardson on the Caribbean island of Antigua, an island that would not gain full independence from British colonial rule until 1981. She was a precocious child and a voracious reader. At 17 years old, she was disillusioned by her family's lack of support for her talents, and moved to New York. Kincaid later became a staff writer for the *New Yorker*. By 1985, writing under her chosen name, she had earned acclaim for two books: *At the Bottom of the River*, a book of short stories, and *Annie John*, a semiautobiographical novel. Using life to inspire fiction, Kincaid cultivated a voice distinct from male Caribbean writers to explore the complexity of relationships, the effects and aftereffects of colonialism, and general alienation.

College and Career Readiness Standards

Focus Standards:

RL.11–12.1 Cite strong and thorough textual evidence to support analysis of what the text says explicitly as well as inferences drawn from the text, including determining where the text leaves matters uncertain.

RL.11–12.5 Analyze how an author's choices concerning how to structure specific parts of a text (e.g., the choice of where to begin or end a story, the choice to provide a comedic or tragic resolution) contribute to its overall structure and meaning as well as its aesthetic impact.

RL.11–12.6 Analyze a case in which grasping a point of view requires distinguishing what is directly stated in a text from what is really meant (e.g., satire, sarcasm, irony, or understatement).

Essay

from "On Seeing England for the First Time"

by **Jamaica Kincaid**

Chunk 1

1 When I saw England for the first time, I was a child in school sitting at a desk. The England I was looking at was laid out on a map gently, beautifully, delicately, a very special jewel: it lay on a bed of sky blue—the background of the map—its yellow form mysterious, because though it looked like a leg of mutton, it could not really look like anything so familiar as a leg of mutton because it was England—with shadings of pink and green, unlike any shadings of pink and green I had seen before, squiggly veins of red running in every direction. England was a special jewel all right, and only special people got to wear it. The people who got to wear England were English people. They wore it well and they wore it everywhere: in jungles, in deserts, on plains, on top of the highest mountains, on all the oceans, on all the seas, in places where they were not welcome, in places they should not have been. When my teacher had pinned this map up on the blackboard, she said, "This is England"—and she said it with authority, seriousness, and adoration, and we all sat up. It was as if she had said, "This is Jerusalem, the place you will go to when you die but only if you have been good." We understood then—we were meant to understand then—that England was to be our source of myth and the source from which we got our sense of reality, our sense of what was meaningful, our sense of what was meaningless—and much about our own lives and much about the very idea of us headed that last list.

Chunk 2

2 At the time I was a child sitting at my desk seeing England for the first time, I was already very familiar with the greatness of it. Each morning before I left for school, I ate breakfast of half a grapefruit, an egg, bread and butter and a slice of cheese, and a cup of cocoa; or half a grapefruit, a bowl of oat porridge, bread and butter and a slice of cheese, and a cup of cocoa. The can of cocoa was often left on the table in front of me. It had written on it the name of the company, the year the company was established, and the words "Made in England." Those words, "Made in England," were written on the box the oats came in too. They would also have been written on the box the shoes I was wearing came in: a bolt of gray linen cloth lying on the shelf of a store from which my mother had bought three yards to make the uniform that I was wearing had written along its edge those three words. The shoes I wore were made in England; so were my socks and cotton undergarments and the satin ribbons I wore tied at the end of two plaits of my hair. My father, who might have sat next to me at breakfast, was a carpenter and cabinet maker. The shoes he wore to work would have been made in England, as were his khaki shirt and brown felt hat. Felt was not the proper material from which a hat that was expected to provide shade from the hot sun should be made, but my father must have seen and admired a

My Notes

mutton: lamb
plaits: braids

ACTIVITY 1.15 continued

4 **FIRST READ:** The passage has been divided into three chunks. Have the class read the first chunk together silently. Ask students to pause at the end of the chunk and address the Making Observation questions. Ask them to write a few words about what stands out to them about the author's childhood in this passage and highlight a detail that captured their attention.

▲ TEXT COMPLEXITY

Overall: Complex
Lexile: 1230L
Qualitative: Moderate Difficulty
Task: Moderate (Analyze)

★ TEACHER TO TEACHER

Some students may need further support with reading and analyzing "On Seeing England for the First Time." Consider referring to Language Workshop 1B: Reading and Writing a Reflective Essay. This workshop includes a **close reading** of the text with extra supports that may be especially beneficial to English language learners. In addition, the workshop provides a more detailed biography of Kincaid to support student understanding of the author's cultural perspective and views on imperialism.

5 Divide students into small groups and have them read chunks 2 and 3 silently together. Ask them to pause after everyone has finished a close reading of each chunk and discuss how their impression of the author's childhood has changed since their initial impression. Remind them to highlight at least one detail in each chunk that captured their attention.

College and Career Readiness Standards

W.11–12.2 Write informative/explanatory texts to examine and convey complex ideas, concepts, and information clearly and accurately through the effective selection, organization, and analysis of content.

Additional Standards Addressed:
RL.11–12.2, RL.11–12.3, RL.11–12.10, W.11–12.2, L.11–12.5, 11–12.5, L.11–12.6

LEVELED DIFFERENTIATED INSTRUCTION

LEVELED DIFFERENTIATED INSTRUCTION

Choral reading can be especially helpful for improving fluency and increasing confidence of English language learners.

Beginning Have students read chunk 1 out loud together. Have them pause after every few sentences and then paraphrase what they just read. Ask them to note any words they do not understand and help them find the meaning in context or use a dictionary, if necessary.

Developing Have students read the entire chunk out loud together. Then, have them paraphrase the chunk. Ask students to help each other define difficult words in context or use a dictionary. Ask them what they think about the author's point of view and what kind of language and literary devices she uses to express that point of view.

Expanding Have students read the chunk out loud in pairs. After they have finished reading, ask them to paraphrase the text. Ask them to share what they think about the author's point of view and discuss what literary and rhetorical devices she uses in the text. Ask them to share any words they find difficult and help one another find the meaning.

Bridging Ask students to explore the idea of reader's theater. A reader's theater is a dramatic performance in which one or more performers read out loud from a text for an audience. Ask the students how they can use intonation and vocal effects to help listeners absorb the author's meaning. Ask them if they think Kincaid's text might be a good one for reader's theater and why. Ask them to think of other texts they might want to read out loud for an audience.

6 As students are reading, monitor their progress. Be sure they are engaged with the text and marking rhetorical strategies.

My Notes

GRAMMAR & USAGE

Clauses

A clause is a group of words that has a subject and a verb. An **independent clause** expresses a complete thought and can stand alone as a sentence. A **dependent clause** does not express a complete thought and cannot stand alone. A sentence with an independent clause and one or more dependent clauses is **a complex sentence**. Complex sentences add variety to writing and establish relationships between ideas. Reread this complex sentence from Kincaid's essay:

"My father, who might have sat next to me at breakfast, was a carpenter and cabinet maker."

The dependent clause—*who might have sat next to me at breakfast*—cannot stand alone as a sentence. It is set off by commas because it is not essential to our understanding of who the father is. The rest of this complex sentence—*My father was a carpenter and cabinet maker*—forms the independent clause.

Find other examples of complex sentences in Jamaica Kincaid's essay. Determine which clauses are independent and which are dependent.

picture of an Englishman wearing such a hat in England, and this picture that he saw must have been so compelling that it caused him to wear the wrong hat for a hot climate most of his long life. And this hat—a brown felt hat—became so central to his character that it was the first thing he put on in the morning as he stepped out of bed and the last thing he took off before he stepped back into bed at night. As we sat at breakfast a car might go by. The car, a Hillman or a Zephyr, was made in England. The very idea of the meal itself, breakfast, and its substantial quality and quantity was an idea from England; we somehow knew that in England they began the day with this meal called breakfast and a proper breakfast was a big breakfast. No one I knew liked eating so much food so early in the day: it made us feel sleepy, tired. But this breakfast business was Made in England like almost everything else that surrounded us, the exceptions being the sea, the sky, and the air we breathed.

Chunk 3

3 At the time I saw this map—seeing England for the first time—I did not say to myself. "Ah, so that's what it looks like." Because there was no longing in me to put a shape to those three words that ran through every part of my life, no matter how small; for me to have had such a longing would have meant that I lived in a certain atmosphere, an atmosphere in which those three words were felt as a burden. But I did not live in such an atmosphere. My father's brown felt hat would develop a hole in its crown, the lining would separate from the hat itself, and six weeks before he thought that he could not be seen wearing it—he was a very vain man—he would order another hat from England. And my mother taught me to eat my food in the English way: the knife in the right hand, the fork in the left, my elbows held still close to my side, the food carefully balanced on my fork and then brought up to my mouth. When I had finally mastered it, I overheard her saying to a friend, "Did you see how nicely she can eat?" But I knew then that I enjoyed my food more when I ate it with my bare hands, and I continued to do so when she wasn't looking. And when my teacher showed us the map, she asked us to study it carefully, because no test we would ever take would be complete without this statement: "Draw a map of England." I did not know then that the statement "Draw a map of England" was something far worse than a declaration of war, for in fact a flat-out declaration of war would have put me on alert, and again in fact, there was no need for war—I had long ago been conquered. I did not know then that this statement was part of a process that would result in my erasure, not my physical erasure, but my erasure all the same. I did not know then that this statement was meant to make me feel in awe and small whenever I heard the word "England": awe at its existence, small because I was not from it. I did not know very much of anything then—certainly not what a blessing it was that I was unable to draw a map of England correctly.

Making Observations

- What visual images came to mind as you were reading this essay?
- What stands out to you the most about this narrator's childhood?

Scaffolding the Text-Dependent Questions

1. What does the repetition of the word "England" in paragraph 1 tell you about the author's point of view? Find the sentences in the first paragraph with the word "England." What kind of words does the author use to describe this England? What effect does that create? What do we know about the author in the first sentences of the paragraph? RL.11–12.6

2. What can you infer from the speaker's tone in the opening paragraph? What images does the author use to describe England? Are those images always flattering to England? How does the author seem to feel about her child self? RL.11–12.4, RL.11–12.5, RL.11–12.6

7 RETURNING TO THE TEXT: Have students answer the text-dependent questions. If they have difficulty, scaffold the questions by rephrasing them or breaking them down into smaller parts. See the Scaffolding the Text-Dependent Questions boxes for suggestions.

Returning to the Text

- Reread the essay to answer these text-dependent questions.
- Write any additional questions you have about the text in your Reader/Writer Notebook.

1. What does the repetition of the word "England" in paragraph 1 tell you about the author's point of view?

As a child, the author was clearly impressed by England. The repetition of the word suggests a

childlike fascination with the place.

2. What can you infer from the speaker's tone in the opening paragraphs?

Kincaid tries to recreate the tone of wonder she had as a child, but it soon slides into a tone

of gentle yet obvious irony, mocking that sense of wonder. Details that describe the map

of England as "a leg of mutton" and England itself as "a special jewel all right" convey that

mocking tone.

3. In Chunk 2, how does the speaker evoke England's presence in her daily life?

Throughout this paragraph the speaker lists in great detail all of the ways that she has come

in contact with England. She lists food, clothing items, and sarcastically notes that even

breakfast was "Made in England like mostly everything around us."

4. In Chunk 3, what rhetorical devices are used and how do they convey Kincaid's attitude toward "seeing England for the first time"?

Kincaid uses an analogy, comparing "Draw a map of England" to a declaration of war. She

compares herself to a conquered land. Her diction ("war," "erasure," "small," "blessing")

also expresses her attitude. She also repeats, the phrase "I did not know..." at the end to

emphasize her ignorance.

5. How does the author's notion of England develop and change over the course of the essay?

As a young child, the author is in awe of England. She learned from her parents that England

is a special place, a source of all good things. Yet as she learns English table manners, she

begins to realize that England is a source of oppression that would lead to her "erasure."

Scaffolding the Text-Dependent Questions

3. In Chunk 2, how does the speaker evoke England's presence in her daily life? What phrase does the author repeat in Chunk 2? What does this reveal about her father? What details does she describe regarding her daily life? How is England related to those details? RL.11–12.3, L.11–12.5

4. In Chunk 3, what rhetorical devices are used, and how do they convey Kincaid's attitude toward "seeing England for the first time"? Look at the words she uses to describe how she sees England. What images are created by those words? What relationship between the author and England is suggested by those words? What phrase does she repeat at the end of the chunk? RL.11–12.4, RL.11–12.5, RL.11–12.6

8 After the reading is complete, organize students in small groups to fill in the chart in the Working from the Text section. Tell them they can reread and review the poems by Kipling and McNeill if necessary.

9 After each group has filled out the chart, have the class compare the groups' charts and come up with a single chart that they all agree is reliable.

10 Ask students to return to their groups and discuss the Check Your Understanding question. Then ask students to respond to the question in two to three sentences.

11 Point out the Grammar & Usage box, and have students scan the text to find examples of dependent and independent clauses. Have them highlight any dependent clauses they find.

12 Lead students in a discussion reflecting on the process of comparing the three literary texts to help prepare them for Embedded Assessment 2.

ASSESS

Review the charts the students filled out comparing the three texts. Note how well students were able to discern each author's tone, intended audience, and perspective about imperialism. Students' charts should show awareness of both cultural and historical context for all three selections.

Use students' responses to the Check Your Understanding to assess how well they synthesized their analyses of the three texts. Look for clear and concise summaries of how analyzing the texts deepened their understanding of imperialism.

ADAPT

If students need additional help evaluating the author's attitude toward imperialism in three texts, have them work in pairs to reread one of the texts and highlight any images, words, or phrases that relate to imperialism. Ask them to discuss the author's ideas informally with their partner.

1.15

Working from the Text

6. With a partner, consider the quotation, "England was a special jewel all right, and only special people got to wear it. The people who got to wear England were English people."

   • Why might the author have included this statement in the first paragraph of her essay?
   • What does this quotation reveal about the narrator's perception of England?
   • How might England's presence in the narrator's every day life cause her to feel like an outsider?

7. Answer each question in the chart that follows. As you fill in the chart think about how each text affects your understanding of the others. Note any ways your ideas or opinions change as you compare and contrast the texts.

Question:	The White Man's Burden	The Poor Man's Burden	On Seeing England for the First Time
What tone does each author use when addressing the reader? Who is the author's intended audience?	The author's tone is very commanding. He is telling other white men like himself what he thinks they should "take up the white man's burden" and colonize other people.	The author's tone is one of outrage and protest. He is writing for wealthy people and people of imperialist nations and telling them that their actions are cruel and immoral.	The author's tone is personal and intimate. She is writing about her childhood. She is writing for a general audience, but many of the details seem to suggest that she thinks her readers will not be completely familiar with her culture.
What does each author believe about imperialism?	The author believes that imperialism is right and should be used to "civilize" non-Western people.	The author believes that wealthy capitalist and imperialists oppress poor and colonized people. He also implies that their actions damage their own societies too.	The author believes that imperialism undermines the respect that colonized people have for their own culture and makes them feel that their values and practices are somehow inferior to those of their oppressors.
What connotations does Western culture have for each author?	The author sees Western culture as a source of all good and "civilized" things.	The author sees Western culture as a system that oppresses poor and colonized people, but also as a system that can potentially be reformed and improved.	The author sees Western culture as something that might not be obviously oppressive or openly brutal, but nevertheless robs colonized people of their own identity and culture.
How does each text reflect the author's cultural and historical context?	The author wrote during the 19th century at a time when Western powers, especially Britain, were expanding their colonial empires.	The author wrote during a time when Western capitalism and imperialism were gaining power, but reform movements in Western culture were also questioning the effects of capitalism on poorer people.	The author wrote during the mid-20th century when many former colonies were free or at least freer than they had been in the 19th century. But it was also a time when the effects of imperialism were still strongly felt in former colonies.

☑ Check Your Understanding

How did analyzing texts from different time periods provide you with a new understanding or perspective of imperialism? Summarize how the texts from Kipling, McNeill, and Kincaid informed your perspective.

Scaffolding the Text-Dependent Questions

5. How does the author's notion of England develop and change over the course of the essay? Summarize the impression the author leaves in each chunk of text. How does she feel about England in each chunk? How does that change over the whole essay? RL.11–12.1, RL.11–12.2

Language Checkpoint: Placing Modifiers

Learning Targets
- Place phrases and clauses correctly in sentences.
- Recognize and correct misplaced and dangling modifiers.

Preview

In this activity, you will develop an understanding of modifiers and how to use them to enhance your writing. Then, you will practice identifying and correctly placing modifiers, before incorporating them into your own writing.

Placing Modifiers Correctly

Part of being an effective writer is placing modifiers so that your meaning is clear. It is also important to know how to revise misplaced and dangling modifiers. A **modifier** is a word, phrase, or clause that makes the meaning of another word or word group more specific. In these examples, the words and word groups in boldface are modifiers:

a beautiful map

the map **of England**

an elegant map **that makes England look like a jewel**

Modifiers should be placed near the word or word group they modify. A **misplaced modifier** can create confusion or accidental humor. The following excerpt is a single sentence that includes many modifiers. If the modifiers were misplaced the reader could easily get confused.

> The England I was looking at was laid out on a map gently, beautifully, delicately, a very special jewel: it lay on a bed of sky blue—the background of the map—its yellow form mysterious, because though it looked like a leg of mutton, it could not really look like anything so familiar as a leg of mutton because it was England—with shadings of pink and green, unlike any shadings of pink and green I had seen before, squiggly veins of red running in every direction.

1. Read the following sentences, and identify the misplaced modifiers. Then rewrite each sentence, placing the modifier correctly. The first one has been done for you.

   a. Jamaica Kincaid was born in 1949 on the colonial island Antigua, <u>who eventually moved to New York and became a famous writer</u>.

   > Jamaica Kincaid, who eventually moved to New York and became a famous writer, was born in 1949 on the colonial island Antigua.

   b. We discussed her reflections on being instructed to draw a map of England <u>during our English class</u>.

   > During our English class, we discussed her reflections on being instructed to draw a map of England.

College and Career Readiness Standards

Focus Standards:

L.11–12.1 Demonstrate command of the conventions of standard English grammar and usage when writing or speaking.

L.11–12.4c Consult general and specialized reference materials (e.g., dictionaries, glossaries, thesauruses), both print and digital, to find the pronunciation of a word or determine or clarify its precise meaning, its part of speech, its etymology, or its standard usage.

W.11–12.5 Develop and strengthen writing as needed by planning, revising, editing, rewriting, or trying a new approach, focusing on addressing what is most significant for a specific purpose and audience.

Additional Standards Addressed:

L.11–12.6, W.11–12.2

PLAN

Materials: students' responses to Activity 1.14 writing prompt
Suggested Pacing: 1 50-minute class period

TEACH

1 Read the Learning Targets, and then introduce the topic by writing this sentence on the board: *Misplaced and dangling, the readers had a great deal of trouble understanding the modifiers.*

2 Ask students what is confusing or humorous about the sentence. Underline *Misplaced and dangling*. Elicit from your students or explain that the phrase seems to modify *readers* rather than *modifiers*. Show them that the sentence can be improved by moving the modifying clause to directly precede *modifiers*.

TEACHER TO TEACHER

Placing modifiers is addressed in a seventh-grade language standard (L.7.1a) but is designated as a Language Progressive Skill. Students may need additional practice applying this skill as the texts they are reading and writing increase in complexity.

3 Briefly review with students the definition of *modifier* and the examples of modifying words, phrases, and clauses on the page. Then have students silently read the explanation and the example sentence from Kincaid's essay.

4 Ask one student to read aloud the original sentence in 1a and another to read aloud the corrected version. Make sure students understand the differences between the two versions.

5 Have students complete 1b and 1c and then share their answers. If time permits, have them discuss what the original sentences meant in a literal sense.

6 Pair students and have them read the Correcting Dangling Modifiers section and complete the exercise. Review their responses and clarify as needed.

 TEACHER TO TEACHER

Students often have more difficulty identifying and correcting dangling modifiers than identifying and correcting misplaced ones. If necessary, explain to students that if they have trouble revising sentences with dangling modifiers, they may need to figure out what information is missing from the sentence. For instance, in example 1e, students need to add a word for the dangling phrase to modify or recast the sentence.

7 Move to the Revising section and remind students that checking for correct use and placement of modifiers is an important step when editing their writing. Have them read the paragraph and revise it to correct misplaced and dangling modifiers. Review answers with students, eliciting and discussing students' different revision choices.

8 Make sure their revision shows that they understand how to place and use modifiers clearly and sensibly.

9 Have students return to the analysis they wrote in Activity 1.14 to check for correct use and placement of modifiers.

SAT® CONNECTIONS

This activity provides practice with this important SAT skill: recognizing and correcting misplaced modifiers in sentences.

LC 1.15

c. She discusses being a child and seeing a map of England <u>sitting at a desk in school</u>.

She discusses being a child sitting at a desk in school and seeing a map of England.

Correcting Dangling Modifiers

A modifier that does not clearly modify any word or word group in a sentence is a dangling modifier. While you can usually correct a misplaced modifier by rearranging the sentence, in the case of a dangling modifier, you may need to add or replace words to clarify your meaning.

Dangling: After reading the essay, a discussion took place. (Did the discussion read the essay?)

Revised: After reading the essay, we discussed it.

Now the phrase modifies *we*.

Dangling: Moving to New York, a career as a writer came next.

In this example, the phrase seems to modify *career*, but that doesn't make sense.

Revised: After Jamaica Kincaid moved to New York, she undertook a career as a writer.

- Read the following sentences, and underline each dangling modifier. Then, rewrite each sentence to make it clear.

d. <u>Coming from a family in an English colony</u>, the author's essay delivers a clear message about identity.

Coming from a family in an English colony, the author delivers a clear message about identity.

e. <u>Struck by the author's memories</u>, the experience seems to have changed her forever.

I was struck by the author's memories and how the experience seems to have changed her forever.

f. <u>Considering her young self conquered</u>, even so, the desire to eat with bare hands never went away.

Considering her young self conquered, the author indicates that, even so, the desire to eat with bare hands never went away.

Revising

Read the paragraph that follows from a student's essay analyzing "On Seeing England for the First Time." Work with a partner to check whether modifiers are placed correctly and whether each clearly modifies a word or word group. Underline any mistakes you notice, and rewrite the paragraph, correcting the mistakes. (Not all sentences include errors.)

[1] <u>Drawn so that it resembled a jewel,</u> the schoolgirl gazed at the map of England. [2] <u>Surprised,</u> it also looked a little like mutton, a popular English meat. [3] At the time, she didn't understand how colonial rule had colored her world and distorted her perception. [4] She would eventually explore what it means to grow up in a colonized Caribbean nation, <u>reflecting on her experiences.</u> [5] <u>No longer a little girl,</u> the essay demonstrates a canny understanding of history and identity.

[1] The schoolgirl gazed at the map of England, drawn so that it resembled a jewel. [2] She was surprised to note that it also looked a little like mutton, a popular English meat. [3] At the time, she didn't understand how colonial rule had colored her world and distorted her perception. [4] Reflecting on her experiences, she would eventually explore what it means to grow up in a colonized Caribbean nation. [5] The work of someone who is no longer a little girl, the essay demonstrates a canny understanding of history and identity.

☑ Check Your Understanding

Imagine you are editing a classmate's writing, and you notice these sentences:

Called Waladii by the native people for hundreds of years, Jamaica Kincaid was born on an island that the Spanish named Antigua. Reading about Antigua, slavery and colonization took a serious toll on the island.

Write an explanation so that your classmate understands the mistakes and how to correct them. Then add a question to your Editor's Checklist to remind yourself to check for correct use of modifiers.

The phrase *Called Waladii . . . years* is a misplaced modifier. The first sentence should be revised so that the phrase modifies *Antigua*. In the second sentence, *Reading about Antigua* is a dangling modifier; the sentence should be revised to indicate who is reading about Antigua or to otherwise clarify the meaning.

Practice

Return to the essay you wrote in Activity 1.13, and check it for correct use and placement of modifiers. Work with a partner, and follow the steps listed.

- Underline any modifying words, phrases, and clauses.
- Check for correct placement and use.
- Rewrite to correct any misplaced or dangling modifiers.

ASSESS

Look for responses to the Check Your Understanding task that show that students understand that modifiers must clearly and sensibly modify a word or word group in the sentence. Students should be able to explain to a classmate why a misplaced or dangling modifier is a mistake and how to fix it. The questions students add to their Editor's Checklists should demonstrate that they know how to look for misplaced and dangling modifiers in their own writing.

ADAPT

If students need additional help understanding misplaced modifiers, provide additional sentences with misplaced modifiers for practice. Include different types of modifiers—words, phrases, and clauses. Write the sentences on strips of paper and cut them so that the misplaced modifier is on a separate strip. Distribute the sentence part strips to small groups of students and have them work together to put the sentences together correctly.

PLAN

Materials: highlighters in three different colors
Suggested Pacing: 2 50-minute class periods

TEACH

1 Read aloud the Learning Targets and Preview with your students. Help them understand that a reflective essay may include multiple events, responses, and reflections, and that these elements do not necessarily occur in chronological order.

2 Direct students to the Organizational Structure of a Reflective Essay section and explain that they will be reading a reflective essay that uses a recursive organizational structure. Go over the three elements of the structure with students. Then, ask them to work with a partner to complete student step 1.

3 Before reading Orwell's essay "Shooting an Elephant," ask students to recall an event that taught them something valuable. Ask students to use the triangle graphic organizer as a prewriting strategy. They should note the event, their response, and their reflection on lessons learned. Students should then draft a quickwrite of the event, including all elements, and think-pair-share responses with a partner.

4 After drafting, ask students to mark the text using three different colors to identify the event, response, and reflection in their drafts. If they are missing a component, provide additional writing time to revise the draft to include that component.

5 Connect the prewriting graphic organizer to the structure of a reflective essay. Students will use this structure when analyzing "Shooting an Elephant" and later to construct a plan for an original reflective essay.

Learning Strategies

Diffusing
Marking the Text
Levels of Questions
Quickwrite
Skimming/Scanning
Think-Pair-Share

My Notes

Learning Targets

- Analyze a reflective essay to explore an author's perspective on imperialism.
- Evaluate how the organizational structure of reflective essay can help you achieve your purpose.
- Draft a reflective essay applying the organizational structure studied.

Preview

In this activity, you will study George Orwell's reflective essay and apply the lens of Cultural Criticism to Orwell's commentary on imperialism. After working with the text, you will turn to your own writing and apply what you have learned about the structure of a reflective essay.

Organizational Structure of a Reflective Essay

A reflective essay is a kind of personal narrative in which the writer reflects on the significance of an incident.

Response
The author describes his or her feelings and thoughts concerning the encounter. This is the initial response, without the benefit of reflection.

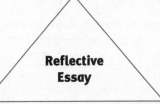

Reflective Essay

Event
The author describes an incident or set of circumstances.

Reflection
The author reflects on the incident. This reflection usually occurs sometime after the event or incident. In the reflection, the author often transitions from describing a situation unique to him or her to a discussion more universal in nature.

1. Look back at the essay "On Seeing England for the First Time" in the previous activity. Work with a partner to try to identify the event, response, and reflection in that essay.

2. **Quickwrite:** Think about an event that taught you something valuable. Use the triangle graphic organizer to brainstorm details about the event, your response, and your reflection on the lessons learned. Then complete a quickwrite that includes these details. You will return to this draft later in the activity.

College and Career Readiness Standards

Focus Standards:

RL.11–12.1 Cite strong and thorough textual evidence to support analysis of what the text says explicitly as well as inferences drawn from the text, including determining where the text leaves matters uncertain.

RL.11–12.4 Determine the meaning of words and phrases as they are used in the text, including figurative and connotative meanings;

analyze the impact of specific word choices on meaning and tone, including words with multiple meanings or language that is particularly fresh, engaging, or beautiful. (Include Shakespeare as well as other authors.)

RL.11–12.5 Analyze how an author's choices concerning how to structure specific parts of a text (e.g., the choice of where to begin or end a story, the choice to provide a comedic or tragic

6 Review the As You Read tasks. To support reading comprehension, remind students to pause at the glossed and footnoted words to check definitions.

7 Ask the students to read the About the Author box. Then ask them what they think Orwell's attitude toward imperialism might be based on the short biography.

8 FIRST READ: Read Chunk 1 aloud. Then ask the students to address the first question in Making Observations. Have them write down one or two sentences describing their first impression of the narrator. Also ask them to summarize the visual scenes in the story so far and the details that seem most important in these scenes.

As You Read

- Use a question mark to note anything you do not understand or any place where you would like more information.
- Circle unknown words and phrases. Try to determine the meaning of the words by using context clues, word parts, or a dictionary.

My Notes

About the Author

George Orwell (1903–1950) was born Eric Blair in what was then British India, where his father was a government official. After an education in England, Orwell worked in the Indian Imperial Police, though he left his position at the age of 24 to turn his hand to writing. Throughout his career, Orwell wrote under his pen name about the poor and working classes in Asia, England, and France. Working for the BBC during and after WWII, he wrote his two most famous works: *Animal Farm*, a satire of collectivism, and *1984*, a stinging critique of totalitarianism. Orwell, who famously said, "Good prose is like a window pane," is considered one of the most influential stylists of the 20th century. He wrote extensively on the art of prose, which he considered a powerful political tool.

Essay

Shooting an Elephant

by **George Orwell**

Chunk 1

1   In Moulmein, in lower Burma, I was hated by large numbers of people—the only time in my life that I have been important enough for this to happen to me. I was subdivisional police officer of the town, and in an aimless, petty kind of way an anti-European feeling was very bitter. No one had the guts to raise a riot, but if a European woman went through the bazaars alone somebody would probably spit betel juice over her dress. As a police officer I was an obvious target and was baited whenever it seemed safe to do so. When a nimble Burman tripped me up on the football field and the referee (another Burman) looked the other way, the crowd yelled with hideous laughter. This happened more than once. In the end the sneering yellow faces of young men that met me everywhere, the insults hooted after me when I was at a safe distance, got badly on my nerves. The young Buddhist priests were the worst of all. There were several thousands of them in the town and none of them seemed to have anything to do except stand on street corners and jeer at Europeans.

bazaars: open-air markets

College and Career Readiness Standards

resolution) contribute to its overall structure and meaning as well as its aesthetic impact.

RL.11–12.6 Analyze a case in which grasping a point of view requires distinguishing what is directly stated in a text from what is really meant (e.g., satire, sarcasm, irony, or understatement).

W.11–12.2 Write informative/explanatory texts to examine and convey complex ideas, concepts,

and information clearly and accurately through the effective selection, organization, and analysis of content.

Additional Standards Addressed:

RL.11–12.2, RL.11–12.10, W.11–12.2, L.11–12.5, L.11–12.6

9 Ask students to read Chunks 2–3 independently and pause after each chunk to address the second question in Making Observations. Ask them to think about the visual images in the story and note what images struck them as interesting, important, or puzzling. Ask them to think about their initial impression of the narrator and how that may have changed.

 TEXT COMPLEXITY

Overall: Complex
Lexile: 1070L
Qualitative: Moderate Difficulty
Task: Moderate (Analyze)

 TEACHER TO TEACHER

For vocabulary practice, you might have students read and discuss the glossed words in this text. Assist students as needed in using context clues, patterns of word changes, and/or reference materials to clarify meaning for these words. Model the correct pronunciation of unfamiliar words, emphasizing the production of sounds. Have students create their own pronunciation guides by marking the text for the sounds of long and short vowels, silent letters, and consonant clusters. Reinforce students' acquisition of new vocabulary through oral reading strategies, such as paired reading, read aloud, and shared readings.

1.16

My Notes

2 All this was perplexing and upsetting. For at that time I had already made up my mind that imperialism was an evil thing and the sooner I chucked up my job and got out of it the better. Theoretically—and secretly, of course—I was all for the Burmese and all against their oppressors, the British. As for the job I was doing, I hated it more bitterly than I can perhaps make clear. In a job like that you see the dirty work of Empire at close quarters. The wretched prisoners huddling in the stinking cages of the lockups, the gray, cowed faces of the long-term convicts, the scarred buttocks of men who had been flogged with bamboos—all these oppressed me with an intolerable sense of guilt. But I could get nothing into perspective. I was young and ill-educated and I had to think out my problems in the utter silence that is imposed on every Englishman in the East. I did not know that the British Empire is dying, still less did I know that it is a great deal better than the younger empires that are going to **supplant** it. All I knew was that I was stuck between my hatred of the empire I served and my rage against the evil-spirited little beasts who tried to make my job impossible. With one part of my mind I thought of the British Raj as an unbreakable tyranny, as something clamped down, in *saecula saeculorum*[1], upon the will of **prostrate** peoples; with another part I thought that the greatest joy in the world would be to drive a bayonet into a Buddhist priest's guts. Feelings like these are the normal by-product of imperialism; ask any Anglo-Indian official, if you can catch him off duty.

Chunk 2

3 One day something happened which in a roundabout way was enlightening. It was a tiny incident in itself, but it gave me a better glimpse than I had had before of the real nature of imperialism—the real motives for which despotic governments act. Early one morning the subinspector at a police station the other end of the town rang me up on the phone and said that an elephant was ravaging the bazaar. Would I please come and do something about it? I did not know what I could do, but I wanted to see what was happening and I got onto a pony and started out. I took my rifle, an old. 44 Winchester and much too small to kill an elephant, but I thought the noise might be useful *in terrorem*[2]. Various Burmans stopped me on the way and told me about the elephant's doings. It was not, of course, a wild elephant, but a tame one which had gone "must." It had been chained up, as tame elephants always are when their attack of "must"[3] is due, but on the previous night it had broken its chain and escaped. Its mahout,[4] the only person who could manage it when it was in that state, had set out in pursuit, but had taken the wrong direction and was now twelve hours' journey away, and in the morning the elephant had suddenly reappeared in the town. The Burmese population had no weapons and were quite helpless against it. It had already destroyed somebody's bamboo hut, killed a cow and raided some fruit stalls and

---

supplant: replace
prostrate: overpowered

[1] *saecula saeculorum*: forever and ever
[2] *in terrorem*: in fright or terror
[3] *must*: a condition of dangerous frenzy
[4] *mahout*: the keeper and driver of an elephant

Scaffolding the Text-Dependent Questions

3. Based on details in paragraphs 1 and 2, what can readers infer about what the narrator is like as a person? How does he respond to the hatred of the Burmese? How does the narrator react to the young men's "sneering faces" in paragraph 1? How does he describe his own feelings about the British Empire and his job in paragraph 2? RL.11–12.1

4. In the first two paragraphs, how does Orwell use imagery to create a contrast between the people of Burma and the narrator? What is the effect on the reader? Look for words that reveal the actions of the people of Burma and the actions taken by the British toward them. RL.11–12.4, RL.11–12.6

10 As students are reading, monitor their progress. Be sure they are engaged with the text and annotating unknown words and places they would like more information.

My Notes

devoured the stock; also it had met the municipal rubbish van and, when the driver jumped out and took to his heels, had turned the van over and inflicted violences upon it.

4 The Burmese subinspector and some Indian constables were waiting for me in the quarter where the elephant had been seen. It was a very poor quarter, a labyrinth of squalid huts, thatched with palm leaf, winding all over a steep hillside. I remember it was a cloudy, stuffy morning at the beginning of the rains. We began questioning the people where the elephant had gone and, as usual, failed to get any definite information. That is invariably the case in the East; a story always sounds clear enough at a distance, but the nearer you get to the scene of events the vaguer it becomes. Some of the people said that the elephant had gone in one direction, some said that it had gone in another, some professed not even to have heard of any elephant. I had made up my mind that the whole story was a pack of lies, when I heard yells a little distance away. There was a loud, scandalized cry of "Go away, child! Go away this instant!" and an old woman with a switch in her hand came round the corner of a hut, violently shooing away a crowd of naked children. Some more women followed, clicking their tongues and exclaiming; evidently there was something the children ought not to have seen. I rounded the hut and saw a man's dead body sprawling in the mud. He was an Indian, a black Dravidian5 coolie,6 almost naked, and he could not have been dead many minutes. The people said that the elephant had come suddenly upon him round the corner of the hut, caught him with its trunk, put its foot on his back, and ground him into the earth. This was the rainy season and the ground was soft, and his face had scored a trench a foot deep and a couple of yards long. He was lying on his belly with arms crucified and head sharply twisted to one side. His face was coated with mud, the eyes wide open, the teeth bared and grinning with an unendurable agony. (Never tell me, by the way, that the dead look peaceful. Most of the corpses I have seen looked devilish.) The friction of the great beast's foot had stripped the skin from his back as neatly as one skins a rabbit. As soon as I saw the dead man I sent an orderly to a friend's house nearby to borrow an elephant rifle. I had already sent back the pony, not wanting it to go mad with fright and throw me if it smelt the elephant.

Chunk 3

5 The orderly came back in a few minutes with a rifle and five cartridges, and meanwhile some Burmans had arrived and told us that the elephant was in the paddy fields below, only a few hundred yards away. As I started forward practically the whole white population of the quarter flocked out of the houses and followed me. They had seen the rifle and were all shouting excitedly that I was going to shoot the elephant. They had not shown much interest in the elephant when he was merely ravaging their homes, but it was different now that he was going to be shot. It was a bit of fun to them, as it would be to an English crowd; besides they wanted the meat. It made me vaguely uneasy.

5 *Dravidian*: belonging to an ancient race in India
6 *coolie*: servant

constables: police officers

Scaffolding the Text-Dependent Questions

5. In paragraph 3, what does the narrator mean when he uses the word "enlightening"? What does the narrator describe as enlightening? What does he learn or understand more clearly as a result of this enlightening occurrence? RL.11–12.4

6. Explain the sequence of events that leads to the narrator being called to "do something about" a rampaging elephant. Reread paragraph 3. Number each event that the narrator describes. What comments in the paragraph reveal different perspectives on those events. RL.11–12.3

7. Paragraph 4 ends very differently than it starts. Describe how the narrator reveals the important details in the paragraph. How do the details at the beginning—and the narrator's reflections on them—differ from the details at the end? How do those differences affect you as a reader? RL.11–12.3, RL.11–12.5

11 Ask students to pause after Chunk 4. Lead a class discussion of situational irony. Ask students to identify significant examples of the narrator's reflection on the events, and discuss their significance to the work as a whole.

1.16

My Notes

I had no intention of shooting the elephant—I had merely sent for the rifle to defend myself if necessary—and it is always unnerving to have a crowd following you. I marched down the hill, looking and feeling a fool, with the rifle over my shoulder and an ever growing army of people jostling at my heels. At the bottom, when you got away from the huts, there was a metaled road and beyond that a miry waste of paddy fields a thousand yards across, not yet plowed but soggy from the first rains and dotted with coarse grass. The elephant was standing eight yards from the road, his left side toward us. He took not the slightest notice of the crowd's approach. He was tearing up bunches of grass, beating them against his knees to clean them, and stuffing them into his mouth.

6 I had halted on the road. As soon as I saw the elephant I knew with perfect certainty that I ought not to shoot him. It is a serious matter to shoot a working elephant—it is comparable to destroying a huge and costly piece of machinery—and obviously one ought not to do it if it can possibly be avoided. And at that distance, peacefully eating, the elephant looked no more dangerous than a cow. I thought then and I think now that his attack of "must" was already passing off; in which case he would merely wander harmlessly about until the mahout came back and caught him. Moreover, I did not want in the least to shoot him. I decided that I would watch him a little while to make sure that he did not turn savage again, and then go home.

Chunk 4

7 But at that moment I glanced round at the crowd that had followed me. It was an immense crowd, two thousand at the least and growing every minute. It blocked the road for a long distance on either side. I looked at the sea of yellow faces above the garish clothes—faces all happy and excited over this bit of fun, all certain that the elephant was going to be shot. They were watching me as they would watch a conjurer about to perform a trick. They did not like me, but with the magical rifle in my hand I was momentarily worth watching. And suddenly I realized that I would have to shoot the elephant after all. The people expected it of me and I had got to do it; I could feel their two thousand wills pressing me forward irresistibly. And it was at this moment, as I stood there with the rifle in my hands, that I first grasped the hollowness, the **futility** of the white man's dominion in the East. Here was I, the white man with his gun, standing in front of the unarmed crowd—seemingly the leading actor of the piece; but in reality I was only an absurd puppet pushed to and fro by the will of those yellow faces behind. I perceived in this moment that when the white man turns tyrant it is his own freedom that he destroys. He becomes a sort of hollow, posing dummy, the conventionalized figure of a sahib[7]. For it is the condition of his rule that he shall spend his life in trying to "impress the natives," and so in every crisis he has got to do what the "natives" expect of him. He wears a mask, and his face grows to fit it. I had got to shoot the elephant. I had committed myself to doing it when I sent for the rifle. A sahib has got to act like a sahib; he has got to appear resolute, to know his own

futility: ineffectiveness

---

[7] *sahib*: native term for a European gentleman

Scaffolding the Text-Dependent Questions

8. What is the narrator's attitude toward shooting the elephant in paragraphs 5 and 6? What language does he use to convey this attitude? Provide evidence from the text to support your answer. How does the narrator describe the elephant's behavior and the importance of the animal in Burma? What does he say about his intentions? RL.11–12.1, RL.11–12.4, L.11–12.5

9. What makes the narrator change his mind about shooting the elephant? What does he understand about himself—as an Englishman and a white man—at the moment of this decision? Return to paragraph 7. Find the sentence in which the narrator states that he realized he will shoot the elephant. What leads up to that realization? RL.11–12.2, RL.11–12.3

mind and do definite things. To come all that way, rifle in hand, with two thousand people marching at my heels, and then to trail feebly away, having done nothing—no, that was impossible. The crowd would laugh at me. And my whole life, every white man's in the East, was one long struggle not to be laughed at.

Chunk 5

8   But I did not want to shoot the elephant. I watched him beating his bunch of grass against his knees, with that preoccupied grandmotherly air that elephants have. It seemed to me that it would be murder to shoot him. At that age I was not squeamish about killing animals, but I had never shot an elephant and never wanted to. (Somehow it always seems worse to kill a large animal.) Besides, there was the beast's owner to be considered. Alive, the elephant was worth at least a hundred pounds; dead, he would only be worth the value of his tusks, five pounds, possibly. But I had got to act quickly. I turned to the experienced-looking Burmans who had been there when we arrived, and asked them how the elephant had been behaving. They all said the same thing; he took no notice of you if you left him alone, but he might charge if you went too close to him.

9   It was perfectly clear to me what I ought to do. I ought to walk up to within, say, twenty-five yards of the elephant and test his behavior. If he charged I could shoot; if he took no notice of me, it would be safe to leave him until the mahout came back. But I also knew that I was going to do no such thing. I was a poor shot with a rifle and the ground was soft mud into which one would sink at every step. If the elephant charged and I missed him, I should have about as much chance as a toad under a steam roller. But even then I was not thinking particularly of my own skin, only of the watchful yellow faces behind. For at that moment, with the crowd watching me, I was not afraid in the ordinary sense, as I would have been if I had been alone. A white man mustn't be frightened in front of "natives"; and so, in general, he isn't frightened. The thought in my mind was that if anything went wrong those two thousand Burmans would see me pursued, caught, trampled on, and reduced to a grinning corpse like that Indian up the hill. And if that happened it was quite probable that some of them would laugh. That would never do.

10   There was only one alternative. I shoved the cartridges into the magazine and lay down on the road to get a better aim. The crowd grew very still, and a deep, low, happy sigh, as of people who see the theater curtain go up at last, breathed from innumerable throats. They were going to have their bit of fun after all. The rifle was a beautiful German thing with cross-hair sights. I did not know then that in shooting an elephant one would shoot to cut an imaginary bar running from earhole to earhole. I ought, therefore, as the elephant was sideways on, to have aimed straight at his earhole; actually I aimed several inches in front of this, thinking the brain would be further forward.

My Notes

_____

_____

_____

_____

_____

_____

_____

_____

_____

_____

_____

_____

Scaffolding the Text-Dependent Questions

10. In paragraph 9, the narrator formulates a logical plan of action that will allow him to avoid shooting the elephant, but he does not follow it. Why not? What persistent thought or worry causes him to prepare to shoot the animal? Think back on what the narrator had "realized" earlier. How does that realization shape his thinking in this paragraph? RL.11–12.3. RL.11–12.6

11. What miscalculation does the narrator make as he prepares to shoot the elephant? How does his error affect what happens next? In paragraph 10, what knowledge guides the narrator in his actions? In what way is that knowledge faulty? What is the direct result of his faulty knowledge? RL.11–12.3, RL.11–12.5

12 Continue the class discussion after Chunk 5, this time focusing on the position of the narrator regarding the shooting of the elephant and what that action suggests about the nature of power in the context of imperialism.

13 As students are reading and annotating, check that they discover the significant event that occurs in Chunk 6.

14 Once students have read Chunk 7, have them answer the second and third Making Observations questions in pairs. If time allows, have each pair share what they felt was most shocking and discuss why they chose that incident or image.

1.16

My Notes

Chunk 6

11 When I pulled the trigger I did not hear the bang or feel the kick—one never does when a shot goes home—but I heard the devilish roar of glee that went up from the crowd. In that instant, in too short a time, one would have thought, even for the bullet to get there, a mysterious, terrible change had come over the elephant. He neither stirred nor fell, but every line of his body had altered. He looked suddenly stricken, shrunken, immensely old, as though the frightful impact of the bullet had paralyzed him without knocking him down. At last, after what seemed a long time—it might have been five seconds, I dare say—he sagged flabbily to his knees. His mouth slobbered. An enormous senility seemed to have settled upon him. One could have imagined him thousands of years old. I fired again into the same spot. At the second shot he did not collapse but climbed with desperate slowness to his feet and stood weakly erect, with legs sagging and head drooping. I fired a third time. That was the shot that did for him. You could see the agony of it jolt his whole body and knock the last remnant of strength from his legs. But in falling he seemed for a moment to rise, for as his hind legs collapsed beneath him he seemed to tower upward like a huge rock toppling, his trunk reaching skywards like a tree. He trumpeted for the first and only time. And then down he came, his belly toward me, with a crash that seemed to shake the ground even where I lay.

12 I got up. The Burmans were already racing past me across the mud. It was obvious that the elephant would never rise again, but he was not dead. He was breathing very rhythmically with long rattling gasps, his great mound of a side painfully rising and falling. His mouth was wide open—I could see far down into caverns of pink throat. I waited a long time for him to die, but his breathing did not weaken. Finally I fired my two remaining shots into the spot where I thought his heart must be. The thick blood welled out of him like red velvet, but still he did not die. His body did not even jerk when the shots hit him, the tortured breathing continued without a pause. He was dying, very slowly and in great agony, but in some world remote from me where not even a bullet could damage him further. I felt that I had got to put an end to that dreadful noise. It seemed dreadful to see the great beast lying there, powerless to move and yet powerless to die, and not even to be able to finish him. I sent back for my small rifle and poured shot after shot into his heart and down his throat. They seemed to make no impression. The tortured gasps continued as steadily as the ticking of a clock.

Chunk 7

13 In the end I could not stand it any longer and went away. I heard later that it took him half an hour to die. Burmans were bringing dahs[8] and baskets even before I left, and I was told they had stripped his body almost to the bones by afternoon.

14 Afterwards, of course, there were endless discussions about the shooting of the elephant. The owner was furious, but he was only an Indian and could do nothing. Besides, legally I had done the right thing, for a mad elephant has to

---

8 *dahs*: bowls

Scaffolding the Text-Dependent Questions

12. Reread Chunk 6 and mark the text for details describing the elephant's collapse. What do these details reveal about the writer's attitude? What specific details does the narrator use to describe each step in the animal's reactions? What feelings do the words evoke? RL.11–12.1. RL.11–12.4

13. What central idea about the value of life in imperial Burma is revealed by the "endless discussions about the shooting of the elephant" in the final paragraph? Look at the responses from each group the narrator identifies, as well as his own reflections. What underlying assumption about the lives of people and elephants do these ideas reflect? RL.11–12.3, RL.11–12.4

be killed, like a mad dog, if its owner fails to control it. Among the Europeans, opinion was divided. The older men said I was right, the younger men said it was a shame to shoot an elephant for killing a coolie, because an elephant was worth more than any Coringhee coolie. And afterwards I was very glad that the coolie had been killed; it put me legally in the right and gave me a sufficient pretext for shooting the elephant. I often wondered whether any of the others grasped that I had done it solely to avoid looking a fool.

My Notes

Making Observations
- What are your first thoughts about the narrator?
- Which details help you visualize the scenes the narrator describes?
- What do you find most shocking in the story?

15 Based on the observations you made during the first reading, you may want to adjust the reading mode for the second reading. For example, you may decide to read aloud certain complex passages, or you may group students differently.

16 RETURNING TO THE TEXT: As students read the essay a second time, have them add annotations noting places where the text reveals the event, the response, and the reflection. Guide students to respond to the text-dependent questions independently. If they have difficulty, scaffold the questions by rephrasing them or breaking them down into smaller parts. See the Scaffolding the Text-Dependent Questions boxes for suggestions.

17 Call on students to share any of their own questions about the essay. Discuss them as a class.

Returning to the Text

- Reread the essay to answer these text-dependent questions.
- Write any additional questions you have about the essay in your Reader/Writer Notebook.

3. Based on details in paragraphs 1 and 2, what can readers infer about what the narrator is like as a person? How does he respond to the hatred of the Burmese?

   The reader can infer that the narrator is a thoughtful, reflective person. He recognizes that, as a European and a police officer, he is a part of a loathed imperialist system: "Imperialism was an evil thing," yet he is still hurt that the Burmese seem to hate him. They target him for insults and "hideous laughter" because he is a representative of the oppressive British Empire.

4. In the first two pragrapgraphs, how does Orwell use imagery to create a contrast between the people of Burma and the narrator? What is the effect on the reader?

   The narrator is unsparing in his description of the Burmese; he describes "the sneering yellow faces of young men," the spitting on European women in the bazaar, the stinking cages in the prisons, and the scars of the men beaten with bamboo. While some Burmese people seem to resent the narrator, he has sympathy for them and the conditions in which they live.

5. In paragraph 3, what does the narrator mean when he uses the word "enlightening"?

   He means that he experienced a moment of sudden understanding and clarity about "the real nature of imperialism" and "the real motives for which despotic governments act." The use of this word lets the reader in on his conflicted thinking.

6. Explain the sequence of events that leads to the narrator being called to "do something about" a rampaging elephant.

   A tame elephant had "gone 'must,'" and after it had broken free from its chains, it "destroyed somebody's hut, killed a cow and raided some fruit stalls." It had also knocked over the local garbage collector's truck.

7. Paragraph 4 ends very differently than it starts. Describe how the narrator reveals the important details in the paragraph.

   The paragraph begins with an observation about the weather and ends with a gruesome description of a man who had been trampled by the elephant. Vivid, descriptive language reveals the important details.

8. What is the narrator's attitude toward shooting the elephant in paragraphs 5 and 6? What language does he use to convey this attitude? Provide evidence from the text to support your answer.

The narrator states clearly that he has "no intention of shooting the elephant" despite having

the elephant gun because, at this point, the elephant is "peacefully" eating grass. In addition,

the narrator understands that it is "a serious matter to shoot a working elephant … and one

ought not to do it if it can possibly be avoided." He has a healthy respect for the animal.

9. What makes the narrator change his mind about shooting the elephant? What does he understand about himself—as an Englishman and a white man—at the moment of this decision?

Once the narrator realizes that thousands of people "expected" him to shoot the animal,

he understands that he "would have to shoot the elephant after all" because he is "only an

absurd puppet pushed to and fro by the will of" the crowd. As "the white man with his gun,"

he must act the part of the "sahib" and "impress the natives" by killing the animal.

10. In paragraph 9, the narrator formulates a logical plan of action that will allow him to avoid shooting the elephant, but he does not follow it. Why not? What persistent thought or worry causes him to prepare to shoot the animal?

The narrator is acutely concerned with not being laughed at by the local people. He states in

paragraph 7 that "every white man's [life] in the East, was one long struggle not to be laughed

at." In paragraph 9, he worries that if the elephant attacked and killed him, "it was quite

probable that someone would laugh," and, the narrator concludes, "that would never do."

11. What miscalculation does the narrator make as he prepares to shoot the elephant? How does his error affect what happens next?

Because the narrator has never shot an elephant before, he "did not know" that he should

"have aimed straight at his earhole." Instead the narrator aims "several inches" away. The

narrator's mistake causes the elephant to die slowly and painfully.

12. Reread Chunk 6 and mark the text for details describing the elephant's collapse. What do these details reveal about the writer's attitude?

Details describing the elephant's collapse include "he sagged flabbily to his knees,"

"desperate slowness to his feet and stood weakly erect," and "legs sagging and head

drooping." The details show that the narrator regards the elephant's death with a horror,

regret, and even shame. He might be drawing a parallel to imperialism.

---

18 Ask students to prepare Levels of Questions using the examples in the Working from the Text section (student step 14) as a model. Ask them to prepare one series of questions for each chunk of the text.

19 Help students think about the essay in light of the Cultural Criticism lens by reviewing the underlying ideas of that perspective from Activity 1.13.

20 Organize students into groups to participate in a Socratic Seminar applying a Cultural Criticism lens and their knowledge of imperialism to the essay. You may consider assigning discussion-group roles to help ensure students address each of the "be sure to" points during their discussion. Be sure students are using the questions they developed in student step 14, as well as discussing any new questions that may come up.

21 Have students complete the Check Your Understanding task with a partner, noting in a discussion the similarities and differences between their annotations for event, response, and reflection. They should explain their own labels and ask respectfully about their partners' labels that are different from their own. Each student should be able to talk about the event, response, and reflection in the text.

22 To extend the discussion, ask how the sequence in which the author presents information affects the impact of the essay. Ask students: *How would the effect change if the narrator described the entire incident and only reflected on it in the final paragraph?*

23 Guide students to understand the difference between formal and informal style explained in the Language & Writer's Craft box. Help students see how a juxtaposition of styles balances Orwell's writing, so that the personal, emotional elements do not overwhelm the cultural insights he is trying to examine with some objectivity. Point out that paragraph 7 combines formal and informal writing ("And it was at this moment ... not to be laughed at."). Encourage students to find other examples.

LEVELED DIFFERENTIATED INSTRUCTION

In this activity, students may need support writing a reflective essay about a significant life event.

Beginning Have students work in pairs to complete the **Narrative Analysis and Writing** graphic organizer as a prewriting activity for their reflective essay. After they have filled in the graphic organizer, have students tell their story to their partner. Then have them support one another in brainstorming additional details.

Developing Have students use the **Narrative Analysis and Writing** graphic organizer as a prewriting activity for their reflective essay. Students should fill in the graphic organizer independently and then work with a partner to think about the overall structure of their essay to brainstorm key images.

Expanding Prior to writing, have students brainstorm a list of vivid and precise language to describe their event in the **Narrative Analysis and Writing** graphic organizer.

---

13. What central idea about the value of life in imperial Burma is revealed by the "endless discussions about the shooting of the elephant" in the final paragraph?

By sharing a range of opinions, the narrator reveals a cold view of the value of life under an

imperialist system. Older Europeans say the narrator "was right" to shoot the elephant, but

younger men say "it was a shame to shoot an elephant for killing a coolie," an attitude that

shows a lack of respect for the lives of other human beings.

Working from the Text

14. Revisit Orwell's essay and write Levels of Questions—literal, interpretative, and universal—to prepare for a Socratic Seminar. Apply a Cultural Criticism lens and your knowledge of imperialism as you develop your questions.

   • **Literal:** Why was the elephant considered a problem?
   • **Interpretive:** What does shooting the elephant mean to Orwell?
   • **Universal:** What kind of forces might cause someone to do something against their conscience or better judgment?

   Literal: _____

   Interpretative: _____

   Universal: _____

15. Discuss your questions with your assigned Socratic Seminar group. During the discussion, be sure to:

   • Explicitly draw on your knowledge of imperialism as well as evidence from the text to support your ideas.
   • Evaluate how cultural context influences the behavior of individuals and how they respond to moral conflicts.
   • Ask thoughtful questions and offer insights that can deepen the group's understanding of the text and help the group move towards its goals.
   • Respond thoughtfully to diverse perspectives and interpretations.
   • Use appropriate eye contact, adequate volume, and clear pronunciation.

☑ Check Your Understanding

Orwell's "Shooting an Elephant" is a reflective essay. Look at your summary of the text for the event, response, and reflection, and compare with a partner. In what order do these three elements occur?

LANGUAGE & WRITER'S CRAFT:
Formal and Informal Style

You have learned that a reflective essay is a type of personal narrative in which the writer reflects on the significance of an incident or set of circumstances. Because such an essay reveals a writer's unique feelings and perceptions, yet also addresses universal issues and insights, the narrator may use a writing style that combines personal and formal elements.

Note how Orwell strikes a balance between the two styles in this example:

Orwell's language and style demonstrate his political intelligence and awareness of the cruelty of imperialism: "hatred of the empire," "unbreakable tyranny," and "upon the will of the prostrate peoples." He conveys a more personal and emotional style when he uses less formal language, such as "evil spirited little beasts" and "into a Buddhist priests' guts."

"All I knew was that I was stuck between my hatred of the empire I served and my rage against the evil spirited little beasts who tried to make my job impossible. With one part of my mind I thought of the British Raj as an unbreakable tyranny, as something clamped down, in saecula saeculorum, upon the will of prostrate peoples; with another part I thought that the greatest joy in the world would be to drive a bayonet into a Buddhist priest's guts."

PRACTICE Return to the Literary writing prompt in Activity 1.13. Analyze your writing and identify whether you used personal elements, formal elements, or a combination of both. In your Reader/Writer notebook, explain the style you used and why. If you would change your style based on what you have learned, explain your reasoning.

✍ Writing Prompt: Literary

Using your quickwrite from the beginning of the activity, write a reflective essay about a significant event in your life that taught you a meaningful lesson. Be sure to:

- Engage the reader by establishing a clear incident, response, progression of events, and reflection.
- Use narrative techniques to develop experiences, events, and/or characters.
- Use precise words and phrases, telling details, and sensory language to convey a vivid picture of the experiences, events, setting, or characters.
- Sequence events to create a coherent narrative that builds toward the outcome.

📦 INDEPENDENT READING LINK
Read and Discuss

Select a point in your independent reading in which a character or the narrator experiences feeling like an outsider. Discuss with a partner or a group how the character reflects on this incident.

My Notes

_____

_____

_____

_____

_____

_____

_____

_____

_____

_____

_____

_____

_____

_____

_____

_____

_____

_____

_____

_____

_____

_____

_____

_____

_____

ACTIVITY 1.16 continued

24 For the writing prompt, ask students to expand on the quickwrites they wrote at the beginning of the activity.

25 When the drafts are completed, ask students to **think-pair-share** what they have written. Ask pairs to mark each other's texts to identify event, response, and reflection. Have them also comment on any language that is imprecise. Provide additional writing time for students to revise the draft.

26 Remind students to read and respond to the Independent Reading Link at the end of the selection.

ASSESS

Monitor the Check Your Understanding discussions to confirm that students can correctly identify the three elements of a reflective essay. Assess how well students are able to discuss those elements in the context of Orwell's essay.

Evaluate students' responses to the writing prompt, which should include an event, a response, and a reflection. The elements should be organized to create a cohesive essay. Look for vivid language, appropriate style, and effective use of transitions.

ADAPT

If students need additional help with the reflective essay organizational structure, provide an outline of an essay that includes all three components. Choose a short essay that can be read and analyzed in a brief reteaching exercise.

✍ WRITING PROMPT: LITERARY

The following standards are addressed in the writing prompt:

- W.11–12.3a
- W.11–12.3b
- W.11–12.3c
- W.11–12.3d
- W.11–12.4

ACTIVITY 1.17

PLAN

Materials: DVD: *Edward Scissorhands* by Tim Burton or another film of your choice (optional)
Suggested Pacing: 2 50-minute class periods

TEACH

1 Read the Learning Targets and Preview with your students. Ask them to think about what being a stranger in the village means and how that might apply to their own lives.

2 Have students read and discuss the Knowledge Question in small groups.

3 Review the As You Read tasks. Help students understand what to annotate by modeling with an example from the beginning of the text. Explain that they will explore the "stranger in the village" theme after reading the text the first time.

4 Have students read the About the Author box. Ask them to think of one question they might want to ask the author based on the short biography.

ACTIVITY
1.17 **Being a Stranger**

Learning Strategies

Brainstorming
Graphic Organizer
Think-Pair-Share

 KNOWLEDGE QUEST

Knowledge Question:

What challenges or difficulties might someone new to a place face?

Across Activities 1.17 and 1.18, you will read two essays and examine the theme of what it means to be a stranger in a new place. While you read and build knowledge about the theme, think about your answer to the Knowledge Question.

My Notes

Learning Targets

- Analyze the thematic concept of "being a stranger in the village."
- Plan and outline a reflective essay that explores a personal experience.
- Draft an informative introduction to a reflective essay based on a personal incident.
- Integrate ideas from multiple texts to build knowledge and vocabulary about thematic concerns regarding being a stranger in a new place.

Preview

In this activity, you will explore the thematic concept of "being a stranger in the village" by analyzing an excerpt from a reflective essay. Then you will reflect on a significant personal event and outline your own reflective essay. A peer will review your outline and provide you with clear feedback. After receiving feedback, you will write a draft.

As You Read

- Underline words, phrases, or sentences that reveal the narrator's ideas about Chinese and British culture.
- Circle unknown words and phrases. Try to determine the meaning of the words by using context clues, word parts, or a dictionary.

About the Author

Xiaolu Guo (b. 1973) is a Chinese-born filmmaker and writer who lives and works in London. She is bilingual in Chinese and English. She was born and raised in a poor rural village in China. At the age of 18 she won a scholarship to the Beijing Film Academy. Unhappy with the repressive atmosphere in China, she moved to London in 2002. Her works have received many awards, including Britain's National Book Circle of Critics Award for her autobiography in 2017. Although not strictly a science-fiction writer, she often employs many elements of that genre in her stories, films, and novels.

College and Career Readiness Standards

Focus Standards:

RL.11–12.2 Determine two or more themes or central ideas of a text and analyze their development over the course of the text, including how they interact and build on one another to produce a complex account; provide an objective summary of the text.

RL.11–12.3 Analyze the impact of the author's choices regarding how to develop and relate elements of a story or drama (e.g., where a story is set, how the action is ordered, how the characters are introduced and developed).

RL.11–12.9 Demonstrate knowledge of eighteenth-, nineteenth- and early-twentieth-century foundational works of American literature, including how two or more texts from the same period treat similar themes or topics.

5 **FIRST READ:** Because this is a long passage, have students read independently.

 TEXT COMPLEXITY

Overall: Accessible
Lexile: 590L
Qualitative: Moderate Difficulty
Task: Moderate (Analyze)

Essay

from "Is this what the west is really like?" How it felt to leave China for Britain

by Xiaolu Guo

Determined to find somewhere she could live and work as she wished, Xiaolu Guo moved from Beijing to London in 2002. But from the weather to the language and the people, nothing was as she expected.

1 By the time I reached my late 20s, I was desperately looking for a way out of Beijing. From 2001 onwards, the city was consumed by preparations for the 2008 Olympics. Every bus route had to be redirected. Every building was covered in scaffolding. Highways were springing up around Beijing like thick noodles oozing from the ground, with complicated U-turns and roundabouts. The city was surrounded by a moonscape of construction sites. Living there had become a visual and logistical torture. For me, as a writer and filmmaker, it was also becoming impossible artistically, with increasing restraints placed on my work.

2 The opportunity to leave came sooner than I could have hoped. I heard that the Chevening scholarship and the British Council were looking for talent in China. I had never heard of Chevening. Someone told me it was a large historical mansion in Kent. My mind was instantly filled with images from The Forsyte Saga – one of the most-watched English television programs on the Chinese internet. The wealthy housewives of Beijing in particular loved the fancy houses and rich people dressed in elegant costumes riding about on white horses. So I applied as a film-maker.

3 Eight months later, after many stressful exams, the British Council in Beijing called me in. "Congratulations! You are one of three people in China this year who've won the scholarship! You beat 500 other candidates!" The English lady brought me a cup of tea with a big smile. She also handed me back my passport with a UK visa in it.

4 When I told my parents the news, they were rather surprised, but both thought it sounded like a great opportunity. "Your father says he is very proud of you!" my mother said. "All your years of studying now make sense." Then she added: "You said the scholarship is from England. Do you mean Great Britain?"

GRAMMAR & USAGE

Punctuating Dialogue

Writers use dialogue—the exact words of the characters—to reveal and develop character, advance the plot, and add life to writing. Direct dialogue is enclosed in quotation marks and set off from the rest of a sentence with a comma, a question mark, or an exclamation point. Commas and periods are always placed inside the quotation marks:

"Your father says he is very proud of you!" my mother said. "All your years of studying now make sense."

Question marks and exclamation points from the dialogue are placed inside the quotation marks:

"Do you have a Chinese passport?" She stared at me with a cold, calm intensity, clutching my British passport.

As you read, notice the way punctuation is used to set off dialogue from the surrounding text. Notice when dialogue is used purposefully to develop the conflict between characters and illuminate the theme.

visa: visitor's permit

College and Career Readiness Standards

W.11–12.2. Write informative/explanatory texts to examine and convey complex ideas, concepts, and information clearly and accurately through the effective selection, organization, and analysis of content.

W.11–12.2b Develop the topic thoroughly by selecting the most significant and relevant facts, extended definitions, concrete details, quotations, or other information and examples appropriate to the audience's knowledge of the topic.

W.11–12.5 Develop and strengthen writing as needed by planning, revising, editing, rewriting, or trying a new approach, focusing on addressing what is most significant for a specific purpose and audience. (Editing for conventions should demonstrate command of Language standards 1–3 up to and including grades 11–12 here.)

Additional Standards Addressed:

RL.11–12.1, RL.11–12.4, RL.11–12.5, SL.11–12.6, L.11–12.4c

6 As students are reading, monitor their progress. Be sure they are engaged with the text and annotating details that reflect the narrator's ideas about Chinese and British culture.

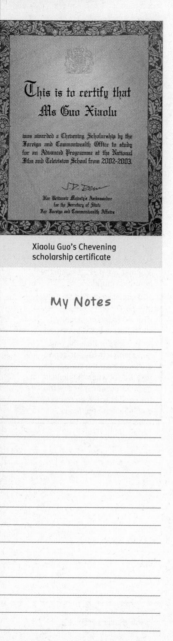

Xiaolu Guo's Chevening scholarship certificate

My Notes

5 "Yes. Great Britain," I confirmed.

6 "That's great. Greater than United States, right?" my mother said, drawing her conclusions from her Maoist education of the 1960s. But I knew that she had no idea about either Britain or America. The only thing she knew about those countries was that they were in the west. "You should take a rice cooker with you. I heard that westerners don't use rice cookers."

7 I remember very well the day I left China. It was 1 April, and the Beijing sandstorm season had begun. I dragged my luggage towards the subway, choking in the sandy soup. This was my chance to escape the world I had grown up in. But that world was trying one last time to keep me.

8 "I will be walking under a gentle and moist English sky soon," I said to myself. "It nurtures rather than hinders its inhabitants. I will breathe in the purest Atlantic sea air and live on an island called Britain." All this was destined to be nothing more than a memory.

9 When I arrived at Heathrow, there was no one to pick me up, and all I had was a reservation letter for a student hostel near Marylebone station in central London. Dragging my luggage, I jumped into a taxi. As I looked out at the streets through the rain-drenched window of the taxi, it smelled damp and soggy. The air clung to my cheeks. The sky was dim and the city drew a low and squat outline against the horizon: not very impressive.

10 We traveled slowly, through unfamiliar, traffic-jammed streets. Everything felt threatening: the policemen moving about the street corner with their hands resting on their truncheons, long queues of grey-faced people at bus stops but no one talking, fire engines shooting through the traffic with howling sirens.

11 I realized that I knew nothing about this country at all. I had planted myself in alien soil. And, most of all, my only tool of communication was a jumble of half-grammatically-correct sentences. In China I had learned that the population of Britain was equal to that of my little province, Zhejiang. Perhaps it was true, since the streets didn't look that grand, especially the motorways, which were even uglier than the ones in China. Everything was one size smaller, or even two. Still, here I was. As the Chinese say, ruxiang suisu – once in the village, you must follow their customs.

12 Before I left China, I was desperately looking for something: freedom, the chance to live as an individual with dignity. This was impossible in my home country. But I was also blindly looking for something connected to the west, something non-ideological, something imaginative and romantic. But as I walked along the London streets, trying to save every penny for buses or food, I lost sight of my previous vision. London seemed no more spiritually fulfilling than home. Instead, I was faced with a world of practical problems and difficulties. Perhaps I was looking for great writers to meet or great books to read, but I could barely decipher a paragraph of English.

13 Now I realized there had been some truth to my own country's communist education: the west was not all milk and honey.

Scaffolding the Text-Dependent Questions

1. What words and details in paragraphs 1–8 reveal the author's perception of China and England? What do these details reveal about her perspective of each country? What is happening in China in paragraph 1? What kind of television shows does the author mention in paragraph 2? What happens right before she leaves China? How does she respond? RL.11–12.1

14 The year I came to England, I was nearing 30. I spent several months in panicked activity as the thought of my age came bearing down on me – to be a 30-year-old woman in China was to be unbearably old. I still remember that celebration in London with some of my classmates from the film school. It was actually the first birthday party I had organized in my entire life. Like most Chinese families at the time, mine never celebrated birthdays. But there I was, cooking Chinese dumplings for my western friends. Everyone declared that 30 was a good age, the age at which you started to know yourself a little, when you were no longer confused and started achieving goals. But I spent that year very confused. I had lost my main tool: language. Here, I was nothing but a witless, dumb, low-class foreigner.

15 At the end of the Chevening scholarship I was supposed to go back to China. But I didn't want to. So I struggled to get all the required paperwork together and managed to extend my visa. Now the crucial question was: how do I make a living in the west? I had to survive somehow. But survival wasn't enough. I wanted dignity. I could only see myself making a living through writing, as I had done in China.

16 I didn't want to risk feeling even lonelier than I had in China. It was not just the physical loneliness, but cultural and intellectual isolation. By the time my 30th birthday party drew to a close, I was clear about my direction: I would have to start writing in another tongue. I would use my broken English, even though it would be extremely difficult.

17 When the birthday party was over, I mopped the floor and did the washing-up. An idea for a novel was already forming in my mind. I would make an advantage out of my disadvantage. I would write a book about a Chinese woman in England struggling with the culture and language. She would compose her own personal English dictionary. The novel would be a sort of phrasebook, recording the things she did and the people she met.

18 I had to overcome the huge obstacle of my poor English. I decided I didn't want to go to language classes because I knew my impatience would kill my will, my threshold for boredom being just too low. Instead, I decided to teach myself. Perhaps this was a huge mistake? As I studied day and night I grew more and more frustrated with English as a language, but also as a culture.

19 The fundamental problem with English for me was that there is no direct connection between words and meanings. In Chinese, most characters are drawn and composed from images. **Calligraphy** is one of the foundations of the written language. When you write the Chinese for sun, it is 太阳 or 日, which means "an extreme manifestation of Yang energy." Yang signifies things with strong, bright and hot energy. So "extreme yang" can only mean the sun. But in English, sun is written with three letters, s, u and n, and none of them suggests any greater or deeper meaning. Nor does the word look anything like the sun! Visual imagination and philosophical understandings were useless when it came to European languages.

Xiaolu Guo came to the United Kingdom in 2002 to spend a year studying documentary film directing.

My Notes

calligraphy: artistic handwriting

Scaffolding the Text-Dependent Questions

2. How does the author's impression of England change over time? What details does she use to describe London when she first arrives? What is her life like? What happens after her 30th birthday? How does that affect her life? RL.11–12.1, RL.11–12.3

My Notes

20 Technically, the foremost difficulty for an Asian writer who wants to write in English is tense. Verb conjugations in English are, quite simply, a real drag. We Chinese never modify verbs for time or person, nor do we have anything like a subjunctive mood. All tenses are in the present, because once you say something, you mean it in your current time and space. There is no past or future when making a statement. We only add specific time indicators to our verbs if we need them. Take the verb "to go." In Chinese it is 走, zou, and you can use zou in any context without needing to change it. But in English the verb has all the following forms: goes, went, gone, going. Mastering conjugations was a serious struggle for me, almost a dialectical critique of the metaphysics of grammar.

21 I particularly detested the past-perfect progressive tense, which I called the Annoying PPP: a continuous action completed at some point in the past. I felt giddy every time I heard the Annoying PPP; I just couldn't understand how anyone was able to grasp something so complex. For example, my grammar book said: "Peter had been painting his house for weeks, but he finally gave up." My immediate reaction, even before I got to the grammatical explanation, was: my God, how could someone paint his house for weeks and still give up? I just couldn't see how time itself could regulate people's actions as if they were little clocks! As for the grammar, the word order "had been" and the added flourishes like "ing" made my stomach churn. They were bizarre decorations that did nothing but obscure a simple, strong building. My instinct was to say something like: "Peter tries to paint his house, but sadness overwhelms him, causing him to lay down his brushes and give up his dream."

22 Another curious realization came when I discovered that I used the first-person plural too much in my everyday speech. In the west, if I said "We like to eat rice," it would confuse people. They couldn't understand who this "we" was referring to. Instead, I should have said "We Chinese like to eat rice." After a few weeks, I swapped to the first-person singular, as in "I like to eat rice." But it made me uncomfortable. After all, how could someone who had grown up in a collective society get used to using the first-person singular all the time? The habitual use of "I" requires thinking of yourself as a separate entity in a society of separate entities. But in China no one is a separate entity: either you were born to a non-political peasant household or to a Communist party household. But here, in this foreign country, I had to build a world as a first-person singular – urgently.

23 Still, the desire and will to work on a first book in English propelled me through the difficulties. Every day, I wrote a detailed diary, filled with the new vocabulary I had learned. The diary became the raw material for my novel, the one I had imagined while mopping the floor after my 30th birthday party: A Concise Chinese–English Dictionary for Lovers.

24 After I finished the novel, I didn't know what to do with it. I knew it would have little chance at ever being published, since I had written it using such broken English in a country awash with BBC voices and the perfect sentences of the Queen. And Britain was not like China, where writers could post their manuscripts directly to publishing houses. While pacing up and

metaphysical: fundamental nature

Scaffolding the Text-Dependent Questions

3. What does the author's discussion of language in paragraph 23 imply about her perceptions of Chinese and Western culture? How does she respond to this difference? What does the author say about pronouns? Which pronouns are most natural to her? RL.11–12.2, RL.11–12.4

4. What does the author's effort to learn English reveal about her character? Do the words "impatient" and "easily bored" really describe her character? What does she do to help herself learn English in paragraph 24? Do you think what she is doing is easy? RL.11–12.1, RL.11–12.3, RL.11–12.4

down in Waterstones one day and wondering how the hell all these books had been published, I happened upon Jung Chang's Wild Swans. I leafed through it. In the acknowledgements, the author thanked her agent.

25 In China, writers don't have agents because, in the world of Chinese socialism, agents have traditionally been viewed as members of the exploiting class. Although I had grown up with this propaganda, I sent my book to Jung Chang's agent that very day. He was a man called Toby Eady, at an address I had gleaned from an internet search. Who was this man, I wondered. What were the chances that he would pay any attention to a manuscript by an unknown Chinese author?

26 A month later, one February morning, I received a call from Eady's office requesting a meeting. After one abortive attempt, we finally managed to meet, and a few months after that, I received an unexpected phone call informing me that Random House wanted to meet me to discuss the book. Leaving my flat at least four hours ahead of the appointed time, I made my way to Pimlico, arriving at the office too early. Sitting on a grey slab outside the publisher's rain-stained brown mansion building, I ate a prawn sandwich.

27 Eventually, I walked into the reception area. Disorientated by the number of floors and having to weave my way around mazes of paper-piled desks, I met some editors. They were very friendly and seemed to know a lot about me. One of them made me a cup of Earl Grey. But I still didn't understand what the meeting was about. By the time I left the office, I didn't even understand that they had already made a good offer for my novel. At that time, even the word "offer" was alien to me. I didn't associate "an offer" with money or buying book rights, I thought it meant "Can I offer you a cup of tea, or a piece of cake?" It took me a whole week to understand that the offer was much bigger than a cup of tea.

28 Some years later, after I had published a number of books in Britain, I managed to finish a novel that I had been laboring on for years. Publication was due in a few months' time, but I began to worry that it would bring me trouble when I next tried to go back to China, since the story concerned the Tiananmen Square massacre of 1989 and the nature of **totalitarianism**. What if I was denied entry because of this book? I decided to make preparations before it came out. So, since I had been living in the UK for nearly 10 years, I applied for a British passport.

29 I spent some months gathering the necessary documents for my **naturalization**. After a drawn-out struggle with immigration forms and lawyers, I managed to obtain my passport. Now, I thought to myself, if there was any trouble with my books and films, I would feel a certain security in being a national of a western country. Now I could go back to visit my sick father and see my family.

30 A week later, I applied for a Chinese visa with my British passport. After waiting at the visa application office in London for about half an hour, I found myself looking at the visa officer through a glass barrier. The woman wore horn-rimmed glasses and had her hair cut short, military-style. She looked like

My Notes

> **totalitarianism:** complete dictatorship by a centralized government
> **naturalization:** process of becoming a citizen

Scaffolding the Text-Dependent Questions

5. How does the author's diction help the reader connect with her reflective essay? How does the author describe herself in paragraph 15? How does the reader react to this description? RL.11–12.1, RL.11–12.3, RL.11–12.4

1.17

My Notes

a resurrected Madame Mao. She took my British passport and scanned me up and down. Her face was stern, the muscles around her mouth stiff, just like all the other Communist officials, seemingly trained to keep their faces this way.

31 "Do you have a Chinese passport?" She stared at me with a cold, calm intensity, clutching my British passport.

32 I took out my Chinese passport and handed it to her through the narrow window.

33 She flipped through its pages. The way she handled it gave me a sudden stomach ache. I sensed something bad was coming.

34 "You know it's illegal to possess two passports as a Chinese citizen?" she remarked in her even-toned, slightly jarring voice.

35 "Illegal?" I repeated. My surprise was totally genuine. It had never occurred to me that having two passports was against Chinese law.

36 The woman glanced at me from the corner of her eye. I couldn't help but feel the judgment she had formed of me: a criminal! No, worse than that, I was a Chinese criminal who had muddied her own Chinese citizenship with that of a small, foreign state. And to top it all, I was ignorant of the laws of my own country.

37 She then flipped through my visa application, which was attached to my British passport, and announced: "Since this is the first time you are using your western passport, we will only issue you a two-week visa for China."

38 "What?" I was speechless. I had applied for a six-month family visit visa. Before I could even argue, I saw her take out a large pair of scissors and decisively cut the corner off my Chinese passport. She then threw it back out at me. It landed before me on the counter, disfigured and invalid.

39 I stared, without comprehension, at this once-trusted document. The enormity of what had just happened slowly began to register. Although I was totally ignorant of most Chinese laws, I knew this for certain: when an embassy official cuts your passport, you are no longer a Chinese citizen. I stared back at Madame Mao with growing anger.

40 "How could you do that?" I stammered, like an idiot who knew nothing of how the world worked.

41 "This is the law. You have chosen the British passport. You can't keep the Chinese one." Case closed. She folded my visa application into my British passport and handed them to another officer, who took it, and all the other waiting passports, to a back room for further processing. She returned her tense face toward me, but she was no longer looking at me. I was already invisible.

42 There I was, standing in front of the Chinese visa office on Old Jewry, near Bank station. I was still struggling to believe what had just happened. Was that it? I had just lost my Chinese nationality? "But I am Chinese, not British," I thought. "I don't feel in any way British, despite my new passport."

Scaffolding the Text-Dependent Questions

6. How does the author explore the theme of identity in the text? Reread paragraphs 43–44. How many different identities does the author mention in those paragraphs? How do those identities define her? RL.11–12.2

7. How does the author's use of a chronological narrative structure contribute to the text's purpose? Think of what happens in the text. How much time passes from the beginning of the essay to the end? What does the author decide to do at the end of the essay? RL.11–12.3, RL.11–12.5

8. How does the metaphor in the last paragraph—"Uproot a tree and it will die; uproot a man and he will survive"—contribute to the author's message? What incidents in the essay show the author's response to British culture? How has she changed at the end of the essay? RL.11–12.4

Little Madame Mao hadn't even asked me which passport I wanted to keep, the British or the Chinese. I suppose from her point of view I had already chosen by applying for another nationality, and in doing so, I had forfeited my birthright. For a few minutes I truly hated her, she became an emblem for everything I detested about my homeland, now no longer my country.

43 My tourist visa was ready a few days later. But for some reason, I never used it. Perhaps because I wasn't sure what I was supposed to do with a two-week stay. From the day I lost my Chinese passport, I came to the simple revelation that nationality did not declare who I was. I was a woman raised in China and in living in exile in Britain. I was a woman who wrote books and made films. I could have applied for a German passport if I had lived in Germany. But a passport and the nationality written on its cover would never define me.

44 As the old Chinese saying goes; "Uproot a tree and it will die; uproot a man and he will survive." I have always agreed with this proverb, especially in the years before I left China. But after the incident at the Chinese visa office, I thought to myself: mere survival is a life without imagination, but a drifter's life with imagination is also a life without substance. As a new immigrant, everything felt intangible: I couldn't integrate fully with the locals, nor penetrate the heart of the western culture that surrounded me. But the only way to overcome these problems was to root myself here, to transplant myself into this land and to grow steadily. So I began to plan a life exactly like every other first-generation immigrant, starting with making myself a proper home.

My Notes

Xiaolu as a new arrival in London in 2002, outside the Houses of Parliament

⌀ Knowledge Quest

- What challenges does the author face that surprise you?
- How does the author's ability to deal with cultural pressures change throughout the essay?

ACTIVITY 1.17 continued

7 Remind students to think about the Knowledge Quest questions as they read. After all the students have finished the first reading, ask them to share with a partner one detail about the author's experience in England they thought someone else might not notice. Have the partners discuss why those details stood out to them.

8 Have the students discuss what happens in the story. If needed, use the **Sequence of Events Time Line** graphic organizer to make sure students understand the order of events. Expand the use of the time line by adding the author's response to each event.

9 **RETURNING TO THE TEXT:** Have students answer the text-dependent questions in small groups. If they have difficulty, scaffold the questions by rephrasing them or breaking them down into smaller parts. See the Scaffolding the Text-Dependent Questions box for suggestions.

10 Direct students' attention to the Grammar & Usage box and have them review the information on punctuating dialogue. Have them make note of Guo's use of dialogue to show the relationship between the author and others. Lead students in a discussion to consider the dialogue's function and its effect on the reader. Ask them to provide examples of quotations that effectively convey the author's point of view and sense of belonging to one culture or another.

11 To transition to a discussion of the thematic concept of "stranger in the village," have students play a drama game. Divide students into two groups, then ask one group to leave the room. Ask the group in the room to create a game. The game should have definite rules, but they should not be readily identifiable. You may want to recommend students alter a familiar game. For example, they might make up rules for baseball with seven bases and home in the middle or hopscotch played by multiple players on a circular grid. Tell them they can think of a name for the game and different words or lingo for scoring, fouls, equipment, etc. Tell students they do not speak the same language as the students outside the room, so they cannot explain the game to the "outsiders" — they are only allowed to use the words and lingo they developed.

Returning to the Text

- Reread the essay to answer these text-dependent questions.
- Write any additional questions you have about the text in your Reader/Writer Notebook.

1. What words and details in paragraphs 1–8 reveal the author's perception of China and England? What do these details reveal about her perspective of each country?

   Guo describes her home city of Beijing as a place of "visual and logistical torture." She sees China as a harsh society that keeps an oppressive hold over its people. By contrast she imagines England to be a gentle and nurturing place where she will breathe "pure Atlantic air."

2. How does the author's impression of England change over time?

   Before Guo arrives in London she has a very idealized image of the city. When she arrives in England she is disappointed how small, gloomy, and "threatening" it seems. She struggles to adjust, but after living in London for a while and learning English, she acquires a more positive view of London. In the end, she decides she wants to become a British citizen.

3. **KQ** What does the author's discussion of language in paragraph 23 imply about her perceptions of Chinese and Western culture? How does she respond to this difference?

   The author notes that she often uses the first person plural "we" because China is a collective society in which the group is more important than the individual. In Western culture the individual is of primary importance and the frequent use of "I" emphasizes this attitude. At first the author feels uncomfortable using "I," but she realizes she must adapt.

4. What does the author's effort to learn English reveal about her character?

   The author comes across as very persistent and determined in her efforts to teach herself English. She is someone who overcomes obstacles to reach her goals. Because she is persistent she is able to make a place for herself in her new "village," even though the cultural differences continue to be challenging and difficult.

5. How does the author's diction help the reader connect with her reflective essay?

The author's diction creates a friendly, conversational tone that engages the reader. She

poses rhetorical questions in paragraphs 22 and 42 that cause the reader to think about the

challenges that the author faces.

6. KQ How does the author explore the theme of identity in the text?

The author struggles to combine her Chinese culture with British culture. Although she

becomes fluent in English, she still feels like she is "living in exile" from her home country.

After she loses her Chinese citizenship she realizes that nationality will never define her as

an individual.

7. How does the author's use of a chronological narrative structure contribute to the text's purpose?

The author uses chronology to show how she changes over time. Each part of the story reveals

how she overcame obstacles. The chronological structure builds tension because the reader is

not sure how it will end. At the conclusion, the reader understands how she gained her insight

into herself as an individual and as a writer.

8. How does the the metaphor in the last paragraph, "Uproot a tree and it will die; uproot a man and he will survive," contribute to the author's message?

This metaphor suggests that people have the ability to adapt to new surroundings and

cultures. Guo puts down "roots" and created a new home in London. She says she has

"transplanted" herself to Britain and "rooted" herself there so she can grow and thrive.

12 Tell the students outside the room to enter the room one by one. Tell them that their job is to join the game. They can attempt to do this in various ways. They can shadow a player, observe, take notes on the different words, draw pictures, or make gestures to communicate with the players. Once they have joined the game they become part of the "village" and the next student enters the room. Eventually all the students should know how to play the game. Then have the students reverse roles. Afterwards, ask them how it felt to try to understand a game whose rules were totally mysterious to them in the beginning. What did they feel like when they finally "got it"?

13 Have partners complete the first three bullets of student step 9 in Working from the Text. Then, use **think-pair-share** and ask students to think about the excerpt from Guo's autobiography and the Orwell essay to respond to the graphic organizer.

 TEACHER TO TEACHER

Consider using a film clip to reinforce the idea of the "stranger in the village." You could use *Edward Scissorhands* for this activity. A good clip to use is 6:00–21:23. Other possibilities for useful film clips include *My Big Fat Greek Wedding*, *Forrest Gump*, and *Toy Story 3*.

14 Ask students to **brainstorm** films and TV shows that capture the "stranger in the village" theme. Students should be able to explain how each example fits this concept.

15 Have students respond to the Check Your Understanding question in a quickwrite.

1.17

Working from the Text

9. With a partner, answer the questions that follow to identify the event, response, and reflection in the passage.

- What is the major incident in Xiaolu Guo's essay?
- How does she respond to this event?
- How does she reflect upon this event?
- Think about how Xiaolu Guo and the narrator of "Shooting an Elephant" are both strangers in their environments. Respond to the first four items in the graphic organizer.

Stranger in the Village	
10. Brainstorm words related to village.	11. What does it mean to be part of the village, the group encountering the unfamiliar?
12. Brainstorm words related to stranger.	13. What does it mean to be the unfamiliar one, the stranger?
14. Listen to the song. How does the artist indicate the "stranger" and the "village"?	15. Brainstorm a list of films which you are familiar with, and for each one discuss this question: Who is the "stranger," and who or what is the "village"?

☑ Check Your Understanding

Based on the texts you have read so far, what does it mean to be a stranger in the village?

16. Review Embedded Assessment 2 and create an outline for your reflective essay. If necessary, come up with ideas by brainstorming, journaling, drawing, or discussion with others. When writing your outline be sure to:

    • Think about what kind of structure you want to use to achieve your purpose. Is there a clear event, response, reflection?
    • Connect the event in your narrative to the concept of being a stranger in a village.

Peer Review

17. Review a peer's outline. When providing feedback address the following questions:

    • Does the outline clearly and effectively address the prompt?
    • Is there a clear and coherent structure?
    • Does the event reflect the theme?

Writing Prompt: Informational

Write a draft of an event in which you or someone you know felt like a "stranger in a village" or were perceived as a stranger. Be sure to:

• Include a effective introduction with a clear event.
• Use precise diction, sensory details, and stylistic devices to describe the event.
• Use transitional phrases and dialogue to connect ideas smoothly.

My Notes

WRITING PROMPT: INFORMATIONAL

The following standards are addressed in the writing prompt:
• W.11–12.2
• W.11–12.2c
• W.11–12.2d
• W.11–12.5

ACTIVITY 1.17 continued

16 Next, ask students to read the directions for the writing prompt. Direct them to prepare an outline for an essay in which they will write about a time they were excluded or treated like a stranger. Let students know that they will write a draft based on this outline after receiving feedback from a peer. Emphasize that they may choose to use this draft as a basis for the Embedded Assessment, so they may want to reread the Embedded Assessment assignment and Scoring Guide.

17 Go over the Peer Review section after students have completed their outlines. Ask students to take notes on their partner's feedback and consult those notes as they revise their outlines.

18 Once they have processed their peers' comments, instruct students to write a draft of the incident or event for the writing prompt.

ASSESS

Evaluate students' responses to the writing prompt to ensure they have depicted a clear event using effective language, details, and style. Check that they show a working understanding of the "stranger in the village" concept. Note how they incorporate dialogue, and check whether they have punctuated dialogue correctly and used speech appropriate to the speakers.

ADAPT

If students need further help understanding the concept of "stranger in the village," review their independent reading with them and ask them to highlight or indicate places that help them understand being a "stranger in the village."

ACTIVITY 1.18

PLAN

Suggested Pacing: 2 50-minute class periods

TEACH

1 Read the Learning Targets and Preview with your students. Point out that the essay explores the concept of being a "stranger in the village," as the title suggests. Explain that this text is divided into chunks, and that they should pause after each chunk to reflect on its significance before moving on to the next.

2 Draw students' attention to the Making Adjustments While Reading section. Remind them they can interact with the text in a variety of ways. Move directly into reviewing the As You Read tasks.

3 Ask students to read the About the Author Box. Ask them what they think James Baldwin might know about being a stranger in the village based on the short biography.

Understanding the Stranger's Perception of the Village

Learning Strategies

Diffusing
Marking the Text
Previewing
Socratic Seminar
Think-Pair-Share

My Notes

Learning Targets

- Analyze the relationships between structure, thematic development, point of view, plot, and character in a reflective essay.
- Participate in a collaborative discussion by asking questions and using textual evidence to evaluate answers and responses.
- Integrate ideas from multiple texts to build knowledge and vocabulary about thematic concerns regarding being a stranger in a new place.

Preview

In this activity, you will read and discuss the essay "Stranger in the Village," analyzing its structure, style, and thematic concepts.

Making Adjustments While Reading

When faced with a complex text, readers sometimes need to pause and make adjustments when their understanding breaks down. When you don't understand something you are reading, try the following adjustments:

- Reread the word, phrase, or sentence that you do not understand. Reread out loud to see if hearing the sentence helps you understand it.
- Use your background knowledge to make sense of what you are reading.
- Ask questions about the text. Jot down questions in the My Notes section and return to them later to see if you know the answer after reading more of the text.
- Use annotations, like metacognitive markers, to note the parts of the text where you have questions or comments.

As You Read

- Make notes using metacognitive symbols (? ! *) to indicate the type of comment you wish to return to.
- Circle unknown words and phrases. Try to determine the meaning of the words by using context clues, word parts, or a dictionary.

About the Author

James Baldwin (1924–1987) was born in Harlem, into a poor household. By his early twenties he was earning a living as a freelance book reviewer and had become friends with many other writers, including the novelist Richard Wright, who encouraged him to write longer works. A grant enabled him to move to Paris in 1948. This move helped provide the critical distance he needed to write *Notes of a Native Son* and his first novel, *Go Tell It on the Mountain*—powerful works about the African American experience. After returning to the United States, he became a leading literary voice for civil rights. While his unsparing view of race issues in the United States drew criticism from his African American and white peers alike, he is now viewed as one of the most significant U.S. writers of the 20th century.

College and Career Readiness Standards

Focus Standards:

RL.11–12.1 Cite strong and thorough textual evidence to support analysis of what the text says explicitly as well as inferences drawn from the text, including determining where the text leaves matters uncertain.

RL.11–12.3 Analyze the impact of the author's choices regarding how to develop and relate elements of a story or drama (e.g., where a story is set, how the action is ordered, how the characters are introduced and developed).

RL.11–12.5 Analyze how an author's choices concerning how to structure specific parts of a text (e.g., the choice of where to begin or end a story, the choice to provide a comedic or tragic resolution) contribute to its overall structure and meaning as well as its aesthetic impact.

Essay

Stranger in the Village

by **James Baldwin**

Chunk 1

1 From all available evidence no black man had ever set foot in this tiny Swiss village before I came. I was told before arriving that I would probably be a "sight" for the village; I took this to mean that people of my complexion were rarely seen in Switzerland, and also that city people are always something of a "sight" outside of the city. It did not occur to me—possibly because I am an American—that there could be people anywhere who had never seen a Negro.

Chunk 2

2 It is a fact that cannot be explained on the basis of the inaccessibility of the village. The village is very high, but it is only four hours from Milan and three hours from Lausanne. It is true that it is virtually unknown. Few people making plans for a holiday would elect to come here. On the other hand, the villagers are able, presumably, to come and go as they please—which they do: to another town at the foot of the mountain, with a population of approximately five thousand, the nearest place to see a movie or go to the bank. In the village there is no movie house, no bank, no library, no theater; very few radios, one jeep, one station wagon; and, at the moment, one typewriter, mine, an invention which the woman next door to me here had never seen. There are about six hundred people living here, all Catholic—I conclude this from the fact that the Catholic church is open all year round, whereas the Protestant chapel, set off on a hill a little removed from the village, is open only in the summertime when the tourists arrive. There are four or five hotels, all closed now, and four or five *bistros*,[1] of which, however, only two do any business during the winter. These two do not do a great deal, for life in the village seems to end around nine or ten o'clock. There are a few stores, butcher, baker, *epicerie*,[2] a hardware store, and a money-changer—who cannot change travelers' checks, but must send them down to the bank, an operation which takes two or three days. There is something called the *Ballet Haus*, closed in the winter and used for God knows what, certainly not ballet, during the summer. There seems to be only one schoolhouse in the village, and this for the quite young children; I suppose this to mean that their older brothers and sisters at some point descend from these mountains in order to complete their

---

[1] *bistros*: small informal restaurants
[2] *epicerie*: French for "grocery store"

KNOWLEDGE QUEST

Knowledge Question:
What challenges or difficulties might someone new to a place face?

My Notes

ACTIVITY 1.18 continued

4 Have students read and discuss the Knowledge Question in small groups.

5 **FIRST READ:** Have students read the text in pairs. Ask the students to read a chunk and compare their annotations before going on to the next chunk. Ask them to mark things that become clearer or questions that are answered as they continue to read.

TEXT COMPLEXITY

Overall: Complex
Lexile: 1400L
Qualitative: High Difficulty
Task: Moderate (Analyze)

College and Career Readiness Standards

RL.11–12.9 Demonstrate knowledge of eighteenth-, nineteenth- and early-twentieth-century foundational works of American literature, including how two or more texts from the same period treat similar themes or topics.

SL.11–12.2 Initiate and participate effectively in a range of collaborative discussions (one-on-one, in groups, and teacher-led) with

diverse partners on grades 11–12 topics, texts, and issues, building on others' ideas and expressing their own clearly and persuasively.

Additional Standards Addressed:

RL.11–12.2, RL.11–12.4, RL.11–12.6, RL.11–12.10, W.11–12.10, L.11–12.4c

6 As students are reading, monitor their progress. Be sure they are engaged with the text, annotating with metacognitive markers, and pausing to summarize each chunk.

LEVELED DIFFERENTIATED INSTRUCTION

In this activity, students may need support comprehending and analyzing a challenging text.

Developing Partner students to read the text together, alternating readers for each paragraph and collaborating to take notes. Provide partners with a copy of the **Narrative Analysis and Writing** graphic organizer to complete in order to demonstrate their understanding of the events, responses, and reflections in the text.

Expanding Have students take notes in the **Narrative Analysis and Writing** graphic organizer as they read the text. Following the reading, have students share their annotations with a partner, and collaborate to write a summary of the text that includes the major incidents, as well as the speaker's response and reflection.

Support Following reading, have students work in groups to label each of the eight chunks in the text, stating whether it mainly focuses on the incident, the speaker's reaction, the speaker's reflection, or a combination.

Extend Ask pairs or groups of students to create a short dramatic sketch highlighting what they believe to be the most compelling reaction the villagers had in response to Baldwin. Ask them to think about whether this response demonstrates discrimination or fascination. After students perform for one another, ask them to discuss their ideas about discrimination versus fascination.

1.18

James Baldwin visted Leukerbad, Switzerland in 1951.

disquietingly: disturbingly
jocularly: jokingly

education—possibly, again, to the town just below. The landscape is absolutely forbidding, mountains towering on all four sides, ice and snow as far as the eye can reach. In this white wilderness, men and women and children move all day, carrying washing, wood, buckets of milk or water, sometimes skiing on Sunday afternoons. All week long boys and young men are to be seen shoveling snow off the rooftops, or dragging wood down from the forest in sleds.

3   The village's only real attraction, which explains the tourist season, is the hot spring water. A disquietingly high proportion of these tourists are cripples, or semi-cripples, who come year after year—from other parts of Switzerland, usually—to take the waters. This lends the village, at the height of the season, a rather terrifying air of sanctity, as though it were a lesser Lourdes.[3] There is often something beautiful, there is always something awful, in the spectacle of a person who has lost one of his faculties, a faculty he never questioned until it was gone, and who struggles to recover it. Yet people remain people, on crutches or indeed on deathbeds; and wherever I passed, the first summer I was here, among the native villagers or among the lame, a wind passed with me—of astonishment, curiosity, amusement and outrage. That first summer I stayed two weeks and never intended to return. But I did return in the winter, to work; the village offers, obviously, no distractions whatever and has the further advantage of being extremely cheap. Now it is winter again, a year later, and I am here again. Everyone in the village knows my name, though they scarcely ever use it, knows that I come from America—though this, apparently, they will never really believe: black men come from Africa—and everyone knows that I am the friend of the son of a woman who was born here, and that I am staying in their chalet. But I remain as much a stranger today as I was the first day I arrived, and the children shout *Neger! Neger!* as I walk along the streets.

Chunk 3

4   It must be admitted that in the beginning I was far too shocked to have any real reaction. In so far as I reacted at all, I reacted by trying to be pleasant—it being a great part of the American Negro's education (long before he goes to school) that he must make people "like" him. This smile-and-the-world-smiles-with-you routine worked about as well in this situation as it had in the situation for which it was designed, which is to say that it did not work at all. No one, after all, can be liked whose human weight and complexity cannot be, or has not been, admitted. My smile was simply another unheard-of phenomenon which allowed them to see my teeth—they did not, really, see my smile and I began to think that, should I take to snarling, no one would notice any difference. All of the physical characteristics of the Negro which had caused me, in America, a very different and almost forgotten pain were nothing less than miraculous—or infernal—in the eyes of the village people. Some thought my hair was the color of tar, that it had the texture of wire, or the texture of cotton. It was jocularly suggested that I might let it all grow long and make myself a winter coat. If I sat in the sun for more than five minutes

---
[3] *Lourdes* is a town in southern France where the Blessed Virgin Mary appeared to St. Bernadette Soubirous in 1858. Today it is a place of pilgrimage and miracles.

Scaffolding the Text-Dependent Questions

1. What is the event described in the first paragraph and why might it be significant? Identify what happens in paragraph 1. Why is that event unusual? How does the event relate to the theme? RL.11–12.2

2. How does Baldwin use setting in paragraphs 2–3 to develop the plot? What details does Baldwin provide about the village? How does he describe the geographical region? How does he feel about being in this village? RL.11–12.3

3. How does Baldwin feel about the village? Why does he keep returning to it? How does his behavior create an inner conflict? How does it contribute to the theme of being a stranger in the village? Consider what Baldwin says about the village in paragraph 3. What reasons does he give for his return the first winter? Do you think those reasons changed in the second winter? Why or why not? RL.11–12.1, RL.11–12.2, RL.11–12.3

some daring creature was certain to come along and gingerly put his fingers on my hair, as though he were afraid of an electric shock, or put his hand on my hand, astonished that the color did not rub off. In all of this, in which it must be conceded there was the charm of genuine wonder and in which there was certainly no element of intentional unkindness, there was yet no suggestion that I was human: I was simply a living wonder.

5   I knew that they did not mean to be unkind, and I know it now; it is necessary, nevertheless, for me to repeat this to myself each time that I walk out of the chalet. The children who shout *Neger!* have no way of knowing the echoes this sound raises in me. They are brimming with good humor and the more daring swell with pride when I stop to speak with them. Just the same, there are days when I cannot pause and smile, when I have no heart to play with them; when, indeed, I mutter sourly to myself, exactly as I muttered on the streets of a city these children have never seen, when I was no bigger than these children are now: *Your* mother *was a nigger.* Joyce[4] is right about history being a nightmare—but it may be the nightmare from which no one *can* awaken. People are trapped in history and history is trapped in them.

Chunk 4

6   There is a custom in the village—I am told it is repeated in many villages—of "buying" African natives for the purpose of converting them to Christianity. There stands in the church all year round a small box with a slot for money, decorated with a black figurine, and into this box the villagers drop their francs. During the carnaval which precedes Lent, two village children have their faces blackened—out of which bloodless darkness their blue eyes shine like ice—and fantastic horsehair wigs are placed on their blond heads; thus disguised, they solicit among the villagers for money for missionaries in Africa. Between the box in the church and blackened children, the village "bought" last year six or eight African natives. This was reported to me with pride by the wife of one of the *bistro* owners and I was careful to express astonishment and pleasure at the solicitude shown by the village for the souls of black folks. The *bistro* owner's wife beamed with a pleasure far more genuine than my own and seemed to feel that I might now breathe more easily concerning the souls of at least six of my kinsmen.

7   I tried not to think of these so lately baptized kinsmen, of the price paid for them, or the peculiar price they themselves would pay, and said nothing about my father, who having taken his own conversion too literally never, at bottom, forgave the white world (which he described as heathen) for having saddled him with a Christ in whom, to judge at least from their treatment of him, they themselves no longer believed. I thought of white men arriving for the first time in an African village, strangers there, as I am a stranger here, and tried to imagine the astounded populace touching their hair and marveling at the color of their skin. But there is a great difference between being the first white man to be seen by Africans and being the first black man to be seen

---

[4] *Joyce*: James Joyce is an important 20th-century Irish author.

My Notes

solicitude: concern

Scaffolding the Text-Dependent Questions

4. What is the significance of the last sentence in paragraph 4? Characterize Baldwin's tone or attitude as he writes about the village. Find diction that contributes to the tone. What words does Baldwin use to describe the villagers and his feelings toward them? Which of these words are particularly connotative? RL.11–12.4

5. How does Baldwin use dashes in Chunks 2 and 3? What impact does this syntax have on the reader? Read a few of the sentences with dashes out loud. What is the function of

the dashes? What stands out to you in those sentences? L.11–12.3

6. What is the irony of the villagers' custom described in Chunk 4? How does Baldwin use irony to reveal cultural differences between him and the villagers? How does Baldwin describe the custom in paragraph 6? Which word choices are particularly telling? What does he say about his own response in the following paragraph? RL.11–12.6

7 Continue monitoring students' progress and evaluating the chosen reading mode. For Chunk 5, guide students to notice the emerging "stranger in the village" theme.

8 **Vocabulary Development:** Discuss the Word Connections with students. Ask students how the words are similar. Then ask them to think of other words that share the prefix *dis-*. As an extension, have students complete the **Roots and Affixes Brainstorm** graphic organizer.

1.18

My Notes

by whites. The white man takes the astonishment as tribute, for he arrives to conquer and to convert the natives, whose inferiority in relation to himself is not even to be questioned; whereas I, without a thought of conquest, find myself among a people whose culture controls me, has even, in a sense, created me, people who have cost me more in anguish and rage than they will ever know, who yet do not even know of my existence. The astonishment with which I might have greeted them, should they have stumbled into my African village a few hundred years ago, might have rejoiced their hearts. But the astonishment with which they greet me today can only poison mine.

8   And this is so despite everything I may do to feel differently, despite my friendly conversations with the *bistro* owner's wife, despite their three-year-old son who has at last become my friend, despite the *saluts* and *bonsoirs* which I exchange with people as I walk, despite the fact that I know that no individual can be taken to task for what history is doing, or has done. I say that the culture of these people controls me—but they can scarcely be held responsible for European culture. America comes out of Europe, but these people have never seen America, nor have most of them seen more of Europe than the hamlet at the foot of their mountain. Yet they move with an authority which I shall never have; and they regard me, quite rightly, not only as a stranger in their village but as a suspect latecomer, bearing no credentials, to everything they have—however unconsciously—inherited.

9   For this village, even were it incomparably more remote and incredibly more primitive, is the West, the West onto which I have been so strangely grafted. These people cannot be, from the point of view of power, strangers anywhere in the world; they have made the modern world, in effect, even if they do not know it. The most illiterate among them is related, in a way that I am not, to Dante, Shakespeare, Michelangelo, Aeschylus, Da Vinci, Rembrandt, and Racine; the cathedral at Chartres says something to them which it cannot say to me, as indeed would New York's Empire State Building, should anyone here ever see it. Out of their hymns and dances come Beethoven and Bach. Go back a few centuries and they are in their full glory—but I am in Africa, watching the conquerors arrive.

Chunk 5

10   The rage of the disesteemed is personally fruitless, but it is also absolutely inevitable: this rage, so generally discounted, so little understood even among the people whose daily bread it is, is one of the things that makes history. Rage can only with difficulty, and never entirely, be brought under the domination of the intelligence and is therefore not susceptible to any arguments whatever. This is a fact which ordinary representatives of the *Herrenvolk*,[5] having never felt this rage and being unable to imagine it, quite fail to understand. Also, rage cannot be hidden it can only be dissembled. This dissembling deludes the thoughtless, and strengthens rage and adds, to rage, contempt. There are,

[5] *Herrenvolk*: German for "master race"

Scaffolding the Text-Dependent Questions

7. **Which details in paragraphs 8–9 does the author use to develop a theme of "stranger in a village"? What idea is conveyed by this phrase?** What does Baldwin connect the Swiss village to in paragraph 9? How does that broader meaning of the "village" underscore his sense of isolation? RL.11–12.2, RL.11–12.4

8. **What does Baldwin mean when he says in paragraph 10 that "the rage of the disesteemed is personally fruitless, but it is also absolutely inevitable"? What feeling does his choice of diction suggest?** Try paraphrasing Baldwin's comment in simpler words. How would his observation have been less powerful if he had used different words? What overall feeling is produced by the words he uses in this sentence? RL.11–12.4, RL.11–12.6

My Notes

no doubt, as many ways of coping with the resulting complex of tensions as there are black men in the world, but no black man can hope ever to be entirely liberated from this internal warfare—rage, dissembling, and contempt having inevitably accompanied his first realization of the power of white men. What is crucial here is that, since white men represent in the black man's world so heavy a weight, white men have for black men a reality which is far from being reciprocal; and hence all black men have toward all white men an attitude which is designed, really, either to rob the white man of the jewel of his naïveté or else to make it cost him dear.

11 The black man insists, by whatever means he finds at his disposal, that the white man cease to regard him as an exotic rarity and recognize him as a human being. This is a very charged and difficult moment, for there is a great deal of will power involved in the white man's naïveté. Most people are not naturally reflective any more than they are naturally malicious, and the white man prefers to keep the black man at a certain human remove because it is easier for him thus to preserve his simplicity and avoid being called to account for crimes committed by his forefathers, or his neighbors. He is inescapably aware, nevertheless, that he is in a better position in the world than black men are, nor can he quite put to death the suspicion that he is hated by black men therefore. He does not wish to be hated, neither does he wish to change places, and at this point in his uneasiness he can scarcely avoid having recourse to those legends which white men have created about black men, the most usual effect of which is that the white man finds himself enmeshed, so to speak, in his own language which describes hell, as well as the attributes which lead one to hell, as being as black as night.

12 Every legend, moreover, contains its residuum of truth, and the root function of language is to control the universe by describing it. It is of quite considerable significance that black men remain, in the imagination, and in overwhelming numbers in fact, beyond the disciplines of salvation; and this despite the fact that the West has been "buying" African natives for centuries. There is, I should hazard, an instantaneous necessity to be divorced from this so visibly unsaved stranger, in whose heart, moreover, one cannot guess what dreams of vengeance are being nourished; and, at the same time, there are few things on earth more attractive than the idea of the unspeakable liberty which is allowed the unredeemed. When, beneath the black mask, a human being begins to make himself felt one cannot escape a certain awful wonder as to what kind of human being it is. What one's imagination makes of other people is dictated, of course, by the laws of one's own personality and it is one of the ironies of black-white relations that, by means of what the white man imagines the black man to be, the black man is enabled to know who the white man is.

13 I have said, for example, that I am as much a stranger in this village today as I was the first summer I arrived, but this is not quite true. The villagers wonder less about the texture of my hair than they did then, and wonder rather more about me. And the fact that their wonder now exists on another level is reflected in their attitudes and in their eyes. There are the children who make those delightful, hilarious, sometimes astonishingly grave overtures of

9 Direct students' attention to paragraph 11. Its topic sentence begins the shift to Baldwin's major argument about African Americans and the American experience.

WORD CONNECTIONS

Roots and Affixes

Attribute comes from the Latin word *attribuere*, which means "to assign." It is related to the word *tribute*, which comes from the Latin word *tribuere*, meaning "to assign, allot, or pay."

naïveté: innocence
malicious: intending to cause harm
residuum: trace

Scaffolding the Text-Dependent Questions

9. How does Baldwin analyze the actions and attitudes of "the white man" in paragraph 11? Use details to support your answer. What explanation does Baldwin give in that paragraph for the complex responses of whites to blacks? Which words and phrases are most important to understanding Baldwin's stance? RL.11–12.1, RL.11–12.4

10. According to the details in paragraph 13, how have the villagers' attitudes changed toward Baldwin over time? What contradictory responses does Baldwin describe? Trace the order of changes Baldwin describes. RL.11–12.1, RL.11–12.2

1.18

Since paragraph 14 is the heart of the essay, you might want to give it additional attention, either at this point or after students have read the entire essay. Ask students to work in pairs and reread this paragraph to determine its meaning and its relationship to the whole essay. (Paragraph 14 connects the first part of the essay about Baldwin being a stranger in Switzerland to the second part of the essay about the more complex and nuanced position Baldwin and African Americans have in American society because they are not "strangers.") Students should paraphrase the last sentence of paragraph 14. Discuss the placement and effect of this last sentence, which is the thesis of the essay.

10 As students read Chunks 6 and 7, ask them to consider how Baldwin shifts the focus of his argument in paragraphs 14 and 15. How does he both connect the Swiss villagers and Americans and underscore their differences in these paragraphs?

My Notes

friendship in the unpredictable fashion of children; other children, having been taught that the devil is a black man, scream in genuine anguish as I approach. Some of the older women never pass without a friendly greeting, never pass, indeed, if it seems that they will be able to engage me in conversation; other women look down or look away or rather contemptuously smirk. Some of the men drink with me and suggest that I learn how to ski—partly, I gather, because they cannot imagine what I would look like on skis—and want to know if I am married, and ask questions about my *métier*.[6] But some of the men have accused *le sale nègre*—behind my back—of stealing wood and there is already in the eyes of some of them the peculiar, intent, paranoiac malevolence which one sometimes surprises in the eyes of American white men when, out walking with their Sunday girl, they see a Negro male approach.

Chunk 6

14   There is a dreadful abyss between the streets of this village and the streets of the city in which I was born, between the children who shout *Neger!* today and those who shouted *Nigger!* yesterday—the abyss is experience, the American experience. The syllable hurled behind me today expresses, above all, wonder: I am a stranger here. But I am not a stranger in America and the same syllable riding on the American air expresses the war my presence has occasioned in the American soul.

15   For this village brings home to me this fact: that there was a day, and not really a very distant day, when Americans were scarcely Americans at all but discontented Europeans, facing a great unconquered continent and strolling, say, into a marketplace and seeing black men for the first time. The shock this spectacle afforded is suggested, surely, by the promptness with which they decided that these black men were not really men but cattle. It is true that the necessity on the part of the settlers of the New World of reconciling their moral assumptions with the fact—and the necessity—of slavery enhanced immensely the charm of this idea, and it is also true that this idea expresses, with a truly American bluntness, the attitude which to varying extents all masters have had toward all slaves.

16   But between all former slaves and slave-owners and the drama which begins for Americans over three hundred years ago at Jamestown, there are at least two differences to be observed. The American Negro slave could not suppose, for one thing, as slaves in past epochs had supposed and often done, that he would ever be able to wrest the power from his master's hands. This was a **supposition** which the modern era, which was to bring about such vast changes in the aims and dimensions of power, put to death; it only begins, in unprecedented fashion, and with dreadful implications, to be resurrected today. But even had this supposition persisted with undiminished force, the American Negro slave could not have used it to lend his condition dignity, for the reason that this supposition rests on another: that the slave in exile yet remains related to his past, has some means—if only in memory—of revering and sustaining the forms of his former life, is able, in short, to maintain his identity.

supposition: belief

[6] *métier*: profession

Scaffolding the Text-Dependent Questions

11. In paragraph 15, what is the new description of the village in which Baldwin is a stranger? What does this say about the history and culture of that village? Look for connotative words and phrases. What does Baldwin describe as the American response to blacks in paragraph 15? RL.11–12.2, RL.11–12.4

12. How does Baldwin use the word "Neger" to examine the nature of racism? Pay attention to how Baldwin connects the Swiss villagers and white Americans. Ask yourself how this comparison helps develop Baldwin's point. RL.11–12.4, L.11–12.3

Chunk 7

My Notes

17 This was not the case with the American Negro slave. He is unique among the black men of the world in that his past was taken from him, almost literally, at one blow. One wonders what on earth the first slave found to say to the first dark child he bore. I am told that there are Haitians able to trace their ancestry back to African kings, but any American Negro wishing to go back so far will find his journey through time abruptly arrested by the signature on the bill of sale which served as the entrance paper for his ancestor. At the time—to say nothing of the circumstances—of the enslavement of the captive black man who was to become the American Negro, there was not the remotest possibility that he would ever take power from his master's hands. There was no reason to suppose that his situation would ever change, nor was there, shortly, anything to indicate that his situation had ever been different. It was his necessity, in the words of E. Franklin Frazier,[7] to find a "motive for living under American culture or die." The identity of the American Negro comes out of this extreme situation, and the evolution of this identity was a source of the most intolerable anxiety in the minds and the lives of his masters.

18 For the history of the American Negro is unique also in this: that the question of his humanity, and of his rights therefore as a human being, became a burning one for several generations of Americans, so burning a question that it ultimately became one of those used to divide the nation. It is out of this argument that the venom of the epithet *Nigger!* is derived. It is an argument which Europe has never had, and hence Europe quite sincerely fails to understand how or why the argument arose in the first place, why its effects are so frequently disastrous and always so unpredictable, why it refuses until today to be entirely settled. Europe's black possessions remained—and do remain—in Europe's colonies, at which remove they represented no threat whatever to European identity. If they posed any problem at all for the European conscience, it was a problem which remained comfortingly abstract: in effect, the black man, *as a man*, did not exist for Europe. But in America, even as a slave, he was an inescapable part of the general social fabric and no American could escape having an attitude toward him. Americans attempt until today to make an abstraction of the Negro, but the very nature of these abstractions reveals the tremendous effects the presence of the Negro has had on the American character.

19 When one considers the history of the Negro in America it is of the greatest importance to recognize that the moral beliefs of a person, or a people, are never really as **tenuous** as life—which is not moral—very often causes them to appear; these create for them a frame of reference and a necessary hope, the hope being that when life has done its worst they will be enabled to rise above themselves and to triumph over life. Life would scarcely be bearable if this hope did not exist. Again, even when the worst has been said, to betray a belief is not by any means to have put oneself beyond its power; the betrayal of a belief is not the same thing as ceasing to believe. If this were not so there would be no

tenuous: fragile or unstable

[7] *E. Franklin Frazier* was an American sociologist who studied race relations.

Scaffolding the Text-Dependent Questions

13. How does Baldwin characterize the "American Negro slave" in paragraph 17? Use details to support your answer. What specific words and phrases does he use to describe the slave in paragraph 17? What point is he trying to make? RL.11–12.1, RL.11–12.4

14. Paraphrase the essential conflict Baldwin presents in paragraphs 19–21. What "beliefs" does Baldwin reference indirectly in paragraph 19? In paragraph 20, what reasons does he give for these ideas being impossible to abandon? RL.11–12.2, RL.11–12.3

11 Consider using a jigsaw strategy for the last ten paragraphs of the text, either during the first read or as part of the second read. Divide students into six groups, and assign them paragraphs to read, providing either A or B group analysis instructions:

- Group A: Assign students to do a shared reading in small groups, using close reading strategies to make meaning from this section of text. This group will chart the organizational structure and discuss the significance of their part to the whole of the essay encountered thus far.

- Group B: Ask students to do a shared reading in small groups, using close reading strategies to make meaning from this section of text. This group will focus on content, style, and craft.

- Group assignments:

  A/B 1: Paragraphs 16–18

  A/B 2: Paragraphs 19–21

  A/B 3: Paragraphs 22–25

12 Have the groups work on their assigned paragraphs and then jigsaw with the other A or B groups (who were assigned the other paragraph clusters). Groups should share and compare understanding of each section and how it contributes to the ending and to the overall essay.

My Notes

shrillness: irritating intensity
pathological: insane

moral standards in the world at all. Yet one must also recognize that morality is based on ideas and that all ideas are dangerous—dangerous because ideas can only lead to action and where the action leads no man can say. And dangerous in this respect: that confronted with the impossibility of remaining faithful to one's beliefs, and the equal impossibility of becoming free of them, one can be driven to the most inhuman excesses. The ideas on which American beliefs are based are not, though Americans often seem to think so, ideas which originated in America. They came out of Europe. And the establishment of democracy on the American continent was scarcely as radical a break with the past as was the necessity, which Americans faced, of broadening this concept to include black men.

20 This was, literally, a hard necessity. It was impossible, for one thing, for Americans to abandon their beliefs, not only because these beliefs alone seemed able to justify the sacrifices they had endured and the blood that they had spilled, but also because these beliefs afforded them their only bulwark[8] against a moral chaos as absolute as the physical chaos of the continent it was their destiny to conquer. But in the situation in which Americans found themselves, these beliefs threatened an idea which, whether or not one likes to think so, is the very warp and woof[9] of the heritage of the West, the idea of white supremacy.

21 Americans have made themselves notorious by the shrillness and the brutality with which they have insisted on this idea, but they did not invent it; and it has escaped the world's notice that those very excesses of which Americans have been guilty imply a certain, unprecedented uneasiness over the idea's life and power, if not, indeed, the idea's validity. The idea of white supremacy rests simply on the fact that white men are the creators of civilization (the present civilization, which is the only one that matters; all previous civilizations are simply "contributions" to our own) and are therefore civilization's guardians and defenders. Thus it was impossible for Americans to accept the black man as one of themselves, for to do so was to jeopardize their status as white men. But not so to accept him was to deny his human reality, his human weight and complexity, and the strain of denying the overwhelmingly undeniable forced Americans into rationalizations so fantastic that they approached the pathological.

22 At the root of the American Negro problem is the necessity of the American white man to find a way of living with the Negro in order to be able to live with himself. And the history of this problem can be reduced to the means used by Americans—lynch law and law, segregation and legal acceptance, terrorization and concession—either to come to terms with this necessity, or to find a way around it, or (most usually) to find a way of doing both these things at once. The resulting spectacle, at once foolish and dreadful, led someone to make the quite accurate observation that "the Negro-in-America is a form of insanity which overtakes white men."

[8] *bulwark*: defense
[9] *warp and woof*: foundation

Scaffolding the Text-Dependent Questions

15. What, according to Baldwin, is the main foundation of the belief in white supremacy? Consider how Baldwin analyzes the origins and content of this "idea" in paragraph 21. Put Baldwin's point of view into your own words.
RL.11–12.2, RL.11–12.6

TEACHER TO TEACHER

You may want to provide students with copies of the **Venn Diagram for Writing a Comparison** graphic organizer and have them use it to compare and contrast the conflicting attitudes of race and culture that Baldwin describes toward the end of the essay. Remind them to distinguish between American and European whites and between African Americans and Africans, as Baldwin sees the experiences of each group as distinct, though interrelated in complex ways.

My Notes

23 In this long battle, a battle by no means finished, the unforeseeable effects of which will be felt by many future generations, the white man's motive was the protection of his identity; the black man was motivated by the need to establish an identity. And despite the terrorization which the Negro in America endured and endures sporadically until today, despite the cruel and totally inescapable ambivalence of his status in his country, the battle for his identity has long ago been won. He is not a visitor to the West, but a citizen there, an American; as American as the Americans who despise him, the Americans who fear him, the Americans who love him—the Americans who became less than themselves, or rose to be greater than themselves by virtue of the fact that the challenge he represented was inescapable. He is perhaps the only black man in the world whose relationship to white men is more terrible, more subtle, and more meaningful than the relationship of bitter possessed to uncertain possessors. His survival depended, and his development depends, on his ability to turn his peculiar status in the Western world to his own advantage and, it may be, to the very great advantage of that world. It remains for him to fashion out of his experience that which will give him sustenance, and a voice. The cathedral at Chartres, I have said, says something to the people of this village which it cannot say to me; but it is important to understand that this cathedral says something to me which it cannot say to them. Perhaps they are struck by the power of the spires, the glory of the windows; but they have known God, after all, longer than I have known him, and in a different way, and I am terrified by the slippery bottomless well to be found in the crypt, down which heretics were hurled to death, and by the obscene, inescapable gargoyles jutting out of the stone and seeming to say that God and the devil can never be divorced. I doubt that the villagers think of the devil when they face a cathedral because they have never been identified with the devil. But I must accept the status which myth, if nothing else, gives me in the West before I can hope to change the myth.

24 Yet, if the American Negro has arrived at his identity by virtue of the absoluteness of his estrangement from his past, American white men still nourish the illusion that there is some means of recovering the European innocence, of returning to a state in which black men do not exist. This is one of the greatest errors Americans can make. The identity they fought so hard to protect has, by virtue of that battle, undergone a change: Americans are as unlike any other white people in the world as it is possible to be. I do not think, for example, that it is too much to suggest that the American vision of the world—which allows so little reality, generally speaking, for any of the darker forces in human life, which tends until today to paint moral issues in glaring black and white—owes a great deal to the battle waged by Americans to maintain between themselves and black men a human separation which could not be bridged. It is only now beginning to be borne in on us—very faintly, it must be admitted, very slowly, and very much against our will—that this vision of the world is dangerously inaccurate, and perfectly useless. For it protects our moral high-mindedness at the terrible expense of weakening our

sustenance: strength
heretics: nonbelievers

Scaffolding the Text-Dependent Questions

16. How does the author reflect on his experience? How does he use this reflection to achieve his purpose? What is the overall structure and purpose of the essay? About what groups does Baldwin draw conclusions? RL.11–12.3, RL.11–12.5

13 As the class reads about Baldwin's arrival, pause and discuss the first Knowledge Quest question. After reading the remaining text for the first time, guide the class in a brief discussion of the second Knowledge Quest question.

14 Direct students to the Focus on the Sentence. Explain that these sentences can help them understand the parts of a reflective essay and how Baldwin has developed his theme.

15 Ask students to work in pairs on the Focus on the Sentence exercise. Have each student complete the sentences and then share their completed sentences with their partner. Ask them to discuss how they have completed the sentences and why.

16 After all the students have finished the Focus on the Sentence section, review their work. Ask if they found any of the sentences to be especially difficult. Note the different answers and help students who need further support understand what they should be looking for in the text to complete the sentences correctly.

My Notes

perpetual: never-ending

grasp of reality. People who shut their eyes to reality simply invite their own destruction, and anyone who insists on remaining in a state of innocence long after that innocence is dead turns himself into a monster.

Chunk 8

25 The time has come to realize that the interracial drama acted out on the American continent has not only created a new black man, it has created a new white man, too. No road whatever will lead Americans back to the simplicity of this European village where white men still have the luxury of looking on me as a stranger. I am not, really, a stranger any longer for any American alive. One of the things that distinguishes Americans from other people is that no other people has ever been so deeply involved in the lives of black men, and vice versa. This fact faced, with all its implications, it can be seen that the history of the American Negro problem is not merely shameful, it is also something of an achievement. For even when the worst has been said, it must also be added that the perpetual challenge posed by this problem was always, somehow, perpetually met. It is precisely this black-white experience which may prove of indispensable value to us in the world we face today. This world is white no longer, and it will never be white again.

✐ Knowledge Quest
• How do the villagers react to Baldwin when he first arrives in Switzerland?
• What strikes you about how the author defines a stranger throughout the passage?

☑ Focus on the Sentence

Use details from the text to complete the sentences that follow. James Baldwin feels like a stranger in the village because the villagers do not see him as an individual African American; instead, they regard him as a stranger because they do not see him as being any part of Western civilization.

James Baldwin feels like a stranger in the village, but he continues to return to the village because he realizes that this gives him a distance from which he can reflect upon his life in America and the history of slavery.

James Baldwin feels like a stranger in the village, so he uses his feelings as an opportunity to explore differences between blacks and whites in Europe and the United States and by saying that, "I am not, really, a stranger any longer for any American alive."

Returning to the Text

- Reread the essay to answer these text-dependent questions.
- Write any additional questions you have about the text in your Reader/Writer Notebook.

1. **What is the event described in the first paragraph and why might it be significant?**

   The event is Baldwin's arrival in a tiny Swiss village. It is significant because he is the first

   African American most of the people there have seen, and his visit provides an opportunity to

   discuss attitudes about race.

2. **How does Baldwin use setting in paragraphs 2–3 to develop the plot?**

   Baldwin uses setting to show the village as a remote place with little connection to the

   outside world and few institutions or sources of entertainment. The village seems strange and

   different to his American hometown. The foreign setting allows him to begin to examine the

   idea of being a "stranger in the village" and what that means.

3. **How does Baldwin feel about the village? Why does he keep returning to it? How does his behavior create an inner conflict? How does it contribute to the theme of being as stranger in the village?**

   Baldwin has mixed feelings about the quiet, affordable village where he is treated as a

   curiosity. As a visitor, he is reluctant to challenge racist assumptions.

4. **KQ What is the significance of the last sentence in paragraph 4? Characterize Baldwin's tone or attitude as he writes about the village. Find diction that contributes to the tone.**

   The sentence is significant because it expresses a complicated thought. Baldwin is not

   angry with the villagers because he understands that their actions are driven by a somewhat

   innocent curiosity. However, at the same time, they were treating him as if he were not human

   but "a living wonder." His tone is one of frustration tempered with human understanding.

© 2021 College Board. All rights reserved.

ACTIVITY 1.18 continued

17 RETURNING TO THE TEXT:
Have students continue to work in pairs to answer the text-dependent questions. If they have difficulty, scaffold the questions by rephrasing them or breaking them down into smaller parts. See the Scaffolding the Text-Dependent Questions boxes for suggestions.

 TEACHER TO TEACHER

The organization of this essay reflects the incident, response, and reflection structure of a reflective essay. Be sure to review with students the incident that inspired Baldwin's meditation on American race relations, Baldwin's complex responses to the incident, and his deep reflections about America's complex relationship to the "black man."

You may also want to highlight the hybrid nature of this text, in which the author intertwines narrative of real events from his life with argumentation and explanation about social and historical issues

5. How does Baldwin use dashes in Chunks 2 and 3? What impact does this syntax have on the reader?

   Baldwin uses dashes to insert commentary and qualify statements. The dashes interrupt the sentences. They cause the reader to pause and draw attention to the commentary.

6. What is the irony of the villagers' custom described in Chunk 4? How does Baldwin use irony to reveal cultural differences between him and the villagers?

   The irony is that the villagers believe they are doing good deeds by collecting money to "buy" Africans in order to convert them to Christianity and save their souls. Baldwin pretends to be pleased and astonished even as he knows the true price his "kinsmen" paid for their introduction to Christianity.

7. KQ Which details in paragraphs 8–9 does the author use to develop a theme of "stranger in a village"? What idea is conveyed by this phrase?

   The author describes an unconscious authority that the villagers have inherited as Europeans that causes him to feel like a stranger not only in the Swiss village but also everywhere in the West. Even though the villagers have never traveled far, he claims that they have the power, authority, and cultural ties that leaves Baldwin feeling like an outsider.

8. What does Baldwin mean when he says in paragraph 10 that "the rage of the disesteemed is personally fruitless, but it is also absolutely inevitable"? What feeling does his choice of diction suggest?

   He means that people who lack self-esteem feel a deep anger that serves no purpose and is unavoidable. He makes the situation sound unbearable.

9. How does Baldwin analyze the actions and attitudes of "the white man" in paragraph 11? Use details to support your answer.

   Baldwin explains that "It is easier" for the white man to keep the black man at a distance than to admit mistakes made by "his forefathers, or his neighbors." This allows the white man to maintain his position of power even though he suspects that "he is hated by black men." Racism is reinforced by accepting legends that describe blackness as sin and "hell."

10. According to the details in paragraph 13, how have the villagers' attitudes changed toward Baldwin over time?

They no longer see him as a wonder but now "wonder rather more about me." Some children try to be his friend, while others that have been taught that "the devil is a black man, scream in genuine anguish" when they see him. Some older women say hello but do not converse with him. Others smirk or look away. The men have accused him of stealing wood.

11. In paragraph 15, what is the new description of the village in which Baldwin is a stranger? What does this say about the history and culture of that village?

Paragraph 15 describes the other "village," America. The history of slavery has made the nation a place where black men and women are still "strangers" to those who cannot really see them as equals.

12. How does Baldwin use the word "Neger" to examine the nature of racism?

When villagers shout the word "Neger" at him, they are expressing "above all, wonder," but this act makes Baldwin think about being a stranger both here in the village and in America. In America, he was not a stranger, but he was also called names, the sound of which "expresses the war" that the presence of black men has caused "in the American soul."

13. How does Baldwin characterize the "American Negro slave" in paragraph 17? Use details to support your answer.

He describes the American slave as someone whose "past was taken from him ... at one blow." Without a past the slave is without an identity. He cannot even imagine that "his situation would ever change" or that it "had ever been different." Cut off from his heritage, the slave had to develop a new identity in order to survive.

14. Paraphrase the essential conflict Baldwin presents in paragraph 19–21?

Baldwin states that white Americans cannot give up the beliefs at the core of American identity, such as equality and democracy. These beliefs, however, threaten white supremacy. If all people are equal, that must include blacks. To avoid acknowledging this, whites subscribe to racist ideas despite how unreasonable or ludicrous those ideas may be.

18 Direct students to the Working from the Text section and ask them to prepare for a **Socratic Seminar** by answering the model seminar questions and then drafting questions of their own using Levels of Questions.

19 Organize students into seminar groups to discuss the text. Encourage them to return to the text repeatedly in order to cite specific evidence when responding to seminar questions.

20 After the groups have completed their Socratic Seminars, reassemble the class as a whole and discuss the groups' main thoughts and conclusions about the text. Invite groups to present any original questions that they developed to the rest of the class.

21 Point out the Independent Reading Checkpoint, and have students respond as a brief check-in of their independent reading from the unit.

1.18

15. What, according to Baldwin, is the main foundation of the belief in white supremacy?

He argues that "the idea of white supremacy rests simply on the fact that white men are the creators of civilization." For that reason, "it was impossible for Americans to accept the black man as one of themselves." According to Baldwin, to accept the black man would diminish the white man's identity.

16. How does the author reflect on his experience? How does he use this reflection to achieve his purpose?

The author reflects on the personal and cultural significance, addressing both his experience in the Swiss village and his experience in the United States. His experiences in Switzerland illustrate some important aspects of U.S. culture. Baldwin believes that Americans' black/ white struggle has better prepared them for a world that is "white no longer."

Working from the Text
- To prepare for a Socratic Seminar, review the pre-seminar questions that follow and use them as a model to create sophisticated questions stemming from your study of Baldwin's essay.
- **Literal:** How does Baldwin compare his interactions with Swiss villagers with his life in America?
- **Interpretive:** What connections does Baldwin make between the historical past, his present day, and the future?
- **Universal:** How can you connect Baldwin's essay to a personal experience or other texts that you have read?

Model Socratic Seminar Questions:
Write your own Socratic Seminar questions. Remember to pose these questions as Levels of Questions, emphasizing interpretive questions more than literal or universal questions.

Literal: _____

_____

Interpretive: _____

_____

Universal: _____

_____

1.18

Knowledge Quest

Think about the challenges that authors Guo and Baldwin describe as strangers in new places. In your small group, discuss the challenges or difficulties someone new to a place might face. Be sure to:

- Draw on your observations as well as evidence from the text to support your ideas.
- Respond thoughtfully to diverse perspectives and interpretations.
- Ask thoughtful questions and build on the ideas of the group to deepen understanding.

 INDEPENDENT READING LINK

You can continue to build your knowledge about the impact of cultural factors on newcomers by reading these and other articles at ZINC Reading Labs. Search for keywords such as *immigration* or *American Dream*.

ZINC

Independent Reading Checkpoint

Review your independent reading and reflect on the characters, events, and ideas in the text using the lens of Cultural Criticism. Write a brief summary of your analysis, taking into consideration cultural factors such as religion, political affiliation, ethnicity, and/or class identification.

ACTIVITY 1.18 continued

22 Return to the Knowledge Question. Have students work in small groups to discuss the questions. Review speaking expectations with students using the "be sure to" points. After groups have had time to discuss the questions, ask each group to share one response.

23 Encourage students to continue building knowledge on this topic as suggested in the Independent Reading Link.

ASSESS

Monitor the Socratic Seminar and evaluate the sophistication of students' questions and the level of thought and attention to the text demonstrated by their answers. Evaluate how well the questions address the overall theme of being a stranger in the village. Monitor to check that students are focusing mostly on interpretive questions and are able to use details and evidence from the text to support their questions and conclusions.

ADAPT

If students need additional help developing Socratic Seminar questions, have them review their notes and their metacognitive markers to focus on the ideas and passages that most interested them. Ask them to think about cultural groups, conflict, and the text's structure as they develop their questions.

Suggested Pacing: 2 50-minute class periods

If you choose to modify this Embedded Assessment by changing the assignment for some or all of your students, be sure that you have properly scaffolded the necessary skills and knowledge.

1 Assignment: With the class, review the assignment and Scoring Guide criteria to ensure they understand the expectations for this assessment.

2 Planning and Prewriting: Students should have preliminary outlines for their reflective essays, as well as a draft of the event part. Allow time for students to review the Planning and Prewriting questions to explore ideas for restructuring the organization of their narrative and to flesh out any additional memories or ideas.

3 Drafting: Students may find it useful to write dialogue on sticky notes and experiment with where in the narrative the participants' actual words would have the most impact. Encourage students to use a variety of stylistic and literary devices. Remind students that showing the connections among ideas will help lend coherence to their draft. Instruct students to write a clear, compelling conclusion that supports the significance of the event shared in their essays.

4 Evaluating and Revising: Remind students to be civil and constructive in their peer reviews. They should provide feedback on the essay without criticizing the writer. Remind students to look at places where the author's meaning seems unclear, to ask questions, and to respond respectfully. Tell them to try to think of ways the author might make the meaning clearer. Perhaps the author needs to choose better words or restructure a section to make a sequence of events more evident. Model turning vague feedback ("This part confuses me") into specific comments ("It would help me understand the interaction between you and this person if you added dialogue").

Writing a Reflective Essay

 ASSIGNMENT

Write and present a reflective essay that illustrates an event in which you or someone you know felt like a "stranger in the village" or were perceived as a stranger by some group.

Planning and Prewriting: Make a plan for writing your essay.	■ What prewriting strategies will you use to explore your memories and capture ideas needed for a reflective essay organized around the concept of "stranger in the village"? ■ How can you best use the general structure of event/response/reflection to plan and organize your reflective essay? ■ What have you learned from literary examples that you've read in this unit that can help you develop your theme? ■ What sorts of tools will you use to record your ideas and structure the essay (for example an outline, or a graphic organizer)? ■ How can you use point of view, setting, plot, and characterization to develop your essay?
Drafting: Determine how you will include the elements of a reflective essay that will assure a successful draft.	■ What stylistic devices (voice, diction, figurative language, detail, and the like) will you include to bring the reader into your reflective essay? ■ What literary devices will you use (imagery, irony, allegory, metaphor/simile, etc.) to develop your theme? ■ How will you identify and use the appropriate tone, voice and vocabulary? ■ How will you review your draft to ensure that your reflective essay's structure includes a clear topic, supporting details, and a strong conclusion?
Evaluating and Revising Your Draft: Review and revise to make your work the best it can be.	■ How can you solicit feedback from others, such as peers, that will help you to know what needs to be improved or revised for clarity, organization, syntax, diction, and rhetorical devices? ■ How will you evaluate transitions within and between sentences? ■ How can you use the Scoring Guide to help guide your revision?
Checking and Editing: Confirm that your final draft is ready for publication and presentation.	■ How will you use print or digital resources to clarify the meaning of words? ■ What style manual will you consult for grammatical correctness, technical accuracy, format, and correct structure? ■ How will you present your work to an audience? (Will you read it out loud? Or will you have a peer read it to you?)

Reflection

After completing this Embedded Assessment, think about how you went about accomplishing this assignment, and respond to the following question:

- How did the structure of the reflective essay help you develop the theme?

College and Career Readiness Standards

Focus Standards:

L.11–12.6 Acquire and use accurately general academic and domain-specific words and phrases, sufficient for reading, writing, speaking, and listening at the college and career readiness level; demonstrate independence in gathering vocabulary knowledge when considering a word or phrase important to comprehension or expression.

W.11–12.2b Develop the topic thoroughly by selecting the most significant and relevant facts, extended definitions, concrete details, quotations, or other information and examples appropriate to the audience's knowledge of the topic.

W.11–12.2c Use appropriate and varied transitions and syntax to link the major sections of the text, create cohesion, and clarify the

SCORING GUIDE

Scoring Criteria	Exemplary	Proficient	Emerging	Incomplete
Ideas	The essay • thoroughly demonstrates a perceptive understanding of the relationship between the event and the thematic concept • uses specific and well-chosen details to create a convincing, compelling text.	The essay • demonstrates a solid understanding of the relationship between the chosen event and the thematic concept • uses specific details to provide support and create a convincing text.	The essay • demonstrates a superficial understanding of the relationship between the event and the thematic concept • underutilizes details, and those included do little to create a convincing text.	The essay • demonstrates no obvious understanding of the relationship between the event and the thematic concept • uses very few details or language to create an engaging or convincing text.
Structure	The essay • shows a perceptive understanding of the relationships among event, response, and reflection • uses transitions to enhance overall coherence and to connect ideas smoothly.	The essay • uses a form or structure that is appropriate to the purpose • uses transitional words, phrases, and clauses to link events and signal shifts between ideas.	The essay • uses a form or structure that shows little understanding of the relationships among event, response, and reflection • may contain minimal use of transitions.	The essay • uses a confusing form or structure that shows a lack of understanding of the relationships among event, response, and reflection • moves between ideas without use of transitions.
Use of Language	The essay • uses diction, syntax, and stylistic devices that are notable and appropriate for the subject, purpose, and audience • demonstrates strong command of the conventions of standard English capitalization, punctuation, spelling, grammar, and usage with few or no errors.	The essay • uses diction, syntax, and other stylistic devices that are appropriate for the subject, purpose, and audience • demonstrates adequate command of standard writing conventions; may contain minor errors that do not interfere with meaning.	The essay • uses vague diction, confusing syntax, and other stylistic devices less effectively for the subject, purpose, and audience • contains errors in standard writing conventions that interfere with meaning.	The essay • uses inappropriate diction, confusing syntax, and other stylistic devices that do not support the subject, purpose, and audience • contains multiple serious errors in standard writing conventions that interfere with meaning.

EMBEDDED ASSESSMENT 2

5 Checking and Editing: Remind students to consult reference materials as needed to ensure that they are using English spelling, grammar, and punctuation correctly.

6 Reflection: Have students respond to the Reflection question, and decide whether you will review responses with students' essays.

TEACHER TO TEACHER

You may choose to manage student presentations in a variety of ways depending on the length and style of the presentations, the number of students per class, and the amount of class time you want to devote to live presenting. There are a number of media resources available online that can facilitate digital video or audio submissions. Video and audio sharing websites can also provide a platform for students to view each other's presentations and leave peer feedback.

7 Portfolio: Be sure students address the reflection question as a separate part of the Embedded Assessment assignment so they can include it separately. All notes for and drafts of the reflective essay should be collected together to show the process students completed in successfully accomplishing the task.

SCORING GUIDE

When you score this Embedded Assessment, you may wish to make copies or download and print copies of the Scoring Guide from SpringBoard Digital. In this way, you can have a copy to mark for each student's work. The Presenting Scoring Guide and Audience Notes and Feedback graphic organizers are available in the Resources section of the student and teacher editions.

College and Career Readiness Standards

relationships among complex ideas and concepts.

W.11–12.2d Use precise language, domain-specific vocabulary, and techniques such as metaphor, simile, and analogy to manage the complexity of the topic.

W.11–12.3a Engage and orient the reader by setting out a problem, situation, or observation and its significance, establishing one or multiple point(s) of view, and introducing a narrator and/or characters; create a smooth progression of experiences or events.

Additional Standards Addressed:
SL.11–12.3, W.11–12.5, W.11–12.6, W.11–12.3e

Planning the Unit

Context

This unit provides an opportunity for students to continue exploring and applying critical perspectives including Archetypal, Feminist, and Marxist literary criticism. Students will be asked to focus their attention on characters, characterizations, and the relationship between and among individuals and groups in a variety of texts including fiction, drama, and nonfiction. This unit not only asks students to examine and analyze texts, but also asks them to consider the social and cultural implications of presenting a text from a particular perspective. By studying texts in this way, students will start to access various textual readings and reflect on how these perspectives enhance their enjoyment and understanding.

Suggested Texts and Materials

You will need the following materials for this unit:

- Activities 2.4–2.11, 2.13: *Pygmalion*, by George Bernard Shaw
- Activity 2.12: Lyrics from Tracy Chapman's "Talkin' 'bout a Revolution" and two additional, teacher-selected songs (optional)
- Activity 2.18: *The Giving Tree*, by Shel Silverstein

Instructional Sequence

The unit begins by establishing an understanding of Archetypal Criticism. Students will then read George Bernard Shaw's *Pygmalion* and analyze its characters, dialogue, subtexts, and plot. With a clear understanding of the text, students will then apply a Marxist critical perspective to further analyze the play. Students will be asked to transform a scene from the play to reflect a specific critical perspective in Embedded Assessment 1.

In the second part of the unit, students will study Feminist Criticism and will apply their understanding to a work of nonfiction, short story, a folk tale, and a children's story. These varied experiences will help students prepare for their individual written analysis of a short story from a feminist perspective in Embedded Assessment 2.

AP® CONNECTIONS

In this unit, students will focus on refining these important skills and knowledge areas for AP/College Readiness:

- Analyzing a variety of texts to deepen knowledge of the ways writers use language to provide meaning and convey pleasure for the reader (Activities 2.3–2.11)
- Analyzing structure, style, and themes, as well as elements such as figurative language, imagery, symbolism, tone, and characterization in literature (Activities 2.4–2.6, 2.8, 2.10, 2.11)
- Analyzing literary works from various genres, periods, perspectives, and cultures (Activities 2.3, 2.4–2.12, 2.17–2.19)
- Writing to interpret, evaluate, and negotiate differing critical perspectives in literature (Activities 2.13, 2.19, Embedded Assessment 2)
- Moving effectively through the stages of the writing process with careful attention to revising and evaluating stylistic techniques that illustrate sophisticated writing skills (Activities 2.7, 2.9, 2.11, LC 2.16)
- Focusing deliberate attention on the craft of sentence-level writing (Activities 2.5, 2.6, 2.12, 2.16, 2.19)

SAT® CONNECTIONS

In this unit, students will practice many important skills that will help them succeed on the SAT and other college readiness exams, including:

- Correctly using punctuation (commas, parentheses, dashes) to set off nonrestrictive and parenthetical sentence elements as well as recognizing and correcting cases in which restrictive or essential sentence elements are inappropriately set off with punctuation (LC 2.16)

Unpacked Embedded Assessments

Embedded Assessment 1: Illuminating *Pygmalion*	Embedded Assessment 2: Applying a Critical Perspective
Skills and Knowledge: • Write a script that conveys a critical perspective. • Understand the genre conventions of a play script. • Understand and apply key themes and components of critical theories. • Use stages of the writing process. • Use guiding questions associated with a variety of literary criticisms. • Apply a sophisticated understanding of the drama. • Understand and apply elements of plot, characterization, dialogue, and subtext. • Reflect on group process of creating, presenting, and making meaning from text.	**Skills and Knowledge:** • Apply the Feminist critical perspective to an unfamiliar text. • Apply close reading strategies to a new text. • Use peer feedback to enhance written products. • Reflect a clear understanding of the connection between summary, thesis, examples, and commentary. • Use appropriate grammar, conventions, and organization.

Cognate Directory

Encouraging students to notice the connections between their primary language and English can help them develop academic vocabulary more quickly. If your class includes Spanish speakers, consider adding the following cognates to the classroom Word Wall. For English Language Learners whose primary language is not Spanish, consider using an online translator or dictionary to support comprehension of vocabulary terms.

Unit 2 Vocabulary Terms with Spanish Cognates

Academic Terms	
English	**Spanish**
genre conventions	convenciones genéricas
patriarchal	patriarcal
subtext	subtexto

Literary Terms	
English	**Spanish**
Archetypal Criticism	crítica de arquetipos
archetype	arquetipo
artistic license	licencia artística
Feminist Criticism	crítica feminista
Marxist Criticism	crítica marxista
motifs	motivos
myth	mito
narrative arc	arco narrativo
satire	sátira

Activity Features at a Glance

The activities in every ELA unit reflect the interconnected nature of reading, writing, listening, speaking, and thinking. The Activity Features at a Glance chart highlights the types of tasks or supports that students and teachers will encounter in each activity.

Writing and Revision	Grammar and Language	Listening, Speaking, and Discussion	Independent Reading	Vocabulary Development	ELL Support	Knowledge Quest	Gaining Perspectives

ELA Activity	Activity Features
2.1	Listening, Independent Reading
2.2	Writing, Listening, Vocabulary, ELL
2.3	Grammar, Listening, Vocabulary, ELL, Knowledge Quest
2.4	Writing, Grammar, Listening, Independent Reading, Vocabulary, ELL
2.5	Writing, Grammar, Listening, Independent Reading, ELL
2.6	Writing, Grammar, Listening, Vocabulary, ELL
2.7	Writing, Listening, Independent Reading, Vocabulary, ELL
2.8	Writing, Listening
2.9	Writing, Listening, Independent Reading, Vocabulary, ELL
2.10	Writing, Grammar, Listening, Vocabulary, ELL

ELA Activity	Activity Features
2.11	Writing, Grammar, Listening, Independent Reading
2.12	Writing, Grammar, Listening, Independent Reading, Vocabulary, ELL
2.13	Writing, Listening, Independent Reading, ELL
2.14	Listening, Independent Reading
2.15	Writing, Listening, Vocabulary, ELL
2.16	Writing, Grammar, Listening, Independent Reading, Vocabulary, Knowledge Quest
LC 2.16	Writing, Grammar, Listening
2.17	Writing, Grammar, Vocabulary, ELL, Knowledge Quest, Gaining Perspectives
2.18	Writing, Listening, Independent Reading, ELL
2.19	Writing, Grammar, Listening, Independent Reading, ELL

Unit Resources at a Glance

Formative Assessment Opportunities	Digital Assessments	Family Connections
Text-dependent questions Writing prompts Check Your Understanding tasks Focus on the Sentence tasks Language Checkpoint exercises Language & Writer's Craft practice	Activity Quizzes 2.2–2.19 Unit Assessment Part 1 Unit Assessment Part 2 **SBD**	Suggestions for Independent Reading Family Letters (English and Spanish) Student Reports **SBD**
English Language Development	**Foundational Skills**	**Independent Reading**
Leveled Differentiated Instruction Graphic Organizers ELD Strategies Language Workshop 2A Language Workshop 2B	Foundational Skills Screening Assessment Observational Look-fors Foundational Skills Workshop	My Independent Reading List Independent Reading Links Independent Reading Checkpoints Independent Reading Log Reader/Writer Notebook Suggestions for Independent Reading

🔘 Suggestions for Independent Reading

This list, divided into the categories of **Literature** and **Nonfiction/Informational Text**, comprises titles related to the themes and content of the unit. For their independent reading, students can select from this wide array of titles, which have been chosen based on complexity and interest. Spanish-language titles are included for those students who can read with greater independence or at a higher grade level in Spanish than in English, since building on their first language literacy can bolster their acquisition of English. Titles on this list have been suggested by teachers and school librarians, but you should be sure to preview texts to assess their appropriateness for your specific students and setting. You can also encourage students to do their own research and select titles that intrigue them.

Unit 2: The Collective Perspective

Literature		
Author	**Title**	**Lexile**
Albee, Edward	*Who's Afraid of Virginia Woolf?*	N/A
Amis, Kingsley	*Lucky Jim*	930L
Austen, Jane	*Sense and Sensibility*	1180L
Bolt, Robert	*A Man for All Seasons: A Play in Two Acts*	N/A
Brontë, Charlotte	*Jane Eyre*	1040L
Butler, Octavia E.	*Parable of the Sower*	710L
Chopin, Kate	*The Awakening*	960L
Fitzgerald, F. Scott	*The Beautiful and the Damned*	1040L
Gilmore, Charlotte Perkins	*The Yellow Wallpaper*	920L
Greene, Graham	*The Quiet American*	800L
Hansberry, Lorraine	*A Raisin in the Sun*	N/A

Harris, Joanne	*Chocolat*	N/A
Homer	*La Iliada*	930L
Homer	*The Illiad*	1330L
Krisher, Trudy	*Uncommon Faith*	N/A
Leiva, Ángel	*El túnel*	920L
Martin, Richard P.	*Myths of the Ancient Greeks*	N/A
O'Neill, Eugene	*Long Day's Journey Into Night*	N/A
Shelley, Mary	*Frankenstein*	1170L
Steinbeck, John	*Grapes of Wrath*	680L
Uhry, Alfred	*Driving Miss Daisy*	N/A
Walker, Alice	*The Color Purple*	670L
Williams, Tennessee	*Cat on a Hot Tin Roof*	N/A
Woolrich, Cornell	*The Cornell Woolrich Omnibus*	N/A

Nonfiction/Informational Text		
Author	**Title**	**Lexile**
Bodanis, David	*E = MC²: A Biography of the World's Most Famous Equation*	1170L
Chesterton, G.K.	*George Bernard Shaw*	N/A
Gray, Richard	*Archetypal Explorations: An Integrative Approach to Human Behavior*	1310L
Iaccino, James F.	*Jungian Reflections Within the Cinema: A Psychological Analysis of Sci-Fi and Fantasy Archetypes*	1510L
Kolbenschlag, Madonna	*Kiss Sleeping Beauty Goodbye*	N/A
Koloski, Bernard	*The Historian's Awakening: Reading Kate Chopin's Classic Novel as Social and Cultural History*	N/A
Levine, Lawrence W.	*The Unpredictable Past: Explorations in American Cultural History*	1460L
Mamet, David	*On Directing Film*	N/A
Murch, Walter	*In the Blink of an Eye: A Perspective on Film Editing*	N/A
Pomerance, Murray	*An Eye for Hitchcock*	1410L
Pratt, Annis	*Archetypal Patterns in Women's Fiction*	1540L
Roller, Judi M.	*The Politics of the Feminist Novel*	1290L
Sayers, Sean	*Marxism and Human Nature*	1250L
Strauss, Rochelle	*One Well: The Story of Water on Earth*	960L
von Franz, Marie-Louise	*Archetypal Patterns in Fairy Tales*	N/A

Unit 2 Instructional Pathways

Instructional Pathways

Teachers can build customized pathways through this unit by making purposeful choices about which resources to use based on students' learning needs. The charts below outline a few possible pathways to show how teachers might integrate digital assessments, Language Workshops, Close Reading Workshops, and Writing Workshops into instruction. Additional planning resources—including detailed standards correlations—are available on SpringBoard Digital.

English Language Arts Unit 2: The Collective Perspective		
Activity	**SBD Digital Assessments**	**Pacing**
Activity 2.1: Previewing the Unit	N/A	1
Activity 2.2: A Closer Look: Archetypal Criticism	Activity Quiz 2.2	1
Activity 2.3: Introducing the Myth	Activity Quiz 2.3	2
Activity 2.4: Viewing the Subjects	Activity Quiz 2.4	1
Activity 2.5: Ladies and Gentlemen	Activity Quiz 2.5	2
Activity 2.6: Language and Satire	Activity Quiz 2.6	1
Activity 2.7: Reading Between the Lines	Activity Quiz 2.7	1
Activity 2.8: Examining Eliza's Options	Activity Quiz 2.8	2
Activity 2.9: Transformations	Activity Quiz 2.9	2
Activity 2.10: What Does Eliza Do?	Activity Quiz 2.10	2
Activity 2.11: Examining the Archetypes	Activity Quiz 2.11	2
Activity 2.12: From a Marxist Perspective	Activity Quiz 2.12	2
Activity 2.13: Money, Power, and Class in *Pygmalion*	Activity Quiz 2.13	1
Embedded Assessment 1: Illuminating *Pygmalion*	**Unit Assessment Part 1**	**1** **1**

Activity	SBD Digital Assessments	Pacing	
Activity 2.14: Unpacking Embedded Assessment 2	Activity Quiz 2.14	1	
Activity 2.15: From a Feminist Perspective	Activity Quiz 2.15	1	
Activity 2.16: A Reversal of Fortune	Activity Quiz 2.16	2	
LC2.16: Language Checkpoint: Using Commas, Parentheses, and Dashes (optional)	Activity Quiz LC 2.16	1	
Activity 2.17: Battle of the Sexes	Activity Quiz 2.17	2	
Activity 2.18: Feminist Critique: The Tree of Life	Activity Quiz 2.18	2	
Activity 2.19: Seeing Beyond Your Own Perspective	Activity Quiz 2.19	3	
Embedded Assessment 2: Applying a Critical Perspective	Unit Assessment Part 2	2	1

Total 50-minute Class Periods: 34–37

Language Development Pathway

Consider using some or all of the Language Workshop and Foundational Skills Workshop activities with English Language Learners or with any student who would benefit from extra support with academic English. More detailed guidance about the timing of Language Workshop and Foundational Skills Workshop activities in relation to the ELA unit and about the purpose of each activity can be found in the Language Workshop teacher edition.

Language Workshop 2A and 2B		
Activity or Workshop		**Pacing**
Activity 2.1: Previewing the Unit		1
Activity 2.2: A Closer Look: Archetypal Criticism		1
Activity 2.3: Introducing the Myth		2
Language Workshop 2A.7: Language Checkpoint		1
Language Workshop 2A.1: Genre Focus		1
Language Workshop 2A.2: Building Knowledge		1
Activity 2.4: Viewing the Subjects		1
Language Workshop 2A.3: Academic Vocabulary		1
Language Workshop 2A.4: Vocabulary Preview and Practice		1
Activity 2.5: Ladies and Gentlemen **OR** **Language Workshop 2A.5:** Close Reading of an Anchor Text*		1
	2	
	Language Workshop 2A.6: Academic Collaboration*	1
Activity 2.6: Language and Satire		1
Activity 2.7: Reading Between the Lines		1
Activity 2.8: Examining Eliza's Options		2
Activity 2.9: Transformations		2
Activity 2.10: What Does Eliza Do?		2
Activity 2.11: Examining the Archetypes		2
Activity 2.12: From a Marxist Perspective		2
Activity 2.13: Money, Power, and Class in *Pygmalion*		1
Embedded Assessment 1: Illuminating *Pygmalion* **OR** Collaborative Embedded Assessment: Illuminating *Pygmalion*	1	4

Activity or Workshop	Pacing
Activity 2.14: Unpacking Embedded Assessment 2	1
Activity 2.15: From a Feminist Perspective	1
Activity 2.16: A Reversal of Fortune	2
LC 2.16: Language Checkpoint: Using Commas, Parentheses, and Dashes (optional)	1
Activity 2.17: Battle of the Sexes	2
Activity 2.18: Feminist Critique: The Tree of Life	2
Language Workshop 2B.1: Genre Focus	1
Language Workshop 2B.2: Building Knowledge	1
Activity 2.19: Seeing Beyond Your Own Perspective	3
Language Workshop 2B.7: Language Checkpoint	1
Language Workshop 2B.3: Academic Vocabulary	1
Language Workshop 2B.4: Vocabulary Preview and Practice	1
Language Workshop 2B.5: Close Reading of an Anchor Text*	1
Language Workshop 2B.6: Academic Collaboration*	1

Embedded Assessment 2: Applying a Critical Perspective	OR	Collaborative Embedded Assessment: Applying a Critical Perspective	2	4

Total 50-minute Class Periods:	34–52

* These activities are available in Spanish.

Foundational Skills Workshop

The Foundational Skills Workshop offers instructional and practice materials for providing small-group instruction to students who are still developing foundational reading skills.

Activity	Pacing
Activity 1: Practicing Letter-Sound Relationships	15 min.
Activity 2: Recognizing Words by Sight	10 min.
Activity 3: Words with Inconsistent but Common Spellings	
Activity 4: Irregularly Spelled Words	
Activity 5: Common Prefixes	
Activity 6: Common Suffixes	35–40 min. per activity
Activity 7: Using Roots and Affixes to Read Multisyllabic Words	
Activity 8: Reading Multisyllabic Words	
Activity 9: Reading Informational Text with Purpose and Understanding	
Activity 10: Reading Poetry with Fluency	

Flexible Pathways

Teachers may build a flexible pathway that focuses on developing students' close reading and writing skills with the Close Reading and Writing Workshops. Each workshop addresses a specific set of standards and includes multiple assessment opportunities to allow students to demonstrate the knowledge and skills that are the focus of that workshop.

Close Reading Workshops

Workshop	Genre Focus	Assessment Opportunities	Pacing
Close Reading Workshop 5: Informational Texts in Social Studies/History	Historical Text Painting Essay	Writing Prompt Debate/Discussion Multimedia Presentation	8

Writing Workshops

Workshop	Genre Focus	Assessment Opportunities	Pacing
Writing Workshop 4: Narrative Writing: Short Story	Short Story	Writing as a Class Writing with a Peer Independent Writing	8
Writing Workshop 5: Literary Analysis: Poem and Short Story	Poetry Short Story	Writing as a Class Independent Writing	7
Writing Workshop 9: Script Writing	Drama	Writing as a Class Writing with a Peer Independent Writing	7

UNIT 2

THE COLLECTIVE PERSPECTIVE

> **Y**ou see, really and truly, apart from the things anyone can pick up (the dressing and the proper way of speaking, and so on), the difference between a lady and a flower girl is not how she behaves, but how she's treated.
>
> —from *Pygmalion*, by George Bernard Shaw

VISUAL PROMPT
How are people transformed through their relationships with others? Do people have a say in how they are perceived by others?

Leveled Differentiated Instruction Directory

For guidance on differentiating tasks for English language learners at various levels of language proficiency, refer to the Leveled Differentiated Instruction suggestions in these activities:

2.2: Use **Conversation for Quickwrite** graphic organizer to encourage students to categorize types of questions they may have on the unit activities.

2.3: Assign students to groups and use **conferencing strategy** so that they discuss and clarify concepts presented in the unit.

2.4: Help students frame their questions about the play.

2.5: Have students use the **Character Map** graphic organizer as a discussion and note-taking tool.

UNIT 2

Read aloud the unit title, "The Collective Perspective," and the quotation. Ask students to mark the text by highlighting words and phrases that will help them determine what the unit will be about. Then ask them to write their interpretations of the quotation and whether or not they agree with the ideas expressed. Support students as they share responses in partner, small-group, or whole-class discussions.

Have students look at the photograph and respond to the visual prompt. You may want to have students think-pair-share to write a short response or discuss their responses as a class.

TEACHER TO TEACHER

You may want to ask students to think about how they are affected by images in films and the way relationships are portrayed in print and film texts. When they read or watch texts, how do they use critical thinking to analyze what they are taking in?

If students are not familiar with the Bechdel Test for Women in Movies, you might search for a current update on YouTube (search "Bechdel Test movies") and show it to students as a discussion starter.

CONTENTS

Have the students skim/scan the activities and texts in this unit. Have them note any texts they have heard about but never read, and any activities that sound particularly interesting.

GOALS

Have students read the goals for the unit and mark any words that are unfamiliar. Have students add these words to the classroom Word Wall, along with definitions.

You may also want to post these goals in a visible place in the classroom for the duration of this unit, allowing you and your students to revisit the goals easily and gauge progress throughout the unit.

UNIT 2

VOCABULARY DEVELOPMENT

Adding to vocabulary knowledge is essential for reading fluency. Students will encounter new vocabulary in this course in multiple ways:

- Academic Vocabulary
- Literary Terms
- Vocabulary in Context (unfamiliar terms glossed in text selections)
- Word Connections
- Oral discussions

Encourage students to use new vocabulary expressively in class discussions and in writing. Have them keep a **Reader/Writer Notebook** in which they record new words, their meanings, and their pronunciations.

See the Resources section for examples of graphic organizers suitable for word study. Having students use word-study graphic organizers will greatly enhance their understanding of new words and their connection to unit concepts and to the broader use of advanced and discipline-based terms.

Have students review the list of academic and literary terms and sort them in a **QHT** chart. Revisit the chart periodically to see how students' understanding progresses throughout the unit.

LANGUAGE DEVELOPMENT

Several recurring SpringBoard features focus on building students' knowledge of grammar and usage concepts. Language & Writer's Craft features guide students to examine a writer's use of a language concept in context before incorporating the concept into their own writing. Grammar & Usage features briefly highlight and explain an interesting grammar or usage concept that appears in a text, both to improve students' reading comprehension and to increase their understanding of the concept. Periodic Language Checkpoints offer in-depth practice with standard English conventions and usage and guide students to revise sample sentences as well as their own work.

UNIT 2

The Collective Perspective

GOALS

- To understand and apply Archetypal, Marxist, and Feminist critical perspectives to drama, nonfiction, and narrative texts
- To use critical theories to analyze ideas in other texts and society at large
- To write an engaging script and an insightful analytical response using genre characteristics and craft
- To write a literary analysis that uses original commentary to support an evaluative response
- To engage in meaningful and respectful discussion with peers, asking questions and acknowledging the validity of other points of view

VOCABULARY

ACADEMIC
enfranchisement
faux pas
genre conventions
patriarchal
subtext

LITERARY
Archetypal Criticism
archetype
artistic license
Feminist Criticism
Marxist Criticism
mise en scène
motifs
myth
narrative arc
satire
subplot

Leveled Differentiated Instruction Directory (continued)

2.6: Use the **Conflict Map** graphic organizer to support students in writing a one-scene script.

2.7: Have students act out dialogue to convey different subtexts.

2.9: Assign students an additional critical framework in order to develop differing perspectives.

2.12: Have students work in small groups to analyze archetypal or stereotypical characteristics.

CONTENTS

*Texts not included in these materials.

 My Independent Reading List

UNIT 2

INDEPENDENT READING

In this unit, students will explore multiple critical perspectives as they read a variety of genres. Their independent reading selections should complement the unit's focus on Archetypal, Marxist, and Feminist Criticism. The Planning the Unit section of the Teacher's Edition and the Resources section of the Student Edition contain reading lists to help you and your students find the right books.

Independent Reading Links in the unit periodically prompt students to reflect on the reading they are doing outside of class and to make connections to the texts, themes, and ideas addressed in the unit.

KNOWLEDGE QUEST

Within the unit, students will engage in two Knowledge Quests. They will read collections of texts about humans playing God and gender equality, building their understanding of the topics and related vocabulary. Each Knowledge Quest begins with a knowledge question and supporting questions that focus student learning. After students read the final text in a set, they will have the opportunity to return to the Knowledge Question and express their growing understanding of the topic by responding to a writing-to-sources prompt or engaging in an academic discussion.

⭐ TEACHER TO TEACHER

The SpringBoard program is designed so that students interact with texts in meaningful ways, such as notetaking and annotating, to facilitate comprehension and analysis. Have students use Reader/Writer Notebooks actively for vocabulary study, answers to text-dependent questions, ideas and questions about texts, reflections, and responses to Independent Reading. The Reader/Writer Notebooks are not listed as part of the materials for each activity, but the expectation is that students will access them frequently.

Leveled Differentiated Instruction Directory (continued)

2.13: Give students the option to create a visual depiction of the interaction of money, power, and social class.

2.14: Work individually with students to locate texts appropriate to their reading levels.

2.15: Give students extra time to locate difficult words associated with Feminist Criticism.

2.16: Group students to work together on passages they find difficult.

2.17: Explain how dialect is used, and support students as they use the **Text Structure Stairs** graphic organizer.

2.18: Work with students in small groups to recast the story.

2.19: Allow students to use the **Text Structure Stairs** graphic organizer to help them see how Dahl builds suspense.

ACTIVITY 2.1

PLAN

Materials: chart paper; markers
Suggested Pacing: 1 50-minute class period

TEACH

1 Read aloud the About the Unit with students. Engage them in a brief discussion of the terms. Based on their prior knowledge, or best guesses, what do they think these terms, in this context, could mean? Review the meaning of the term literary criticism if needed.

2 Have students **think-pair-share** responses to the three Essential Questions. Students will revisit these questions throughout the unit to develop a deeper understanding of these ideas.

3 Guide students to unpack the first Embedded Assessment. Ask them to find the Embedded Assessment 1 Assignment and Scoring Guide. Lead students through a **close reading** of the prompt, steps, and Scoring Guide criteria. Have students **mark the text** by underlining or highlighting places that mention skills or knowledge necessary to succeed on the Embedded Assessment.

4 Help students prepare for independent reading, including selecting appropriate texts. Some examples of novels that have been adapted for film include *The Grapes of Wrath*, *The Awakening*, and *The Color Purple*. Guide students in previewing texts by analyzing the visuals and text on the front and back covers.

ASSESS

Instruct students to **summarize/ paraphrase** with a partner or small group what they will need to know for the Embedded Assessment. As you conduct a large-group discussion, create a web **graphic organizer** that lists the knowledge and skills students hope to hone or gain.

ADAPT

Revisit the web graphic organizer throughout the unit to reinforce the purpose of each activity. You may want to enlarge the Embedded Assessment web graphic organizer to provide a visual in the classroom throughout the course of the unit.

ACTIVITY 2.1 Previewing the Unit

Learning Strategies

Discussion Groups
Graphic Organizer
Marking the Text
Summarizing
Think-Pair-Share

My Notes

Learning Targets

- Preview the big ideas for the unit.
- Identify and analyze the skills and knowledge needed to complete Embedded Assessment 1 successfully.
- Create a plan for reading independently.

Preview

- In this activity, you will the explore the big ideas and tasks of the unit to come and make plans for your independent reading.

About the Unit

In this unit, you will focus on analyzing literary works through multiple critical perspectives. You will explore three theories: Archetypal Criticism, Marxist Criticism, and Feminist Criticism. The first half of the unit focuses on Archetypal Criticism and Marxist Criticism and the second half focuses on Feminist Criticism. Using these lenses, you will analyze the social and cultural implications of a variety of texts, including fiction and drama. As part of your study, you will write a script for a dramatic scene and a literary analysis of a short story, using a critical perspective.

Essential Questions

Based on your current knowledge, respond to the Essential Questions.

1. How do writers develop great characters?
2. How does a person's environment affect his or her identity?
3. How does power affect people's interactions and relationships?

Unpacking Embedded Assessment 1

Read the following assignment for Embedded Assessment 1.

Work with a partner to write a script that transforms a scene from *Pygmalion* so that it reflects one of the critical perspectives you have studied. You will also write a reflection analyzing and evaluating your process and product.

Summarize in your own words what you will need to know for this assessment. With your class, create a graphic organizer that represents the skills and knowledge you will need to complete the Embedded Assessment. To help you complete your graphic organizer, be sure to review the criteria in the Scoring Guide.

Planning Independent Reading

In this unit, you will read a play that has been adapted into a film. Collaborate with your peers to compile a list of texts that have also been made into film. For your independent reading, discuss how you might compare the original text and the film. Which narrative elements will you compare? Consider dialogue, exposition, and the interpretations of the characters. Consider the elements available to the filmmaker but not the author, such as music and special effects. How do these elements change the telling of the story?

College and Career Readiness Standards

Focus Standards:

RL.11–12.1 Cite strong and thorough textual evidence to support analysis of what the text says explicitly as well as inferences drawn from the text, including determining where the text leaves matters uncertain.

RL.11–12.10 By the end of grade 12, read and comprehend literature, including stories, dramas, and poems, at the high end of the grades 11-CCR text complexity band independently and proficiently.

L.11–12.5 Demonstrate understanding of figurative language, word relationships, and nuances in word meanings.

Additional Standards Addressed:

W.11–12.10

A Closer Look: Archetypal Criticism

Learning Targets

- Collaborate with peers to understand and apply the definition of archetype.
- Analyze a series of photographs to draw conclusions about common archetypes and their universal meaning.

Preview

In this activity, you will learn about archetypes and collaboratively write definitions of common archetypes found in society. You then will identify recurring archetypes and motifs in photographs. Finally, you'll consider how archetypes shape perspective and give deeper meaning to texts.

How Is My Perspective Shaped?

Reading and viewing are not passive activities. You bring certain levels of engagement to your reading and viewing, just as you bring biases, experiences, and prior knowledge to any text you read.

Reading drama can be demanding because most often there is no narrative point of view to help the reader understand the action. To interpret meaning fully, readers and viewers have to pay attention to the usual literary elements, as well as dramatic elements such as stage directions, costume, and set design.

At the same time, you can layer on a critical perspective or lens through which to interpret and understand the larger ideas of the drama. In this way you can challenge and critique the ideas and opinions presented in the drama. Examining texts through multiple literary theories provides you the opportunity to sharpen your analytical skills as you consider alternative ways to view texts.

What Is an Archetype?

An archetype is a universal symbol, image, or character. Archetypal Criticism focuses on analyzing recurring archetypes found in the literature of widely diverse cultures. For example, most cultures have stories that present a hero's journey. Using Archetypal Criticism to analyze a text requires the reader or viewer to slow down and read closely. Using an archetypal critical lens, readers analyze and evaluate the following:

- recurring images that share a common interpretation across cultures, such as water, the sun, or fire, and settings such as a garden or a desert
- characters that recur across cultures, such as the hero, the trickster, the great mother, the sculptor, or the prodigal son
- motifs that recur across cultures, including creation stories, quests, journeys, initiations, and voyages to the underworld

Learning Strategies

Marking the Text
Note-taking
Quickwrite
Think-Pair-Share
Visual/Auditory Prompts

VOCABULARY

LITERARY

An **archetype** is a universal symbol that recurs in the myths, dreams, oral traditions, songs, literature, and other texts of peoples widely separated by time and place.

Motifs are words, characters, objects, images, or ideas that recur in a literary work or works. A motif is almost always related to the theme of a work of literature.

Archetypal Criticism deals with symbols and patterns that recur in the literature of widely diverse cultures.

WORD CONNECTIONS

Roots and Affixes

An archetype is an original pattern or prototype. It derives from the Greek word parts *arche*, meaning "first," and *type*, meaning "a mark."

College and Career Readiness Standards

Focus Standards:

RL.11–12.1 Cite strong and thorough textual evidence to support analysis of what the text says explicitly as well as inferences drawn from the text, including determining where the text leaves matters uncertain.

RI.11–12.7 Integrate and evaluate multiple sources of information presented in different media or formats (e.g., visually, quantitatively) as well as in words in order to address a question or solve a problem.

L.11–12.5 Demonstrate understanding of figurative language, word relationships, and nuances in word meanings.

ACTIVITY 2.2

PLAN

Materials: poster paper
Suggested Pacing: 1 50-minute class period

TEACH

1 Start the activity by reading aloud the Learning Targets and the Preview. Give students time to read "How Is My Perspective Shaped?" independently. Then review Reader-Response and Cultural Criticism in preparation for building on their understanding of other critical perspectives.

2 Review the definitions of archetype and Archetypal Criticism with students. Ask them to mark the text for unfamiliar words as they read What is an Archetype?

3 **Vocabulary Development:** Have students read the definition for the literary term *motif*. Ask students to name a few examples from books, films, or television, and briefly discuss whether those examples fit the definition provided here.

4 If your class includes English language learners, consider using a cognate bridge strategy for the word *archetypal*. Add cognates that include the word root *arche* and the suffix *type* to the class word wall to create a bridge between English vocabulary terms and their cognates in other languages. Spanish cognates include *arquetipo*, *arquitectura*, and *monarca*.

⭐ TEACHER TO TEACHER

You may want to show one or two advertisements for this activity. If so, look for elements of Archetypal Criticism as presented in this activity. Preview the clips for appropriateness and note the length as you plan your instruction. Make sure clip the adequately presents an archetype.

5 Activate prior knowledge by asking students if they know of any archetypes. Explain that archetypes can be used to help transfer information to an audience. In pairs have student closely analyze the images and respond to the questions in student step 1.

6 As they work through the questions about each photograph, circulate to make sure they are noting all relevant details.

7 In a class discussion, elicit from students the details that they found most telling when considering the symbols in each photograph.

2.2

My Notes

Images as Archetypes

1. The use of archetypes in imagery can quickly convey a vast amount of information to an audience. Closely analyze the images to infer each photograph's meaning. Consider what you have learned about Archetypal Criticism and recurring images, symbols, and characters.

What universal symbols do you notice in this photo? What do these symbols mean to most viewers?

What kinds of messages could be easily conveyed through this photo?

College and Career Readiness Standards

SL.11–12.1b Work with peers to promote civil, democratic discussions and decision-making, set clear goals and deadlines, and establish individual roles as needed.

Additional Standards Addressed:
RL.11–12.2, L.11–12.4c, SL.11–12.3

My Notes

What universal symbols do you notice in this photo? What do these symbols mean to most viewers?

What kinds of messages could be easily conveyed through this photo?

LEVELED DIFFERENTIATED INSTRUCTION

Many students will benefit from informally discussing the archetypes and making notes of their thoughts before conducting On the Spot Research on the archetypes.

Beginning Support students who are at an early stage in their English language development by having them work in groups to complete the activity. Monitor them as they use the conferencing strategy to collaboratively fill in gaps in knowledge.

Developing Assemble students into small groups and have them complete the **Conversation for Quickwrite** graphic organizer as prewriting support. Review the prompt as a group, clarifying the ways in which adjectives describe nouns.

Expanding Pair students and have them complete the **Conversation for Quickwrite** graphic organizer as prewriting support. As partners restate the prompt, clarify and answer questions as needed.

Support Model completing the **Quickwrite** graphic organizer as prewriting support. Then assemble students into small groups and have them discuss the archetypes. Ask each group to make notes of their ideas and questions. Monitor groups and answer questions as needed.

Extend Pair students and have them research Carl Jung and the twelve common archetypes. Have pairs choose four of these twelve for their On the Spot Research. In addition to completing the graphic organizer, have students write and reflect on which archetype they find most compelling in literary texts.

My Notes

What universal symbols do you notice in this photo? What do these symbols mean to most viewers?

What kinds of messages could be easily conveyed through this photo?

2.2

What universal symbols do you notice in this photo? What do these symbols mean to most viewers?

_____

_____

_____

What kinds of messages could be easily conveyed through this photo?

_____

_____

_____

_____

My Notes

_____

_____

_____

_____

_____

_____

_____

_____

_____

_____

_____

_____

_____

_____

_____

_____

_____

_____

_____

_____

_____

_____

_____

_____

_____

_____

_____

_____

_____

_____

_____

_____

_____

ACTIVITY 2.2 continued

8 Review the definition of archetype and discuss the idea of universal symbols (e.g., water, tree). Choose one symbol, such as trees, and have students brainstorm meanings and symbolic uses in different cultures (tree of life, totem poles, family trees).

9 Divide students into small groups and provide them with four archetypes to conduct their On the Spot Research.

 TEACHER TO TEACHER

The caregiver, explorer, hero, and creator archetypes are presented in the photographs on the student page. Give each group one of these archetypes and consider selecting the additional archetypes for each group from Jung's 12 archetypes.

10 Have students jot down **notes** about their archetypes, then brainstorm works of literature, film, or television that incorporate this archetype. Based on their findings, each group should summarize their four archetypes.

11 Have each group create a poster. Encourage them to be visually creative in their designs. When they have finished, ask each group to present their poster to the class. As each group presents, students should take notes so that they have a list of all 12 archetypes.

12 To encourage discussion of the archetypes, ask the following questions: What commonalities do you see? Are these ideas universal? Why do individuals have a shared understanding?

13 Ask students to respond to the Check Your Understanding in writing.

ASSESS

For Check Your Understanding, be sure that students give clear examples of how Archetypal Criticism has provided them with a new understanding of advertising. They should point to details in photographs that clue them in to which archetype is being used, and what universal desires or values the archetype represents. For example, a great mother archetype might be used to evoke values of safety, security, and love. Check photographs for clear, relevant examples and characteristics of archetypes.

ADAPT

If students need additional help with archetypes, have them select a text from Unit 1 to which they can apply Archetypal Criticism. One option would be the archetype of the nature god in Cummings' "[in just-]."

2.2

2. With your discussion group, share your observations of the four photographs. Be sure to use details from the photos to support your analysis.

On the Spot Research

3. Conduct research on the four archetypes your teacher has assigned to your group. Jot down key words relating to the archetypes in the notes column of the graphic organizer.

   Discuss your findings, and work collaboratively to add a list of examples of this archetype to your graphic organizer. Consider characters in movies and other works of fiction. Then use your notes and list of examples to write a definition of each archetype.

Notes	Examples	Definition

4. Share your definitions with the other groups in your class, so you have a complete list of 12 common archetypes.

5. Return to the photographs as you respond to the following questions. Use evidence from the photographs and apply your definitions to support your responses.

   - What archetype is presented in each photo?
   - How do the images diverge from or alter the archetype?
   - How do you think the creator of each image used knowledge of the archetype to make artistic choices?

☑ Check Your Understanding

Consider your initial analysis to each photograph. Were your inferences informed by universal symbols and archetypes? How does Archetypal Criticism provide you with a new understanding of each photograph that you have studied?

Introducing the Myth

Learning Targets

- Analyze and compare the key ideas and archetypes presented in two literary texts.
- Summarize the texts, concentrating on the most important elements.
- Examine how an author draws on and transforms ideas from other works.
- Integrate ideas from multiple texts to build knowledge and vocabulary about the concept of playing creator.

Preview

In this activity, you will analyze and compare two texts from different literary periods. You will read a myth and draw connections to the archetypes presented in the classic novel, *Frankenstein*. Then, you will summarize your new understanding of the texts in a written response.

As You Read

- Highlight words or phrases in the myth that reveal the main character's attributes.
- Circle unknown words and phrases. Try to determine the meaning of words by using context clues, word parts, or a dictionary.

Learning Strategies

Drafting
Marking the Text
Note-taking
Paraphrasing
Summarizing
Visualizing

LITERARY

A myth is a traditional story, passed down from generation to generation, that explains beliefs, customs, or natural phenomena through the actions of gods or heroes. These stories often focus on supernatural beings or events.

VOCABULARY

My Notes

About the Author

The Roman poet Ovid, born Publius Ovidius Naso (43 BC– AD 17) is best known for *Metamorphoses*, a collection of myths describing transformation. He was born into a well-to-do family in Sulmo, a small town near Rome, and was considered a great orator. Ovid worked for a time in a minor judicial post, honoring his father's wish for him to pursue a traditional career. He soon abandoned this life to pursue his interest in poetry full time. Ovid's early work centered on love, beauty, and amorous intrigue, reflecting the pleasure-seeking, sophisticated circles in which he moved. The humor, sympathy, and vividness of Ovid's writing, in particular *Metamorphoses*, influenced many writers and artists of Ovid's time period and beyond, including Geoffrey Chaucer, William Shakespeare, and George Bernard Shaw.

College and Career Readiness Standards

Focus Standards:

RL.11–12.2 Determine two or more themes or central ideas of a text and analyze their development over the course of the text, including how they interact and build on one another to produce a complex account; provide an objective summary of the text.

RL.11–12.7 Analyze multiple interpretations of a story, drama, or poem (e.g., recorded or live production of a play or recorded novel or poetry), evaluating how each version interprets the source text. (Include at least one play by Shakespeare and one play by an American dramatist.)

ACTIVITY 2.3

PLAN

Materials: *Pygmalion*, Act I, by George Bernard Shaw
Suggested Pacing: 2 50-minute class periods

TEACH

1 Read through the Preview with students. Ask students to name two works of literature or two films they have read or seen that utilize the same archetypes (for example, the warrior, the great mother, the artist, the mad scientist) in different ways. Engage them in a discussion comparing two selected works.

2 Return students to Activity 2.2 to review the definition of Archetypal Criticism. Ask students to select a familiar story such as "Pinocchio" for discussion and identify main characters in the archetype.

3 **Vocabulary Development:** Review the meaning of the term *myth* with students. Have them work in pairs to define the term in their own words and think of both examples and non-examples.

4 For English learner students, consider using a cognate bridge strategy. Add to the class Word Wall cognates that include the word root myth to create a bridge between English vocabulary terms and their cognates in other languages. Spanish cognates include *mito*, *mítica*, and *mitología*. Add *motivo*, the Spanish word for motif.

5 Direct students to the As You Read. Go over methods for determining which words to highlight and how to look at the text surrounding an unknown word for context clues.

6 Direct students to the Knowledge Question. Lead the class in a brief discussion about what they think it means to "play creator." Then have small groups discuss their responses to the Knowledge Question.

7 Have students read the About the Author and ask them to mark any facts about the authors they feel may be significant to understanding their work.

8 **FIRST READ:** Read aloud the first two sentences of *Orpheus Sings: Pygmalion and the Statue*. Then pose the question: who are "they?" Refer to the first Making Observations question, and ask students how they feel about Pygmalion's view of women and his response to the statue. What does it say about him?

TEXT COMPLEXITY

Overall: Complex
Lexile: 1070L
Qualitative: Moderate Difficulty
Task: Moderate (Analyze)

9 Then have students pair up to read the remainder of the myth. Have students pause after reading the second paragraph to answer the remaining Knowledge Quest questions.

10 As students are reading, monitor their progress. Be sure they are engaged with the text and annotating words and phrases that show aspects of character. Evaluate whether the selected reading mode is effective.

11 Based on the observations you made during the first reading, you may want to adjust the reading mode. For example, you may decide for the second reading to read aloud certain complex passages, or you may group students differently.

2.3

KNOWLEDGE QUEST

Knowledge Question:
Why do people believe the price of playing creator outweighs the gains?
In Activity 2.3, you will read a myth and an excerpt from a novel that examine the theme of humans "playing God." While you read and build knowledge about the theme, think about your answer to the Knowledge Question.

Pygmalion working on Galatea, a beautiful statue of a woman, made out of ivory.

Myth

Orpheus Sings: Pygmalion and the Statue

by **Ovid**

from *Metamorphoses*, Book X

1 Pygmalion had seen them, spending their lives in wickedness, and, offended by the failings that nature gave the female heart, he lived as a bachelor, without a wife or partner for his bed. But, with wonderful skill, he carved a figure, brilliantly, out of snow-white ivory, no mortal woman, and fell in love with his own creation. The features are those of a real girl, who, you might think, lived, and wished to move, if modesty did not forbid it. Indeed, art hides his art. He marvels: and passion, for this bodily image, consumes his heart. Often, he runs his hands over the work, tempted as to whether it is flesh or ivory, not admitting it to be ivory. He kisses it and thinks his kisses are returned; and speaks to it; and holds it, and imagines that his fingers press into the limbs, and is afraid lest bruises appear from the pressure. Now he addresses it with compliments, now brings it gifts that please girls, shells and polished pebbles, little birds, and many-coloured flowers, lilies and tinted beads, and the Heliades'[1] amber tears, that drip from the trees. He dresses the body, also, in clothing; places rings on the fingers; places a long necklace round its neck; pearls hang from the ears, and cinctures[2] round the breasts. All are fitting: but it appears no less lovely, naked. He arranges the statue on a bed on which cloths dyed with Tyrian murex[3] are spread, and calls it his bedfellow, and rests its neck against soft down, as if it could feel.

2 The day of Venus's festival[4] came, celebrated throughout Cyprus, and heifers, their curved horns gilded, fell, to the blow on their snowy neck. The incense was smoking, when Pygmalion, having made his offering, stood by the altar, and said, shyly: "If you can grant all things, you gods, I wish as a bride to have …" and not daring to say "the girl of ivory" he said "one like my ivory girl." Golden Venus, for she herself was present at the festival, knew what the prayer meant, and as a sign of the gods' fondness for him, the flame flared three times, and shook its crown in the air. When he returned, he sought out the image of his girl, and leaning over the couch, kissed her. She felt warm: he pressed his lips to her again, and also touched her breast with his hand. The ivory yielded to his touch, and lost its hardness, altering under his fingers, as the bees' wax

---

[1] The *Heliades* were daughters of Helios and turned into poplar trees.
[2] A *cincture* is a belt or sash.
[3] *Tyrian murex* is an expensive purple dye made often reserved for royalty.
[4] In Roman times, *Venus's festival* celebrated the goddess of love and desire.

College and Career Readiness Standards

W.11–12.2 Write informative/explanatory texts to examine and convey complex ideas, concepts, and information clearly and accurately through the effective selection, organization, and analysis of content.

Additional Standards Addressed:

RL.11–12.1, RL.11–12.2, RL.11–12.3, RL.11–12.4, RL.11–12.6, RL.11–12.10, L.11–12.5, SL.11–12.1

of Hymettus[5] softens in the sun, and is molded, under the thumb, into many forms, made usable by use. The lover is stupefied, and joyful, but uncertain, and afraid he is wrong, reaffirms the fulfillment of his wishes, with his hand, again, and again.

3   It was flesh! The pulse throbbed under his thumb. Then the hero, of Paphos,[6] was indeed overfull of words with which to thank Venus, and still pressed his mouth against a mouth that was not merely a likeness. The girl felt the kisses he gave, blushed, and, raising her bashful eyes to the light, saw both her lover and the sky. The goddess attended the marriage that she had brought about, and when the moon's horns had nine times met at the full, the woman bore a son, Paphos, from whom the island takes its name.

🖉 Knowledge Quest

- What are your initial thoughts about Pygmalion's relationship with the statue?
- What imagery could you picture in your mind?
- What do you notice in this myth that someone skimming over it might miss?

About the Author

Mary Shelley (1797–1851) is most known for her famous and enduring novel *Frankenstein, or The Modern Prometheus*. Mary Shelley met the well-known Romantic poet Percy Shelley when she was 16, and they married a year later. In the summer of 1816, Mary and Percy, along with friends, including the poet Lord Byron, gathered at the Villa Diodati on the shores of Lake Geneva in Switzerland. The weather was rainy and unpleasant, so they amused themselves by inventing ghost stories, providing the genesis for *Frankenstein*. Shelley published *Frankenstein* when she was 21 years old. Her novel is often considered the world's first science fiction novel and has become the inspiration for many 20th-century films.

[5] *Hymettus* was a famous source of honey near Athens, Greece.
[6] *Paphos* is the mythical birthplace of Aphrodite.

WORD CONNECTIONS

Roots and Affixes
To be stupefied is to be shocked or stunned in amazement. The word derives from the Latin *stupere*, "to be stunned," and *facere*, "to make." Other related words are *stupefaction*, *stupid*, and *stupendous*.

My Notes

stupefied: stunned

ACTIVITY 2.3 continued

12 Direct students to the Roots and Affixes Word Connections box.

13 Have students read the About the Author for Mary Shelley and ask them to mark any facts about the author they think may be significant to understanding her work.

⊕ TEACHER TO TEACHER

There is a common misconception that Mary Shelley's famous monster is named Frankenstein. Before reading the excerpt, explain to students that the narrator's name is Victor Frankenstein. This will help students articulate their thoughts about the narrator during the first and second read of the excerpt.

14 Review the Knowledge Question with students. Remind them to think about their answer to the Knowledge Question as they read and build knowledge about the topic.

15 FIRST READ: Read aloud the first paragraph of *Frankenstein*. Ask students to note the details they found most compelling. Then have them remain in pairs to read the remainder of the excerpt. Remind pairs to review the Word Connections box before reading paragraph 3.

 TEXT COMPLEXITY

Overall: Very complex
Lexile: 1020L
Qualitative: Moderate Difficulty
Task: Challenging (Evaluate)

2.3

KNOWLEDGE QUEST

Knowledge Question:
Why do people believe the price of playing creator outweighs the gains?

My Notes

WORD CONNECTIONS

Roots and Affixes
Traverse comes from a combination of the Latin words *trans*, meaning "across," and *versus*, meaning "turned." It shares a common root with the word *travel* and means "to move across or back and forth."

ardour: passion
traversing: moving across
lassitude: tiredness
livid: bluish gray

Novel Excerpt

from *Frankenstein, or the Modern Prometheus*

by **Mary Shelley**

excerpt from Chapter 5

1 It was on a dreary night of November that I beheld the accomplishment of my toils. With an anxiety that almost amounted to agony, I collected the instruments of life around me, that I might infuse a spark of being into the lifeless thing that lay at my feet. It was already one in the morning; the rain pattered dismally against the panes, and my candle was nearly burnt out, when, by the glimmer of the half-extinguished light, I saw the dull yellow eye of the creature open; it breathed hard, and a convulsive motion agitated its limbs.

2 How can I describe my emotions at this catastrophe, or how delineate the wretch whom with such infinite pains and care I had endeavoured to form? His limbs were in proportion, and I had selected his features as beautiful. Beautiful! Great God! His yellow skin scarcely covered the work of muscles and arteries beneath; his hair was of a lustrous black, and flowing; his teeth of a pearly whiteness; but these luxuriances only formed a more horrid contrast with his watery eyes, that seemed almost of the same colour as the dun-white sockets in which they were set, his shrivelled complexion and straight black lips.

3 The different accidents of life are not so changeable as the feelings of human nature. I had worked hard for nearly two years, for the sole purpose of infusing life into an inanimate body. For this I had deprived myself of rest and health. I had desired it with an ardour that far exceeded moderation; but now that I had finished, the beauty of the dream vanished, and breathless horror and disgust filled my heart. Unable to endure the aspect of the being I had created, I rushed out of the room and continued a long time traversing my bedchamber, unable to compose my mind to sleep. At length lassitude succeeded to the tumult I had before endured, and I threw myself on the bed in my clothes, endeavouring to seek a few moments of forgetfulness. But it was in vain; I slept, indeed, but I was disturbed by the wildest dreams. I thought I saw Elizabeth, in the bloom of health, walking in the streets of Ingolstadt. Delighted and surprised, I embraced her, but as I imprinted the first kiss on her lips, they became livid with the hue of death; her features appeared to change, and I thought that I held the corpse of my dead mother in my arms; a shroud enveloped her form, and I saw the grave-worms crawling in the folds of the flannel. I started from my sleep with horror; a cold dew covered my forehead, my teeth chattered, and every limb became convulsed; when, by the dim and

---

Scaffolding the Text-Dependent Questions

1. In the first sentence, Ovid writes, "Pygmalion had seen them, spending their lives in wickedness …" Whom is Ovid writing about when he uses the pronoun "them?" How does Pygmalion feel in the first sentence? In the next sentence, what does Pygmalion make? How does his creation result from his feelings about women? RL.11–12.4, L.11–12.3

2. Reread the description of Pygmalion's statue in lines 4–7. What is the dual meaning of "art hides his art"? What are the two meanings of art? How do Pygmalion's actions relate to the statue as a piece of art? What do the meanings of art say about Pygmalion? RL.11–12.4, L.11–12.5

yellow light of the moon, as it forced its way through the window shutters, I beheld the wretch—the miserable monster whom I had created. He held up the curtain of the bed; and his eyes, if eyes they may be called, were fixed on me. His jaws opened, and he muttered some inarticulate sounds, while a grin wrinkled his cheeks. He might have spoken, but I did not hear; one hand was stretched out, seemingly to detain me, but I escaped and rushed downstairs. I took refuge in the courtyard belonging to the house which I inhabited, where I remained during the rest of the night, walking up and down in the greatest agitation, listening attentively, catching and fearing each sound as if it were to announce the approach of the demoniacal corpse to which I had so miserably given life.

4 Oh! No mortal could support the horror of that countenance. A mummy again **endued** with animation could not be so hideous as that wretch. I had gazed on him while unfinished; he was ugly then, but when those muscles and joints were rendered capable of motion, it became a thing such as even Dante[7] could not have conceived.

5 I passed the night wretchedly. Sometimes my pulse beat so quickly and hardly that I felt the palpitation of every artery; at others, I nearly sank to the ground through **languor** and extreme weakness. Mingled with this horror, I felt the bitterness of disappointment; dreams that had been my food and pleasant rest for so long a space were now become a hell to me; and the change was so rapid, the overthrow so complete!

⊘ Knowledge Quest
- Which part of this excerpt stands out to you? Why?
- What details do you notice about the narrator?

My Notes

---

[7] _Dante Alighieri_ (1265–1321) was an Italian poet whose epic poem _The Divine Comedy_ is considered the greatest poem of the Middle Ages and one of the greatest works of world literature in history. Dante's poem depicts the Christian conception of the afterlife and is especially known for its colorful and vivid depiction of hell.

endued: given or provided
languor: fatigue

ACTIVITY 2.3 continued

16 After reading the text for the first time, guide the class in a discussion by asking the Knowledge Quest questions. Check students' general comprehension of the text based on their observations, asking follow-up questions if needed.

★ TEACHER TO TEACHER

There are many film versions of the classic _Frankenstein_ story, and a viewing of scenes from one or more of these could lead to an engaging discussion of how character archetypes are portrayed in each. Consider having the class watch the famous "birth of the creature" scene from the classic film _Frankenstein_ (1931) and compare it with the same scene in Mel Brooks's celebrated spoof, _Young Frankenstein_ (1974).

Scaffolding the Text-Dependent Questions

3. Describe Pygmalion at the beginning of the story. How has he changed or not changed by the end of the story? What does Pygmalion think of women and marriage at the beginning of the story? What has he done by the end of the story? Has his opinion of all women changed? RL.11–12.2, RL.11–12.3

4. How does the main character's vanity as the creator drive the events of the plot? What is Pygmalion's biggest personality flaw? How does this flaw affect his behavior? What does it cause him to do? RL.11–12.2, RL.11–12.3

Victor Frankenstein's scientific experiment produces life—but not in the way he had envisioned.

Scaffolding the Text-Dependent Questions

5. What task is the narrator trying to complete in the first paragraph? What is his reaction once he achieves his goal? Does the narrator's experiment go as planned? What details show this? What realization does he have? What details convey his state of mind? RL.11–12.1, RL.11–12.2

6. What comparison is the author making in paragraph 4? What purpose does it serve?

Identify the words in the paragraph that show comparison (like, as). Does the comparison create a vivid image? RL.11–12.1, RL.11–12.4, RL.11–12.6

7. What is the significance of the narrator's dream? What "message" is the dream sending him? Is the dream pleasant or unpleasant? What details in the dream show Frankenstein's subconscious fears? RL.11–12.2, RL.11–12.3

2.3

Returning to the Text

- Reread the myth and novel excerpt to answer these text-dependent questions.
- Write any additional questions you have about the text in your Reader/Writer Notebook.

Metamorphoses, Book X

1. In the first sentence, Ovid writes, "Pygmalion had seen them, spending their lives in wickedness ..." Whom is Ovid writing about when he uses the pronoun "them"? Use text evidence in your answer.

   Ovid adds that Pygmalion was "offended by the failings that nature gave the female heart"

   and "lived as a bachelor, without a wife." Pygmalion also creates a statue of an "ideal" woman

   and falls in love with it. "Them" must refer to women.

2. **KQ** Reread the description of Pygmalion's statue in lines 4–7. What is the dual meaning of "art hides his art"?

   Pygmalion's art, or artistic skill, hides the fact that the statue is a work of art and not real.

   Ovid uses this phrase to explain that Pygmalion is creating a physical statue and a fantasy of

   the perfect woman.

3. Describe Pygmalion at the beginning of the story. How has he changed or not changed by the end of the story?

   At the beginning of the story, Pygmalion thinks all women are wicked and weak, and he has

   no desire to marry one. By the end of the story, he has married the woman who used to be the

   statue he carved. Although he and Venus together created his perfect woman, it is unlikely he

   revised his opinion of all women.

4. **KQ** How does the main character's vanity as the creator drive the events of the plot?

   The plot hinges on Pygmalion's desire to create the perfect woman. In the myth, the perfect

   woman is defined by her physical attributes. He is consumed by vanity and "marvels" at his

   own skill so intensely that he begins to see the statue as real rather than ivory.

ACTIVITY 2.3 continued

17 RETURNING TO THE TEXT: Guide students to answer the text-dependent questions. Assign students to pairs or small groups to reread the texts and respond to the questions. Remind them to use text evidence in their responses.

18 Move from group to group. If students have difficulty, scaffold the questions by rephrasing them or breaking them down into smaller parts. See the Scaffolding the Text-Dependent Questions boxes for suggestions.

Scaffolding the Text-Dependent Questions

8. Which words or phrases in paragraph 3 show that the narrator is afraid of the moral and ethical consequences of his experiment? Cite the text and explain your answer. What is the narrator's reaction to his monster? How does he describe the monster's appearance? RL.11–12.1, RL.11–12.4

9. What connections might Shelley and Ovid be making to the concept of playing God? What is the outcome of Frankenstein's experiment? Do the authors portray the creations in a positive or negative light? RL.11–12.1, RL.11–12.2, RL.11–12.6

Frankenstein, or the Modern Prometheus

5. **What task is the narrator trying to complete in the first paragraph? What is his reaction once he achieves his goal?**

   The narrator is trying to restore life in a corpse. Despite working on his creation for two years, and selecting "beautiful" features such as "lustrous black hair" and pearly white teeth, the scientist is immediately disillusioned. In paragraph 3, he says, "... now that I had finished, the beauty of the dream vanished, and breathless horror and disgust filled my heart."

6. **What comparisons is the author making in paragraph 4? What purpose does it serve?**

   In paragraph 4, Shelley compares the monster to a "mummy endued with animation" and alludes to the depiction of Hell in *The Divine Comedy*, through the phrase "such as even Dante could not have conceived." These comparisons vividly bring the grotesque monster to life and add an element of drama and exaggeration to the text.

7. **What is the significance of the narrator's dream? What "message" is the dream sending him?**

   In the dream, Elizabeth (who from the context is, or once was, the narrator's paramour), turns from a woman in the bloom of youth to a corpse as he kisses her. The dream reminds the narrator that death is inevitable, and that his efforts to cheat death through scientific means will lead to anguish and horror.

8. **KQ Which words or phrases in paragraph 3 show that the narrator is afraid of the moral and ethical consequences of his experiment? Cite the text and explain your answer.**

   After an encounter with the creature, the narrator describes himself as "catching and fearing each sound as if it were to announce the approach of the demoniacal corpse..." The way the narrator describes himself as the creator who "miserably" gave life demonstrates regret. He implies that his experiment violates ethical standards.

9. **KQ What connections might Shelley and Ovid be making to the concept of playing God?**

   Shelley's story warns of the pursuit of science for its own ends and a desire to "play God" without considering the ethical consequences of those pursuits. Pygmalion's apparent success only leaves his limited view of women unchallenged.

2.3

Working from the Text

10. The myth of Pygmalion and the story of *Frankenstein* give us the opportunity to compare tales in which characters who represent similar archetypes experience drastically different outcomes for their behavior. Work with a partner to answer the questions. Refer to your notes on archetypes and the two texts as needed.

    - What are the character's goals?
    - What is the outcome of the story?
    - Are both characters based on the same archetype? Why or why not?
    - What are the character's positive qualities?
    - What are the character's tragic flaws?

11. Use the graphic organizer to compare the characters of Victor Frankenstein and Pygmalion.

Character	Goal	Outcome of "experiment"	Positive personality traits	Tragic flaw	Possible archetypes
Pygmalion	To create the perfect woman	The statue is given life by Aphrodite. Pygmalion falls in love with the woman that he created and they marry	Talented sculptor; creative and imaginative	Superficial; narcissistic	The artist; the creator; the narcissist
Victor Frankenstein (narrator)	To instill life into the dead (ostensibly for betterment of humankind)	The creature turns out to be ugly and monstrous; Dr. Frankenstein is consumed by horror	Intelligent; initially believes his experiment will benefit humanity	Obsessive; failure to consider the moral implications of his work	The artist; the creator; the mad scientist

19 WORKING FROM THE TEXT: Allow students to discuss the Pygmalion archetype (e.g., a transformation story where an external force seeks to change someone else). Ask them to draw a connection between "Pygmalion and the Statue" and the excerpt from *Frankenstein*. Encourage them to think about how the archetypal characters in each text might relate to the images they viewed in the previous activity.

20 Have students work in pairs to answer the questions and fill in the graphic organizer. Then have them share their answers in a group discussion.

21 Revisit the unit's first Essential Question: How do writers develop great characters?

LEVELED DIFFERENTIATED INSTRUCTION

Many students will find it helpful to have an informal conversation so that they can work through and discuss their thoughts before responding to written questions.

Beginning Support students who are at an early stage in their English language development by having them work in groups to complete the Working from the Text activity. Have them use the conferencing strategy so that knowledge gaps can be addressed.

Developing Group students and have them complete the **Conversation for Quickwrite** graphic organizer as prewriting support. Review the prompt as a group, clarifying that adjectives are describing words.

22 Review the Language & Writer's Craft guidelines for writing a summary. Explain to students that being able to write a summary of a text is an important step in incorporating evidence into a written response. Have them practice by writing a brief summary of the Pygmalion myth.

2.3

My Notes

LANGUAGE & WRITER'S CRAFT: Summarizing

Good writers know how to express themselves concisely. When writing a summary of a literary or informational text, the goal is to condense the main idea and details into a concise paragraph or paragraphs. Use these guidelines for writing an effective summary:

- Begin the summary with a statement of the main idea.
- Include only the most significant details about the setting, characters, and events presented in the story.
- Keep the details in a logical order.
- Write in complete but concise sentences.
- Make no interpretive or analytical statements, and objectively report the main plot points.
- Paraphrase using your own words.

PRACTICE Using these guidelines, summarize Ovid's myth "Pygmalion and the Statue" in a single paragraph.

Knowledge Quest

Think about the two texts. Which was greater: the price of playing creator or the gains? Write an argumentative text answering this question. Be sure to:

- Cite evidence from both texts to support your argument.
- Use reasoning to develop your ideas and connect your claim to your evidence.
- Use precise language and topic-specific vocabulary.

INDEPENDENT READING LINK

You can continue to build your knowledge about the concept of playing creator by reading related fiction at ZINC Reading Labs.

Select the **fiction** filters and type *playing God* in the **Search all ZINC articles** field.

ZINC

☑ Check Your Understanding

Many stories from different world cultures feature elements of Ovid's myth. Why do you think this myth exists in different cultures? How and why do you think authors draw inspiration from archetypes and modify them to tell new stories? Write a short paragraph explaining your ideas.

ACTIVITY 2.3 continued

23 Return to the Knowledge Question. Review writing expectations with students using the "be sure to" points. Ask volunteers to paraphrase them to ensure class understanding.

24 Encourage students to continue building knowledge on this theme as suggested in the Independent Reading Link. Have students complete the Check Your Understanding.

ASSESS

Check that students' summaries include the main ideas and archetypal characteristics shared by Pygmalion and Frankenstein. Are they able to state these ideas clearly? Are they using comparative sentences, such as: *Both Frankenstein and Pygmalion are _____, but Frankenstein _____.*

Check that students' summaries follow the guidelines provided in the Language & Writer's Craft. Review their responses to the writing prompt to assess their understanding of themes in the myth, such as the vanity of the artist.

ADAPT

If students need additional help writing short summaries of "Pygmalion and the Statue" and *Frankenstein*, group students and have them share and respond to one another's papers.

If students are unclear about how to compare and contrast two texts, have them look back at the graphic organizer in the Working from the Text and practice writing sentences that summarize the information contained in it. You may want to help out by providing sentence frames. Possible examples include: *While Pygmalion _____, Victor Frankenstein _____. Like Pygmalion, Victor Frankenstein _____. However, in Pygmalion's case _____. Both texts explore themes of _____ and _____. However, _____.*

PLAN

Suggested Pacing: 1 50-minute class period

TEACH

1 Read the Preview with students. Help them understand how the play *Pygmalion* connects to the archetypal elements established in Ovid's myth.

2 Have students **brainstorm** other play and film adaptations which incorporate the archetypes of a myth or older story into a more modern setting. Examples could include various Shakespeare plays or folktales that have been adapted into films. Taken together, these texts demonstrate the construction of archetypes that endure across cultures and time periods.

3 Review the pyramid diagram and **discuss** the structure of the dramatic arc. Have students work in pairs to answer the questions. Observe students' responses to ensure that they understand how to identify plot elements.

4 Vocabulary Development: Discuss the Literary Vocabulary with students. Ask them to work with a partner to brainstorm words to define the concept of *mise en scène*.

Learning Strategies

Brainstorming
Discussion Groups
Note-taking
Visual/Auditory Prompts

My Notes

Learning Targets

- Analyze the composition and use of archetypes in a visual medium.
- Collaboratively make inferences about a story's plot and theme based on images.
- Analyze how setting, plot, and characterization work together to communicate a central theme.

Preview

In this activity, you will begin reading George Bernard Shaw's play, *Pygmalion*. Before reading, you will review the parts of a five-act play and make inferences about the play by closely analyzing film stills. Then you will read and reflect on Act I of the play, giving you an opportunity to confirm or correct your judgments and analyze the author's use of archetypes.

Reviewing the Five-Act Play

1. The structure pyramid depicts the traditional "dramatic arc" of a five-act play. This is often used to create an effective plot. In addition to drama, the pyramid is found in novels, short stories, films, television shows, and even individual scenes.

   With a partner, discuss how the major plot points of Ovid's myth can be broken into a five-act structure.

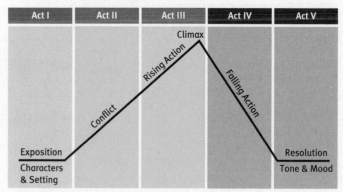

Making Inferences

2. Analyze the film stills from *My Fair Lady*, directed by George Cukor, and complete the descriptions of each image.

   - Describe the mise en scène (scene composition) of the photo. Consider where the characters are in relation to one another and within the setting.
   - Describe the subjects—the characters. Consider costume, facial expression, and body language. For example, look at the first photo. What additional context can you draw from the title, *My Fair Lady*? What time period do you think this film takes place in?

VOCABULARY

LITERARY

Mise en scène is a French expression used to describe a film or theater production's composition and setting. This includes everything presented to the viewer, such as the costumes, makeup, props, lighting, background scenery, and the actors' positioning, facial expressions, and behavior.

College and Career Readiness Standards

Focus Standards:

RL.11–12.2 Determine two or more themes or central ideas of a text and analyze their development over the course of the text, including how they interact and build on one another to produce a complex account; provide an objective summary of the text.

RL.11–12.3 Analyze the impact of the author's choices regarding how to develop and relate elements of a story or drama (e.g., where a story is set, how the action is ordered, how the characters are introduced and developed).

RL.11–12.7 Analyze multiple interpretations of a story, drama, or poem (e.g., recorded or live production of a play or recorded novel or poetry), evaluating how each version interprets the source text. (Include at least one play by Shakespeare and one play by an American dramatist.)

a.

Description of *Mise en Scène:*

_____

_____

Description of Character:

_____

_____

_____

b.

Description of *Mise en Scène:*

_____

_____

Description of Character:

_____

_____

_____

c.

Description of *Mise en Scène*:

_____

_____

Description of Character:

_____

_____

_____

d.

Description of *Mise en Scène:*

_____

_____

Description of Character:

_____

_____

_____

5 Have students work in pairs or groups to examine the film stills from *My Fair Lady*. Ask them to make note of what they think are the most important details in each image. What do they notice about the setting? The style of dress? After they've reviewed the images and made notes about the details, ask them to share their inferences about storyline, characters, and setting.

6 Advise students that as they read the play, they will return to the stills, as well as video or audio segments from the 1938 original film adaptation of *Pygmalion*, to compare these adaptations with the play and the myth. You may also consider presenting clips from a contemporary adaptation such as *She's All That*. Ask students to identify some of the differences they might expect to see as they examine multiple interpretations of the play.

College and Career Readiness Standards

L.11–12.3 Apply knowledge of language to understand how language functions in different contexts, to make effective choices for meaning or style, and to comprehend more fully when reading or listening.

SL.11–12.1 Initiate and participate effectively in a range of collaborative discussions (one-on-one, in groups, and teacher-led) with

diverse partners on grades 11–12 topics, texts, and issues, building on others' ideas and expressing their own clearly and persuasively.

Additional Standards Addressed:

L.11–12.4c, L.11–12.6, SL.11–12.1b, SL.11–12.1d, SL.11–12.2

7 Have students share their inferences with the class, and then discuss visual context. Were they able to begin identifying the characters corresponding to those of the Pygmalion myth?

TEACHER TO TEACHER

This would be a good opportunity for students to return to their Reader/Writer Notebooks. Have them record their insights into what the play will be about; they may want to write down the significant details or even do drawings of the film stills to return to later.

8 Ask students to silently read the About the Author. Point out the significant social issues Shaw featured in his writing. Ask students which they think might feature heavily in *Pygmalion*.

9 Read aloud Reading *Pygmalion* and the two guiding questions. Ask for volunteers to take on roles in the reading of Act I.

10 After line 11, pause to review the Grammar & Usage box on idioms. Remind students to use context clues to help them understand idioms. Ask volunteers to review how to use context clues such as assessing the overall meaning of a sentence or paragraph. Explain the way that context can provide clues about the use of idioms. Point out that in the example of "throw one's hat in the ring," there might be no other mention of a hat in the scene since the hat is being used figuratively. SImilarly, in the example of Freddy looking for a cab, the references to "love" and "money" are not related to the rest of the conversation, since they are not used literally. These context clues can help students recognize idioms in a text. Ask students to keep their eyes out for idioms in the rest of the act.

11 As students are reading, monitor their progress. Be sure they are engaged with the text and annotating with a star those lines that connect to the archetypal characters of "the creator" and "the created."

2.4

My Notes

_____

_____

_____

_____

_____

_____

_____

_____

_____

_____

_____

GRAMMAR & USAGE

Idioms

An **idiom** is an expression that means something different from the literal meaning of the words. An idiom such as "throw one's hat into the ring" does not refer literally to throwing a hat into a ring; it can mean announcing you plan to enter a contest. With this and other idioms, context can help you understand the phrase. Many idioms are used only in informal English.

Notice how in Act I, line 11, Freddy states, "there's not one [cab] to be had for love or money." The idiom "for love or money" is always used in negative statements to indicate something that cannot be accomplished for anything. In this case, Freddy uses it to express how impossible it is to find a cab.

Try to find two more examples of idioms in *Pygmalion* and explain their meaning to a partner.

3. Based on your observations of the photos, make inferences about elements of the play:

- Where might the play take place?
- What kind of characters might be in the play?
- What do you think is the relationship between the various characters?
- What do you think the play is about?

4. Ovid gives us a written version of the myth, which derives from the oral tradition of the early Greeks and Romans. Revisit the myth to look for archetypal characters: the creative person, the object of his affection, and the being who grants his wish. How are these characters represented in the images you viewed?

5. **Discussion Groups:** Share your preliminary ideas and discuss connections or differences between your inferences and the inferences of your peers. Based on the photos, what do you think the plot structure will be? Make sure to express your ideas clearly and build on others' ideas in a focused response.

Reading *Pygmalion*

As you read Act I, identify the characters, define the conflicts, and apply the archetypal perspective to gain understanding of the characters' relationships.

- Use sticky notes to identify textual evidence that will help you answer this question: Which archetypal characters do you recognize?
- Circle unknown words or phrases. Try to determine the meaning of the words by using context clues, word parts, or a dictionary.

About the Author

George Bernard Shaw (1856–1950) was an Irish playwright and a cofounder of the London School of Economics. He was a prolific journalist, essayist, novelist, short story writer, and dramatist. He wrote more than 60 plays. Shaw often used wit and satire in writings about significant social issues such as education, marriage, religion, government, and class differences. He is the only person to have been awarded both a Nobel Prize in Literature (1925) and an Oscar (1938, for his work on the film *Pygmalion*).

Reflecting on Act I

6. Read the following lines from Act I, and then answer the following questions:

   THE NOTE-TAKER: You see this creature with her kerbstone English: the English that will keep her in the gutter to the end of her days. Well, sir, in three months I could pass that girl off as a duchess at an ambassador's garden party.

   - What is the significance of language? Why does the note-taker believe that the flower girl's dialect hinders her ability to transform her station in life?
   - Consider contemporary, real-life parallels to this idea. Can you think of a situation where people are judged by their accents, dialect, or style of speaking?

7. Revisit the film stills and compare the director's interpretation in *My Fair Lady* with *Pygmalion* after reading Act I. If you had been the director, what would you have done differently? Why?

 **Check Your Understanding**

Now that you've read Act I, confirm or correct your ideas about the play's setting, characters, and major plot points. Use your revised notes to write a brief statement explaining the archetypes presented and the developing theme in Act I.

 INDEPENDENT READING LINK

Read and Research

Using your understanding of Archetypal Criticism, analyze the characters presented in the text you are reading. Which archetypes or universal symbols do you notice in your independent reading? How does identifying archetypes deepen your understanding of the text? Write a brief response in your Reader/Writer Notebook.

ACTIVITY 2.4 continued

12 After the first read, have students work together in established groups or in pairs to answer the questions under Reflecting on Act I. Have students share their thoughts in a class discussion.

13 Have students respond to the Check Your Understanding in the form of a Quickwrite.

14 Play corresponding scenes for students using video or audio clips from the 1938 original film adaptation or a modern-day equivalent. Have students share their impressions of these interpretations.

15 Remind students to complete the Independent Reading Link.

LEVELED DIFFERENTIATED INSTRUCTION

Some students may benefit from the use of sentence frames and suggested language. Write on the board question frames and lists of adjectives/adverbs/verbs students can incorporate into their writing.

Expanding Have students work independently to write a description of each of the film stills. Encourage them to use adjectives, figurative language, and specific detail in their writing.

Extend Have students choose one of the film stills and write an expanded description.

ASSESS

Discuss students' responses to the Check Your Understanding task. Be sure that students updated their inferences and are able to articulate at least one theme of the play.

ADAPT

If students need additional help making connections between the photographs, their inferences, and the developing themes of the play, you may want to have them work in pairs to respond to the writing prompt.

PLAN

Materials: *Pygmalion*, Acts II and III; sticky notes
Suggested Pacing: 2 50-minute class periods plus homework

TEACH

1 Read aloud the Learning Targets and Preview. Engage students in a discussion of what constitutes text evidence. Model annotating the first page of the script, highlighting dialogue or stage directions that show character.

2 Revisit Act I of *Pygmalion*. Ask students what they have learned about the characters and their relationships so far.

3 As they read Act II, have students mark the text (with sticky notes, if necessary), noting any lines that reveal significant characterization of the five characters listed in the graphic organizer. They should especially look for the elements of characterization.

4 Have small groups **think-pair-share** to complete the **graphic organizer.** Use the suggested responses in the graphic organizer for modeling. Explain to students that they can make many other inferences about the characters.

Ladies and Gentlemen

Learning Strategies

Discussion Groups
Graphic Organizer
Think-Pair-Share

Learning Targets

- Analyze the interactions between setting, dialogue, point of view and characterization.
- Evaluate and discuss how characters' motivations act as a driving force in advancing the plot.
- Write a comparative analysis of characters from two different texts

Preview

In this activity, you will read Act II of *Pygmalion*. As you reflect on this act, you will collect text evidence to inform your analysis of each character, and then you will discuss the traits of the various characters and what motivates them. Finally, you will complete a written response drawing connections between Shaw's *Pygmalion* and Ovid's *Metamorphoses*.

Reading *Pygmalion*: Act II

As you read Act II, identify each character's significant attributes. Jot down notes on how the playwright develops the characters in the play.

- Use sticky notes to identify elements of characterization: dialogue, dramatic action, or point of view.
- Circle unknown words or phrases. Try to determine the meaning of the words by using context clues, word parts, or a dictionary.

1. Based on your reading, list three to five adjectives that describe each of the characters and select evidence from the text to support your ideas.

Character	Characteristics	Textual Evidence
Eliza	proud, uneducated	"Well, I ain't come here to ask for any compliment; and if my money's not good enough I can go elsewhere."
Higgins	rude, pompous	"… shall we ask this baggage to sit down or shall we throw her out of the window?"
Pickering	humble	"I rather fancied myself because I can pronounce twenty-four distinct vowel sounds; but your hundred and thirty beat me."
Mrs. Pearce	concerned, bold	"You must be reasonable, Mr. Higgins: really you must. You can't walk over everybody like this."
Mr. Doolittle	manipulative, cynical	"Is this reasonable? Is it fair to take advantage of a man like this? The girl belongs to me."

College and Career Readiness Standards

Focus Standards:

RL.11–12.3 Analyze the impact of the author's choices regarding how to develop and relate elements of a story or drama (e.g., where a story is set, how the action is ordered, how the characters are introduced and developed).

RL.11–12.5 Analyze how an author's choices concerning how to structure specific parts of a text (e.g., the choice of where to begin or end a story, the choice to provide a comedic or tragic resolution) contribute to its overall structure and meaning as well as its aesthetic impact.

2.5

☑ Focus on the Sentence

Using what you know about the characters, turn the following fragments into complete sentences. Use correct punctuation and capitalization.

My Notes

higgins treats

Higgins treats Eliza like a science experiment rather than a person.

_____

disagrees with

Mrs. Pearce disagrees with Higgins's abrasive and unpleasant attitude.

_____

eliza's appearance

While Mrs. Pearce transforms Eliza's appearance, it is not enough to make her a

"true lady."

doolittle reveals

Mr. Doolittle reveals that he isn't interested defending his daughter's honor.

Reflecting on Act II

2. In your discussion groups, discuss your preliminary responses to the questions in preparation for a collegial discussion. Come to the discussion group prepared with relevant, insightful questions and well-reasoned ideas. Be sure to use evidence from the text to support your analysis and remain open to interpretations offered by your peers.

   • How is Eliza made to conform at Professor Higgins's home?

   • What will Eliza need to change about herself to be considered a "lady"?

   • How does the setting of Victorian England influence the plot and character development?

   • Does social class play a significant role in characterization? Explain.

☑ Check Your Understanding

Based on what you have read so far, what appears to motivate each of the characters?

College and Career Readiness Standards

W.11–12.2 Write informative/explanatory texts to examine and convey complex ideas, concepts, and information clearly and accurately through the effective selection, organization, and analysis of content.

Additional Standards Addressed:

RL.11–12.1, RL.11–12.2, RL.11–12.7, W.11–12.2a, W.11–12.2b, W.11–12.2c, W.11–12.2d, W.11–12.2e, W.11–12.2f, W.11–12.5, W.11–12.7

LEVELED DIFFERENTIATED INSTRUCTION

In this activity, students may need support identifying character details.

Beginning In small groups, have students use the **Character Map** graphic organizer as a discussion and note-taking tool. Guide small-group discussions by asking, "Does Eliza wear expensive clothes? Is she polite or is she loud? How does she speak? What does Higgins say about her?"

Developing Distribute the **Character Map graphic organizer** to pairs and assign either Eliza or Higgins to each student. Remind students to include how the character dresses and speaks, and how other characters feel about him or her.

Expanding Assign a character to each student. Have them use the **Character Map** graphic organizer to identify character details. Next, group students to discuss what appears to motivate each character.

5 Have students respond to Focus on the Sentence. Remind them to base their answers on what they have read about the characters so far.

 TEACHER TO TEACHER

The Focus on the Sentence activity provides a good opportunity to review sentence structures. Review subordinating conjunctions such as *while*, *because*, *although*, and *since*, and challenge students to use one or more of them when writing their sentences.

6 Maintaining the established groups, have students briefly preview and discuss the questions in Reflecting on Act II to prepare for a larger group discussion.

7 After the small groups have previewed the questions, engage in a class discussion on these questions.

8 Ask students to describe the motivations of the characters at this point in the play. Then have them respond to the Check Your Understanding prompt.

9 Review the Language & Writer's Craft guidelines for organizing information. Explain the organization of a compare-and-contrast essay in which students organize by topic or point rather than by character. Analyze the Model Text, pointing out movement of organization from topic 1, Professor Higgins and then Pygmalion, to topic 2, first discussing Higgins and then Pygmalion, to topic 3, again first discussing Higgins and then Pygmalion. Also, call attention to the textual evidence and commentaries that explain the significance of the evidence. Last, highlight the transition words and phrases that add fluency to the paragraph.

10 Direct students to the practice in Language & Writer's Craft, in which they will need to make a comparison of their own. Have students record responses in their Reader/Writer Notebooks or on a separate sheet of paper.

2.5

My Notes

LANGUAGE & WRITER'S CRAFT: Organizing Information

When organizing a text that compares two literary works, an important step is identifying the points of comparison and creating a thesis statement to focus your writing. Then, for each point, cite textual evidence and explain the significance of the evidence. As you develop your ideas, use appropriate and varied transitions to link the major sections of the text.

Study this model text, which compares Ovid's character, Pygmalion, to Shaw's Professor Higgins. With your discussion groups, analyze the organizational structure.

- What is the thesis statement?
- What are the points of comparison?
- How does the writer use transitions to provide smooth links between these points?

Model Text

In Shaw's *Pygmalion*, Professor Higgins exhibits drive and passion for creating beauty just as Ovid's Pygmalion does. Both characters have rejected women. Professor Higgins proudly boasts in Act II that he is "a confirmed old bachelor," while Pygmalion, "offended by the failings that nature gave the female heart," lives as a bachelor. However, each takes on the task of shaping or transfiguring a woman. Higgins tells Colonel Pickering that the chore of transforming Eliza is "almost irresistible. She's so deliciously low—so horribly dirty." Like Higgins, Pygmalion desires to carve a beautiful figure that he can manipulate and beautify. In their actions, the two characters demonstrate their desires for control and manipulation. In addition, both characters dress and beautify their "works." Higgins tells Mrs. Pearce to take Eliza's clothes and burn them and to buy her new ones appropriate for her new station. Similarly, Pygmalion "dresses the body, also, in clothing; places rings on the fingers; places a long necklace round its neck." Both characters manipulate and control the women, perhaps to enhance their own feelings of power.

PRACTICE Find one other point of comparison the writer could have used in the model text. Write a sentence or two explaining the comparison, with text evidence, and mark the model text to show where you would add this information so it is logically organized.

2.5

 Writing Prompt: Informational

Compare the character of Eliza with the statue in the original Pygmalion myth. How is each described by the author? What relationships do they have to the other main characters in the stories? In what ways are they acted upon, and in what ways are they the source of action? Be sure to:

- Begin with a concise comparative thesis statement.
- Develop the topic using direct quotations and specific examples to support your analysis.
- Use a coherent structure to organize information with appropriate transitions that highlight similarities and differences.
- Use precise vocabulary to convey your ideas in a clear and interesting way.
- Provide an engaging conclusion that summarizes your comparisons while examining their implications and significance.
- Maintain an engaging, formal, and objective tone, while using the standard English conventions of mechanics and usage.

INDEPENDENT READING LINK

Read and Recommend

Write a brief review and recommendation of your independent reading text based on what you have read so far. In your review, summarize what the text is about, explain how the author expresses ideas using archetypes, and provide commentary about why you would or would not recommend the text to your peers.

ACTIVITY 2.5 continued

11 Direct students to the writing prompt and ask them to respond individually, either during class or as homework. Direct them to complete a self evaluation or peer evaluation using the bulleted points of the prompt. For each point, have students analyze their response as you demonstrated with the model text in the Language & Writer's Craft.

12 Remind students to respond to the Independent Reading Link.

ASSESS

Discuss students' responses to the Check Your Understanding task. Be sure that students have considered the motivations of the characters they read about in Act II. Remind students how they used the graphic organizer to make inferences based on textual evidence. Check their responses to the writing prompt and their self or peer evaluations to determine how well they adhered to the bulleted guidelines in the prompt. Verify that they correctly identified thesis statements.

ADAPT

If students need additional help understanding character motivation, have them work with a partner or small group to act out a scene from the play. Encourage them to consider how the characters feel and why they behave as they do. You may wish to have partners or groups perform the scene for the class. To support students' self or peer evaluations of the writing prompt, consider having them transform the points in the bulleted list into a basic rubric, which they can then use to assess their own or their peers' writing.

 WRITING PROMPT: INFORMATIONAL

The following standards are addressed in the writing prompt:
- RL.11–12.3
- W.11–12.2a
- W.11–12.2b
- W.11–12.2c
- W.11–12.2d
- W.11–12.2e
- W.11–12.2f

PLAN

Materials: *Pygmalion*, Act III
Suggested Pacing: 1 50-minute class period

TEACH

1 Review the Learning Targets and Preview with students.

2 Read aloud Reading *Pygmalion*: Act III. Before students read Act III, revisit the definition of the Archetypal Perspective. Discuss the archetypes students have identified so far in the play. Make sure students understand what literary elements they should be paying attention to as they analyze the comedic effect Shaw has tried to create.

3 Define the term *faux pas* as an embarrassing social gaffe. Direct students to the Word Connections entry in the sidebar.

4 Have students review the annotations they will make as they read *Pygmalion* Act III. Engage students in a brief discussion about other transformative characters they have recently encountered in their reading who also face early challenges and commit significant mistakes.

5 Conduct a shared reading of Act III.

6 Have students work in small groups to discuss and compare their annotations and text evidence. Encourage students to help one another with unknown words and phrases. Move from group to group as students are working and remind them to use textual evidence in their responses.

7 Instruct students to work individually to complete the sentences in Focus on the Sentence. If any students are having trouble understanding the relationship between the conjunction and the specific information needed to complete the sentence, go over the rules governing conjunctions and subordinate clauses. Discuss their responses as a class.

Language and Satire

Learning Strategies

Discussion Groups
Marking the Text
Note-taking
Sharing and Responding
Skimming/Scanning
Think-Pair-Share

VOCABULARY

ACADEMIC

A *faux pas* is an embarrassing act or remark in a social situation.

WORD CONNECTIONS

Etymology

The term faux pas is an example of a "loan" phrase—one borrowed from another language that becomes, over time, adopted into common use. The literal translation of *faux pas* from French is "false step," but it has been used in English since the 17th century.

My Notes

Learning Targets

- Analyze how an author creates a satirical effect.
- Evaluate and discuss the significance of language, including diction and syntax, as a means of conveying tone and theme.
- Analyze the genre conventions and structure of a script and apply them by writing a scene.

Preview

In this activity, you will read Act III of *Pygmalion* and analyze how the author uses literary elements like tone to advance the plot and create a comedic effect. Then, you'll write a short script for a scene using characteristics of the genre.

Reading *Pygmalion*: Act III

In Act III, Eliza faces a challenge. The character undergoing a transformation must often face a test early in the training process and usually commits a significant mistake.

- Mark the text for evidence that helps you answer this question: What faux pas does Eliza commit, and how does this experience contribute to the plot and her development as a character?
- Circle unknown words or phrases. Try to determine the meaning of the words by using context clues, word parts, or a dictionary.

☑ Focus on the Sentence

Use information from the play to complete the sentences. Consult a dictionary to learn more about the term *faux pas*, if needed.

Eliza commits a faux pas because <u>she doesn't realize that the story about her aunt</u> <u>is embarrassing.</u>

Eliza commits a faux pas, but <u>Freddy is awe-struck by her "new small talk."</u>

Eliza commits a faux pas, so <u>Higgins signals that she should remove herself</u> <u>from the situation.</u>

College and Career Readiness Standards

Focus Standards:

RL.11–12.2 Determine two or more themes or central ideas of a text and analyze their development over the course of the text, including how they interact and build on one another to produce a complex account; provide an objective summary of the text.

RL.11–12.6 Analyze a case in which grasping a point of view requires distinguishing

what is directly stated in a text from what is really meant (e.g., satire, sarcasm, irony, or understatement).

L.11–12.3a Vary syntax for effect, consulting references (e.g., Tufte's Artful Sentences) for guidance as needed; apply an understanding of syntax to the study of complex texts when reading.

2.6

1. **Quickwrite:** Have you come across archetypal characters that undergo a transformation in any of the texts or films that you've encountered outside of class? Did the character commit a humorous faux pas? Compare their experience to Eliza's.

My Notes

Pygmalion performance at the Garrick Theatre in London, 2011

Reflecting on Author's Craft in Act III

2. Shaw uses satire in his work to expose humanity's vices and shortcomings in a comedic way. Review a few writing techniques often found in satirical texts:

- **Exaggeration / Caricature:** to distort an individual's prominent characteristics to the point of making that individual appear ridiculous.
- **Parody:** to imitate a work with the intent of ridiculing the author, ideas, or work.
- **Irony:** to use words or events to convey a reality opposite to appearance or expectation. The recognition by the audience often produces a comic effect.

LITERARY

Satire describes a manner of writing that mocks social conventions, actions, or attitudes with wit and humor.

VOCABULARY

ACTIVITY 2.6 continued

8 Give students time to complete the Quickwrite, and then have volunteers **share** their responses with the class.

9 Engage students in a discussion about the photo from a *Pygmalion* performance at the Garrick Theatre. Invite students to guess which scene is shown in the photo and ask them to cite text evidence to support their ideas.

10 Vocabulary Development: Direct students to the Literary Vocabulary. Read aloud the definition of *satire*. Then engage students in a brief discussion of this term, asking them to apply it to a well-known text or popular movie.

11 Have students read Reflecting on Author's Craft in Act III, and then discuss the terms *exaggeration*, *parody*, and *irony*. Make sure students understand the difference between satire and parody. Engage students in a discussion in which they brainstorm examples of these techniques from popular comedy films or television shows (such as *The Simpsons*, *Saturday Night Live*, or *Bob's Burgers*.)

12 After they complete student step 4, gauge student comprehension by having them complete the Check Your Understanding.

13 Have students work in pairs or in small groups to complete the graphic organizer. Circulate among the groups to make sure they understand and are able to identify the satirical techniques used in the play.

College and Career Readiness Standards

W.11–12.3d Use precise words and phrases, telling details, and sensory language to convey a vivid picture of the experiences, events, setting, and/or characters.

Additional Standards Addressed:
RL.11–12.1, RL.11–12.3, RL.11–12.4, RL.11–12.5, SL.11–12.3, W.11–12.4, W.11–12.5, W.11–12.10, L.11–12.4a

14 Have students read the vocabulary feature and work with a partner to paraphrase the definitions. Engage students in a brief discussion about the narrative arc in other fictional texts they have read.

15 Review the genre conventions of writing a play script. Lead students in a discussion about the function and importance of these elements in creating a successful scene. Encourage students to consult references, such as Tufte's Artful Sentences, for guidance on varying syntax in their scenes.

 TEACHER TO TEACHER

This is a good time to reference Writing Workshop 9: Script Writing. Consider using the graphic organizer from the workshop to introduce the parts of a play script to students.

LEVELED DIFFERENTIATED INSTRUCTION

In this activity, students may need support writing their one-scene script and may benefit from a **think-pair-share** in which to brainstorm ideas.

Expanding Distribute the **Conflict Map** graphic organizer. Model how to develop a clearly stated conflict based on a social blunder. For example: "Once, I tagged my friend online when she didn't want to be tagged. She didn't like the picture, so she was upset with me."

Bridging Allow students to work collaboratively to complete the **Conflict Map** graphic organizer as prewriting support. Remind them to choose a faux pas as the basis for the conflict in their scenes.

Extend If some students finish writing one-scene scripts and are ready for an additional challenge, ask them to work together to perform each other's scenes. Have them record video or audio of their performances.

2.6

3. Skim Act III to identify the satirical techniques that Shaw employs. Notice his use of syntax and diction and the effects of these choices.

Satirical Technique	Text Evidence

4. Discuss with your group the specific character trait or flaw Shaw is satirizing in the scene. In your discussion, evaluate and answer the following:
   - What message is Shaw sending to the audience through his use of satire?
   - How does the social setting of Victorian England influence the plot?
   - How is Shaw making a statement about society through his use of satire?

☑ Check Your Understanding

Write a brief response explaining how Shaw uses satire throughout his play. What techniques does he primarily use and why might an audience find this funny?

Writing a Play Script

5. Writing a script for a play involves using certain conventions and dramatic elements, in order to give an audience context for the story that is taking place. Consider the following genre conventions of writing a play script.
   - **Title:** The name of the play
   - **List of Characters:** The people in the play; may include a brief description of each
   - **Setting:** Where and when the scene takes place; usually included at the beginning of each scene
   - **Dialogue:** The words spoken on stage, the primary vehicle through which the audience learns about the characters and conflicts. Writers use dialogue to advance the plot. Also, writers can add meaning or style through the language they choose.
   - **Conflict:** The problem that complicates the lives of the characters until the problem is resolved.
   - **Narrative Arc:** A clear and logical progression from one event or experience to the next.
   - **Stage Directions:** Language separate from dialogue that indicates the time and place of the action, entrances, exits, movement, and subtext. Stage directions also indicate what the characters are doing on stage as well as provide clues as to how actors should deliver their lines.

VOCABULARY

ACADEMIC

Genre conventions are the defining features of a specific type of writing, such as short story, poetry, or script.

LITERARY

The **narrative arc** is the story line of a text, which includes a beginning (the exposition), a middle (the rising action), a climax (the highest point of tension), and an end (the falling action and resolution). As part of the narrative arc, characters grow, change, and face conflicts.

2.6

☑ Check Your Understanding

Return to the beginning of *Pygmalion*, Act I. Annotate the text to identify the details from Act I that illustrate each of the conventions described here, and label the text accordingly.

📝 Writing Prompt: Literary

Think about a faux pas you have committed or can imagine someone committing. Write a one-scene script with at least two characters that satirizes the situation. Consider how you will incorporate the use of satire and archetypes. Be sure to:

- Include the conventions of a play script: setting, dialogue, conflict, narrative arc, and stage directions.
- Incorporate humor through word choice and diction.
- Incorporate one or more of the four elements of satire—exaggeration, incongruity, reversal, and parody.

My Notes

WRITING PROMPT: LITERARY

The following standards are addressed in the writing prompt:

- W.11–12.2d
- W.11–12.4
- L.11–12.3a
- L.11–12.5

ACTIVITY 2.6 continued

16 Have students complete the Check Your Understanding before turning to the writing prompt. The length of the scenes is not important, as long as the finished product provides ample opportunity for students to incorporate the various elements of a play script.

17 Place students in small groups to share their scenes. Encourage them to provide feedback on how effectively they followed the conventions of writing a play script.

ASSESS

Student responses to the Check Your Understanding should demonstrate that they have a full grasp of the different satirical techniques. They should understand the difference between parody and irony, for example, and should be able to find text evidence in the play that shows use of the technique.

ADAPT

If students are still confused by the definitions/examples of satirical techniques, have them work in pairs to look through examples you have selected from *The Onion* and find articles that exemplify each technique. Have each pair explain why they chose their example. Encourage students to find specific words or details that demonstrate a technique—for example, unusual diction or very hyperbolic language.

PLAN

Materials: *Pygmalion*, Acts II and III; sticky notes

Suggested Pacing: 1 50-minute class period

TEACH

1 With students, read the Learning Targets.

2 **Vocabulary Development:** Review the meaning of the term *subtext* with students. Have them work in pairs to define the term in their own words and think of both examples and non-examples.

3 Read through the Preview and make sure students understand what they are going to do in this activity. Engage them in a discussion of whether they think *how* a line is performed is more important, less important, or equally important as *what* is said.

TEACHER TO TEACHER

You may want to increase understanding of subtext by showing short scenes of dialogue between two characters from movies or television shows, in which a character's gestures, facial expressions, behavior and tone of voice convey as much or more than his or her actual lines.

4 For student step 1, have two pairs of students plan and present an oral interpretation of the dialogue contained in the text boxes on the student page. Give the pairs different subtexts (without sharing these with the rest of the class). The first pair will present the dialogue as though A is a child giving his or her report card to a parent, B. The second pair will present the dialogue as though A is presenting B with a wrapped gift.

5 As the two pairs perform their interpretations, the rest of the class should try to identify the subtext of each performance, completing the **graphic organizer** and comparing the two performances for meaning and effect.

Learning Strategies

Close Reading
Graphic Organizer
Note-taking
Oral Reading
Skimming / Scanning
Think-Aloud

VOCABULARY

ACADEMIC

Subtext is the unspoken meaning or context that can be inferred from what is directly stated. Written and spoken texts in many domains may include subtext. For example, a political speech may carry meaning in what is not stated as well as in what is stated. When studying drama, readers look for this implied meaning in order to understand a play on a deeper level.

Learning Targets

- Infer the subtext of dramatic dialogue by analyzing the impact of a speaker's delivery of lines.
- Analyze and annotate text to indicate how to present an oral reading of dialogue.
- Revise an original script to improve its impact on the audience.

Preview

In this activity, you discover how the delivery of lines can bring additional layers of meaning to a text. You will perform a dialogue using voice, tone, gestures, and other dramatic elements to bring different meanings and emotions to the text. With a group, you will analyze and discuss possible hidden meanings and different interpretations of a scene from *Pygmalion*. Finally, you will revise your script from the previous activity to include subtext.

Creating Subtext

1. This chart contains a dialogue between two characters, A and B. With your classmates, you will perform the dialogue with different scenarios in mind. During your performance, use your voice, facial expressions, and body language to give the dialogue a specific meaning. As you watch the other groups, try to identify the subtext.

   - What can you infer from the way a line is spoken?
   - Record notes about the way the tone of voice, pacing, body language and word emphasis provide clues.

My Notes

College and Career Readiness Standards

Focus Standards:

L.11–12.3 Apply knowledge of language to understand how language functions in different contexts, to make effective choices for meaning or style, and to comprehend more fully when reading or listening.

SL.11–12.6 Adapt speech to a variety of contexts and tasks, demonstrating a command of formal English when indicated or appropriate. (See grades 11–12 Language standards 1 and 3 here for specific expectations.)

2.7

Text	Performance 1 (What clues help you figure out the subtext?)	Performance 2 (What clues help you figure out the subtext?)
A. Well, here it is.		
B. Is that what I think it is?		
A. I think so.		
B. Are you sure?		
A. See for yourself, if you don't believe me.		
B. Okay, what now?		

My Notes

_____
_____
_____
_____
_____
_____
_____
_____
_____
_____
_____
_____
_____
_____
_____
_____
_____
_____
_____
_____
_____
_____

INDEPENDENT READING LINK

Read and Respond

Infer the subtext in a scene from your independent reading text. What lines in the dialogue give clues to the subtext? Does the author provide stage directions or other commentary to clarify the subtext? Record your analysis in your Reader/Writer Notebook.

Analyzing Dialogue

Skim Acts II and III paying close attention to dialogue that implies meaning underlying the text. For example, consider the lines from Act I:

> THE DAUGHTER. If Freddy had a bit of gumption, he would have got one at the theatre door.
>
> THE MOTHER. What could he have done, poor boy?

College and Career Readiness Standards

W.11–12.4 Produce clear and coherent writing in which the development, organization, and style are appropriate to task, purpose, and audience.

Additional Standards Addressed:

RL.11–12.1, RL.11–12.2, RL.11–12.5, W.11–12.5, L.11–12.5, L.11–12.5b

ACTIVITY 2.7 continued

6 In a general class discussion, ask students to verbalize what clues allowed them to determine the subtext, since the words spoken in both performances are the same. These clues may include which words were stressed, the pitch of the speaker's voice, the pacing of the lines, actions the readers performed, the readers' facial expressions, and any props the readers used.

LEVELED DIFFERENTIATED INSTRUCTION

Students may need additional support recognizing subtext and working with unfamiliar vocabulary.

Beginning To reinforce the idea of subtext and help with vocabulary, have students work in small groups and provide them with a list (and definitions if necessary), such as *secretive*, *dishonest*, *delighted*, *ironic*, *disgusted*, and so on. Then have them act out lines of dialogue to convey the different emotions through tone of voice, body language, etc.

Developing Have small groups act out lines of dialogue with different subtexts. In each group, have a pair of students act out the lines, while the others write down what subtext they think is being conveyed, and at least one reason why they think this (i.e., "She rolled her eyes on the word, which indicated she didn't believe what she was saying").

Expanding Pair advanced students and have them write their own short original dialogue, along with stage directions indicating how the lines should be performed. They should write at least two different sets of stage directions, to indicate different subtexts; for example, one could indicate an ironic delivery of the lines while the other indicates a more straightforward interpretation.

7 In Analyzing Dialogue, point out the additional stage directions with the scene from Act III, and discuss how they add meaning and affect The Daughter's delivery. How do these directions change the implications of the subtext?

8 Have students read The Mother's line, emphasizing various words. Allow them to discuss the reflective questions.

9 Ask students to consider subtext as they continue reading *Pygmalion*. There are several conversations in Acts II and III in which the characters misunderstand each other. Lead the class in a **close reading** of a scene they have already read—for example, the conversation in Act II, when the Flower Girl asks Higgins to teach her proper English.

10 Ask students to use sticky notes to record their ideas about the subtext of a line. Model the process using a **think-aloud**. For example:

- **HIGGINS:** Pickering: shall we ask this baggage to sit down, or shall we throw her out of the window?
- **YOUR THINK-ALOUD:** Higgins may be speaking rudely because he is embarrassed that someone so far beneath him socially is trying to hire him as a teacher.

11 Ask students to respond to the Check Your Understanding task.

12 Have students respond to the Independent Reading link.

ASSESS

Review students' responses to the Check Your Understanding. Ensure that partners marked up a few lines of the script to show how they would direct actors to deliver lines to convey subtext.

ADAPT

For students who need additional help understanding subtext, find subtext-rich passages in the play and read them aloud. Ask students to rephrase each line to reveal subtext.

2.7

My Notes

Notice the absence of stage directions for these lines. When a playwright decides not to include stage directions, it is sometimes to emphasize the characters' words.

- Consider the effects of adding stage directions. How do the stage directions effect your understanding of these lines?

THE DAUGHTER. *[snarling and growling]* If Freddy had a bit of gumption, he would have got one at the theatre door.

Snarling and growling adds the element of anger in the daughter's voice. She is obviously mad at Freddie.

- Now consider the line with this stage direction, which adds not only vocal but physical emphasis:

THE DAUGHTER. *[speaking rapidly and eagerly; jumping up and down]* If Freddy had a bit of gumption, he would have got one at the theatre door.

Rapidly and eagerly and *jumping up and down* imply that the girl is agitated. How the mother responds might be to calm the daughter, and this would show in the mother's tone of voice.

- Read the next line aloud three times. The first time, emphasize the word *what*. Next, emphasize *could*. Then, emphasize *done*, and note how these three different ways of speaking influence your impression of how the mother is responding to the daughter.

THE MOTHER. What could he have done, poor boy?

2. With your discussion group, consider these questions:
   - How does the addition of stage directions affect the delivery of lines?
   - Why do playwrights sometimes omit these directions, and why do they sometimes include them?
   - Choose a line or two of dialogue from the play that does contain stage directions. Why do you think stage directions were given here by the playwright?
   - What is the subtext created by each of the three readings of "What could he have done, poor boy?" Return to Act I, Scene 1. Reread this scene and think about what subtexts Shaw might have had in mind.

☑ Check Your Understanding

Return to the one-scene script about a faux pas that you wrote in the previous activity. Working with a partner, revise your script to show how you would direct actors to deliver the lines to convey the subtext.

Examining Eliza's Options

Learning Targets

- Analyze character development within a play to write an original script using genre characteristics and craft.
- Use logical arguments and text evidence to make a compelling argument, while acknowledging counterclaims.

Learning Strategies

Debating
Graphic Organizer
Sharing and Responding
Summarizing/Paraphrasing
Think-Pair-Share

Preview

In this activity, you will reflect on the character development in Act III of *Pygmalion*. You will collaboratively write and perform an original script based on what you have learned about the characters. Then you will read Act IV of the play and engage in a class debate.

Reflecting on Act III

1. With a small group, summarize how Eliza, Higgins, or Pickering has evolved along with the plot. Compare the character's behavior before and after the ball.

The Character: _____

How does the character typically behave and speak? Use adjectives and adverbs to describe these behaviors. Cite textual evidence.	How does the character feel now that the ball is over? Cite textual evidence from Act III to support your position.

2. Now that you have discussed and taken notes on one of the characters with your small group, you will work with another group to create a dialogue among all three characters. Remember that the subtext is often even more important than the words that are spoken, so include any subtext that seems appropriate by noting it in parentheses at the end of the corresponding line.

My Notes

_____

College and Career Readiness Standards

Focus Standards:

RL.11–12.1 Cite strong and thorough textual evidence to support analysis of what the text says explicitly as well as inferences drawn from the text, including determining where the text leaves matters uncertain.

RL.11–12.3 Analyze the impact of the author's choices regarding how to develop and relate

elements of a story or drama (e.g., where a story is set, how the action is ordered, how the characters are introduced and developed).

SL.11–12.1b Work with peers to promote civil, democratic discussions and decision-making, set clear goals and deadlines, and establish individual roles as needed.

ACTIVITY 2.8

PLAN

Materials: *Pygmalion*, Acts III and IV; student-generated notes
Suggested Pacing: 2 50-minute class periods plus homework

TEACH

1 Begin this lesson with a review by asking students to **summarize** how Eliza has won Higgins' bet for him. You might do this as a class discussion or you might ask students to write a brief summary.

2 Have a volunteer read the Learning Targets and Preview.

3 Divide the class into three groups. Each group will focus on one character (Eliza, Higgins, or Pickering). Have students **think-pair-share** responses to the questions about their character.

4 Ask students to use the two-column chart on the student page. Jigsaw students so that the new groups have at least one student expert on each of the three characters. Have these groups share their notes on their characters and then create a dialogue among Higgins, Pickering, and Eliza that might have taken place after the party. They should write in parentheses any appropriate subtext for the lines.

5 Ask students to share and respond to the dialogues they have written.

TEACHER TO TEACHER

Give students ample encouragement and opportunity to act out their original lines of dialogue as well as the lines of dialogue from the play. Encourage them to enthusiastically take on their chosen roles—perhaps even using British accents—and considering how best to play the part.

6 Have the class read Act IV, marking the text for evidence that supports or does not support their imagined scenes. If needed, model a think-aloud showing the thought process for finding relevant evidence.

7 When they are finished reading Act IV, direct students to Reflecting on Act IV. Have them respond to these questions either individually or in small groups. As they brainstorm Eliza's options, remind students that they should include the options Higgins states in Act IV, the ones Eliza states, and any others that they can think of.

8 Have students respond to the Check Your Understanding in the My Notes area. Based on their ideas of what Eliza should do next, select one possible option to **debate** as a class.

9 Ask students to read the bulleted points in student step 7, and have them make notes as you review these steps with them. Invite volunteers to share examples of a claim. Provide input to help with clarity as needed. Remind students that the line of reasoning is their argument and evidence from the text should support that argument. Ask students what types of evidence they might use (explicit and inferential examples, direct quotations, clear connections). Encourage students to anticipate and discuss counterclaims in their small groups as they prepare for the debate.

10 Give students time in small groups to prepare for the class debate. Assign each group a character and have students prepare for the class debate, using the bulleted points in student step 7.

11 Divide small groups into pro/con debate groups. Each small group will present the view of one character, for or against the chosen option. Ask students to define speaking roles, including opening and closing statements, for as many members of the group as possible. Reassign students who do not have speaking roles in the debate to be members of a council who will decide the winner of the debate.

2.8

My Notes

Reading *Pygmalion*: Act IV

Before reading Act IV, compare the dialogues your class has created. For your comparisons, consider the following and record notes in the My Notes area.

- Based on textual evidence of events of characters from Acts I–III, which imagined scene is the most plausible?
- What qualities of plot and character make your selection most authentic?

3. As you read Act IV:

- Mark the text for evidence that either supports or does not support your imagined scene.
- Circle any unknown words and phrases. Try to determine the meaning of the words by using context clues, word parts, or a dictionary.

Reflecting on Act IV

4. After you have read Act IV, compare how the conversation Shaw created is similar to and different from the one you and your group created.

5. How are Eliza's choices limited by the setting in Victorian England? How does this affect her behavior? How do Eliza's and Higgins' social classes impact their actions?

6. In Act IV, Eliza asks, "Where am I to go? What am I to do? What's to become of me?" What are Eliza's options, given the setting of the play? Using a T-graphic organizer, brainstorm Eliza's options and the pros and cons of each option.

College and Career Readiness Standards

SL.11–12.4 Present information, findings, and supporting evidence, conveying a clear and distinct perspective, such that listeners can follow the line of reasoning, alternative or opposing perspectives are addressed, and the organization, development, substance, and style are appropriate to purpose, audience, and a range of formal and informal tasks.

Additional Standards Addressed:
RL.11–12.2

2.8

☑ Check Your Understanding

Now that you have read Act IV, you have a clear picture of Higgins's and Pickering's attitudes toward their "project." Think about what Eliza should do next and jot down your ideas in the My Notes area. Keep the following in mind as you brainstorm ideas:

- The setting: Victorian England
- Eliza's personality
- Eliza's social class

Class Debate

7. Prepare for a class debate with your group. You will take on the persona of one of the characters in the play (Higgins, Pickering, or Eliza) and present an argument stating what you (the character) believe Eliza's next steps should be. Prepare to explain your reasoning using text evidence. Address counterarguments. Speak clearly and expressively in presenting your position. Prepare a well-organized presentation so that your viewpoint is clear to your audience.

   - Introduce a clear arguable claim as to what Eliza's next steps should be.
   - Logically present your reasoning and evidence.
   - Support your position with relevant evidence from Acts I–IV.
   - Acknowledge counterclaims made by others as part of the discussion.
   - Conclude by reminding the audience of how you proved your argument.

8. **Quickwrite:** Reflect on what you initially thought Eliza's next steps should be. Did the class debate present evidence that affects your opinion of what Eliza should do?

My Notes

12 Prompt the debate participants to begin with brief opening statements. As students debate Eliza's next steps, make sure they provide textual support. Encourage them to acknowledge and refute the other side's claims.

13 Give students with opposing viewpoints the opportunity to make counterclaims. Ensure that students are respectful and wait for others to finish making points before speaking.

14 Give students time to reflect on the ideas shared in the debate. During this time, the members of the council will discuss their decision. Each member of the council should provide a part of the reasoning for their ruling, referencing the points made in the debate, the evidence used to support it, or the discussion of counterclaims.

ASSESS

For this activity, you have three options for assessment: (1) the dialogue writing; (2) the **graphic organizer**; (3) the debate. Students should provide textual evidence to support their responses in all three. For the dialogue writing, make sure students have included subtext in parentheses. For the graphic organizer, check that students are thoughtfully incorporating adjectives and adverbs in a way that enhances their ideas. For the debate, make sure students present their ideas effectively, citing textual evidence.

ADAPT

If students need additional help to form an opinion about what Eliza should do next, have them use sentence starters to state their opinion:

- *I agree with your point about _____, but it is also important to consider _____.*
- *I disagree with your point about _____, and would like to counter with the idea that _____.*
- *You made a good point about _____, but have you considered _____?*

PLAN

Materials: *Pygmalion*, Act V
Suggested Pacing: 2 50-minute class periods

TEACH

1 After reading through the Learning Targets and Preview with students and making sure they understand what the activity will entail, engage students in a discussion of transformation.

2 Have students brainstorm films, stories, books and television shows where the main character undergoes a transformation. For example, the character of Anakin Skywalker undergoes a dramatic transformation in the Star Wars films, becoming Darth Vader.

3 Have students choose a character from the discussion and write a short description of his or her transformation. Ask them, *What type of transformation was this? What prompted the transformation? How did conflict spur transformation? Were these transformations permanent? How did the transformation affect the people around the character?*

4 Vocabulary Development: Before students read Act V, discuss the term *subplot*. Have them work in pairs to define this term in their own words and think of both examples and non-examples.

5 *Explain that there can be more than one subplot in a text. Engage the class in a discussion of the concept. Ask Is there a subplot in* Pygmalion? *Is there more than one? Whom does it involve? How does the subplot enhance our understanding of the characters, main plot, or themes of the play?*

6 Have students work in pairs to complete student step 1 in the Reading *Pygmalion*: Act V feature. Then have them share their responses with the class. To guide discussion, note the different traits pairs have focused on in describing the characters.

Learning Strategies

Close Reading
Graphic Organizer
Self-editing/Peer Editing

VOCABULARY

LITERARY
A **subplot** is a secondary plot in a fictional text, such as a play, short story, or television show. Authors often use this technique to support the main plot by driving part of the conflict, adding tension, or providing information or insight about the characters.

📖 INDEPENDENT READING LINK

Read and Connect
Analyze how one or more characters change in your independent reading. How has the character evolved or transformed over time? What contributed to the change? How does the transformation affect the character's point of view and relationships with other characters? Create a two-column graphic organizer in your Reader/Writer Notebook to describe the changes that take place in characters.

Learning Targets
- Analyze how an author develops dynamic characters.
- Write an original script that reflects your working knowledge of critical theory and genre characteristics.
- Use the writing process to improve the clarity and organization of your writing.

Preview

In this activity, you will analyze how the main characters of a play undergo a transformation. You will discuss the parallels and differences between characters in order to anticipate the resolution of the play. Based on your new understanding, you will write an alternate ending for *Pygmalion*.

Reading *Pygmalion*: Act V

1. To begin your study of character transformations between Acts I and V, focus on two characters. For these two major characters—Eliza and Alfred Doolittle—create a two-column graphic organizer to list their characteristics in Act I. Try to include at least five adjectives to describe each character.

2. As you read Act V:
   - Draw a star any place you notice a transformation in Eliza or Alfred Doolittle.
   - Circle any unknown words and phrases. Try to determine the meaning of the words by using context clues, word parts, or a dictionary.

Reflecting on Act V

3. In Act V, Eliza's father, Alfred Doolittle resurfaces. Like Eliza, Doolittle has been transformed. Use a Venn diagram or other graphic organizer to compare these two transformations. You should consider these points, as well as any others that occur to you:
   - What, specifically, about each character has changed? Refer to the adjectives that you listed in Step 1. What comparisons to these adjectives can you identify? How did the transformation occur?
   - How might the transformation affect each character's future?
   - What is each character's attitude toward the transformation?
   - What role does social class play in each of their transformations?

4. Now that you have read Act V, discuss your Venn diagram with a partner.
   - How is Alfred Doolittle's transformation a **subplot** in *Pygmalion*?
   - How are the characters' transformations similar, and how do they differ?

College and Career Readiness Standards

Focus Standards:

RL.11–12.3 Analyze the impact of the author's choices regarding how to develop and relate elements of a story or drama (e.g., where a story is set, how the action is ordered, how the characters are introduced and developed).

W.11–12.3b Use narrative techniques, such as dialogue, pacing, description, reflection, and multiple plot lines, to develop experiences, events, and/or characters.

5. Answer the questions after closely rereading the end of *Pygmalion* (beginning when Pickering and Doolittle exit for the wedding, leaving Higgins and Eliza alone).

	Henry	Eliza
Primary motivation at beginning of play/behavior:	To win a bet by proving he can transform Eliza by improving her speech and manners	To escape poverty by allowing Higgins to use her for an experiment
Primary motivation at end of play:	To get Eliza back—Higgins has fallen in love with Eliza	To be independent; to take control of her own destiny
Conflict:	Discovery that Eliza has walked out on him and won't bend to his wishes	She protests being treated like property and demands respect

6. The play ends with Higgins laughing at the thought of Eliza marrying Freddy. Based on Shaw's portrayal of these characters, what do you imagine becomes of Eliza and of Higgins?

_____

_____

7. Review Reader Response Critical Theory, Cultural Criticism, and Archetypal Criticism. Select one of these critical perspectives and write three questions that will help you understand *Pygmalion*. You may use the questions here as models to craft your own questions:

- Reader Response: As a reader, what attitudes am I bringing to understanding this text?
- Cultural Criticism: What is Shaw saying about the differences in social customs and expectations in this play?
- Archetypal Criticism: Why does Higgins take on the role of the creator or transformer? What's in it for him?

☑ **Check Your Understanding**

Share your questions with a partner but do not reveal the critical perspective you chose. After reading the questions out loud, have your partner guess which critical perspective relates to the questions. Then take turns responding to the questions briefly.

College and Career Readiness Standards

W.11–12.3d Provide a conclusion that follows from and reflects on what is experienced, observed, or resolved over the course of the narrative.

Additional Standards Addressed:
RL.11–12.5, RL.11–12.7, W.11–12.3c, W.11–12.5, W.11–12.9, W.11–12.10

ACTIVITY 2.9 continued

7 Have the class read Act V, marking the text for evidence that demonstrates the characters' transformations. If needed, model a think-aloud showing the thought process for finding relevant evidence.

8 After they have finished reading Act V, direct students to Reflecting on Act V. Have them work with a partner to share the Venn diagrams or other methods they used as they read. Direct them to answer the questions and complete the chart on the page.

9 Have students read through student step 7 and choose which type of critical framework they will use to formulate their questions. If necessary, review the definitions of these different critical perspectives.

10 Have students respond to the Check Your Understanding in their Reader/Writer notebooks. Then, have pairs share the perspective they chose and share their answers with the class.

11 Have students respond to the writing prompt. The length of the scenes is not important. The finished scene should demonstrate an identifiable critical perspective, as well as attention to and understanding of the elements of craft.

12 Instruct students to **self-edit** their papers. Then, have them write a second draft in which they change at least one element—they may add dialogue, add more stage direction, rewrite to make the critical perspective clearer, or delete one or more lines.

13 Invite partners to exchange second drafts and edit them based on the criteria. Finally, have students create a final draft that incorporates their partner's notes and feedback.

14 Ensure that students understand and respond to the Independent Reading Link, found on the first page of the activity.

LEVELED DIFFERENTIATED INSTRUCTION

Students may benefit from other methods, such as visuals, to engage with the text and support or extend the literary writing prompt.

Developing Before they respond to the writing prompt, have students brainstorm and fill in a **graphic organizer** that lists elements of Eliza's motivation, her current situation, and her possibilities for the future.

Expanding Have students rewrite their ending scene as a short story or flash fiction. Have them incorporate description—for example, describing the physical space where the action unfolds—as well as exposition as needed.

Extend Have students choose an additional critical lens and write a second possible ending for the play that reflects this critical perspective. Challenge them to consider whether this lens will alter the basic trajectory of the ending.

ASSESS

For the Check Your Understanding, partners should be able to guess the critical lens that one another used in writing questions. If either partner guessed the wrong lens, review the questions to assess which of the two partners needs greater support understanding how to apply a critical lens.

Review students' scripts and be sure that students have followed the guidance outlined in the bulleted points. To reinforce the activity, ask students to explain the critical lens through which they believe their script should be interpreted.

ADAPT

If students need additional help with the concept of critical perspectives, have them work in groups to write questions and answers about all three critical perspectives. Use a piece of student-written dialogue to model analysis of its relationship with one of the critical perspectives.

2.9

My Notes

🅒 Writing Prompt: Literary

Write an alternate ending that adheres to the conventions of a play script, addresses the changes in Eliza's character in the first half of Act V, and reflects one critical theory. Use well-chosen details and a well-structured event sequence to provide a logical conclusion for the story. You may want to review the elements of script writing in Activity 2.6. Be sure to:

- Use the genre characteristics of a script, including a narrative arc, subtext, and stage direction.
- Write dialogue that reflects your interpretation of the play through one critical perspective.
- Provide a conclusion that resolves the problem or situation of the story.
- Use consistent voice and purposeful vocabulary.

Self-Editing and Peer Editing

After you have responded to the writing prompt, use these questions to review your script.

- Which critical perspective is evident in this alternate ending?
- How has Eliza's transformation led to this alternate ending?

Share your draft with your writing partner. Using the checklist, jot down notes about your partner's script, recording your ideas in the My Notes section. Then expand your notes into clear and concise feedback. Be sure to use the feedback from your partner to revise your draft.

- ☐ **Form:** Are these elements present: title, act and scene numbers, list of characters, description of setting?
- ☐ **Dialogue:** Does the dialogue help create a logical resolution?
- ☐ **Problem:** Since this scene ends the play, how is the problem or conflict between Eliza and Professor Higgins resolved?
- ☐ **Stage Directions:** How do the stage directions suggest delivery of dialogue or movement of characters in a way that makes clear their final intentions?

📝 WRITING PROMPT: LITERARY

The following standards are addressed in the writing prompt:
- RL.11–12.7
- W.11–12.3
- W.11–12.4
- W.11–12.5

What Does Eliza Do?

Learning Targets

- Draw on evidence from a source text to adapt a plot summary into a play script.
- Analyze how the structure of the play incorporates or departs from a traditional dramatic structure.
- Cite textual evidence in a discussion to evaluate an author's choices.

Preview

In this activity, you'll read Shaw's sequel to *Pygmalion* and evaluate and discuss the structure of the play. You then will transform Shaw's sequel into a cohesive script. You will complete a peer review activity with a partner to give and receive constructive feedback and improve the quality of your writing.

Analyzing the Plot Structure

1. Work with a partner to examine the dramatic arc in *Pygmalion*. Create a graphic organizer and jot down key details from each act. Does the play follow a traditional five-act structure? Review the structure of a five-act play in Activity 2.4 if needed.

2. Discuss the following with a partner to evaluate Shaw's decisions:

   - What elements does Shaw present to orient the reader to the story? How does the environment affect a person's identity?
   - Does the play have a clear rising and falling action? How do these elements advance the plot?
   - What message is Shaw conveying to his audience by omitting a detailed scene at the Ambassador's party?
   - What is the climax of the story? How does it advance the plot?
   - Is there a clear conclusion to the play's plot? Is it clear if the main characters achieve their goals?

   Why do you think Shaw chose to structure the play the way he did? What purpose does this allow him to achieve?

Reading *Pygmalion*: The Sequel

3. As you read the sequel to *Pygmalion*, visualize what Shaw is telling the readers.

   - Annotate with a star those lines you are able to visualize most easily.
   - Circle unknown words and phrases. Try to determine the meaning of words by using context clues, word parts, or a dictionary.

4. Consider the following quotation from Shaw's sequel to *Pygmalion*. Do you agree or disagree with Shaw's interpretation of what Eliza would do? With your discussion group, explain why you would defend or challenge Shaw's ending.

   "This being the state of human affairs, what is Eliza fairly sure to do when she is placed between Freddy and Higgins? ... Unless Freddy is biologically repulsive to her, and Higgins biologically attractive to a degree that overwhelms all her other instincts, she will, if she marries either of them, marry Freddy. And that is just what Eliza did."

Learning Strategies

Brainstorming
Drafting
Note-taking
Visualizing

GRAMMAR & USAGE

Commas

Writers often use commas to slow readers down, which leads them to pay closer attention to certain parts of the sentence. Reread this sentence from *Pygmalion*, focusing on Shaw's placement of commas: "Unless Freddy is biologically repulsive to her, and Higgins biologically attractive to a degree that overwhelms all her other instincts, she will ... marry Freddy."

Notice that the commas before "and" and after "instincts" are not required. Why does Shaw include them? Try reading the sentence again without those commas. How does the pacing change?

Find another example in *Pygmalion* that uses commas, and practice saying those lines out loud to see how the punctuation changes the pacing and emphasis of the words.

My Notes

_____

_____

_____

_____

_____

_____

_____

College and Career Readiness Standards

Focus Standards:

RL.11–12.3 Analyze the impact of the author's choices regarding how to develop and relate elements of a story or drama (e.g., where a story is set, how the action is ordered, how the characters are introduced and developed).

RL.11–12.5 Analyze how an author's choices concerning how to structure specific parts of a text (e.g., the choice of where to begin or end a story, the choice to provide a comedic or tragic resolution) contribute to its overall structure and meaning as well as its aesthetic impact.

ACTIVITY 2.10

PLAN

Materials: *Pygmalion*, sequel
Suggested Pacing: 2 50-minute class periods

TEACH

1 Begin by reading through the Learning Targets and Preview. If necessary, review traditional dramatic structure with students by drawing a pyramid diagram on the board and having students label the different points of the dramatic arc.

2 Read aloud one section from the sequel, asking students to be sure to **visualize** as they read along with you. Ask them to **take notes**, identifying the parts they can visualize most clearly.

3 For Analyzing the Plot Structure, pair more advanced students with students who need extra guidance. Suggest that they consider drawing a pyramid or using another visual method in order to analyze the play structure. Have students report their findings to the larger group.

4 Before they begin reading *Pygmalion*: The Sequel, direct students' attention to the quotation (in student step 4), which is an example of Shaw's advancement of the plot by summary. Ask students whether or not they agree or disagree with Shaw's interpretation of what Eliza would do. Then ask them how they would apply the theory of Cultural Criticism to this statement.

5 As students are reading, monitor their progress. Be sure they are engaged with the text and annotating with a star those lines that they are able to visualize most easily. Evaluate whether the selected reading mode is effective.

6 Point students to the Grammar & Usage box in the sidebar. Review rules for comma use with appositives and elements that interrupt a sentence. Discuss why the commas surrounding the phrase "and Higgins biologically attractive to a degree that overwhelms all her other instincts" are not grammatically required. Point out that Shaw uses them to enhance meaning and to give the reader further insight into what Eliza is thinking.

7 Vocabulary Development: Before students respond to the writing prompt, have them work with a partner to brainstorm words to define the concept of *artistic license*.

8 Have students analyze the photo of Cukor on the movie set with the actors. Ask them what they can tell about Cukor from the picture; for example, have them list traits conveyed by his body language. Guide student discussion to include some ways in which the director of a play works with actors in the same or in different ways than the director of a film would. Direct students to review their notes about the sequel to inform their writing.

9 Remind students to adhere to the genre conventions of a play script as they complete the writing prompt. Reiterate that students will build to a conclusion that thoughtfully reflects on what the characters have experienced and resolved in the story. Also remind them to be faithful to the plot Shaw spelled out, even though they will need to employ artistic license to create the dialogue.

10 Gauge student understanding of the material in this activity by having them complete Check Your Understanding and then share their postscripts with the class.

ASSESS

Review students' responses to the Check Your Understanding task. Make sure students are using details to convey their ideas. Check that they have incorporated a mix of exposition, description, and dialogue.

ADAPT

Consider placing students in pairs or small groups to help each other. Model how to complete the first few sections of the graphic organizer. When students have completed the task, encourage them to read aloud.

WRITING PROMPT: LITERARY

The following standards are addressed in the writing prompt:
- W.11–12.3
- W.11–12.5
- W.11–12.4

2.10

My Notes

VOCABULARY

LITERARY

Artistic license describes the practice of rewording dialogue, alteration of language, or reordering of plot of a text created by another artist. The purpose of using artistic license is to give a different approach to a text or to enhance the text.

Writing Prompt: Literary

Think about the dialogue that would be shared during this scene. Using artistic license, write a script that reflects Shaw's version of the play's ending. Consider key points in the plot that would have an impact on the ending. How does Shaw's ending resolve the conflict of the story? Be sure to:

- Follow Shaw's version of the story's resolution.
- Structure the ending so that it follows from and reflects on what has been experienced by the characters in the story.
- Use appropriate diction and tone that reflect the characters' personalities and conditions.
- Correctly use subtext and genre characteristics of a play.

Use a separate paper to brainstorm ideas for your script. Consider the following elements of a script as you brainstorm ideas.

- Title and List of Characters
- Setting
- Problem/Dialogue
- Narrative Arc
- Stage Directions

Director George Cukor coaches actors Audrey Hepburn and Rex Harrison during the musical production of *My Fair Lady*, 1964.

Check Your Understanding

How can an author or director stay true to a source material while also using artistic license?

College and Career Readiness Standards

W.11–12.3 Write narratives to develop real or imagined experiences or events using effective technique, well-chosen details, and well-structured event sequences.

Additional Standards Addressed:
RL.11–12.9, SL.11–12.1a, W.11–12.3b, W.11–12.3c, W.11–12.3d, W.11–12.3e, W.11–12.4, W.11–12.5

Examining the Archetypes

Learning Targets
- Draw connections between the key plot elements and archetypes presented in a myth and a play.
- Analyze how an author uses characterization, setting, and dialogue to communicate specific meanings and themes.
- Write an argument evaluating an author's interpretation of a myth.

Preview

In this activity, you will read excerpts from the play *Pygmalion* and make connections to archetypal elements found in Ovid's myth. You will then evaluate the effectiveness of the author's choices in the form of an argumentative essay.

Appling Archetypal Criticism

1. Reread the excerpts from Shaw's *Pygmalion*, considering how each excerpt does or does not represent the archetypes present in Ovid's myth. As you read the excerpts, put a star next to lines that connect to the archetypal characters of the creator and the created.

Act I Excerpts:

- THE NOTE TAKER. You see this creature with her kerbstone English: the English that will keep her in the gutter to the end of her days. Well, sir, in three months I could pass that girl off as a duchess at an ambassador's garden party. I could even get her a place as a lady's maid or shop assistant, which requires better English.

- HIGGINS. Yes, you squashed cabbage leaf, you disgrace to the noble architecture of these columns, you incarnate insult to the English language: I could pass you off as the Queen of Sheba.

Act II Excerpts:

- HIGGINS. *[carried away]* Yes: in six months—in three if she has a good ear and a quick tongue—I'll take her anywhere and pass her off as anything. We'll start today: now! this moment! Take her away and clean her, Mrs. Pearce.

- HIGGINS. *[deftly retrieving the handkerchief and intercepting her on her reluctant way to the door]* You're an ungrateful wicked girl. This is my return for offering to take you out of the gutter and dress you beautifully and make a lady of you.

- HIGGINS. What! That thing! Sacred, I assure you. *[Rising to explain]* You see, she'll be a pupil; and teaching would be impossible unless pupils were sacred. I've taught scores of American millionairesses how to speak English: the best-looking women in the world. I'm seasoned. They might as well be blocks of wood. *I* might as well be a block of wood.

Act III Excerpts:

- HIGGINS. Oh, I can't be bothered with young women. My idea of a lovable woman is something as like you as possible. I shall never get into the way of seriously liking young women: some habits lie too deep to be changed. *[Rising abruptly and walking about, jingling his money and his keys in his trouser pockets]* Besides, they're all idiots.

Learning Strategies

Paraphrasing
Peer Editing
Rereading
Revising
Summarizing

My Notes

College and Career Readiness Standards

Focus Standards:

RL.11–12.2 Determine two or more themes or central ideas of a text and analyze their development over the course of the text, including how they interact and build on one another to produce a complex account; provide an objective summary of the text.

RL.11–12.3 Analyze the impact of the author's choices regarding how to develop and relate elements of a story or drama (e.g., where a story is set, how the action is ordered, how the characters are introduced and developed).

PLAN

Materials: *Pygmalion*; students' summaries from Activity 2.4
Suggested Pacing: 2 50-minute class periods

TEACH

1 Remind students that the Pygmalion myth is an archetype. Explain that its characters and motif are repeated in many stories around the world.

2 Have students discuss stories they have encountered in independent readings that present archetypes and motifs also found in the Pygmalion myth.

3 Read through the Learning Targets and Preview with students. Discuss connections to the archetypal elements established in Ovid's myth.

4 Have students volunteer or assign them to read aloud the excerpts from the play. As each excerpt is read aloud, circulate around the room and make sure students are following along and marking the text as necessary. Then have students share their responses with the class.

5 In groups, instruct students to answer the questions in Working from the Text. All groups should then complete student step 3.

6 Point out the Grammar & Usage box in the sidebar. Remind students that a clause must contain a subject and a verb and that an independent clause must be able to stand alone and make sense by itself.

2.11

Compound Sentences

Compound sentences have two or more independent clauses. When Shaw writes, "I shall never get into the way of seriously liking young women: some habits lie too deep to be changed," he creates a compound sentence. In this case, a colon joins the two clauses. Independent clauses can also be joined by a semicolon or by a comma and a coordinating conjunction (e.g., *for*, *and*, *but*).

Find and underline two more examples of compound sentences in the text.

My Notes

_____

_____

_____

_____

_____

_____

_____

_____

_____

_____

_____

_____

_____

_____

_____

_____

_____

_____

_____

Act V Excerpts:

- LIZA. *[continuing]* It was just like learning to dance in the fashionable way: there was nothing more than that in it. But do you know what began my real education?

  PICKERING. What?

  ELIZA. *[stopping her work for a moment]* Your calling me Miss Doolittle that day when I first came to Wimpole Street. That was the beginning of self-respect for me.

  [She resumes her stitching] And there were a hundred little things you never noticed, because they came naturally to you. Things about standing up and taking off your hat and opening doors—

- ELIZA. I know. I am not blaming him. It is his way, isn't it? But it made such a difference to me that you didn't do it. You see, really and truly, apart from the things anyone can pick up (the dressing and the proper way of speaking, and so on), the difference between a lady and a flower girl is not how she behaves, but how she's treated. I shall always be a flower girl to Professor Higgins, because he always treats me as a flower girl, and always will; but I know I can be a lady to you, because you always treat me as a lady, and always will.

- ELIZA. You never thought of the trouble it would make for me.

  HIGGINS. Would the world ever have been made if its maker had been afraid of making trouble? Making life means making trouble. There's only one way of escaping trouble; and that's killing things. Cowards, you notice, are always shrieking to have troublesome people killed.

- HIGGINS. *[wondering at her]* By George, Eliza, I said I'd make a woman of you; and I have.
  I like you like this.

Working from the Text

2. After reading the excerpts, respond to the following questions in your Reader/Writer Notebook:

   - Act I: What is Higgins's (the Note Taker's) opinion of himself and of Eliza? What textual clues reveal this opinion?

   - Act II: Through most of the myth, Pygmalion's ideal woman is ivory, not human. She fits the archetype of the created. How do Higgins's words echo this aspect of the myth?

   - Act III: How was Eliza's transformation different from what she expected?

   - Act V: How does Higgins's ego affect his point of view and perception of Eliza?

3. Return to the summary of Ovid's myth that you wrote for Activity 2.3. Review the text of the myth and your summary. Working with a writing partner, answer these reflective questions:

   - How has Shaw included the character of the creator?

   - How has Shaw included the character of the created?

   - How has Shaw defined the relationship between the creator and the creation?

   - How has Shaw defined the nature of the transformation?

College and Career Readiness Standards

W.11–12.1 Write arguments to support claims in an analysis of substantive topics or texts, using valid reasoning and relevant and sufficient evidence.

Additional Standards Addressed:

RL.11–12.1, RL.11–12.7, SL.11–12.1c, W.11–12.1a, W.11–12.1b, W.11–12.1c, W.11–12.1d, W.11–12.1e, W.11–12.5, W.11–12.9

2.11

☑ Check Your Understanding

How effectively does Shaw adapt or alter the original Pygmalion myth? Use text evidence to support your response.

✒ Writing Prompt: Argumentative

Review your summary of Ovid's version of the myth and your notes on these excerpts. To what extent does Shaw adhere to or depart from the Pygmalion archetype? How does recognizing the archetype advance or complicate the reading? Write an argumentative essay to defend your analysis of Shaw's use of the Pygmalion archetype. Be sure to:

- Introduce an analytical claim that is specific, clear, and compelling.
- Include convincing and relevant examples from both Ovid and Shaw to support your claim.
- Establish and maintain a formal style and objective tone.
- Observe the conventions of academic writing.
- Strategically use transitions to connect ideas and explain the relationship between the claim and the evidence.
- Provide a concluding statement that summarizes the argument presented.

Revising and Editing

After you have completed your draft, collaborate with a writing partner to enhance your drafts. Complete these next two steps of the writing process:

- REVISE: Review the content by considering the supporting evidence and logical organization of the essay. Evaluate the introduction, development, and conclusion of the argument based on the bullets in the writing prompt.
- EDIT: Correct any grammar, usage, mechanical, or spelling errors. Give special attention to syntax, correctly punctuating compound sentences.

Peer Review Checklist

You may want to use a checklist to guide your peer sharing and responding to produce a well-organized, well-supported essay demonstrating maturity of language and insight into Archetypal Criticism.

☐ Is the claim clearly stated in an engaging way?

☐ Is there plenty of convincing and relevant evidence, with multiple examples from both Ovid and Shaw?

☐ Is the relationship between the claim and the evidence logical and are ideas well-connected?

☐ Is the tone consistently interesting, formal, and impartial?

☐ Is the essay well-structured, with an effective introduction, well-developed claim, and a strong conclusion that summarizes the argument?

My Notes

📖 INDEPENDENT READING LINK

Read and Discuss

Review your notes from your independent reading plan in Activity 2.1. Watch a film adaption of your independent reading text. Jot down how narrative elements are presented in the original text and film versions respectively. Compare how the author and filmmaker handled dialogue, character, exposition, and the interpretations of the characters. If you were the filmmaker, what might you have done differently? Discuss your observations with a peer and record notes of your discussion in your Reader/Writer Notebook.

✒ WRITING PROMPT: ARGUMENTATIVE

The following standards are addressed in the writing prompt:

- W.11–12.1
- W.11–12.1a
- W.11–12.1b
- W.11–12.1c
- W.11–12.1d
- W.11–12.1e

ACTIVITY 2.11 continued

7 Have students respond to the Check Your Understanding.

8 As students turn to the writing prompt, remind them to use their notes to help them form their opinion about whether Shaw adhered to or departed from the Pygmalion archetype.

9 Identify pairs of students for **peer editing** and sharing and responding. For editing purposes, encourage students to focus on sentence variety and correct use of the compound sentence.

10 After students have made their editing checklists, pair them up to allow them to compare their checklists with a partner.

11 Have students complete the Independent Reading Link at home (watching a film version of their text).

ASSESS

Review students' responses to the Check Your Understanding for an evaluative statement about Shaw's use of archetypes that effectively compares the play and the myth. Use the writing prompt to determine whether students thoughtfully defend their opinion about Shaw's use of the Pygmalion archetype. Student essays should introduce a thesis, defend that thesis in body paragraphs, and conclude with a summary of their argument's main points.

ADAPT

If students need additional help stating and defending their opinion in writing, have students work in small groups to review the components of their earlier debate experience. Encourage them to consider how textual evidence supported a strong argument in debate, and how that could inform their approaches to a written argument.

© 2021 College Board. All rights reserved.

PLAN

Materials: "Talkin' 'bout a Revolution" by Tracy Chapman; lyrics for two additional songs (teacher-selected)

Suggested Pacing: 2 50-minute class periods

TEACH

1 Read through the Learning Targets and Preview with students.

2 Read aloud Marxist Criticism, pausing to make connections to students' prior knowledge in history and economics, and also referencing the Vocabulary sidebar. Have students paraphrase the definition of Marxist Criticism. Engage students in a discussion of the meaning of this definition and the context in which it is used. Then have students conduct a close reading of the assumptions and common questions associated with a Marxist critical perspective.

3 Vocabulary Development: Direct students to the Word Connections box. Have students consider the etymology of the word *economics* and then engage them in a brief discussion. Ask how they think economics is like "managing a house"? Guide students to briefly discuss and take notes on the insights the etymology of the word gives them into the concept of economics.

 TEACHER TO TEACHER

You may want to show a film clip to demonstrate ideas about Marxist Criticism. *Nine to Five*, Scene 2: "A New Job" (start at 2:33, stop at 6:47) is a good possibility. This clip can help anticipate issues raised using a Marxist critical perspective. After the viewing, ask students to share their initial responses to the clip in a Quickwrite.

ACTIVITY 2.12
From a Marxist Perspective

Learning Strategies

Discussion Groups
Graphic Organizer
Paraphrasing
SOAPSTone
Summarizing
Quickwrite

WORD CONNECTIONS

Etymology
Economics is the science that deals with the production, distribution, and consumption of wealth. The term came into usage in 1792, derived from the adjective *economic*. The word comes from the ancient Greek *oikonomos*, a combination of *oikos*, "house," and *nemein*, "to manage."

VOCABULARY

LITERARY
Marxist Criticism asserts that economics provides the foundation for all social, political, and ideological reality. Economic inequality is a power structure that drives history and influences differences in religion, race, ethnicity, and gender.

Learning Targets

- Conduct research and synthesize information from multiple sources to develop an understanding of Marxist Criticism.
- Analyze an author's message and draw connections to society's economic structures.

Preview

In this activity, you will read about Marxist critical theory and its influence on ideas about economics, culture, and society. You will then apply your understanding by analyzing song lyrics through a Marxist lens. Finally, you will collaboratively research the implications of social and economic class and share your findings with your peers.

Marxist Criticism

Karl Marx lived from 1818 to 1883. During his life, he was a philosopher, economist, political theorist, historian, and author whose work focused on how social classes struggle and how the accumulation of wealth and power enables an economic minority to dominate a working-class majority. He proposed that social conditions result from economic and political conditions. According to Marxist critics, economic conditions heavily influence a culture's literature.

Marxist Criticism asserts that economics is the foundation for all social, political, and ideological reality. Marxist critics would argue that economic inequalities create a power structure that drives history and influences differences in religion, race, ethnicity, and gender. The following are common principles of Marxist Criticism:

- Human relations are based on the struggle for economic power.
- The basic struggle in human society is between the "haves" and the "have nots."

Marxist Literary Criticism looks at ways in which a text reveals the oppression of the working class or poor by a dominant economic elite. Analyzing a text from a Marxist perspective helps the reader to evaluate how social class affects a story. Among questions that might be asked when analyzing a text through a Marxist Criticism lens are the following:

- Whose viewpoint is represented in the text (that of the poor, middle class, or wealthy)—that is, whose story gets told?
- What values are represented for each of the social classes (poor, middle class, wealthy)?
- What economic and social values do the main characters hold?
- Who is the audience, and what does the text suggest about their values?
- Who is the author and how might the author's own class or background influence the telling of the story?

College and Career Readiness Standards

Focus Standards:

RL.11–12.2 Determine two or more themes or central ideas of a text and analyze their development over the course of the text, including how they interact and build on one another to produce a complex account; provide an objective summary of the text.

W.11–12.8 Gather relevant information from multiple authoritative print and digital sources, using advanced searches effectively; assess the strengths and limitations of each source in terms of the task, purpose, and audience; integrate information into the text selectively to maintain the flow of ideas, avoiding plagiarism and overreliance on any one source and following a standard format for citation.

✅ Focus on the Sentence

Write two complete sentences in response to what you have learned so far about Marxist Criticism. The first should be a statement that paraphrases the definition of Marxist Criticism in your own words. The second should be a question you have about Marxist Criticism.

Statement: Marxist criticism is a formal way of questioning the class struggles
presented in literature.

Question: Can you apply Marxist criticism to all texts?

Applying Marxist Criticism

1. To begin your study of Marxist Criticism, read the lyrics to Tracy Chapman's song "Talkin' 'bout a Revolution." As you use SOAPSTone to analyze the lyrics, try to keep in mind the principles of Marxist Criticism.

Speaker	The speaker could be a "have," for she uses the pronoun "they." Or the speaker could be a "have not" who is speaking about other "have nots."
Occasion	The speaker is warning the "haves" that the "have nots" are ready to revolt, to "rise up and take what's theirs."
Audience	The audience is most likely the "haves."
Purpose	The purpose could be to warn the "haves" that the "have nots" are ready to revolt.
Subject	Poor people are tired of economic disparity and are ready to "rise up."
Tone	threatening cautionary

2. Based on your analysis, how effective is the songwriter's message? Do you think her audience found her message to be compelling?

🔵 INDEPENDENT READING LINK

Read and Research

Apply your research from this activity to your independent reading text. Consider the economic values and attitudes of the characters in your independent reading. Add your notes to the chart you started in this activity to broaden your understanding of how such perspectives and attitudes are conveyed in literature.

My Notes

_____

_____

_____

_____

_____

_____

_____

_____

_____

_____

_____

_____

_____

_____

_____

_____

_____

_____

_____

_____

_____

_____

4 Have students work individually to complete the Focus on the Sentence activity. If any students are having trouble coming up with a statement or a question, have them reread the definition of Marxist Criticism and practice restating the paragraph in their own words.

5 Next, provide students the lyrics to "Talkin' 'bout a Revolution" by Tracy Chapman (available online). Once students have completed their analysis using the **SOAPSTone** chart, organize small groups to employ Marxist Criticism to analyze the text of the lyrics.

6 Ask the groups to report back for a class discussion. Encourage discussion by asking, *What connections can be made between Tracy Chapman's song lyrics and Marxist Criticism?* To extend students' discussion of tone and how Marxist Criticism deals with it, Chapman's recording creates an interesting contrast to the tone of the lyrics themselves.

7 To help students clarify their own thoughts about the importance of money and power, you could provide them with lyrics to at least two other songs. It would be best if you chose songs that present opposing viewpoints; for example, you might present "Can't Buy Me Love" in contrast with "Money (That's What I Want)."

LEVELED DIFFERENTIATED INSTRUCTION

Extend Break students into small groups and have each group choose a song lyric from among those presented in the activity. Using the **On-the-Spot Research** graphic organizer, have members of each group collaborate on identifying how the speaker in the song exhibits archetypal or stereotypical characteristics.

College and Career Readiness Standards

Additional Standards Addressed:
RL.11–12.3, RL.11–12.7, SL.11–12.1d, W.11–12.7, L.11–12.6

8 Discuss the On the Spot Research prompt with students. You may want to set aside time in the computer lab or media center for students to do research. Help them identify appropriate search terms. For general information, students may want to search on terms such as *wealth* and *poverty* or *wealth* and *power*. The idea of the hidden rules in society that guide social and economic behavior has been popularized by author Ruby Payne. To explore this topic and its connections to Archetypal and Marxist Criticism, have students conduct an online search using the phrase *hidden rules of poverty*.

9 After students complete their research and their **graphic organizers**, ask them to respond to the bulleted questions.

10 Have students compile their lists for the Check Your Understanding prompt and share them with a partner.

11 Remind students to complete the Independent Reading Link.

ASSESS

Review students' lists of key elements in Marxist Criticism in the Check Your Understanding task. They should have accurately synthesized several of the elements of Marxist Criticism introduced in this activity.

ADAPT

If students need additional help relating Marxist Criticism to the content in their graphic organizers, prompt them to look for words such as *wealth*, *poverty*, *privilege,* or phrases such as "haves" and "have nots."

2.12

On the Spot Research

3. Marxist Criticism considers characters' perspectives in terms of economic and social status. It looks at the "hidden rules" that are characteristic of each economic and social class. With a partner, conduct research on the concept of "hidden rules" to describe attitudes of each of these groups toward the topics listed in the following graphic organizer.

	Poor	Middle Class	Wealthy
Money			
Use of Time			
Education			
Family Structure			
Language			

4. Respond to the following questions, using the information from your research.

- What are the "hidden rules" for each social or economic class? Do you agree that these rules are hidden? Why or why not?

- What connections can you make between these rules and Marxist Criticism?

- Are these differences archetypal or stereotypical? Explain.

☑ Check Your Understanding

In your own words write a list of the key elements and considerations of Marxist Criticism. Use your Focus on the Sentence response as a starting point. Share your list with a partner.

Money, Power, and Class in *Pygmalion*

Learning Strategies

Discussion Groups
Graphic Organizer
Think-Pair-Share

Learning Targets

- Analyze characterization and plot development through the Marxist perspective.
- Collaboratively analyze the effects of social class, power, and money on characters in the text.
- Explain how a critical perspective affects a reader's understanding of the meaning of a text.

Preview

In this activity, you will analyze and discuss the ways in which social class, wealth, and power dynamics impact the plot and character development of Shaw's *Pygmalion*. You will then reflect on the text from a Marxist critical perspective and explain your new understanding in the form of a written response.

Power

1. Create a graphic to illustrate the hierarchy of power in *Pygmalion*. In other words, visually represent a ranking of who has the most power to who has the least power. In addition to the major characters (Higgins, Pickering, and Eliza), be sure to include the minor characters, such as Mrs. Pearce, Mrs. Higgins, Mr. Doolittle, Freddy, Clara, and Mrs. Eynsford Hill. Include on your graphic an explanation as to why some of the characters have power while others do not.

Money

2. Create a graphic ranking the characters in *Pygmalion* according to their degree of power (highest to lowest), their social class (highest to lowest), and their wealth (richest to poorest). As you work to rank the characters, note whether the degree of wealth a character has correlates to their power. Does power always correlate with greater wealth and higher social class?

Social Class

3. With your discussion group analyze how social class, distribution of wealth, and power dynamics are represented through the characters in *Pygmalion*. Identify the social classes represented in *Pygmalion*.

- Who is in each class?
- What do you think Shaw thought of class divisions?
- What in the text makes you think this?
- If you need additional support, refer to your notes from the previous activity about how to apply Marxist Criticism.

My Notes

ACTIVITY 2.13

PLAN

Materials: *Pygmalion*; chart paper; markers/crayons
Suggested Pacing: 1 50-minute class period

TEACH

1 Read through the Learning Targets and Preview with students. Briefly review what they learned about Marxist Criticism in the previous activity.

2 Divide students into small groups.

3 Have each group read through the questions, or create a **graphic organizer**, as directed in student steps 1–3. Invite groups to consider how intertwined the three concepts are.

4 Ask the groups to prepare short presentations, supporting their graphic illustrations with explanations (**think-pair-share**). These presentations will help students see the connections among power, money, and social class.

5 Students should now return to the definition of Marxist Criticism and apply it to Shaw's play. Lead the class in a discussion of their discoveries.

6 Continue the discussion by asking what other qualities can confer power. Gender? Intelligence? Talent? Have students brainstorm other sources of power, and then connect them to social class and money. Are they ever independent of these things? Are they sometimes independent?

 TEACHER TO TEACHER

As you approach the end of the unit, consider showing several scenes from Cukor's 1964 musical adaptation of *Pygmalion*, *My Fair Lady*, that illustrate the different critical frameworks discussed in class. Good choices include the Ascot race scene, the ball, and Alfred Doolittle's return.

College and Career Readiness Standards

Focus Standards:

RL.11–12.3 Analyze the impact of the author's choices regarding how to develop and relate elements of a story or drama (e.g., where a story is set, how the action is ordered, how the characters are introduced and developed).

W.11–12.2 Write informative/exploratory texts to examine and convey complex ideas, concepts, and information clearly and accurately through the effective selection, organization, and analysis of content.

Additional Standards Addressed:

RL.11–12.2, RL.11–12.6, W.11–12.2a, W.11–12.2b, W.11–12.2c, W.11–12.2d, W.11–12.2e, W.11–12.2f, SL.11–12.1b

7 Ask students to complete Check Your Understanding. Invite volunteers to share their responses with the class.

8 Before students write responses to the writing prompt, remind them of Marxist Criticism and its assumptions.

9 Have students complete the Independent Reading Checkpoint.

LEVELED DIFFERENTIATED INSTRUCTION

These activities can be used to support students in synthesizing key concepts in Marxist Criticism.

Beginning Before writing, have students come up with three to five questions that they think a person would ask when approaching a text using a Marxist framework.

Developing Encourage students to look up Marxist terminology (such as "bourgeoisie," "commodity," "worker") and incorporate these words into their responses.

Expanding Students may benefit from creating a SIFT examining stylistic elements, symbolism, and imagery in a chosen passage of text.

ASSESS

In student responses to the writing prompt, look for a clearly written thesis statement supported by textual evidence that relates Marxist Criticism to literature, incorporating proper terminology and academic vocabulary.

ADAPT

If students need additional help to analyze literature through a Marxist lens, have pairs review their close read of *Pygmalion* from Activity 2.11. Model the process by considering how lines such as "Take her away and clean her, Mrs. Pearce" show class conflict.

2.13

My Notes

☑ Check Your Understanding

Select one of the characters that you have analyzed and summarize the transformation the character undergoes over the course of the play. Consider how the following factors affect the character:

- external factors (money, historical context, and social class)
- internal factors (psychology, personality)

✍ Writing Prompt: Informational

In this activity, you analyzed *Pygmalion* from a Marxist perspective to evaluate how money, power, and social class are represented. How can applying critical perspectives create a new understanding of a literary work? Explain how using a critical lens changes or enhances a reader's understanding of the play. Be sure to:

- Introduce a clear thesis and continue to build on the thesis, using ideas, concepts, and information to create a unified whole.
- Organize your ideas clearly, using transitional words and phrases to connect the ideas.
- Use precise language to convey ideas and manage the complexity of the subject.
- Maintain an engaging, formal, and objective tone, while using the standard English conventions of mechanics and usage.
- Cite relevant textual evidence to support your explanation.
- Provide a logical conclusion that summarizes the new insights gained from applying Marxist Criticism.

⏱ Independent Reading Checkpoint

Review your independent reading and consider which critical perspective would provide the most interesting analysis of the reading (Reader Response Criticism, Cultural Criticism, Archetypal Criticism, or Marxist Criticism). How might you apply this perspective to transform your reading into a staged play? Record your ideas in your Reader/Writer Notebook.

✍ WRITING PROMPT: INFORMATIONAL

The following standards are addressed in the writing prompt:

- RL.11–12.1
- RL.11–12.2
- W.11–12.2a
- W.11–12.2b
- W.11–12.2c
- W.11–12.2d
- W.11–12.2e
- W.11–12.2f

Illuminating *Pygmalion*

© 2021 College Board. All rights reserved.

☑ ASSIGNMENT

Work with a partner to write a script that transforms a scene from *Pygmalion* so that it reflects one of the critical perspectives you have studied. You will also write a reflection analyzing and evaluating your process and product.

Planning and Prewriting: Read and choose a scene to transform.	■ Which scene from *Pygmalion* gives the best opportunities to convey a clear and interesting interpretation of the text? ■ Which of the critical perspectives that you have encountered so far (Reader Response Criticism, Cultural Criticism, Archetypal Criticism, or Marxist Criticism) is the best choice for the scene you have selected? ■ What elements of the play will you change to emphasize the critical perspective, and how will it affect that scene? ■ What parts of using a critical lens to create a script are especially challenging?
Drafting: Write a draft of your script.	■ How will you approach your writing so that your script has both dialogue and subtext (two columns, for instance, or subtext in parentheses)? ■ How will you use dialogue to show new elements and perspectives that address your chosen critical perspective? ■ What can you include to help demonstrate the subtext of the scene (tone of voice, placement of actors, body language, and so on)? ■ How can you use your thinking as you plan and draft as part of your reflective analysis and evaluation? ■ How can you use technology to enhance your formatting and presentation of the script?
Evaluating and Revising Your Draft: Review and improve your draft.	■ How well do the changes that you made to the scene help to highlight your chosen critical perspective? ■ How can you work with peers and with the Scoring Guide to help you determine what needs to be added or changed?
Checking and Editing for Publication: Confirm that your final draft is technically accurate.	■ How will you review your work to make sure that you have followed the genre conventions of a play script? ■ What resources can you use to correct errors in spelling, conventions, grammar, style, and formatting?

Reflection

In this assignment, you were asked to transform a dramatic scene. Drama is a deeply interactive process between the writer and the audience; how effective is drama as a way to present ideas? How can different staging and acting choices create a new interpretation of a play? How does an audience's perspective mold and affect an interpretation or understanding of ideas?

College and Career Readiness Standards

Focus Standards:

W.11–12.3 Write narratives to develop real or imagined experiences or events using effective technique, well-chosen details, and well-structured event sequences.

W.11–12.4 Produce clear and coherent writing in which the development, organization, and style are appropriate to task, purpose, and audience.

W.11–12.5 Develop and strengthen writing as needed by planning, revising, editing, rewriting, or trying a new approach, focusing on addressing what is most significant for a specific purpose and audience. (Editing for conventions should demonstrate command of Language standards 1–3 up to and including grades 11–12 here.)

EMBEDDED ASSESSMENT 1

Suggested Pacing: 1 50-minute class period

⭐ TEACHER TO TEACHER

If you want or need to modify this Embedded Assessment by changing the assignment for some or all of your students, be sure that you have properly scaffolded the necessary skills and knowledge.

1 Assignment: Review the assignment with the class, and have students mark the text to identify all the requirements.

2 Planning and Prewriting: Encourage students to review all the critical perspectives before choosing one.

3 Drafting: Remind students that the critical perspective they've selected is not set in stone. If they find that the lens is not working as they draft, they can restart using another.

4 If needed, conduct writing conferences to ensure appropriate responses. Consider mini-lessons in writing dialogue, applying a particular critical perspective, and inclusion of all four elements of a dramatic script: format, dialogue, problem, stage directions.

5 Evaluating and Revising: Remind students to use the Scoring Guide criteria to ensure they have met the expectations for this assessment.

6 Checking and Editing: Direct students to revisit the Word Wall to examine newly acquired vocabulary. Have them incorporate those words into their drafts. Encourage students to review their drafts to ensure that they are using and spelling basic vocabulary words correctly.

7 Reflection: Have students respond to the reflection questions. Decide whether to collect their responses as part of the assignment.

8 Portfolio: All notes for and drafts of the script should be collected and presented together to show the process students completed in successfully accomplishing the task.

SCORING GUIDE

When you score the Embedded Assessment, you may wish to download and print copies of the Scoring Guide from Springboard Digital. This way, you can have a copy to make for each student's work.

SCORING GUIDE

Scoring Criteria	Exemplary	Proficient	Emerging	Incomplete
Ideas	The script • portrays a scene that lends itself well to the chosen critical perspective. • transforms the scene, revealing sophisticated understanding of the critical perspective. • offers thorough and well-considered reflection about choices made and insights into how the perspective affects the drama.	The script • portrays an appropriate scene for the chosen critical perspective. • transforms the scene in a way that shows adequate comprehension of the critical perspective. • includes some reflection that considers choices made and how the perspective affects the drama.	The script • portrays a scene that incompletely fits well with the chosen critical perspective. • changes the scene in ways that shows minimal understanding of the critical perspective. • includes a reflection that provides limited discussion of choices made and shows a vague grasp of how the perspective affects the drama.	The script • portrays a scene that does not fit well with the chosen critical perspective. • does not change the scene to show an understanding of the critical perspective and • does not include a reflection.
Structure	The script • follows an organization that clearly identifies dialogue, stage directions, and subtext. • smoothly incorporates new elements into the scene while maintaining an engaging plot. • includes an insightful reflection.	The script • follows an organization that adequately separates dialogue from stage directions and subtext. • incorporates new elements into the scene while maintaining a coherent plot. • includes some reflection.	The script • is not organized to show clear distinctions between dialogue, stage directions, and subtext. • includes changes that make the scene difficult to follow. • includes a weak or superficial reflection.	The script • is disorganized and does not show clear distinctions between dialogue, stage directions, and subtext. • is missing elements that make the scene difficult to follow • includes no reflection.
Use of Language	The script • crafts dialogue that maintains consistent character voice from the original text. • incorporates creative techniques to enhance meaning and add interest. • demonstrates strong control and mastery of standard writing conventions.	The script • includes dialogue that largely maintains character voice from the original text. • incorporates some creative techniques to add interest. • demonstrates control of writing conventions but may contain minor errors that do not interfere with meaning.	The script • includes dialogue that varies from the original text. • does not successfully incorporate creative techniques to add interest; techniques used may interfere with meaning. • contains frequent errors in standard writing conventions that interfere with meaning.	The script • includes dialogue that does not match the text or fit the scene. • does not creatively use techniques to add interest. • contains numerous errors in standard writing conventions that interfere with meaning.

College and Career Readiness Standards

W.11–12.9 Draw evidence from literary or informational texts to support analysis, reflection, and research.

W.11–12.10 Write routinely over extended time frames (time for research, reflection, and revision) and shorter time frames (a single sitting or a day or two) for a range of tasks, purposes, and audiences.

Unpacking Embedded Assessment 2

Learning Targets

- Reflect on big ideas for the second half of the unit.
- Create a plan for reading independently.
- Identify and analyze the skills and knowledge needed to complete Embedded Assessment 2 successfully.

Preview

In this activity, you will review the Essential Questions and create an independent reading plan for the second half of the unit.

Learning Strategies

Close Reading
Graphic Organizer
Marking the Text
Summarize
Think-Pair-Share

My Notes

Making Observations

You have considered archetypes, power struggles, and wealth while examining and transforming a text. You have considered the social and cultural implications of presenting a text from a particular perspective. In the second half of this unit, you will expand your toolbox of critical theories by practicing analysis from another critical perspective: Feminist Criticism. In addition, you will encounter examples of how that theory is applied to a familiar story and a film, as models for applying that perspective to another work of literary merit.

Essential Questions

Review the Essential Questions for this unit. How would you answer them now?

1. How do writers develop great characters?
2. How does a person's environment affect his or her identity?
3. How does power affect people's interactions and relationships?

Unpacking Embedded Assessment 2

Closely read the assignment for Embedded Assessment 2: Applying a Critical Perspective and summarize the major elements in your Reader/Writer Notebook.

Your assignment is to write an analytical essay applying the Feminist Critical Perspective to a short story. You have two stories to read and choose from, "The Story of an Hour" by Kate Chopin and "The Chaser" by John Collier.

What knowledge must you have to succeed on Embedded Assessment 2? Summarize in your own words what you will need to know for this assessment. With your class, create a graphic organizer that represents the skills and knowledge you will need to accomplish this task. To help you complete your graphic organizer, be sure to review the criteria in the Scoring Guide.

Planning Independent Reading

Select a text for independent reading that lends itself to analysis from a feminist perspective. Authors for consideration might include Jane Austen, F. Scott Fitzgerald, Margaret Atwood, and Alice Walker, among others. Once you have selected a text, research the author's background and write a short reflection about how the author's circumstances may influence his or her writing.

College and Career Readiness Standards

Focus Standards:

RI.11–12.4 Determine the meaning of words and phrases as they are used in a text, including figurative, connotative, and technical meanings; analyze how an author uses and refines the meaning of a key term or terms over the course of a text (e.g., how Madison defines faction in Federalist No. 10).

W.11–12.10 Write routinely over extended time frames (time for research, reflection, and revision) and shorter time frames (a single sitting or a day or two) for a range of tasks, purposes, and audiences.

Additional Standards Addressed:

SL.11–12.1b, W.11–12.7

PLAN

Materials: poster paper or display for unpacking Embedded Assessment 2
Suggested Pacing: 1 50-minute class period

TEACH

1 Ask students to **think-pair-share** responses to the Essential Questions, considering how their answers may have changed.

2 Ask a volunteer to read aloud the Making Observations section. Ask everyone to write down one question they have about Feminist Criticism.

3 Ask students to find the Embedded Assessment 2 assignment and Scoring Guide. Lead them through a **close reading** of the assignment, steps, and Scoring Guide criteria. Have students **mark the text** by underlining the places in the text that mention a skill or knowledge necessary to succeed on the Embedded Assessment.

4 Instruct students to **summarize/ paraphrase** with a partner or small group what they have underlined. As you conduct a large-group discussion, create a web **graphic organizer** that lists the knowledge and skills.

5 Revisit the web graphic organizer throughout the unit to reinforce and practice skills.

6 Direct the students to the Planning Independent Reading section. Remind them that they will be writing about the text from a feminist perspective.

ASSESS

Ensure that students understand the expectations, skills, and knowledge they will need to complete the assessment by reviewing summaries with the students. Evaluate how closely their summaries capture the skills and knowledge necessary for the Embedded Assessment.

ADAPT

If students need help writing a reflection about their independent reading selection, let them work in pairs to ask and answer questions of each other before writing.

From a Feminist Perspective

PLAN

Suggested Pacing: 1 50-minute class period

TEACH

1 Review the Learning Targets with students.

2 Read aloud the Preview. Tell students that they will be using a **KWHL** chart in this activity. Remind them to keep track of the L column.

3 Ask students to **activate prior knowledge** about writing from a feminist perspective. Summarize that knowledge as a class.

4 Vocabulary Development: Discuss the Word Connections with students. Ask them how the words are similar. Then ask them to think of other words that share the Latin word *femina*. As an extension, have students complete the **Roots and Affixes Brainstorm** graphic organizer.

5 Introduce the phrase "feminist lens" and ask students what they think using a feminist lens means.

6 Ask the students to form small **discussion groups** to talk about the points in the Feminist Criticism section. Ask them to share one example from a text they have read or from real life.

7 As part of a **think-pair-share** activity, have students complete student step 1 individually. Then ask students to work in pairs and share their paraphrases. Ask partners to note any missed concepts or paraphrases that may not be clear.

8 After they have worked in pairs, ask the students if there were any points they found especially difficult or challenging to paraphrase. Have students share these points and see if the class can come up with a way to paraphrase them.

Learning Strategies

Activating Prior Knowledge
Discussion Groups
KWHL
Marking the Text
Quickwrite
Think-Pair-Share

Learning Targets

- Develop and apply an understanding of key concepts and vocabulary related to the study of Feminist Criticism.
- Conduct research to answer self-generated questions about Feminist Criticism.
- Deliver a logically structured oral presentation of research.

Preview

In this activity, you will learn about the feminist critical perspective. You will collaboratively develop questions for informal research and synthesize your findings in the form of a summary. Then you will share your response with your peers and reflect on how the feminist lens can be used to analyze texts.

VOCABULARY

LITERARY
Feminist Criticism focuses on relationships between genders. It examines the patterns of thought, behavior, values, enfranchisement, and power in relations between and within the sexes.

ACADEMIC
A **patriarchal** society is one in which men have greater power and influence than women.
Enfranchisement means having the rights of citizenship, such as the right to vote.

WORD CONNECTIONS

Word Relationships
Feminist is an adjective derived from the Latin word *femina*, meaning "woman." Other words derived from *femina* include *feminine*, *femininely*, *feminineness*, *femininity*, and *female*.

Feminist Criticism

The perspective that you will study in this half of the unit is Feminist Criticism, which focuses on relationships between genders. It evaluates the impact of patriarchy on both men and women. It also analyzes how the lack of enfranchisement may limit the role women play in public and economic life. Feminist criticism encourages an examination of the patterns of thought, behavior, values, and power in relations between and within the sexes. For example, a feminist reading of *Pygmalion* may emphasize the idea of power relationships between the men and women of the play. Following are some key concepts in Feminist Criticism:

- A pervasively patriarchal society conveys the notion of male dominance through the images of women in its texts.
- Many literary texts lack complex female figures, as they are written from a masculine point of view.
- Issues of gender and sexuality are central to artistic expression.
- Without enfranchisement, the choices open to women may be limited and narrow.
- Fictional portrayals of female characters often reflect and reinforce stereotypical attitudes toward women.
- The feminine point of view has often been devalued by society.
- Texts created by women may have different viewpoints than texts created by men.

1. **Quickwrite:** Briefly paraphrase the key concepts of Feminist Criticism in your own words.

College and Career Readiness Standards

Focus Standards:

RL.11–12.2 Determine two or more themes or central ideas of a text and analyze their development over the course of the text, including how they interact and build on one another to produce a complex account; provide an objective summary of the text.

L.11–12.6 Acquire and use accurately general academic and domain-specific words and phrases, sufficient for reading, writing, speaking, and listening at the college and career readiness level; demonstrate independence in gathering vocabulary knowledge when considering a word or phrase important to comprehension or expression.

2. Use the key concepts information and your prior knowledge to add notes to your KWHL chart.

- K: What do you know about feminist criticism? Add what you know based on your reading and prior knowledge to column "K."
- W: What do you want to know about feminist criticism? Add your questions to column "W." These will serve as preliminary research questions.

Feminist Criticism			
K: What Do I Know?	**W: What Do I Want to Know?**	**H: How Can I Learn More?**	**L: What I Have Learned?**
	Are men and women equally represented in texts?	Conduct research on the Bechdel test to understand how women are represented in film.	

College and Career Readiness Standards

SL.11–12.1 Initiate and participate effectively in a range of collaborative discussions (one-on-one, in groups, and teacher-led) with diverse partners on grades 11–12 topics, texts, and issues, building on others' ideas and expressing their own clearly and persuasively.

W.11–12.7 Conduct short as well as more sustained research projects to answer a question (including a self-generated question) or solve a problem; narrow or broaden the inquiry when appropriate; synthesize multiple sources on the subject, demonstrating understanding of the subject under investigation.

Additional Standards Addressed:

SL.11–12.6, W.11–12.4

LEVELED DIFFERENTIATED INSTRUCTION

Some students may need additional support speaking and writing about Feminist Criticism.

Beginning Have students consult the English/Spanish glossary in the Resources section (or a dictionary in their primary language) to clarify vocabulary words and other terms. Consider using activities from this unit's corresponding Language Workshop to help students develop vocabulary more deeply.

Developing Ask students who are challenged by the Quickwrite to work with another student using the **Conversation for Quickwrite** graphic organizer. Tell them to listen to one another summarize Feminist Criticism and write down any key words they think are important. After they have finished their independent summaries, review their work and discuss the use of their keywords.

Extend Have students write a journal entry in which they discuss the feminist perspective and what it means to them in their own lives.

9 Draw the students' attention to the KWHL chart. Ask them to list at least one question in the W column that encourages further inquiry. Tell them to review the points of Feminist Criticism if they need help focusing in on an issue that intrigues or challenges them.

10 After they have formulated their questions, have the students return to their discussion groups for the On the Spot Research. Remind them that everyone in the group should participate. Point out that the discussion can give them insights to add to their L column.

11 Have groups review the numbered points in On the Spot Research. Remind students to evaluate if their group's questions need to be more focused or expanded. Ask volunteers to explain what makes a source reliable. Have students complete steps 3 through 5.

12 After students have selected a resource, direct them to **mark the text**, making notes or highlighting parts of their chosen resource as they read it. Again, remind them that their resource can help them fill in the L column.

13 With their research groups, have students discuss the main points they plan to include in their summaries. Encourage groups to ask questions to help group members sharpen their summaries and clarify understanding.

14 As students prepare to share their findings with their group, remind groups to assess whether the research clearly addresses the question. Before the students make their oral presentation, briefly review the elements of a good oral presentation. Ask the students to keep those elements in mind as they listen to one another.

15 Have students complete Check Your Understanding individually.

ASSESS

Check students' responses to the Check Your Understanding task to see how they have used new academic and literary terms and determine whether their understanding of Feminist Criticism has deepened.

ADAPT

Have students who are challenged by oral presentations pair off with a partner and give their presentations one on one. Ask the partners to provide feedback.

2.15

On the Spot Research

3. With your research group discuss your preliminary research questions. Discuss your questions and give one another feedback. Note how the feedback helps you revise or answer your questions. Collaborate with your group to identify at least one research question for each group member.

4. In the "H" column of your KWHL chart, list search terms that you might use and types of sources that you might find online to answer your question(s). As you compile your list note the following:

   • Where is this source located?
   • How reliable is the source?
   • Do you notice any explicit or implicit biases in the source?
   • How does the information drawn from various sources provide an answer to your question?
   • Is the information from various sources consistent and complementary?

5. Select the best resources based on your evaluation of their credibility.

6. Evaluate what you have learned from your research and decide how to best summarize your findings.

7. Share your findings with your research group. Prepare your findings in a brief summary to present to the class. When you present, be sure to:

   • Use information from your research to explain how Feminist Criticism is applied.
   • Use appropriate eye contact, adequate volume, clear pronunciation, and appropriate register.

☑ Check Your Understanding

Review your response to the quickwrite earlier in this activity. How would you revise your response, based on what you've learned about Feminist Criticism from your individual research and your classmates' presentations?

A Reversal of Fortune

Learning Targets
- Evaluate how an author builds an argument in a work of literary criticism.
- Formulate and collaboratively discuss your critique of an author's argument.
- Analyze key details in a text and draw connections to Marxist and Feminist Critical Perspectives.
- Integrate ideas from multiple texts to build knowledge and vocabulary about gender equality.

Preview
In this activity, you will read an example of literary criticism and analyze the author's critical interpretation of a famous fairy tale. Then you will write an analysis of how the author develops an argument over the course of the text.

As You Read
- Mark paragraphs that connect to Feminist Criticism with an "F" and paragraphs that connect to Marxist Criticism with an "M."
- Circle unknown words and phrases. Try to determine the meaning of the words by using context clues, word parts, or a dictionary.

About the Author

An author, educator, and activist, Madonna Kolbenschlag (1935–2000) wrote six books on feminism and spirituality. A member of the Catholic Sisters of Humility, Kolbenschlag earned PhDs in both literature and clinical psychology. *Kiss Sleeping Beauty Goodbye* (1979) uses fairy tale and myth to explore contemporary female psychology. *Eastward Toward Eve* (1996) explores the connections between gender, culture, and psychology.

Literary Criticism

Cinderella, the Legend

from *Kiss Sleeping Beauty Goodbye*
by **Madonna Kolbenschlag**

1   Cinderella, the best-known and probably best-liked fairy tale, is above all a success story. The rags-to-riches theme perhaps explains its equal popularity among boys as well as girls. It is a very old fairy tale having at least 345 documented variants and numerous unrecorded versions. The iconic focus of the tale on the lost slipper and Cinderella's "perfect fit" suggest that the story may have originated in the Orient where the erotic significance of tiny feet has been a popular myth since ancient times.

Learning Strategies

Discussion Groups
Marking the Text
SOAPSTone
Think-Pair-Share

⊘ KNOWLEDGE QUEST

Knowledge Question:
Why is gender equality important?
Across Activities 2.16 and 2.17, you will read a literary criticism essay and a folktale that examine the topic of gender equality. While you read and build knowledge about the topic, think about your answer to the Knowledge Question.

⊕ INDEPENDENT READING LINK

Read and Respond
In your Reader/Writer Notebook, note how the female characters are portrayed in your independent reading. Using evidence from the text, write a paragraph explaining how the author develops a feminist perspective through one or more of the characters.

iconic: culturally significant

ACTIVITY 2.16

PLAN

Materials: vocabulary reference sources (dictionary, thesaurus)
Suggested Pacing: 2 50-minute class periods plus homework

TEACH

1 Read the Learning Targets and Preview together with your students. Ask them to activate prior knowledge and quickly summarize the Marxist and Feminist perspectives. Tell them they will be identifying these perspectives as they read a text.

2 Direct students to the Knowledge Question. Ask volunteers to explain what gender equality means. Have small groups discuss responses to the Knowledge Question.

3 Read the As You Read section aloud. Then read the first paragraph of the essay out loud. Pause at the end and ask the students to note in the margin whether they think the paragraph connects to Marxist Criticism, Feminist Criticism, or both. Ask the students what category they chose and note on the blackboard how many students "voted" for each. Discuss the results with the class. Have the students explain their choice using evidence from the paragraph.

4 Ask students to read the About the Author individually. Lead a brief class discussion about how feminism and spirituality might intersect. From that discussion, you might also ask students what a book titled *Kiss Sleeping Beauty Goodbye* might be about.

College and Career Readiness Standards

Focus Standards:

RI.11–12.5 Analyze and evaluate the effectiveness of the structure an author uses in his or her exposition or argument, including whether the structure makes points clear, convincing, and engaging.

RI.11–12.6 Determine an author's point of view or purpose in a text in which the rhetoric is particularly effective, analyzing how

style and content contribute to the power, persuasiveness or beauty of the text.

SL.11–12.1c Propel conversations by posing and responding to questions that probe reasoning and evidence; ensure a hearing for a full range of positions on a topic or issue; clarify, verify, or challenge ideas and conclusions; and promote divergent and creative perspectives.

5 **FIRST READ:** This is a complex passage of literary criticism. Begin by reading the first few paragraphs aloud while students follow along silently.

 TEXT COMPLEXITY

Overall: Complex
Lexile: 1070L
Qualitative: High difficulty
Task: Challenging (Evaluate)

6 Explain that "Cinderella, the Legend" is an excerpt from a book of literary criticism in which Madonna Kolbenschlag analyzes well-known fairy tales from a feminist perspective.

7 As you read, move about the classroom, ensuring students are engaged with the text and annotating paragraphs that connect to Feminist Criticism with an "F" and paragraphs that connect to Marxist Criticism with an "M." Students should also be putting a star next to allusions in the text. Evaluate whether the selected reading mode is effective.

8 If their comprehension is good, ask a strong reader to take over. Other students should continue to mark the text as before.

2.16

My Notes

2   The basic motifs of the story are well-known: an ill-treated heroine, who is forced to live by the hearth; the twig she plants on her mother's grave that blossoms into a magic tree; the tasks demanded of the heroine; the magic animals that help her perform the tasks and provide her costume for the ball; the meeting at the ball; the heroine's flight from the ball; the lost slipper; the shoe test; the sisters' mutilation of their feet; the discovery of the true bride and the happy marriage. The variants retain the basic motifs; while differing considerably in detail, they range more widely in their origins than any other fairy tale: Asiatic, Celtic, European, Middle-Eastern and American Indian versions numbered among them.

3   The Horatio Alger quality of the story helps to explain its special popularity in **mercantile** and capitalistic societies. As a parable of social mobility, it was seized upon by the writers of the new "literature of aspiration" in the seventeenth and eighteenth centuries as a basic plot for a new kind of private fantasy—the novel. Our literary world has not been the same since Pamela and all her orphaned, governess sisters. Most Anglo-American novels, early and late, are written in the shadow of Pamela and the Cinderella myth. Even Franklin's *Autobiography*, the **seminal** work in the success genre, owes much to the myth. The primary "moral" of the fairy tale—that good fortune can be merited—is the very essence of the Protestant Ethic.

4   At the personal and psychological level, Cinderella evokes intense identification. It is a tale of sibling rivalry (and subliminally, of sex-role stereotyping)—a moral fable about socialization. Very few themes could be closer to the inner experience of the child, an emerging self enmeshed in a family network. …

5   The personality of the heroine is one that, above all, accepts *abasement* as a prelude to and precondition of *affiliation*. That abasement is characteristically expressed by Cinderella's servitude to **menial** tasks, work that diminishes her. This willing acceptance of a condition of worthlessness and her expectation of rescue (as reward for her virtuous suffering) is a recognizable **paradigm** of traditional feminine socialization. Cinderella is deliberately and systematically excluded from meaningful achievements. Her stepmother assigns her to meaningless tasks; her father fails her as a helpful mentor. Her sisters, inferior in quality of soul, are preferred before her.

6   Like most fairy tales, Cinderella dramatizes the passage to maturity. Her **sojourn** among the ashes is a period of grieving, a transition to a new self. On the explicit level of the story, Cinderella is literally grieving for her dead mother. Grimm's version of the tale preserves the sense of process, of growth that is symbolized in the narrative. Instead of a fairy godmother—*deus ex machina*[1]—Cinderella receives a branch of hazel bush from her father. She plants the twig over her mother's grave and cultivates it with her prayers and tears. This is her contact with her past, her roots, her essential self. Before one

mercantile: business-oriented
seminal: first important
abasement: lowering of status
affiliation: connection with a group
menial: lowly or degrading
paradigm: pattern; archetype
sojourn: temporary stay

---
[1] Literally meaning "god from the machine," *deus ex machina* comes from the Greek and Roman practice of introducing a god into a play suddenly to solve a problem that couldn't be solved otherwise.

College and Career Readiness Standards

W.11–12.2 Write informative/explanatory texts to examine and convey complex ideas, concepts, and information clearly and accurately through the effective selection, organization, and analysis of content.

Additional Standards Addressed:
RI.11–12.1, RI.11–12.2, RI.11–12.3, RI.11–12.4, L.11–12.5a, L.11–12.4c, L.11–12.5, W.11–12.5, W.11–12.10

can be transformed one must grieve for the lost as well as the possible selves, as yet unfulfilled—Kierkegaard's existential anguish. …

7   The Perrault version places great emphasis on the "midnight" prohibition given to Cinderella. The traditional connotation would, of course, associate it with the paternal mandate of obedience, and a threat: if the heroine does not return to domesticity and docility at regular intervals she may lose her "virtue" and no longer merit her expected one. Like the old conduct manuals for ladies, the moral of the tale warns against feminine excursions as well as ambition. Too much time spent "abroad" may result in indiscreet sex or unseemly hubris, or both. …

8   The slipper, the central icon in the story, is a symbol of sexual bondage and imprisonment in a stereotype. Historically, the virulence of its significance is born out in the twisted horrors of Chinese foot binding practices. On another level, the slipper is a symbol of power—with all of its accompanying restrictions and demands for conformity. When the Prince offers Cinderella the lost slipper (originally a gift of the magic bird), he makes his kingdom hers.

9   We know little of Cinderella's subsequent role. In Grimm's version she is revenged by the birds which pluck out the eyes of the envious sisters. But Perrault's version celebrates Cinderella's kindness and forgiveness. Her sisters come to live in the palace and marry two worthy lords. In the Norse variant of the tale, Aslaug, the heroine, marries a Viking hero, bears several sons, and wields a good deal of power in Teutonic[2] style. (She is the daughter of Sigurd and Brynhild.) But in most tales Cinderella disappears into the vague region known as the "happily ever after." She changes her name, no doubt, and—like so many women—is never heard of again.

Walt Disney's *Cinderella* was inspired by Charles Perrault's folktale written in 1697.

---

[2] *Teutonic* refers either to the Teutons, an ancient northern European tribe, or more generally to Germany, Germans, or the German language.

WORD CONNECTIONS

Roots and Affixes
Virtue comes from the Anglo-French *vertu*, meaning "moral strength or excellence." Other related words include *virtuoso* and *virtuosity*, which both refer to highly valued technical skill.

WORD CONNECTIONS

Cognates
The English word mandate functions both as a noun meaning "a formal command" and a verb meaning "to require or direct." The Spanish noun *mandato* and verb *mandar* are cognates of *mandate*—words that sound similar and have the same or similar meanings in both languages.

My Notes

_____

docility: passive obedience
hubris: excessive pride
virulence: harmfulness
conformity: following strict rules

9 Vocabulary Development: After paragraph 7, pause to discuss the Word Connections boxes. Have students identify how the word *mandate* is used in the text. Then ask them about the author's possible intent for using the word. Elicit other words that the author could have used.

10 When the passage has been read, pose the Knowledge Quest questions. Ask students to think about their initial reaction to the author's argument.

Scaffolding the Text-Dependent Questions

1. What in the Cinderella story suggests its origin, according to the author? What evidence from the text explains why her theory is uncertain? Which ancient culture valued women with small feet? How many versions of the story have there been? Where did the many versions come from? RI.11–12.1, RI.11–12.4

2. What details from the fairy tale support the author's claim that the Cinderella story fits the Protestant ethic? How does the author connect the "moral" of the story to the Protestant ethic? How do Cinderella's stepmother and stepsisters treat her? Does it change the way she works? In what ways does she earn her good fortune? RI.11–12.1

3. What details from the paragraph and the fairy tale explain what the author means by the "paradigm of traditional feminine socialization?" How does Cinderella react to having to do menial tasks? How does she expect life to improve? How are her expectations fulfilled? RI.11–12.3, RI.11–12.4

11 **RETURNING TO THE TEXT:** Divide the class into small groups to answer the text-dependent questions. You can have each group answer one or two of the questions depending on the size of the class and number of groups. Remind them to use evidence from the text to support their conclusions.

12 Visit each group and scaffold the question(s) for them if they are having difficulty. See the Scaffolding the Text-Dependent Questions boxes for suggestions. Have each group collaborate on a short, written answer to their question(s). After all the groups are finished, have each group share its answer(s) with the class.

13 Use the **SOAPSTone** strategy to help students understand the essay and reach conclusions about the author's audience, purpose, and tone.

2.16

⊘ Knowledge Quest
- What aspects of the author's argument stand out to you?
- Which version of the story of Cinderella is most surprising to you? Why?
- What are your first thoughts about how the author presents men and women in the text?

Returning to the Text
- Reread the literary criticism to answer these text-dependent questions.
- Write any additional questions you have about the text in your Reader/Writer Notebook.

1. **What in the Cinderella story suggests its origin, according to the author? What evidence from the text explains why her theory is uncertain?**

   According to the author, the focus on the slipper perfectly fitting Cinderella's foot (which was smaller than her sisters') suggests that the story may have originated in East Asia, where small feet were highly valued. However, with 345 known variations of the story, and many more never recorded, it is impossible to know for certain where it originated.

2. **What details from the fairy tale support the author's claim that the Cinderella story fits the Protestant Ethic?**

   The author defines the moral of the story, "that good fortune can be merited," as the essence of the Protestant Ethic. The claim is supported by the evidence of Cinderella's hard work even when her family treats her badly—hard work which leads directly to her happy ending. In this way, the story implies that hard work and personal effort will end in reward.

3. **KQ** **Reread paragraph 5. What details from the paragraph and the fairy tale explain what the author means by the "paradigm of traditional feminine socialization"?**

   The author writes that Cinderella accepts being devalued and expects to be rescued. She is "excluded from meaningful achievements." In the fairy tale, Cinderella is rewarded for suffering without protest; she is rescued. The "paradigm of traditional feminine socialization" is the patriarchal attitude that women should be passive, not be assertive.

4. **KQ** **What is the "midnight prohibition" in the fairy tale? How does it reinforce the "paradigm of traditional feminine socialization"?**

   The phrase "midnight prohibition" suggests the image of Cinderella running from the ball and leaving one shoe behind. The word "prohibition" reinforces that women were expected to be obedient follow rules. Preventing women from being out on their own at night was patriarchal society's way of keeping women tied to domestic life and the home.

Scaffolding the Text-Dependent Questions

4. What is the "midnight prohibition" in the fairy tale? How does it reinforce the "paradigm of traditional feminine socialization"? In the fairy tale, what would happen if Cinderella stayed at the ball past midnight? What is the societal effect of requiring women to be home at night? RI.11–12.2, RI.11–12.4, L.11–12.4c

5. How does the author use the glass slipper as a symbol to convey a feminist perspective? What is the dual, or paradoxical, nature of the slipper in the story? How did Chinese culture take this idea to an extreme? What does the prince do when he offers Cinderella the slipper? Does this power have a catch? RI.11–12.4, RI.11–12.5, RI.11–12.6, L.11–12.5

5. How does the author use the glass slipper as a symbol to convey a feminist perspective? What is the dual, or paradoxical, nature of the slipper in the story? Use details from the text to explain your answer.

The author calls the slipper a symbol of "bondage" and connects it to the "horrors of Chinese

foot binding practices." In this context the slipper is a symbol of feminine submission. When

the Prince puts the slipper on Cinderella's foot and "makes the kingdom hers," the slipper is a

symbol of power with "accompanying restrictions."

6. What reasons does the author give throughout the article for the popularity of the Cinderella tale? How does this affect her argument?

Cinderella is a "rags-to-riches theme" that appeals to "boys as well as girls" (paragraph 1). In

paragraph 4, the author explains, "At the personal and psychological level, Cinderella evokes

intense identification." It is a "tale of sibling rivalry," and "very few themes could be closer to

the inner experience of the child." These examples explain the appeal of the tale.

Working from the Text

7. With your group, use SOAPSTone to analyze the author's purpose in this text. How does she develop her ideas over the course of the text for her specific purpose?

Speaker:

Occasion:

Audience:

Purpose:

Subject

Tone:

8. In paragraph 3, the author makes four allusions: three to works of literature (Horatio Alger, Pamela, Franklin's Autobiography) and one to a religious ideal (Protestant Ethic). Research each allusion. What is her purpose in uniting these seemingly disparate references in one paragraph?

9. Reread the last two sentences of paragraph 9. Why is this comment a statement of Feminist Criticism? Look back at your annotations for Feminist and Marxist Criticism throughout the text. With a discussion group, articulate why each statement you marked connects to either Feminist or Marxist Criticism.

ACTIVITY 2.16 continued

14 Have students revisit the text to find the four allusions mentioned in student step 8 before conducting quick research. Remind them that when they read texts, they should put a star next to capitalized names or ideas that might be allusions.

 TEACHER TO TEACHER

The essay has many allusions: Grimm, Perrault, Horatio Alger, Pamela, Ben Franklin's *Autobiography*, and Kierkegaard. You might consider asking students to do some quick online research to help them understand the allusions in the text. Have them put a star next to capitalized names or other allusions and then research and discuss these references.

15 Ask the students to return to their discussion groups to respond to the remaining question in the Working from the Text. When each group is finished have it share its answer with the class.

Scaffolding the Text-Dependent Questions

6. What reasons does the author give throughout the article for the popularity of the Cinderella tale? How does this affect her argument? What does the author write about the story's popularity in paragraphs 1 and 3? What attributes of the story described in paragraph 4 could help make it popular? RI.11–12.5, RI.11–12.6

16 Review Critiquing the Author's Argument with the students. Have the students work on this section independently. Remind them to use more than a "yes" or "no." (The questions are phrased in a way that might make that type of answer seem adequate, but they should be able to support their "yes" or "no.")

17 After students have addressed all the elements in the Critiquing the Author's Argument section, have them return to their **discussion groups** and share their work with the group. After they have discussed their work with the group, ask each student to note one new thing they learned from the other students' answers or one new question they have about the author's argument.

18 Check for understanding by having students write Kolbenschlag's thesis in their own words. Their responses will vary, but they should be able to produce a reasonable statement of the essay's thesis before they go on to complete the writing prompt.

19 Ask students to work in pairs to complete the Focus on the Sentence. Have students share their sentences with one another and evaluate how well they think the subordinate clause was used in each sentence. Ask them to revise their sentences, if needed, after feedback.

Critiquing the Author's Argument

10. Now that you have evaluated Kolbenschlag's work, critique how effectively she builds her argument. Review the following questions and jot down notes in your Reader/Writer Notebook to help you formulate your opinion. Cite evidence from the text to support your thoughts.

   - **Claim:** What is the author's claim? Is it stated directly and clearly?
   - **Evidence:** Are the examples and evidence used believable, logical and sufficient? Are you persuaded by her argument?
   - **Counterclaims:** Has the author overlooked any possible opposition?
   - **Language:** How does the author's diction influence her credibility?
   - **Appeal:** What are the most effective components of the text? What, if any, do you think are its weaknesses?

11. Share your critique of Kolbenschlag's work with your discussion group. Listen to your classmate's critiques to gain new insights about how the author builds an argument.

 Focus on the Sentence

After your group discussion, reflect on your own critique of Kolbenschlag's argument as well as the ideas your classmates shared. Write two sentences starting with subordinating conjunctions.

While Kolbenschlag suggests that the story of Cinderella may have originated in East Asia, this claim cannot be proven.

Before James pointed out the positive effects of Kolbenschlag's use of allusion, these examples seemed to distract from the author's argument.

LANGUAGE & WRITER'S CRAFT:
Punctuating Lists

Notice that the first sentence in the second paragraph of Kolbenschlag's essay has a list introduced by a colon. When creating a list followed by a colon, you typically use commas to separate items. However, as seen in this list, it is necessary to separate items with a semicolon if the items already have commas within them.

For example, the first item in the list has a comma within it, which separates the descriptive clause ("who is forced to live by the hearth") from the word it modifies ("an ill-treated heroine"). In order to make the rest of the list clear, semicolons separate all the following items in the list.

PRACTICE Write a sentence that contains a list of other common elements in fairy tales. Be sure to practice proper placement of colons, commas, and semicolons.

Writing Prompt: Rhetorical Analysis

Write a response in which you explain how Kolbenschlag builds an argument to persuade her audience. As you write, consider how she uses persuasive elements to develop, support, and connect her ideas. Be sure to:

- Discuss how Kolbenschlag's feminist interpretation strengthens the logic and persuasiveness of her argument.
- Support your analysis by citing textual evidence.
- Use a clear and logical organizational structure.
- Use standard English conventions and proper punctuation.

WRITING PROMPT: RHETORICAL ANALYSIS

The following standards are addressed in the writing prompt:

- RI.11–12.5
- RI.11–12.6
- W.11–12.2a
- W.11–12.2b
- W.11–12.2c
- W.11–12.2d

ACTIVITY 2.16 continued

20 Language & Writer's Craft presents a good opportunity for students to focus on the use of parallelism in lists. Show them the following sentence: "I looked through my closet and found the following items: a shoe without laces, a shirt with a hole, a belt without a buckle, a book with a ragged cover, and a torn dollar covered with ink doodles." Explain that the base parts of the list are parallel nouns. Ask students to create and share their own sentences using parallelism.

21 Have students complete the writing prompt. They can use their restatement of Kolbenschlag's thesis as a jumping-off point from which to analyze her argument.

22 Remind students to complete the Independent Reading Link.

ASSESS

Review the completed essays to assess if students' work reflects a solid understanding of Feminist Criticism. Evaluate how well the students have identified and analyzed the ways in which the author uses Feminist Criticism to build her argument.

ADAPT

If students need additional help, have them outline the development of Kolbenschlag's essay, listing the claim(s), support, and evidence. Additional essays you might use for this activity include Margaret Atwood's "The Curse of Eve—Or, What I Learned in School," Gloria Steinem's satirical essay "If Men Could Menstruate," and "I Want a Wife" by Judy Syfers.

PLAN

Materials: student responses to questions in Activity 2.16
Suggested Pacing: 1 50-minute class period

TEACH

1 Introduce the topic of punctuating nonrestrictive elements by writing this sentence on the board without the parentheses: "Nonessential information (information that adds to a sentence but is not essential to the sentence's basic meaning) is often set off with commas, parentheses, or dashes."

2 Before revising the sentence, review the Learning Targets and Preview for the activity, making references to the example sentence on the board.

3 Ask students whether the sentence is clear as it is written. Then ask whether adding punctuation would make it clearer. Underline information that adds to a sentence but is not essential to the sentence's basic meaning. Elicit from your students or explain that using commas, parentheses, or dashes to set off the phrase would make the sentence clearer.

SAT® CONNECTIONS

This activity provides practice with this important SAT skill: punctuation to set off nonrestrictive elements. Using punctuation correctly is designated as a Language Progressive Skill. Students may need additional practice applying this skill as the texts they are reading and writing increase in complexity.

4 Model using commas, then parentheses, then dashes to set off the phrase. Ask students how each punctuation mark affects emphasis.

5 Have students read aloud the restrictive examples in the chart. Then have them reread each example with the restrictive elements left out. Guide students to understand that without the restrictive element, we do not know which realm or which version is meant.

Language Checkpoint:
Using Commas, Parentheses, and Dashes

Learning Targets

- Identify essential and nonessential elements in sentences in order to improve sentence fluency.
- Use a style guide to determine how nonessential elements are set off correctly.
- Work with a partner to evaluate how well you convey both essential and nonessential elements in a sentence.

Preview

In this activity you will learn to distinguish between essential and nonessential information in your writing, and how to punctuate that information correctly. Then you will have the opportunity to practice your new knowledge on your own writing.

Identifying Essential and Nonessential Information

Words, phrases, and clauses that are not essential to the basic meaning of a sentence are nonrestrictive elements. Nonrestrictive elements are set apart from the rest of the sentence with punctuation. Words, phrases, and clauses that are essential to the basic meaning of a sentence are restrictive elements. Restrictive elements do not need any special punctuation.

Restrictive	Nonrestrictive
In most versions, Cinderella disappears into the realm **known as "the happily ever after."**	**Known all around the world**, the Cinderella story is a coming-of-age tale.
The version that **I read as a child** includes a fairy godmother.	I like Grimm's version, **which I read as a child**.

1. Read the following sentences and decide whether the bolded words are restrictive or nonrestrictive.

   In the Norse version of the tale, Aslaug, **the Cinderella character**, wields a good deal of power.

   nonrestrictive

   In the Norse version of the tale, the character **Aslaug** wields a good deal of power.

   restrictive

2. With a partner, write a few sentences explaining how you decided whether the bolded words in each sentence are restrictive or nonrestrictive.

   In the first sentence, the phrase "the Cinderella character" adds extra information. The sentence would be complete without it, so it is nonrestrictive. In the second sentence, Aslaug identifies which character. Without the name, the basic meaning of the sentence would change, so it is restrictive.

College and Career Readiness Standards

Focus Standards:

W.11–12.5 Develop and strengthen writing as needed by planning, revising, editing, rewriting, or trying a new approach, focusing on addressing what is most significant for a specific purpose and audience.

L.11–12.2 Demonstrate command of the conventions of standard English capitalization, punctuation, and spelling when writing.

Punctuating Nonrestrictive Elements

Nonrestrictive elements are set off by punctuation (usually commas, parentheses, or dashes).

Punctuation	Examples
Comma: Most of the time, writers use commas to set off nonrestrictive elements. A nonrestrictive element in the middle of a sentence is set off with a comma before and after.	Madonna Kolbenschlag, **the writer of the essay**, discusses Cinderella. **Using fairy tales and myths**, she explores contemporary female psychology.
Parentheses: Using parentheses to set off nonrestrictive elements suggests that the information is extra or separate from the surrounding information.	One theme of the tale is social mobility **(the ability to move out of one class and into another)**.
Dash: A dash or pair of dashes can be used to signal a pause that calls attention to information.	She changes her name, no doubt, and—**like so many women**—is never heard of again.

3. For each of the following sentences, underline the nonrestrictive element, and add punctuation to set it off from the rest of the sentence.

    One moral of the story that good fortune can be merited is a popular idea in Western countries

One moral of the story (that good fortune can be merited) is a popular idea in Western countries. (Commas or dashes are also acceptable.)

    Some versions have a gruesome finale birds pluck out the stepsisters' eyes.

Some versions have a gruesome finale—birds pluck out the stepsisters' eyes.

4. Remember that restrictive elements do not have to be set off with punctuation. Extra punctuation can confuse readers. For the following sentence, delete any unnecessary punctuation around restrictive elements.

    Foot-binding, which disfigured many girls and women, began to die out as a result of a twentieth-century campaign, discouraging the practice.

Foot binding, which disfigured many girls and women, began to die out as a result of a twentieth-century campaign discouraging the practice.

6. Have students read aloud the nonrestrictive examples in the chart. Then have them reread each example with the nonrestrictive elements left out. Help students understand that even without the nonrestrictive element, the meaning of the sentences is complete.

7. Have pairs of students work through steps 1 and 2 on the student page. Check that students understand that the bolded elements serve different purposes in each sentence.

8. After reviewing the chart in Punctuating Nonrestrictive Elements, encourage students to experiment with changing the punctuation marks used in the examples. Ask students how the meaning or tone of the sentence changes depending on the punctuation. Then have them complete student steps 3 and 4.

9. Move to Revising and remind students that checking for correct use of punctuation is an important step when editing. Have them read the paragraph, correcting punctuation of restrictive and nonrestrictive elements.

10. Direct students to the Check Your Understanding. Make sure their answers show that they understand the rules for punctuating nonrestrictive elements.

11. Have students return to their written responses from Activity 2.16 to check for correct punctuation of restrictive and nonrestrictive elements.

ASSESS

Look for responses to the Check Your Understanding task that show that students understand the underlying rules, not just that they recognize mistakes. For example, "The name *Little Red Riding Hood* should not be set off with commas because it is essential to the sentence's meaning." Be sure students are able to recognize the dependent clause, "Studying the fairy tale Little Red Riding Hood," and explain why it is set off with a comma.

ADAPT

If students need additional practice, have them use the adding strategy, inserting new restrictive and nonrestrictive elements to their writing to add detail to their own sentences.

Revising

Read the following student summary of part of "Cinderella, the Legend." Work with a partner to check whether restrictive and nonrestrictive elements are punctuated correctly. Mark the text to correct the mistakes.

Choice of punctuation may vary, but students should set off each nonrestrictive element.

[1] The essay, "Cinderella the Legend" was published as part of the book *Kiss Sleeping Beauty Goodbye.*[2] Madonna Kolbenschlag, the author, is a writer, educator, and activist.[3] Discussing and interpreting the Cinderella tale, Kolbenschlag covers a lot of ground.[4] The essay says that the story is very old and has hundreds of variants (at least 345 recorded ones). [5] The story's most prominent motifs, which include the young woman who sleeps near a hearth and who is treated as a servant, appear in many cultures.[6] Many versions also include the problematic symbol of the tiny slipper (how does anyone even walk in a glass slipper?) and the prince.[7] The main thing, that I will remember about this essay, is just how complex a "simple" fairy tale can be.

☑ Check Your Understanding

Imagine you are editing a classmate's writing and you notice this sentence:

> Studying the fairy tale, Little Red Riding Hood I realized how strange how very, very strange a familiar story can be when you examine it closely.

Write a note to the writer describing why the original sentence is confusing. Help the writer understand how to correctly punctuate the sentence. Make sure your instructions are clear and your comments are succinct. After writing the note, add a question to your Editor's Checklist to remind yourself to check for correct punctuation of nonrestrictive elements.

Without the punctuation, it is hard to tell how the ideas are related.

The comma after "tale" should be deleted. The phrase "how very, very strange" should be set off with dashes or parentheses.

Are commas, parentheses, and dashes used correctly to set off nonessential information?

Practice

Return to the essay you wrote in the previous activity, analyzing Kolbenschlag's argument. Check that you used punctuation correctly to set apart nonrestrictive elements. Consult a style guide if necessary. Be sure to:

- Use standard English conventions to punctuate nonrestrictive elements with commas, parentheses, or dashes.
- Revise any sentences that incorrectly use punctuation to improve sentence fluency.

Battle of the Sexes

Learning Targets

- Evaluate a folktale and literary critique through a feminist perspective.
- Collaboratively discuss an author's message and draw connections to your personal perspective.
- Synthesize your analysis of two texts in the form of an explanatory essay.
- Integrate ideas from multiple texts to build knowledge and vocabulary about gender equality.

Preview

In this activity, you will read a folktale using the ideas of Feminist Criticism to help you understand the author's message. With your discussion group, you will compare ideas about men and women presented in a folktale with the ideas presented in "Cinderella, the Legend," by Kolbenschlag. Finally, you will synthesize your understanding of the texts in a written response.

As You Read

- As you read, use metacognitive markers to monitor your comprehension and interact with the text.
- Circle unknown words and phrases. Try to determine the meaning of the words by using context clues, word parts, or a dictionary.

About the Author

Zora Neale Hurston (1891–1960) is known for her powerful portrayals of African American life and culture in the rural South. An anthropologist, folklorist, novelist, civil rights activist, and journalist, she was a leading member of the Harlem Renaissance. Born in Florida, Hurston moved to New York in her twenties and studied anthropology at Barnard College and Columbia University. She became one of the first African American anthropologists to collect the folktales of the rural South and Haiti. These stories provided inspiration for her short fiction and novels. Her best-known work is the novel *Their Eyes Were Watching God* (1937). *Barracoon: The Story of the Last Black Cargo*, is based on her interviews with a survivor of the African slave trade. The manuscript was discovered by researchers among her papers in the Howard University Archives and published for the first time in 2018.

Learning Strategies

Close Reading
Discussion Groups
Graphic Organizer
Metacognitive Markers
Oral Reading
Summarizing
Questioning the Text

My Notes

College and Career Readiness Standards

Focus Standards:

RL.11–12.2 Determine two or more themes or central ideas of a text and analyze their development over the course of the text, including how they interact and build on one another to produce a complex account; provide an objective summary of the text.

SL.11–12.1 Initiate and participate effectively in a range of collaborative discussions (one-on-one, in groups, and teacher-led) with diverse partners on grades 11–12 topics, texts, and issues, building on others' ideas and expressing their own clearly and persuasively.

ACTIVITY 2.17

PLAN

Suggested Pacing: 2 50-minute class periods

TEACH

1 Read the Learning Targets and Preview with your students. Help them understand that folktales are brief, simple stories that are handed down from generation to generation, and that that they often teach social values or family responsibilities. Ask students if they are familiar with any folktales.

2 Direct students to the Knowledge Question. Ask students how they think feminism relates to gender equality. Have students discuss their ideas in small groups. Invite volunteers to share their ideas.

3 Read the As You Read instructions as a class. If needed, briefly review metacognitive markers. You can mention a few students might use or ask students to name some they think might be applicable.

4 Ask students to read the About the Author section. After they have finished, ask them to name one thing they find interesting or significant about Zora Neale Hurston. Ask them how they might find out more about her background and her works.

5 Remind students to keep the feminist perspective in mind as they read and make notes in the margins.

6 Before beginning the selection, read and discuss the Grammar & Usage box on dialect to help prepare students for what they'll encounter in the passage.

7 FIRST READ: The dialect in this passage may be challenging to students who need additional support with reading comprehension. If you are able to read the passage convincingly, read it aloud—or at least the first 2 chunks.

 TEXT COMPLEXITY

Overall: Accessible
Lexile: 970L
Qualitative: Moderate Difficulty
Task: Moderate (Analyze)

8 After Chunk 2, ask the students to pause and write down in their notes the first thing they noticed about the text. Remind them to write spontaneously. They may only write a word or two or a phrase. You want them to give their first and most immediate reaction.

9 If students seem to be comprehending well, let them read the rest in small groups, taking turns reading aloud. Acknowledge that the dialogue may seem awkward to some of them. Encourage them to read in a natural tone of voice. Their reading can be lively and expressive, but they don't have to use an exaggerated tone of voice or imitate what they think a Black southern accent may be.

2.17

 **KNOWLEDGE QUEST**

Knowledge Question:
Why is gender equality important?

GRAMMAR & USAGE

Dialect
Languages change over time and spoken language can sound dramatically different according to geography. You might notice dialect in the ways people from different places and social backgrounds use words or phrases. Writers sometimes choose to write in dialect to provide authenticity when representing a certain time, place, or social group. Oftentimes dialect is spelled phonetically, or how the words sound when spoken aloud. For example, in the first paragraph of Chunk 3, the character uses words like *de*, *Heben*, *yo'*, *tole*, and *Ah'm*.

Find two more examples of the ways in which the author uses unconventional spelling to convey dialect and consider the impact it has on your understanding of the text.

Folktale

Why Women Always Take Advantage of Men

by **Zora Neale Hurston**

from *Mules and Men*

Chunk 1

1 "Don't you know you can't git de best of no woman in de talkin' game? Her tongue is all de weapon a woman got," George Thomas chided Gene. "She could have had mo' sense, but she told God no, she'd ruther take it out in hips. So God give her her ruthers. She got plenty hips, plenty mouf and no brains."

2 "Oh, yes, womens is got sense too," Mathilda Moseley jumped in. "But they got too much sense to go 'round braggin' about it like y'all do. De lady people always got de advantage of mens because God fixed it dat way."

3 "Whut ole black advantage is y'all got?" B. Moseley asked indignantly. "We got all de strength and all de law and all de money and you can't git a thing but whut we jes' take pity on you and give you."

4 "And dat's jus' de point," said Mathilda triumphantly. "You do give it to us, but how come you do it?" And without waiting for an answer Mathilda began to tell why women always take advantage of men.

Chunk 2

5 You see in de very first days, God made a man and a woman and put 'em in a house together to live. 'Way back in them days de woman was just as strong as de man and both of 'em did de same things. They useter get to fussin' 'bout who gointer do this and that and sometime they'd fight, but they was even balanced and neither one could whip de other one.

6 One day de man said to hisself, "B'lieve Ah'm gointer go see God and ast Him for a li'l mo' strength so Ah kin whip dis 'oman and make her mind. Ah'm tired of de way things is." So he went on up to God.

7 "Good mawnin', Ole Father."

8 "Howdy man. Whut you doin' 'round my throne so soon dis mawnin'?"

9 "Ah'm troubled in mind, and nobody can't ease mah spirit 'ceptin' you."

10 God said: "Put yo' plea in de right form and Ah'll hear and answer."

11 "Ole Maker, wid de mawnin' stars glitterin' in yo' shinin' crown, wid de dust from yo' footsteps makin' worlds upon worlds, wid de blazin' bird we call

---

College and Career Readiness Standards

W.11–12.2 Write informative/explanatory texts to examine and convey complex ideas, concepts, and information clearly and accurately through the effective selection, organization, and analysis of content.

Additional Standards Addressed:
RL.11–12.1, RL.11–12.3, RL.11–12.4, RL.11–12.5, RL.11–12.6, RL.11–12.10, L.11–12.2, L.11–12.4c, L.11–12.5, W.11–12.5, W.11–12.10

My Notes

de sun flyin' out of yo' right hand in de mawnin' and consumin' all day de flesh and blood of stump-black darkness, and comes flyin' home every evenin' to rest on yo' left hand, and never once in all yo' eternal years, mistood de left hand for de right, Ah ast you please to give me mo' strength than dat woman you give me, so Ah kin make her mind. Ah know you don't want to be always comin' down way past de moon and stars to be straightenin' her out and its got to be done. So give me a li'l mo' strength, Ole Maker and Ah'll do it."

12 "All right, Man, you got mo' strength than woman."

Chunk 3

13 So de man run all de way down de stairs from Heben till he got home. He was so anxious to try his strength on de woman dat he couldn't take his time. Soon's he got in de house he hollered "Woman! Here's yo' boss. God done tole me to handle you whichever way Ah please. Ah'm yo' boss."

14 De woman flew to fightin' 'im right off. She fought 'im frightenin' but he beat her. She got her wind and tried 'im agin but he whipped her agin. She got herself together and made de third try on him vigorous but he beat her every time. He was so proud he could whip 'er at last, dat he just crowed over her and made her do a lot of things she didn't like. He told her, "Long as you obey me, Ah'll be good to yuh, but every time yuh rear up Ah'm gointer put plenty wood on yo' back and plenty water in yo' eyes."

15 De woman was so mad she went straight up to Heben and stood befo' de Lawd. She didn't waste no words. She said, "Lawd, Ah come befo' you mighty mad t'day. Ah want back my strength and power Ah useter have."

16 "Woman, you got de same power you had since de beginnin'."

17 "Why is it then, dat de man kin beat me now and he useter couldn't do it?"

18 "He got mo' strength than he useter have. He come and ast me for it and Ah give it to 'im. Ah gives to them that ast, and you ain't never ast me for no mo' power."

19 "Please suh, God, Ah'm astin' you for it now. Jus' gimme de same as you give him."

20 God shook his head. "It's too late now, woman. Whut Ah give, Ah never take back. Ah give him mo' strength than you and no matter how much Ah give you, he'll have mo'."

Chunk 4

21 De woman was so mad she wheeled around and went on off. She went straight to de devil and told him what had happened.

22 He said, "Don't be dis-incouraged, woman. You listen to me and you'll come out mo' than conqueror. Take dem frowns out yo' face and turn round and go right on back to Heben and ast God to give you dat bunch of keys hangin' by de mantel-piece. Then you bring 'em to me and Ah'll show you what to do wid 'em."

WORD CONNECTIONS

Roots and Affixes

Dis-incouraged is not a word you'll find in the dictionary, but you can still decode it using roots and affixes. The Latin root *cur* means "heart" and is the base of the word courage. The prefix *en-* (here written *in-*) means "to make" or "to cause," and the prefix *dis-* means "to deprive." Hurston intentionally adds these two conflicting prefixes to create a word with complex meaning.

Scaffolding the Text-Dependent Questions

1. How does the author use language and dialogue in Chunk 1 to reveal how men see the relative advantages of men and women? What words and phrases do the men use in Chunk 1 to describe men's and women's advantages? What is one advantage George Thomas gives women in the first paragraph? What three advantages does B. Moseley describe in the third paragraph? RL.11–12.1, RL.11–12.2, RL.11–12.4

2. How does using the word "triumphantly" to describe Mathilda's speech at the end of Chunk 1 create surprise and set up the folktale? How does this word shape the reader's anticipation of what will come next? What has B. Moseley said just before Mathilda speaks "triumphantly?" Does he expect her to reply that way? How does this exchange echo the balance of power in the folktale? RL.11–12.4, RL.11–12.5

 TEACHER TO TEACHER

Nora Zeale Hurston uses African American vernacular English (AAVE) in this story. It is important that students know this is a legitimate form of English and that they treat it with respect. You may want to explain to students what vernacular means and point out that there are many forms of vernacular English used in the United States both today and in the past. Ask students why they think Hurston used it in this story.

There are many resources for AAVE. PBS has a discussion of Hurston's use of dialect at "The Power of Prose: African American Women."

The University of Hawaii includes a page on AAEV on their Language Varieties site.

Portland State University also has a page on AAVE.

Finally, the Dictionary of American Regional English Online, maintained by the University of Wisconsin, can help students explore different dialects and regional phrases both past and present.

10 As students are reading, monitor their progress. Be sure they are engaged with the text and annotating using metacognitive markers. Evaluate whether the selected reading mode is effective.

11 Based on the observations you made during the first reading, you may want to adjust the reading mode. For example, you may decide for the second reading to read aloud certain complex passages, or you may group students differently.

12 Vocabulary Development: Discuss the Word Connections with students. Then ask them to think of other words that share the root *cur* and the prefixes *dis-* and *en-*. As an extension, have students complete the **Roots and Affixes Brainstorm** graphic organizer

LEVELED DIFFERENTIATED INSTRUCTION

Students may need support closely reading and comprehending the dialect used in this text.

Developing Use the About the Author section to preview the text before students' first reading. Explain that the text is written in *dialect*, so that words are spelled to mimic how they sound. Distribute the **Text Structure Stairs graphic organizer**. Have students perform a choral reading of the first few paragraphs. Check understanding by asking: *What event happened in this chunk of the story?* Have students record their answers on the organizer.

Expanding Distribute the **Text Structure Stairs graphic organizer** for students to use as a note-taking tool. Have pairs take turns reading the text aloud to one another, pausing after each chunk to answer the question: *What important event happened in this chunk of the story?* Have students record their answers on the organizer.

Bridging Assign students into pairs or small groups and have them take turns reading the story aloud to one another. After each chunk of text, have students define any difficult-to-understand words. Then have them use the **Text Structure Stairs graphic organizer** to record the major events in the story.

Support Model reading the first chunk of the text aloud. Point out the use of dialect in the first paragraph and summarize its meaning. Have students underline all other occurrences of dialect in Chunk 1. Then ask pairs to work together to summarize what each speaker is saying. Invite pairs to share their summaries. Provide clarification as needed.

Extend Have students write their own folktale using a form of African American vernacular English. The folktales should represent a conflict between men and women.

My Notes

23 So de woman climbed back up to Heben agin. She was mighty tired but she was more out-done that she was tired so she climbed all night long and got back up to Heben agin. When she got befo' de throne, butter wouldn't melt in her mouf.

24 "O Lawd and Master of de rainbow, Ah know yo' power. You never make two mountains without you put a valley in between. Ah know you kin hit a straight lick wid a crooked stick."

25 "Ast for whut you want, woman."

26 "God, gimme dat bunch of keys hangin' by yo' mantel-piece."

27 "Take 'em."

28 So de woman took de keys and hurried on back to de devil wid 'em. There was three keys on de bunch. Devil say, "See dese three keys? They got mo' power in 'em than all de strength de man kin ever git if you handle 'em right. Now dis first big key is to de do' of de kitchen and you know a man always favors his stomach. Dis second one is de key to de bedroom and he don't like to be shut out from dat neither and dis last key is de key to de cradle and he don't want to be cut off from his generations at all. So now you take dese keys and go lock up everything and wait till he come to you. Then don't you unlock nothin' until he use his strength for yo' benefit and yo' desires."

29 De woman thanked 'im and tole 'im, "If it wasn't for you, Lawd knows whut us po' women folks would do."

30 She started off but de devil halted her. "Jus' one mo' thing: don't go home braggin' 'bout yo' keys. Jus' lock up everything and say nothin' until you git asked. And then don't talk too much."

Chunk 5

31 De woman went on home and did like de devil tole her. When de man come home from work she was settin' on de porch singin' some song 'bout "Peck on de wood make de bed go good."

32 When de man found de three doors fastened what useter stand wide open he swelled up like pine lumber after a rain. First thing he tried to break in cause he figgered his strength would overcome all obstacles.

33 When he saw he couldn't do it, he ast de woman, "Who locked dis do'?"

34 She tole 'im, "Me."

35 "Where did you git de key from?"

36 "God give it to me."

37 He run up to God and said, "God, woman got me locked 'way from my vittles, my bed and my generations, and she say you give her the keys."

Scaffolding the Text-Dependent Questions

3. Why does the man tell God he needs more strength than the woman at the end of Chunk 2? What does this reveal about his character and the power dynamics in the society in which he lives? What patriarchal attitude does his request reflect? What is the structure of a patriarchal society? How do men hold on to power in such a society? Which of the man's words to God reflect this attitude? RL.11–12.2, RL.11–12.4

13 When students have read the entire story, pose the Knowledge Quest questions.

My Notes

38 God said, "I did, Man, Ah give her de keys, but de devil showed her how to use 'em!"

39 "Well, Ole Maker, please gimme some keys jus' lak 'em so she can't git de full control."

40 "No, Man, what Ah give Ah give. Woman got de key."

41 "How kin Ah know 'bout my generations?"

42 "Ast de woman."

43 So de man come on back and submitted hisself to de woman and she opened de doors.

44 He wasn't satisfied but he had to give in. Way after while he said to de woman, "Le's us divide up. Ah'll give you half of my strength if you lemme hold de keys in my hands."

45 De woman thought dat over so de devil popped and tol her, "Tell 'im, naw. Let 'im keep his strength and you keep yo' keys."

46 So de woman wouldn't trade wid 'im and de man had to **mortgage** his strength to her to live. And dat's why de man makes and de woman takes.

47 You men is still braggin' 'bout yo' strength and de women is sittin' on de keys and lettin' you blow off till she git ready to put de bridle on you.

48 B. Moseley looked over at Mathilda and said, "You just like a hen in de barnyard. You cackle so much you give de rooster de blues."

49 Mathilda looked over at him archly and quoted:

50 Stepped on a pin, de pin bent.

51 And dat's de way de story went.

⊘ Knowledge Quest
- What emotions do you feel while reading the speech in this folktale?
- What is your first impression of the gender issues raised in this folktale?

---

mortgage: hand over the rights of

Scaffolding the Text-Dependent Questions

4. In Chunk 4, how does the devil's explanation of the keys add irony to the folktale? What are the keys for? How are the keys different from what the man received? RL.11–12.6

14 Return to the Knowledge Question. Have students work with a partner to brainstorm ideas in response to the prompt. Encourage students to take notes to help them with the writing task. Review writing expectations with students using the "be sure to" points. Ask volunteers to paraphrase them to ensure class understanding.

15 Encourage students to continue building knowledge on this topic as suggested in the Independent Reading Link.

2.17

INDEPENDENT READING LINK

You can continue to build your knowledge about gender equality by reading other articles at ZINC Reading Labs. Search for keywords such as gender equality.

 ZINC

Knowledge Quest

Think about how Kolbenschlag and Hurston address gender equality. Choose "Cinderella, the Legend" or "Why Women Always Take Advantage of Men," and write a paragraph explaining how the conflict between men and women as explored in your reading is relevant today in gender equality issues. Be sure to:

- Clearly introduce the central idea and logically organize your ideas.
- Use significant and relevant examples, details, or quotations that thoroughly develop and explain the topic.
- Provide an engaging conclusion that supports the central idea and examines its implications.

Scaffolding the Text-Dependent Questions

5. What does the image of the keys suggest? What does this statement show about how men see the power of women? What view of women's power can be inferred from this statement? What do the keys represent in the story? How is the devil traditionally characterized? What can be inferred from this about women's power? RL.11–12.4, RL.11–12.6

6. What is the cause of the conflict between the man and the woman in the folktale? How do the characters contribute to that conflict? **What does this imply about men and women?** What did the man and woman argue about when they both had the same strength? What happened when they fought? What does this imply about the equal division of power between men and women? RL.11–12.2, RL.11–12.3

16 **RETURNING TO THE TEXT:** During the second reading, students will be returning to the text to answer the text-dependent comprehension questions. Have them work in pairs. Ask them to discuss each question and then write down the answer they have agreed on.

Returning to the Text

- Reread the folktale to answer these text-dependent questions.
- Write any additional questions you have about the text in your Reader/Writer Notebook.

1. How does the author use the language and dialogue in Chunk 1 to reveal how men see the relative advantages of men and women? Use details from the text to support your answer.

In the first paragraph, George Thomas says a woman's tongue is a "weapon," and women have "plenty mouf and no brains." In the third paragraph, B. Moseley says men have all the "strength," "law" (legal rights), and "money," and women "can't git a thing but whut we jes' take pity on you and give you."

2. How does the use of the word "triumphantly" to describe Mathilda's speech at the end of Chunk 1 create surprise and set up the folktale? How does this word shape the reader's anticipation of what will come next?

Moseley thinks he has spoken the last word about men's advantages over women. However, when Mathilda speaks "triumphantly" in reply, it reveals the surprise that he has played right into her argument. The exchange echoes how the woman in the folktale uses the man's power to her advantage.

3. **KQ** Why does the man tell God he needs more strength than the woman at the end of Chunk 2? What does this reveal about his character and the power dynamics in the society in which he lives?

The man asks for more strength "so Ah kin make her mind" and so God doesn't have to always "be straightenin' her out." This shows the man believes it is right and natural that he be stronger than women and that women need to be kept in line by men. As God gives the man more strength, it can be inferred that this power dynamic was widely accepted.

4. In Chunk 4, how does the Devil's explanation of the keys add irony to the folktale?

The Devil explains that the keys are for three simple things: the kitchen, the bedroom, and the cradle. The irony is that the man received physical strength to control the woman, whereas the woman only needed three keys to control the man.

Scaffolding the Text-Dependent Questions

7. How does Hurston's choice to present the folktale as part of a conversation between men and a woman change the effect of the story and its impact on the reader? What do the men and Mathilda discuss before she tells the story? How does the folktale connect to their conversation? How would the effect be different if the folktale were presented without the conversation around it? RL.11–12.3, RL.11–12.6

8. What themes are expressed in the last six paragraphs of the story? How do they interact to create a view of the power balance between men and women? What two statements does Mathilda make about men and women at the end? What themes about power do these statements express? Are men or women more powerful? RL.11–12.2, RL.11–12.3, RL.11–12.5

17 Tell students to note any questions that seem challenging or difficult to them. Visit with each group and scaffold the difficult questions by rephrasing them or breaking them down into smaller parts. See the Scaffolding the Text-Dependent Questions boxes for suggestions.

2.17

5. In Chunk 5, God says, "I did, Man, Ah give her de keys, but de devil showed her how to use 'em!" What does the image of the keys suggest? What does this statement show about how men see the power of women?

The keys suggest power. Although God gave the woman the keys, to gain power over the man, it was the Devil who taught her how to use them. Traditionally the Devil is cunning and deceptive, implying that women's power is calculated and requires scheming rather than brute force.

6. What is the cause of the conflict between the man and the woman in the folktale? How do the characters contribute to that conflict? What does this imply about men and women?

When the man and the woman had the same amount of strength, they fought about who was going to do what. Because they were equally strong, neither of them could win in a fight. They each had to seek a way of gaining power over the other. This implies that men and women can't get along when power is divided equally between them.

7. How does Hurston's choice to present the folktale as part of a conversation between men and a woman change the effect of the story and its impact on the reader?

The folklore's lesson is echoed in conversations Mathilda and the men have at the beginning and end of the folktale. The conversation makes the lesson feel more immediate and connects it to real life rather than being just an abstract lesson. The informal speech and imagery help the reader both "see" and "hear" the story as it unfolds.

8. **KQ** What themes are expressed in the last six paragraphs of the story? How do they interact to create a view of the power balance between men and women?

The phrases "de man makes" and "You men is still braggin' 'bout yo' strength" express the theme that men think they have all the power, while "de woman takes" and "de women is sittin' on de keys ... till she git ready to put de bridle on you" express the theme that although women seem less powerful in society, they are actually in control of men's power.

2.17

Gaining Perspectives

In the folktale, the woman has two interpersonal conflicts, which also happen in real life. In one instance, physical harm occurs, and in the other, there is a battle of wits. With a partner, discuss how the woman handles the situations she encounters. What other ways could someone in her situation prevent or resolve an interpersonal conflict where violence is involved? Based on your community, what options do people have if they need to ask for help? Who can a person reach out to if she or he is in this situation? Family? Friends? Healthcare workers? In your Reader/Writer notebook, write about some strategies for how to handle this situation.

Working from the Text

9. Think about the gender issues raised by the authors of the essay "Cinderella, the Legend" and the folktale "Why Women Always Take Advantage of Men." Use a Venn diagram to compare and contrast the issues raised by each author and those shared by both. As you fill out the diagram, make sure your commentary and summaries are supported by the texts. Share the information in your diagram with the rest of your group in a discussion.

"Cinderella, the Legend" **Both** **"Why Women Always Take Advantage of Men"**

The female is forced to perform menial tasks and to serve others and is excluded from meaningful achievements. The female is required to obey the paternal expectation of returning home before midnight. The female loses individual identity when she marries.

The texts present social attitudes toward women that are different but arguably both stereotypical. Cinderella is presented as obedient and subservient. Mathilda is presented as manipulative and talkative.

The male holds physical power over the female.

The female holds the "keys" to coexistence with a male.

18 Draw students' attention to the Gaining Perspectives feature. Have partners discuss how citizens in a community can handle a situation where violence is involved. Then have students write the strategies they discussed in their Reader/Writer notebooks.

19 Turn to the Working from the Text section. Divide students into small groups. Direct each group to discuss the feminist issues raised by Zora Neale Hurston's folktale "Why Women Always Take Advantage of Men" and Madonna Kolbenschlag's essay "Cinderella, the Legend." Groups should use the graphic organizer on this page to compare and contrast the issues raised in the two texts and to guide their discussion.

20 Each group should summarize its discussion and findings. Select a representative from each group to present the group's discussion summary to the whole class.

21 Ask students to complete the first two columns of the graphic organizer on the student page. To do so, they may first need to reread or skim the Kolbenschlag selection. For each of the assumptions common to a feminist critical perspective, students must indicate whether they believe these authors would agree or disagree with the assumption.

22 Solicit oral responses and discuss how students matched the assumptions to the authors.

23 Prompt students to share evidence from the essay or folktale that they believe supports their responses.

24 Before students complete the final column, ask them to review and consider the assumptions one more time. Then they should use the final column to indicate whether they agree with the assumptions of Feminist Criticism.

25 Have students complete the Check Your Understanding by summarizing their groups' responses to the graphic organizer.

26 Have students work individually or in pairs to respond to the writing prompt.

ASSESS

Assess the paragraphs the students have produced in response to the writing prompt. Evaluate how well they compare and contrast the authors' treatment of a key idea of Feminist Criticism. Assess whether or not students used at least two details, one from each text, to support their thesis statements. Make sure students have used punctuation and grammar correctly. Sentences should reflect what students learned about dependent clauses in the previous activity. Their conclusions should follow naturally from the thesis statement.

ADAPT

If students need additional help using a feminist critical lens to compare and contrast these two texts, model explaining an assumption of Feminist Criticism for them. Use a character from their previous reading. You might use Eliza Doolittle from *Pygmalion* or ask a student to name a character from the independent reading in Activity 2.14. Have the student briefly summarize the character and plot. Discuss that character from a feminist point of view with the group.

2.17

10. Consider some of the key ideas of Feminist Criticism. Based on your reading and discussion of "Cinderella, the Legend" and "Why Women Always Take Advantage of Men," decide whether Kolbenschlag and Hurston would tend to agree or disagree with the ideas here. Use evidence from the texts to support your views. Then decide whether you agree or disagree with the same statements and record your thinking in the last column.

Key Ideas Related to the Use of Feminist Critical Perspective	Kolbenschlag		Hurston		You	
	Agree	Disagree	Agree	Disagree	Agree	Disagree
The relationship between men and women has almost always been unequal.						
The female reader is an outsider who must assume male values.						
Gender issues are central in our society.						
Fictional portrayals of women are often stereotypical.						
Texts authored by women may have different viewpoints from those authored by men.						

WORD CONNECTIONS

Etymology
The Latin root of the word assumption is *sumere*, meaning "take." When we assume, or make an assumption, we take on a responsibility, an idea, or other item.

☑ **Check Your Understanding**

Reflect on the points that your group has made about each idea. Write a paragraph briefly summarizing some of the significant points of your group's discussion.

> **Writing Prompt: Informational**
>
> Write a detailed response explaining a key idea of Feminist Criticism from the graphic organizer you completed in this activity. Evaluate how Kolbenschlag and Hurston explore this idea in their writing. Be sure to:
>
> - Write a clear thesis that compares how each author addresses the key idea associated with the critical perspective.
> - Include direct quotations and specific evidence from both texts to support your thinking.
> - Introduce and punctuate all quotations correctly, using varied syntax.
> - Use a coherent organizational structure and employ transitions effectively to highlight similarities and differences.

✍ WRITING PROMPT: INFORMATIONAL

The following standards are addressed in the writing prompt:

- W.11–12.2a
- W.11–12.2b
- W.11–12.2c
- L.11–12.2
- L.11–12.6

Feminist Critique: The Tree of Life

Learning Targets
- Analyze a picture book through a feminist perspective.
- Develop claims and support them with textual evidence.

Preview

In this activity, you will review the general assumptions you have learned about Feminist Criticism. Then you will analyze character relationships presented in a picture book. Finally, you will write a literary analysis to reflect your new understanding of the text, viewed through a feminist perspective.

Feminist Criticism

1. Think about the description and definition of Feminist Criticism in Activity 2.15, then answer the following questions about the lens.

   - If a matriarchal society is the opposite of a patriarchal society, what is the basis of the difference?

   - What is one statement Feminist Criticism makes about patriarchal societies?

   - What assumption does Feminist Criticism make about the treatment of female characters in literary texts?

   - How can a literary character both reflect and reinforce stereotypes?

   - What perspective does Feminist Criticism present about texts authored by men versus those authored by women?

Learning Strategies
Activate Prior Knowledge
Discussion Groups
Graphic Organizer
Paraphrasing
Summarizing

📖 INDEPENDENT READING LINK

Read and Connect

Think about the analytical questions you have applied to your in-class reading. Use the questions to consider the perspective of Feminist Criticism in your independent reading. Create a Venn diagram in your Reader/Writer Notebook to explore the connections between the texts you have read independently and in class. How do the authors portray gender roles and relationships between men and women?

My Notes

College and Career Readiness Standards

Focus Standards:

RL.11–12.2 Determine two or more themes or central ideas of a text and analyze their development over the course of the text, including how they interact and build on one another to produce a complex account; provide an objective summary of the text.

RL.11–12.4 Determine the meaning of words and phrases as they are used in the text, including figurative and connotative meanings; analyze the impact of specific word choices on meaning and tone, including words with multiple meanings or language that is particularly fresh, engaging, or beautiful. (Include Shakespeare as well as other authors.)

PLAN

Materials: *The Giving Tree* by Shel Silverstein
Suggested Pacing: 2 50-minute class period

TEACH

1 Have a volunteer read the Learning Targets and Preview for this activity. Mention that the picture book will be *The Giving Tree*. Give students a few minutes to share some memories about the book. If none have heard of it, ask for volunteers to make inferences about the story from the title.

2 Ask students to reread the description of Feminist Criticism from Activity 2.15. Organize students in pairs to review Feminist Criticism by answering the questions on the student page.

3 In the Opening Writing Prompt, have students activate prior knowledge by asking them to think about the tree of life. Read the prompt aloud. Have students first discuss the various art, literary, or other works in which they have encountered the Tree of Life archetype and what it symbolizes. Some students may mention the tree of life as part of the Adam and Eve/Garden of Eden story in Genesis. Explain that the tree of life appears in the mythology and literature of a number of cultures as an archetypal symbol.

4 Discuss the About the Author section. Then read aloud *The Giving Tree* to acquaint students with the plot and characters. Ask for a volunteer to summarize the characters, conflict, and plot.

5 Afterward, give students a few moments to return to the questions in student step 1. Ask them if there is anything they would change or add to their earlier answers. If time allows, have them share their answers in discussion groups.

6 Next, ask students to critique the story from their own perspective. Have them identify the subject, theme, and the author's point of view.

7 Direct students' attention to the **graphic organizer** that follows. Ask students to form pairs to complete the organizer. Have one member of the pair write down a quotation from the text for the other to analyze. Then have them switch roles until the organizer is complete. If time allows have the pairs share their organizers with the class.

8 Point out the Independent Reading Link and remind students to record their responses in their Reader/Writer Notebooks.

9 In your second reading, show the class the pictures as you read aloud. Pause after each page and ask students to consider the questions and record their answers in the graphic organizer. Use the annotations on the reduced Student Edition page to model the process.

10 As the story continues, pull back from modeling and ask students to start interpreting the text and completing the graphic organizer on their own or in small groups.

11 When the students have completed their graphic organizers, ask them to report their findings for each page. Consider focusing on some of the following ideas:

- The boy uses the tree for enjoyment/pleasure and she gets nothing in return.
- The female is trapped by the promise of emotional attachment.
- The boy loves her, even carving his love into her, but his love is not permanent, while hers is.
- As the boy grows older, the tree is alone without the man. He even flaunts his infidelity by carving a new name in the tree.
- The tree is willing to give away her fruit and her ability to grow to fulfill the man's desires. Her happiness is through him.
- Not until the tree gives the man everything does she realize that she is not happy. However, she is joyful again when the man returns to her one last time.

My Notes

Opening Writing Prompt

Think about the phrase "the tree of life" and respond to the following question.

The tree of life is an archetype. What do you know about this phrase and its meaning? Are there any examples of this archetype that you can connect to texts, films, or artwork that you've read or viewed?

About the Author

Sheldon Allan "Shel" Silverstein (1930–1999) was an American author, cartoonist, songwriter, and playwright from Chicago. While Silverstein won multiple Grammy awards as a songwriter and musician, he is best known for his children's books and poetry collections. His first major poetry collection, *Where the Sidewalk Ends* (1974), is full of inventive characters and dark humor. His children's books, which he also illustrated, have been translated into more than 30 languages and have sold more than 20 million copies. Works including *The Giving Tree* and *Falling Up* are still cherished by children and adults alike.

The Giving Tree

You will read a picture book that allows you to analyze the phrase "the tree of life" from the perspective of Feminist Criticism. A cornerstone of Feminist Criticism is the examination of the portrayal of gender roles and relationships between men and women.

2. As your teacher reads aloud Shel Silverstein's *The Giving Tree*, listen for evidence that supports a feminist critique of the book, and record your ideas in the My Notes column. Consider the following:

   a. From whose point of view do we see this story?

   b. How are women presented in the text? How are men presented in the text?

   c. How does the author use imagery to convey ideas about men and women?

   d. How is the relationship between men and women presented?

   e. To what extent does the portrayal of men and women support a patriarchal view of the world?

   f. How do the characters' behaviors influence the theme?

3. Use the following graphic organizer to analyze the story. Write a quotation in the left column, and, using the questions from Step 2, write your analysis and commentary in the right column. Your teacher will model the completion of the first few passages.

College and Career Readiness Standards

W.11–12.2 Write informative/explanatory texts to examine and convey complex ideas, concepts, and information clearly and accurately through the effective selection, organization, and analysis of content.

Additional Standards Addressed:
RL.11–12.1, RL.11–12.5, SL.11–12.6, W.11–12.5, W.11–12.9. L.11–12.3, L.11–12.6

Quotation	Answers and Analysis
a. "Once there was a tree … and she loved a little boy."	The tree here is presented as female. The idea of a tree is productive, nurturing, and a provider of shelter. In relation to the boy, the tree becomes the caregiver.
b. "And every day the boy would come and he would gather her leaves …"	The tree is presented with arms outstretched offering to embrace the male character and offer him a safe and secure area. While the tree (female) offers safety, the boy (male) takes that which provides safety and sustenance.
c. "… and make them into crowns and play king of the forest."	Here the tree's loss is the boy's gain. While the tree is presented as giving and nurturing the boy's wishes, the boy immediately establishes power as the "king of the forest" and, implicitly, her.
d.	
e.	
f.	

LEVELED DIFFERENTIATED INSTRUCTION

Some students may be still challenged by the idea of "recasting" the story from a feminist perspective. They can work in groups, in pairs, or alone to do this.

Developing Work with students in a small group to have them brainstorm about how they would approach recasting the story. Remind them about point of view. Ask them if they can retell the story from the tree's point of view. Ask if they would draw different pictures to accompany the text. In a picture book, pictures can sometimes illustrate something that is not in the text itself. For instance, a picture might give the reader a different perspective on what the tree is thinking or feeling. If students are challenged by English, they can use a combination of words and images to recast the story.

Expanding Have the students work in pairs to recast the story from a feminist point of view. Suggest that one student come up with list of questions to ask the tree and have the other student respond as they think the tree might. Then have them switch roles and one student come up with a list of questions for the boy. Remind them that the questions should touch upon issues related to gender and sexual stereotypes. Have them use their questions and answers to develop a new version of the story that reflects a feminist perspective.

Bridging If students are ready to work alone have them experiment with different approaches for recasting the story. They may, for instance, tell it from the tree's point of view, create dialogue, or add commentary—a sort of hypertext in the margins—that gives the reader an alternative point of view as they read the story. Ask them to think of other children's stories they could recast from a feminist point of view.

12 After students have reported their ideas, ask them to respond to the Check Your Understanding.

⭐ TEACHER TO TEACHER

This is a good place to remind students of the task for Embedded Assessment 2. Conduct a reflection of skills they have developed so far that will help them be successful with this task. Responses may include some of the following:

- defining Feminist Criticism
- recognizing elements of Feminist Criticism in text
- identifying textual evidence that supports understanding
- using the SOAPSTone strategy to define a writer's point of view
- writing a summary
- studying the organization and thesis of a critical analysis model

13 Ask students to complete the writing prompt either in class or for homework.

ASSESS

When reviewing responses to the Check Your Understanding, be sure that students mention at least one new understanding that emerged when they read *The Giving Tree* from a feminist perspective.

Make sure that responses to the writing prompt contain a clear thesis and effective textual support. Ask students to share their claims. Use student responses to the writing prompt to assess their ability to apply Feminist Criticism in support of their own opinion.

ADAPT

If students need additional help perceiving *The Giving Tree* through a feminist lens, model completing a **SMELL** graphic organizer, paying particular attention to the character of the tree. Alternatively, ask students to complete a feminist reading of a familiar text or film, and write a brief response explaining what new understandings emerged.

2.18

My Notes

☑ Check Your Understanding

Based on your analysis and discussion of *The Giving Tree*, what is one new understanding that emerges when reading the story from a feminist perspective? How could you recast *The Giving Tree* as a feminist story?

✍ Writing Prompt: Informational

Consider the final line of the story: "And the tree was happy." Write an explanation of why the tree would or would not be happy. How could a feminist analysis of this story give the reader a new or different understanding? Consider the author's portrayal of men and women in the text and the relationship between them as you incorporate principles of Feminist Criticism in your explanation. Be sure to:

- Begin with a clear thesis statement.
- Include relevant quotations and examples from the text to support your analysis and commentary.
- Use a coherent organizational structure and employ transitions effectively to make connections between ideas.
- Use academic and purposeful vocabulary.

WRITING PROMPT: INFORMATIONAL

The following standards are addressed in the writing prompt:

- W.11–12.2a
- W.11–12.2b
- W.11–12.2c
- W.11–12.2d
- W.11–12.9
- L.11–12.3
- L.11–12.6

Seeing Beyond Your Own Perspective

Learning Targets

- Evaluate the author's craft in a short story and present your views in a collegial discussion.
- Compare multiple texts, from across genres, using a feminist perspective.
- Apply the feminist lens by writing a literary analysis of a short story.

Preview

In this activity, you will closely read a short story and develop analytical questions to actively participate in a Socratic Seminar. Then, using a feminist perspective, you will compare the short story to texts previously read in this unit. You will synthesize your new understanding in a written response.

As You Read

- As you read, underline instances where you feel the author is building a sense of foreshadowing or suspense.
- Circle unknown words and phrases. Try to determine the meaning of the words by using context clues, word parts, or a dictionary.

About the Author

Roald Dahl (1916–1990) was a prolific 20th-century writer who worked in a variety of genres. He is best known for his children's books, but he also wrote novels and short stories for adults, screenplays, and autobiographies. Born in Wales, UK, to Norwegian parents, Dahl was educated in Britain and became a British citizen. He joined the Royal Air Force during World War II and published his first short stories soon after the war in 1946. Dahl was known for his sense of irony and dark humor. His stories often end with a surprise twist. Among his most famous works are *Matilda*, *The Witches*, *James and the Giant Peach*, and *Charlie and the Chocolate Factory*.

Learning Strategies

Close Reading
Levels of Questions
Marking the Text
Socratic Seminar

My Notes

ACTIVITY 2.19

PLAN

Materials: index cards
Suggested Pacing: 3 50-minute class periods

TEACH

1 Read the Learning Targets and Preview with your students. Help them understand this will be a **close reading** of a short story with the aim of analyzing it from a feminist perspective.

2 Review the rules of a **Socratic Seminar**. Tell the students that they will be asking and answering one another's questions.

3 Go over the As You Read with students. Ask them to define *foreshadowing* in their own words.

4 Read About the Author with your students. Ask them about previous Roald Dahl books they've read or film adaptations they've seen. Write a list on the board of common attributes of Dahl stories. Ask one or two students to volunteer inferences about the story in this activity, based on these common characteristics.

College and Career Readiness Standards

Focus Standards:

RL.11–12.3 Analyze the impact of the author's choices regarding how to develop and relate elements of a story or drama (e.g., where a story is set, how the action is ordered, how the characters are introduced and developed).

W.11–12.9 Draw evidence from literary or informational texts to support analysis, reflection, and research.

SL.11–12.1c Propel conversations by posing and responding to questions that probe reasoning and evidence; ensure a hearing for a full range of positions on a topic or issue; clarify, verify, or challenge ideas and conclusions; and promote divergent and creative perspectives.

5 FIRST READ: While this is a fairly straightforward short story, it also contains a definite mood of suspense that might be best conveyed by a read-aloud. Ask students to volunteer to read parts of the story aloud. You may want to divide the story into chunks. Tell students to think of how the story builds suspense.

 TEXT COMPLEXITY

Overall: Complex
Lexile: 790L
Qualitative: Low Difficulty
Task: Challenging (Evaluate)

6 You might model the **levels of questions** strategy before students begin reading. Remind them of the three types of questions with these suggestions for the first two paragraphs:

- **Literal:** What is the weather like when Billy arrives in Bath?
- **Interpretive:** What does the author imply when he describes the air as "deadly cold" and the wind like "a flat blade of ice" on Billy's cheeks?
- **Universal:** What does it feel like to arrive alone at night in a place you have never been before?

2.19

My Notes

Short Story

The Landlady

by **Roald Dahl**

1 Billy Weaver had travelled down from London on the slow afternoon train, with a change at Swindon on the way, and by the time he got to Bath it was about nine o'clock in the evening and the moon was coming up out of a clear starry sky over the houses opposite the station entrance. But the air was deadly cold and the wind was like a flat blade of ice on his cheeks.

2 "Excuse me," he said, "but is there a fairly cheap hotel not too far away from here?"

3 "Try The Bell and Dragon," the porter answered, pointing down the road. "They might take you in. It's about a quarter of a mile along on the other side."

4 Billy thanked him and picked up his suitcase and set out to walk the quarter mile to The Bell and Dragon. He had never been to Bath before. He didn't know anyone who lived there. But Mr. Greenslade at the Head Office in London had told him it was a splendid city. "Find your own lodgings," he had said, "and then go along and report to the Branch Manager as soon as you've got yourself settled."

5 Billy was seventeen years old. He was wearing a new navy-blue overcoat, a new brown trilby hat, and a new brown suit, and he was feeling fine. He walked briskly down the street. He was trying to do everything briskly these days. Briskness, he had decided, was the one common characteristic of all successful businessmen. The big shots up at Head Office were absolutely fantastically brisk all the time. They were amazing.

6 There were no shops on this wide street that he was walking along, only a line of tall houses on each side, all them identical. They had porches and pillars and four or five steps going up to their front doors, and it was obvious that once upon a time they had been very swanky residences. But now, even in the darkness, he could see that the paint was peeling from the woodwork on their doors and windows, and that the handsome white façades were cracked and blotchy from neglect.

7 Suddenly, in a downstairs window that was brilliantly illuminated by a street-lamp not six yards away, Billy caught sight of a printed notice propped up against the glass in one of the upper panes. It said BED AND BREAKFAST. There was a vase of yellow chrysanthemums, tall and beautiful, standing just underneath the notice.

8 He stopped walking. He moved a bit closer. Green curtains (some sort of velvety material) were hanging down on either side of the window. The chrysanthemums looked wonderful beside them. He went right up and peered through the glass into the room, and the first thing he saw was a bright

College and Career Readiness Standards

W.11–12.1 Write arguments to support claims in an analysis of substantive topics or texts, using valid reasoning and relevant and sufficient evidence.

Additional Standards Addressed:
RL.11–12.1, RL.11–12.2, RL.11–12.4, RL.11–12.5, RL.11–12.6, W.11–12.5, W.11–12.1a, W.11–12.1b, W.11–12.1c, W.11–12.1d, W.11–12.1e, SL.11–12.1b

fire burning in the hearth. On the carpet in front of the fire, a pretty little dachshund was curled up asleep with its nose tucked into its belly.

9   The room itself, so far as he could see in the half-darkness, was filled with pleasant furniture. There was a baby-grand piano and a big sofa and several plump armchairs; and in one corner he spotted a large parrot in a cage. Animals were usually a good sign in a place like this, Billy told himself; and all in all, it looked to him as though it would be a pretty decent house to stay in. Certainly it would be more comfortable than The Bell and Dragon.

10   On the other hand, a pub would be more congenial than a boarding-house. There would be beer and darts in the evenings, and lots of people to talk to, and it would probably be a good bit cheaper, too. He had stayed a couple of nights in a pub once before and he had liked it. He had never stayed in any boarding-houses, and, to be perfectly honest, he was a tiny bit frightened of them. The name itself conjured up images of watery cabbage, rapacious landladies, and a powerful smell of kippers in the living-room.

11   After dithering about like this in the cold for two or three minutes, Billy decided that he would walk on and take a look at The Bell and Dragon before making up his mind. He turned to go. And now a queer thing happened to him. He was in the act of stepping back and turning away from the window when all at once his eye was caught and held in the most peculiar manner by the small notice that was there. BED AND BREAKFAST, it said. BED AND BREAKFAST, BED AND BREAKFAST, BED AND BREAKFAST. Each word was like a large black eye staring at him through the glass, holding him, compelling him, forcing him to stay where he was and not to walk away from that house, and the next thing he knew, he was actually moving across from the window to the front door of the house, climbing the steps that led up to it, and reaching for the bell.

12   He pressed the bell. Far away in a back room he heard it ringing, and then at once—it must have been at once because he hadn't even had time to take his finger from the bell-button—the door swung open and a woman was standing there.

13   Normally you ring the bell and you have at least a half-minute's wait before the door opens. But this dame was a like a jack-in-the-box. He pressed the bell—and out she popped! It made him jump.

14   She was about forty-five or fifty years old, and the moment she saw him, she gave him a warm welcoming smile.

15   "Please come in," she said pleasantly. She stepped aside, holding the door wide open, and Billy found himself automatically starting forward into the house. The compulsion or, more accurately, the desire to follow after her into that house was extraordinarily strong. "I saw the notice in the window," he said, holding himself back.

16   "Yes, I know."

17   "I was wondering about a room."

My Notes

_____

_____

_____

_____

_____

_____

_____

_____

conjured up: brought to mind
rapacious: extremely greedy
dithering about: pausing indecisively
compulsion: overwhelming urge

ACTIVITY 2.19 continued

7 Prompt students to engage with the three **levels of questions** using these suggestions for paragraphs 10–11:

- **Literal:** Why does Billy think a pub might be better than a boarding house?
- **Interpretive:** What does the author imply when he says that "each letter was like a large black eye staring at him..."?
- **Universal:** What does it feel like to be compelled to do something by forces you don't understand?

8 Pause after paragraph 12 to address the first two Making Observations bullets. Also remind students to note their emotions as they read.

9 Support comprehension by using the vocabulary support provided throughout the story, such as vocabulary glossed in the passage and footnotes.

Scaffolding the Text-Dependent Questions

1. How is Billy described in the first few paragraphs of this story (paragraphs 1–5)? What does this reveal about his character? Use evidence to support your answer. How is Billy dressed? How does he move? How does he feel? What details reveal these things? RL.11–12.1, RL.11–12.3

2. What does Billy observe about the Bed and Breakfast in paragraphs 8–9? What details stand out about the description of the Bed and Breakfast? How do these details make Billy feel? RL.11–12.3, RL.11–12.6

10 Pause after paragraph 27. Ask students what details stand out to them about the boarding house. How do these details add to the sense of suspense?

2.19

My Notes

18 "It's all ready for you, my dear," she said. She had a round pink face and very gentle blue eyes.

19 "I was on my way to The Bell and Dragon," Billy told her. "But the notice in your window just happened to catch my eye."

20 "My dear boy," she said, "why don't you come in out of the cold?"

21 "How much do you charge?" "Five and sixpence a night, including breakfast."

22 It was fantastically cheap. It was less than half of what he had been willing to pay.

23 "If that is too much," she added, "then perhaps I can reduce it just a tiny bit. Do you desire an egg for breakfast? Eggs are expensive at the moment. It would be sixpence less without the egg."

24 "Five and sixpence is fine," he answered. "I should like very much to stay here."

25 "I knew you would. Do come in."

26 She seemed terribly nice. She looked exactly like the mother of one's best schoolfriend welcoming one into the house to stay for the Christmas holidays. Billy took off his hat, and stepped over the threshold.

27 "Just hang it there," she said, "and let me help you with your coat."

28 There were no other hats or coats in the hall. There were no umbrellas, no walkingsticks—nothing.

29 "We have it all to ourselves," she said, smiling at him over her shoulder as she led the way upstairs.

30 "You see, it isn't very often I have the pleasure of taking a visitor into my little nest."

31 The old girl is slightly dotty, Billy told himself. But at five and sixpence a night, who gives a damn about that?—"I should've thought you'd be simply swamped with applicants," he said politely.

32 "Oh, I am, my dear, I am, of course I am. But the trouble is that I'm inclined to be just a teeny weeny bit choosy and particular—if you see what I mean."

33 "Ah, yes."

34 "But I'm always ready. Everything is always ready day and night in this house just on the off-chance that an acceptable young gentleman will come along. And it is such a pleasure, my dear, such a very great pleasure when now and again I open the door and I see someone standing there who is just exactly right." She was half-way up the stairs, and she paused with one hand on the stair-rail, turning her head and smiling down at him with pale lips. "Like you," she added, and her blue eyes travelled slowly all the way down the length of Billy's body, to his feet, and then up again.

Scaffolding the Text-Dependent Questions

3. How does Billy feel about choosing between living in a boarding house and above a pub? What does this reveal about his perspective of men and women? Reread paragraph 10. What words does the author use to describe a pub? What words does he use to describe a boarding house? How do these words relate to places that are stereotypically male or female? RL.11–12.3, RL.11–12.6

4. Describe the mood in paragraph 11. How does the author create this mood? What words does the author use to describe what Billy sees in this paragraph? What words does he use to describe Billy's inner state? RL.11–12.3, RL.11–12.4

5. What is strange about the landlady when Billy rings the doorbell? What is the sequence of actions after Billy rings the doorbell? What effect do those actions create? RL.11–12.3

11 Continue helping students to engage with the text using levels of questions. Pause after paragraph 45. Ask students to note one thing that stands out to them about Billy's interaction with the landlady.

My Notes

35 On the first-floor landing she said to him,

36 "This floor is mine."

37 They climbed up a second flight. "And this one is all yours," she said. "Here's your room. I do hope you'll like it." She took him into a small but charming front bedroom, switching on the light as she went in.

38 "The morning sun comes right in the window, Mr. Perkins. It is Mr. Perkins, isn't it?"

39 "No," he said. "It's Weaver."

40 "Mr. Weaver. How nice. I've put a waterbottle between the sheets to air them out, Mr. Weaver. It's such a comfort to have a hot water-bottle in a strange bed with clean sheets, don't you agree? And you may light the gas fire at any time if you feel chilly."

41 "Thank you," Billy said. "Thank you ever so much." He noticed that the bedspread had been taken off the bed, and that the bedclothes had been neatly turned back on one side, all ready for someone to get in.

42 "I'm so glad you appeared," she said, looking earnestly into his face. "I was beginning to get worried."

43 "That's all right," Billy answered brightly. "You mustn't worry about me." He put his suitcase on the chair and started to open it.

44 "And what about supper, my dear? Did you manage to get anything to eat before you came here?"

45 "I'm not a bit hungry, thank you," he said. "I think I'll just go to bed as soon as possible because tomorrow I've got to get up rather early and report to the office."

46 "Very well, then. I'll leave you now so that you can unpack. But before you go to bed, would you be kind enough to pop into the sitting-room on the ground floor and sign the book? Everyone has to do that because it's the law of the land, and we don't want to go breaking any laws at this stage in the proceedings, do we?" She gave him a little wave of the hand and went quickly out of the room and closed the door.

47 Now, the fact that his landlady appeared to be slightly off her rocker didn't worry Billy in the least. After all, she was not only harmless—there was no question about that—but she was also quite obviously a kind and generous soul. He guessed that she had probably lost a son in the war, or something like that, and had never got over it.

48 So a few minutes later, after unpacking his suitcase and washing his hands, he trotted downstairs to the ground floor and entered the living-room. His landlady wasn't there, but the fire was glowing in the hearth, and the little dachshund was still sleeping in front of it. The room was wonderfully warm and cosy. I'm a lucky fellow, he thought, rubbing his hands. This is a bit of all right.

Scaffolding the Text-Dependent Questions

6. What juxtaposition does the author create to suggest to the reader that Billy's perception of the landlady is not quite accurate? How does the author describe Billy's first impression of the landlady? Read paragraph 18 and then read paragraph 34. What do you notice about the landlady's eyes in each of these paragraphs? RL.11–12.2, RL.11–12.4, RL.11–12.5

My Notes

49 He found the guest-book lying open on the piano, so he took out his pen and wrote down his name and address. There were only two other entries above his on the page, and, as one always does with guest-books, he started to read them. One was a Christopher Mulholland from Cardiff. The other was Gregory W. Temple from Bristol. That's funny, he thought suddenly. Christopher Mulholland. It rings a bell. Now where on earth had he heard that rather unusual name before?

50 Was he a boy at school? No. Was it one of his sister's numerous young men, perhaps, or a friend of his father's? No, no, it wasn't any of those. He glanced down again at the book. Christopher Mulholland, 231 Cathedral Road, Cardiff. Gregory W. Temple, 27 Sycamore Drive, Bristol. As a matter of fact, now he came to think of it, he wasn't at all sure that the second name didn't have almost as much of a familiar ring about it as the first.

51 "Gregory Temple?" he said aloud, searching his memory. "Christopher Mulholland? …"

52 "Such charming boys," a voice behind him answered, and he turned and saw his landlady sailing into the room with a large silver tea-tray in her hands. She was holding it well out in front of her, and rather high up, as though the tray were a pair of reins on a frisky horse.

53 "They sound somehow familiar," he said.

54 "They do? How interesting."

55 "I'm almost positive I've heard those names before somewhere. Isn't that queer? Maybe it was in the newspapers. They weren't famous in any way, were they? I mean famous cricketers or footballers or something like that?"

56 "Famous," she said, setting the tea-tray down on the low table in front of the sofa. "Oh no, I don't think they were famous. But they were extraordinarily handsome, both of them, I can promise you that. They were tall and young and handsome, my dear, just exactly like you."

57 Once more, Billy glanced down at the book.

58 "Look here," he said, noticing the dates.

59 "This last entry is over two years old."

60 "It is?"

61 "Yes, indeed. And Christopher Mulholland's is nearly a year before that—more than three years ago."

62 "Dear me," she said, shaking her head and heaving a dainty little sigh. "I would never have thought it. How time does fly away from us all, doesn't it, Mr Wilkins?"

63 "It's Weaver," Billy said. "W-e-a-v-e-r."

64 "Oh, of course it is!" she cried, sitting down on the sofa. "How silly of me. I do apologise. In one ear and out the other, that's me, Mr. Weaver."

65 "You know something?" Billy said. 'Something that's really quite extraordinary about all this?"

66 "No, dear, I don't."

67 "Well, you see—both of these names, Mulholland and Temple, I not only seem to remember each one of them separately, so to speak, but somehow or other, in some peculiar way, they both appear to be sort of connected together as well. As though they were both famous for the same sort of thing, if you see what I mean—like … like Dempsey and Tunney, for example, or Churchill and Roosevelt."

68 "How amusing," she said. "But come over here now, dear, and sit down beside me on the sofa and I'll give you a nice cup of tea and a ginger biscuit before you go to bed."

69 "You really shouldn't bother," Billy said. "I didn't mean you to do anything like that." He stood by the piano, watching her as she fussed about with the cups and saucers. He noticed that she had small, white, quickly moving hands, and red finger-nails.

70 "I'm almost positive it was in the newspapers I saw them," Billy said. "I'll think of it in a second. I'm sure I will."

71 There is nothing more **tantalizing** than a thing like this which lingers just outside the borders of one's memory. He hated to give up.

72 "Now wait a minute," he said. "Wait just a minute. Mulholland ... Christopher Mulholland ... wasn't that the name of the Eton schoolboy who was on a walking-tour through the West Country, and then all of a sudden ..."

73 "Milk?" she said. "And sugar?"

74 "Yes, please. And then all of a sudden ..."

75 "Eton schoolboy?" she said. "Oh no, my dear, that can't possibly be right because my Mr. Mulholland was certainly not an Eton schoolboy when he came to me. He was a Cambridge undergraduate. Come over here now and sit next to me and warm yourself in front of this lovely fire. Come on. Your tea's all ready for you." She patted the empty place beside her on the sofa, and she sat there smiling at Billy and waiting for him to come over. He crossed the room slowly, and sat down on the edge of the sofa. She placed his teacup on the table in front of him.

76 "There we are," she said. "How nice and cosy this is, isn't it?"

77 Billy started sipping his tea. She did the same. For half a minute or so, neither of them spoke. But Billy knew that she was looking at him. Her body was half-turned towards him, and he could feel her eyes resting on his face, watching him over the rim of her teacup. Now and again, he caught a whiff of a peculiar smell that seemed to **emanate** directly from her person. It was not in the least unpleasant, and it reminded him—well, he wasn't quite sure what it reminded him of. Pickled walnuts? New leather? Or was it the corridors of a hospital?

My Notes

tantalizing: fascinating
emanate: flow from

Scaffolding the Text-Dependent Questions

7. What can the reader infer, using evidence from the text, about the two boys that are missing? Based on this information, what conclusion can be drawn about Billy's fate? Read paragraphs 68–73. What do you notice about the way the landlady speaks to Billy? How does this shape the relationship between them? RL.11–12.1

My Notes

trifle: little bit

78 "Mr. Mulholland was a great one for his tea," she said at length. "Never in my life have I seen anyone drink as much tea as dear, sweet Mr. Mulholland."

79 "I suppose he left fairly recently," Billy said. He was still puzzling his head about the two names.

80 He was positive now that he had seen them in the newspapers – in the headlines.

81 "Left?" she said, arching her brows. "But my dear boy, he never left. He's still here. Mr. Temple is also here. They're on the third floor, both of them together."

82 Billy set down his cup slowly on the table, and stared at his landlady. She smiled back at him, and then she put out one of her white hands and patted him comfortingly on the knee. "How old are you, my dear?" she asked.

83 "Seventeen."

84 "Seventeen!" she cried. "Oh, it's the perfect age! Mr. Mulholland was also seventeen. But I think he was a trifle shorter than you are, in fact I'm sure he was, and his teeth weren't quite so white. You have the most beautiful teeth, Mr. Weaver, did you know that?"

85 "They're not as good as they look," Billy said.

86 "They've got simply masses of fillings in them at the back."

87 "Mr. Temple, of course, was a little older," she said, ignoring his remark. "He was actually twenty-eight. And yet I never would have guessed it if he hadn't told me, never in my whole life. There wasn't a blemish on his body."

88 "A what?" Billy said.

89 "His skin was just like a baby's."

90 There was a pause. Billy picked up his teacup and took another sip of his tea, then he set it down again gently in its saucer. He waited for her to say something else, but she seemed to have lapsed into another of her silences. He sat there staring straight ahead of him into the far corner of the room, biting his lower lip.

91 "That parrot," he said at last. "You know something? It had me completely fooled when I first saw it through the window from the street. I could have sworn it was alive."

92 "Alas, no longer."

93 "It's most terribly clever the way it's been done," he said. "It doesn't look in the least bit dead. Who did it?"

94 "I did."

95 "You did?"

96 "Of course," she said. "And have you met my little Basil as well?" She nodded towards the dachshund curled up so comfortably in front of the fire.

Billy looked at it. And suddenly, he realised that this animal had all the time been just as silent and motionless as the parrot. He put out a hand and touched it gently on the top of its back. The back was hard and cold, and when he pushed the hair to one side with his fingers, he could see the skin underneath, greyish-black and dry and perfectly preserved.

97 "Good gracious me," he said. "How absolutely fascinating." He turned away from the dog and stared with deep admiration at the little woman beside him on the sofa. "It must be most awfully difficult to do a thing like that."

98 "Not in the least," she said. "I stuff all my little pets myself when they pass away. Will you have another cup of tea?"

99 "No, thank you," Billy said. The tea tasted faintly of bitter almonds, and he didn't much care for it.

100 "You did sign the book, didn't you?"

101 "Oh, yes."

102 "That's good. Because later on, if I happen to forget what you were called, then I can always come down here and look it up. I still do that almost every day with Mr. Mulholland and Mr ... Mr..."

103 "Temple," Billy said. "Gregory Temple. Excuse my asking, but haven't there been any other guests here except them in the last two or three years?"

104 Holding her teacup high in one hand, inclining her head slightly to the left, she looked up at him out of the corners of her eyes and gave him another gentle little smile. "No, my dear," she said. 'Only you.'

My Notes

Making Observations

- What details do you notice about the landlady's living room?
- What emotions do you feel when reading this short story?

GRAMMAR & USAGE

Complex Sentences

A complex sentence has one independent clause and one or more dependent clauses.

Independent Clause: *There were no shops on this wide street that he was walking along*

Dependent Clause: *only a line of tall houses on each side*

Dependent Clause: *all them identical*

Using a complex sentence structure enables a writer to show complex relationships between and among ideas.

Find one more example of a complex sentence in the story and note how it shows a complex idea.

ACTIVITY 2.19 continued

12 Pause at the end of the story. Ask students to look over the last few paragraphs and underline the place where they first became aware of Billy's fate and what would happen to him after the story ended.

13 Direct students' attention to the Grammar & Usage box. Discuss the box with students and have them complete the practice.

14 **RETURNING TO THE TEXT:** During the second reading, students will be returning to the text to answer the text-dependent comprehension questions. Have the students read independently. Students will have an opportunity to discuss their responses in small groups.

15 Following the reading, have partners think-pair-share to discuss their Making Observations notes. Listen in on group discussions to gauge comprehension.

Scaffolding the Text-Dependent Questions

8. What is the author implying when the landlady says, "...I stuff all my little pets myself when they pass away. Will you have another cup of tea?" Reread the end of the story. What does the narrator say? What does he not say? What effect does that create? Does the reader know for sure? What does the reader assume? RL.11–12.1, RL.11–12.3, RL.11–12.4

16 Have students complete the Focus on the Sentence to check their comprehension of the text.

17 After the students have finished reading, have them break up into small groups to discuss their answers to the text-dependent questions. Circulate around the room, asking the students to note any questions they find difficult. Scaffold the questions by rephrasing them or breaking them down into smaller parts. See the Scaffolding the Text-Dependent Questions boxes for suggestions.

2.19

My Notes

☑ Focus on the Sentence

Use details from the short story to complete the following sentences.

The landlady "seemed terribly nice" because

she "looked exactly like the mother of one's best schoolfriend welcoming one into the house to stay for the Christmas holidays."

The landlady "seemed terribly nice," so

Billy decided to stay at her bed and breakfast even though she also seemed "slightly dotty."

The landlady "seemed terribly nice," but

the story ends with an ominous implication that Mr. Weaver will become her next victim.

Returning to the Text

- Reread the story to answer these text-dependent questions.
- Write any additional questions you have about the text in your Reader/Writer Notebook.

1. How is Billy described in the first few paragraphs of this story (paragraphs 1–5)? What does this reveal about his character? Use evidence to support your answer.

   Billy is a teenager, who strives to be a successful businessman. He is wearing "a new navy trilby hat, and a new brown suit." These details, coupled with the fact that "he was trying to do everything briskly these days," suggest that Billy is trying to appear more mature than he actually is. His desire to move briskly, even in new territory, reveals his naivety.

2. What does Billy observe about the Bed and Breakfast in paragraphs 8–9?

   Based on what Billy can see from outside, the Bed and Breakfast appears to have "pleasant furniture," and a "pretty little dachshund curled up," in front of the fire place. He reasons that animals are a good sign, and "all in all, it looked to him as though it would be a pretty decent house to stay in. Certainly it would be more comfortable than The Bell and Dragon."

3. How does Billy feel about choosing between living in a boarding house and above a pub? What does this reveal about his perspective of men and women?

   At first Billy thinks he would rather live above a pub because it is a friendly atmosphere with typical male activities like "beer and darts." He is a "bit frightened" of boarding houses. He has never stayed in one but thinks he would find only "watery cabbage and rapacious landladies." This suggests that he feels that women are predatory.

4. Describe the mood in paragraph 11. How does the author create this mood?

   The mood is ominous and threatening. The use of capitalization puts the reader on alert and indicates that danger lies ahead. The Bed and Breakfast sign is described as a "large black eye" that is "compelling" Billy to the front door. This diction suggests that there is a dark and almost supernatural force drawing Billy.

LEVELED DIFFERENTIATED INSTRUCTION

Distribute the **Text Structure Stairs** graphic organizer and explain that it will help students understand how Dahl increases the level of suspense throughout the story.

Beginning Divide the story into chunks for the students. Possible divisions might be: Billy's arrival in Bath and his first observations of the boarding house (paragraphs 1–11); Billy's first encounter with the landlady (paragraphs 12–45); and the final scene between Billy and the landlady (paragraphs 46–102).

Developing After the students finish the first read, distribute the graphic organizer and guide student pairs or small groups to work through the story. For each chunk, ask them to paraphrase what happens in that chunk, paying particular attention to events, words and images that add to their sense of suspense. Have them note those things in the organizer. After they have filled out the organizer, have them discuss the end of the story and how they feel about it.

Expanding Arrange students into pairs or small groups and distribute the graphic organizer. Then ask them to reread the story together and fill in each step of graphic organizer. Ask them to discuss their reactions as readers after they fill in each step. Have them discuss the end of the story and why they think Dahl did not want to spell it out for the reader.

Bridging Before students move on to the Second Read questions, have them complete the steps of the graphic organizer for The Landlady. Then ask them to use a blank copy of the organizer to help structure an original story that relies on developing a sense of foreboding in the reader. Have them think of how they will end their story. If they wish they can write the story on their own time and add it to their notebooks or portfolios.

5. **What is strange about the landlady when Billy rings the doorbell?**

The narrator emphasizes the speed at which the landlady answers the door. The landlady

answers the door before Billy takes his finger off the bell, which startles him. Her eagerness to

answer the door foreshadows her ulterior motives.

6. **What juxtaposition does the author create to suggest to the reader that Billy's perception of the landlady is not quite accurate?**

Dahl uses the phrase "terribly nice" to describe Billy's first impression of the landlady. This

contradictory phrase hints that the woman may not be as kind as she appears. The landlady

is described as having "very gentle blue eyes," but Dahl later contrasts this by describing her

eyes traveling "slowly all the way down the length of Billy's body."

7. **What can the reader infer, using evidence from the text, about the two boys that are missing? Based on this information, what conclusion can be drawn about Billy's fate?**

The reader senses that what Billy is trying to remember is important. The landlady interrupts

him, which builds suspense and distracts him from completing his thought. Her interruptions

give her control over the conversation and Billy himself.

8. **What is the author implying when the landlady says, "... I stuff all my little pets myself when they pass away. Will you have another cup of tea?"**

Dahl is implying that the landlady not only performs taxidermy on small animals, but that she

also stuffs the young men who stay at her bed and breakfast. By posing the question, "Will

you have another cup of tea?" Dahl is creating a cliff hanger. The reader is left wondering if the

tea is poisonous and if it will ultimately lead to Billy's demise.

2.19

Working from the Text

9. Review your questions in the My Notes section. To prepare for a Socratic Seminar meet with your reading group. Share your list of questions with your group and work collaboratively to select 8–10 questions that deeply question the story from a Feminist perspective. Respectfully listen to your classmates' opinions. Record your group's questions in the chart.

Socratic Seminar Questions	

10. Using the index cards provided by your teacher, write one question per card; on the reverse side, cite textual evidence that can support responses. Divide the cards among members of the group equally. Be prepared to refer to these cards during the seminar discussion.

11. Socratic Seminar: Listen closely to your peers' questions during the Socratic Seminar. Contribute relevant questions to the discussion and record notes from the discussion in the graphic organizer provided in step 12.

18 Transition to a discussion of the text from a feminist perspective by having students respond to the Working from the Text questions. Explain that this preparation is important for effective discussion during the Socratic Seminar.

19 Have students share their levels of questions and select the ten to twelve questions that best probe for understanding. After they have added these questions to the chart on the student page, have them write the questions and the text evidence that supports responses to them on index cards.

20 When students have prepared their questions, they are ready to participate in a Socratic Seminar discussion of this story. So that students effectively support their claims with textual evidence, encourage them to refer to their index cards and the story's text as references. You might begin this discussion with the question *How does a feminist reading of "The Landlady" lead to your understanding of the short story?*

21 After the Socratic Seminar, ask students to write a reflective summary of their understanding of Feminist Criticism. Alert them that they must apply this perspective independently to a short story as they complete Embedded Assessment 2.

 TEACHER TO TEACHER

This activity is intended to provide gradual release for students, preparing them to work independently as they complete Embedded Assessment 2. You have directed the activities of reading the folktale, literary criticism and the play; this activity calls for students to work cooperatively to analyze a text from one perspective, Feminist Criticism.

22 Direct students to clarify their understanding of Feminist Criticism assumptions by reviewing previous texts. The graphic organizer in student step 12 will help them review four texts that they have studied, require them to review the textual evidence, and identify the feminist assumptions evident in each text.

23 Before students begin, model the completion of the graphic organizer with one text. Suggested answers are provided on the reduced student page.

24 Have students jigsaw these texts in groups, with one student working with one text. As each person presents, the listening students take notes to complete their graphic organizers.

25 Check for understanding when groups have completed their sharing by asking students to identify what they know about Feminist Criticism. Discuss how the reading and viewing of the texts from a feminist perspective adds to the understanding of each text.

12. In previous activities, you have studied two texts written by women: "Cinderella, the Legend" and "Why Women Always Take Advantage of Men." You also have applied the feminist critical perspective to a text written by a man: *Pygmalion*. "The Landlady" is written by a man and the main character is a young man. To review how to apply Feminist Criticism, think about the works you have read, how you have applied the feminist perspective in each, and what attitudes and details you might expect to discover while applying this lens.

Work Studied	Plot Conflict, Character, or Values Commentary that Illustrate Feminist Perspective	Implications of Feminist Perspective
"Cinderella, the Legend"	The female is rescued from her plight by a male.	patriarchal dominance, female author's viewpoint
"Why Women Always Take Advantage of Men"	God, presumably a man, agrees to give man more strength than he gives woman.	patriarchal dominance, central gender issues
Pygmalion	Eliza first appears ignorant, unsophisticated; Higgins "fixes" her.	patriarchal dominance, central gender issues, female assuming male values
"The Landlady"	Billy, the naïve male protagonist, is entrapped by a murderous woman.	male assumptions about women's capabilities based on stereotypical gender roles

My Notes

LANGUAGE & WRITER'S CRAFT: Citing Textual Evidence

For Embedded Assessment 2, you must include textual evidence and commentary to support your thesis statement. As you write the textual evidence on your index cards, practice three important skills of citing textual evidence:

- introducing the citation with a clearly written and appropriate lead-in.
- defining the source (In this case, cite paragraph or section number since the text is in your book)
- supporting the citation by providing original commentary and explanation

Examples:

Billy initially assumes the landlady is the stereotypical maternal older woman. He finds her to be warm and friendly and even thinks that she looks, "exactly like the mother of one's best schoolfriend welcoming one in the house to stay for the Christmas holidays" (paragraph 25).

Lead-in: Billy initially assumes the landlady is the stereotypical maternal older woman. He finds her to be warm and friendly and even thinks that she looks,

Textual evidence: "exactly like the mother of one's best schoolfriend welcoming one in the house to stay for the Christmas holidays"

Source: (paragraph 25)

In the parlor, Billy begins to wonder about other young men. His puzzlement and inability to remember make him a little unsure of himself in his surroundings. The landlady, on the other hand, begins to assert her control even further. When she tells him to come and sit by her, "He crossed the room slowly, and sat down on the edge of the sofa" (Paragraph 73).

Commentary: In the parlor, Billy begins to wonder about other young men. His puzzlement and inability to remember make him a little unsure of himself in his surroundings. The landlady, on the other hand, begins to assert her control even further

Lead-in: When she tells him to come and sit by her,

Textual evidence: "He crossed the room slowly, and sat down on the edge of the sofa"

Source: (Paragraph 73)

PRACTICE After finding your first piece of textual evidence to write on your index cards, follow the example to practice the skills mentioned for citing textual evidence: introduce with appropriate lead-in, define the source, and comment with an explanatory statement.

26 For Language & Writer's Craft, have students work in pairs. Ask them to review one another's index cards and give each other feedback. Remind them to make sure that they can identify the lead-in, text evidence, and source. Tell them to point out anything that seems unclear or inaccurate. If necessary, the students should revise their work based on their partner's feedback.

27 Have students complete the writing prompt either in class or as homework. Briefly discuss the skills and knowledge they will need to complete the prompt and highlight how it connects to the Embedded Assessment. Reiterate that a thesis statement will clearly focus on the topic and the body of the essay will use ideas and evidence to support that topic. Review how to organize the literary analysis and connect the major components as noted in the student steps. Remind students that relevant evidence directly supports their analysis and reflection while addressing counterclaims, or what someone who opposes their interpretation might say.

28 Direct students to the Independent Reading Checkpoint. Ask them to note one new thing they have learned about Feminist Criticism from their reading and share it with the class. Decide when they should conclude their independent reading for this unit.

ASSESS

Evaluate student responses to the writing prompt and assess whether or not each essay includes a clear thesis that presents the writer's interpretation of the relationship between Billy and the landlady, applying a feminist perspective. Check that they organized their analysis logically and cohesively. Note how they used dialogue as evidence and ensure that all evidence is relevant. Verify punctuation is used correctly.

ADAPT

If students need additional help with the writing prompt, first ensure that their thesis statement is clear, specific, and defensible. Ask them if they have encountered examples of sexual stereotypes in their own experience or independent reading. Ask students to respond to these questions: What does Dahl imply about Billy and the landlady through their interactions? What larger issues about men, women, and power are suggested?

2.19

My Notes

📝 Writing Prompt: Argumentative

Write an analytical essay to explain the relationship between Billy and the landlady in "The Landlady," analyzing the story from a Feminist Perspective. In what ways do Billy and the landlady demonstrate characteristics stereotypical of men and women? In what way are the characters different? What is the balance of power between the sexes in this story and how is that power expressed? Use textual evidence to support and clarify your thinking. Be sure to:

- Begin with a clear thesis that states your primary interpretation of Dahl's story.
- Organize your analysis by logically sequencing your interpretation, counterclaims, reasons, and evidence.
- Use transitions strategically to link your ideas.
- Cite textual evidence to provide reasons to support your interpretation.
- Introduce and punctuate all quotations and nonrestrictive elements correctly.

📗 Independent Reading Checkpoint

Review your independent reading and any notes you have taken. What have you learned about Feminist Criticism and how to analyze a text from a feminist perspective? Discuss your learning with classmates, clarify your understanding of Feminist Criticism, and add new insight to your notes. How can this information help you complete the upcoming Embedded Assessment?

📝 WRITING PROMPT: ARGUMENTATIVE

The following standards are addressed in the writing prompt:

- W.11–12.2a
- W.11–12.2b
- W.11–12.2c
- W.11–12.2d
- W.11–12.2e
- W.11–12.9

Applying a Critical Perspective

 ASSIGNMENT

Your assignment is to write an analytical essay applying the Feminist Critical Perspective to a short story. You have two stories to read and choose from, "The Story of an Hour" by Kate Chopin or "The Chaser" by John Collier. (Both stories are included.)

Planning and Prewriting: Read critically and collect your evidence.	■ Which of the two stories resonates with you on a personal level? ■ What questions are asked about a text when it is read from a feminist perspective? ■ How will you collect your initial ideas to create a focus on feminist perspective of these stories? (e.g., brainstorming, a graphic organizer)? ■ How will you determine which ideas should go into your draft? ■ Who is the audience for your essay? How much do you think this audience knows about feminist issues and feminist criticism?
Drafting: Craft your analysis.	■ How much summary is necessary to introduce the story to the audience? How can you summarize and paraphrase the text in a way that keeps the author's original meaning? ■ How will you use both evidence from the text and your own words to support your feminist perspective? ■ How can you make sure that your writing is clear and engaging to the reader (e.g., using appeals, sentence variety, transitions between ideas)?
Evaluating and Revising Your Draft: Review and improve to make your work the best it can be.	■ How can you determine if your syntax and use of language helps the reader understand your feminist analysis? ■ How will you determine if your sentence structure and transitions present your ideas in the best way? ■ How can you use your peers' insights and the Scoring Guide to help evaluate your draft and guide your revision?
Checking and Editing for Publication: Confirm that your final draft is ready.	■ How will you check for grammatical and technical accuracy? ■ What tools are available to you to create a technically sound text (e.g., dictionary or format guide, spell check)?

Reflection

After completing this Embedded Assessment, think about how you went about accomplishing this assignment, and respond to the following:

- How did your understanding of Feminist Criticism shape your analysis of the short story?

College and Career Readiness Standards

Focus Standards:

RL.11–12.2 Determine two or more themes or central ideas of a text and analyze their development over the course of the text, including how they interact and build on one another to produce a complex account; provide an objective summary of the text.

W.11–12.1 Write arguments to support claims in an analysis of substantive topics or texts, using valid reasoning and relevant and sufficient evidence.

W.11–12.9 Draw evidence from literary or informational texts to support analysis, reflection, and research.

Materials: student-selected short story from the two provided; students' notes on Feminist Criticism
Suggested Pacing: 2 50-minute class periods plus homework

TEACHER TO TEACHER

If you want or need to modify this Embedded Assessment by changing the assignment for some or all of your students, be sure that you have properly scaffolded the necessary skills and knowledge.

1 Assignment: Review the assignment with the class. Students should mark the text to identify all the requirements and review their notes from Activity 2.14.

2 Planning and Prewriting: Encourage students to read both short stories, choosing the one that appeals most to them since both can be read from a feminist critical perspective.

3 Drafting: Have students review the Language & Writer's Craft in Activities 2.4 and 2.19 to refresh their understanding of how to write a summary and cite textual evidence.

4 Evaluating and Revising: Peers should read through each other's drafts to offer suggestions on sequencing the analysis. Remind students to use the Scoring Guide criteria to ensure they have met the expectations for this assessment.

5 Checking and Editing: Remind your students to use their Editing Checklists as they revise their drafts. They should specifically check for the grammar topics covered in this unit, including use of commas, parentheses, and dashes. Reinforce the need for appropriate punctuation when citing textual evidence.

6 Reflection: Have students respond to the reflection question after they have completed the assignment.

EMBEDDED ASSESSMENT 2

7 **Portfolio:** Be sure students address the Reflection question as a separate part of the Embedded Assessment assignment, so they can include it separately. All notes for and drafts of the analytical essay should be collected and presented together to show the process students completed in successfully accomplishing the task.

SCORING GUIDE

When you score this Embedded Assessment, you may wish to download and print a copy of the Scoring Guide from SpringBoard Digital. This way, you can have a copy to mark for each student's work.

 TEACHER TO TEACHER

If any of your students need support with English language development, you may wish to preview the Embedded Assessment text, "The Story of an Hour," with the corresponding Language Workshop 2B activities available on SpringBoard Digital. Built around Kate Chopin's short story, these activities offer a scaffolded approach to developing academic language through vocabulary study, guided close reading, and collaborative academic discussion.

SCORING GUIDE

Scoring Criteria	Exemplary	Proficient	Emerging	Incomplete
Ideas	The essay • demonstrates a thorough understanding of feminist issues in the short story. • perceptively applies the Feminist Critical perspective to the text. • uses well-chosen details that support the main ideas of the analysis.	The essay • demonstrates an understanding of the feminist issues in the short story. • appropriately applies the Feminist Critical perspective to the text. • analyzes the work with appropriate details that support the main ideas.	The essay • demonstrates a superficial understanding of the feminist issues in the short story. • contains an underdeveloped application of Feminist Criticism. • contains too few examples or details, possibly replaced by excessive and unorganized summary.	The essay • demonstrates little understanding of the feminist short story. • does not apply Feminist Criticism. • contains few examples or details and may repeat some details unnecessarily.
Structure	The essay • follows an exceptionally clear organization. • uses sentence structure and transitions effectively and creatively to move smoothly from one idea to the next.	The essay • organizes ideas clearly so that they are easy to follow. • uses sentence structure adequately and some transitions to move between ideas.	The essay • organizes ideas in ways that are difficult to follow. • uses weak sentence structure and few transitions or jumps too rapidly between ideas.	The essay • is disorganized or uses a confusing organization. • uses poor or awkward sentence structure and few or no transitions to move between limited ideas.
Use of Language	The essay • crafts language to enhance the analysis and consistently convey an academic voice. • successfully weaves in textual evidence from the story. • demonstrates strong control and mastery of standard writing conventions.	The essay • uses language clearly to communicate the analysis and demonstrate an appropriate academic voice. • accurately weaves in textual evidence from the story. • demonstrates control of standard writing conventions; may contain minor errors that do not interfere with meaning.	The essay • uses language that does not clearly communicate the analysis or demonstrate an academic voice. • awkwardly or inaccurately incorporates evidence from the story. • contains frequent errors in standard writing conventions that interfere with meaning.	The essay • does not clearly communicate the analysis or use an academic voice. • inaccurately uses a few details from the story. • contains numerous errors in standard writing conventions that seriously impede understanding.

College and Career Readiness Standards

W.11–12.5 Develop and strengthen writing as needed by planning, revising, editing, rewriting, or trying a new approach, focusing on addressing what is most significant for a specific purpose and audience.

Additional Standards Addressed:

RL.11–12.1, RL.11–12.3, RL.11–12.4, RL.11–12.5, W.11–12.1a, W.11–12.1b, W.11–12.1c, W.11–12.1d, W.11–12.1e

TEXT COMPLEXITY

Overall: Accessible
Lexile: 960L
Qualitative: Moderate Difficulty
Task: Moderate (Analyze)

My Notes

About the Author

A native of St. Louis, Missouri, Kate Chopin (1850–1904) became a keen observer of New Orleans culture after her marriage to Oscar Chopin of Louisiana. She depicted the regional flavor and racial tensions of Creole and Cajun people in the short story collections *Bayou Folk* (1894) and *A Night in Acadie* (1897). Her best-known work is *The Awakening* (1899), a novel that explores the emotional growth of a dissatisfied New Orleans wife and mother. Contemporary critics condemned *The Awakening* for its frank treatment of sexuality and women's independence.

Short Story

The Story of an Hour

by **Kate Chopin**

1   Knowing that Mrs. Mallard was afflicted with a heart trouble, great care was taken to break to her as gently as possible the news of her husband's death.

2   It was her sister Josephine who told her, in broken sentences; veiled hints that revealed in half concealing. Her husband's friend Richards was there, too, near her. It was he who had been in the newspaper office when intelligence of the railroad disaster was received, with Brently Mallard's name leading the list of "killed." He had only taken the time to assure himself of its truth by a second telegram, and had hastened to forestall any less careful, less tender friend in bearing the sad message.

3   She did not hear the story as many women have heard the same, with a paralyzed inability to accept its significance. She wept at once, with sudden, wild abandonment, in her sister's arms. When the storm of grief had spent itself she went away to her room alone. She would have no one follow her.

4   There stood, facing the open window, a comfortable, roomy armchair. Into this she sank, pressed down by a physical exhaustion that haunted her body and seemed to reach into her soul.

5   She could see in the open square before her house the tops of trees that were all aquiver with the new spring life. The delicious breath of rain was in the air. In the street below a peddler was crying his wares. The notes of a distant song which someone was singing reached her faintly, and countless sparrows were twittering in the eaves.

6   There were patches of blue sky showing here and there through the clouds that had met and piled one above the other in the west facing her window.

My Notes

7   She sat with her head thrown back upon the cushion of the chair, quite motionless, except when a sob came up into her throat and shook her, as a child who has cried itself to sleep continues to sob in its dreams.

8   She was young, with a fair, calm face, whose lines bespoke repression and even a certain strength. But now there was a dull stare in her eyes, whose gaze was fixed away off yonder on one of those patches of blue sky. It was not a glance of reflection, but rather indicated a suspension of intelligent thought.

9   There was something coming to her and she was waiting for it, fearfully. What was it? She did not know; it was too subtle and elusive to name. But she felt it, creeping out of the sky, reaching toward her through the sounds, the scents, the color that filled the air.

10   Now her bosom rose and fell tumultuously. She was beginning to recognize this thing that was approaching to possess her, and she was striving to beat it back with her will—as powerless as her two white slender hands would have been. When she abandoned herself a little whispered word escaped her slightly parted lips. She said it over and over under her breath: "free, free, free!" The vacant stare and the look of terror that had followed it went from her eyes. They stayed keen and bright. Her pulses beat fast, and the coursing blood warmed and relaxed every inch of her body.

11   She did not stop to ask if it were or were not a monstrous joy that held her. A clear and exalted perception enabled her to dismiss the suggestion as trivial. She knew that she would weep again when she saw the kind, tender hands folded in death; the face that had never looked save with love upon her, fixed and gray and dead. But she saw beyond that bitter moment a long procession of years to come that would belong to her absolutely. And she opened and spread her arms out to them in welcome.

12   There would be no one to live for during those coming years; she would live for herself. There would be no powerful will bending hers in that blind persistence with which men and women believe they have a right to impose a private will upon a fellow-creature. A kind intention or a cruel intention made the act seem no less a crime as she looked upon it in that brief moment of illumination.

13   And yet she had loved him—sometimes. Often she had not. What did it matter! What could love, the unsolved mystery, count for in the face of this possession of self-assertion which she suddenly recognized as the strongest impulse of her being!

14   "Free! Body and soul free!" she kept whispering.

15   Josephine was kneeling before the closed door with her lips to the keyhole, imploring for admission. "Louise, open the door! I beg; open the door—you will make yourself ill. What are you doing, Louise? For heaven's sake open the door."

16   "Go away. I am not making myself ill." No; she was drinking in a very elixir of life through that open window.

TEXT COMPLEXITY

Overall: Accessible
Lexile: 700L
Qualitative: Moderate Difficulty
Task: Moderate (Analyze)

My Notes

17 Her fancy was running riot along those days ahead of her. Spring days, and summer days, and all sorts of days that would be her own. She breathed a quick prayer that life might be long. It was only yesterday she had thought with a shudder that life might be long.

18 She arose at length and opened the door to her sister's importunities. There was a feverish triumph in her eyes, and she carried herself unwittingly like a goddess of Victory. She clasped her sister's waist, and together they descended the stairs. Richards stood waiting for them at the bottom.

19 Someone was opening the front door with a latchkey. It was Brently Mallard who entered, a little travel-stained, composedly carrying his grip-sack and umbrella. He had been far from the scene of the accident, and did not even know there had been one. He stood amazed at Josephine's piercing cry; at Richards' quick motion to screen him from the view of his wife.

20 When the doctors came they said she had died of heart disease—of the joy that kills.

About the Author

John Collier (1901–1980) was a British-born author and screenplay writer. Collier was educated by his uncle in London and decided in his late teens that he wanted to be a writer. Writers and artists of the 1920s influenced Collier as he was drawn to modern literary styles, visual images, and ideals. He is best known for his short stories, many of which appeared in *The New Yorker*. His story collection *Fancies and Goodnights* won the International Fantasy Award in 1951.

Short Story

The Chaser

by **John Collier**

1 Alan Austen, as nervous as a kitten, went up certain dark and creaky stairs in the neighborhood of Pell Street, and peered about for a long time on the dime landing before he found the name he wanted written obscurely on one of the doors.

2 He pushed open this door, as he had been told to do, and found himself in a tiny room, which contained no furniture but a plain kitchen table, a rocking chair, and an ordinary chair. On one of the dirty buff-coloured walls were a couple of shelves, containing in all perhaps a dozen bottles and jars. An old man sat in the rocking chair, reading a newspaper. Alan, without a word, handed him the card he had been given.

My Notes

3 "Sit down, Mr. Austen," said the old man very politely.

4 "I am glad to make your acquaintance."

5 "Is it true," asked Alan, "that you have a certain mixture that has—er—quite extra ordinary effects?"

6 "My dear sir," replied the old man, "my stock in trade is not very large. I don't deal in laxatives and teething mixtures but such as it is, it is varied. I think nothing I sell has effects which could be precisely described as ordinary."

7 "Well, the fact is …" began Alan.

8 "Here, for example," interrupted the old man, reaching for a bottle from the shelf. "Here is a liquid as colourless as water, almost tasteless, quite imperceptible in coffee, wine, or any other beverage. It is also quite imperceptible to any known method of autopsy."

9 "Do you mean it is a poison?" cried Alan, very much horrified.

10 "Call it a glove-cleaner if you like," said the old man indifferently. "Maybe it will clean gloves. I have never tried. One might call it a life-cleaner. Lives need cleaning sometimes."

11 "I want nothing of that sort," said Alan.

12 "Probably it is just as well," said the old man. "Do you know the price of this? For one teaspoonful, which is sufficient, I ask five thousand dollars. Never less. Not a penny less."

13 "I hope all your mixtures are not as expensive," said Alan apprehensively.

14 "Oh dear, no," said the old man. "It would be no good charging that sort of price for a love potion, for example. Young people who need a love potion very seldom have five thousand dollars. Otherwise they would not need a love potion."

15 "I am glad to hear that," said Alan.

16 "I look at it like this," said the old man. "Please a customer with one article, and he will come back when he needs another. Even if it is more costly. He will save up for it, if necessary."

17 "So," said Alan, "you really do sell love potions?"

18 "If I did not sell love potions," said the old man, reaching for another bottle, "I should not have mentioned the other matter to you. It is only when one is in a position to oblige that one can afford to be so confidential."

19 "And these potions," said Alan. "They are not just—just—er …"

20 "Oh, no," said the old man. "Their effects are permanent, and extend far beyond the mere casual impulse. But they include it. Oh, yes they include it. Bountifully, insistently. Everlastingly."

21 "Dear me!" said Alan, attempting a look of scientific detachment. "How very interesting!"

22 "But consider the spiritual side," said the old man.

23 "I do, indeed," said Alan.

24 "For indifference," said the old man, "they substitute devotion. For scorn, adoration. Give one tiny measure of this to the young lady—its flavour is imperceptible in orange juice, soup, or cocktails and however gay and giddy she is, she will change altogether. She will want nothing but solitude and you."

25 "I can hardly believe it," said Alan. "She is so fond of parties."

26 "She will not like them any more," said the old man. "She will be afraid of the pretty girls you may meet."

27 "She will actually be jealous?" cried Alan in a rapture. "Of me?"

28 "Yes, she will want to be everything to you."

29 "She is, already. Only she doesn't care about it."

30 "She will, when she has taken this. She will care intensely. You will be her sole interest in life."

31 "Wonderful!" cried Alan.

32 "She will want to know all you do," said the old man. "All that has happened to you during the day. Every word of it. She will want to know what you are thinking about, why you smile suddenly, why you are looking sad."

33 "That is love!" cried Alan.

34 "Yes," said the old man. "How carefully she will look after you! She will never allow you to be tired, to sit in a draught, to neglect your food. If you are an hour late, she will be terrified. She will think you are killed, or that some siren has caught you."

35 "I can hardly imagine Diana like that!" cried Alan, overwhelmed with joy.

36 "You will not have to use your imagination," said the old man. "And, by the way, since there are always sirens, if by any chance you should, later on, slip a little, you need not worry. She will forgive you, in the end. She will be terribly hurt, of course, but she will forgive you in the end."

37 "That will not happen," said Alan fervently.

38 "Of course not," said the old man. "But, if it did, you need not worry. She would never divorce you. Oh, no! And, of course, she will never give you the least, the very least, grounds for uneasiness."

39 "And how much," said Alan, "is this wonderful mixture?"

40 "It is not as dear," said the old man, "as the glove-cleaner, or life-cleaner, as I sometimes call it. No. That is five thousand dollars, never a penny less. One has to be older than you are, to indulge in that sort of thing. One has to save up for it."

41 "But the love potion?" said Alan.

My Notes

My Notes

42 "Oh, that," said the old man, opening the drawer in the kitchen table, and taking out a tiny, rather dirty-looking phial. "That is just a dollar."

43 "I can't tell you how grateful I am," said Alan, watching him fill it.

44 "I like to oblige," said the old man. "Then customers come back, later in life, when they are better off, and want more expensive things. Here you are. You will find it very effective."

45 "Thank you again," said Alan. "Goodbye."

46 "Au revoir," said the man.

Planning the Unit

Context

William Shakespeare's *The Tragedy of Othello, the Moor of Venice* has been performed for more than 400 years, and its characters and conflicts continue to be relevant to every age and country in which his plays are produced. Unit 3 asks students to apply multiple critical lenses to Shakespeare's *Othello,* which yields rich perspectives on this canonical play. Students will read, listen to, watch and perform the drama, which will allow them to make meaning and truly own their interpretations of the text. Students will understand the play as performers, and they will consider its ever-evolving interpretations.

Suggested Texts and Materials

You will need the following materials for this unit:

- Activities 3.2, 3.5–3.18: *The Tragedy of Othello, the Moor of Venice,* by William Shakespeare
- Activity 3.3: Lyrics for "The Right to Love" by Gene Lees, recording of "The Right to Love" by Gene Lees and Lalo Schifrin
- Activity 3.4: Props (student choice)
- Activity 3.6: Project Brabantio's speech to model annotating the text
- Activities 3.8, 3.12, 3.12, 3.15, (optional) 3.20: Film versions of *Othello* to help students examine performance choices and form interpretations (see film recommendations at the end of this Planning the Unit section)
- Activity 3.14: Cards labeled with critical perspectives
- Activity 3.22: Playbills from stage performances

Instructional Sequence

Throughout their reading and study of *Othello,* students will have opportunities to practice performing and staging Shakespeare's drama. They will also apply critical perspectives to scenes in anticipation of their own interpretive performances. Viewing and comparing film and filmed stage versions of *Othello* allows students to see a variety of interpretations. The sequence of instruction begins with a reading and analysis of *Othello,* culminating in Embedded Assessment 1 with a written analysis in which students apply a critical perspective to *Othello.*

At the end of the unit, students will read an essay that traces multiple interpretations of *Othello* over time. They will then plan and stage their own performance of a scene for Embedded Assessment 2: Staging an Interpretation.

AP® CONNECTIONS

In this unit, students will focus on refining these important skills and knowledge areas for AP/College Readiness:

- Grounding interpretation of a text in its historical and social setting (Activities 3.5, 3.7, 3.9, 3.10, 3.14, 3.17)
- Comparing and evaluating artistic interpretations of text (Activities 3.13, 3.14, 3.15)
- Developing textually substantiated interpretations of text (Activities 3.6, 3.8, 3.12, Embedded Assessment 1)
- Writing a well-organized, cohesive essay that includes a defensible claim about an interpretation of literature supported with evidence and reasoning (Activity 3.6, 3.7, 3.8, 3.15)
- Focusing deliberate attention on the craft of sentence-level writing (Activities 3.3, 3.6, 3.7, 3.9)

SAT® CONNECTIONS

In this unit, students will practice many important skills that will help them succeed on the SAT and other college readiness exams, including:

- Recognizing and correcting inappropriate shifts in verb tense, voice, and mood within and between sentences (LC 3.20)

Unpacked Embedded Assessments

Embedded Assessment 1: Writing a Literary Analysis	Embedded Assessment 2: Staging an Interpretation
Skills and Knowledge: • Develop a clearly defined thesis that makes an assertion about a character. • Provide valid reasoning and relevant and sufficient evidence to support the analysis. • Organize the essay so that ideas move smoothly. • Choose a critical perspective and analyze a character through that critical lens. • Solicit and incorporate feedback for revision. • Use transitions for coherence.	**Skills and Knowledge:** • Read and interpret the selected scene from *Othello*. • Select and apply a relevant critical perspective. • Collaborate in planning, rehearsing, and presenting the scene. • Reflect on the process, including the acting company's collaboration on scene analysis and interpretation during rehearsals. • Compose correspondence to the audience that explains the message behind the dramatic interpretation.

Cognate Directory

Encouraging students to notice the connections between their primary language and English can help them develop academic vocabulary more quickly. If your class includes Spanish speakers, consider adding the following cognates to the classroom Word Wall. For English Language Learners whose primary language is not Spanish, consider using an online translator or dictionary to support comprehension of vocabulary terms.

Unit 3 Vocabulary Terms with Spanish Cognates

Academic Terms	
English	**Spanish**
components	componentes
scenario	escenario

Literary Terms	
English	**Spanish**
blocking	bloqueo
dramatic irony	ironía dramática
epithet	epíteto
Historical Criticism	crítica histórica
monologue	monólogo
situational irony	ironía situacional
soliloquy	soliloquio
verbal irony	ironía verbal

Activity Features at a Glance

The activities in every ELA unit reflect the interconnected nature of reading, writing, listening, speaking, and thinking. The Activity Features at a Glance chart highlights the types of tasks or supports that students and teachers will encounter in each activity.

 Writing and Revision   **Grammar and Language**   **Listening, Speaking, and Discussion**   **Independent Reading**   **Vocabulary Development**   **ELL Support**   **Knowledge Quest**   **Gaining Perspectives**

ELA Activity	Activity Features
3.1	🗣️ 📦
3.2	✍️ 🗣️
3.3	✍️ G 🗣️ V ELL
3.4	✍️ 🗣️ V
3.5	✍️ G 🗣️ 📦 V ELL
3.6	✍️ G 🗣️ 📦 V ELL
3.7	✍️ G 🗣️ V ELL
3.8	✍️ G 🗣️ 📦 V ELL
3.9	✍️ G 🗣️ V ELL 🧭
3.10	✍️ 🗣️ 📦
3.11	🗣️ 📦 V ELL
3.12	✍️ 🗣️ 📦 ELL

ELA Activity	Activity Features
3.13	✍️ 🗣️ V ELL 🌱
3.14	✍️ 🗣️ 📦 ELL
3.15	✍️ 🗣️ ELL
3.16	🗣️ V ELL
3.17	🗣️ ELL
3.18	✍️ 🗣️ 📦 ELL
3.19	🗣️ 📦
3.20	✍️ 🗣️ V ELL 🧭
LC 3.20	G 🗣️
3.21	✍️ 🗣️ 📦 ELL
3.22	✍️ 🗣️ 📦

Unit Resources at a Glance

Formative Assessment Opportunities	Digital Assessments	Family Connections
Text-dependent questions Writing prompts Check Your Understanding tasks Focus on the Sentence tasks Language Checkpoint exercises Language & Writer's Craft practice	Activity Quizzes 3.2–3.22 Unit Assessment Part 1 Unit Assessment Part 2 (SBD)	Suggestions for Independent Reading Family Letters (English and Spanish) Student Reports (SBD)
English Language Development	**Foundational Skills**	**Independent Reading**
Leveled Differentiated Instruction Graphic Organizers ELD Strategies Language Workshop 3A Language Workshop 3B	Foundational Skills Screening Assessment Observational Look-fors Foundational Skills Workshop	My Independent Reading List Independent Reading Links Independent Reading Checkpoints Independent Reading Log Reader/Writer Notebook Suggestions for Independent Reading

⊕ Suggestions for Independent Reading

This list, divided into the categories of **Literature** and **Nonfiction/Informational Text,** comprises titles related to the themes and content of the unit. For their independent reading, students can select from this wide array of titles, which have been chosen based on complexity and interest. Spanish-language titles are included for those students who can read with greater independence or at a higher grade level in Spanish than in English, since building on their first language literacy can bolster their acquisition of English. Titles on this list have been suggested by teachers and school librarians, but you should be sure to preview texts to assess their appropriateness for your specific students and setting. You can also encourage students to do their own research and select titles that intrigue them.

Unit 3: Evolving Perspectives

Literature		
Author	**Title**	**Lexile**
Atwood, Margaret	*The Handmaid's Tale*	750L
Bellow, Saul	*Herzog*	850L
Brontë, Charlotte	*Jane Eyre*	1040L
Brontë, Charlotte	*Jane Eyre (Spanish)*	1040L
Coetzee, J.M.	*Waiting for the Barbarians*	930L
Dostoevsky, Fyodor	*The Eternal Husband and Other Stories*	N/A
Hardy, Thomas	*Tess of the D'Urbervilles*	1110L
Hosseini, Khaled	*The Kite Runner*	840L
Kafka, Franz	*The Metamorphosis*	1340L
Lester, Julius	*Othello: A Novel*	770L
Lloyd, Rosemary	*Closer and Closer Apart: Jealousy in Literature*	1600L

Morrison, Toni	The Bluest Eye	920L
Naslund, Sena Jeter	Ahab's Wife: Or, The Star-gazer: A Novel	N/A
Robbe-Grillet, Alain	Jealousy	N/A
Roy, Arundhati	The God of Small Things	840L
Shakespeare, William	Otelo: el moro de Venecia	NP
Soyinka, Wole	Death and the King's Horseman: A Play	NP
Stevenson, Robert Louis	El extraño caso del doctor Jekyll y el señor Hyde	1110L
Stevenson, Robert Louis	The Strange Case of Dr. Jekyll and Mr. Hyde	1060L
Stoppard, Tom	Rosencrantz and Guildenstern Are Dead	NP

Nonfiction/Informational		
Author	**Title**	**Lexile**
Andraka, Jack	Breakthrough: How One Teen Innovator Is Changing the World	940L
Berger, Arthur A.	Cultural Criticism: A Primer of Key Concepts	N/A
Bernard, Jacqueline	Journey Toward Freedom: Sojourner Truth	N/A
Cooper, Alex	Saving Alex: When I Was Fifteen I Told My Mormon Parents I Was Gay, and That's When My Nightmare Began	N/A
de Pizan, Christine	The Treasure of the City of Ladies	N/A
Gladwell, Malcolm	The Tipping Point: How Little Things Can Make a Big Difference	1160L
Grandin, Temple	Animals in Translation	1130L
Harper, Hill	Letters to a Young Brother: Manifest Your Destiny	N/A
Hodgdon, Barbara	The Shakespeare Trade: Performances and Appropriations	N/A
Janik, Vicki (editor)	Fools and Jesters in Literature, Art, and History	1380L
Johnson, David	Shakespeare and South Africa	1640L
Kerrigan, John (editor)	Motives of Woe: Shakespeare and 'Female Complaint'	1330L
Loomba, Ania and Martin Orkina (editors)	Post-Colonial Shakespeares	N/A
Maolem, Sharon	Inheritance: How Our Genes Change Our Lives - and Our Lives Change Our Genes	N/A
O'Hagan, Andrew	The Secret Life: Three True Stories of the Digital Age	N/A
Suzman, Janet	Not Hamlet: Meditations on the Frail Position of Women in Drama	N/A
Tannen, Deborah	Gender and Discourse	1270L
Wells, Stanley (editor)	Shakespeare in the Theater: An Anthology of Criticism	1360L
Winoker, Jon	The Big Book of Irony	N/A
Woolf, Virginia	A Room of One's Own	1220L

Unit 3 Instructional Pathways

Instructional Pathways

Teachers can build customized pathways through this unit by making purposeful choices about which resources to use based on students' learning needs. The charts below outline a few possible pathways to show how teachers might integrate digital assessments, Language Workshops, Close Reading Workshops, and Writing Workshops into instruction. Additional planning resources—including detailed standards correlations—are available on SpringBoard Digital.

English Language Arts Unit 3: Evolving Perspectives

Activity	SBD Digital Assessments	Pacing
Activity 3.1: Previewing the Unit	N/A	1
Activity 3.2: Creating Acting Companies	Activity Quiz 3.2	1
Activity 3.3: Cultural Criticism	Activity Quiz 3.3	3
Activity 3.4: Building a Plot and Bringing It to Life: Irony	Activity Quiz 3.4	2
Activity 3.5: Viewing a Cast of Characters through a Marxist Lens	Activity Quiz 3.5	2
Activity 3.6: A Father's Reaction: Performing and Defending an Interpretation	Activity Quiz 3.6	2
Activity 3.7: The Moor: Character Analysis through a Cultural Lens	Activity Quiz 3.7	1
Activity 3.8: Critiquing a Monologue	Activity Quiz 3.8	2
Activity 3.9: A Historical Look at the Moor	Activity Quiz 3.9	1
Activity 3.10: Desdemona: From a Feminist Perspective	Activity Quiz 3.10	2
Activity 3.11: Honest Iago: The Dramatic Speech	Activity Quiz 3.11	1
Activity 3.12: Demystifying Emilia: Questioning through a Critical Lens	Activity Quiz 3.12	1
Activity 3.13: Staging Iago's Lies: Blocking for Effect	Activity Quiz 3.13	1
Activity 3.14: One Scene, Many Perspectives	Activity Quiz 3.14	1
Activity 3.15: "Talk You of Killing?": Defending a Perspective	Activity Quiz 3.15	1
Activity 3.16: A Minor Folly: Analyzing Roderigo	Activity Quiz 3.16	1
Activity 3.17: Evolving Perspectives	Activity Quiz 3.17	1
Activity 3.18: Evaluating an Essay: Rubric Creation	Activity Quiz 3.18	1
Embedded Assessment 1: Writing a Literary Analysis	Unit Assessment Part 1	2	1

Activity	🔵 Digital Assessments	Pacing	
Activity 3.19: Unpacking Embedded Assessment 2	Activity Quiz 3.19	1	
Activity 3.20: *Othello* through Time	Activity Quiz 3.20	2	
LC3.20: Language Checkpoint: Understanding Verb Voice and Mood (optional)	Activity Quiz LC 3.20	1	
Activity 3.21: Staging a Performance	Activity Quiz 3.21	1	
Activity 3.22: Playbill: *Othello*	Activity Quiz 3.22	1	
Embedded Assessment 2: Staging an Interpretation	**Unit Assessment Part 2**	**3**	**1**

Total 50-minute Class Periods: 35–38

Language Development Pathway

Consider using some or all of the Language Workshop and Foundational Skills Workshop activities with English Language Learners or with any student who would benefit from extra support with academic English. More detailed guidance about the timing of Language Workshop and Foundational Skills Workshop activities in relation to the ELA unit and about the purpose of each activity can be found in the Language Workshop teacher edition.

Language Workshop 3A and 3B		
Activity or Workshop		**Pacing**
Activity 3.1: Previewing the Unit		1
Activity 3.2: Creating Acting Companies		1
Activity 3.3: Cultural Criticism		3
Activity 3.4: Building a Plot and Bringing It to Life: Irony		2
Activity 3.5: Viewing a Cast of Characters through a Marxist Lens		2
Activity 3.6: A Father's Reaction: Performing and Defending an Interpretation		2
Language Workshop 3A.1: Genre Focus		1
Language Workshop 3A.2: Building Knowledge		1
Language Workshop 3A.3: Academic Vocabulary		1
Language Workshop 3A.4: Vocabulary Preview and Practice		1
Activity 3.7: The Moor: Character Analysis through a Cultural Lens	**OR** **Language Workshop 3A.5:** Close Reading of an Anchor Text*	1
		Language Workshop 3A.6: Academic Collaboration*	1
Activity 3.8: Critiquing a Monologue		1

Activity or Workshop		Pacing	
Activity 3.9: A Historical Look at the Moor		1	
Language Workshop 3A.7: Language Checkpoint		1	
Activity 3.10: Desdemona: From a Feminist Perspective		2	
Language Workshop 3B.3: Academic Vocabulary		1	
Language Workshop 3B.4: Vocabulary Preview and Practice		2	
Activity 3.11: Honest Iago: The Dramatic Speech	Language Workshop 3B.5: Close Reading of an Anchor Text*	1	1
	Language Workshop 3B.6: Academic Collaboration*		1
Activity 3.12: Demystifying Emilia: Questioning through a Critical Lens		1	
Activity 3.13: Staging Iago's Lies: Blocking for Effect		1	
Activity 3.14: One Scene, Many Perspectives		1	
Activity 3.15: "Talk You of Killing?": Defending a Perspective		1	
Activity 3.16: A Minor Folly: Analyzing Roderigo		1	
Activity 3.17: Evolving Perspectives		1	
Activity 3.18: Evaluating an Essay: Rubric Creation		1	
Embedded Assessment 1: Writing a Literary Analysis	Collaborative Embedded Assessment: Writing an Analysis of a Drama	2	4
Activity 3.19: Unpacking Embedded Assessment 2		1	
Language Workshop 3B.1: Genre Focus		1	
Language Workshop 3B.2: Building Knowledge		1	
Activity 3.20: Othello through Time		2	
Language Workshop 3B.7: Language Checkpoint		1	
LC 3.20: Language Checkpoint: Understanding Verb Voice and Mood (optional)		1	
Activity 3.21: Staging a Performance		1	
Activity 3.22: Playbill: Othello		1	
Embedded Assessment 2: Staging an Interpretation	Collaborative Embedded Assessment: Performing a Shakespearean Play	3	7
	Total 50-minute Class Periods:	35–55	

* These activities are available in Spanish.

Foundational Skills Workshop

The Foundational Skills Workshop offers instructional and practice materials for providing small-group instruction to students who are still developing foundational reading skills.

Activity	Pacing
Activity 1: Practicing Letter-Sound Relationships	15 min.
Activity 2: Recognizing Words by Sight	10 min.
Activity 3: Words with Inconsistent but Common Spellings	
Activity 4: Irregularly Spelled Words	
Activity 5: Common Prefixes	
Activity 6: Common Suffixes	35–40 min. per activity
Activity 7: Using Roots and Affixes to Read Multisyllabic Words	
Activity 8: Reading Multisyllabic Words	
Activity 9: Reading Informational Text with Purpose and Understanding	
Activity 10: Reading Poetry with Fluency	

Flexible Pathways

Teachers may build a flexible pathway that focuses on developing students' close reading and writing skills with the Close Reading and Writing Workshops. Each workshop addresses a specific set of standards and includes multiple assessment opportunities to allow students to demonstrate the knowledge and skills that are the focus of that workshop.

Close Reading Workshops

Workshop	Genre Focus	Assessment Opportunities	Pacing
Close Reading Workshop 4: Shakespeare	Drama Visual Text Poetry	Writing Prompt Debate/Discussion Multimedia Presentation	8

Writing Workshops

Workshop	Genre Focus	Assessment Opportunities	Pacing
Writing Workshop 10: Procedural Texts: Project Proposals	Procedural Texts	Writing as a Class Writing with a Peer Independent Writing	7

Film Versions of *Othello*

Title	Director	Actors	Year	Notes
The Tragedy of Othello: The Moor of Venice	Orson Welles	Orson Welles, Micheál MacLiammóir, Suzanne Cloutier	1952	Black and white; very cinematic; many scenes moved around, added, and omitted
Othello	Stuart Burge	Laurence Olivier, Frank Finlay, Maggie Smith	1965	Filmed stage production; Olivier in blackface makeup
Othello	Jonathan Miller	Anthony Hopkins, Bob Hoskins, Penelope Wilton	1981	BBC version, filmed onstage
Othello	Franco Zeffirelli	Placido Domingo	1986	Opera by Verdi; very cinematic, with subtitles
Othello	Janet Suzman	John Kani, Richard Haddon Haines, Joanna Weinberg	1989	South African version, filmed onstage; directed by a woman and staged during South Africa's time of apartheid
Othello	Trevor Nunn	Willard White, Ian McKellen, Imogen Stubbs	1990	Royal Shakespeare Company, filmed onstage
Othello	Oliver Parker	Laurence Fishburne, Kenneth Branagh, Irene Jacob	1995	Maintains Shakespeare's language and setting, yet is very cinematic; rated R
Othello	Geoffrey Sax	Eamonn Walker, Christopher Eccleston, Keeley Hawes	2002	Masterpiece Theater, set in contemporary England; uses Shakespeare's characters and the basic plotline, but is revised in many ways
Othello	Wilson Milam	Eamonn Walker, Tim McInnerny, Zoe Tapper	2007	Filmed onstage at Shakespeare's Globe Theater; audience highly visible

Recommended Scenes for Activity 3.8

Title/Director	Clock Counter	Notes
Othello/Burge	15:30–18:40	Olivier tries to infuse humor into the scene.
Othello/Milam	Disc 1, 20:20–22:42	Brabantio is angry and fairly unsympathetic. The audience laughs when the Duke says, "I think this tale would win my daughter, too."
Othello/Miller	18:37–21:35	Othello keeps his back to Brabantio nearly the whole time; when he does look at him, Brabantio seems to grudgingly admit that he had been (and still may be) intrigued by Othello's tales of travel.
Othello/Nunn	18:50–22:00	Several shots of the Duke and senators show their reactions to Othello's speech.
Othello/Parker	12:43–14:27	The romance is shown through flashback with voiceover.
Othello/Suzman	15:28–17:50	Othello is presented as an exotic, skilled storyteller who is respectful of the frail Brabantio.
Othello/Welles	9:28–12:26	Desdemona is in the room listening to Othello's speech.
Otello/Zeffirelli	23:34–26:51	Othello does not make his speech before the Duke; the stories of their courtship and of Othello's sad history are told through flashback. Desdemona is clearly the initiator.

Recommended Scenes for Activity 3.13

Title/Director	Clock Counter	Notes
Othello/Burge	1:39:11–1:53:57	Filmed stage production. The trance is at 1:41:50.
Othello/Milam	Disc 2, 0:01:30–0:08:08	Filmed stage production. The audience seems to be inches away from Othello while he is in the trance.
Othello/Miller	Part 2, 0:00–15:33	Film adaptation.
Othello/Parker	1:07:43–1:19:18	Film adaptation. The viewer "sees" Othello's thoughts during the trance.
Othello/Suzman	1:52:15–2:04:30	Filmed stage production.
Othello/Welles	49:38–55:59, 58:26–1:00:25	Film. Welles changes the sequence of events and uses stylized cinematic techniques to present the trance.
Otello/Zeffirelli	1:17:54–1:27:45	Cinematic opera. The order of some of the sequences is changed; Othello's trance is at 1:33:00.

Matching Cards for Activity 3.17

Below are the cards you will need for the matching activity. You will need to make enough copies so that each student receives one card.

Cultural Criticism	Race, gender, and ethnicity play a role in the way characters are depicted or treated as an "other" or as part of the dominant culture.	Shakespeare uses the character of Othello, to explore racial attitudes in Venetian society.
Archetypal Criticism	Certain images, characters, and motifs that share a common interpretation recur in the texts of peoples widely separated by time and place.	Othello fulfills the archetype of the tragic hero. Jealousy and insecurity are two of his tragic flaws.
Marxist Criticism	The issue of social class is central to the plot of the play.	Iago is motivated by his desire to elevate himself to a higher social class. He seeks revenge against Othello because Cassio was chosen for a promotion.
Feminist Criticism	In order to understand the text, one should consider the roles of the men and women.	Desdemona defies patriarchal authority by eloping with Othello. However, she still must abide by traditional marriage rules.

UNIT 3

VISUAL PROMPT
What do you notice about the figures in this painting? How would you characterize their relationship? What might be the artist's message?

EVOLVING PERSPECTIVES

O! beware, my lord, of jealousy;
It is the green-ey'd monster which doth mock
The meat it feeds on.

—from *Othello*, by William Shakespeare

Leveled Differentiated Instruction Directory

For guidance on differentiating tasks for English language learners at various levels of language proficiency, refer to the Leveled Differentiated Instruction suggestions in these activities:

3.3: In order to facilitate clear comparison and contrast between a poem and a song from different time periods, the **Venn Diagram for Writing a Comparison** may be helpful.

3.5: Use the **Unknown Word Solver** graphic organizer to support students in determining the meaning of unknown words.

3.6: Provide an audio version of the text to support comprehension and model pronunciation and intonation.

UNIT 3

Read aloud the unit title, "Evolving Perspectives," and engage students in a brief discussion. What factors might make an individual's perspective on some topic change? What about collective perspectives? How might those evolve over time, and why?

Read the quotation aloud and then have students examine the painting. Guide students to answer the questions in the visual prompt and to use those answers to understand how the image relates to the quote.

 **TEACHER TO TEACHER**

You may want to ask students to think about their experience with Shakespeare's work. Have they read poems by Shakespeare? Have they read or heard any popular quotes from Shakespeare's plays applied to personal or modern experiences? Which plays, if any, have they read or seen performed in whole or in part? Have they seen any modern film adaptations of Shakespeare's works? Ask them why they think his works endure. If students hesitate or seem perplexed by this question, ask them if they are familiar with any well-known characters (such as Romeo, Juliet, and Macbeth) or with the themes of some of his most well-known plays, such as *King Lear* and *A Midsummer Night's Dream*.

CONTENTS

Have the students **skim/scan** the activities and texts in this unit. Have them note any texts they have heard about but never read, and any activities that sound particularly interesting.

GOALS

Have students read the goals for the unit and mark any words that are unfamiliar. Add these words to the classroom Word Wall, along with definitions.

You may also want to post these goals in a visible place in the classroom for the duration of this unit, allowing you and students to revisit the goals easily and gauge progress throughout the unit.

UNIT 3

VOCABULARY DEVELOPMENT

Adding to vocabulary knowledge is essential for reading fluency. Students will encounter new vocabulary in this course in multiple ways:

- Academic Vocabulary
- Literary Terms
- Vocabulary in Context (unfamiliar terms glossed in text selections)
- Word Connections
- Oral Discussions

Encourage students to use new vocabulary expressively in class discussions and in writing. Have them keep a **Reader/Writer Notebook** in which they record new words, their meanings, and their pronunciations.

See the Resources section for examples of graphic organizers suitable for word study. Having students use word-study graphic organizers will greatly enhance their understanding of new words and their connection to unit concepts and to the broader use of advanced and discipline-based terms.

Have students review the list of academic and literary terms and sort them in a **QHT** chart. Revisit the chart periodically to see how students' understanding progresses throughout the unit.

LANGUAGE DEVELOPMENT

Several recurring SpringBoard features help build students' knowledge of grammar and usage concepts. Language & Writer's Craft features guide students to examine a writer's use of a language concept in context before incorporating the concept into their own writing. Grammar & Usage features briefly highlight and explain an interesting grammar or usage concept that appears in a text, both to improve students' reading comprehension and to increase their understanding of the concept. Periodic Language Checkpoints offer in-depth practice with standard English conventions and usage and guide students to revise sample sentences as well as their own work.

UNIT 3 Evolving Perspectives

GOALS

- To apply critical perspectives to drama and poetry
- To evaluate the use of dramatic elements in a play
- To analyze the ways in which historical and social context have influenced staged performances
- To evaluate and critique multiple interpretations of a Shakespearean tragedy
- To plan and perform dramatic interpretations of selected scenes

VOCABULARY

ACADEMIC
components
rationale
scenario
unconventional

LITERARY
aside
blocking
dramatic irony
epithet
Historical Criticism
monologue
situational irony
soliloquy
verbal irony

Leveled Differentiated Instruction Directory (continued)

3.8: Use the **Persuasive/Argument Writing Map** graphic organizer and the **Venn Diagram for Writing a Comparison** to support planning and writing argument essays about film interpretations of *Othello*.

3.9: Use the **Collaborative Dialogue** graphic organizer to help prepare students for a Socratic Seminar.

3.12: Model how to complete one column of a graphic organizer to help students analyze text.

3.13: Offer a kinesthetic option to explore the concept of blocking.

3.14: Assign students who need extra support an archetypical critical perspective, modeling how to write an analysis using this lens.

CONTENTS

Texts not included in these materials.

🔲 My Independent Reading List

UNIT 3

INDEPENDENT READING

In this unit, students will use different critical perspectives to explore a drama. Their independent reading selections should complement the unit's focus on developing the skills needed to evaluate multiple interpretations of a play using critical perspectives in historical and social contexts. The Planning the Unit section of the Teacher's Edition and the Resources section of the Student Edition contain reading lists to help you and your students find the right books.

Independent Reading Links in the unit periodically prompt students to reflect on the reading they are doing outside of class and to make connections to the texts, themes, and ideas addressed in the unit.

KNOWLEDGE QUEST

Within the unit, students will engage in two Knowledge Quests. They will read collections of texts about racial stereotypes and *Othello* through time, building their understanding of the topics and related vocabulary. Each Knowledge Quest begins with a knowledge question and supporting questions that focus student learning. After students read the final text in a set, they will have the opportunity to return to the Knowledge Question and express their growing understanding of the topic by responding to a writing-to-sources prompt or engaging in an academic discussion.

⭐ TEACHER TO TEACHER

The SpringBoard program is designed so that students interact with texts in meaningful ways, such as notetaking and annotating, to facilitate comprehension and analysis. Have students use Reader/Writer Notebooks actively for vocabulary study, answers to text-dependent questions, predictions and questions about texts, reflections, and responses to Independent Reading Links. The Reader/Writer Notebooks are not listed as part of the materials for each activity, but the expectation is that students will access them frequently.

Leveled Differentiated Instruction Directory (continued)

3.15: To help students analyze dramatic elements, model how to use a graphic organizer.

3.16: Use visual interpretations to support students in analyzing the impact of a subplot.

3.17: Use a thesis statement stem to help students convey a compelling new idea about *Othello*.

3.18: Provide an exemplar essay with the thesis statement, paragraphs, and claims labeled in order to help students plan their own essays.

3.20: Chunk readings to highlight the most relevant concepts.

3.21: Help students map out story events by providing them with the **Text Structure Stairs** graphic organizer.

ACTIVITY 3.1

PLAN

Materials: chart paper; markers; Embedded Assessment 1
Suggested Pacing: 1 50-minute class period

TEACH

1 To introduce the purpose of Activity 3.1, read aloud the Learning Targets and Preview.

2 Then, read the About the Unit section as a class. Pause occasionally to ask a volunteer to paraphrase the text.

3 Place students in pairs. Have pairs read and discuss the Essential Questions. Expand the discussion to the entire class by writing each Essential Question on a piece of chart paper. Record student responses. Students will revisit their answers to the Essential Questions as they work through the unit.

4 Ask students to locate the Embedded Assessment 1 assignment and Scoring Guide. Lead students through a close reading of the prompt, steps, and Scoring Guide criteria.

5 Have students mark the text by underlining or highlighting places in the text that mention a skill or knowledge necessary to succeed on Embedded Assessment 1.

Learning Strategies

Discussion Groups
Note-taking
Sharing and Responding
Visualizing

My Notes

Learning Targets
- Preview the big ideas for the unit.
- Create a plan for reading independently.
- Identify and analyze the skills and knowledge needed to complete Embedded Assessment 1 successfully.

Preview
In this activity, you will explore the big ideas and tasks of the unit and make plans for your independent reading.

About the Unit
In this unit, you will deepen your understanding of critical perspectives as you apply literary theories to Shakespeare's *The Tragedy of Othello, The Moor of Venice*. This play has been in continuous production for more than 400 years. In addition to its role as a drama, two operas, several ballets, and other plays have been derived from *Othello*. Shakespeare's works continue to be relevant today because they speak to universal themes that are still present in many people's lives. As you read *Othello* you will be introduced to Historical Criticism as a means to analyze the drama and the characters from a historical perspective.

Essential Questions
Based on your current knowledge, respond to the following Essential Questions.

1. What role does literature play in examining recurring social issues?

2. How can an original text be adapted for different audiences?

Unpacking Embedded Assessment 1
Closely read the following assignment for Embedded Assessment 1: Writing a Literary Analysis.

 Select a character from Othello and write a literary analysis about him or her using one of the critical lenses that you have studied (choose among Feminist, Marxist, Cultural, Historical, or Archetypal for this assignment). You will support your analysis with valid reasoning and sufficient evidence from your reading, observations, and previous written work.

With your class, create a graphic organizer that includes the skills and knowledge you will need to write an in-depth literary analysis. Summarize the major elements in your Reader/Writer Notebook.

College and Career Readiness Standards

Focus Standards:

RL.11–12.1 Cite strong and thorough textual evidence to support analysis of what the text says explicitly as well as inferences drawn from the text, including determining where the text leaves matters uncertain.

RL.11–12.10 By the end of grade 12, read and comprehend literature, including stories, dramas, and poems, at the high end of the grades 11-CCR text complexity band independently and proficiently.

W.11–12.10 Write routinely over extended time frames (time for research, reflection, and revision) and shorter time frames (a single sitting or a day or two) for a range of tasks, purposes, and audiences.

Additional Standards Addressed:

SL.11–12.1

3.1

🎲 Planning Independent Reading

The focus of this unit is the play *Othello* by William Shakespeare. For independent reading, consider a novel or play that connects to one or more themes from *Othello*, such as race, identity, jealousy, or deceit. Make a reading plan and decide which themes you'd like to explore. Discuss your plan and list of potential texts with a group of peers. Listen attentively and offer feedback on text selections and how to make your reading plans more effective.

Previewing Embedded Assessment 2

In this unit, you will be building skills and knowledge relevant to both Embedded Assessment 1 and Embedded Assessment 2 at the same time. Before diving in to study of *Othello*, it may be beneficial to also read the Embedded Assessment 2 assignment and Scoring Guide.

My Notes

_____
_____
_____
_____
_____
_____
_____
_____
_____
_____
_____
_____
_____
_____
_____
_____
_____
_____
_____
_____
_____
_____
_____
_____
_____
_____
_____
_____
_____
_____
_____

ACTIVITY 3.1 continued

6 Review the Planning Independent Reading box with students. Give students time to research possible texts for their independent reading. A librarian may be able to recommend titles to students based on interest and reading level.

ASSESS

Review students' summaries from their Reader/Writer Notebooks for evidence that they have identified and included the key skills and knowledge needed for writing a literary analysis.

ADAPT

If students need additional help summarizing the skills and knowledge, model doing so using the completed graphic organizer. Though students will not unpack Embedded Assessment 2 now, they should skim/scan the assignment and Scoring Guide in order to make informed choices about a scene they will perform.

ACTIVITY 3.2

PLAN

Materials: *The Tragedy of Othello, The Moor of Venice* by William Shakespeare; poster paper
Suggested Pacing: 1 50-minute class period

TEACH

1 Introduce the activity by reading the Learning Targets and Preview as a class. Ask a volunteer to paraphrase the Preview section.

2 Place students in discussion groups. Mix students with differing learning styles and abilities. Explain to students that they will be working in this group to complete Embedded Assessment 2.

3 Direct groups to read the first paragraph of All the World's a Stage, and then to choose a name for their acting company. Allow groups to share their names with the entire class when they have finished.

4 Read the second and third paragraphs of All the World's a Stage as a class. Ensure that students understand that their goal is to work as a group to make preliminary decisions in preparation for performing a scene in Embedded Assessment 2.

5 Then, have groups read about and choose group roles.

Learning Strategies

Discussion Groups
Marking the Text
Quickwrite

My Notes

Learning Targets

- Work collaboratively to examine the requirements for a staged interpretation of a scene from *Othello*.
- Examine scenes in the play to prepare a group performance.

Preview

In this activity, you will work with your group to create an acting company. You will familiarize yourself with the theatrical roles commonly found in a staged performance and collaborate to assign a role to each member of your group.

All the World's a Stage

1. In Shakespeare's day, acting companies named themselves, sometimes honoring their patron. Shakespeare belonged first to the Lord Chamberlain's Men and later to the King's Men. Choose a name for your acting company.

2. For the second Embedded Assessment, you and your acting group will stage an interpretation of a scene from *Othello* that you find demonstrates a critical perspective. Work with your acting company to make a preliminary scene selection from the list of suggested scenes on pages 255–256.

3. In Shakespeare's day, an acting company included a director, a dramaturge, and a company of actors. With the other members of your company, collaboratively assign roles for each member of the company for this activity. It is not absolutely necessary that gender dictate your casting choices. Make preliminary decisions about the following roles within your acting company:

   - **Director:** Leads rehearsals, working collaboratively with the group. Assumes responsibility for all of the theatrical elements: a set diagram, a plan for lighting and sound, props, and a complete script of the scene. Writes and memorizes an engaging introduction to the performance and delivers it to the audience on performance day.

   - **Dramaturge:** Conducts research to support the critical perspective the group has decided to apply to the scene and answers questions. Writes a concluding statement about the scene that explains how the group applied a critical perspective and how research supported the performance and recites this statement at the end of the performance.

   - **Actors:** Study the play, paying particular attention to their characters' motivations and relationships to other characters, and take notes. Collaborate with the director and the other actors to plan a performance. During the performance, use appropriate vocal delivery, tone, gestures, movement, props, and costumes to convey nuances of each character.

College and Career Readiness Standards

Focus Standards:

RL.11–12.1 Cite strong and thorough textual evidence to support analysis of what the text says explicitly as well as inferences drawn from the text, including determining where the text leaves matters uncertain.

RL.11–12.2 Determine two or more themes or central ideas of a text and analyze their development over the course of the text,

including how they interact and build on one another to produce a complex account; provide an objective summary of the text.

RL.11–12.6 Analyze how an author's choices concerning how to structure specific parts of a text (e.g., the choice of where to begin or end a story, the choice to provide a comedic or tragic resolution) contribute to its overall structure and meaning as well as its aesthetic impact.

3.2

Scene	Description	Characters	First line and approximate length
Act I, Scene I	Iago and Roderigo awaken Brabantio and inform him that his daughter has eloped.	Iago Roderigo Brabantio	RODERIGO: Tush, never tell me! 206 lines (Companies could opt to do only part of the scene.)
Act I, Scene III Lines 197–335	Desdemona admits her love for Othello; the Duke dispatches them to Cyprus.	Duke Desdemona Othello First senator (only one line)	DUKE: I think this tale would win my daughter too. 139 lines
Act I, Scene III Lines 344–447	Iago continues to take advantage of Roderigo's affection for Desdemona.	Roderigo Iago	RODERIGO: Iago— IAGO: What say'st thou, noble heart? 104 lines
Act II, Scene I Lines 197–307	Desdemona welcomes Othello to Cyprus; Iago convinces Roderigo to attack Cassio.	Othello Desdemona Iago Roderigo	OTHELLO: O my fair warrior! 111 lines
Act II, Scene III Lines 14–124	With Iago's encouragement, Cassio gets drunk.	Cassio Iago Montano Gentleman (only one line, which could be given to Montano)	CASSIO: Welcome, Iago. We must to the watch. 111 lines
Act II, Scene III Lines 125–265	A drunken brawl ends with Othello demoting Cassio.	Iago Montano Cassio Roderigo	IAGO [*to Montano*]: You see this fellow that is gone before. 141 lines

College and Career Readiness Standards

SL.11–12.1c Propel conversations by posing and responding to questions that probe reasoning and evidence; ensure a hearing for a full range of positions on a topic or issue; clarify, verify, or challenge ideas and conclusions; and promote divergent and creative perspectives.

Additional Standards Addressed:
RL.11–12.10, L.11–12.4c, L.11–12.5, W.11–12.2, SL.11–12.1b

ACTIVITY 3.2 continued

6 Give groups time to read the descriptions of *Othello* scenes in the chart. Have them discuss which scenes they would like to interpret. Ask each group to rank their top three choices.

TEACHER TO TEACHER

Line-number references for the suggested scenes mentioned throughout the unit refer to the Folger Shakespeare Library edition of *Othello*. This edition is easily searchable and downloadable online (www.folgerdigitaltexts.org).

Scene	Description	Characters	First line and approximate length
Act III, Scene III Lines 1–99	Desdemona tries to convince Othello to reinstate Cassio.	Desdemona Emilia Cassio Othello Iago	DESDEMONA: Be thou assured, good Cassio ... 99 lines
Act III, Scene III Lines 100–240	Iago plants the seed of doubt in Othello's mind.	Othello Iago	OTHELLO: Excellent wretch! 141 lines
Act III, Scene IV Lines 39–115	Othello demands to see the handkerchief, while Desdemona tries to change the subject by pleading Cassio's case.	Othello Desdemona	OTHELLO: How do you, Desdemona? 77 lines
Act IV, Scene II Lines 128–201	Desdemona seeks advice from Iago, while Emilia curses the person who planted the thought of infidelity in Othello's mind.	Iago Desdemona Emilia	IAGO: What is your pleasure, madam? 74 lines
Act IV, Scene III Lines 11–117	Desdemona and Emilia discuss infidelity.	Desdemona Emilia	EMILIA: How goes it now? 107 lines
Act V, Scene I Lines 1–151	Roderigo attacks Cassio.	Iago Roderigo Cassio Gratiano Lodovico Bianca Emilia	IAGO: Here, stand behind this bulk. 151 lines
Act V, Scene II Lines 131–301	Emilia tells Othello the truth.	Emilia Othello Desdemona Montano	OTHELLO: What's the matter with thee now? 171 lines

4. Once you have come to an agreement, sign and turn in a contract to your teacher. You may use the following template:

We, the _____ (name of acting company),

pledge to plan, rehearse, and perform _____

(act and scene) **from William Shakespeare's** *The Tragedy of Othello*.

Cast:

(Name of student) **as** (name of character)

Director:

Dramaturge:

☑ **Check Your Understanding**

Quickwrite: Explain how you will help your troupe achieve the goal of interpreting a scene of *Othello*. How will your role impact the audience based on your understanding of the roles of a director, a dramaturge, and actors?

My Notes

7 When the acting companies have completed their initial planning, have students write and sign an agreement regarding their participation. If they wish, students may model their agreements on the example in student step 4. Next, have students complete the Check Your Understanding independently and discuss their responses in their groups.

ASSESS

Circulate while students are forming their acting companies, choosing roles, and selecting a scene. Ensure that they distinguish among roles and can explain their purpose in choosing particular roles. Look for consensus in each group about the chosen scene and the role each member will play in it. Assess students' quickwrites for evidence they understand the most important unit ideas about analyzing a play and planning the performance of a scene.

ADAPT

If students need additional help choosing a scene or individual roles, you may want to assign them based on which scene or role will best fit individual students.

To extend learning, ask students to summarize the reasons for the role and scene selections they have made for their company. If student quickwrites are vague on the unit concepts of critical perspectives and dramatic elements, a reiteration of these may be helpful. Use a **Conversation for Quickwrite** in a think-pair-share to guide students in completing their quickwrites about the main ideas of the unit.

PLAN

Materials: lyrics for "The Right to Love" by Gene Lees; recording of "The Right to Love" by Gene Lees and Lalo Schifrin

Suggested Pacing: 2 50-minute class periods

TEACH

1 Ask a student to read aloud the Learning Targets and Preview. Make sure students understand that they will be comparing how two different works comment on social issues.

2 Vocabulary Development: Read the Academic Vocabulary box and the Word Connections: Roots and Affixes box as a class. Then, direct students to review the *components* and assumptions of Cultural Criticism and its examination of diversity in a society. Have students highlight terms important to Cultural Criticism as they read. Explain that they will be returning to Cultural Criticism throughout the unit.

3 Ask a student to read aloud the Focus on the Sentence prompt, and then give students time to write a statement and question independently. Have students share their responses with a partner.

Learning Strategies

Graphic Organizer
Marking the Text
Summarizing

VOCABULARY

ACADEMIC

Components are the parts that make up a whole. They can be steps in a process, ingredients in a recipe, or aspects of a critical perspective.

WORD CONNECTIONS

Roots and Affixes

The word **components** contains the Latin prefix *com-*, which means "with" or "together." The Latin root of *component* is *ponere*, which means "to place." Related words include *comport*, *compose*, *composer*, and *composite*.

My Notes

Learning Targets

• Compare and contrast the development of a theme in song lyrics and a poem.
• Analyze two texts through a critical perspective to make connections to a social issue.
• Evaluate the use of meter and form in two texts.

Preview

In this activity, you will review the elements of Cultural Criticism and apply the lens to compare how two authors address similar themes. You will make pointed observations about the similarities and differences in how each writer has crafted their work to comment on a recurring social issue.

Cultural Criticism

1. Review the components of Cultural Criticism. Use this critical perspective as your lens as you carefully consider two texts that follow.

   Cultural Criticism examines how differing religious beliefs, ethnicities, class identifications, political beliefs, and individual viewpoints affect how texts are created and interpreted. What it means to be a part of—or excluded from—a specific group contributes to and affects our understanding of texts in relation to culture.

   Some common assumptions in the use of Cultural Criticism are as follows:

   • Ethnicity, religious beliefs, political beliefs, and customs are crucial components in formulating plausible interpretations of texts.
   • An examination or exploration of the relationship between dominant cultures and the marginalized groups is essential to understanding a text.

☑ Focus on the Sentence

Write two complete sentences in response to what you have learned so far about Cultural Criticism. The first should be a statement that paraphrases the definition of Cultural Criticism in your own words. The second should be a question you have about the lens.

Statement: Cultural Criticism is a formal way to analyze how marginalized groups are represented in a given text.

Question: How does the study of dominant cultures overlap with Marxist Criticism?

College and Career Readiness Standards

Focus Standards:

RL.11–12.2 Determine two or more themes or central ideas of a text and analyze their development over the course of the text, including how they interact and build on one another to produce a complex account; provide an objective summary of the text.

RL.11–12.6 Analyze a case in which grasping a point of view requires distinguishing what is directly stated in a text from what is really meant (e.g., satire, sarcasm, irony, or understatement).

Additional Standards Addressed:

RL.11–12.1, RL.11–12.3, RL.11–12.4, RL.11–12.6, L.11–12.4c L.11–12.6, W.11–12.2, W.11–12.10, SL.11–12.2

2. Listen to the song "The Right to Love," written by Gene Lees and Lilo Schifrin in the 1960s. As you listen, follow along with the printed lyrics. After listening to the song, write a one-sentence summary of what the song is about. Then read the following poem.

_____

_____

As You Read
- Underline words and phrases that connect to the song lyrics.
- Circle unknown words and phrases. Try to determine the meaning of the words by using context clues, word parts, or a dictionary.

About the Author

Born to a prosperous Catholic family in London at a time when anti-Catholic sentiment abounded, John Donne (1572–1631) had a promising career as a diplomat but spent most of his fortune on leisure and pleasure. He secretly married Anne More, much to the disapproval of her father, and she gave birth to 12 children, dying with the last birth. In 1615, at the king's order, he became an Anglican priest and was later dean of St. Paul's Cathedral. His life was influenced by spiritual conflict, and Donne is best known as a metaphysical poet whose writings are laden with rich religious symbolism, metaphor, and unexpected imagery.

Poetry

The Canonization

by **John Donne**

For God's sake hold your tongue, and let me love;
    Or chide my palsy, or my gout;
My five gray hairs, or ruin'd fortune flout;
    With wealth your state, your mind with arts improve;
5   Take you a course, get you a place,
      Observe his Honour, or his Grace;
Or the king's real, or his stamp'd face
    Contemplate; what you will, approve,
    So you will let me love.

WORD CONNECTIONS

Etymology
The word canonization, in the Roman Catholic Church, refers to the act of formally recognizing a saint. The term comes from the Late Latin *canon*, meaning "church law," which later referred to a list of texts considered holy by the church. To *canonize* is to treat something as sacred.

chide: scold
flout: openly disregard

4 Divide the class into small groups and provide each discussion group with a copy of the lyrics for the song "The Right to Love" by Gene Lees and Lalo Schifrin. Play a recording of the song, and ask students to write a one-sentence summary. Have students share their summaries in small groups.

5 Read the About the Author box as a class. Ask students to underline details that convey John Donne's cultural background.

6 Then ask students to read the Word Connections box independently. Ask a volunteer to restate the meaning of *canonization*. Ask students to work in pairs or small groups to skim the poem. Ask students to discuss how Donne's background may have influenced his writing. Ask students how Cultural Criticism might help them interpret Donne's poetry.

7 Ask a volunteer to read the As You Read section.

8 FIRST READ: Read the poem as a class, pausing after each stanza to annotate the text. Ask a student to paraphrase difficult lines, using the vocabulary boxes for reference.

Scaffolding the Text-Dependent Questions

3. What clues in the poem indicate the message the author wishes to convey? To whom is he addressing his comments? What tone is the author taking as indicated in the first two lines? How does he direct his critics to find fault? RL.11–12.1, RL.11–12.2

9 After reading, divide students into small groups. Give students time to help each other understand complex vocabulary, using dictionaries if necessary. Then, ask students to discuss words or phrases in the poem that connect to the song. Have groups share and discuss any questions they recorded as they read.

3.3

My Notes

10   Alas! alas! who's injured by my love?

        What merchant's ships have my sighs drown'd?

    Who says my tears have overflow'd his ground?

        When did my colds a forward spring remove?

            When did the heats which my veins fill

15   Add one more to the plaguy bill?

    Soldiers find wars, and lawyers find out still

        Litigious men, which quarrels move,

        Though she and I do love.

    Call's what you will, we are made such by love;

20   Call her one, me another fly,

    We're tapers too, and at our own cost die,

        And we in us find th' eagle and the dove.

            The phoenix riddle hath more wit

            By us; we two being one, are it;

25   So, to one neutral thing both sexes fit.

        We die and rise the same, and prove

        Mysterious by this love.

    We can die by it, if not live by love,

        And if unfit for tomb or hearse

30   Our legend be, it will be fit for verse;

        And if no piece of chronicle we prove,

            We'll build in sonnets pretty rooms;

            As well a well-wrought urn becomes

    The greatest ashes, as half-acre tombs,

35   And by these hymns, all shall approve

        Us canonized for love.

    And thus invoke us, "You, whom reverend love

        Made one another's hermitage

    You, to whom love was peace, that now is rage;

litigious: quarrelsome
tapers: candles
canonized: marked
invoke us: call upon us for help
hermitage: hideaway or retreat

Scaffolding the Text-Dependent Questions

4. What context clues reveal the meaning of "the plaguy bill" in line 15? How might a plague, or illness, connect to the word "heat" in line 14? What could be the "bill" of a plague? RL.11–12.1, RL.11–12.4

5. How does the speaker use rhetorical questions in lines 10–15 to make his point? What does the speaker mean in line 10? How do the following questions illustrate the point introduced in line 10? RL.11–12.3, RL.11–12.6

6. What images does Donne create in the lines "Call her one, me another fly, / We're tapers too, and at our own cost die" to compel his audience? How long do flies live? How long do candles burn? In this imagery, how might they die at their own cost? RL.11–12.4, RL.11–12.5, RL.11–12.6

3.3

40   Who did the whole world's soul contract, and drove

        Into the glasses of your eyes;

        So made such mirrors, and such spies,

    That they did all to you epitomize—

        Countries, towns, courts beg from above

45   A pattern of your love!"

My Notes

Making Observations
- What is the speaker asking his audience?
- What imagery do you notice in the poem?
- How would you describe the speaker's relationship?

epitomize: represent

Scaffolding the Text-Dependent Questions

7. What does the title of the poem reveal about the speaker's descriptions of himself and his lover in lines 28–36? How does the theme of love develop over the course of the poem? What does the speaker think will happen to the story of his love after he dies? RL.11–12.3, RL.11–12.4, RL.11–12.6

8. What does the speaker say about the value of the criticisms leveled against his love by the end of the poem? What does canonization have to do with this specific idea of love? How could people's poems lead to canonization? How does the speaker compare the story of his love to his critics in terms of the future? RL.11–12.3, RL.11–12.4, RL.11–12.6

ACTIVITY 3.3 continued

10 Finally, ask students to answer the Making Observations questions individually, before giving them time to discuss their answers in small groups. Circulate as students discuss to ensure comprehension of the poem.

11 Return to the components and assumptions of Cultural Criticism that were discussed in relation to the song. In what way do they also apply to Donne's poem? Have students share their initial responses to the poem in discussion and then with a quickwrite.

TEACHER TO TEACHER

Several recordings of the song "The Right to Love" can be found online by artists including Tony Bennett, Nancy Wilson, and k.d. lang. Try searching for the song title plus the artist's name to narrow results.

12 Next, you might consider having students break into discussion groups and use TP-CASTT to analyze the poem.

Title: What inferences can students make based on the title of the poem?

Paraphrase: Having students paraphrase certain parts of the poem, especially the first 15 lines, will give them confidence that they can understand the poem at a comprehension level.

Connotation: Which significant words in the poem have a connotation that needs to be examined?

Be sure to discuss the idea of "canonization" and "phoenix" in relation to this poem as a love poem.

Attitude: What is the attitude of the speaker toward the topic? How does the speaker feel about his love?

Shift: Where (if anywhere) does a shift in the tone, speaker, or topic take place in the poem?

Theme: What statement is the poem making about the topic?

Title again: What new meanings can be found in the title?

13 RETURNING TO THE TEXT: Have students answer the text-dependent questions. If they have difficulty, scaffold the questions by rephrasing them or breaking them down into smaller parts. See the Scaffolding the Text-Dependent Questions box for suggestions.

3.3

Returning to the Text

- Reread the poem to answer these text-dependent questions.
- Write any additional questions you have about the text in your Reader/Writer Notebook.

3. What clues in the poem indicate the message the author wishes to convey?

The first two lines, "hold your tongue, and let me love" and "Or chide my palsy, or my gout" indicate that the speaker feels the need to defend his right to his relationship. The poem concludes with the statement that the legend of his love will, through canonization, outlast death and its critics.

4. What context clues reveal the meaning of "the plaguy bill" in line 15?

"[T]he heats which my veins fill" in line 14 suggests the heat of a fever, caused either by love or by an illness. The word "plaguy" probably refers to an illness like a plague, the symptoms of which include a fever. The phrase "the plaguy bill" refers to a list of the people an illness has killed.

5. How does the speaker use rhetorical questions in lines 10–15 to emphasize his point?

The speaker uses rhetorical questions to make the point his relationship is not hurting anyone, first directly through the lines "Alas! Who's injured by my love?" and then by listing the things his love does not affect, including ships, floods, spring, and whom the plague kills.

6. What images does Donne create in the lines "Call her one, me another fly, / We're tapers too, and at our own cost die" to compel his audience?

Donne juxtaposes images of insects attracted to the flame of a candle to die by flying into it with the burning of tapers (candles) for light, even though they consume themselves in doing so. The two images placed together invoke the brevity and intensity of love.

7. What does the title of the poem reveal about the speaker's descriptions of himself and his lover in lines 28–36?

The speaker suggests love binds the two of them together so that after their deaths, their story will be immortalized in poetry—"Our legend ... will be fit for verse" (line 30). Out of this poetry their story will inhabit "pretty rooms" (line 32), and everyone who reads this poem will agree this love is the standard by which an ideal love should be judged.

14 • Have student groups work together to complete the graphic organizer.

15 • After students have had time to record their ideas in the graphic organizer, lead a brief class discussion about the implications of each text regarding relationships that fall outside a culture's general expectations.

8. What does the speaker say about the value of the criticisms leveled against his love by the end of the poem?

The speaker reminds his critics of their relative insignificance at the end of the poem, as he

says the future will see many admirers transformed by the perfect (saintly) power of his love

("Countries, towns, courts beg from above / A pattern of your love!").

Working from the Text

9. Work with your discussion group to analyze the texts using Cultural Criticism. Respond to the questions in the following graphic organizer and conduct On the Spot Research, as needed, to learn more about the author or singer's background or the time period in which each text was written.

"The Right to Love"	Applying Cultural Criticism	"The Canonization"
	Who is the speaker? What is the situation? How might the cultural context affect the meaning of the text?	
	Is the point of view of the speaker from a marginalized or dominant perspective?	
	What does the author suggest about the experience of people who have been ignored, under-represented, or misrepresented in history (such as women, people of color)?	
	How does this literary work add to our understanding of the human experience of love in the time and place in which it is set?	
	How might this work be received differently by today's audience than it was by the audience of the time it was written?	
	Does the text have relevance to contemporary life?	

16 Have students respond to the Check Your Understanding question.

17 Prompt students to consider the first Essential Question in the context of this activity: What role does literature play in examining recurring social issues?

18 Ask students to review the definition of *meter* in the Language & Writer's Craft. Then have them read aloud the lines from "The Canonization." Write the lines on the board, and work with students to mark the text to show stressed and unstressed syllables as you reread the lines.

19 Have students work in pairs to mark the text from *Othello*. Regroup the class and demonstrate iambic pentameter by marking out the 10 iambic syllables in each line. Then have students complete the Practice independently.

3.3

My Notes

☑ Check Your Understanding

How has Cultural Criticism provided you with insight into the authors' purposes and the circumstances surrounding the creation of "The Canonization" and "The Right to Love"?

LANGUAGE & WRITER'S CRAFT: Rhythm and Meter

Meter refers to a repeating pattern of stressed and unstressed syllables in spoken or written language. By placing an emphasis on certain syllables, an author is able to create rhythm. Look at these lines from the poem "The Canonization" by John Donne:

> Alas! Alas! Who's injured by my love?
>
> …
>
> Who says my tears have overflow'd his ground?
>
> When did my colds a forward spring remove?

These lines consist of a number of metrical feet, which in this case contain one unstressed and one stressed syllable. This pattern of unstressed-stressed creates iambic meter, the most common rhythm in English verse. Some say it sounds like a heartbeat:

> da-DUM, da-DUM, da-DUM, da-DUM, da-DUM

Much of *Othello* is written in blank verse, which is iambic pentameter (10 syllables to a line) that does not rhyme. Mark up the lines spoken by Othello to show meter. Write a symbol like this (˘) over each unstressed syllable and one like this (') over each stressed syllable.

> She loved me for the dangers I had passed,
>
> And I loved her that she did pity them.
>
> This only is the witchcraft I have used.
>
> Here comes the lady; let her witness it.

Notice how the slight variations in the rhythm prevent the lines from becoming too singsong, even though most of the lines are in iambic pentameter.

PRACTICE Revisit a section of John Donne's poem of interest to you and mark the text to identify the meter.

3.3

 Writing Prompt: Informational

Write a comparative analysis paragraph that examines the rhythm and meter in the song lyrics and the poem. Be sure to:

- Identify the rhythm and meter of song lyrics.
- Support your analysis by providing examples from each text.
- Use the third-person point of view and a formal academic tone.

My Notes

ACTIVITY 3.3 continued

20 Direct students to write a paragraph analyzing and comparing the rhythm and meter in the song and the poem.

LEVELED DIFFERENTIATED INSTRUCTION

Some students may require support comparing the two texts.

Support If students have difficulty comparing and contrasting how the poem and song thematically relate to the issue of social acceptance, break the class into small groups using the **Venn Diagram for Writing a Comparison**. Circulate among groups to ascertain how students are analyzing concepts in the poem and song.

ASSESS

Assess students' understanding of "The Right to Love" and "The Canonization" by reviewing their responses to the Check Your Understanding. Are students able to identify several ways in which their understanding of the poem and song changed when they applied Cultural Criticism?

Check students' annotations of meter. Use students' responses to the writing prompt to assess their understanding of how rhythm and meter are used in both the song and the Donne poem.

ADAPT

If students need additional help showing effective use of meter and rhythm, model marking up another section of "The Canonization" and ask students to read aloud in pairs, stressing the iambic meter. Student pairs can work together to mark up and read aloud self-selected sections.

To extend learning, have students mark up the lyrics to "The Right to Love" or other song lyrics of their choosing according to meter and rhythm. If the meter and rhythm are altered, is meaning also altered?

WRITING PROMPT: INFORMATIONAL

The following standards are addressed in the writing prompt:

- RL.11–12.1
- RL.11–12.2
- RL.11–12.5
- RL.11–12.7
- W.11–12.2

PLAN

Materials: props (student choice)
Suggested Pacing: 2 50-minute class periods

TEACH

1 Read the Learning Targets, the Preview, and the Academic Vocabulary box to introduce students to the activity. Ask a volunteer to read aloud student step 1 in Analyzing the Plot and Themes.

2 Assign pairs of students one of the outcomes for the scenario. Direct them to visualize what the scene may look and sound like on the stage, considering how a character's perceptions, background and social position might influence the assumptions that character brings to a given situation.

3 Have students investigate how characters with different backgrounds, perceptions, or social positions might interact in a way that produces misunderstandings that complicate a situation.

Building a Plot and Bringing It to Life: Irony

Learning Strategies

Drafting
Visualizing

VOCABULARY

ACADEMIC
Something **unconventional** does not follow the accepted ways of acting in a situation. Interracial marriages were uncommon in Shakespeare's time.

The word **scenario** refers to a hypothetical situation or specific possibility. As used here, it indicates the outline of a dramatic scene.

Learning Targets

- Demonstrate your understanding of dramatic, situational, and verbal irony through preparation and performance of a scene.
- Interpret a scenario considering the characters' background and underlying motivations.

Preview

In this activity, you will examine the effects of verbal, situational, and dramatic irony. You will then collaborate with your group to present a scenario and one of the outcomes to the class. Then write an essay in a group describing how one of the other scenarios presented irony and subtext.

Analyzing the Plot and Themes

1. Although it is likely you have not encountered Shakespeare's *Othello* in your previous English classes, its plot and the theme—jealousy, leading to passion and betrayal—are universally appealing literary themes. In order to jump into the timeless story of an **unconventional** marriage and the jealousy that complicates it, visualize the **scenario** that follows and the outcome assigned to you by your teacher.

Scenario	Character 1 tells Character 2 that Character 2's romantic partner is cheating on him. Character 1 then produces "evidence." However, the story is untrue; Character 1 is actually lying.
Outcome A	Character 2 does not believe the story and turns on Character 1.
Outcome B	Character 2 considers the story as a possibility but then, after much investigation, decides it is not true.
Outcome C	Character 2 believes the story, is filled with jealousy, and wants revenge.

My Notes

College and Career Readiness Standards

Focus Standards:

L.11–12.3 Apply knowledge of language to understand how language functions in different contexts, to make effective choices for meaning or style, and to comprehend more fully when reading or listening.

SL.11–12.3 Evaluate a speaker's point of view, reasoning, and use of evidence and rhetoric, assessing the stance, premises, links among ideas, word choice, points of emphasis, and tone used.

SL.11–12.6 Adapt speech to a variety of contexts and tasks, demonstrating a command of formal English when indicated or appropriate.

3.4

2. Review the definitions of the types of irony in the Literary Terms box. How is **dramatic**, **verbal**, or **situational** irony used in the scenario? How can you make irony a significant part of your plot?

   - What is the character's motivation? Your identification of character backgrounds and motivations is an important aspect of the subtext of this scene.
   - How will you use dialogue to advance the plot?
   - What physical evidence will serve as "proof" of cheating? Knowledge of the truth by one character and not the other creates dramatic irony.

3. Work with your group to draft the scenario. As you review your draft, ask yourselves these questions:

   - Is the language and word choice precise and engaging enough to keep listeners interested?
   - Are your sentences varied?
   - What adaptations have you made in order to present to your literary peers?

4. Rehearse and present the scenario to your classmates, employing eye contact, a reasonable speaking volume, and gestures that help your audience fully understand and appreciate your scenario. Think about the way your delivery of lines or the way you stand or move will enhance the performance.

5. Thoughtfully and respectfully attend the performances of the scenes developed by your classmates, and take note of how each scene makes use of the dramatic elements. Use the chart that follows to take notes on the performances you view.

LITERARY

VOCABULARY

Dramatic irony is a situation in which the audience knows more about the circumstances or future events in a story than the characters within it; as a result, the audience can see a discrepancy between characters' perceptions and the reality they face.

Verbal irony occurs when a character says one thing but means something very different.

Situational irony is like a surprise ending—your audience expects one thing to happen, but something completely different takes place.

Performance Notes	
What clues were given to indicate the type of irony being displayed?	
What is the climactic aspect of the scene?	
How was subtext used to create irony?	

College and Career Readiness Standards

W.11–12.4 Produce clear and coherent writing in which the development, organization, and style are appropriate to task, purpose, and audience.

Additional Standards Addressed:
L.11–12.4.C, W.11–12.5

ACTIVITY 3.4 continued

4 **Vocabulary Development:** Review the different types of *irony* (dramatic, verbal, and situational) with students. Have them work in pairs to define the term in their own words and think of both examples and non-examples.

5 Direct students to work through student step 2 to prepare for the presentation of their scene to the class. Have them use a chart to note the dramatic elements they used to demonstrate irony as a tool with which to create subtext. Remind students to build to a conclusion that thoughtfully reflects on what the characters have experienced and resolved in the scenario.

6 Ask students to review student step 3 within their groups. Invite volunteers to paraphrase each question. Clarify that students can vary the length of their sentences so their pace and tempo will also be varied. Remind students to adjust their speech based on their characters and assigned outcomes.

7 Arrange the class into groups of two or three student pairs. Explain that each pair will present to their small group, while other students in the small groups take notes in the Performance Notes graphic organizer. If students are viewing more than one performance, give them time to create additional Performance Notes graphic organizers on paper.

8 When pairs have finished performing, give groups time to discuss their performance notes.

9 After the discussion, have students work independently to respond to the Check Your Understanding task.

10 Direct students to the writing prompt and ask them to respond with their group. Have groups exchange and evaluate their paragraphs by directing them to the bulleted points of the prompt.

ASSESS

Check students' quickwrites to ensure they have a clear understanding of dramatic, verbal, and situational irony.

Use students' responses to the writing prompt to assess their ability to analyze irony and subtext in their classmates' performances. Students should cite specific examples to support their answers and should make clear how motivations, ideas, and irony were conveyed in the performance.

ADAPT

If students need additional help understanding irony or writing dialogue, pair them with another student and assign Outcome A. Remind them of the expression "Don't blame the messenger" and ask them to flesh out what happens (and why it is potentially ironic) when Character 2 blames Character 1.

3.4

My Notes

☑ **Check Your Understanding**

What did you learn about analyzing irony, writing dialogue, and performing a short scene?

📝 **Writing Prompt: Informational**

With your group, write a paragraph to analyze how one of the other groups conveyed irony and subtext in their performance. Be sure to:

- Identify the group and give a brief summary of its performance.
- Include specific examples from the performance that convey a particular type of irony.
- Use a coherent organizational structure and make connections between specific words, images, and ideas conveyed.

 WRITING PROMPT: INFORMATIONAL

The following standards are addressed in the writing prompt:

- W.11–12.2
- W.11–12.5
- SL.11–12.3
- L.11–12.3

Viewing a Cast of Characters through a Marxist Lens

Learning Targets
- Use a Marxist critical lens to analyze the relationships between characters.
- Make effective use of academic vocabulary in writing and discussions.

Preview
In this activity, you will evaluate the social status of each character in *Othello* based on their cast descriptions. Then, you will use the Marxist perspective to write an essay explaining how the economic context of the setting influences the dynamics between characters.

Setting the Stage
Knowledge of the social and class structure within *Othello* is essential to analyzing the characters and their motivations from a Marxist perspective. The social hierarchy, which senators and their families presided over, was divided into basic groups according to wealth (land, education, and resources), familial ancestry, and occupation.

The categories of this hierarchy are:

Upper Class: Political, judicial, and economic rule was consolidated in the comprehensive rights and responsibilities firmly retained by a few ruling noble families of the senators, called Signori. These families not only made and enforced all the rules of society and government, patronized the arts, and contributed to the church, but they also maintained personal armies to enforce social order, defend the city, and support their elite positions.

Middle Class: The middle classes had varying degrees of wealth gained through enterprise. It is largely from this class that a young man aspired to gain patronage from a powerful Signori to improve his status. These young men often served the upper-class nobility as advisors, military sub-commanders, and financial managers.

Labor Class: This class provided services required by the higher classes and individuals were bound by the craft skills passed down from father to son. Marriage was expected to follow the traditional occupation or service of the family; in other words, the daughter of a shoemaker was expected to marry a shoemaker. This group held occupations such as house managers, semi-skilled servants, porters, or farmers.

Poor: At the bottom of the hierarchy, the poor did just about any task no one else wanted to do. The poor often included destitute women, children, people of advanced age, and people with disabilities.

Learning Strategies
Discussion Groups
Drafting
Graphic Organizer

WORD CONNECTIONS

Etymology
The Italian word **signori** comes from the Latin root *senior*. The term *signori* indicates a man accomplished as both a scholar and a military leader. An elder signori could "adopt" a promising and gifted young man (especially in the military ranks) and sponsor not only his education, but also his advancement to a higher status.

My Notes

ACTIVITY 3.5

PLAN
Materials: *Othello*, Act I Cast of Characters; poster paper
Suggested Pacing: 2 50-minute class periods

TEACH

1 Ask students to revisit their responses to Essential Question 2: *What role does literature play in examining recurring social issues?*

2 Explain how their interpretation of the scene in the previous activity was likely from a Reader Response critical perspective. If students considered cultural elements (for example, religious or language barriers that created tension) when formulating their scene, bring their attention to the idea that they have approached the scene through the lens of Cultural Criticism, which is only one of several lenses that can be applied to a text.

3 Review the assumptions and definition of Marxist Criticism from the previous unit. Have students read Setting the Stage independently. As students read, they will likely make some assumptions about social class in Venetian (or Elizabethan) society.

4 **Vocabulary Development:** Direct students to the Word Connections box. Ask them to work with a partner to brainstorm words to define the concept of *signori*. Then have them discuss how age and rank help establish the role of a signori in his society.

College and Career Readiness Standards

Focus Standards:

RL.11–12.3 Analyze the impact of the author's choices regarding how to develop and relate elements of a story or drama (e.g., where a story is set, how the action is ordered, how characters are introduced and developed).

L.11–12.1b Consult general and specialized reference materials (e.g., dictionaries, glossaries, thesauruses), both print and digital, to find the pronunciation of a word or determine or clarify its precise meaning, its part of speech, its etymology, or its standard usage.

L.11–12.4 Determine or clarify the meaning of unknown and multiple-meaning words and phrases based on grades 11–12 reading and content, choosing flexibly from a range of strategies.

5 Circulate as students complete the Independent Reading Link peer discussion. Make sure students can give examples to explain why a certain critical perspective might be useful in analyzing their texts.

6 Have students read the Cast of Characters section and consider the *Othello* cast in relation to their understanding of Venetian social classes. Direct students to the Venetian Social Hierarchy Graphic Organizer so that they can begin analyzing the text from a Marxist critical perspective. This will give students an opportunity to discuss social status and power in terms of class divisions in society.

7 Direct discussion groups to explore the relationships between characters in the Cast of Characters. Students should either use the graphic organizer or create their own that shows these relationships in a visual way.

3.5

INDEPENDENT READING LINK
Read and Discuss
Discuss with peers how a Marxist critical perspective would or would not illuminate your independent reading text. Give examples from your text and then discuss with a peer which critical perspectives might offer a useful way to analyze the characters and their behavior.

My Notes

Cast of Characters

1. Examine the list of characters from the play *Othello*, which follows. Use your new understanding of Venetian social hierarchy during the 1600s to determine the social class of each character. What evidence can you find to make your determinations?

2. As a group, discuss what information the character descriptions provide about each character's social status. What conflicts may arise from the characters' relationships?

Othello
Cast of Characters

- **Othello**, a Moorish general in the Venetian army
- **Desdemona**, a Venetian lady, Othello's wife, Brabantio's daughter
- **Brabantio**, a Venetian senator, Desdemona's father
- **Iago**, Othello's standard-bearer, or "ancient"
- **Emilia**, Iago's wife, Desdemona's attendant
- **Cassio**, Othello's second-in-command, or lieutenant
- **Roderigo**, a wealthy Venetian gentleman
- Duke of Venice
- **Lodovico and Gratiano**, Venetian gentlemen, kinsmen to Brabantio
- Venetian senators
- **Montano**, the governor of Cyprus
- **Bianca**, a courtesan, who is in love with Cassio
- **Clown**, a comic servant to Othello and Desdemona
- Gentlemen of Cyprus
- Sailors
- Servants, Attendants, Officers, Messengers, Herald, Musicians, Torchbearers

3. Use the graphic organizer to write the names of the characters in the category to which they may belong. Use arrows to connect those characters you believe may interact and note whether you think they will cause conflict in doing so.

College and Career Readiness Standards

W.11–12.2 Write informative/explanatory texts to examine and convey complex ideas, concepts, and information clearly and accurately through the effective selection, organization, and analysis of content.

Additional Standards Addressed:

W.11–12.5, W.11–12.10, L.11–12.4a, L.11–12.4b, L.11–12.4c, L.11–12.4d

Venetian Social Hierarchy Graphic Organizer

My Notes

8 You may wish to have students engage in pair or small group discussion to reflect on how Marxist Criticism might analyze characters' relationships as dictated by their social status. Ask students to respond to the Check Your Understanding before moving to the next segment of the activity.

☑ **Check Your Understanding**

Reflect on where the characters are positioned according to status in their society. How might using a Marxist lens inform your understanding of how the characters in the play might respond to each other?

9 Guide students through the Language & Writer's Craft feature on determining the meaning of the word *decorum*. Have students consider which of the decoding strategies works best for them. Pair students and have pairs use a decoding strategy with two unknown words. Invite volunteers to paraphrase the meaning of one of the words and explain the strategy they used. Use a dictionary to confirm definitions. Have students complete the practice. Use student responses to assess understanding.

LEVELED-DIFFERENTIATED INSTRUCTION

In this activity, students might need support determining the meaning of unknown words.

Beginning Distribute copies of the **Unknown Word Solver** graphic organizer to pairs of students and model using it with the word *criticism*. Then have them work together using the graphic organizer with another academic vocabulary term from the unit.

Developing Have small groups use the **Unknown Word Solver** graphic organizer to find the meaning of *decorum* and *implored*, using the suggested strategies from the Language & Writer's Craft. Encourage students to use the organizer to define additional academic words.

Expanding Students who readily grasp the meanings of these words might be directed to write a paraphrase of a passage of dialogue between two characters in Act II, Scene I that illuminates the relationship between the two characters. They could indicate tone of voice, pauses, and body language cues to amplify the dynamics of the exchange.

3.5

My Notes

LANGUAGE & WRITER'S CRAFT: Decoding the Meaning of Words

When you are reading a text and come across a word you do not know, there are several ways to determine the word's meaning.

Example: What does the word *decorum* mean in the following text?

> In their tragedies they acted with appropriate *decorum*; in these they caused tears not only by their speaking but also by their action.

One way to figure out the meaning of the word is to use patterns of word changes that indicate different meanings. You might already be familiar with the words *decor* or *decorate*. You might also recognize that *-um* is a suffix that is usually used with noun forms. By using these clues, you may be able to tell the meaning of *decorum*.

Another way to determine a word's meaning is to look for context clues. What meanings and connotations do the surrounding words and sentences provide? Here, the words *appropriate* and *action* provide strong context clues.

Sometimes you need to use a dictionary to be sure you understand a word's denotation (definition) and its connotations (associations). If you look up the definition of *decorum*, you will learn that it means "correct behavior." You can also research a word's etymology (history) to learn how it has evolved. *Decorum* was originally a theater term regarding the appropriateness of part of an artistic performance within the larger artwork.

PRACTICE Read the following text. What does the word *implored* mean?

> After explaining that the missing handkerchief had been a precious gift from his dying mother, Othello *implored* Desdemona to tell him where it could be.

First, jot notes based on context clues and your knowledge of word parts and changes. Then look up the word in a dictionary and record its definition.

My Notes

Writing Prompt: Informational

Write a paragraph that explains how Marxist Criticism can inform analysis of characters in the play. Take into consideration how each character interacts with others from the various social hierarchies. Be sure to:

- Begin with a topic sentence summarizing your understanding of the ways in which Marxist Criticism highlights the social hierarchy of characters.
- Cite relevant textual evidence to support your explanation.
- Use words, phrases, and clauses to link major sections of the text and explain relationships between your analysis and new understandings.
- Maintain an engaging, formal, and objective tone, while using the standard English conventions of mechanics and usage.
- Use precise, accurate language to explain your perspective on the topic.
- Consult a dictionary or other reference materials to clarify the meanings of unknown words.
- Provide a logical conclusion that summarizes the new insights gained from applying Marxist Criticism.

WRITING PROMPT: INFORMATIONAL

The following standards are addressed in the writing prompt:

- RL.11–12.1
- RL.11–12.2
- L.11–12.4c
- W.11–12.2

ACTIVITY 3.5 continued

10 Have students work together with their discussion groups to respond to the writing prompt. Students will be reading lines from the end of Act I, Scene I, in the next activity. Consider assigning the first scene as homework.

ASSESS

Review students' inferences from the Check Your Understanding. They should mention that the characters' different social and economic rankings might cause misunderstandings or conflict.

Use the students' responses to the writing prompt to assess their understanding of how the conflict in the play may be read through a Marxist critical lens. Evaluate whether their topic sentences are supported by evidence.

ADAPT

If students need additional help, point out specific aspects of Venetian society depicted in *Othello*. If titles such as "standard-bearer," "attendant," "gentleman," or "lady" are not clear, provide students with resources to help them place those terms in context.

ACTIVITY 3.6

PLAN

Materials: projection of Brabantio's speech

Suggested Pacing: 2 50-minute class periods

TEACH

1 Students should have read Act I, Scene I, prior to this activity. Before starting the activity, ask students to summarize the events of Act I, Scene I.

2 Read the Academic Vocabulary box, Learning Targets, and Preview as a class. Emphasize that underlining words and phrases that indicate Brabantio's emotional state will help with planning the performance and will also facilitate the use of the Marxist Critical lens.

3 Vocabulary Development: Discuss the Word Connections with students. Ask students how the words are similar. Then ask them to think of other words that share the prefix *ad-*, the root *notare*, or the suffix *-tion*. As an extension, have students complete the **Roots and Affixes Brainstorm** graphic organizer.

4 Group students and have them read the About the Author. Ask them to discuss which social class Shakespeare belonged to, using details from About the Author and their prior knowledge to support their opinions.

5 Encourage students to use online or print dictionaries to define unfamiliar words. As students are reading, monitor their progress. Be sure they are engaged with the text. They should be annotating words and phrases that indicate Brabantio's emotional state and jotting down notes about how a director might go about conveying the emotion of the scene.

A Father's Reaction: Performing and Defending an Interpretation

Learning Strategies

Drafting
Drama Games
Graphic Organizer
Marking the Text

VOCABULARY

ACADEMIC

A *rationale* is an explanation. A rationale can tell why a particular interpretation of a play is effective.

WORD CONNECTIONS

Roots and Affixes

The Latin root *notare*, meaning "note" or "mark," and the prefix *ad-*, meaning "to," form the base of the word *annotate*. A related noun is formed by adding the suffix *-tion*. Words from the same root include *notary*, *notable*, and *notation*.

Learning Targets

- Revise a scene with added subtext to convey an alternate tone in performance.
- Write a character analysis describing different, sometimes conflicting character traits.
- Analyze a performance of a Shakespearean scene using two critical perspectives.

Preview

In this activity, you will reread Act I, Scene I (lines 178–206). Then you will annotate the lines and perform the scene with your acting company. You will also write and share a rationale for your interpretation from a Marxist perspective.

As You Read

- Underline words and phrases that indicate Brabantio's emotional state.
- Circle unknown words and phrases. Try to determine the meaning of the words by using context clues, word parts, or a dictionary.

About the Author

British poet and playwright William Shakespeare (1564–1616) is perhaps the most famous writer of all time. Shakespeare began his theatrical life as an actor and writer. He eventually started an acting troupe and opened his own theatre, The Globe, in London. Shakespeare was a favorite playwright of many royals and noblemen, yet his work was also beloved by the common people. After his death, speculation grew as to whether or not one man could have written such eloquent and varied works. Nevertheless, Shakespeare has remained one of the most widely read, published, and studied authors of all time.

College and Career Readiness Standards

Focus Standards:

RL.11–12.3 Analyze the impact of the author's choices regarding how to develop and relate elements of a story or drama (e.g., where a story is set, how the action is ordered, how the characters are introduced and developed).

L.11–12.1a Apply the understanding that usage is a matter of convention, can change over time, and is sometimes contested.

L.11–12.1b Resolve issues of complex or contested usage, consulting references (e.g., Merriam-Webster's Dictionary of English Usage, Garner's Modern American Usage) as needed.

Play

from *The Tragedy of Othello: The Moor of Venice*

by **William Shakespeare**

Enter Brabantio in his nightgown, with Servants and Torches.

BRABANTIO: It is too true an evil. Gone she is;

And what's to become of my despised time

180 Is naught but bitterness. Now, Roderigo,

Where didst thou see her?—O, unhappy girl!—

With the Moor, say'st thou?—Who would be a
father?—

How didst thou know 'twas she?—O, she deceives

185 me

Past thought!—What said she to you?—Get more
tapers.

Raise all my kindred.—Are they married, think
you?

190 RODERIGO: Truly I think they are.

BRABANTIO: O heaven! How got she out? O treason of the blood!

Fathers, from hence trust not your daughters' minds

By what you see them act.—Is there not charms

By which the property of youth and maidhood

195 May be abused? Have you not read, Roderigo,

Of some such thing?

RODERIGO: Yes, sir, I have indeed.

BRABANTIO: Call up my brother.—O, would you had had her!—

Some one way, some another.—Do you know

200 Where we may apprehend her and the Moor?

RODERIGO: I think I can discover him, if you please

To get good guard and go along with me.

GRAMMAR & USAGE

Complex Sentences

Even though the English of Shakespeare's day is somewhat different from the language we use today, much of the sentence structure remains the same.

Note Roderigo's sentence, "I think I can discover him, if you please to get good guard and go along with me."

This is a complex sentence, meaning that it begins with an independent clause (*I think I can discover him*) and ends with a dependent clause (*if you please to get good guard and go along with me*). This subordinate clause is introduced by the conjunction *if*, and since it modifies the verb *discover* it can be considered an adverbial clause. An adverbial clause gives details about the verb.

Find another complex sentence from *Othello* and annotate it for independent clause, dependent clause, conjunction, and adverbial clause where appropriate.

ACTIVITY 3.6 continued

6 **FIRST READ:** Choose two talented students to read the passage, one taking Brabantio's lines, the other Roderigo's. Encourage the other students to visualize how characters reveal their thoughts and feelings and to think about how they (as actors or directors) might convey those thoughts and feelings onstage. As they conduct a think-pair-share, call their attention to the opening stage directions for clues about the time and location of the scene.

7 Have students read and follow the instructions in the Grammar & Usage box. Circulate as students work to monitor comprehension. Invite volunteers to share the complex sentence they found and identify the independent clause, dependent clause, and the conjunction.

College and Career Readiness Standards

W.11–12.1 Write arguments to support claims in an analysis of substantive topics or texts, using valid reasoning and relevant and sufficient evidence.

Additional Standards Addressed:

RL.11–12.1, RL.11–12.2, RL.11–12.4, RL.11–12.5, SL.11–12.1, SL.11–12.3, SL.11–12.4, W.11–12.1a, W.11–12.1b, W.11–12.1c, W.11–12.1d, L.11–12.3, L.11–12.5

8 Have student volunteers respond verbally to the Making Observations questions. Discuss with the class various initial thoughts students might have about Brabantio's reaction.

9 Have students read the Grammar & Usage box. Before students complete the practice, ask why it is important to have command of standard English conventions. Guide students to understand that standard conventions help facilitate clear communication. Lead students in a brief discussion of how language changes over time. Ask students if they can think of other examples of how language has changed over time. Remind students of the importance of choosing words that are appropriate to context and purpose. Ask them why a word might get contested and how to determine who is right. Prompt students to use resources such as Merriam-Webster's *Dictionary of English Usage* or Garner's *Modern American Usage*. Have students complete the practice and invite volunteers to share their responses.

10 Direct students to use details from the passage to complete the Focus on the Sentence task.

3.6

GRAMMAR & USAGE

Language Change
The English language has changed quite a bit in the 500 years since Shakespeare wrote his famous plays. Words such as *naught*, *hence*, *maidhood*, and *tapers* have dropped from common usage but can still be understood through **context**. Some usages are no longer modern, but people still understand them, as is the case with the word *treason* in "treason of the blood."

Other words such as *didst* and *say'st* can show us how verb forms have changed since Shakespeare's era. We have dropped the *-st* from our versions of these words.

Find two examples in the text of words that seem to have changed since Shakespeare's time and update them with modern language.

My Notes

_____

_____

_____

_____

_____

_____

_____

_____

_____

_____

BRABANTIO: Pray you lead on. At every house I'll call.

I may command at most.—Get weapons, ho!

205 And raise some special officers of night.—

On, good Roderigo. I will deserve your pains.

They exit.

Iago and Roderigo inform Brabantio of Othello and Desdemona's marriage.

Making Observations
- What news does Roderigo share with Brabantio?
- What are your initial thoughts about Brabantio's reaction?
- What questions do you have about this scene?

☑ Focus on the Sentence
Use details from the passage to complete the sentences:

Brabantio is frantic because <u>he has just received word that Desdemona and Othello are married.</u>

Brabantio is frantic, but <u>Roderigo is trying to remain calm.</u>

Brabantio is frantic, so <u>the orders he gives are extreme and incoherent.</u>

Scaffolding the Text-Dependent Questions

1. What evidence in Brabantio's first speech shows how he is feeling? How does Brabantio describe the event? How does he feel about his "despised time"? What conflicting thoughts and his feelings about them do his phrases separated by pauses convey in lines 4–9? RL.11–12.1, RL.11–12.3, RL.11–12.4

2. What earlier phrase shows what Brabantio means when he says to "Call up my brother" the third time he speaks? Remember the time period in which Shakespeare was writing. What does Brabantio ask regarding his family the first time he speaks? What other way may someone be "called up"? L.11–12.5, RL.11–12.5

3.6

Returning to the Text

- Reread the play to answer these text-dependent questions.
- Write any additional questions you have about the text in your Reader/Writer Notebook.

1. What evidence in Brabantio's first speech shows how he is feeling?

   In the first three lines, "And what's to become of my despised time / Is naught but bitterness" shows Brabantio is heartbroken and expects this "evil" event to ruin the rest of his life. In the next six lines, he speaks a series of disconnected thoughts separated by pauses, seeming panicked and unable to put a full thought together.

2. What earlier phrase shows what Brabantio means when he says to "Call up my brother" the third time he speaks?

   Brabantio already has commanded Roderigo to "Raise all my kindred," which Roderigo can accomplish only by running to each household where these extended family members reside, waking a servant to open the door, and explaining why Brabantio needs help. Next, his lord commands Roderigo to run specifically to get his brother.

3. Speak aloud the sentence, "At every house I'll call" from Brabantio's last speech. How does the unusual sentence structure affect the emphasis?

   Putting the verb at the end of the sentence, after the noun and the adverb phrase, places it on a stressed beat in the meter and makes it the last word in the sentence the audience hears. This puts the emphasis on the action rather than what is being acted upon.

4. Which details give clues to the meaning of the word *pains* in the last line of the excerpt?

   Earlier, Brabantio tells Roderigo "Raise all my kindred," indicating he wants Roderigo to alert his brother and ask him for help. The word *pains* here describes the effort of providing that help.

5. What phrases in Brabantio's speech indicate his speed and urgency?

   Toward the end of the scene, Brabantio shifts from asking Roderigo if he "has read of some such thing" to abruptly saying, "Some one way, some another" as if ordering servants to search the immediate premises for his daughter. He hardly pauses before again asking Roderigo "Do you know where we may apprehend her and the Moor?"

Scaffolding the Text-Dependent Questions

3. Speak aloud the sentence "At every house I'll call" from Brabantio's speech. How does the unusual sentence structure affect the emphasis? How is the structure of the sentence unusual? What is the effect of emphasizing the verb in by placing it at the end of the sentence? L.11–12.3, RL.11–12.4

4. Which details give clues to the meaning of the word *pains* in the last line of the excerpt? What actions has Brabantio asked Roderigo to take? What meaning of *pains* could describe these actions? L.11–12.1a

5. What phrases in Brabantio's speech indicate his speed and urgency? Does he wait for an answer to his questions before asking the next one? How are these questions related? How do his questions combine with his comments or speculations to suggest the physical actions accompanying them? RL.11–12.3, RL.11–12.4

---

11 **RETURNING TO THE TEXT:** During the second reading, direct students to answer the text-dependent questions in small groups. If they have difficulty, scaffold the questions by rephrasing them or breaking them down into smaller parts. See the Scaffolding the Text-Dependent Questions box for suggestions.

12 In preparation for students' work in Planning an Interpretation, model how to annotate Brabantio's lines. Some sample annotations are provided on the reduced student page. Have a student volunteer to come to the front of the class and follow the directions you suggest. Elicit student responses about anything in the language that may suggest Brabantio's distraught state. Be sure to inform them that the dashes indicate that Brabantio is addressing a different person; your notes should suggest how the actor might make the changes clear.

13 Have students work with their acting companies to mark the rest of Brabantio's lines to convey his heartbreak. Allow a volunteer or two to demonstrate how the group decided Brabantio should deliver the rest of his lines.

14 Still working with their acting companies, have students mark the text with a different reaction in mind; they should indicate how an actor might convey a sense of anger in these lines. Model annotating the text where appropriate.

LEVELED DIFFERENTIATED INSTRUCTION

Some students may benefit from hearing a performance of the scene.

Beginning To support students who are at an early stage of English language development, consider using the passage audio for *Othello*, available on SpringBoard Digital. Reading along as they listen to the audio can boost students' comprehension of the text. Additionally, the audio performance provides a clear model for pronunciation and intonation.

Bridging Have students looking for an additional challenge conceptualize what the scene would look and sound like if Brabantio and Roderigo swapped social positions without changing the words of the text. What opportunities for irony could be realized if Brabantio were Roderigo's servant?

Support Have students watch a video clip of Othello, depicting the scene in the passage as well as what happens immediately before and after to provide visual context and enhance understanding. Organize students into small groups and assign each group Brabantio or Roderigo. Ask groups to brainstorm observations about their assigned character. Then have groups share their observations.

Extend Pair students who need an extra challenge and have them rewrite the scene in present-day language and context. Remind students to retain the characters' emotions and preserve the core content of the scene. Invite pairs to read a portion of their rewrite for the class.

3.6

My Notes

Planning an Interpretation

6. Follow along as your teacher models how to annotate the text in order to guide an actor delivering Brabantio's lines. Consider how the delivery the can reveal Brabantio's characteristics.

7. Based on your assigned subtext, annotate the text to include how the actor should move on stage to convey the emotional tone of the scene.

BRABANTIO: It is too true an evil. Gone she is,

And what's to become of my despised time

Is naught but bitterness.—Now, Roderigo,

Where didst thou see her?—O, unhappy girl!—

With the Moor, say'st thou?—Who would be a father?—

How didst thou know 'twas she?—O, she deceives me

Past thought!—What said she to you?—Get more tapers.

Raise all my kindred.—Are they married, think you?

RODERIGO: Truly, I think they are.

BRABANTIO: O heaven! How got she out? O treason of the blood!

Fathers, from hence trust not your daughters' minds

By what you see them act.—Is there not charms

By which the property of youth and maidhood

May be abused? Have you not read, Roderigo,

Of some such thing?

RODERIGO: Yes, sir, I have indeed.

BRABANTIO: Call up my brother.—O, would you had had her!—

Some one way, some another.—Do you know

Where we may apprehend her and the Moor?

RODERIGO: I think I can discover him, if you please

To get good guard and go along with me.

BRABANTIO: Pray you lead on. At every house I'll call.

I may command at most.—Get weapons, ho!

And raise some special officers of night.—

On, good Roderigo. I will deserve your pains.

8. With your acting company, rehearse the lines for a performance. Ensure that the performance includes strong stage presence, including eye contact and pacing.

Applying Critical Perspectives

9. Consider interpreting the text through the application of critical lenses. How might you adjust the scene so that it lends itself to a strong analysis from either a cultural or Marxist perspective? Review the assumptions of Cultural and Marxist Criticism as needed.

Critical Perspective	Delivery of Lines, Staging (characters' actions), Blocking (characters' movements)
Cultural	
Marxist	

15 Have each acting company choose parts, rehearse, and then act out the scene for another acting company. One student in each company might be the director. If time permits, you might allow some groups to present to the class.

16 Explain to students that these activities approached the scene from a Reader Response critical perspective. Ask them to consider how they would interpret the scene from a Cultural and Marxist critical perspective. They should work with their discussion groups to complete the graphic organizer.

17 Remind students to complete the Independent Reading Link. Pair students to share their marked-up texts and observations about conflict.

18 Have students complete the Check Your Understanding, referring to their acting company's marked-up scene and notes if necessary.

19 Ask students to respond to the writing prompt. Point out that completing the writing prompt assignment will help them prepare for Embedded Assessment 1, in which they will write a full Literary Analysis.

ASSESS

Review students' explanations for how they made decisions about conveying the scene in the Check Your Understanding task. Engage the whole class in a discussion about each acting company's rationale and approaches to a scene.

Use students' responses to the writing prompt to assess their ability to apply a critical lens to the scene and the character. The lens students choose should provide meaningful insight into Brabantio's character. Students should defend their claims with specific evidence and demonstrate an understanding of the Cultural or Marxist critical perspective.

ADAPT

If students need additional help responding to the text through different critical lenses, place students in small groups and have them review the definitions of Reader Response, Cultural, and Marxist Criticism. Assign each student one critical lens to define for the rest of the group, using examples from this scene. Model using examples where appropriate.

3.6

INDEPENDENT READING LINK
Read and Connect

As you read the texts you have chosen, think about the conflicts that arise between characters. Choose one strong example of a conflict. If possible, choose an excerpt that includes dialogue. Mark up the text as you would a dramatic scene for a performance. Then share your observations and marked-up text with a peer, comparing it to what you have read in *Othello*.

☑ Check Your Understanding

Think about the decisions your acting company made about how to convey the scene onstage. How did you adapt the original text for your current audience? Explain the rationale—or reasons—behind those decisions.

✍ Writing Prompt: Literary Analysis

Write a brief character analysis of Brabantio from either a Cultural or a Marxist critical perspective. Choose the lens that best illuminates Brabantio's character in this scene, and state your claim at the beginning of your paragraph. Be sure to:

- Provide a well-reasoned claim that incorporates the critical lens.
- Establish the significance of your claim, distinguishing it from alternate or opposing choices made by others.
- Use varied syntax, such as adverb clauses, and proper grammar.

WRITING PROMPT: INFORMATIONAL

The following standards are addressed in the writing prompt:

- W.11–12.1a
- W.11–12.1b
- W.11–12.1c
- W.11–12.1d
- W.11–12.9

The Moor: Character Analysis Through a Cultural Lens

Learning Targets
- Examine and analyze how the descriptions of Othello reflect cultural and social attitudes of the time period.
- Write a character analysis based on the assumptions of Cultural Criticism.

Preview

In this activity, you will closely analyze the characters in Act I of *Othello*. Then you will use Cultural Criticism to write a character sketch about the main character.

Reflecting on *Othello*: Act I, Scene I

1. Whether endearing or irritating, the way others refer to us says a great deal about our culture—its values, beliefs, attitudes, and expectations. The use of an epithet, such as "so-and-so's daughter" or a "quarterback on team X," can reveal a culture's attitudes about family legacy or social expectations. With a partner, think of a few additional examples of epithets.

2. Skim and scan the first scene of *Othello*, paying particular attention to the ways in which the characters refer to Othello. Mark the text to indicate where epithets are used.

3. Throughout the first scene, no character uses Othello's name, although all three characters refer to him several times. Use your annotations to decide what each speaker is suggesting about Othello, and whether each term is complimentary or derogatory. Also, decide what the descriptive terms reveal about the speaker in each case. Use the graphic organizer on the following page to record your ideas.

Othello speaks before Brabantio and Venetian Senators.

Learning Strategies
Graphic Organizer
Quickwrite
Think-Pair-Share

LITERARY

An **epithet** is a descriptive word or phrase used in place of or along with a name. For instance, Shakespeare is sometimes simply called "the Bard." Detroit is known as "Motor City." Alexander III of Macedon is commonly called "Alexander the Great."

My Notes

_____

_____

_____

_____

_____

_____

_____

_____

_____

WORD CONNECTIONS

Word Relationships
A **derogatory** term conveys a lack of respect for a person or thing. Its synonym *belittling* describes making someone feel small, and to be *contemptuous* is to treat a person with hate or scorn. *Complimentary* is an antonym that describes speaking well about someone.

PLAN

Materials: *Othello*, Act I, Scenes I–II
Suggested Pacing: 1 50-minute class period

TEACH

1 Read the Learning Targets and Preview as a class. Explain that students will scan Act I, Scene I for instances of other characters referring to Othello without using his name. Pair students and give them time to complete the steps in Reflecting on *Othello*: Act I, Scene I.

2 Orient students to the activity by reading as a class the Literary Vocabulary box.

3 Use a **think-pair-share** to generate student thoughts about the significance of their names. Elicit student responses about how names can reflect a culture. One's name—and nicknames—can reveal something about the background of the individual and those who use the terms. Students may recall certain works in which a character's name is central to the conflict and the culture—for example, the Capulets and Montagues in *Romeo and Juliet* and the Cunninghams, Ewells, and Finches in *To Kill a Mockingbird*.

4 Vocabulary Development: Ask students to review the Word Connections box. Have them clarify the precise meaning for each word using the dictionary. Then have them discuss the connotation of each word with a partner.

College and Career Readiness Standards

Focus Standards:

RL.11–12.3 Analyze the impact of the author's choices regarding how to develop and relate elements of a story or drama (e.g., where a story is set, how the action is ordered, how the characters are introduced and developed).

L.11–12.2 Demonstrate command of the conventions of standard English capitalization, punctuation, and spelling when writing.

L.11–12.5 Demonstrate understanding of figurative language, word relationships, and nuances in word meanings.

5 As pairs work, circulate to ensure students are moving from textual references to draw conclusions in the last two columns of the graphic organizer.

6 Check that students are citing specific textual evidence to support their inferences about each speaker as they complete their graphic organizers.

7 To prepare students to complete student step 4, read aloud Act I, Scene II, stopping to model and discuss thoughts about Othello's response to the accusations. Allow students time to complete the graphic organizer individually, before completing student steps 5 and 6 with their partners or in small groups.

3.7

Reference to Othello	Who is speaking? (line number)	How does the phrase exhibit an attitude toward Othello?	How is the character of speaker revealed in his use of the phrase?
Example: "his Moorship's"	Iago (line 35)	He's ironically compared to royalty.	Iago uses verbal irony here; he doesn't think of Othello as royalty. Despite Othello's rank, Iago looks down on him.
"the Moor"	Iago (lines 42, 63, 130, and 164) Brabantio (line 182 and 200)	He's an outsider, a foreigner.	The speaker is suspicious of outsiders.
"the thick lips"	Roderigo (line 72)	Stereotypical physical description	Roderigo follows Iago's lead and buys into the stereotype.
"thieves, thieves"	Roderigo (line 89)	He has stolen Brabantio's daughter.	He thinks that outsiders are not to be trusted.
"black ram"	Iago (line 97)	He is compared to an animal.	Iago believes that the relationship is like a relationship between animals.
"the devil"	Iago (line 100)	He is compared to someone who is purely evil.	Iago attributes evil motives to the outsider.

Reading Othello: Act I, Scene II

4. As you read Act I, Scene II, make note of Othello's responses to the accusations against him.

Accusation	Accuser	Othello's Response	What does Othello's response indicate about him?
Lines 8–10: According to Iago, he has spoken "against your honor" in an insulting way.	Brabantio	Let Brabantio do his worst. I am descended from as fine a folk as he is.	He is proud, confident, unashamed.
Lines 82: "foul thief" That Othello "hast enchanted her."	Brabantio	I will not fight; I will go to answer your charges.	self-assured, not easy to anger

College and Career Readiness Standards

W.11–12.2 Write informative/explanatory texts to examine and convey complex ideas, concepts, and information clearly and accurately through the effective selection, organization, and analysis of content.

Additional Standards Addressed:

RL.11–12.1, RL.11–12.6, SL.11–12.1b, SL.11–12.4, SL.11–12.6, W.11–12.2a, W.11–12.2b, W.11–12.2e, W.11–12.5

5. Discuss with a group how other characters' descriptions of Othello reveal the cultural attitudes of the time period. Why might they use derogatory phrases instead of referring to Othello by name or title?

☑ Focus on the Sentence

Given the subject, write a sentence using an appositive to describe the subject.

Brabantio

Brabantio, a rich Venetian statesman, believes that Othello has "stolen"

Desdemona by marrying her without his consent.

Desdemona

Desdemona, a beautiful and fair maiden, defies her father's and society's

expectations by entering an interracial marriage.

Othello

Despite his accolades, Othello, an experienced Venetian military leader, is

subjected to racism and treated as an outsider.

✒ Writing Prompt: Literary Analysis

Write a character analysis of Othello that describes him from the Cultural Criticism perspective. Consider your own observations and the insights from your group discussion. Use the following character analysis of Brabantio, Desdemona's father, as a model for your writing. Be sure to:

- Include a thesis statement that applies the perspective of Cultural Criticism.
- Include specific details and textual evidence about Othello that describe the character.
- Use correct punctuation, such as dashes and commas.

Brabantio, Desdemona's father in William Shakespeare's *Othello*, is a statesman and respected member of Venetian society. He disapproves of his daughter's marriage to the Moor. Brabantio is unable to conceive of anything—aside from spells and witchcraft—that could move his dear Desdemona to commit this "treason of the blood" (I.i.191). In spite of his having placed a great deal of trust in Othello—enough to honor Othello with frequent visits to his own home—Brabantio laments that "[Desdemona] is abused, stol'n from me, and corrupted" (I.iii.73). His views of his daughter as his property and of the valiant military man as an outlandish choice for his daughter's hand in marriage show Brabantio to be a nobleman who shares prejudices common in his culture. His inability to accept or honor the choices of others may help explain his grief at his daughter's elopement.

GRAMMAR & USAGE

Appositives

Appositives are nouns or noun phrases that rename, add emphasis to, clarify, or even contradict the meanings of other nouns; they are placed near to the nouns they are intended to qualify. An example of an appositive is given in the sentence, "Dan, the waiter, always gives us free dessert."

GRAMMAR & USAGE

Dashes

This sketch shows an example of how a writer can use dashes to amplify a point or to explain. Notice the writer's use of dashes in this sentence to offer an explanation:

Brabantio is unable to conceive of anything—aside from spells and witchcraft—that could move his dear Desdemona …

Commas, parentheses, or colons can provide a similar effect, but here dashes slow the reader down enough to understand what the writer means by "anything."

Try revising another sentence from this sketch that uses dashes by replacing them with commas, parentheses, or a colon. Consider how your revision changes the way you read the sentence.

WRITING PROMPT: INFORMATIONAL

The following standards are addressed in the writing prompt:

- W.11–12.2a
- W.11–12.2b
- W.11–12.2e
- RL.11–12.1
- RL.11–12.3
- L.11–12.2

ACTIVITY 3.7 continued

8 Point out the Grammar & Usage boxes on the student page. Give students more details about dashes:

- A sentence should not have more than two dashes.
- In dialogue, a dash or dashes can be used to indicate a sudden break in thought. For example: "Will the president—*should* the president—sign that bill?" asked Marcus.

9 Explain and model examples of appositives. Have students practice writing several appositive sentences.

10 Assign the character sketch to students, explaining that their description of Othello should apply a Cultural Criticism perspective. Ask them to apply the Grammar & Usage instruction on dashes and use appositives appropriately to enhance their character sketches.

ASSESS

Review the character sketches students create in response to the writing prompt. Students' sketches should include descriptions of several of Othello's character traits and how those traits are shown through what other characters say about him. Check to make sure student writing includes a thesis statement and a clear application of the Cultural Criticism lens. Students should include specific details and textual evidence to support their ideas and should use correct punctuation.

ADAPT

If students need additional help with character sketches for analysis, allow them to think-pair-share their thoughts about differing or conflicting personality traits of people in their personal experiences as a way to tie into Othello's character. Have them practice writing sentences with appositives or dashes.

PLAN

Materials: *Othello*, Act I, Scene III; two filmed versions of *Othello*— Oliver Parker (1995) and Orson Welles (1952) versions suggested
Suggested Pacing: 2 50-minute class periods

TEACH

1 Review the Learning Targets and Preview with students.

2 **Vocabulary Development:** Review the meaning of the Literary Vocabulary *monologue* with students. Have them work in pairs to define this term in their own words and think of both examples and non-examples. Then explain how a monologue is used by the playwright in advancing the action of a play.

3 Have students give examples of a work of literature that they have read and then seen on film before having them respond to the Opening Writing Prompt.

4 Before students read the monologue individually, point out the instructions in the As You Read section. Encourage them to read the glossary near the end of the passage before they read.

5 **FIRST READ:** Instruct your students to read the passage individually; as they do, circulate to view their annotations and ensure comprehension. Have them circle any challenging vocabulary words or phrases.

Critiquing a Monologue

Learning Strategies

Activating Prior Knowledge
Drafting
Graphic Organizer
Oral Reading
SOAPSTone

VOCABULARY

LITERARY
A **monologue** is a speech that is delivered by a single character. This literary device is used to reveal a character's thoughts and underlying motivations. The character usually speaks directly to the audience, or to another character.

My Notes

bade me: told me to
wherein: in which
imminent: approaching

Learning Targets

• Analyze the role of a monologue in advancing the action of a play.
• Evaluate and critique the effectiveness of delivery of the same monologue in two film adaptations.

Preview

In this activity, you will closely read and practice delivering lines from a monologue. Then you will compare two film adaptations of the text and evaluate the director's choices and how effectively the lines are delivered. Finally, you will write an analysis of the director's thematic and interpretive choices.

📝 Opening Writing Prompt

Analyzing literature and film is a specialized form of rhetorical analysis that requires critical analysis and evaluation. However, you have done this type of analysis if you have ever seen a movie version of a novel or short story you have read. Think of a time when you watched a film adaptation of a narrative that you had read, and then respond to the Essential Question: How can an original text be adapted for different audiences?

As You Read

• Underline the claims Othello makes about other characters in the play.
• Circle unknown words and phrases. Try to determine the meaning of the words by using context clues, word parts, or a dictionary.

Monologue

from Act I, Scene III

Her father loved me; oft invited me,
150 Still questioned me the story of my life
From year to year—the battles, sieges, fortunes
That I have passed.
I ran it through, even from my boyish days
To th' very moment that he **bade me** tell it,
155 **Wherein** I spake of most disastrous chances:
Of moving accidents by flood and field;
Of hairbreadth 'scapes i' th' **imminent** deadly
   breach,

College and Career Readiness Standards

Focus Standards:

RL.11–12.7 Analyze multiple interpretations of a story, drama, or poem (e.g., recorded or live production of a play or recorded novel or poetry), evaluating how each version interprets the source text. (Include at least one play by Shakespeare and one play by an American dramatist.)

L.11–12.1a Apply the understanding that usage is a matter of convention, can change over time, and is sometimes contested.

L.11–12.1b Resolve issues of complex or contested usage, consulting references (e.g., Merriam-Webster's Dictionary of English Usage, Garner's Modern American Usage) as needed.

Of being taken by the insolent foe

160 And sold to slavery; of my redemption thence

And portance[1] in my travel's history,

Wherein of antres[2] vast and deserts idle,

Rough quarries, rocks, and hills whose heads
    touch heaven

165 It was my hint to speak—such was the process—

And of the Cannibals that each other eat,

The Anthropophagi[3] and men whose heads

Do grow beneath their shoulders. This to
    hear

170 Would Desdemona seriously incline:

But still the house-affairs would draw her thence,

Which ever as she could with haste dispatch

She'd come again, and with a greedy ear

Devour up my discourse. Which I, observing,

Took once a *pliant* hour, and found good means

To draw from her a prayer of earnest heart

That I would all my pilgrimage *dilate*,

Whereof by parcels she had something heard,

But not intentively. I did consent,

180 And often did *beguile* her of her tears

When I did speak of some distressful stroke

That my youth suffered. My story being done,

She gave me for my pains a world of sighs.

She swore, in faith, 'twas strange, 'twas passing

185   strange,

'Twas pitiful, 'twas wondrous pitiful.

She wished she had not heard it, yet she wished

That heaven had made her such a man. She thank'd
    me,

My Notes

pliant: flexible
dilate: expand
beguile: charm

[1] *portance*: bearing or carriage; figuratively, behavior
[2] *antres*: caves
[3] *Anthropophagi* is a Greek word that means "cannibals."

College and Career Readiness Standards

L.11–12.3 Apply knowledge of language to understand how language functions in different contexts, to make effective choices for meaning or style, and to comprehend more fully when reading or listening.

Additional Standards Addressed:

RL.11–12.1, RL.11–12.2, RL.11–12.3, RL.11–12.4, RL.11–12.5, RI.11–12.6, SL.11–12.2, W.11–12.2a, W.11–12.2b, W.11–12.10, L.11–12.4c

6 Pair students and have them discuss their responses to the Making Observations questions.

3.8

My Notes

190 And bade me, if I had a friend that loved her,

I should but teach him how to tell my story.

And that would woo her. Upon this hint I spake.

She loved me for the dangers I had passed,

And I loved her that she did pity them.

195 This only is the witchcraft I have used.

Here comes the lady: let her witness it.

An illustration of French actor Mounet-Sully as Othello, 1899

Making Observations
• What details about Othello's life stand out to you?
• How would you describe Othello's relationship with Desdemona?

Returning to the Text

- Reread the monologue to answer these text-dependent questions.
- Write any additional questions you have about the text in your Reader/Writer Notebook.

1. What tone does Othello take to defend himself? What words or phrases at the beginning of the monologue contribute to this tone?

Othello's tone is calm and sincere. He calmly explains with phrases such as "Her father loved

me; oft invited me" to tell "the story of my life" and "I ran it through, even from boyish days."

He is telling his story, much like he did to Desdemona and her father.

2. How do Othello and Desdemona's differences in background contribute to them falling in love? Provide support from the text.

Desdemona is fascinated by the events of Othello's life, listening with a "greedy ear" to

stories of his travels, which are exotic to her as a Venetian noble. The stories engage her

sympathies; she cries and sighs and calls them "wondrous pitiful." Othello says, "She loved

me for the dangers I had passed, / And I loved her that she did pity them."

3. What does Shakespeare reveal about Othello's character through this monologue? Use text evidence to support your answer.

Based on this speech, Othello appears honest and honorable. When he is accused, he calmly

defends himself by describing how his relationship with Desdemona developed. According

to Othello, he did not press himself on Desdemona but instead waited for her to hint at her

feelings for him. He is confident she will confirm his account.

7 RETURNING TO THE TEXT: As students reread the text, encourage them to paraphrase the lines in the My Notes section. Consider giving students space to quietly read the monologue to themselves to better understand the speaker's tone and mood.

8 Have students answer the text-dependent questions in small groups. If they have difficulty, scaffold the questions by rephrasing them or breaking them down into smaller parts. See the Scaffolding the Text-Dependent Questions box for suggestions.

Scaffolding the Text-Dependent Questions

1. What tone does Othello take to defend himself? What words and phrases at the beginning of the monologue contribute to this tone? Why might he chronicle the progression of events and how he interpreted them leading to his elopement with Desdemona? RL.11–12.1, RL.11–12.4

2. How do Othello's and Desdemona's differences in background contribute to them falling in love? Provide support from the text. What does Desdemona think of Othello's stories? Why are they exotic to her? How does she react when she hears them? When did he profess his love to Desdemona? RL.11–12.1, RL.11–12.3

9 Have students discuss in pairs what effect they imagine Othello wants to have when he gives this speech. Which critical lens would produce this interpretation? Ask them to mark the text to show how they would have Othello deliver these lines to achieve this effect based on their chosen critical perspective. Then, have pairs complete the steps in Working from the Text, using the **SOAPSTone** strategy as they analyze the monologue using the chart in Working from the Text.

10 Ask some pairs to present for the whole class using the **Oral Interpretation** strategy. Discuss the vocal delivery and movement and how they further the desired interpretation. Lead the class in a discussion of the reception Othello receives from the Duke and the Senators, both before and after his speech. Students should consider the words they use to describe Othello, what they say about him, and what they say to him.

11 Direct students to respond to the Check Your Understanding prompt.

12 Show students two film interpretations of this speech and have them take notes in the **Venn Diagram for Writing a Comparison** graphic organizer. Explain to students that by comparing the two film interpretations, they are evaluating how dramatic elements are used to interpret the original scene by Shakespeare.

 TEACHER TO TEACHER

The best film choices—because of their differences—are the Oliver Parker (1995) and Orson Welles (1952) interpretations. Wide variations between the interpretations make this scene interesting for comparisons. You may want to start the scene earlier to see Brabantio's accusation. As with any film clip, be sure you preview in order to determine its appropriateness for your students.

3.8

My Notes

Working from the Text

4. With a partner, use the SOAPSTone graphic organizer provided by your teacher to analyze how the monologue builds. Use your notes from the first reading of the text to help support your answers.

Introducing the Strategy: Oral Interpretation

An **oral interpretation** is reading aloud a literary text with expression. The purpose is to share with an audience the reader's personal insight into a text through voice, fluency, and tone. The oral interpretation requires careful analysis of a text to determine appropriate rate (speed), inflection (emphasis on specific words for effect), and tone (speaker's attitude toward the subject).

5. Discuss how you would have Othello deliver these lines in a performance by your acting company. As you discuss the planning of your performance, highlight lines that you find particularly important in conveying how Othello's past experiences led him to his present circumstances.

6. Use the lines that you have highlighted to practice giving an oral interpretation of Othello's monologue with your acting company. Listen attentively and provide feedback on each other's use of enunciation, volume, rate, tone, pauses, and gestures.

☑ Check Your Understanding

How will your performance of this scene differ according to the chosen critical perspective? Highlight a few lines from Othello's speech and perform them based on your chosen lens.

7. As you view different interpretations of Othello's speech, take notes in the graphic organizer that follows. Evaluate the elements listed to analyze the effectiveness of each adaptation.

Scaffolding the Text-Dependent Questions

3. **What does Shakespeare reveal about Othello's character through this monologue? Use text evidence to support your answer.** What kind of logic does Othello use to defend himself? What evidence is there in his speech that indicates whether or not he expects to be believed? RL.11–12.1, RL.11–12.3

Film version 1	Film version 2
Delivery of lines	
Actions/gestures/facial expressions	
Interactions among characters	
Props/costumes	
Set	
Dramatic/ Theatrical elements	

13 Jigsaw the groups or have a whole-class discussion about each of the six aspects on the graphic organizer so that each student can complete the graphic organizer. Have students use their notes to respond to the Check Your Understanding prompt with a partner.

14 Review the Language & Writer's Craft box. Encourage students to list some of the words and types of changes they have noticed in the play. Challenge students to determine the meanings of archaic words from context before consulting reference materials. Some archaic words and meanings students might research in Act I, Scene III include *oft* (149), *bade* (154), *wherein* (155), *spake* (155), *scapes* (157), *thence* (159), *portance* (160), *antres* (161), and *'twas* (181). Consult a dictionary or other references as needed.

15 Direct students to write a rhetorical analysis by following the Writing Prompt directions, using the **Persuasive/Argument Writing Map**.

16 Pair students to discuss the prompt in the Independent Reading Link. Have students choose a few specific sections of text to focus on for the discussion.

LEVELED DIFFERENTIATED INSTRUCTION

In this activity, students might need support planning and writing their responses to the Rhetorical Analysis Writing Prompt.

Beginning Have students needing additional support meet in mixed-level small groups to form a thesis for their rhetorical argument using the **Venn Diagram for Writing a Comparison**. Have students write a statement, such as *The film version (a or b) of Othello is the most effective at interpreting Shakespeare's play because a) _____ b) _____ and c) _____.*

Developing Guide students independently or in small groups as they engage the **Venn Diagram for Writing a Comparison** to provide support in stating a thesis and following a logical progression to a conclusion.

Bridging Students adept in developing a rhetorical analysis might be challenged by making an argument *against* the interpretation of one of the films based on their observations using the **Venn Diagram for Writing Comparison**; they may then present them to the class.

ASSESS

Review students' literary analysis responses to the two film versions of Othello's monologue. Make sure students include a clear thesis and cite specific dramatic features from both clips that will affect an audience's experience of the monologue.

ADAPT

If students need additional help analyzing the film representations, consider having them make suggestions on what they think the film directors might have done to change the effect Othello's speech had on the other characters and the audience, and why.

INDEPENDENT READING LINK

Read and Discuss

Based on what you've read so far, discuss with a partner the aspects of your text that would lend themselves to a film interpretation. How would you convey narrative elements visually? Would modifying the original text enhance or diminish the audience's ability to comprehend and appreciate the text?

My Notes

---

8. Discuss with a partner which film adaptation you find more effective. Use your notes from the graphic organizer and the following questions to guide your discussion:

- How do the set, costumes, and theatrical elements affect the viewer?
- Which film adaptation evokes an emotional response from the viewer?
- How effective is the actor's delivery of the lines in helping the audience connect to Othello's life story?
- Which film adaption best illuminates Othello's honor and nobility?

LANGUAGE & WRITER'S CRAFT: Language Change

Language changes over time because of shifts in culture, geography, and trends. Although we can still read and understand Shakespeare, we can also see that certain words from his era are not in use anymore or that they are used in different ways. We also know that there are many words and usages that have evolved since Shakespeare's time. As language changes, rules about how to use language change, too.

For example, read the following sentence from Act I:

Her father loved me; oft invited me;
Still questioned me the story of my life

Oft has the same usage as our modern *often*, indicating a language change. Another difference appears in the structure of "still questioned me the story of my life," which is not how someone might say it today, though we still understand its meaning.

Who gets to decide what usage is correct, or **standard**? As new words and usages appear to fill new communication needs, they may become more popular. People who create dictionaries and usage guides then decide which new usages to include and which to get rid of. Over time, a consensus arises about what the new words and usages mean and how to use them effectively. This means that standard usage is largely a matter of cultural consensus, or convention.

PRACTICE Skim a few scenes from *Othello*. In your Reader/Writer notebook, list a few words that are not commonly used today or that are used differently now. Look them up in a dictionary of etymology such as the *Oxford English Dictionary* or etymonline.com. Then create a chart with the categories *then* and *now* to show how the meanings have shifted.

Writing Prompt: Rhetorical Analysis

Think about the film interpretations of *Othello* you have viewed. Evaluate how the features of each clip affect how the audience experiences the drama. Write a paragraph comparing the directors' thematic and interpretive choices to the scene. Be sure to:

- Include a comparative statement in your thesis.
- Identify the interpretive approach of each film and explain how it conveys the character of Othello.
- Support your commentary by citing examples of imagery and cinematic techniques used in each film.

WRITING PROMPT: RHETORICAL ANALYSIS

The following standards are addressed in the writing prompt:

- RL.11–12.1
- RL.11–12.7
- W.11–12.2a
- W.11–12.2b

A Historical Look at the Moor

Learning Targets

- Closely read and analyze an author's claims in a literary criticism text.
- Participate in a discussion to analyze a character through the lens of Historical Criticism.
- Integrate ideas from multiple texts to build knowledge and vocabulary about stereotypes and racial prejudice.

Preview

In this activity, you will learn about Historical Criticism and then closely analyze an excerpt from a book of literary criticism. You will work collaboratively to generate discussion questions to participate in a Socratic Seminar.

Historical Criticism

1. Previously, you learned about critical theories and used them to understand and interpret various texts. Review the critical perspectives with a partner, taking turns to identify and define the perspectives until you have reviewed all those you have studied. In your Reader/Writer Notebook, sketch a picture suitable to represent each critical perspective.

2. Another critical perspective is **Historical Criticism**. Historical Criticism considers the time period in which a work was created and how that time period may have influenced the work. For example, an interpretation of *Things Fall Apart* by Chinua Achebe may be enhanced by an understanding of the effects of colonialism in present-day African life. Likewise, an interpretation of *The Crucible*, which is set in 17th-century New England, may be enhanced by an understanding of political developments in the 1950s, when Arthur Miller wrote the play. The major principles of Historical Criticism are as follows:

   - A text cannot be separated from its historical context, which is a web of social, cultural, personal, and political factors.
   - An understanding of a text is enhanced by the study of cultural norms and of artifacts such as diaries, films, paintings, and letters in existence when the text was created.

   Historical Criticism suggests that we examine how the historical context in which a text is created or set might influence the text's themes, characters, events, ideas, and structure. With drama, the time period in which a drama is reimagined and performed adds another layer of interpretation of historical significance. For instance, in South Africa under apartheid, producing *Othello*—a drama about an interracial marriage—was an act of social, cultural, and historical significance.

   Historical performances of *Othello* give modern audiences a peek into the minds of people in generations past and inspire us to imagine how future generations might perform and receive this play.

3. Add Historical Criticism to your list of critical theories. In your Reader/Writer Notebook, sketch a symbol or picture suitable to represent this critical perspective.

Learning Strategies

Levels of Questions
Marking the Text
Paraphrasing
Sketching
Socratic Seminar

LITERARY

Using **Historical Criticism**, the reader recognizes the significance of historical information in interpreting literature. This perspective assumes that texts both influence and are influenced by the times in which they were created.

VOCABULARY

My Notes

ACTIVITY 3.9

PLAN

Materials: *Othello*, Act I
Suggested Pacing: 1 50-minute class period

TEACH

1 Orient students to the activity by reading as a class the Literary Vocabulary box. Ask students to give examples of literary works that strongly reflect and are influenced by historical context and setting. Read the Learning Targets and Preview as a class. Then, briefly review the previously studied critical perspectives—Marxist, Feminist, Cultural, Reader Response, and Archetypal.

2 Introduce Historical Criticism to students, asking them to read and annotate the description, explanation, and assumptions. Give students time to add Historical Criticism to their Reader/Writer Notebooks.

College and Career Readiness Standards

Focus Standards:

RI.11–12.1 Cite strong and thorough textual evidence to support analysis of what the text says explicitly as well as inferences drawn from the text, including determining where the text leaves matters uncertain.

RI.11–12.2 Determine two or more central ideas of a text and analyze their development over the course of the text, including how they interact and build on one another to provide a complex analysis; provide an objective summary of the text.

RI.11–12.3 Analyze a complex set of ideas or sequence of events and explain how specific individuals, ideas, or events interact and develop over the course of the text.

3 Have students complete the Focus on the Sentence to summarize what they have learned about Historical Criticism. Give students time to read the About the Author section.

TEACHER TO TEACHER

It is important for students to realize that although authors are influenced by their cultural and historical contexts, their writings do not always reflect the times in which they lived. The reading passage provides background about what Shakespeare's contemporaries thought about the Moors. Students can determine for themselves after reading the play whether Shakespeare agreed with commonly held opinions of his time.

4 Read the As You Read section with your students. Help them understand the metacognitive markers such as question marks, asterisks, exclamation points, and underlining they should use to annotate the text.

3.9

My Notes

☑ Focus on the Sentence

Use what you have learned about Historical Criticism to turn the following fragments into complete sentences.

Historical Criticism interprets a text based on

Historical Criticism interprets a text based on the historical time period in which it was written.

to study *Othello* with Historical Criticism

To study *Othello* with Historical Criticism, it is necessary to learn about Elizabethan England.

can shed light on the historical context of the play

A production set in a time different from a play's original setting can shed light on the historical context of the play.

As You Read

- Use **metacognitive markers** to annotate the text to help you monitor your own understanding of the author's argument.

    ?   Use a question mark to signal confusion or question an idea.

    *   Use an asterisk for comments about the text.

    !   Use an exclamation point for reactions to the text.

    _   Underline the key idea or topic sentence in each paragraph.

- Circle unknown words and phrases. Try to determine the meaning of the words by using context clues, word parts, or a dictionary.

About the Author

Jack D'Amico (b. 1939) was born the son of a musician in Buffalo, New York, and earned his PhD from the State University of New York in 1965. He served as the English Department Chair of Canisius College in Buffalo, New York, from 2000–2002. In addition to *The Moor in English Renaissance Drama* (1991), D'Amico has written *Shakespeare and Italy: The City and the Stage* (2001).

College and Career Readiness Standards

SL.11–12.1 Initiate and participate effectively in a range of collaborative discussions (one-on-one, in groups, and teacher-led) with diverse partners on grades 11–12 topics, texts, and issues, building on others' ideas and expressing their own clearly and persuasively.

Additional Standards Addressed:

RI.11–12.4, RI.11–12.5, RI.11–12.6, SL.11–12.6, W.11–12.1a, W.11–12.1b, W.11–12.1e, W.11–12.9

Literary Criticism

from **The Moor in English Renaissance Drama**

by Jack D'Amico

Chunk 1

1 Relations between England and Morocco were extremely complex, and the opinions generated by those relations were as varied. What we find is not one image of the Moroccan, but many images, from the dangerously inscrutable alien to the exotically attractive ally. I have reviewed the experiences of these men in this chapter because, it seems to me, theater has the ability to re-create for its audience the encounter with an alien culture and to force an imaginative assessment of likeness and difference. Through this kind of experience some prejudices may be confirmed, while in other ways spectators may come to see themselves and their world differently.

2 The positive and negative characterizations that emerge from the first fifty years of trade and diplomacy can with ease be related to the specific historical perspectives of trade, war, and diplomacy. But traditional images of the Moor as black devil, Islamic infidel, or oriental despot were certainly drawn on to articulate what the traders and diplomats experienced. Optimistic prospects, disappointment and frustrations, and strong prejudices against Catholic Spain were by turn equally strong. Dramatic contexts, too, reflect a give-and-take of opinion, a frequent counter-balancing of prejudices, the interplay of abstract stereotypes and the more complex shadings of experience.

3 The theatrical representation of the Moor, while shaped in part by the traditional anti-Islam polemic, or the characterization of the black man as devil, also reshapes those traditions. Along with the stereotypes we will find subtler explorations of the problems that beset individuals from different cultures as they attempt to judge one another. Stereotypes often provide a convenient mask the dramatist can use to identify a character. But under the pressure of dramatic experience that character will move often closer to the context of the observer's world, exhibiting the same needs, frustrations, and perceptions that shape "our" experience. As with the diversity of opinion about Moors and Morocco represented by the reports of traders and diplomats, we must follow the complex, and at times tangled, dramatic interplay of ideas, opinions, stereotypes, and fresh characterizations within the plays. Even if the spectator does not come away from the dramatic experience with a fuller understanding of another culture and its people, in most instances seeing the familiar world set in a different perspective leads to an expansion of imaginative experience.

****

KNOWLEDGE QUEST

Knowledge Question:

How do stereotypes affect the social issue of racial prejudice? In Activity 3.9, you will read literary criticism that examines the topic of stereotypes. While you read and build knowledge about the topic, think about your answer to the Knowledge Question.

GRAMMAR & USAGE

Modifiers

A **free modifier** is a phrase or clause that modifies the main clause. Pay attention to the bolded part of the following sentence, which is a free modifier: *But under the pressure of dramatic experience that character will often move closer to the context of the observer's world,* **exhibiting the same needs, frustrations, and perceptions that shape 'our' experience.**

Notice how this **participial phrase** modifies the subject, "character."

Find another example of a free modifier in this text, and diagram how it modifies the subject.

inscrutable: mysterious
despot: tyrant
polemic: argument

5 Direct students to the Knowledge Question. Ask students to share examples of stereotypes in literature. Lead the class in a brief discussion about how and why stereotypes are formed. Then have small groups discuss responses to the Knowledge Question. Ask groups to think about how stereotypes could have a positive effect by forcing us to confront prejudice.

6 **FIRST READ:** Consider switching the reading mode after each chunk for gradual release: read Chunk 1 as a class, Chunk 2 in pairs, and Chunk 3 individually. Have pairs discuss the first Making Observations question after they finish reading Chunk 2.

7 Direct students' attention to the Grammar & Usage box and answer any questions they have about free modifiers. Suggest that students wait until they reread to look for and diagram another example from the text.

 TEXT COMPLEXITY

Overall: Very Complex
Lexile: 1430L
Qualitative: High Difficulty
Task: Challenging (Evaluate)

Scaffolding the Text-Dependent Questions

4. What historical connection does the author focus on in Chunk 1? How are the two cultures connected? What differences separate them? What contradiction existed in the image of Moroccans? What key words does he use to convey these contradictions? RI.11–12.5

5. What two stereotypes of Moroccans (or Moors) does the author give in the first paragraph? Which stereotype most closely applies to the character of Othello? What historical factors are mentioned? RI.11–12.2

6. In paragraph 3, what two points does the author make about stereotypes in theatrical presentations? How can stereotypes lead to a richer theater experience? What does he say about the exchange of ideas in theatre? RI.11–12.2

8 As students are reading, monitor their progress. Be sure they are engaged with the text and annotating sections of the text to which they have specific reactions.

 TEACHER TO TEACHER

Remind students that Shakespeare wrote during the English Elizabethan period (during which Elizabeth I was Queen), which is also known as the English Renaissance.

3.9

My Notes

Chunk 2

4   Yet the representation of the Moor could also lead the dramatist and the audience beyond a comfortable sense of **superiority** or the superficial **titillation** provided by a darkly alien villain. The Moor could become a dramatic symbol of the many stereotypes and masks that divide society and alienate the individual. The process by which a character is reduced to a type and the consequences of that reduction became a central dramatic issue. The representation of the Moor, whether motivated by a desire to make theatrical capital of a famous event, such as the Battle of Alcazar, or by a desire to discover and explore difference, opened up the question of what resulted from the contact between different cultures, religions, and races.

5   Dramatic interest also seemed naturally to focus on the question of the kind of power the isolated individual sought within a society of others. Power could mean destroying or mastering that society, controlling its women and tricking its men into acts of blind self-destruction. Or power could be sought in ways acceptable to society, as was the case for Othello, who could seem "fair" both within his dark exterior and within the Venetian state because of his military **prowess**. Audiences and dramatists were drawn to the Moor as a type because the character provided a way to examine some of the most difficult questions of division and alienation. The audience that witnessed the struggle for self-control and the **insidious** powers that transform Othello would confront the destructiveness of its own collective perceptions of race, religion, and cultural difference. In this case, the audience would engage in an exchange of something other than a coin for the sight of a dead Indian; the living character required that the audience engage in an emotional and intellectual exchange. And that giving, which is the life of theater, certainly drew the audience into some understanding of the tragic divisions within their own world as mirrored in the story of a character such as Othello, the Moor of Venice.

6   Our imaginative journey into the dramatic world of these plays fosters respect for the willingness and ability of Renaissance dramatists to do more than trade in dead stereotypes. Most of the plays created for their audience a complex dramatic encounter with the Moor. The audience identified the otherness of the type and to the extent that individual members of that audience saw difference as essential to human experience, they were connected to the outsider. Working within the conventions of Western theater and poetry, the dramatist could use the open stage of Shakespeare's age to explore inner perspectives and challenge easy assumptions about difference and inferiority. The poet-dramatist was provided with a further connection between the Moor, or the alien, and the role of the artist within society.

****

Chunk 3

7   Shakespeare more than any other dramatist of the English Renaissance used theater to create an important political perspective that framed the

---

superiority: thinking themselves better than others

titillation: excitement

prowess: skill and accomplishments

insidious: sneakily harmful

Scaffolding the Text-Dependent Questions

7. How does the author introduce and develop a key idea in paragraph 4? What is the Moor's function in the second sentence? How is the process examined? What question does it suggest to audiences? RI.11–12.3, RI.11–12.5

8. What clues to the meaning of "dead stereotype" does the author provide at the end of paragraph 5? **Does Othello fit this description?** What striking image does the author give in paragraph 5? How could the image relate to a "dead stereotype?" Is Othello a flat or engaging character? How might the theater experience either support or defy a "dead stereotype?" RI.11–12.1, RI.11–12.4

encounter between different cultures. On the Moor he focused the problems that any state would face when it moved from a relatively closed condition to the open expansion that generates contact and conflict with other civilizations. Around the Moor he built those conflicts which test a society's sense of the natural rightness of its particular cultural traditions. He saw that with the kind of political expansion that characterized Renaissance Venice and ancient Rome came the problem of absorbing the outsider and the fear of being absorbed. The opposition between Roman reason and the darkly feminine otherness and fertility of Egypt is but one variation on this conflict between different conceptions of power and order. Shakespeare could also identify with a Moor of military virtú who is fearful of the erotic femininity of Venice, a European city as exotic for him as Alexandria was for the Romans. For the modern, cosmopolitan state that thrives on the exchange of goods and images with other nations and cultures, this conflict persists in the struggle between a closed national identity and the need for intercourse with others.

8 … Shakespeare wrote for a society that saw its contact with other people increase, while it struggled to define for itself the kind of government and religion it would have. Traditional definitions of Western norms and of the others who deviated from those norms provided a groundwork for curiosity, or a base of operations for exploration and exploitation. But the ground was and always is shifting as experience and traditional values interact. What may have seemed strange turns out to be familiar, as when Clem finds that courts in Morocco and England are much the same; and what is native may, upon closer examination, turn out to be more monstrous than the strangest alien. As we have seen with Tamburlaine[1], an outsider who became a projection of new political ambition, the imaginative contact with the outsider became a way of dramatizing the need to create new categories. The Moor's difference was something established by tradition, and the Moor was a sign of spatial distance, a creature from a distant place. But for the English Renaissance stage the Moor could also be identified with the newness of discovery, exploration, and trade. This experience, real or theatrical, might confirm or challenge the tradition. Since the Moor was often portrayed as isolated and in rebellion against Western society, the type might conveniently channel opposition to traditional structures. If the old definitions fixed the character in safe inferiority, the new experience created an emotionally and intellectually charged encounter with a figure who required the audience to reflect on and to question its own values.

9 The plays certainly trade in what were, and still are, trusted assumptions about the Moor, Islam, and cultural difference. And they also draw upon our fascination with how another culture can make the familiar world seem strange. It is unsettling and also exciting to feel the ground of assumptions shift, as is the case in travel, when the norm is not your norm, when dress, speech, food, and the details of life reflect a difference that places you at the margin, reduced to a sign of deviation from the norm. That sense of

---

[1] *Tamburlaine* is a character who had high political aspirations, from the play of the same name by Christopher Marlowe.

WORD CONNECTIONS

Roots and Affixes
The word cosmopolitan contains the Greek prefix *cosmo-*, meaning "world" or "universe." Someone who is *cosmopolitan* is not bound by any local or national customs or prejudices. Other words beginning with this prefix include *cosmonaut*, *cosmology*, and *cosmopolis*.

My Notes

conceptions: ideas
exploitation: using for their own benefit
spatial: physical
deviation: departure

9 **Vocabulary Development:** After paragraph 7, pause to discuss the Word Connection box. Ask students to determine the meaning of the other words based on what they have learned about the Greek prefix *cosmo-*.

Scaffolding the Text-Dependent Questions

9. In paragraph 6, what opinion does the author express about Renaissance dramatists? In the first two sentences, whom does the author respect and why? How might the condition of an open stages and poetic conventions challenge "easy assumptions about difference and inferiority?" RI.11–12.1, RI.11–12.6

10. In paragraph 7, what historical changes do Shakespeare's plays reflect? How are the conflicts that arise from changes reflected in modern cultural exchanges? What phrase does the author use to describe the nature of the "modern, cosmopolitan state?" What does this cultural dynamic thrive on? What conflicts arise when cultural traditions are challenged? Where and why do we see these conflicts today? RI.11–12.1, RI.11–12.3

10 After the First Read, pose the Knowledge Quest questions. Ask students to think about their initial reaction to the author's claims about stereotypes.

3.9

My Notes

disorientation was projected into an Eleazar[2] who speaks of the finger of scorn pointed at him, or Othello who fears the accusing gesture that will destroy his reputation. What is most disturbing for the outsider is the sense that the secret, unwritten codes are being used to degrade one's true image. As a group, sharing language, a national and racial identity, and an inherited set of theatrical conventions, the audience would have been like those Venetians or Spaniards who share a culture the Moor can never understand. And yet the individual spectator might retain a sense of separateness and know what it is like to be the object of open scorn, or what is worse, to feel the unspoken isolation of one who is reduced to a mere sign of the abnormal.

Knowledge Quest
- Which of the author's claims stand out to you the most?
- What questions do you have after reading this essay?
- What are your first thoughts about the relationship between stereotypes and racial prejudice after reading the article?

---

[2] *Eleazar* is a villainous Moor in an English Renaissance drama called *Lust's Dominion.*

Scaffolding the Text-Dependent Questions

11. **What character in** *Othello* **could fit the description "what is native may … turn out to be more monstrous than the strangest alien?"** What kind of man is Othello? Which native of Venice is the "monstrous" one in the play? RI.11–12.4

12. **How can traditional themes of being a cultural outsider, such as those described** **by the author, connect with people watching plays today?** Why might watching a play like this have been uncomfortable in Shakespeare's time? How might a play that highlighted cultural differences make the audience feel today? RI.11–12.1, RI.11–12.2, RI.11–12.6

11 RETURNING TO THE TEXT: Have students answer the text-dependent questions. If they have difficulty, scaffold the questions by rephrasing them or breaking them down into smaller parts. See the Scaffolding the Text-Dependent Questions boxes for suggestions.

Returning to the Text

- Reread the literary criticism to answer these text-dependent questions.
- Write any additional questions you have about the text in your Reader/Writer Notebook.

Chunk 1

4. What historical connection does the author focus on in Chunk 1? How are the two cultures connected? What differences separate them?

The author begins by explaining that the image of Moroccans in Shakespeare's time was a

complex contradiction between a dangerous other and an exotic ally in trade. He states that

the medium of theater is an ideal one through which to present these kinds of conflicting

perceptions.

5. KQ What two stereotypes of Moroccans (or Moors) does the author give in the first paragraph? Which stereotype most closely applies to the character of Othello?

The author says views of Moroccans (or Moors) range from that of the "dangerously

inscrutable alien" to the "exotically attractive ally." In paragraphs 2 and 3, stereotypes such

as the "black devil" and "Islamic infidel" only support the dangerous alien view, but in Act I

of the play, Othello is clearly the exotic ally.

6. KQ In paragraph 3, what two points does the author make about stereotypes in theatrical presentations? How can stereotypes lead to a richer theater experience?

The author says theatrical presentations are "shaped in part" by stereotypes; however,

the theater "reshapes those traditions" through "explorations of the problems that beset

individuals from different cultures as they attempt to judge one another." By presenting

different perspectives, plays can entice audiences to re-examine their prejudices.

Chunk 2

7. How does the author introduce and develop a key idea in paragraph 4?

In the second sentence, the author introduces the idea that the dramatic character of the Moor

may initially function as a focus for superiority or "superficial titillation." However, he goes on

to say that thoughtful characterization of such a person brings up the question of what results

"from the contact between different cultures, religions, and races."

8. **KQ** What clues to the meaning of "dead stereotype" does the author provide at the end of paragraph 5? Does Othello fit this description?

The author presents the image of "a dead Indian" as what the audience may expect from Othello's character—a flat and lifeless stereotype. What the play's audience gets instead is an inside glimpse from within a tragedy of "a living character" with whom they can "engage in an emotional and intellectual exchange."

9. In paragraph 6, what opinion does the author express about Renaissance dramatists?

The author respects the way most dramatists avoid "dead stereotypes" and create "a complex dramatic encounter with the Moor" by exploring "inner perspectives" presented on the open stages in Shakespeare's era. D'Amico asserts that this condition encourages some audience members to reexamine "easy assumptions about difference and inferiority."

Chunk 3

10. In paragraph 7, what historical changes do Shakespeare's plays reflect? How are the conflicts that arise from changes reflected in modern cultural exchanges?

The author states that Shakespeare writes about trade, which thrives on "the exchange of goods and images." This tests a society's self-image and identity. The arrival of foreigners creates the "problem of absorbing the outsider and the fear of being absorbed." Today conflict between "national identity" and international exchange continues.

11. What character in *Othello* could fit the description "what is native may ... turn out to be more monstrous than the strangest alien"?

This description calls to mind the character of Iago, who is a native of Venice and the scheming villain of the play, while Othello, the Moor outsider, displays honor and integrity.

12. How can traditional themes of being a cultural outsider, such as those described by the author, connect with people watching plays today?

The author writes about the experience of seeing a play like *Othello*, which causes the audience to "question its own values" as the play depicts outsiders in unconventional roles. People watching plays today can connect to the idea of being a cultural outsider (in one or many ways) or insider to challenge their ways of viewing the world.

Knowledge Quest

The author of this essay explores the way theater can lead "the individual spectator" to look closer at stereotypes and re-examine prejudices. Think about a contemporary film and write an informative text explaining how the film uses stereotypes to affect racial prejudice. Be sure to:

- Provide a well-reasoned claim that is clearly stated.
- Use significant and relevant examples, details, or quotations from the film that thoroughly develop and support your claim.
- Provide an engaging conclusion that supports the claim and examines its implications.

 INDEPENDENT READING LINK

You can continue to build your knowledge about the effects of stereotypes and racial prejudice by reading other articles at ZINC Reading Labs. Search for keywords such as *stereotypes* and *racial prejudice*.

ZINC

Working from the Text

13. Your teacher will assign chunks of the excerpt from *The Moor in English Renaissance Drama* to various individuals in your group. Reread your assigned chunk to write levels of questions in preparation for a Socratic Seminar. Locate textual evidence from Act I of Othello that helps address your questions, or that confirms or counters D'Amico's assertions.

14. Using the lens of Cultural Criticism, write Levels of Questions to explore the preceding text. Choose at least one question for each chunk to pose during the Socratic Seminar. With your group, review the levels of questions for each chunk.

Literal: _____

_____

_____

Interpretive: _____

_____

_____

Universal: _____

_____

_____

12 Return to the Knowledge Question. Have students work with a partner to discuss the film they have in mind and how it uses stereotypes to confront prejudice. Encourage students to take notes to help them with the writing task. Review writing expectations with students using the "be sure to" points.

13 Encourage students to continue building knowledge on this topic as suggested in the Independent Reading Link.

14 After students have finished the Knowledge Quest, break students into discussion groups to address the Working from the Text steps. Assign one section of the text to each group member and ask them to write leveled questions about their section.

15 Have each group prepare at least one question from each section to pose during the Socratic Seminar.

16 Conduct a Socratic Seminar with students using their notes for support. Open with one of the Essential Questions for this unit:

What role does literature play in examining recurring social issues? How do the various characters' assessments of Othello in Act I reflect (or contradict) the commonly held beliefs of Shakespeare's times?

17 Before the Socratic Seminar comes to an end, make sure to address the bulleted questions on the student page.

18 Have students complete the Check Your Understanding task independently.

LEVELED DIFFERENTIATED
INSTRUCTION

In this activity, students may need support preparing for a Socratic Seminar.

Beginning Distribute the **Collaborative Dialogue** graphic organizer to each student. Prior to the discussion, have partners complete the organizer by adding their Socratic Seminar questions. Then have the pairs rehearse for the Socratic Seminar with the support of the graphic organizer and sentence frames for academic discussion: *What in the text makes you say that? Based on _____, I think that _____. Another example of _____ is _____.*

Developing Have partners complete the **Collaborative Dialogue** graphic organizer prior to the whole group discussion. Have students use the organizer to record and practice clarifying, paraphrasing, and extending questions, such as: *I have a question about _____. In other words, are you saying that _____? The idea of _____ is important because _____. I'd like to add _____.*

ASSESS

Monitor the Socratic Seminar to ensure students understand how English Renaissance poets and playwrights represented the Moors in literature. Students should also cite explicit evidence as they engage with D'Amico's assertions.

ADAPT

If students need additional help preparing for the Socratic Seminar, model writing a question and answer that would address the ideas under discussion. Students may also work in groups to generate levels of questions for each chunk. After discussing Level 1 questions as a whole class, use the best Level 2 questions as a basis for a Socratic Seminar on one of the remaining chunks that you think would be of greatest benefit to students.

My Notes

15. Participate in a Socratic Seminar, making sure to address the following questions:

- How do English Renaissance poets and playwrights represent the Moors in their literature?
- What evidence from Act I of the play supports or contradicts D'Amico's assertions about Othello as a character?

Remember to listen attentively, evaluating evidence and reasoning that may modify or change your own understanding of the text.

☑ Check Your Understanding

Use your new understanding of Historical Criticism to respond to the following question in the form of a quickwrite: How can a playwright impact an audience's perspective of social and cultural stereotypes?

Desdemona: From a Feminist Perspective

Learning Targets

- Analyze the portrayal of women in a scene from *Othello*.
- Research the historical and social context of a play to analyze character development.
- Explain various interpretations of a scene based on differing critical perspectives.

Preview

In this activity, you will analyze the character of Desdemona through a feminist lens. You will also conduct research to better understand how cultural and historical context influence character development. Finally, you will join your acting company to interpret and perform a scene through a feminist critical perspective.

Learning Strategies

Double-Entry Journal
Quickwrite
Revisiting Prior Work

My Notes

_____

_____

_____

_____

_____

_____

_____

_____

_____

_____

Revisiting Feminist Critical Perspective

1. Review the principles of Feminist Criticism. In what light has Desdemona's character been cast in Act I of *Othello*? How does she fulfill or resist societal and familial expectations?

On the Spot Research

How different are the rules of courtship, marriage, and filial duty to one's parents, in Shakespeare's time (1600s) from those of today?

Conduct research into how women of different social strata were expected to perform their duties in society. Use print and digital information from reputable sources, such as academic journals or established encyclopedias. Remember that a Wiki source is not guaranteed to be reliable or authoritative. However, one way to use it is to search key words and access the bibliography for titles of books or articles that touch on your topic of interest.

2. Quickwrite: What are the most striking differences in the expectations of marriageable noble women in Shakespeare's Elizabethan England (such as Desdemona) and young women of today?

Othello and Desdemona in Venice, by Théodore Chassériau (1850)

ACTIVITY 3.10

PLAN

Materials: *Othello*, Act II, Scene I
Suggested Pacing: 2 50-minute class periods

TEACH

1 Ask students to review the attributes of feminist critical perspective by revisiting prior work and the definitions of key terms. Then, give students time to read the Learning Targets and Preview independently. Ask a volunteer to summarize the Preview for the class.

2 Direct students in a discussion to recall how Desdemona's character has been represented in Act I. Then allow them a few minutes to think-pair-share their thoughts about how Desdemona's character and actions contribute to the conflict that propels the plot of the play.

⊕ TEACHER TO TEACHER

Students may note that the conflict has arisen primarily because of Desdemona's bold action in marrying Othello, revealing Desdemona's independent spirit. Students may also note that Brabantio assumes from the beginning that Desdemona was the passive victim of Othello's deception. They may also note that she asserts her confidence in having married him and pleads to be near him during his battle rather than be "a moth of peace" (I.III.ll 255–259).

3 Ask students if they think Desdemona is a much more assertive woman than students may recall encountering in previous Shakespeare plays, such as Juliet (who also married contrary to her father's wishes), or Ophelia and Gertrude in *Hamlet*.

4 Direct students to conduct On the Spot Research into how women of different social classes were expected to conduct themselves in Shakespeare's time. Ask them to consult print and/or online resources. Then, have students use their research to complete the quickwrite.

College and Career Readiness Standards

Focus Standards:

RL.11–12.3 Analyze the impact of the author's choices regarding how to develop and relate elements of a story or drama (e.g., where a story is set, how the action is ordered, how the characters are introduced and developed).

SL.11–12.1b Work with peers to promote civil, democratic discussions and decision-making,

set clear goals and deadlines, and establish individual roles as needed.

SL.11–12.1d Respond thoughtfully to diverse perspectives; synthesize comments, claims, and evidence made on all sides of an issue; resolve contradictions when possible; and determine what additional information or research is required to deepen the investigation or complete the task.

5 Ask students to read Act II, Scene I. If one of the acting companies has chosen this scene for their Embedded Assessment 2 staging, ask them to read the scene aloud to the class. When students arrive at line 108, tell them to begin noting the references to women in the text.

6 When a character shares a perception of women between lines 108–179 (beginning with Cassio's line "Good ancient, you are most welcome" and ending when Cassio takes Desdemona by the hand), direct students to record the quotation and response in the double-entry journal.

7 As students read, encourage them to check the explanatory notes in their text, discuss word meanings, and use a diffusing strategy by substituting synonyms learned from peer discussion or reference texts.

8 Ask each group to perform a few chosen lines of the "banter" in this scene as interpreted through the feminist lens. Encourage one group to perform it in front of the class. Discuss the tone of the scene. Ask students to record their written responses to each performance.

3.10

3. As you read Act II, Scene I, pay attention to the ways women are referred to in the text. When you encounter a character's perception of women in lines 108–179, record the quotation and your response in the following double-entry journal. Include the line numbers.

Quotation	Response

4. How might someone view this scene from a Feminist critical perspective?

5. How do Desdemona and Emilia simultaneously "comply and defy" restrictions on their lives and behaviors?

6. In what ways do you find Feminist Criticism overlaps considerations inherent in Historical, Cultural, or Marxist critical perspectives?

College and Career Readiness Standards

Additional Standards Addressed:

RL.11–12.1, RL.11–12.2, RL.11–12.5, W.11–12.5, W.11–12.7, W.11–12.8, RI.11–12.7, SL.11–12.2

3.10

Interpreting the Lines

7. Choose a few lines to perform as an acting company. Discuss how you would interpret the lines through a feminist lens, taking into considering your research on courtship. As a group, determine the tone of each of the characters and of the conversation as a whole.

8. Pay attention to how tone of voice, body language, timing, and setting complement the relationships women have with men in the scene.

9. Now select a different critical perspective through which to examine the scene. Describe how the dramatic elements of the scene change when performed through a different lens.

☑ Check Your Understanding

How can a critical perspective be conveyed in a dramatic performance? How has this lesson strengthened your understanding of the way literary theories can shape a staged scene?

📖 INDEPENDENT READING LINK

Read and Discuss

With a partner discuss the main or supporting female characters in your text. Explain how someone might analyze the characters from a Feminist critical perspective. Work together to list the similarities and differences between how the two authors' portrayals of women.

My Notes

ACTIVITY 3.10 continued

9 Ask groups to read the scene with a different interpretation, such as Cultural Criticism or Historical Criticism. Choose one representative group to present to the class. Discuss the tone of the scene. Have students record a written response to the Check Your Understanding.

10 Pair students to discuss the prompt in the Independent Reading Link. Students can use a three-column chart to note similarities and differences in how their texts portray women.

11 Ask students to consider the first Essential Question at the conclusion of this activity. Use this as an opportunity to check for student understanding.

12 Assign students to read Act II, Scenes II and III as homework to prepare for the activities of the next class period.

ASSESS

Review student responses to the Quickwrite to check their understanding of how expectations were different for women in Elizabethan England or in Europe at this time. Use students' responses to the Check Your Understanding to determine how well they understand the way a feminist critical perspective reveals explicit and implicit motivations in a dramatic scene.

ADAPT

If students need additional help answering the lesson questions correctly, consider having them think-pair-share or gather in small groups to discuss expectations of women in modern society compared to those of Shakespeare's time, citing evidence they find in the reading.

To extend learning, ask students to write a brief essay in which they identify insights gleaned from considering the scene through a feminist critical lens.

ACTIVITY 3.11

PLAN

Materials: *Othello*, Act II; Passage audios for *Othello*, Act II, Scenes 1–3, available on SpringBoard Digital
Suggested Pacing: 1 50-minute class period

TEACH

1 Review with the class the explanations of *soliloquy* in the Literary Vocabulary box. Read the Learning Targets and Preview as a class.

2 Remind students that *dramatic irony* occurs when the audience knows something that a character does not. Explain that sometimes characters make assumptions or decisions based on faulty or incomplete information, leading to tragic conclusions. Ask students to provide examples from their own life experiences. Ask students to explain how Shakespeare uses dramatic irony in Act II to convey Iago's untrustworthiness.

3 Have students sketch or use another graphic organizer to show understanding of the related but distinct terms *monologue*, *soliloquy*, and *aside*. To check for understanding, ask students to explain which of these kinds of speeches by a character are intended for the audience only to hear, and which are meant to also be heard by other characters. Then, read the Word Connections box to reinforce the meaning of *soliloquy*.

ACTIVITY
3.11

Honest Iago: The Dramatic Speech

Learning Strategies

Graphic Organizer
Marking the Text
Paraphrasing
Think-Pair-Share

My Notes

VOCABULARY

LITERARY

A **soliloquy** is a long speech delivered by a character alone on the stage. The audience hears the character's internal thoughts.

An **aside** is a short speech spoken by an actor directly to the audience and unheard by other actors on stage.

Learning Targets

- Analyze a character's motivations and traits by closely reading a soliloquy.
- Interpret a scene and evaluate how the delivery of lines can be used to amplify dramatic irony.

Preview

In this activity, you will review three dramatic elements and evaluate how they can be used to convey a specific message to an audience. You will then conduct a close reading of a character's speech and work with your acting group to interpret and deliver the lines.

Dramatic Elements

1. Revisit the definition of dramatic irony from Activity 3.4. How is dramatic irony already evident in *Othello*?

2. What do you recall about the dramatic elements known as soliloquies and monologues from your previous study of plays? Refer to print or digital sources for examples and definition of a soliloquy to sharpen your understanding of this dramatic device.

Soliloquies and monologues are speeches given by an actor on stage. Soliloquies are directed to the character, voicing his or her own thoughts. Sometimes the character is aware of the audience, and sometimes the viewers are an "omniscient witness" to the internal, secret thoughts of the character. Monologues, by contrast, are directed to other characters. Monologues may reveal the character's secret thoughts, but other characters, whether or not the speaker is aware, overhear those voiced ideas.

An aside also allows a character to reveal his or her thoughts to the audience. However, asides are much shorter and are spoken while others are on stage, often in reaction to another character's words or actions. An aside lets the audience in on information that the other characters are not able to hear, so the audience is in a privileged position of knowing something hidden from others. For this reason, asides are a good set up for dramatic irony. Asides and soliloquies can be used as dramatic devices in three ways:

- directly to the audience, or to the camera (if filmed)
- as if the character is simply talking to himself
- as a voice-over, while the actor appears to be lost in thought

---

College and Career Readiness Standards

Focus Standards:

RL.11–12.6 Analyze a case in which grasping a point of view requires distinguishing what is directly stated in a text from what is really meant (e.g., satire, sarcasm, irony, or understatement).

RL.11–12.7 Analyze multiple interpretations of a story, drama, or poem (e.g., recorded or live production of a play or recorded novel or poetry), evaluating how each version interprets the source text. (Include at least one play by Shakespeare and one play by an American dramatist.)

© 2021 College Board. All rights reserved.

304 SpringBoard® English Language Arts **English IV**

Reading *Othello*: Act II

3. With your acting company, conduct a close reading of one of Iago's asides or soliloquies. As you read, annotate the places that reveal Iago's motivations and emotions and convey the tone and mood of the speech. Choose one of the following scenes:

Scene A: Act II, Scene I, lines 182–193 ("He takes her by the palm ...")

Scene B: Act II, Scene III, lines 49–66 ("If I can fasten but one cup ...")

Scene C: Act II, Scene III, lines 356–382 ("And what's he, then, that says ...")

- Set the scene: what has happened before this speech?

- How does the aside or soliloquy use irony?

- What phrases and words in the speech reveal Iago's secret motivations leading to his actions?

- How does the speech advance the plot of the drama?

WORD CONNECTIONS

Roots and Affixes
The word **soliloquy** comes from the Latin for "talking to oneself," from the roots *solus* ("alone") and *loqui* ("speak"). Other words from the roots *solus* include *sole*, *solitary*, and *desolate*, and *loqui* forms words such as *eloquence* and *ventriloquist*.

4 Assign each acting company (discussion group) a close reading of one of Iago's asides or speeches (the speeches will be used more than once).

Have groups reread the speech and skim the surrounding text in order to answer the guiding questions about the meaning of the speech and its importance.

5 Once each acting company has a clear understanding of its assigned speech, group members should demonstrate understanding by planning a delivery of the speech. Direct students to rewrite the speech and to mark it as they did for Brabantio's words in Activity 3.6. Each student should **rehearse** the speech in the manner the group agrees upon. Rearrange the groups using a jigsaw so that each student presents his or her group's assigned speech to a different small group.

6 **Vocabulary Development:** Discuss the Word Connections with students. Ask students how the words are similar. Then ask them to think of other words that share the roots *solus* or *loqui*. As an extension, have students complete the **Roots and Affixes Brainstorm** graphic organizer.

College and Career Readiness Standards

SL.11–12.3 Evaluate a speaker's point of view, reasoning, and use of evidence and rhetoric, assessing the stance, premises, links among ideas, word choice, points of emphasis, and tone used.

Additional Standards Addressed:

RL.11–12.2, RL.11–12.3, RL.11–12.4, RL.11–12.5, SL.11–12.1b, SL.11–12.1c, W.11–12.2d, W.11–12.5, W.11–12.10

7 Direct students' attention to the Comparing Interpretations. Remind students that audio texts and in-class performances are both interpretations of the original text that students can react to. Pause after playing the audio recording of each scene and have students share their evaluations of each interpretation. Also, ask students to compare their initial interpretation with the interpretation presented by the actor. For example, the actor may speak the lines with different intonation, pacing, or word emphasis than the student applied in independent reading or in performance. Through varied approaches and multiple readings, students learn to evaluate and compare interpretations.

8 Have students respond to the Check Your Understanding in the form of a quickwrite.

9 As pairs discuss the Independent Reading Link, encourage them to consider points of comparison between the character's internal thoughts and external dialogue.

 TEACHER TO TEACHER

Use the remaining class time in this lesson to show a film version of Act II, Scenes I–III. Ask students to consider the continual use of dramatic irony in their reading of Act II, Scene III, and be prepared to discuss Iago's continued ability to dupe those around him, using examples from the reading, in the next class.

ASSESS

Circulate while students present their speeches to the small groups, noting whether or not students comprehend the speech in relation to the play as a whole. The presentation should clearly convey what students want the audience to understand about the character.

ADAPT

If students need additional help to ensure their presentation conveys what they wish, offer to coach students in vocal delivery, staging, and blocking.

INDEPENDENT READING LINK

Read and Discuss

Reflect on the internal thoughts and dialogue between characters in your independent reading. Discuss with a partner how this external or internal dialogue gave you more insight into the character's motivations.

My Notes

Interpreting the Lines

4. Now that you have annotated the text, work as a group to decide how to best represent Iago's character traits. Each member of the group will deliver the speech and provide feedback to one another on the delivery. Take these questions into consideration as you reread the text and plan your presentation:

- What do you want the audience to understand about the play and about Iago?
- How will the character's vocal delivery, staging (gestures, acting choice), and blocking (movement) convey an interpretation of Iago's character?
- Are any other actors on the stage? If so, what are they doing?
- Do you see the opportunity for staging to enhance irony in the speech? How could you prepare the delivery or setting to optimize the impact of the irony?

Comparing Interpretations

5. Listen to the audio recording of the same three scenes performed by each acting company in your class. As you listen, compare and contrast each recording with the interpretation presented by your peers. Then evaluate both performances against the original play. Jot down your ideas and observations in the My Notes section.

✓ Check Your Understanding

Reflect on the dramatic elements your acting company incorporated. How did these elements affect the meaning and delivery of the lines?

Demystifying Emilia: Questioning Through a Critical Lens

Learning Targets

- Analyze how a minor character in *Othello* influences the plot.
- Apply a critical perspective to gain new insights about a minor character.

Preview

In this activity, you will analyze how one character's actions and motives influence the moral dilemmas and advance the plot of *Othello*. You will then use your analysis to write a short story from the character's point of view.

Learning Strategies

Discussion Groups
Graphic Organizer
Jigsaw
Levels of Questions
Summarizing
Web Organizer

Reading *Othello*: Act III

1. Though Emilia is a minor character in *Othello* and her marriage to the antagonist Iago is secondary to that of Othello and Desdemona, the drama unfolds around and in some ways because of her.

   Where does Emilia's loyalty lie—to her honest lady, Desdemona, or to her husband, Iago? As you read Act III, consider Emilia's duty to Iago and Desdemona.

2. Preview the following graphic organizer, and then read closely the short scene assigned to your group. What does the scene reveal about Emilia? You may begin to make your determinations about this character by questioning the text. How is she characterized? What is her relationship to other characters? What are her motivations? Use the graphic organizer for your notes.

Scene	What the Scene Reveals About Emilia	Textual Evidence
Act III, Scene I, lines 46–64, Emilia & Cassio (Begins with EMILIA: Good morrow ... and goes to the end of Scene I)		
Act III, Scene III, lines 344–368, Emilia & Iago (Begins with IAGO: How now? What do you here alone? and ends when Emilia exits)		

ACTIVITY 3.12

PLAN

Materials: *Othello*, Act III
Suggested Pacing: 1 50-minute class period

TEACH

1 Read the Learning Targets and Preview aloud. You may conduct a brief whole-class discussion on the role minor characters play in plot development and on the challenges that might arise when writing from a fictional character's point of view.

2 Engage students by asking them to complete a quickwrite in which they recall a personal experience of making a difficult choice. Read the paragraph prior to discussing Emilia's predicament. Read aloud Reading *Othello: Act III*.

3 Assign each acting company (**discussion group**) a scene from the **graphic organizer**. Each scene features Emilia, Iago's wife. Have groups complete the graphic organizer by rereading the scene and recording what the scene reveals about the character of Emilia. Remind students to justify their opinions with specific textual evidence, which they will also record in the graphic organizer.

College and Career Readiness Standards

Focus Standards:

RL.11–12.1 Cite strong and thorough textual evidence to support analysis of what the text says explicitly as well as inferences drawn from the text, including determining where the text leaves matters uncertain.

RL.11–12.3 Analyze the impact of the author's choices regarding how to develop and relate elements of a story or drama (e.g., where a

story is set, how the action is ordered, how the characters are introduced and developed).

W.11–12.3 Write narratives to develop real or imagined experiences or events using effective technique, well-chosen details, and well-structured event sequences.

Additional Standards Addressed:

RL.11–12.6, W.11–12.5

LEVELED DIFFERENTIATED INSTRUCTION

Some students may benefit from having one column of their graphic organizer filled in by the teacher; students who finish quickly may complete the graphic organizer for other characters.

Developing Consider assisting students who need extra support by providing at least one brief example in the textual support column of their graphic organizer and then having them fill in what the supporting evidence reveals about the character.

Expanding Have students who accurately complete their graphic organizer about Emilia move on to develop similar assessments of the other characters in their assigned scene. If time allows, they can share their thoughts with the students who read the same scene.

4 Jigsaw small groups with the same text to share their responses. Allow time for students to share their revelations about Emilia.

5 Remind students of the essay they will be writing in Embedded Assessment 1. Consider revisiting the unpacked assessment from Activity 3.1 to mark the skills and knowledge students have acquired.

6 Pair students and ask them to formulate questions about the same scene through two different critical lenses. Direct students to **question the text**, first in pairs and then individually, using two different critical perspectives.

TEACHER TO TEACHER

Whether you assign pairs from the current jigsaw groups or from original acting companies, consider pairing students so that stronger students extend their knowledge by clarifying the task to a student who needs more support. Mixed groups often allow for strengthening and supporting of both students in a pair.

3.12

Scene	What the Scene Reveals About Emilia	Textual Evidence
Act III, Scene IV, lines 23–34, Emilia & Desdemona (Begins with DESDEMONA: Where should I lose that handkerchief, Emilia? and ends when Othello enters)		

3. With a partner, choose one critical perspective (Archetypal, Marxist, Feminist, Reader-Response, Cultural, or Historical). Draft one literal, one interpretive, and one universal question through that lens to explore the character of Emilia. For example, using a Cultural critical lens:

- **Literal:** Why does Emilia give Iago the handkerchief?
- **Interpretive:** Is Emilia torn between her duty to Desdemona and Iago?
- **Universal:** How can the powerless be coerced into other people's schemes?
- You should focus your questions on the character of Emilia. When you have checked your work with another group, repeat the process for a different critical perspective, this time on your own.

Act/Scene/Lines: _____

    Critical Perspective: _____

    Literal: _____

    Interpretive: _____

    Universal: _____

Act/Scene/Lines: _____

    Critical Perspective: _____

    Literal: _____

    Interpretive: _____

    Universal: _____

Invite students to share their responses to the activity. Which critical frames did students feel yielded the most interesting questions? What new insights did they gain about Emilia or about the play? Address student questions before turning to the writing prompt.

Remind students to complete the Independent Reading Link.

ASSESS

Review student responses to the writing prompt. Students will create a short story written from Emilia's point of view. The short story should apply the textual support students collected in their graphic organizer. It should also provide enough detail for a reader unfamiliar with the situation to understand the moral dilemma Emilia faces.

ADAPT

If students need additional help with organizing their short stories, have them start with a **web organizer**. Prompt them to summarize Emilia's dilemma in the center circle. Have students work in pairs to brainstorm Emilia's feelings about the dilemma and jot them in the outer circles.

 Writing Prompt: Literary

Write a short story from the perspective of Emilia talking to a close friend in person. Explain the moral dilemma that you, the character, are having and how you feel about it. Use your analysis of the character and your assigned scene to inform how you shape the character's point of view. Be sure to:

- Summarize conflict in the play and clearly present Emilia's point of view.
- Use narrative techniques, such as dialogue and pacing, to develop the story.
- Organize the events in your story so the relationship between them is evident.
- Use appropriate register and tone to reflect the moral dilemma.
- Develop descriptive details that convey a realistic picture of Emilia and what she thinks and experiences.
- Provide a conclusion that reflects on the resolution.

 INDEPENDENT READING LINK

Read and Respond

Think about the reading you are doing independently. Jot a few notes in your Reader/Writer Notebook about which critical perspective best illuminates your reading, and why.

 WRITING PROMPT: LITERARY

The following standards are addressed in the writing prompt:

- RL.11–12.1
- RL.11–12.3
- W.11–12.3

ACTIVITY 3.13

PLAN

Materials: *Othello*, Act IV, Scene I; filmed versions, including a filmed stage production, if possible
Suggested Pacing: 1 50-minute class period

TEACH

1 Read aloud the Learning Targets and Preview. Conduct a brief whole-class discussion in which students connect this activity with prior knowledge by comparing different versions or adaptations of films they may have seen. Remind students that multiple interpretations may present contrasting views even though they are based on the same source text.

2 Before reading Act IV, Scene I, have students revisit their work in Activity 3.4, and connect the activity to *Othello*, as described in student step 1. Explain that they should discuss the three outcomes in that activity and find lines from *Othello* that mirror those outcomes.

3 Ask students to infer the extremes to which Iago will go to convince Othello that his wife is unfaithful.

4 If the edition of *Othello* that your students are using provides a summary for each scene, have them read the summary for Act IV, Scene I. If not, have students read this scene in their acting companies (**discussion groups**) and summarize the scene as part of the Working from the Text section.

5 **Vocabulary Development:** Direct students' attention to the Literary Vocabulary box and point out that blocking is important in this scene. Have students work with a partner to brainstorm words to define the concept of *blocking*.

Staging Iago's Lies: Blocking for Effect

Learning Strategies

Drafting
Drama Games
Graphic Organizer
Revisiting Prior Work
Sketching
Summarizing

Learning Targets

- Evaluate two directors' use of dramatic elements in their interpretations of a scene.
- Apply a critical interpretation to the staging of a scene.
- Make informed decisions about blocking to convey a particular effect on the audience.

Preview

In this activity, you will compare, evaluate, and critique how the same scenarios—and even the same characters and lines—can change based on the setting, the staging strategies, and the actors' approaches to the material.

Reading *Othello*: Act IV, Scene I

1. Revisit your work from Step 1 in Activity 3.4. The scenario and outcomes in that activity reflect the events in *Othello*. Discuss your scenario with your acting company and take notes on connections between it and Shakespeare's play.

Scenario: Character 1 tells Character 2 that Character 2's romantic partner is cheating on him. Character 1 then produces "evidence." However, the story is untrue; Character 1 is actually lying.

Outcomes	How my acting company (or another company in my class) presented the outcome	How Shakespeare presents the situation in *Othello*
Outcome A Character 2 does not believe the story and turns on Character 1.		
Outcome B Character 2 considers the story as a possibility but then, after much investigation, decides it is not true.		
Outcome C Character 2 believes the story, is filled with jealousy, and wants revenge.		

College and Career Readiness Standards

Focus Standards:

RL.11–12.1 Cite strong and thorough textual evidence to support analysis of what the text says explicitly as well as inferences drawn from the text, including determining where the text leaves matters uncertain.

RL.11–12.2 Determine two or more themes or central ideas of a text and analyze their development over the course of the text, including how they interact and build on one another to produce a complex account; provide an objective summary of the text.

RL.11–12.7 Analyze multiple interpretations of a story, drama, or poem (e.g., recorded or live production of a play or recorded novel or poetry), evaluating how each version interprets the source text. (Include at least one play by Shakespeare and one play by an American dramatist.)

Reflecting on *Othello*: Act IV, Scene I

2. Summarize the key events of Act IV, Scene I, in the space provided.

3. Summarize lines 91 (IAGO: Stand you awhile apart) to 120 (IAGO: How do you, lieutenant?).

4. The moment when Othello falls into a trance is important, but it can be challenging to stage. How would your acting company present Othello's trance in a way that would not create an inadvertently humorous effect? With your acting company, read Act IV, Scene I, lines 1–89 on your feet, pausing to discuss and determine the most effective way to block this scene. In the space that follows, describe how you will stage the scene.

5. Working with a partner, choose one of the critical perspectives (Archetypal, Feminist, Marxist, Cultural, or Historical) and develop a literal question, an interpretive question, and a universal question about Act IV, Scene I.

6. The conversation that follows in Act IV, Scene I (lines 120–180) can be tricky to stage. Othello must be visible to the audience but not to Cassio. The audience needs to see how Othello could misinterpret Cassio's comments about Bianca, knowing all the while, of course, how Iago has orchestrated this misunderstanding.

Block this scene by using paper as the set and X's and arrows to indicate characters and blocking. Or use trinkets to represent characters in a "shoebox" set, with arrows to show blocking. Be prepared to explain your choices regarding blocking and the effects you intend to create through characters' movements on stage.

VOCABULARY

LITERARY
In drama, **blocking** is the way actors position themselves in relation to one another, the audience, and the objects on the stage. Directors carefully consider blocking to create an intended dramatic effect.

My Notes

_____

_____

_____

_____

_____

_____

_____

_____

_____

_____

_____

_____

_____

_____

_____

_____

_____

_____

_____

_____

_____

_____

College and Career Readiness Standards

SL.11–12.6 Adapt speech to a variety of contexts and tasks, demonstrating a command of formal English when indicated or appropriate.

Additional Standards Addressed:
RL.11–12.3, SL.11–12.1b, W.11–12.9

ACTIVITY 3.13 continued

6 To support students as they complete the Working from the Text section, suggest that acting companies read aloud the scene (through line 88) while standing. Encourage students to try out different ways of staging the scene.

7 Have the students to go back to their scene summary and elaborate on their summary of the portion of the scene between lines 89 and 120.

8 Have the students work with a partner to develop a literal, an interpretive, and a universal question about the text (**questioning the text**). Encourage pairs to develop questions that might inform their choices on how to stage the scene.

9 Clarify which conversation student step 6 in Working from the Text is referring to and have students work individually or with their acting companies to block the scene.

LEVELED DIFFERENTIATED INSTRUCTION

Support Many students, including those at various stages of language acquisition or mastery, can benefit from using trinkets to block the scene rather than doing the work on paper. Offering this kinesthetic option to the whole class will allow students to choose the method that works best for them.

10 Lead the class in a discussion of their choices and the justifications for those choices. If time permits, allow volunteers to present parts of the scene to demonstrate the choices they made.

TEACHER TO TEACHER

Shakespeare's Globe website (shakespearesglobe.com) includes an interactive tool called *Staging It*. The tool allows students to view segments of a scene delivered multiple times by professional actors, each time with different blocking, subtext, and emotional tone. They can select the interpretations they like the most and put them together to create a complete scene. Consider giving students time in your school's media lab to explore this or similar resources as they plan their scenes.

11 Explain that seeing different productions of a play is an opportunity to explore multiple interpretations of it. Using the bulleted questions, guide a discussion of the advantages of film and stage versions. Show students a cinematic version and a filmed stage production of this scene. Have students record their ideas in the **graphic organizer**.

12 Have students complete the Gaining Perspectives discussion. Ask students to share their responses. Invite volunteers to role-play an alternate scene between Othello and Desdemona or Othello and Iago, using their responses.

13 Have students respond to the Check Your Understanding prompt. Once they have discussed their ideas and decided which interpretation creates a stronger effect on the viewer, have students complete a **quickwrite** paragraph stating and supporting their opinions.

LEVELED DIFFERENTIATED INSTRUCTION

In this activity, students may need support explaining and defending their opinions about which version of the scene creates the strongest effect on the viewer.

Expanding Provide students with the **Opinion Builder** graphic organizer to use during the small-group discussion. Remind students to use their viewing notes from the charts to identify supporting evidence for their opinions.

Bridging Provide students with the **Opinion Builder** graphic organizer to complete as they discuss the Check Your Understanding prompt. Encourage them to use the organizer not only to brainstorm reasons for their own opinions but also to cite specific examples from the filmed interpretations.

3.13

Film Study: Evaluating Act IV, Scene I

You will view two versions of this scene: one a filmed version and the other a stage production. How effective are the filmed and staged productions?

- What advantages might a film version have?
- What advantages might a stage version have?

Film version—Director: Miller, Parke, or Welles	How is it presented?	What is the effect?
Dialogue between Iago and Othello, up to the trance		
The trance		
Dialogue between Iago and Cassio, observed by Othello		
Dialogue between Cassio and Bianca, observed by Othello		
Dialogue between Othello and Iago, after Cassio and Bianca exit		
Othello striking Desdemona		

Filmed stage version—Director: Burge, Milam, or Suzman	How is it presented?	What is the effect?
Dialogue between Iago and Othello, up to the trance		
The trance		
Dialogue between Iago and Cassio, observed by Othello		
Dialogue between Cassio and Bianca, observed by Othello		
Dialogue between Othello and Iago, after Cassio and Bianca exit		
Othello striking Desdemona		

7. With your peers, discuss the effectiveness of the scenes in the film and staged productions. Evaluate the directors' use of dramatic or cinematic elements.

Gaining Perspectives

You have learned that Iago is a master at manipulating people, especially Othello, and people like Iago often create interpersonal conflicts between people for their own personal gain or enjoyment without worrying about the consequences. With a partner, imagine that Othello and Desdemona are a real-life modern couple that you know. What types of conflict resolution skills would help a contemporary Othello and Desdemona resolve the problem in an effective way? What strategies would help a modern Othello work effectively with a twenty-first century Iago?

☑ Check Your Understanding

In discussion groups, determine which film interpretation of the scene creates the strongest effect on the viewer. Then, explain your selection in a quickwrite with appropriate examples to support your opinion.

ACTIVITY 3.13 continued

Support Before the small-group discussion, provide students with the **Opinion Builder** graphic organizer to assemble ideas. Then direct students to use the graphic organizer during the discussion to record ideas.

Extend Encourage students who need an extra challenge to use the insights from their **Opinion Builder** graphic organizer to write a brief critique of one of the interpretations they found inferior and include it for comparison purposes in their Check Your Understanding paragraph.

14 Tell students to read Act IV, Scenes II–III prior to the next class.

ASSESS

Review student responses to the Check Your Understanding task. Ensure they offer a clearly stated claim with rationale and specific support as well as evidence from the text. They should be able to explain why they chose the interpretation of the scene that they did, citing examples from the interpretation to justify why they found it to be the most effective version of the scene. The explanations should flow clearly from notes in their graphic organizer and should include references to concepts such as blocking.

ADAPT

If students need additional help with film critique, place them in small groups and have them review film terms and discuss their work on the graphic organizers before responding to the Check Your Understanding prompt. Monitor these discussions and review students' charts to ensure they are prepared to respond to the prompt.

To extend learning, ask students to create a Venn diagram or other graphic organizer to compare the character of Othello in Act IV, Scene I, to the character of Othello in Act II, Scene III. Share out, as time permits.

PLAN

Materials: *Othello*, Act IV; note cards, one per group, each labeled with a critical perspective (excluding Reader Response)
Suggested Pacing: 1 50-minute class period

TEACH

1 Read aloud the Learning Targets and Preview. To draw students into the activity, you may conduct a whole class brainstorm to review what students know about each critical perspective.

2 Provide students time to respond in small groups to the text they have read outside class. Circulate among groups to hear points about plot, characters, conflict, or setting that students found interesting.

3 Help students consider how a scene from Othello could reflect a particular critical perspective. Model the process of applying the archetypal critical perspective to Act IV, Scene II, lines 1–110, in the **graphic organizer**. Help students understand how an awareness of the temptress archetype, for example, might have influenced Shakespeare as he wrote the scene. Discuss how the archetype might influence Othello as he grapples with the idea of his wife's infidelity, as well as how it influences the students themselves as they read.

LEVELED DIFFERENTIATED INSTRUCTION

Some students may have a more difficult time applying a critical perspective to the text while others will easily grasp how to interpret material through a different lens. These modifications should help address those differences.

Developing Consider assigning the archetypal critical perspective to students who need extra support, which will allow them to use your modeled response as a starting point.

One Scene, Many Perspectives

Learning Strategies

Graphic Organizer
Note-taking
Oral Interpretation
Rehearsing

Learning Targets

- Analyze a scene through multiple critical perspectives and evaluate how each lens affects the interpretation of the scene.
- Rehearse and perform a dramatic interpretation of a text while using a critical perspective.

Preview

In this activity, you will analyze a scene from *Othello* from multiple critical perspectives. You will then work with your acting company to present the scene from a specific critical perspective. Then you will write an essay stating which critical lens provides the strongest insight into the scene.

Reading *Othello*: Act IV

1. Now that you have read through Act IV, Scene III, select a quotation from scene II or III that you find to be especially interesting or significant. Share the quote and your commentary with your acting company. Be sure to use evidence from the text to support your comments.

2. Examine Scene II (lines 1–110) through each critical perspective. Use evidence from the text to support your analysis through the different lenses.

Critical Perspective	What is revealed by analyzing the text through this Critical Perspective?
Archetypal Criticism might suggest that an archetype such as the temptress (a woman who uses her power—intellect, magic, or beauty—to make men weak) is essential to understanding this scene.	Consider how Othello seems torn between his love for Desdemona and his sense of betrayal. He says Desdemona is both fair and foul and compares her to a prostitute.
Feminist Criticism might suggest that the male-female power relationships that come into play in this scene are the most important influence on our understanding of it.	Students may consider the fact that Desdemona has little recourse against Othello's rage. She turns to a man, Iago, for help.
Marxist Criticism might suggest that we must examine the issues of class or social standing in order to fully understand this scene.	Emilia, though outraged at Othello's rough treatment of Desdemona, has no right to intervene because she is a servant.
Reader response Criticism might suggest that what you bring to the scene will determine its significance.	Students' personal responses should connect personal experience to the text and include relevant textual evidence.
Cultural Criticism might suggest that we must consider such issues as ethnicity, religious beliefs, and customs to understand this scene.	An understanding of Desdemona's religious beliefs lends insight into her mindset about adultery.
Historical Criticism might suggest that the historical context plays a significant role in a modern reader's understanding the scene.	Desdemona's acceptance of Othello's curses and her mention of losing her father may be grounded in the Elizabethan practice of arranged marriages.

College and Career Readiness Standards

Focus Standards:

RL.11–12.1 Cite strong and thorough textual evidence to support analysis of what the text says explicitly as well as inferences drawn from the text, including determining where the text leaves matters uncertain.

SL.11–12.1c Propel conversations by posing and responding to questions that probe reasoning and evidence; ensure a hearing for a full range of positions on a topic or issue; clarify, verify, or challenge ideas and conclusions; and promote divergent and creative perspectives.

W.11–12.1a Introduce precise, knowledgeable claim(s), establish the significance of the claim(s), distinguish the claim(s) from alternate or opposing claims, and create an organization that logically sequences claim(s), counterclaims, reasons, and evidence.

Interpreting the Scene

3. Your teacher will assign you one of the critical perspectives from the list. With your acting company, determine how the interpretation of Act IV, Scene II, lines 1–110 from this perspective would translate into staging this scene. Record your ideas in the space that follows. Also add some notes, with support and references from your previous responses to convey how your ideas reflect the perspective your company has been assigned.

Critical Perspective: _____

Vocal Delivery (rate, volume, and the general tone this character should convey):

Othello: _____

_____

_____

Emilia: _____

_____

_____

Desdemona: _____

_____

_____

Staging (gestures, mannerisms each character will use):

Othello: _____

_____

_____

Emilia: _____

_____

_____

_____

Desdemona: _____

_____

_____

Blocking (the position of the actors on stage in relation to one another, the set, and the props): Illustrate your plan for blocking on separate paper.

College and Career Readiness Standards

W.11–12.1b Develop claim(s) and counterclaims fairly and thoroughly, supplying the most relevant evidence for each while pointing out the strengths and limitations of both in a manner that anticipates the audience's knowledge level, concerns, values, and possible biases.

Additional Standards Addressed:

RL.11–12.3, RL.11–12.5, RL.11–12.7, SL.11–12.1b, W.11–12.1e, W.11–12.5

Extend For students who need an extra challenge, ask them to write a paragraph that details the critical perspective most evident in one of the film versions from the previous activity, using specific examples from the film to support their point of view.

4 For the remaining five perspectives, have students work with their acting companies (**discussion groups**) to discuss and take notes on how each perspective applies to this particular scene.

TEACHER TO TEACHER

If time allows, you may want to share some information on how plays were staged in Shakespeare's time and how staging has evolved. The Folger Shakespeare Library provides a podcast (https://www. folger.edu/shakespeare-unlimited/ costume-scenery-design) on the subject.

5 Distribute one note card to each group. Make sure each is labeled with one of the critical perspectives (excluding Reader Response). Give students time to plan and rehearse their characters' vocal delivery, staging, and blocking to reflect their assigned critical perspective.

TEACHER TO TEACHER

During the rehearsal process, remind students that the assigned director in each group should make notes on the actors' tone, timing, and other dramatic elements and suggest changes as needed.

6 As acting companies perform their scenes, allow the audience to determine the critical perspective being used. Briefly discuss the groups' choices and presentation.

7 Once students have examined the scene through the various perspectives, ask them to decide which one helped them understand the scene most fully. Have them respond individually in a brief written response.

8 As an extension of the Check Your Understanding task, ask students to complete the writing prompt either in class or for homework.

9 Assign reading through Act V, Scene I, for homework, and remind students to complete the Independent Reading Link.

10 If time permits, model the Independent Reading Link using one of the key themes from *Othello*.

LEVELED DIFFERENTIATED INSTRUCTION

Extend Consider asking students who need an extra challenge to write a paragraph about which critical perspective is reflected most strongly in their independent reading material. Paragraphs should cite specific examples from the text to support their point of view.

ASSESS

Before they begin the writing prompt, review students' responses to the Check Your Understanding task. They should articulate which performance provided the best insight into the play, and why. The argumentative paragraph for the writing prompt should include a strong thesis statement supported by evidence that demonstrates understanding of the critical perspective chosen. The concluding statement should support and reiterate the paragraph's claim without introducing new ideas or being overly repetitive.

ADAPT

If students need additional help explaining which critical lens made the scene stand out most for them, have them work in small groups to discuss the aspects of each version of the scene. Encourage them to remind one another about the types of critical lenses through which they interpreted the scene, and to explore why each was or was not powerful.

3.14

🔲 INDEPENDENT READING LINK

Read and Respond

Write a paragraph analyzing one of the key themes presented in your independent reading. Be sure to include a thesis statement that makes an assertion about that theme, a direct quotation from the text, and a strong concluding sentence.

4. Assign roles and rehearse the scene according to your notes. Choose one individual to play the role of director to guide speaking and moving and to ensure that actors are conveying the assigned interpretation. Rehearse your scene before presenting it to the class.

☑ Check Your Understanding

Reflect on the vocal, staging, and blocking choices that your acting company made. How did your assigned critical perspective inform your decisions? Did the critical perspective lend itself to a rich interpretation of the text?

📝 Writing Prompt: Argumentative

Write an argumentative paragraph about the critical lens that provides the most interesting perspective for the scene. Explain how interpreting the scene through this lens provides the most compelling understanding of the scene. Be sure to:

- Include a claim that states which critical lens provides the best insight into Othello.
- Include relevant evidence from the stages interpretations and the text demonstrating how of critical lenses can help shape dramatic elements.
- Provide a concluding statement that supports your key claim.

📝 WRITING PROMPT: ARGUMENTATIVE

The following standards are addressed in the writing prompt:

- W.11–12.1a
- W.11–12.1b
- W.11–12.1e
- RL.11–12.1

"Talk You of Killing?": Defending a Perspective

Learning Targets
- Make predictions about how the plot and subplots of the play will be resolved.
- Evaluate and critique the dramatic elements used in two film interpretations of *Othello*.
- Defend one film interpretation and the corresponding critical perspective it uses in an argumentative essay.

Preview
In this activity, you will read Act V of *Othello* and watch two film adaptions of the final act of the play. After comparing the dramatic elements in the films, you will write an argument stating which version best expresses the themes of the play through the use of a critical perspective.

Reading *Othello*: Act V

1. **Quickwrite:** It is no surprise that a Shakespearean tragedy ends ... tragically. Now that you have read Act V, Scene I, predict the action in the final scene. Will Othello learn the truth? Will Iago be brought to justice? How will the conflict ultimately be resolved?

2. Act V, Scene II of *Othello* is the climax of the tragedy. As you read Desdemona's last conversation with her husband, visualize the set, costumes, actions, lighting, and music. Make notes in your Reader/Writer Notebook.

3. Now that you have completed the play, reflect on your predictions about the final scene. How accurate were your predictions? Why do you think Shakespeare chose to end the play this way?

4. Using the same critical lens you chose in the last activity, write one literal, one interpretive, and one universal question about Act V. Be sure your interpretive and universal questions are written in a way that requires literary analysis as well as support from the text. Here are some examples written from the cultural perspective:

   Literal: What is Desdemona's fate?

   Interpretive: What drives Othello to commit such an act?

   Universal: How can jealousy and revenge cloud a person's judgement?

Learning Strategies
Drafting
Graphic Organizer
Levels of Questions
Note-taking

My Notes

ACTIVITY 3.15

PLAN
Materials: *Othello*, Act V, Scene II; two film versions of Othello; sticky notes
Suggested Pacing: 1 50-minute class period

TEACH

1 Read aloud the Learning Targets and Preview. Clarify that students will be analyzing connections between the play, class performances, and critical perspectives. You may want to review students' previous experience with comparing film versions in Activity 3.8.

2 Ask students to quickwrite their predictions of what they think will happen in the final scene of the play.

3 Distribute sticky notes to students to record their visualization of the theatrical elements of the final scene as they read Act V, Scene II.

4 Conduct a brief whole-class discussion on students' predictions and thoughts on the play's resolution.

5 Instruct students to question the text by writing one literal, one interpretive, and one universal question about Act V. As a class, discuss the examples in the Student Edition and brainstorm possible answers for each question. Record students' answers on the board. Be sure responses demonstrate literary analysis and use supporting evidence from the text.

College and Career Readiness Standards

Focus Standards:

RL.11–12.7 Analyze multiple interpretations of a story, drama, or poem (e.g., recorded or live production of a play or recorded novel or poetry), evaluating how each version interprets the source text. (Include at least one play by Shakespeare and one play by an American dramatist.)

W.11–12.1a Introduce precise, knowledgeable claim(s), establish the significance of the claim(s), distinguish the claim(s) from alternate or opposing claims, and create an organization that logically sequences claim(s), counterclaims, reasons, and evidence.

6 Direct acting companies to divide the theatrical elements on the graphic organizer so that each student is responsible for one to three elements to record during the viewing. Show the students one film version of the scene and allow time for them to share their recorded elements with the entire group. Ask students to switch theatrical elements for the viewing of the second film version. Again, allow time for sharing and discussion. Ask volunteers to summarize contrasting views from the two film interpretations. Lead the class in a brief discussion about what is emphasized or absent in each version.

LEVELED DIFFERENTIATED INSTRUCTION

Beginning For students who need extra support, consider modeling one or two responses on a graphic organizer to assist them in analyzing dramatic elements.

Discuss with students the critical perspective that they see reflected through each director's interpretation. Be sure students can support these perspectives with evidence from the viewings. Check for student understanding by having students think-pair-share about which interpretation of the final scene they think best conveys the play's themes.

 TEACHER TO TEACHER

Students will use this essay as a tool to create a rubric for the scoring of literary analysis in Activity 3.18. Ask students to label their essays with a number or student ID and to omit their names from the writing. This way you will be able to use the essays as samples while still protecting students' privacy.

3.15

Film Study

5. Your class will watch two versions of the final act of *Othello*. As you view two versions of the film, take notes in the following graphic organizer.

Dramatic Element:	Film Version 1 Director: Year:	Film Version 2 Director: Year:
The set (Consider use of space, etc.)		
Sound (Think about how music and other sounds influence the production.)		
Delivery (What is the impact of the actors' delivery of the line?)		
Mood (Consider how elements including lighting, props, costumes, and more work together to create mood.)		
Critical perspective reflected in the film adaptation		

College and Career Readiness Standards

W.11–12.1b Develop claim(s) and counterclaims fairly and thoroughly, supplying the most relevant evidence for each while pointing out the strengths and limitations of both in a manner that anticipates the audience's knowledge level, concerns, values, and possible biases.

W.11–12.1e Provide a concluding statement or section that follows from and supports the argument presented.

Additional Standards Addressed:
RL.11–12.1, RL.11–12.2, RL.11–12.3, SL.11–12.1b, SL.11–12.3

Write your own caption: _____

Check Your Understanding

Which interpretation of the final scene best conveys the tragic themes of the play? What dramatic elements does your chosen version use most effectively to communicate with the audience and bring the play to a close?

📝 Writing Prompt: Argumentative

Select one of the themes presented in *Othello*. Write an argumentative essay explaining which film adaptation of *Othello* best illuminates one of the themes presented in the play through its use of dramatical elements. Consider using your Check Your Understanding response as a starting point. Be sure to:

- Include a clear claim about a theme in the play.
- Use specific evidence from the text and one or more film interpretations to reinforce your claim about the connection between the play and film.
- Provide a concluding statement that supports your key claim.

📝 WRITING PROMPT: ARGUMENTATIVE

The following standards are addressed in the writing prompt:

- RL.11–12.7
- W.11–12.1
- W.11–12.1a
- W.11–12.1b
- W.11–12.9

ACTIVITY 3.15 continued

7 Prompt students to examine the image depicting the final scene. Discuss students' observations and have students write their own captions. Have volunteers share their captions.

8 Give students time in class to draft an argument about the most effective film interpretation of the final scene in *Othello*. Direct students to determine which interpretation they feel is most effective based on how well each conveys a theme. Remind students that their argumentative essay should assert which critical perspective was most evident in the film version they selected.

ASSESS

Before they begin the writing prompt, review student responses to the Check Your Understanding task. They should note which interpretation best conveys tragedy and how theatrical elements communicate tragedy to the audience.

Students' argumentative essays should articulate a specific theme from the play and use evidence from the text and at least one film adaptation to write about how the director used dramatic elements such as set, sound, lighting, and props to increase viewers' understanding of the theme.

ADAPT

If students need additional help articulating their ideas about how the tragedy unfolds through the use of theatrical elements, model the process with a specific example from their graphic organizers. Repeat the modeling process using one of the critical perspectives.

ACTIVITY 3.16

PLAN

Materials: selected scenes from *Othello* named in the graphic organizer for this activity; chart paper for groups to display their final timelines

Suggested Pacing: 1 50-minute class period

TEACH

1 Read aloud the Learning Targets and Preview. If the version of the play that you are using provides a description of Roderigo, review it with students. If not, lead a whole-class discussion to develop a description of the character.

2 Vocabulary Development: Review the meaning of the term *subplot* with students. Have them provide examples from material previously covered in class to illustrate the meaning of the term.

 TEACHER TO TEACHER

Since this activity does not require acting, consider splitting up acting companies into different groups to allow students the opportunity to work with others.

3 Instruct students to close read the scenes assigned to their discussion group. Review the concept of character motivation and make suggestions on how students might mark the text if needed.

Learning Strategies

Marking the Text
Note-taking
Rereading
Skimming/Scanning

VOCABULARY

LITERARY

A **subplot** is a feature in a work of fiction, especially in a drama, that comments on the main plot of the story. Subplots may either complement or present an opposition to the main plot in a narrative.

Learning Targets

- Closely analyze a scene from a play to summarize a character's underlying motives and actions.
- Identify, evaluate, and critique a subplot in *Othello*.
- Collaboratively create a pictorial timeline that illustrates a subplot found in *Othello*.

Preview

In this activity, you will evaluate and critique Shakespeare's use of subplot in *Othello*. You will work collaboratively to summarize how Roderigo's actions and words contribute to plot and subplot within the play.

Reviewing Subplot

1. A **subplot** is a secondary or minor story that unfolds in a narrative text. Authors often use a subplot to add complexity to characters and conflicts within a story. Think of a novel you've read or a film that you have watched. Did it have a subplot? How did the subplot contribute to the action in the story?

My Notes

2. Reread your assigned scene and mark the text to indicate how the subplot contributes to or advances the plot in the play. Consider the following questions as you read:

- What is Roderigo's motivation?
- How is he persuaded by Iago?
- What is the result of Roderigo's actions?
- What conflict or dilemma does he create?

"Othello. Act V, Scene I" by Felix Octavius Carr Darley (1895)

College and Career Readiness Standards

Focus Standards:

RL.11–12.3 Analyze the impact of the author's choices regarding how to develop and relate elements of a story or drama (e.g., where a story is set, how the action is ordered, how the characters are introduced and developed).

RL.11–12.5 Analyze how an author's choices concerning how to structure specific parts of a text (e.g., the choice of where to begin or end a story, the choice to provide a comedic or tragic resolution) contribute to its overall structure and meaning as well as its aesthetic impact.

SL.11–12.1b Work with peers to promote civil, democratic discussions and decision-making, set clear goals and deadlines, and establish individual roles as needed.

Additional Standards Addressed:

RL.11–12.1, RL.11–12.2, W.11–12.10

3. With your group, write a brief summary of Roderigo's actions and the impact on the overall action in the play. As you complete the graphic organizer, include text evidence to strengthen your summary.

Scene	Summary	Impact on the Plot
Act I, Scene I–II	Roderigo is shocked to hear that Desdemona has run off with Othello. He is upset because he had feelings for Desdemona. He quickly goes with Iago to tell her father the news and eagerly tells Brabantio, "I think I can discover him, if you please, to get good guard and go along with me."	Alerting Brabantio of Desdemona's actions spurs the first conflict in the play.
Act II, Scene III	Taking cues from Iago, Roderigo provokes a fight with the inebriated Cassio. "Beat me?" Iago cries as he runs across the room, causing a spectacle in front of Montano and the other guards.	This fight sullies Cassio's name and seemingly confirms the false rumors that Iago has spread about Cassio's drinking. This event spurs Cassio and Desdemona's private conversation and leads to many of the misunderstandings between Desdemona and Othello.
Act IV, Scene II	Roderigo is easily convinced by Iago to kill Cassio. While he questions the logic behind this plan, he is hopeful that getting rid of Cassio will bring him one step closer to Desdemona.	This exchange sets in motion the action in the final act of the play.
Act V, Scene II	Roderigo attempts to kill Cassio despite having "no great devotion to the deed." When Roderigo fails to carry out the plan, Iago takes matters into his own hands and strikes Cassio with a sword. In order to cover up his part in the attack, Iago fatally wounds Roderigo.	Roderigo's actions cause Othello to believe that Cassio has died. Roderigo's actions propel the action in this scene and Othello reluctantly kills Desdemona, leading to the play's tragic end.

ACTIVITY 3.16 continued

4 Direct students to work with their group to summarize their assigned scenes and articulate the scenes' impact on the play as a whole. Remind students to use evidence from the text. Note that they can also pull evidence from scenes not assigned to them.

5 Have students jigsaw with other groups to share insights about their assigned scenes. During these jigsaw group discussions, students should listen, ask questions to gather additional information as needed, and use their graphic organizers to take notes on the scenes assigned to other groups.

6 Regroup students into their original groups for this activity to create a timeline on chart paper of the scenes that feature Roderigo. The timeline should also illustrate the scenes' impact on the play's plot as a whole. Students should use words, symbols, and drawings to visualize and record this information.

7 As a group, students should discuss the subplots evident on their timeline and answer the questions presented in student step 6.

8 Instruct students to focus on one subplot in the paragraph they write for Check Your Understanding.

LEVELED DIFFERENTIATED INSTRUCTION

Some students may benefit from conferring with their peers.

Developing If students need extra support, allow them time to review the timelines created by other groups. Seeing other visual interpretations may help them solidify their ideas about the impact of a specific subplot. Students may also benefit from you providing a suggestion of the subplot that should be the focus of their paragraph.

Extend Ask students who need an extra challenge to work in a group to create a similar timeline for another character in the play, such as Emilia, that indicates evidence of another subplot and its impact on the play as a whole.

ASSESS

Review the graphic organizers created by students and the timelines created by the groups before students begin the Check Your Understanding. Students' Check Your Understanding paragraph should focus on a specific subplot and how it contributes to the development of the story as a whole. The paragraph should also explain how the subplot adds depth and meaning to the work and use evidence from the text to support ideas.

ADAPT

If students need extra support to complete the Check Your Understanding, conduct a whole-class discussion to identify and articulate the subplots in the play.

3.16

4. Be prepared to share your summary in a group discussion. Listen to your classmates' summaries of the remaining scenes and jot down notes in your graphic organizer. Ask insightful questions to capture the following information about each scene:

   • What happens in the scene?

   • What motivates Roderigo in each scene?

   • How do Roderigo's actions in the scene contribute to or advance the main plot of the play?

5. With your group, create a timeline of the scenes you have discussed. Use drawings, symbols, and words to demonstrate the action in each scene. In addition, consider how you can show the scene's impact on the overall plot.

6. As a group, critique and evaluate how these subplots contribute to and advance the action in the play. How effective are the scenes in making the play move forward? Which of Roderigo's actions is most critical to driving other action in the play?

☑ Check Your Understanding

Write a paragraph explaining how Shakespeare uses a subplot to advance the action in *Othello*. What does this technique add to the play?

Evolving Perspectives

Learning Targets
- Review characteristics of various critical perspectives and apply those characteristics to the plot and other elements of a text.
- Work collaboratively to present your analysis of a character.

Preview
In this activity, you will work in groups to apply a specific critical perspective to a character in *Othello*. Then you will create a class presentation to share your findings with your peers.

Applying Critical Perspectives

1. You will complete a matching activity to review the critical perspectives and how each one might apply to *Othello*. Once you receive a card from your teacher, you will need to find two classmates with cards that have the same critical perspective. Of the three cards, one will have the name of the critical perspective, another will have a brief note about that critical perspective, and the third card will show a statement about one of the main characters that has been filtered through that critical perspective. Once you find the other members of your group, you will be asked to focus on the critical perspective you have on your cards. See the example cards.

> ### HISTORICAL CRITICISM

> Text cannot be separated from its historical context; situating a text in its time period helps the reader understand the text.

> Othello feels isolated from Venetian society because of prevailing views about race and culture at that time and place in history.

Learning Strategies
Discussion Groups
Drafting
Graphic Organizer
Note-taking

My Notes

_____

_____

_____

_____

_____

_____

_____

_____

_____

_____

_____

_____

_____

_____

_____

_____

_____

_____

_____

ACTIVITY 3.17

PLAN
Materials: cards for matching activity (located in the Planning the Unit section)
Suggested pacing: 1 50-minute class period

TEACH
1 Read over the Learning Targets and Preview with your students to orient them to the activity.

⭐ TEACHER TO TEACHER
The text for this activity's cards is located in the Unit 3 Planning the Unit section, and the directions for the activity follow. Make copies of the manipulatives page from the Planning the Unit, and cut along the lines to make sets of 15 cards. Make enough sets so that each student will receive one card. An example of the cards is included on the student page to help explain the activity to the class. *Note: If you use more than one set of the cards, then adjust your explanation so students understand that two or more people may have the same card.*

2 Use the cards as **manipulatives** to review the critical perspectives and how each one might apply to *Othello* and/or one or more of its characters. Include Cultural Criticism in your review, even though it is not included in the manipulatives.

3 Give every student a card, and explain that they are to find the other students whose cards are associated with the same critical perspective as theirs.

4 Allow students to find their group members. Assign each group to focus on the critical perspective they have on their cards.

College and Career Readiness Standards

Focus Standards:

RL.11–12.1 Cite strong and thorough textual evidence to support analysis of what the text says explicitly as well as inferences drawn from the text, including determining where the text leaves matters uncertain.

SL.11–12.1 Initiate and participate effectively in a range of collaborative discussions (one-on-one, in groups, and teacher-led) with diverse partners on grades 11–12 topics, texts, and issues, building on others' ideas and expressing their own clearly and persuasively.

5 After students have found their matches, ask the groups to discuss their assigned critical perspective and complete the graphic organizer. Depending on the size of your class, you may want to use more than one set of cards. If so, create subgroups with the same criticism so that all students in each group have a chance to participate in discussions.

6 As the groups work, monitor their discussions, questioning assumptions and offering suggestions as needed. Remind groups to use language and word choices that are precise and engaging enough to keep listeners interested. Have groups review what they have written to ensure they have avoided slang and filler words.

7 Next, jigsaw students or have each small group present their findings to the class. As each group presents, other students should take notes on the graphic organizer. After all the presentations have been given, engage students in a whole-class discussion on the various perspectives.

8 Remind students that this discussion of the applicability of the various perspectives needs to be applied to *Othello* as a whole and/or one or more of the play's characters, depending on the instructions given at the beginning of this activity.

3.17

2. With your group, complete the graphic organizer on the following page as you use the perspective on your cards to analyze *Othello*.

Critical Perspective:	
Paraphrase the definition and position of this critical perspective.	
How does this perspective provide insight into a particular theme?	
How does thinking about this perspective affect your understanding of the characters' behaviors?	
How does thinking about this perspective affect your understanding of the setting?	
Which aspects of the plot best lend themselves to an interpretation from this critical perspective? Explain.	

3. Each group will present its findings. In planning the presentation, assign roles within your group or divide the group's notes from the graphic organizer to ensure everyone is actively involved in the presentation.

College and Career Readiness Standards

SL.11–12.4 Present information, findings, and supporting evidence, conveying a clear and distinct perspective, such that listeners can follow the line of reasoning, alternative or opposing perspectives are addressed, and the organization, development, substance, and style are appropriate to purpose, audience, and a range of formal and informal tasks.

Additional Standards Addressed:

RL.11–12.3, SL.11–12.3

4. As you view other groups' presentations, use the following graphic organizer to take notes and record questions or comments about their presentations in your Reader/Writer Notebook.

Notes on the Play	
Which critical perspective lends itself to a deep analysis of *Othello*?	
What does the critical perspective reveal about the themes, characters, setting, and plot?	Textual support for your ideas:

5. Be prepared to use your notes on your own and your classmates' presentations in a class discussion of the way an examination of a text through multiple perspectives can impact understanding of the character.

☑ **Check Your Understanding**

After listening to your classmates' presentations, identify the most compelling new idea to emerge from the analysis. Draft a thesis statement to sum up the idea.

9 Allow students time to respond to the Check Your Understanding.

LEVELED DIFFERENTIATED INSTRUCTION

Students might need support drafting their thesis statements to sum up a compelling new idea about the play.

Beginning You may provide a thesis statement stem to students whose language skills are still developing.

Developing Review students' graphic organizers from student step 4 to ensure they have sufficient information to formulate a solid thesis statement. If students are having difficulty, model a response and its accompanying supporting evidence.

Bridging Encourage students to draft a complex thesis statement that goes beyond summing up the idea by explaining what makes it compelling in its interpretation of the play. If students' initial thesis statements are simplistic, model a more sophisticated thesis using a different critical perspective.

ASSESS

Review students' responses to the Check Your Understanding. Students' thesis statements should have a clear connection to their notes from the graphic organizers and should show that students drew insight from the discussion in student step 5.

ADAPT

If students need additional help identifying a compelling idea for the Check Your Understanding task, have pairs review their group discussion notes. Students can agree on one idea and develop support together.

ACTIVITY 3.18

PLAN

Materials: student portfolios with graded/evaluated essays; plain, half sheets of letter-sized paper for essay evaluations (3 per student)

Suggested Pacing: 1 50-minute class period

TEACH

1 Read the Learning Targets and Preview with your students.

2 Allow students time to revisit prior work by reviewing several past assignments in their writing portfolios (or collected essays from this year). Have them do a quickwrite to record feedback.

 TEACHER TO TEACHER

Consider making portfolio reviews a regular activity in the classroom. Reviews often make good transitions between units.

3 Direct students to close read the assignment and steps for Embedded Assessment 1, using the information to generate key categories for a rubric.

LEVELED DIFFERENTIATED INSTRUCTION

This activity should help students at all levels evaluate their own work more effectively.

Beginning You may provide students whose language skills are still developing a simplified version of the Standard for Writing a Literary Analysis section or a rubric with some of the key categories already identified.

Developing Students who have difficulty dissecting the parts of a literary analysis may benefit from seeing an example essay that has all the parts—thesis, body paragraphs, etc.—labeled.

Expanding Provide students who are proficient at self-editing two sample papers of comparable quality and encourage them to look at nuances in language usage and other finer points to determine which should score higher.

Learning Strategies

Close Reading
Graphic Organizer
Quickwrite
Revisiting Prior Work

My Notes

Learning Targets
- Collaboratively construct a rubric that effectively evaluates the ideas, organizational structure, and style of a written response.
- Closely evaluate and critique the characteristics of your own argumentative writing and that of your peers.

Preview

In this activity, you will prepare for Embedded Assessment 1 by analyzing the Assignment and Scoring Guide. With your group, you will create a rubric and use it to evaluate previous writing assignments you and your classmates have completed, paying close attention to the quality of the thesis statements, supporting evidence, and conclusions.

Revisiting Prior Work

1. **Quickwrite:** Review some of the essays you wrote earlier in the year. What kind of feedback did you receive? Write some of the comments about your writing in the following space.

2. In relying on the teacher to assess written work, you may not have considered your own ability to assess your writing. The process of writing is ongoing, and getting in the habit of planning your writing will strengthen your ability to make an effective argument.

   In order to create a standard for evaluating your writing, you need to be fully aware of the criteria. With your acting company or discussion group, closely read the Assignment and Steps for Embedded Assessment 1: Writing a Literary Analysis. Identify the key categories in column 1 that, according to the Assignment and Steps, need to be mastered in this assessment.

Rubric

Key Categories			

College and Career Readiness Standards

Focus Standards:

SL.11–12.1a Come to discussions prepared, having read and researched material under study; explicitly draw on that preparation by referring to evidence from other texts and other research on the topic or issue to stimulate a thoughtful, well-reasoned exchange of ideas.

W.11–12.4 Produce clear and coherent writing in which the development, organization, and style are appropriate to task, purpose, and audience.

W.11–12.5 Develop and strengthen writing as needed by planning, revising, editing, rewriting, or trying a new approach, focusing on addressing what is most significant for a specific purpose and audience.

Key Categories			

How to Write a Literary Analysis

3. Writing a literary analysis requires you to break down a text into smaller components and carefully examine these different elements of a literary text to reach new understandings about the text and its significance. Read the following standards for writing a literary analysis. Is there anything missing from your rubric?

Standard for Writing a Literary Analysis: A literary analysis examines how elements such as setting, characters, plot, literary devices, and theme come together to tell a story. There are many ways to approach writing an analytical essay, but here are some elements all literary analyses should include:

- A thesis statement that makes some sort of assertion about one or more of the literary elements of the text.
- Body paragraphs that each begin with a topic sentence and contain evidence and details from the text and other relevant sources that support the topic sentence and the essay's overall thesis. Your body paragraphs should address specific literary elements such as theme, plot, and characters.
- Transitional words, phrases, and clauses as well as varied syntax that link the major sections of the text, create cohesion, and clarify the relationships between the thesis, topic sentences, and supporting details and evidence.
- A formal style and use of an appropriate tone for your purpose, audience, and topic.
- A concluding statement or section that follows from and supports the argument presented.

4. Your teacher will distribute your essays from a previous activity. Skim the essays, noting the apparent strengths and weaknesses of each. Use the sample papers to guide you as you construct the scoring guidelines for your essay. What constitutes the highest-quality paper in each of the key categories?

5. Write a thorough explanation of the level of mastery for each category, quoting examples from the sample essays where possible and appropriate.

Bridging Consider asking advanced students to provide supplemental support—including a second reading or discussion of revision options—to students who need additional help. Multiple peer readings are often necessary to ensure that all students receive high-quality feedback to help them improve their writing.

4 Distribute the student essays from Activity 3.11 or 3.15. For privacy, be sure these essays are identified by a number and omit the student name. Ask each discussion group member to take turns skimming the essays. Students should make notes about strengths and weaknesses they see in the essays.

5 As a class, create a rubric that includes a description of the mastery level for each category and examples from the sample essays. Ask students to determine key words designating the "quality" of the papers in the top row of the rubric. Prompt them to defend their reasons. You may also ask each group to create guidelines for one row and then share with the class. After class, type a master copy of the rubric to distribute to students as they complete Embedded Assessment 1.

6 Direct students to use their rubric to evaluate at least two other students' essays. Distribute sheets of paper for them to write their scores and answer the five questions in student step 6.

7 Once students have evaluated their peers' essays, collect the papers and distribute each to its original author. Students will complete the same evaluation for their own papers. Assign students to make revisions according to their own and their peers' feedback.

8 Have students complete the Independent Reading Checkpoint.

ASSESS

Apply the rubric for the Embedded Assessment to some of the sample papers you distributed. Conduct a whole-class discussion in which students compare and contrast how they evaluated the papers with how you evaluated them. Ask students to identify key changes they can make to improve their writing.

ADAPT

If students need support evaluating peer essays, allow them to work in pairs to apply the rubric to the essays. Provide students with constructive ways to offer feedback, such as sentence frames:

- Your thesis statement would be stronger if _____ .
- You do a good job with _____ , but _____ needs more work.

3.18

My Notes

6. Using your established guidelines, evaluate at least two sample essays. If you do not have multiple copies of the rubric, use abbreviations and a number system to score each essay on a separate sheet of paper. In addition to giving a score, answer the following questions about each:

- Does this paper have a clear thesis?
- What is the strongest sentence in the paper? Why?
- What is the writer's most effective argument in support of his or her thesis?
- How does this paper's conclusion give it a sense of closure?
- One suggestion for improvement to this essay is...

7. After your teacher has collected and redistributed essays to their owners, evaluate your essay using the rubric and questions **before** viewing others' feedback about your writing.

Independent Reading Checkpoint

Write a paragraph analyzing one of the characters in your text using one of the critical lenses that you have studied. Using your rubric as a guide, include a clear thesis statement, supporting evidence from the text and a conclusion that provides a sense of closure.

Writing a Literary Analysis

 ASSIGNMENT

Select a character from *Othello* and write a literary analysis about him or her using one of the critical lenses that you have studied (choose Feminist, Marxist, Cultural, Historical, or Archetypal for this assignment). You will support your analysis with valid reasoning and sufficient evidence from your reading, observations, and previous written work.

Planning and Prewriting: Take time to plan ideas and structure.	■ How will you evaluate the different critical perspectives and decide which will provide a strong analysis of one of the characters? ■ How will you go about collecting textual evidence that supports your thesis? ■ How will you analyze the character's behaviors and motivations? ■ What sorts of tools will you use to record your ideas and structure the essay (for instance, an outline or a graphic organizer)?
Drafting: Select evidence to support your thesis and develop body paragraphs that analyze the literary elements of the play while supporting your thesis.	■ How can you craft a single thesis statement so that it makes a clear assertion about a character through a specific critical lens? ■ How will you use the evidence you selected to support your thesis and clarify your thinking? ■ Which literary elements will you analyze and how will they contribute to supporting your thesis? ■ How can you conclude your work in a way that follows naturally from the ideas while avoiding unnecessary repetition?
Evaluating and Revising: Get feedback from peers and revise to improve structure, transitions, and coherence.	■ How will you make sure that the evidence you include clearly and consistently supports your position? ■ How will you make sure you avoid oversimplifying the critical perspective you are using to analyze your character? (For example, "from a Feminist critical perspective, all men are bad")? ■ What kinds of feedback from peers and the Scoring Guide can you use to guide your revision?
Checking and Editing for Publication: Make your work the best it can be.	■ How will you ensure that your essay maintains an academic, formal tone; that it seamlessly embeds quotations within the text; and that it uses varied syntax? ■ How will you check for grammatical and technical accuracy? ■ What sort of outside resources can help you to check your draft? ■ How will you publish and present your essay to its intended reader or readers in a format that reflects its content and purpose?

Reflection

After completing this Embedded Assessment, think about how you went about accomplishing this assignment, and respond to the following:

• How were you able to consider your audience when crafting your thesis, anticipating what information they would need, and what potential questions they might have?

College and Career Readiness Standards

Focus Standards:

RL.11–12.1 Cite strong and thorough textual evidence to support analysis of what the text says explicitly as well as inferences drawn from the text, including determining where the text leaves matters uncertain.

RL.11–12.3 Analyze the impact of the author's choices regarding how to develop and relate elements of a story or drama (e.g., where a story is set, how the action is ordered, how the characters are introduced and developed).

RL.11–12.5 Analyze how an author's choices concerning how to structure specific parts of a text (e.g., the choice of where to begin or end a story, the choice to provide a comedic or tragic resolution) contribute to its overall structure and meaning as well as its aesthetic impact.

EMBEDDED ASSESSMENT 1

Materials: *Othello*; essay rubrics from Activity 3.18; access to computers for word processing (optional)

Suggested Pacing: 2 50-minute class periods

1 Planning and Prewriting: Encourage students to use a graphic organizer or other note-taking method while doing a thorough review of the writing they've already done for this unit. Ask students to carefully evaluate textual evidence and choose those facts, details, examples, and quotations that directly support and help them develop their claim. Reiterate the importance of creating an organization that logically sequences claims, counterclaims, reasons, and evidence. Also remind students to identify their audience for this essay to help them prepare for the reflection question.

2 Drafting: Remind students that a clear thesis statement is essential to structuring an effective essay. Ask students to think about how to create a thesis that introduces a compelling claim. Remind them that the claim should be clearly arguable, with a purposeful position. Suggest they also draft topic sentences for each body paragraph to assist them in collecting and organizing sufficient and relevant evidence for their ideas. Review the importance of fairly and thoroughly pointing out the strengths and limitations of evidence found in each counterclaim.

3 Evaluating and Revising: If you wish to use peer editing, remind students that the scoring guide should be used to evaluate work. Provide students with sentence stems to aid them in formulating effective critiques of peer work.

4 Checking and Editing for Publication: Remind students of print and online resources available to them as they prepare to publish their work. For example, encourage them to use a thesaurus to find appropriate alternatives for words used frequently in their essays.

5 **Portfolio:** At this point you may want to ask students to go to their portfolios and find previous unit reflection responses so that they might get a sense of their growth as academic thinkers and producers. You may also ask students to compare their literary analysis with a literary analysis essay from a previous unit. Can they implement any feedback from the scoring process to improve their *Othello* essay?

6 **Reflection:** Be sure students address the Reflection question as a separate part of the Embedded Assessment assignment so they can submit it separately.

SCORING GUIDE

When you score this Embedded Assessment, you may wish to make copies or download and print copies of the Scoring Guide from SpringBoard Digital. This way you can have a copy to mark for each student's work.

SCORING GUIDE

Scoring Criteria	Exemplary	Proficient	Emerging	Incomplete
Ideas	The essay • offers a clear thesis statement supported by strong evidence and provides valuable insight into the text • offers an insightful and thorough analysis of the chosen critical perspective • demonstrates a sophisticated understanding of the perspective and the dramatic elements of the play • offers in-depth analysis of a specific character, considering that character in light of the theme and plot.	The essay • provides a solid thesis statement that is supported by adequate evidence and shows some level of analysis of the text • offers a reasonable analysis of the chosen critical perspective • demonstrates an adequate understanding of the perspective and of the dramatic elements used in the play • offers analysis of a specific character that extends beyond summary of the text.	The essay • struggles to articulate a clear thesis and support, often relying on summary or paraphrase instead of specific evidence • offers a less-than-thorough understanding of the task and an inadequate treatment of the chosen critical perspective • overlooks or understates the complexity of the perspective and the text's use of dramatic elements • offers analysis of a specific character that relies on summary and generalization.	The essay • does not articulate a clear thesis and support, often relying on summary or paraphrase instead of specific evidence • offers a tenuous understanding of the task and an inadequate treatment of the chosen critical perspective • does not address the complexity of the perspective or adequately analysis any dramatic elements in the play • offers little or no analysis of a specific character.
Structure	The essay • is organized exceptionally, so that ideas move smoothly • uses transitions effectively to enhance the essay's coherence.	The essay • has an organization that is clear and easy to follow • includes transitions that help readers move between ideas.	The essay • is difficult to follow and may jump too rapidly between ideas • lacks transitions between ideas.	The essay • is confusing and difficult to follow, moving back and forth among different ideas • lacks transitions between ideas.
Use of Language	The essay • uses diction, syntax, and other stylistic devices that are notable and appropriate for the subject, purpose, and audience • demonstrates command of standard English conventions, with few or no errors.	The essay • uses diction, syntax, and other stylistic devices that are appropriate for the subject, purpose, and audience • contains few errors in standard writing conventions; minor errors do not interfere with meaning.	The essay • uses diction, syntax, and other stylistic devices inconsistently for the subject, purpose, and audience • contains errors in standard writing conventions that seriously interfere with meaning.	The essay • uses diction, syntax, and other stylistic devices ineffectively or inappropriately for the subject, purpose, and audience • contains numerous errors in standard writing conventions that seriously interfere with meaning.

College and Career Readiness Standards

RL.11–12.7 Analyze multiple interpretations of a story, drama, or poem (e.g., recorded or live production of a play or recorded novel or poetry), evaluating how each version interprets the source text. (Include at least one play by Shakespeare and one play by an American dramatist.)

W.11–12.1 Write arguments to support claims in an analysis of substantive topics or texts,

using valid reasoning and relevant and sufficient evidence.

W.11–12.5 Develop and strengthen writing as needed by planning, revising, editing, rewriting, or trying a new approach, focusing on addressing what is most significant for a specific purpose and audience.

Additional Standards Addressed:

RL.11–12.2

Unpacking Embedded Assessment 2

Learning Targets

- Reflect on and make connections between literature, performance, and critical perspectives.
- Identify and analyze the skills and knowledge needed to complete Embedded Assessment 2 successfully.

Preview

In this activity, you will explore the big ideas and tasks of the second half of the unit and make plans for your independent reading.

Making Connections

Think about the events in *Othello* and how you might perform them. In this part of the unit, you will deliver a dramatic interpretation of a scene from *Othello*. Staging a scene will make the play come alive for you and your classmates. As part of the assessment, you will also craft a note to your audience explaining the reasons your company chose to interpret the material through a specific critical lens.

Essential Questions

Review your answers to the essential questions based on your current knowledge.

1. What role does literature play in examining recurring social issues?

2. How can an original text be adapted for different audiences?

Unpacking Embedded Assessment 2

Closely read the assignment for Embedded Assessment 2: Staging an Interpretation.

🔊 Your assignment is to interpret a scene from *Othello* to emphasize the principles of one of the critical perspectives you have studied, then plan, rehearse, and perform the scene. With your acting company write a letter to the audience explaining the message your interpretation is trying to convey.

With your classmates, identify the skills and knowledge you will need to complete this assessment successfully. With your class, create a graphic organizer to represent the skills and knowledge you will need to complete the tasks identified in the Embedded Assessment.

Learning Strategies

Close Reading
Graphic Organizer
Paraphrasing
Summarizing
Think-Pair-Share

📦 **INDEPENDENT READING LINK**

Read and Respond

Reflect on the plot of your independent reading and the unit's Essential Questions. Write a paragraph explaining what aspects of your text connect to recurring social issues. What is the social issue? What message is the author trying to convey to his or her audience about this issue? Use textual evidence to support your response.

My Notes

College and Career Readiness Standards

Focus Standards:

RL.11–12.7 Analyze multiple interpretations of a story, drama, or poem (e.g., recorded or live production of a play or recorded novel or poetry), evaluating how each version interprets the source text. (Include at least one play by Shakespeare and one play by an American dramatist.)

SL.11–12.1b Work with peers to promote civil, democratic discussions and decision-making, set clear goals and deadlines, and establish individual roles as needed.

Additional Standards Addressed:

RL.11–12.2, SL.11–12.1c, SL.11–12.1d, SL.11–12.4

ACTIVITY 3.19

PLAN

Materials: chart p... Embedded Assessm... arkers; **Suggested Pacing:** 1 ... period ...te class

TEACH

1 Read aloud the Learning ... and Making Connections. To ... students into the activity, enco... them to make connections to film versions of *Othello* that they have viewed in class.

2 Have students **think-pair-share** to review the Essential Questions and see how their responses developed during the unit.

3 Ask students to find the Embedded Assessment 2 assignment and Scoring Guide. Guide them through a **close reading** of the prompt, steps, and Scoring Guide criteria. Instruct students to mark the text by underlining or highlighting the places that mention skills or knowledge necessary to succeed on the Embedded Assessment.

4 Instruct students to summarize with a partner or small group the skills and knowledge they have marked. With the class, create a **web graphic organizer** that lists the knowledge and skills required for Embedded Assessment 2.

5 Instruct students to complete the Independent Reading Link, using a text they have read previously if their current independent reading text does not clearly address a recurring social issue.

ASSESS

Review students' responses to the Essential Questions. Their answers should reveal an understanding of the role of literature in the examination of social issues based on your discussions of critical perspectives and *Othello*.

ADAPT

If students need additional help unpacking the embedded assessment, model the initial steps using the completed graphic organizer.

PLAN

Materi...llo; film adaptation
...ional); highlighters
of *Oth*...**acing:** 2 50-minute class

Su...

...H

1 Based on the title of this essay ...d their observations, students should consider how the character of Othello might be portrayed on the stage and screen. Give acting companies (**discussion groups**) time to brainstorm the traits of Othello that come to mind. Ask one representative from each group to stand and share the list of traits they associate with Othello. As one representative reads his group's list, other groups should check off any traits they also have on their lists. Students sit when all their ideas have been shared out. Make a class list on the board or on poster paper to record students' ideas.

2 Read the Learning Targets, Preview, As You Read, and About the Author sections with students. Help them understand they will be reading a critical essay tracing multiple interpretations of *Othello*.

 TEACHER TO TEACHER

Consider leading a whole-class discussion that elaborates on the similarities and differences between how Othello was portrayed in some of the film and staged versions you viewed in class to help frame students' thinking about the essay's topic. The film version of *Othello* directed by Geoffrey Sax (2002) is set in a modern-day London police department. Consider showing a few scenes from the film, and then discussing the adaptations using a historical critical perspective.

 TEXT COMPLEXITY

Overall: Complex
Lexile: 1370L
Qualitative: High Difficulty
Task: Moderate (Analyze)

Learning Strategies

Close Reading
Discussion Groups
Marking the Text
Paraphrasing
Skimming/Scanning
Summarizing

My Notes

Learning Targets

- Trace the use of critical perspectives in an essay.
- In an argumentative essay, apply one's own perspective to a contemporary staging of *Othello*.
- Integrate ideas from multiple texts to build knowledge and vocabulary about changing interpretations of *Othello* over time.

Preview

In this activity, you will read an essay that traces multiple interpretations of *Othello* over time. Then, after listening to your peers' opinions, you will consider how the interpretation of the character of Othello has changed over time. Finally, you will write more broadly about the merits of modifying an original text.

As You Read

- Highlight phrases that help answer the guiding question, *How has the lead character of* Othello *been portrayed throughout history?*
- Circle unknown words and phrases. Try to determine the meaning of the words by using context clues, word parts, or a dictionary.

About the Author

Sylvan Barnet (1926–2016) was a professor of English and former director of writing at Tufts University. Barnet served as general editor for the Signet Classic Shakespeare series, aimed at making the writer's work more accessible to college students. Barnet's writing remains significant in the field of English literature. This essay was first published in 1963.

 KNOWLEDGE QUEST

Knowledge Question:
What do differences in the interpretations of Othello's character over time express about culture and society?

In Activity 3.20 you will read an essay that traces multiple interpretations of *Othello* over time. The author explains how society and culture impact the way the character of Othello is interpreted. As you read and build knowledge about the topic, think about your answer to the Knowledge Question.

Essay

Othello on Stage and Screen

by **Sylvan Barnet**

1 The earliest mention of a performance of *Othello*, in an account of 1604, reports only that the play was acted before James I at Whitehall Palace. Next come two references to performances in 1610, one telling us that it was acted at the Globe in April, the other telling us that it was acted in September at Oxford. The reference to the Oxford production is especially valuable, since it provides one of the very few glimpses we have of early seventeenth-century acting and of an audience's response to a performance. The relevant passage, in Latin, may be translated thus:

> In their tragedies they acted with appropriate decorum; in these they caused tears not only by their speaking, but also by their action. Indeed

College and Career Readiness Standards

Focus Standards:

RI.11–12.1 Cite strong and thorough textual evidence to support analysis of what the text says explicitly as well as inferences drawn from the text, including determining where the text leaves matters uncertain.

RI.11–12.5 Analyze and evaluate the effectiveness of the structure an author uses

in his or her exposition or argument, including whether the structure makes points clear, convincing, and engaging.

Additional Standards Addressed:

RI.11–12.2, RI.11–12.3, RI.11–12.4, RI.11–12.6, L.11–12.5, W.11–12.1a, W.11–12.1b, W.11–12.2, W.11–12.4

Desdemona, although greatly successful throughout, moved us especially when at last, lying on her bed, killed by her husband, she implored the pity of the spectators in her death with her face alone.

2 This may not seem like much, but it is more than we have for all but a few of Shakespeare's other plays, and it is especially valuable as a reminder that the Renaissance boy actors—a boy played Desdemona—were highly skilled performers.

3 There are only a few additional references to performances in the first half of the seventeenth century, but a very large number of rather general references to the play (as opposed to specific performances) allows us to conclude that the play must have been popular on the stage. From 1642 to 1660 the theaters were closed by act of Parliament, but when the theaters reopened in 1660, *Othello* was staged almost immediately. Samuel Pepys saw it in 1660:

> To the Cockpit to see *The Moor of Venice*, which was well done. [Nathaniel] Burt acted the Moor: by the same token, a very pretty lady that sat by me called out, to see Desdemona smothered.

4 He saw it again in 1669, this time with less pleasure:

> To the King's playhouse, and there in an upper box … did see *The Moor of Venice*: but ill acted in most parts; [Michael] Mohun which did a little surprise me not acting Iago's part by much so well as [Walter] Clun used to do … nor, indeed, Burt doing the Moor's so well as I once thought he did.

5 During this period, the great interpreter of the title role was Thomas Betterton, who performed it from 1684 to 1709. Although he was the leading Othello of the period and was much praised, the only informative contemporary account of his performance in the role tells us little more than that his

aspect was serious, **venerable**, and majestic. … His voice was low and grumbling, though he could lime it by an artful climax, which enforced attention. … He kept this passion under, and showed it most.

6 Betterton's successor as Othello was James Quin, who played the part from 1722 to 1751. Wearing a white wig and the white uniform (including white gloves) of a British officer, he was said to have presented an impressive appearance, but his acting was characterized as statuesque, even stiff, lacking in tenderness, pathos, fire, and any suggestion of inner pain. Quin was eclipsed in 1745 by David Garrick, whose Othello was quite different: the complaint now was that this Othello lacked dignity. The accusation was not merely a glance at Garrick's relatively short stature (he sought to compensate for his height by adding a turban to the costume of an officer in the British army), or even at his bold restoration of the fainting episode (4.1.45), which had been cut by his predecessors. Rather, it was directed at Garrick's violent gestures, which suggested to one critic that Othello seemed afflicted with St. Vitus' dance. Garrick defended his interpretation by arguing that Shakespeare

My Notes

venerable: worthy of respect

3 **FIRST READ:** A whole-class chunking of the text may be the best approach for this essay if students need extra support. In this approach, each discussion group closely reads one chunk of the text. Then, groups share their observations with the entire class. Create a timeline or other graphic organizer to record the insights from all groups.

Scaffolding the Text-Dependent Questions

1. **Shakespeare died in 1616. What can the reader infer about his vision for *Othello* from the performance described in paragraph 1?** What was the date of the performance described in paragraph 1? What can we infer about Shakespeare's influence and vision? What details show how he wanted it acted? RI.11–12.1

2. **What inference can a reader make about society's views on race based on the quoted passage at the end of paragraph 6?** How can we paraphrase or summarize this quotation using modern-day English? What is its main idea? RI.11–12.1, RI.11–12.2

4 Remind students to make their own observations from the text as they read. As students are reading, monitor their progress. Be sure they are engaged with the text and underlining words and phrases that help answer the guiding question, "How has the lead character of Othello been portrayed throughout history?"

3.20

My Notes

had shown us white men jealous in other pieces, but that their jealousy had limits, and was not so terrible. … [In] Othello he had wished to paint that passion in all its violence, and that is why he chose an African in whose being circulated fire instead of blood, and whose true or imaginary character could excuse all boldness of expression and all exaggerations of passion.

7   Garrick's rival, Quin, was not convinced. Of Garrick's Othello, Quin said: "Othello! … psha! no such thing. There was a little black boy … fretting and fuming about the stage; but I saw no Othello."

8   A reader can scarcely overlook the racism in these remarks, and something should be said about attitudes toward Moors. There is no doubt that most Elizabethans regarded Moors as vengeful—largely because they were not Christians. That Moors were black—the color of the devil—was thought to be a visible sign of their capacity for endless evil. (In fact, Shakespeare specifies that Othello is a Christian, and this is only one of several ways in which Othello departs from the stereotype.) Othello's physical blackness, by the way, seems not to have been doubted until the early nineteenth century. Certainly Quin and Garrick played him in blackface, and presumably so did their predecessor Betterton. And there is no doubt that on the Elizabethan stage Othello was very black. The only contemporary illustration of a scene from Shakespeare shows another of Shakespeare's Moors, Aaron in *Titus Andronicus*, as having an inky complexion. But in the early nineteenth century one finds expressions of distinct discomfort at the thought that Othello is black rather than, say, bronzed, or (to use an even loftier metaphor) golden. Even the best critics were not exempt from the racist thinking of their times. Thus, in 1808 Charles Lamb, picking up Desdemona's assertion that she judged Othello by his mind rather than by his color, argued that although we can share her view when we read the play, we cannot do so when we see a black Othello on the stage:

She sees Othello's color in his mind. But upon the stage, when the imagination is no longer the ruling faculty, but we are left to our poor unassisted senses, I appeal to every one that has seen Othello played, whether he did not, on the contrary, sink Othello's mind in his color; whether he did not find something extremely revolting in the courtship and wedded caresses of Othello and Desdemona, and whether the actual sight of the thing did not over-weigh all that beautiful compromise which we make in reading. …

9   At about the time that Lamb offered his comment on Othello, Lamb's friend Coleridge made some notes to the effect that Shakespeare could not possibly have thought of Othello as a black:

Can we suppose [Shakespeare] so utterly ignorant as to make a barbarous *negro* plead royal birth? Were negroes then known but as slaves; on the contrary, were not the Moors the warriors? … No doubt Desdemona saw Othello's visage in his mind; yet, as we are constituted, and most

Scaffolding the Text-Dependent Questions

3. How do cultural attitudes toward black people change between Shakespeare's time and Coleridge's (paragraphs 6–10)? What stereotypes of black Moors do Elizabethans hold? How is Othello viewed in the play? How does Coleridge view black people? RI.11–12.1, RI.11–12.2

ACTIVITY 3.20 continued

5 Prompt students to use context clues to determine the meaning of any unknown words or phrases and to refer to the vocabulary terms glossed alongside the text.

surely as an English audience was disposed in the beginning of the seventeenth century, it would be something monstrous to conceive this beautiful Venetian girl falling in love with a veritable negro. It would argue a disproportionateness, a want of balance in Desdemona, which Shakespeare does not appear to have in the least contemplated.

10   Given Coleridge's certainty that Othello could not possibly have been black, it is well to reiterate that the Elizabethans thought of Moors as black. True, there are a few references in Elizabethan literature to "tawny" Moors, but there is no evidence that the Elizabethans distinguished between tawny and black Moors, and in any case, if they did, various passages in *Othello* indicate that the protagonist is surely a black Moor. Admittedly, most of the references to Othello's Negroid features are made by persons hostile to him—Roderigo calls him "the thick-lips" (1.1.63), for instance, and Iago speaks of him as "an old black ram" (1.1.85)—but Othello himself says that his name "is now begrimed and black / As mine own face" (3.3.384–5). Of course "black" is sometimes used in the sense of brunette, but there really cannot be any doubt that Othello is black in the most obvious modern sense, and to call him tawny or golden or bronzed, or to conceive of him as something of an Arab chieftain, is to go against the text of the play.

11   When Spranger Barry, the actor who displaced Garrick as Othello in the middle of the eighteenth century (he was said to have not only the passion of Garrick but also the majesty that in Quin was merely stiffness), the question of color seems not to have come up, nor did it come up when the role in effect belonged to John Philip Kemble, the chief Othello at the turn of the eighteenth century (he played his first Othello in 1785, his last in 1805). Kemble, tall and stately, acted in what can be called a classic rather than romantic manner, a style suited more to, say, Brutus than to Othello. His interpretation of the role was criticized for its superabundance of dignity and for its lack of variety and fire, but not for its blackness. But when Edmund Kean played the role in 1814 he is said to have used a light brown makeup in place of the usual burnt cork. Oddly, there is some uncertainty about this—most critics of the period did not comment on the novelty—but putting aside the question of who made the change, and exactly when, about this time the color changed. By 1827 Leman Thomas Rede's *The Road to the Stage* (a book on makeup) could report that "A tawny tinge is now the color used for the gallant Moor." Here it is evident that the makeup no longer uses burnt cork. Most of the Othellos of the rest of the century were tawny, their bronze skin suggesting that they were sons of the desert, but Henry Irving's Othello of 1881 was conspicuously dark (darker than his "bronze" Othello of 1876), and, as we shall see, in the twentieth century dark Othellos have been dominant, especially in our own generation, when American blacks have often played the part.

My Notes

___

Scaffolding the Text-Dependent Questions

4. What details from paragraph 8 explain what the author means by "bronzed, (or to use an even loftier metaphor) golden"? What is the main idea of the paragraph? What did "blackness" represent to Elizabethans? How did they reconcile their desired societal image of Othello to Shakespeare's Othello? RI.11–12.2, RI.11–12.4

My Notes

12 Putting aside the point that Kean's Othello was lighter than usual, it was exceptional for its power and its pathos. If Kemble is the paradigm of classical acting, Kean—passionate, even spasmodic—is the paradigm of romantic acting. Coleridge wrote: "Seeing [Kean] act was like reading Shakespeare by flashes of lightning." Another great romantic writer, William Hazlitt, at first found Kean too passionate. In the following passage Hazlitt complains that the fault in the performance is not in the color of Kean's face, or in Kean's relatively short stature:

> Othello was tall, but that is nothing; he was black, but that is nothing. But he was not fierce, and that is everything. It is only in the last agony of human suffering that he gives way to his rage and despair. … Mr. Kean is in general all passion, all energy, all relentless will. … He is too often in the highest key of passion, too uniformly on the verge of extravagance, too constantly on the rack.

13 Kean later moderated the passion, perhaps under Hazlitt's influence, but, curiously, Hazlitt regretted the change, remarking: "There is but one perfect way of playing Othello, and that was the way … he used to play it." Equally compelling is the tribute to Kean offered by the American actor Junius Brutus Booth, who in England in 1817–18 played Iago to Kean's Othello. Booth said that "Kean's Othello smothered Desdemona and my Iago too." Kean's triumph in the role was undoubted, but in 1825, two weeks after he had been proved guilty of adultery, public opinion turned against him, denouncing the hypocrisy of an adulterer who dared to play the outraged husband lamenting his wife's infidelity. Still, he continued in the role, playing Othello almost to the day of his death. His last performance was in this role, in 1833, when he collapsed on the stage and died a few weeks later.

14 Other nineteenth-century actors have made their mark in the role—for instance William Macready (he sometimes played Iago against Kean's Othello) and Samuel Phelps—but here there is space to mention only four, Ira Aldridge, Edwin Booth, Tommaso Salvini, and Henry Irving. Aldridge, a black, was born in New York in 1807. As a very young man he determined to be an actor, but seeing no possibility of a career as an actor in America, he went to London in 1824 and never returned to the United States. At least one black actor, James Hewlett, had already played Othello in America, but that was with the all-black African Company, and Aldridge's ambition was to be accepted as an actor, not as a black actor, an ambition impossible to fulfill in the United States, where there were no interracial companies. He performed throughout the British Isles and also on the Continent, playing not only Othello but also (with white makeup) such roles as Richard III, Shylock, Hamlet, Macbeth, and Lear.

15 In America, Edwin Booth (son of Junius Brutus Booth) acted Othello almost annually from 1826 to 1871. From time to time he changed his performance, sometimes working in the violent style associated with Tommaso Salvini, hurling his Iago to the ground, but sometimes he played with

Scaffolding the Text-Dependent Questions

5. What might be the author's purpose behind mentioning aspects of Kean's personal life in paragraph 13? What does it mean that "public opinion" turned on Kean? What prompted the shift? RI.11–12.6

6. Based on Edwin Booth's advice on how to play Iago in paragraph 15, why was his Iago more "terrifyingly evil" than others'? How does Booth say Iago should not act? What does this imply about how other actors played the role? How should Iago act? How is that scarier? RI.11–12.1, RI.11–12.6

restraint—occasionally he even omitted striking Desdemona at IV.i.240— and he was especially praised for his tender passion. Most critics, however, preferred his Iago, which seemed genial, sincere, and terrifyingly evil; he was widely regarded as the greatest Iago of the later nineteenth century. (Among the performers with whom he alternated the roles of Othello and Iago were Henry Irving and James O'Neill, Eugene O'Neill's father; and he played Iago to Salvini's Othello. Here is his advice on how to play Iago:

> Don't *act* the villain, don't *look* it or *speak* it (by scowling and growling, I mean), but *think* it all the time. Be genial, sometimes jovial, always gentlemanly. Quick in motion as in thought; lithe and sinuous as a snake. A certain bluffness (which my temperament does not afford) should be added to preserve the military flavor of the character; in this particular I fail utterly, my Iago lacks the soldierly quality.

16 Henry Irving played Othello only in 1876 and 1881. Although he had already achieved success in the roles of Hamlet, Macbeth, and Lear, his Othello did not find equal favor. It was not especially violent, but it was said to lack dignity (apparently there was much lifting up of hands and shuffling of feet), and after the attempt in 1881 Irving decided to drop the role. Still, some things about the 1881 performance should be mentioned. The makeup was very black, the costume exotic (a white jeweled turban, an amber robe), and the killing of Desdemona very solemn—until Desdemona tried to escape, at which point he flung her on the bed. The play ended with Othello's suicide, the curtain descending as he fell at Gratiano's feet. Iago (played by Booth) stood by, smiling malignantly.

17 By common consent the greatest Othello of the later nineteenth century was Tommaso Salvini, who acted in Italian—even when in England or the United States, with the rest of the company speaking English. Some Victorians regarded Salvini as too savage, too volcanic, too terrifying to arouse pity—he seized Iago by the throat and hurled him to the floor, and put his foot on Iago's neck, and of course he did not hesitate to strike Desdemona—but most audiences were deeply moved as well as terrified by his performance. We are told that especially in the first three acts, where some of the love play seemed almost to be high comedy, his Othello was "delightful" and "delicate." Still, the overall effect was that of enormous energy, though not of mere barbarism. Henry James was among Salvini's greatest admirers:

> It is impossible to imagine anything more living, more tragic, more suggestive of a tortured soul and of generous, beneficent strength changed to a purpose of destruction. With its tremendous force, it is magnificently quiet, and from the beginning to the end has not a touch of rant or crudity.

18 Actors of note who played Othello or Iago in the early twentieth century include Johnston Forbes-Robertson, Oscar Asche, and Beerbohm Tree, but none of these was widely regarded as great. Indeed, the standard opinion is

My Notes

lithe: moving easily
bluffness: frankness

Scaffolding the Text-Dependent Questions

7. In paragraph 16, the author says that "some things about the 1881 performance should be mentioned." What are they and why are they noteworthy? Which three ways is Othello portrayed differently in 1881 than a number of past performances? Do the changes move Othello further from or closer to Shakespeare's text? RI.11–12.1, RI.11–12.5

8. Based on context clues and word parts, what is the meaning of *malignantly* at the end of paragraph 16? What does *malignantly* describe? What other phrase describes Edwin Booth as Iago? Does the root sound familiar if the *-ly* suffix is removed? L.11–12.5

6 Vocabulary Development: After paragraph 18, pause and discuss the Word Connections box. Ask students how the words are similar. Then ask them to think of other words that share the root *litera* or the prefix *ob-*. As an extension, have students complete the **Roots and Affixes Brainstorm** graphic organizer.

3.20

WORD CONNECTIONS

Roots and Affixes
The verb *obliterate* originates from the Latin root *littera*, meaning "letter," combined with the prefix *ob-*, meaning "against" or "in the way of." *Obliterating* something means removing it or obscuring it so it cannot be seen or understood. Other words from *littera* include *literature*, *alliteration*, *literal*, and *letter*.

My Notes

that the twentieth century did not have a great Othello until Paul Robeson, an African American, played the role in 1943. But Robeson was not primarily an actor. As a college student at Rutgers he distinguished himself not to theatrics but in athletics (all-American end in football in 1918, and letters in several varsity sports) and in scholarship (Phi Beta Kappa). He next prepared for a career in the law, taking a law degree at Columbia University, but while at Columbia in 1921 he performed in his first amateur production. He soon began to appear in some professional productions, including *Showboat*, where his singing of "Ol' Man River" led to a career as a concert singer, especially of spirituals and work songs, though he returned to the stage to play Othello in 1930 in England, in 1942 in Cambridge, Boston, and Princeton, in 1943 in New York, and in 1959 at Stratford-upon-Avon. Observers agree that the 1959 performance was poor; Robeson had been weakened by an attack of bronchitis, his political beliefs had been shaken (earlier he had praised Stalin, but now the crimes of the Stalin era were evident), and, perhaps worst of all, the director's presence was too strongly felt, for instance in a distracting fog that supposedly was the result of the storm at Cyprus. Many scenes were so dark that spectators could not see the actors' faces, and there seems no reason to doubt the accuracy of those reviewers who accused the director of obliterating the principal actors.

19 Robeson's first Othello—indeed, his first performance in a play by Shakespeare, in 1930—was much more enthusiastically received. The London *Morning Post* said: "There has been no Othello on our stage for forty years to compare with his dignity, simplicity, and true passion." But not all of the reviewers were entirely pleased. James Agate, the leading theater critic of the period, said that Robeson lacked the majesty that Shakespeare insists on early in the play, for instance in such lines as

> I fetch my life and being
>
> From men of royal siege,   (I.ii.20–21)

and

> Were it my cue to fight, I should have known it
>
> Without a prompter,   (82–83)

and

> Keep up your bright swords, for the dew will
>
> rust them.   (58)

20 The majesty displayed in such passages, Agate said, tells us how Othello must behave when he puts down Cassio's drunken brawl, but according to Agate, Robeson (despite his height—six feet, three inches) lacked this majesty. Thus, when Robeson's Othello said "Silence that dreadful bell! It frights the isle/ From her propriety" (II.iii.174–75), he showed personal annoyance rather than the "passion for decorum" (Agate's words) that the line reveals. Agate found Robeson best in the third and fourth acts, where he captured the jealousy of the part, but weak (lacking in dignity) in the last act, where he failed to perform the murder with a solemn sense of sacrifice.

Scaffolding the Text-Dependent Questions

9. How did the circumstances in which black actors portrayed Othello change over time? Scan the article to find information about the portrayal of Othello by black or African American actors. Which occurred first? In what types of companies have black actors played Othello? RI.11–12.2

10. In paragraph 20, how do Agate's criticisms of Robeson's performance suggest a critical lens? What does Agate think Robeson lacks?

What part of the role does Agate feel Robeson captures best? How does this echo stereotypes? RI.11–12.1, RI.11–12.2

11. Based on the description of Robeson's 1943 New York production of Othello at the end of paragraph 21, did the audience agree with the critics? How do you know? How does the public react to Robeson's production? Is this consistent with the criticisms? RI.11–12.1, RI.11–12.3

7 It may be helpful to provide some essential information about Lawrence Olivier to help students place paragraphs 24–28 in context.

21 Despite the reservations of Agate and others, there was some talk of bringing the production to the United States, but nothing came of it, doubtless because of uncertainty about how American audiences (and perhaps performers?) would respond to a company that mixed whites and blacks. In 1938 Margaret Webster again raised the topic, but she was discouraged by the Americans with whom she talked. It was acceptable for a black actor—a real black man, not a white man in blackface—to kiss a white girl in England, but not in the United States. Fortunately, however, Webster later persuaded the Theatre Guild to invite Robeson to do *Othello* in the United States in 1942, if not on Broadway at least as summer stock, with José Ferrer as Iago and Uta Hagen as Desdemona. The production was enthusiastically received, but Robeson's concert commitments prevented it from going to New York until the fall of 1943. When it did open in New York, the reviews were highly favorable, but some of them contained reservations about Robeson's ability to speak blank verse and to catch the grandeur of the role. In any case, the production was an enormous success, running for 296 continuous performances. The previous record for a New York *Othello* had been 57.

22 Robeson inevitably was asked to discuss his conception of the role; equally inevitably, he said different things at different times, and perhaps sometimes said what reporters wanted to hear—or perhaps the reporters heard only what they wanted to hear. Sometimes he was reported as saying that the matter of color is secondary, but on other occasions he is reported as saying: "The problem [of *Othello*] is the problem of my own people. It is a tragedy of racial conflict, a tragedy of honor, rather than of jealousy."

23 Until Robeson, black actors in the United States were in effect limited to performing in all-black companies. With Robeson, a black actor played Othello with an otherwise white company. His appearance as Othello in 1943 was an important anticipation of the gains black actors were to make in later decades. Earle Hyman, Moses Gunn, Paul Winfield, William Marshall, and James Earl Jones are among the black actors who have played impressive Othellos in mixed-race companies. More important, however, as the careers of these actors show, a black may now also play a role other than Othello, as Ira Aldridge did a hundred and fifty years ago, though he had to cross the Atlantic to do it.

24 Before looking at Laurence Olivier's Othello in 1964, mention should be made of Olivier's Iago in a production of 1937, directed by Tyrone Guthrie at the Old Vic. Olivier and Guthrie talked to Ernest Jones, friend of Sigmund Freud, and came away with the idea that Iago's hatred for Othello was in fact based on a subconscious love for Othello. That Iago protests "I hate the Moor" means nothing, for he is unaware of his true emotions. Ralph Richardson was Othello in this production, but Guthrie and Olivier decided not to shock him (remember, this was 1937) by any such unconventional idea, and so, the story goes, Richardson could never quite understand what Olivier was making out of the role. (What Olivier apparently made out of it was something like this: Iago is manic because he cannot face his true feelings.) The critics, like Richardson

Paul Robeson and Uta Hagen as Othello and Desdemona on Broadway, 1943

My Notes

_____
_____
_____
_____
_____
_____
_____
_____
_____
_____
_____
_____
_____
_____
_____
_____
_____
_____
_____

Scaffolding the Text-Dependent Questions

12. In paragraph 24, how did Freud inspire the new interpretation of Iago in the 1930s? What is the effect of this interpretation, and how was the performance received? What do Olivier and Guthrie think of Iago's hatred after talking with Freud's friend? How does Olivier apply that to his performance of Iago? How is it received? RI.11–12.1, RI.11–12.3

13. In paragraph 25, what two cultural influences were reflected in Eliot's and Leavis's new interpretation of Othello? What evidence shows these influences? How does Othello value himself in Eliot's and Leavis's interpretation? What is he in denial about? What is Othello under the "veneer of civilization"? RI.11–12.1, RI.11–12.2, RI.11–12.3

My Notes

and the general public, were in the dark, and the production was poorly reviewed. Guthrie himself later called the production "a ghastly, boring hash," and Olivier has said that he no longer subscribes to Jones's interpretation.

25 In 1964 Olivier played Othello, with Frank Finlay as Iago, and Maggie Smith as Desdemona, in a production directed by John Dexter. (This production was later filmed, and most of what is true of the stage production is true also of the film.) Far from suggesting that Othello was some sort of desert chief, Olivier emphasized the Negroid aspects, or at least the white man's stock ideas of Negroid aspects. Thus, Othello's skin was very dark, his lips were red and sensuous, and his lilting voice had something of a West Indian accent. He rolled his eyes a good deal, and he walked (barefooted and adorned with ankle bracelets) with a sensuous sway. More important (worse, some viewers felt), was the idea behind this Othello, which was indebted to some thoughts by T. S. Eliot and F. R. Leavis. For Eliot (in an essay called "Shakespeare and the Stoicism of Seneca," first published in 1927) and for Leavis (in an essay first published in a journal in 1937 but more readily available, in reprinted form, in Leavis's *The Common Pursuit*), Othello is not so much a heroic figure—the noble Moor who gains our sympathy despite the terrible deed he performs—as a **fatuous** simpleton, a man given to egotistical self-dramatizing. The playbill included some passages from Leavis's essay, which the director in effect summarized when he told the cast that

> Othello is a pompous, word-spinning, arrogant black general. … The important thing is not to accept him at his own valuation. … He isn't just a righteous man who's been wronged. He's a man too proud to think he could ever be capable of anything as base as jealousy. When he learns he can be jealous, his character changes. The knowledge destroys him, and he goes berserk.

26 Thus, Olivier delivered "Farewell the tranquil mind" (3.3.345)—a speech customarily delivered reflectively—in a frenzy. It's probably fair to say that the gist of the idea underlying this production is fairly odd: Othello is a barbarian with a thin veneer of civilization. Thus, the early speeches were delivered with easy confidence because Othello had no understanding of how simple and how volatile he really was. The change from civilized man to barbarian was marked by Othello tearing off a crucifix he wore, an effective enough bit of business but one at odds with two aspects of the end of Shakespeare's play: Othello (who just before he kills Desdemona is careful to urge her to make her peace with God; "I would not kill thy soul" (5.2.32) murders Desdemona partly because he believes she has been false to the highest ideals. Second, when he comes to understand the horror of his action he executes justice upon himself. Still, although much in the conception could be faulted, it was widely agreed that Olivier's acting was a triumph—a triumph won, among other things, at the expense of an **unprepossessing** Iago and a **negligible** Desdemona.

> **fatuous:** foolish
> **unprepossessing:** unappealing
> **negligible:** unimportant

27 The film with Olivier (1965), directed by Stuart Burge, was made in a sound studio, using sets that were essentially those of the stage production—even for scenes set out-of-doors—but it was not simply a filmed version of what a spectator sitting in the third row center would have seen. For instance, because close-ups are used for all of Iago's soliloquies, Iago becomes considerably more prominent in the film than he was on the stage.

28 Olivier said that the backgrounds in the film were minimal because he was concerned with "offering as little visual distraction as possible from the intentions of Shakespeare—or our performance of them." For a film of the opposite sort, a film that does not hesitate to introduce impressive visual effects not specified in the text, one should look at Orson Welles's *Othello*, a black and white film begun in 1951 and completed and released in 1955, with Welles in the title role. The film was shot on location, chiefly in Morocco and Venice, but what especially strikes a viewer is not that the camera gives us a strong sense of the real world, but that the camera leads us into a strange, shadowy world of unfamiliar and puzzling appearance. The film begins with Welles reading a passage from Shakespeare's source while we see a shot of the face of the dead Othello. The camera rises above the bier, which is carried by pallbearers, and we then see Desdemona's body, also being borne to the grave. We see the two funeral processions converge, and then we see Iago, in chains, thrust into a cage and hoisted above the crowd. From above—Iago's viewpoint—we look down on the bodies of Othello and Desdemona. All of this is presented before we see the credits for the film. The film ends with a dissolve from the dying Othello to a shot of the funeral procession and then to shots of the fortress at Cyprus, the cage, and Venetian buildings and ships. Between this highly cinematic beginning and ending, other liberties are taken with the text. The murder of Roderigo, for instance, is set in a steamy bathhouse. Welles had intended to shoot the scene in a street, but because he had run out of money and didn't have costumes, he set it in a steam bath, where a few towels were all the clothing that was needed. In short, Welles's *Othello* is not for the Shakespeare purist (too much is cut and too much is added), but it is imaginative and it often works. Admirers will want to see also *Filming "Othello,"* a film memoir (1978) in which Welles and others discuss the work.

29 The BBC television version of *Othello*, directed by Jonathan Miller and released in 1981, is, like Olivier's film, somewhat in the Eliot-Leavis tradition. In the introduction to the printed text of the BBC version, Miller says that the play does not set forth "the spectacle of a person of grandeur falling." Rather,

> what's interesting is that it's not the fall of the great but the disintegration of the ordinary, of the representative character. It's the very ordinariness of Othello that makes the story intolerable.

30 Miller is insistent, too, that the play is not about race. "I do not see the play as being about color but as being about jealousy—which is something we are all vulnerable to." In line with this emphasis on the ordinary, Othello (Anthony

My Notes

Scaffolding the Text-Dependent Questions

14. In paragraphs 29 and 30, what clues show what Miller means by "It's the very ordinariness of Othello that makes the story intolerable"? What does Miller say the play is about in paragraph 30? Whom does Othello represent? What implications does that have for the people represented? RI.11–12.1, RI.11–12.2, RI.11–12.4

15. What organizational pattern does Barnet use in his essay? How does it aid his purpose? Why do you think the author is using historical reviews? What time frame do the performances in this essay cover? RI.11–12.5

My Notes

Hopkins) is relatively unheroic, though he is scarcely as commonplace as Miller suggests, since he is full of energy and rage. More successful is Iago (Bob Hoskins), a bullet-headed hood who delights in Othello's anguish. The sets, in order to reduce any sense of heroism or romance, are emphatically domestic; no effort was made to take advantage of the camera's ability to record expansive space. Interestingly, however, the domestic images on the screen are by no means ordinary; notably beautiful, they often remind us of Vermeer.

31 During the course of this survey it has been easy to notice racist implications in the remarks of certain actors and critics. And it was racism, of course, that kept blacks from acting in *Othello* and in other plays) along with whites. One point that has not been raised till now is this: Does it matter if a black plays Othello? When Robeson played the part, some theatergoers found that the play made more sense than ever before, partly because Robeson (whatever his limitations as an actor) was a black [man]. Others found that it was distracting for a black to play the part; it brought into the world of *Othello* irrelevant issues of twentieth-century America. Jonathan Miller, holding the second position, puts it thus:

> When a black actor does the part, it offsets the play, puts it out of balance. It makes it a play about blackness, which it is not. … The trouble is, the play was hijacked for political purposes.

32 Many things can be said against this view, for instance that when the white actor Olivier played Othello he expended so much energy impersonating a black that a spectator was far more conscious of the performer's blackness than one is of, say, James Earl Jones's. In any case, Miller has not said the last word on this topic, which will continue to be debated.

> *Bibliographic Note*: For a modern edition of *Othello* prefaced with a long stage history, and equipped with abundant footnotes telling how various actors delivered particular lines, see Julie Hankey, *Othello* (1987), a volume in a series entitled Plays in Performance.

33 For a survey of *Othello* on the stage, see Marvin Rosenberg, *The Masks of "Othello"* (1961); for a brief study of five recent productions (including Robeson in 1943, Olivier in 1964, and the BBC television version of 1981), see Martin L. Wine, *"Othello": Text and Performance* (1984). Errol Hill's *Shakespeare in Sable* (1984), a history of black actors of Shakespeare, contains much information about *Othello*. Other items especially relevant to the productions discussed above include: Arthur Colby Sprague, *Shakespearian Players and Performances* (1953), for Kean's Othello and Edwin Booth's Iago; Daniel J. Watermeier, "Edwin Booth's Iago," *Theatre History Studies* 6 (1986): 32–55; Kenneth Tynan, ed., *"Othello" by William Shakespeare: The National Theatre Production* (1966), on Olivier; *The BBC TV Shakespeare: "Othello"* (1981), on the version directed

by Jonathan Miller. On Robeson, see Susan Spector, "Margaret Webster's *Othello*," *Theatre History Studies 6* (1968): 93–108. For film versions, see Jack J. Jorgens, *Shakespeare on Film* (1977), and, for Welles's film only, see Michael MacLiammoir, *Put Money in Thy Purse* (1952).

Laurence Fishburne and Irene Jacob as Othello and Desdemona, in the 1995 film adaptation

⊘ Knowledge Quest

- What example of staging *Othello* could you picture most vividly as you read Barnet's essay?
- Which interpretation of Othello stands out to you the most as being influenced by society and culture? Why?

My Notes

9 Have students jot down responses to the Knowledge Quest questions so that they will be prepared to share them during class discussion.

10 Spend class time discussing students' findings about the history of *Othello* on stage and in film. If your students read the assignment independently as homework, you will want to spend more time in discussion.

11 Discuss how critical perspectives inform the staging of a play. Be sure students see the connection between how Othello has been portrayed or received and the critical perspective guiding that production.

12 RETURNING TO THE TEXT:
During the second reading, students will be answering the text-dependent questions. If you have chosen to have students read the text in their discussion groups, you may want to introduce a jigsaw approach to answering questions. Have students divide questions among their discussion group members and encourage students who need assistance with their responses to work with other members of their group. If they have difficulty, scaffold the questions by rephrasing them or breaking them down into smaller parts. See the Scaffolding the Text-Dependent Questions box for suggestions.

3.20

Returning to the Text

- Return to the essay as you respond to the following questions. Use text evidence to support your responses.
- Write any additional questions you have about the text in your Reader/Writer Notebook.

1. Shakespeare died in 1616. What can the reader infer about his vision for *Othello* from the performance described in paragraph 1?

   The Oxford production in 1610 would have been heavily influenced by him. Readers can infer that the description of that performance provides a small window into his vision for the performance. The actors display "appropriate decorum," so they are dignified, but they also "[cause] tears" by their speaking and acting, so they display passion.

2. KQ What inference can a reader make about society's views on race based on the quoted passage at the end of paragraph 6?

   In the mid-1700s, most members of the audience probably viewed Africans as more prone to jealousy and passionate violence, which is why Shakespeare chose to depict Othello as an African, according to the quote.

3. KQ How do cultural attitudes toward black people change between Shakespeare's time and Coleridge's (paragraphs 6–10)?

   Cultural biases toward black people grow to be more extreme from Shakespeare's time to Coleridge's. In the Elizabethan era, black Moors are viewed as "evil" and "vengeful," but *Othello* demonstrates they could still be viewed as (nearly) equal members of society who can earn respect. Coleridge, in a later time, cannot imagine a black person not being a slave.

4. KQ What details from paragraph 8 explain what the author means by "bronzed, (or to use an even loftier metaphor) golden"?

   The author explains that Elizabethans thought the blackness of Moors represented "a visible sign of their capacity for endless evil." To remedy their inability to accept Othello as black, they portrayed him in some cases as "bronzed" and in others, "golden," which was optimal for audiences of the time as this represented a positive connotation.

5. What might be the author's purpose behind mentioning aspects of Kean's personal life in paragraph 13?

   This addition provides context about the audience and reveals the conservative views during this time period. The details also serve to draw the reader in because they illustrate irony of what the audience is willing to accept in a staged performance versus real life.

6. Based on Edwin Booth's advice on how to play Iago in paragraph 15, why was his Iago more "terrifyingly evil" than others'?

Edwin Booth says not to act, look, or speak like the villain, but instead to act friendly and

funny and polite, but think like the villain "all the time." This advice implies other actors

tended to play Iago as the villain quite explicitly, making him more of a caricature. Booth also

adds the mannerism of moving quickly and smoothly, bringing to mind a snake.

7. In paragraph 16, the author says that "some things about the 1881 performance should be mentioned." What are they and why are they noteworthy?

The author lists as notable the black makeup, Othello's exotic costume, the solemnity of

Desdemona's murder, and the staging at the end of the play. These elements seem to signal a

return to Shakespeare's original conception of Othello as an exotic foreigner and a man with

some control.

8. Based on context clues and word parts, what is the meaning of *malignantly* at the end of paragraph 16?

Malignantly describes the smile of Edwin Booth's Iago, who is "terrifyingly evil," indicating

it means "in a very evil way." Removing the *-ly* suffix, *malignant* may also be familiar in a

medical context, where it describes a dangerous cancer.

9. KQ How did the circumstances in which black actors portrayed Othello change over time?

Opportunities for black actors to play Othello slowly became more common. The first black

actor mentioned is James Hewlett, who played in an all-black company. Concern about

American reactions kept him from playing in America until 1942. After that, several black

actors played Othello in mixed-race companies.

10. In paragraph 20, how do Agate's criticisms of Robeson's performance suggest a critical lens?

Agate criticizes Robeson for lacking majesty and dignity in his performance and feels he best

captures the jealousy in the role. Agate seems to find Robeson, who is black, most convincing

when he plays to the cultural stereotype, suggesting a Cultural Criticism lens.

LEVELED DIFFERENTIATED INSTRUCTION

Before beginning the Returning to the Text section, students may need support identifying key ideas and supporting details.

Beginning For students with emerging language skills, conduct a read aloud of a shortened version of the essay or have it translated into students' native language for their first read.

Developing For students who need extra support, provide a shortened version of the essay, focusing on the material from the twentieth century. Edit the Returning to the Text questions as needed.

Expanding Chunk the text into eight sections. Group students, and assign two sections of reading accordingly. Have students use the **Key Idea and Details Chart** graphic organizer as a note-taking tool as they read their assigned sections in pairs.

Support Pair students of varying abilities and have them use the **Key Idea and Details Chart** graphic organizer as a note-taking tool. Assign half of the reading to one student and half to the other. Next, have pairs use the graphic organizers as they answer the text-dependent questions. Then have students compare answers with another pair. Ask each group of four to work together to resolve discrepancies.

Extend Pair students who need an extra challenge and have them summarize three key ideas from the essay. Ask them to individually write two new questions and answers per key idea. Have students exchange and answer the questions. Have students evaluate the questions to ensure they align with each key idea. Then ask pairs to compare and discuss their responses.

13 Consider taking the opportunity to model using context clues to find the meaning of *malignantly* at the end of paragraph 16. Prompt students to consider the word's different definitions and which one best fits the context of the paragraph.

3.20

11. Based on the description of Robeson's 1943 New York production of *Othello* at the end of paragraph 21, did the audience agree with the critics? How do you know?

The audience did not seem to share the critics' concerns about Robeson's lack of "grandeur" at all. The production ran for 296 consecutive performances, blowing away the previous record for *Othello*.

12. In paragraph 24, how did Freud inspire the new interpretation of Iago in the 1930s? What is the effect of this interpretation, and how was the performance received?

Freud, inventor of psychoanalysis, inspires Laurence Olivier to play Iago as motivated by his subconscious love for Othello. This causes Olivier to play Iago as "manic because he cannot face his true feelings," which confuses the cast, critics, and audience. The production is poorly reviewed.

13. KQ In paragraph 25, what two cultural influences were reflected in Eliot's and Leavis's new interpretation of Othello? What evidence shows these influences?

The new interpretation of Othello by Eliot and Leavis contains traces of both self-obsession and racism. Othello is egotistical—you can't "accept him at his own valuation"—and he is in denial about being "capable of anything as base as jealousy." Once the "veneer of civilization" is stripped away, he reverts to being a "barbarian," echoing racist views.

14. In paragraphs 29 and 30, what clues show what Miller means by "It's the very ordinariness of Othello that makes the story intolerable"?

Miller says Othello is the "representative character" and that the play is about "jealousy— which is something we are all vulnerable to." If Othello represents the capacity for jealousy in everyone, it means that his "disintegration" could also happen to any one of us, which is difficult to confront.

15. What organizational pattern does Barnet use in his essay? How does it aid his purpose?

Barnet relies heavily on primary documents in the form of critical reviews, which is effective in this essay on how depictions of Othello have changed through time. He also uses chronological order when presenting these documents to create a credible timeline.

Knowledge Quest

In analyzing the staging of *Othello* over time, the author connects artistic choices to the prevailing social and cultural perspectives regarding race at various times. Imagine a contemporary production of *Othello* in a particular American city. What do you believe are the prevailing social and cultural perspectives regarding race that would affect the production? With your small group, discuss the context in which a contemporary staging of *Othello* would be presented. How might this influence the decisions of the director and actors working on a modern production? Be sure to:

- Prepare by reviewing what you have learned about how society and culture have influenced the way the character of Othello has been interpreted to date.
- Ask and respond to questions to clarify details, evidence, and ideas.
- Acknowledge perspectives and reasoning that are different from your own.

INDEPENDENT READING LINK

You can continue to build your knowledge about changing interpretations of *Othello* over time by reading other articles at ZINC Reading Labs. Search for keywords such as *Othello* or *Shakespeare*.

 ZINC

My Notes

14 Return to the Knowledge Question. Have students work with a small group to discuss the changes in the way Othello has been presented over time. Ask pairs to discuss the way they think a contemporary production would present *Othello*. Have small groups share out and remind students to incorporate different views from their own as they outline their responses. Encourage students to take notes to help them with the writing task. Review writing expectations with students using the "be sure to" points.

15 Encourage students to continue building knowledge on this topic by reading additional texts as suggested in the Independent Reading Link.

16 Break students into groups and have them discuss the first Working from the Text question using Cultural Criticism. How does that lens affect their thinking about whether African American actors should play Othello?

Working from the Text

16. Through today's critical lens of Cultural Criticism, do you think the answers to "Does it matter if a black plays Othello?" (paragraph 31) would be different? Why or why not?

It may still make more sense to a modern American audience for Othello to be played by an African American since racial and cultural differences are a part of the play as Shakespeare wrote it. A few may still feel, as Miller does, that a black Othello pulls modern racial issues into the theater with him. However, audiences today are more accustomed to minorities playing many different roles in dramas of all formats, and it seems unlikely many would share Miller's view.

17 Have students do a quickwrite answering the bulleted questions on the student page, considering which critical perspective they think most applies to a modern audience. Then allow them some time to discuss within their acting companies.

18 Check for student understanding by having them discuss or write a response about the proper role of a director in a performance.

19 Direct students to complete the writing prompt.

ASSESS

Discuss students' responses to the Check Your Understanding task. Be sure that students acknowledge that directors see their roles differently, and discuss the possible outcomes of those varying perspectives. Review students' responses to the Returning to the Text Questions to monitor their comprehension of the essay and their use of supporting evidence for their answers. Responses to the writing prompt should include a clear thesis, well-chosen textual support, and an effective conclusion.

ADAPT

If students need additional help seeing how the director's role in a production might affect the performance of the actors, group them together to do a short skit. Have one student play the part of director, changing his or her approach and demonstrating how it affects the actors.

3.20

My Notes

17. **Quickwrite:** Answer the following questions then discuss your responses with your acting company. Use evidence from the text to support your claims:

- What is Barnet's primary claim in his essay?
- Does he make that claim convincingly, or do you challenge any of his points?
- What questions does he leave unanswered?
- Do Barnett's thesis, evidence, commentary, and conclusion all support his purpose?

☑ **Check Your Understanding**

Sylvan Barnet's review pointed out that observers of one production noted "the director's presence was too strongly felt." What is the proper role of a director in a performance? How can you use this information to guide your staging of a scene from *Othello*?

📝 **Writing Prompt: Argumentative**

At this point, you have seen or read about various stage and screen interpretations of *Othello*. Combining what you've learned about *Othello* with your prior knowledge about stage and screen adaptations, explain how modifying an original text can affect the audience's perception. Be sure to:

- Begin a clear thesis to present your position.
- Support your claims with engaging details and examples.
- Include a conclusion that reinforces your thesis in a convincing way without introducing any new ideas.

✍ **WRITING PROMPT: ARGUMENTATIVE**

The following standards are addressed in the writing prompt:

- W.11–12.1a
- W.11–12.1b
- W.11–12.1e

Language Checkpoint: Understanding Verb Voice and Mood

Learning Targets
- Understand verb voice and mood.
- Revise writing to correct inappropriate shifts in verb voice and mood.

Preview

In this activity you will learn about appropriate use of voice and mood to enhance your writing. Then you will practice revising for consistency in voice and mood.

Reviewing Verb Voice and Mood

Verbs are the engines of sentences. They express action (run, jump, think) or a state of being (is, was). Verbs have qualities called **voice** and **mood** that provide additional information.

Verb voice refers to whether the verb is active or passive. In a sentence using active voice, the subject of the sentence performs the action expressed by the verb. In a sentence using passive voice, the subject of the sentence receives the action.

Passive Voice: The title role was performed by Tim Betterton from 1684 to 1790.

Active Voice: Thomas Betterton performed the title role from 1684 to 1709.

Active voice is more direct and less wordy than passive voice, so you should use active voice in most cases. In some cases, though, the passive voice may be preferable. For instance, a writer might want to emphasize the recipient of the action or may want to avoid naming who or what performs an action.

Verb mood expresses a writer's or speaker's attitude. Indicative mood, the most common mood, is used to make statements or ask questions. Imperative mood is used to give a command or make a request. Subjunctive mood is used to express doubt or discuss hypothetical situations.

Indicative Mood: The performance is popular in several major cities.

Imperative Mood: Take me to go see the performance!

Subjunctive Mood: If I were you, I would be excited to watch the performance.

Exploring Verb Voice

1. Writers use active voice most of the time. Read the following sentence, which uses active voice. Then briefly describe why you think the writer chose the active voice.

   I wrote a negative review of the play.

College and Career Readiness Standards

Focus Standards:

L.11–12.1 Demonstrate command of the conventions of standard English grammar and usage when writing or speaking.

L.11–12.3 Apply knowledge of language to understand how language functions in different contexts, to make effective choices for meaning or style, and to comprehend more fully when reading or listening.

L.11–12.6 Acquire and use accurately general academic and domain-specific words and phrases, sufficient for reading, writing, speaking, and listening at the college and career readiness level; demonstrate independence in gathering vocabulary knowledge when considering a word or phrase important to comprehension or expression.

LC 3.20

PLAN

Materials: writing prompt responses from Activity 3.20
Suggested Pacing: 1 50-minute class period

TEACH

1 Introduce or review the topic of verb voice by selecting some sentences from the essay in Activity 3.20 that use active voice and some that use passive voice. In a whole-class discussion, identify the distinctions between the verbs in active and passive sentences.

2 Have students use print or online dictionaries to look up the words *indicative*, *imperative*, and *subjunctive*. Discuss as a class how these three definitions might apply to verbs.

3 Read aloud the Language Checkpoint title and ask students to read the Learning Targets and Reviewing Verb Voice and Mood.

TEACHER TO TEACHER

Before students complete the Language Checkpoint practice, pause for a whole-class discussion in which students share additional examples of sentences with indicative, imperative, and subjunctive verbs to check for understanding.

4 Have students pair with their peer editing partner so that they will be ready to complete items 1 and 2. Direct students to answer the questions under Exploring Verb Voice. Ask volunteers to share their responses.

SAT® CONNECTIONS

This activity provides practice with this important SAT skill: correctly using active or passive voice and indicative, imperative, or subjunctive mood.

5 Before students complete the next two steps, explain that shifting between active and passive voice can be confusing to the reader and can also make writing awkward. Provide some examples to illustrate.

6 Direct students to complete items 3 and 4 and ask volunteers to share their responses.

7 Pause to briefly discuss why academic writing often uses indicative mood.

8 Direct students to complete the items under Exploring Verb Mood and Avoiding Unnecessary Shifts in Mood. Remind them to work with the same partner throughout the activity. Ask volunteers to share their responses.

LC 3.20

2. Now read this sentence, which is written in passive voice. How does the passive voice change the meaning and effect of the sentence?

   The play was negatively reviewed.

Avoiding Unnecessary Shifts in Voice

Writers may choose to use active and passive voice for different effects, but they should avoid unnecessary shifts in voice.

3. Look at this sentence from a student's essay about *Othello*. Underline the verbs.

   The critic recalls the play, and Salvini's terrifying portrayal of Othello is remembered.

4. What do you notice about the verbs in these two clauses? With a partner, look at the sentence, and make an observation about the verbs' voice.

Exploring Verb Mood

5. The indicative mood is used most often. But there are specific situations when other verb moods are useful. Read the following sentence, which is in the imperative mood, and describe briefly when you would use this mood.

   Go watch the play!

College and Career Readiness Standards

W.11–12.5 Develop and strengthen writing as needed by planning, revising, editing, rewriting, or trying a new approach, focusing on addressing what is most significant for a specific purpose and audience.

6. Now read this sentence, which is in the subjunctive mood. Describe briefly when you would use this mood.

If I were you, I would have played the part of Iago.

Avoiding Unnecessary Shifts in Mood

7. Look at this sentence from "Othello on Stage and Screen." Underline the verbs.

The critic is entertained, but he does not understand Othello's complexity.

8. Continue examining the same sentence from the text, and determine the mood of the verbs you identified. With a partner, write a new sentence that uses the same mood.

9. Look at this sentence from a student's essay about "Othello on Stage and Screen." Underline the verbs.

Think about the critic's review. Imagine his perspectives.

10. What mood are these verbs in? With a partner, write a new sentence that uses the same mood.

9 After students have completed the items in the Editing section, have them check a partner's work. Review the answers as a class.

10 Have students work independently to complete the Check Your Understanding. Ask volunteers to share their responses. Make sure that their Editor's Checklist questions include verb voice and mood.

11 Students should work individually to revise their writing as directed in the practice, underlining every verb in order to ensure a complete review of their use of verb voice and mood. Circulate while the students work in order to provide feedback and additional support.

12 After students have revised their responses to the Activity 3.20 writing prompt, as described in the practice section, ask them to review a classmate's writing.

ASSESS

Students' work should show that they understand the difference between active and passive voice and can use each appropriately in writing. Similarly, students' work should show understanding and appropriate use of verb mood. Review students' revised work from the practice section to ensure their revisions demonstrate understanding of the concepts.

ADAPT

If students need additional practice, consider opportunities to continue practicing these skills when the students read other texts within the unit. As you prepare instruction, provide opportunities for students to identify verbs and evaluate their use of voice and mood. Continue to address effective use in the students' original writing.

Consider introducing the "by zombies" method of identifying passive voice (https://www.archives.gov/open/plain-writing/tips/passive-voice.html).

LC 3.20

Editing

Read the following passage and revise the underlined words as needed to correct inappropriate shifts in voice or mood. If the sentence has no unnecessary shifts, write "no change."

11. The audience <u>watched</u> the play and warmly receives Robeson's performance.

   watches

12. If the survey <u>were</u> correct, American audiences would not have welcomed a black actor playing Othello in the United States.

   no change

13. Surprisingly, Robeson's Othello is a success and the audience <u>watched</u> the performance.

   the audience watches the performance.

☑ Check Your Understanding

Imagine you are editing a classmate's writing, and you notice these sentences:

What would you do if you are cast as Iago in the play? You could act like a villain, or acting friendly.

Write an explanation so that your classmate understands how to correct the unnecessary shifts. Add an item to your Editor's Checklist to help you remember to check for verb voice when revising your own work.

Practice

Using what you have learned about verb usage in this lesson, revisit what you wrote for the writing prompt in Activity 3.19. Be sure to:

• Check for appropriate verb voice and mood.
• Revise any inappropriate shifts between voices and moods.

Staging a Performance

Learning Targets

- Determine the theme of a play from its dramatic structure.
- Apply dramatic elements to a performance to reveal theme and reflect a critical perspective.

Preview

In this activity, you will identify a universal theme found in *Othello* and analyze it through multiple critical perspectives. Then you will prepare for Embedded Assessment 2 by planning and rehearsing your staged interpretation of a scene from the play.

Learning Strategies

Graphic Organizer
Note-taking
Rehearsal
Think-Pair-Share
Visualizing
Visual Response

Staging a Dramatic Scene

1. What do you know about the dramatic structure of a play? Share your ideas about this term with a partner.

2. Thinking back to one of the stage or film versions of *Othello*, how does this structure and other dramatic elements such as the actors' and director's use of space advance the plot of the play? Be sure to consider secondary characters like Emilia when sharing thoughts with a partner or your acting company.

3. How would you map the plot of *Othello*? Think back to the events that took us from Othello and Desdemona's marriage to the tragic ending. Create mental images of Othello's transformation throughout the play. Plot the key events with your acting company. Be prepared to share your visual with the class.

Timeless Themes

A text conveys meaning in multiple ways. Consider, for example, how theme is developed through dramatic structure. Sometimes, determining the theme of a work is easier when you simplify the plot. Suppose you were to wrap up the plot of *Othello* in as few as nine words (three 3-word sentences). For *Romeo and Juliet*, a literal 3 x 3 might look like this:

Montague loves Capulet.

Feud complicates love.

Miscommunication brings death.

In order to derive theme from the literal events, let's substitute thematic ideas for the specific ones in the previous 3 x 3.

Adolescents defy boundaries.

Emotions go unchecked.

Interference complicates reality.

Our "literary 3 x 3" now leads us to some general truths about life. What is Shakespeare saying about the unchecked emotions of adolescence, or of the unchecked emotions of adults engaged in an ancient quarrel? Could we also safely infer from the text that adults' interference in the lives of young people invites—rather than prevents—complications that are a natural part of growing up?

My Notes

College and Career Readiness Standards

Focus Standards:

RL.11–12.2 Determine two or more themes or central ideas of a text and analyze their development over the course of the text, including how they interact and build on one another to produce a complex account; provide an objective summary of the text.

RL.11–12.5 Analyze how an author's choices concerning how to structure specific parts of a text (e.g., the choice of where to begin or end a story, the choice to provide a comedic or tragic resolution) contribute to its overall structure and meaning as well as its aesthetic impact.

ACTIVITY 3.21

PLAN

Materials: chart paper; markers
Suggested Pacing: 1 50-minute class period

TEACH

1 Read aloud the Learning Targets and Preview.

2 Activate prior knowledge of dramatic structure in a **think-pair-share.** Discuss dramatic structure. List the essential elements of dramatic structure on the board: exposition, rising action, climax, falling action, and resolution.

3 Ask acting companies to create a diagram of the dramatic structure of *Othello*. This may resemble a line with peaks at high points in the text. Students may reflect the structure in various ways. Invite volunteers to explain their diagrams.

LEVELED DIFFERENTIATED INSTRUCTION

In this activity, students may need support mapping out story events to use when staging a dramatic scene.

Beginning Provide students with the **Text Structure Stairs** graphic organizer. Provide cues on some "stairs" to suggest which key events should be included. Have students work in pairs to map the most important events from the play onto the organizer. Help facilitate discussions by asking: *What changes do Othello, Iago, and Desdemona undergo during the play? How does each act end? How does the play itself end?*

Developing Provide students with the **Text Structure Stairs** graphic organizer. Have them work in pairs to map the most important events from the play onto the organizer. If the version of the play you are using does not include a summary, consider providing a summary for students who may need extra support when identifying key events.

4 Use the sample 3 × 3s for *Romeo and Juliet* as a guide for the creation of literal and literary 3 × 3s for *Othello*. After each group has created a literal 3 × 3, which should reference specific characters and plot events, allow groups to share their ideas. Have the students help you determine the best combination of meaningful words to express the dramatic structure of *Othello*.

5 Once all students have written the class 3 × 3, ask each acting company to use it to create a literary 3 × 3, which should reflect the big ideas of the text. Again, share out groups' responses.

3.21

My Notes

4. Work with your acting company to "wrap up" the dramatic structure of *Othello* in a literal 3 x 3.

5. Write your class's combined "best" in the space provided.

   Othello marries Desdemona.

   Iago wants revenge.

   Manipulation and betrayal triumph over truth.

6. Now move from the literal to capture the themes at work in *Othello* in a literary 3 x 3.

   Love defies boundaries.

   Evil finds weakness.

   Love cannot hold.

7. Write a thematic statement from your 3 x 3 in the space provided.

   Students should construct thematic statements about topics such as race, jealousy, and manipulation.

Make It Work for You

8. Keeping in mind the theme that you identified from your work with 3 x 3s, now consider your assigned scene for Embedded Assessment 2: Staging an Interpretation. Where does your scene fit in the dramatic structure of the play? Revisit your dramatic structure visual from the beginning of this activity, and plot it on your "map." Then, apply the theme from your 3 x 3 to your assigned scene.

9. How does your acting company's scene connect to the themes of the work? How would the themes of the work impact how the actors in your company portray the characters? Explain the relationship in a quickwrite.

   Suppose a theme identified in the 3 x 3 relates to the role of jealousy in destroying a relationship. Scene III.III is the beginning of Iago's attempt to plant suspicious thoughts in the mind of Othello. He plants the "root" of jealousy in this scene. So Iago should come across as trustworthy and convincing in this scene. Othello may begin the scene with a skeptical air that begins to dissolve a little as the scene progresses.

10. How can you apply a critical perspective to the scene? Considering the scene's place in the dramatic structure and its connection to a theme of the work as a whole, what are some lenses through which you can view the scene? Begin with Marxist, Cultural, and Feminist Criticism, and add any others that offer a suitable lens for viewing the scene.

    Marxist: Iago's attempts to destroy Othello through suspicions and jealousy are rooted in his anger at being passed over for a better paying (and higher profile) position.

College and Career Readiness Standards

SL.11–12.1b Work with peers to promote civil, democratic discussions and decision-making, set clear goals and deadlines, and establish individual roles as needed.

W.11–12.5 Develop and strengthen writing as needed by planning, revising, editing, rewriting, or trying a new approach, focusing on addressing what is most significant for a specific purpose and audience. (Editing for conventions should demonstrate command of Language standards 1-3 up to and including grades 11-12 here.)

Additional Standards Addressed:
RL.11–12.3, RL.11–12.4, RL.11–12.6

Cultural: Iago's attempts to destroy Othello are rooted in his prejudiced attitudes about Moors, associating Othello's dark skin with a less-than-worthy military man and husband.

My Notes

Feminist: One may consider Desdemona's role in pleading for Cassio's position with her husband a demeaning task that depends on her beauty and her private relationship with her husband. Rather than Cassio speaking on his own behalf with an appeal to logic, he relies on the emotional appeal of a woman to be reinstated. Of course this route to getting what he wants provides the perfect avenue for Iago to use to plant seeds of suspicion in Othello.

11. As an acting company, come to an agreement about the critical perspective that offers the most engaging interpretation of the scene for a staged performance.

12. Now it's time to consider how to blend the play's literary elements and the dramatic elements you will use while staging your assigned scene to reflect a specific critical perspective in a performance. The dramatic and literary elements will vary depending on your scene. For example, if your scene includes a soliloquy, you might need to consider how the actor who delivers the lines can stand or act apart from the other actors onstage to maintain the audience's focus. Use the graphic organizer to plan your presentation. Use the additional rows for other categories/characters.

Scene:

_____

Connection to Theme:

_____

_____

Critical Perspective:

_____

_____

_____

6 Direct students to write a sentence expressing a theme of the play. Be sure each student's theme is written in a complete declarative sentence and expresses a defensible theme of *Othello*.

7 Students will now connect their understanding of their scene to the "big ideas" of the play as they explore how their scene connects to the theme of the work. Allow time for acting company discussions.

8 Have students provide specific examples that show *Othello* through Marxist, cultural, and feminist perspectives.

9 Next, students will need to explore the way their scene could be examined from various critical perspectives. Be prepared to assist students as they consider how a character's role may be enacted differently when portrayed through a feminist lens versus a Marxist lens, for example. Acting companies need to determine the most engaging interpretation of their scene.

10 Direct students to complete the **graphic organizer** to help them plan the presentation of their scenes. Then have them complete the final script preparations and rehearse the scene.

3.21

	Creating the Desired Effect	Notes Create notes and suggest changes during rehearsal.
Timing	Work with the actors and the director to plan out movements and gestures to increase the impact of dialogue.	
Mood	Decide on the appropriate mood for the scene and adjust sound, music, props, etc. to evoke the desired mood.	
Space	Work together to block the scene in a way that uses the space effectively. How will the movement on stage enhance your interpretation?	
Language	Consider how the actors will deliver their lines. How will they use body language and tone of voice? Will you adjust the script or deliver the lines as written?	
Other	Consider props, use of music, lighting, etc. How will the props and music enhance your interpretation?	

Make Final Preparations

13. Print your script and annotate the scene for your vocal delivery, gestures, use of space, etc. Rehearse your scene and accept constructive criticism from your director to help you convey a convincing performance. Be sure to keep in mind the critical perspective you are applying to the scene and adjust your character's performance to reflect that interpretation.

☑ Check Your Understanding

Review the Assignment, Steps, and Scoring Guide from Embedded Assessment 2 with your acting company. Discuss which components of the assignment may need further preparation. How will you work together as a group to complete any remaining steps?

INDEPENDENT READING LINK

Read and Discuss

Select a point in your independent reading in which a character or the narrator experiences feeling like an outsider. Discuss with a partner or a group how the character reflects on this incident.

ACTIVITY 3.21 continued

11 Have students complete the Check Your Understanding. Remind students to revisit the assignment, steps, and Scoring Guide for Embedded Assessment 2 to ensure they are meeting the criteria for their staged performance of a scene from *Othello*.

12 Remind students to complete the Independent Reading Link. If time permits, have students share their responses with the class as a mini book report of sorts.

TEACHER TO TEACHER

While students may be able to complete some of their script annotations independently, this activity will require at least one class period for students to collaborate on their desired effect and the theatrical elements that will create that effect. They will need time, probably more than one day, to rehearse their scenes prior to their staged performances.

ASSESS

Meet individually with acting companies to ensure clear understanding of the critical perspective they have chosen and its proper application to the scene they will present. Review their graphic organizers for necessary presentation notes. For instance, notes should include specific ideas on how students plan to block their performance. Review students' notes on completion plans for any remaining steps. The action plans should include specific tasks and divide remaining work equitably between members of the acting company.

ADAPT

To support groups who are not yet adequately prepared for the upcoming performance, review their roles and responsibilities to ensure they have a plan in place to complete the remaining steps and polish their performance.

To extend learning, have students review film clips they have viewed in this unit as inspiration for their own presentation choices.

ACTIVITY 3.22

PLAN

Materials: *Othello*; playbills from staged performances (any); access to computers

Suggested Pacing: 1 50-minute class period

TEACH

1 Read aloud the Learning Targets and Preview. Then ask for volunteers to explain in their own words what they will be doing for this activity.

2 Group students to view examples of playbills at playbill.com. You can also print examples of playbills to provide to students or bring playbills to class. Consider contacting high school, college, and community theater groups and asking for playbills from previous shows.

3 While the students study the playbills, direct them to list the kinds of information typically included in a playbill. They should include information about the cast, the director, the play itself, advertisements, and graphics or artwork.

4 Ask research groups to share their observations about the content and point of view in the playbills they researched. They may note that detailed, personalized descriptions of the actors reveal that the actors themselves had input into the creation of the biography, but the descriptions are written in the third-person point of view.

Learning Strategies

Close Reading
Round Table Writing
Sketching
Skimming/Scanning

My Notes

Learning Targets

- Research, plan, and produce a playbill that follows formatting and writing conventions.
- Contribute to the creation of a performance guide for a staged performance.
- Collaboratively write a playbill, or theatre program, that explains the use of a critical perspective

Preview

In this activity, you will analyze the graphics and textual content in a variety of playbills, and then work with your acting company to create a playbill for your interpretation of *Othello*. Collaboratively, you will write a letter to your audience about your acting company's use of a specific critical perspective to drive your interpretation.

Planning a Playbill

1. Use the Internet and your school's library to research playbills used for theater performance. You can view playbills online at playbill.com. To help you plan your company's playbill, jot down notes to answer the following questions:

   - How is a playbill typically structured?
   - What kind of information is included in a playbill based on the examples you viewed?

2. Playbills generally include the background and acting experience of the performers. Take the time to closely read a description of a cast member.

   - What information is included in the description?
   - What point of view is used in the description?
   - What does the actor or production company want a reader to know?

3. A synopsis is another staple of a playbill.

   - How is it structured?
   - How much detail does it provide?

4. Share the notes from your research with your acting company. Then make a list of the key sections that are consistent to all playbills. Note special sections that appear for a single production. As you make your observations, discuss the possible reasons the creator of the playbill chose to include the information and place it accordingly.

College and Career Readiness Standards

Focus Standards:

RI.11–12.3 Analyze a complex set of ideas or sequence of events and explain how specific individuals, ideas, or events interact and develop over the course of the text.

SL.11–12.2 Integrate multiple sources of information presented in diverse formats and media (e.g., visually, quantitatively, orally) in order to make informed decisions and solve problems, evaluating the credibility and accuracy of each source and noting any discrepancies among the data.

5 Have students work with their acting company to complete the graphic organizer in student step 5.

6 Give students time to review their notes about the artwork and layout of playbills. Then, ask them to speculate about the reasons for those choices.

7 If you have multiple playbills per group, allow acting companies to compare the copy, structure, and graphics in a discussion. Or you may rotate playbills among groups so that students may see various renditions.

8 Direct students to note the kinds of advertisements used in the playbill. Students may make observations about the audience as well.

5. With your group, complete the graphic organizer to plan the basic structure of your company's playbill.

Key sections	Notes on each section	New ideas and additions to your playbill

6. Next, look at the graphics and/or artwork incorporated in the playbill.

_____

_____

7. What images from the play did the artist choose to represent? Why?

_____

_____

8. What message might the production company want to send through the print and graphics used in the publication?

Do you think the purpose was achieved? Why or why not?

_____

_____

If you have more than one playbill, what differences do you notice in design, artwork, and (copy) text? If you were to choose one of the performances to attend, which would it be? Why?

_____

_____

9. How are advertisements incorporated into the playbill?

_____

_____

College and Career Readiness Standards

W.11–12.4 Produce clear and coherent writing in which the development, organization, and style are appropriate to task, purpose, and audience.

W.11–12.9 Draw evidence from literary or informational texts to support analysis, reflection, and research.

9 Assign students the creation of a collaboratively written playbill to accompany their production of a scene from *Othello*. Have students follow the instructions in student steps 10 and 11. Groups should make sure each member has clear responsibilities and tasks.

10 Require that students submit the playbill to you prior to the performance to allow you time to make copies for the class.

3.22

Designing the Playbill

10. Your group is responsible for creating a playbill to accompany your performance of *Othello*. Your playbill should enhance your performance and your audience's understanding of the critical perspective that informs your interpretation. Imitate the playbills you viewed in class to guide your content and structure.

As you design your playbill, be sure to:

- Include a creative design with the artwork, graphics, and advertisements presented.
- Adhere to the message and literary theory pursued through the staged performance.
- Use a computer program to produce a visually appealing and technically sound publication.
- Share the responsibilities of designing the playbill by listing all of its components and then assigning an individual to each task.

11. Sketch a plan for the playbill's design in the space provided. Then, have each member of the group develop a brief, written plan to complete the task. Share plans among the company and make any constructive suggestions that could help others improve their plan and accomplish the task in the most effective way.

Playbill design for the 1943 Broadway production of *Othello*, featuring Paul Robeson

☑ Check Your Understanding

In the form of quickwrite, explain how an author can strategically use organizational design and graphic elements when creating a playbill to inform and engage the audience.

✍ Writing Prompt: Informational

With your acting company, draft a professional letter to the audience explaining the interpretation of the scene you will produce. In your letter, describe the message the adaptation is trying to convey by interpreting the work through a specific critical lens. You will finalize your letter for Embedded Assessment 2. Be sure to:

- State which cultural perspective is providing the framework for your production and explain the lens in a way that will clarify its impact on the presentation.
- Follow the formatting conventions and structure of professional letters.
- Use appropriate register and vocabulary.

🕮 Independent Reading Checkpoint

Review your independent reading. Suppose you were going to design a playbill for your text. What kind of information would you include? What design elements would you make or use that reflect aspects of your text? Which actors might you choose as performers? Share your ideas with a group.

✍ WRITING PROMPT: INFORMATIONAL

The following standards are addressed in the writing prompt:
- RI.11–12.3
- SL.11–12.2
- W.11–12.4
- W.11–12.9

---

11 After students have completed their plans, ask them to respond individually to the Check Your Understanding.

12 To prepare students for the writing prompt, find an example of a letter to the audience that has been included in a professional playbill and review it with students. Review the parts of a professional letter or similar form of professional correspondence.

13 Have acting companies work collaboratively to complete the letter to the audience detailed in the writing prompt. Consider having each group use round table writing to revise and edit the text of the letter. One student can check for clarity, one can check for spelling, one can check for punctuation, and one can check for varied syntax.

14 Have students complete the Independent Reading Checkpoint.

ASSESS

Check student playbills for creativity, coherence, and adept use of technology in creating the final draft. Review each group's professional letter. Look for proper formatting, tone, and other evidence of understanding of the writing conventions for playbills. The letter should also include a clear explanation of the group's chosen critical perspective written for an audience member who might view their production.

ADAPT

To support learning, provide playbill templates based on sample playbills and stock images and advertisements for students to use.

To extend learning, have students produce mock advertisements that are appropriate to the critical lens of their performance.

EMBEDDED ASSESSMENT 2

Materials: *Othello*; student-annotated scripts

Suggested Pacing: 3 50-minute class periods

1 Planning and Prewriting: Remind students of their assigned roles and responsibilities. Make adjustments, as needed.

2 Drafting: Be sure students are mindful of Shakespeare's original stage directions, but assure them that contemporary directors add their own, as necessary. Remind them to make their own stage directions clear and concise.

3 Evaluating and Revising: If you wish to record rehearsals so students can self- and peer-evaluate, discuss student use of video technology with your school's media specialist. Remind students to use the Scoring Guide as a basis for feedback on rehearsals.

4 Checking and Editing for Performance: Remind students of the resources available to them as they edit their scripts for errors.

5 Have students turn in all drafts of their scripts.

6 Reflection: Be sure students address the Reflection question as a separate part of the Embedded Assessment assignment so they can include it separately.

7 Portfolio: At this point you may want to ask students to go to their portfolios and find previous unit reflection responses so that they might get a sense of their growth as academic thinkers and producers.

All notes for and drafts of the script should be collected and presented together to show the process students completed in successfully accomplishing the task.

Staging an Interpretation

 ASSIGNMENT

Your assignment is to interpret a scene from *Othello* to emphasize the principles of one of the critical perspectives you have studied, and then plan, rehearse, and perform the scene. With your acting company, write a letter to the audience explaining the message your interpretation is trying to convey.

Planning and Prewriting: Take time to plan ideas and the structure of your scene.	■ How will you determine which critical perspective will best apply to your scene? ■ What message is your production planning to convey? How explicitly will you state this message in your communication to the audience? ■ How can your acting company bring to life the principles or core ideas of the critical perspective you've chosen? ■ How will you divide the various tasks among group members?
Drafting: Create all elements needed for an effective performance.	■ How can you integrate dramatic elements into your scene? ■ What changes do you need to make to your scene (delete or change lines, alter the setting or gender of characters) in order to apply your selected critical perspective? Will you detail some or all of these changes in your letter to the audience? ■ How can you ensure that the group works successfully to maintain its purpose and achieve its goals?
Evaluating and Revising: Obtain feedback and revise to make your work the best it can be.	■ How can you use practice and rehearsal to prepare and evaluate your presentation (videotape a rehearsal, ask another group to provide feedback)? ■ How can you use the Scoring Guide as a resource to evaluate your draft? ■ Are you being faithful to Shakespeare's original within your interpretation?
Checking and Editing for Performance: Polish your written materials and your vocal delivery.	■ How will you check for grammatical and technical accuracy in your written materials? ■ Are you prepared to provide feedback to other acting companies as well as to accept constructive criticism for your own performance? ■ How will you structure the feedback to ensure it is fair and useful?

Reflection

After completing this Embedded Assessment, think about how you went about accomplishing this assignment, and respond to the following:

- The goal of applying a critical perspective to a text is to bring out a new, deeper understanding of the work. How did you manage the challenge of making changes to your scene in order to highlight the chosen critical perspectives without completely altering the scene's original meaning?

College and Career Readiness Standards

Focus Standards:

SL.11–12.1 Initiate and participate effectively in a range of collaborative discussions (one-on-one, in groups, and teacher-led) with diverse partners on grades 11–12 topics, texts, and issues, building on others' ideas and expressing their own clearly and persuasively.

SL.11–12.4 Present information, findings, and supporting evidence, conveying a clear and distinct perspective, such that listeners can follow the line of reasoning, alternative or opposing perspectives are addressed, and the organization, development, substance, and style are appropriate to purpose, audience, and a range of formal and informal tasks.

EMBEDDED ASSESSMENT 2

SCORING GUIDE

When you score this Embedded Assessment, you may wish to make copies or download and print copies of the Scoring Guide from SpringBoard Digital. This way you can have a copy to mark for each student's work.

SCORING GUIDE

Scoring Criteria	Exemplary	Proficient	Emerging	Incomplete
Ideas	The interpretation • reveals an insightful analysis and mature understanding of the scene • insightfully interprets the scene and applies the critical perspective • shows strong understanding of the historical context of the play and the critical lens of the interpretation • clearly communicates the intended effect through dramatic elements • (the letter) effectively explains how a critical lens is reflected in the performance.	The interpretation • demonstrates clear analysis and understanding of the scene • plausibly interprets the scene and applies the critical perspective • shows understanding of the historical context of the play and the critical lens of the interpretation • communicates the intended effect through dramatic elements • (the letter) adequately explains how a critical lens is reflected in the performance.	The interpretation • reveals a limited analysis and understanding of the scene • interprets the scene and applies the critical perspective with limited success • shows limited understanding of the historical context of the play and the critical lens of the interpretation • inadequately communicates the intended effect; dramatic elements are ineffective • (the letter) inadequately explains how a critical lens is reflected in the performance.	The interpretation • reveals little analysis or understanding of the scene • attempts to interpret the scene but does not successfully apply a critical perspective • does not show understanding of the historical context of the play and the critical lens of the interpretation • does not communicate the intended effect; dramatic elements are absent or ineffective • does not explain how a critical lens is reflected in the performance.
Structure	The interpretation • skillfully uses dramatic elements and effective vocal delivery • demonstrates equal and appropriate sharing of responsibility.	The interpretation • uses adequate dramatic elements and vocal delivery • demonstrates mostly balanced sharing of responsibility.	The interpretation • offers few dramatic elements and vocal delivery that detract from the quality of the scene • demonstrates an unequal division of responsibilities.	The interpretation • offers a disorganized scene with few to no dramatic elements and vocal delivery that detracts from the performance • demonstrates an unequal division of responsibilities that affects the performance.
Use of Language	The interpretation • includes written materials that advance the group's ideas • demonstrates command of oral and written English with few or no errors.	The interpretation • includes written materials that adequately support the group's ideas • demonstrates good usage of oral and written English with few errors.	The interpretation • ineffectively supports the group's ideas in written material • attempts to use appropriate oral and written language but contains errors that interfere with meaning.	The interpretation • contains inadequate support in written materials • contains serious errors in language use or inappropriate language.

College and Career Readiness Standards

SL.11–12.6 Adapt speech to a variety of contexts and tasks, demonstrating a command of formal English when indicated or appropriate.

W.11–12.2 Write informative/explanatory texts to examine and convey complex ideas, concepts, and information clearly and accurately through the effective selection, organization, and analysis of content.

W.11–12.5 Develop and strengthen writing as needed by planning, revising, editing, rewriting, or trying a new approach, focusing on addressing what is most significant for a specific purpose and audience.

W.11–12.9 Draw evidence from literary or informational texts to support analysis, reflection, and research.

Additional Standards Addressed:
RI.11–12.1, SL.11–12.3

Planning the Unit

Context

This unit asks students to apply critical lenses to real-world events in order to understand the underlying tensions that can cause an event to resonate with a society. Students analyze print and nonprint journalistic texts and their own reactions to them. They also consider how personal and cultural experiences, assumptions, and biases influence perspectives on what is "true" about an event, becoming filters that strongly influence how we interpret the world. By studying how a single event is reported by different sources, students will explore how the critical lenses they have examined influence the way we define truth.

Suggested Texts and Materials

The unit is built around texts that explore the many issues surrounding the 2005 storm, Hurricane Katrina. These texts and documentaries should be used to model investigation into a significant issue, since students will find their own issue to investigate for the Embedded Assessments.

- Activity 4.4: Online video segments or online articles from two different sources covering the same subject from different perspectives
- Activity 4.6: Trailer from *Trouble the Water*, directed by Tia Lessin and Carl Deal (available online); a podcast episode reporting the aftermath of Hurrican Katrina
- Activity 4.9: MLA style manuals
- Activity 4.12: video clip of George W. Bush's speech at Warren Easton Charter High School on the 10th Anniversary of Hurricane Katrina, or another teacher-selected video of a speech
- Activity 4.13: clip from a television news magazine show, such as 60 Minutes or Frontline (optional)
- Activity 4.14: video clip of a speech, documentary or news story on the topic of charter schools

Instructional Sequence

The unit begins with several close-reading activities that ask students to examine journalistic texts to identify the critical perspectives that inform them and to analyze how information and rhetoric (verbal or visual) are used to influence our understanding of the meaning of things. Students will then examine a collection of journalistic texts about Hurricane Katrina and examine the coverage through multiple critical lenses. Students will then transfer this knowledge to a collaborative investigation and analysis of an issue or controversy of their choice. Students will work in groups to do this analysis, but each group member will individually craft an essay that examines how a critical lens or perspective shapes (or can be exposed within) the coverage of the subject for Embedded Assessment 1.

In the later part of the unit, students will shift from analyzing others' texts to creating their own. Students will study speeches and their conventions in preparation for Embedded Assessment 2: Presenting an Argument, which asks students to present an argument in a medium of their choice.

AP® CONNECTIONS

In this unit, students will focus on refining these important skills and knowledge areas for AP/College Readiness:

- Conducting analyses based on close reading through a variety of critical perspectives (Activities 4.5, 4.6, 4.7)
- Identifying the components of the rhetorical situation and making strategic choices appropriate to an intended audience (Activities 4.5, 4.7, 4.8, 4.12, 4.13)
- Developing or addressing an alternative perspective by considering and responding to relevant evidence (4.8, Embedded Assessment 1 and 2)
- Focusing deliberate attention on the craft of sentence-level writing (Activities 4.2, 4.4, 4.11)

SAT® CONNECTIONS

In this unit, students will practice many important skills that will help them succeed on the SAT and other college readiness exams, including:

- Recognizing and correcting cases in which unlike terms are compared (LC 4.7)

Unpacked Embedded Assessments

Embedded Assessment 1: Examining How an Issue Is Presented in Media Texts	Embedded Assessment 2: Presenting an Argument
Skills and Knowledge: • Apply a critical lens to the meaning and significance of a real world event. • Develop a clear thesis. • Evaluate textual passages for use as evidence in support of an interpretive claim. • Synthesize sources in support of an interpretive argument. • Use organization to enhance the persuasiveness of an argument.	**Skills and Knowledge:** • Manipulate the genre conventions of a vocal performance for rhetorical effect. • Demonstrate a thorough investigation and deep understanding of the topic. • Create a script that reveals insightful analysis. • Organize ideas in an appropriate and polished order. • Use precise language.

Cognate Directory

Encouraging students to notice the connections between their primary language and English can help them develop academic vocabulary more quickly. If your class includes Spanish speakers, consider adding the following cognates to the classroom Word Wall. For English Language Learners whose primary language is not Spanish, consider using an online translator or dictionary to support comprehension of vocabulary terms.

Unit 4 Vocabulary Terms with Spanish Cognates

Academic Vocabulary	
English	**Spanish**
agenda	agenda
annotated bibliography	bibliografía anotada
conventions	convenciones
documentary	documental
media	medios de comunicación
media channel	canales mediaticos
rhetorical context	contexto retórico

Activity Features at a Glance

The activities in every ELA unit reflect the interconnected nature of reading, writing, listening, speaking, and thinking. The Activity Features at a Glance chart highlights the types of tasks or supports that students and teachers will encounter in each activity.

 Writing and Revision

 Grammar and Language

 Listening, Speaking, and Discussion

 Independent Reading

 Vocabulary Development

 ELL Support

 Knowledge Quest

 Gaining Perspectives

ELA Activity	Activity Features
4.1	🗣 📖 V ELL
4.2	✏ G 🗣 V ELL
4.3	✏ G 🗣 V ELL
4.4	✏ G 🗣 V ELL 🧭
4.5	✏ 🗣 📖 V ELL 🌿
4.6	✏ 🗣 📖 V ELL
4.7	✏ G 🗣 V ELL 🧭
LC 4.7	✏ G 🗣

ELA Activity	Activity Features
4.8	✏ 🗣
4.9	📖 V
4.10	🗣 📖
4.11	✏ G 🗣 V ELL
4.12	🗣
4.13	🗣 📖 V ELL
4.14	✏ 🗣 📖 V

Unit Resources at a Glance

Formative Assessment Opportunities	Digital Assessments	Family Connections
Text-dependent questions Writing prompts Check Your Understanding tasks Focus on the Sentence tasks Language Checkpoint exercises Language & Writer's Craft practice	Activity Quizzes 4.2–4.14 Unit Assessment Part 1 Unit Assessment Part 2 (SBD)	Suggestions for Independent Reading Family Letters (English and Spanish) Student Reports (SBD)
English Language Development	**Foundational Skills**	**Independent Reading**
Leveled Differentiated Instruction Graphic Organizers ELD Strategies Language Workshop 1A Language Workshop 1B	Foundational Skills Screening Assessment Observational Look-fors Foundational Skills Workshop	My Independent Reading List Independent Reading Links Independent Reading Checkpoints Independent Reading Log Reader/Writer Notebook Suggestions for Independent Reading

Suggestions for Independent Reading

This list, divided into the categories of **Literature** and **Nonfiction/Informational Text**, comprises titles related to the themes and content of the unit. For their independent reading, students can select from this wide array of titles, which have been chosen based on complexity and interest. Spanish-language titles are included for those students who can read with greater independence or at a higher grade level in Spanish than in English, since building on their first language literacy can bolster their acquisition of English. Titles on this list have been suggested by teachers and school librarians, but you should be sure to preview texts to assess their appropriateness for your specific students and setting. You can also encourage students to do their own research and select titles that intrigue them.

Unit 4: Creating Perspectives

Literature		
Author	**Title**	**Lexile**
Adichie, Chimamanda Ngozi	*Americanah*	N/A
Brown, Don	*Drowned City*	920L
Calvino, Italo	*Invisible Cities*	1290L
Coelho, Paulo	*The Alchemist*	910L
Egger, Dave	*Zeitoun*	840L
Golding, William	*El señor de las moscas*	760L
Hawkins, Paula	*The Girl on the Train*	760L
Henriques, Diana	*The Wizard of Lies: Bernie Madoff and the Death of Trust*	N/A

Kessler, Lauren	Clever Girl	N/A
McCann, Colum	Let the Great World Spin	N/A
McLean, Bethany and Elkind, Peter	The Smartest Guys in the Room: The Amazing Rise and Scandalous Fall of Enron	N/A
Mitchell, David	Ghostwritten	N/A
Moore, Alan	The Watchmen	N/A
Morrison, Toni	Song of Solomon	870L
Pérez, Ashley Hope	Out of Darkness	660L
Volponi, Paul	Hurricane Song	850L
Ward, Jesmyn	Salvage the Bones	890L
Woolf, Virginia	To the Lighthouse	1030L

Nonfiction/Informational

Author	Title	Lexile
Atkins, Larry	Skewed: A Critical Thinker's Guide to Media Bias	N/A
Baum, Dan	Nine Lives: Mystery, Magic, Death, and Life in New Orleans	N/A
Bowden, Mark	The Finish Line	N/A
Brinkley, Douglas	The Great Deluge: Hurricane Katrina, New Orleans, and the Mississippi Gulf Coast	N/A
Dineen, Jacqueline	Huracanes y tifones (Hurricanes and Typhoons)	
Diamond, Jared	Guns, Germs, and Steel: The Fates of Human Societies	1440L
Donovan, Sandy	Media: From News Coverage to Political Advertising	1150L
Fink, Sheri	Five Days at Memorial	N/A
Foster, Thomas C.	How to Read Literature Like a Professor	820L
Goldberg, Bernard	A Slobbering Love Affair: The True (And Pathetic) Story of the Torrid Romance Between Barack Obama and the Mainstream Media	N/A
Greenwald, Glenn	No Place to Hide: Edward Snowden, the NSA, and the U.S. Surveillance State	N/A
Konnikova, Maria	Mastermind: How to Think Like Sherlock Holmes	N/A
Krakauer, Jon	Into Thin Air	
Lule, Jack	Globalization and Media: Global Village of Babel	N/A
Momaday, N. Scott	The Way to Rainy Mountain	890L
Moore, Wes	The Other Wes Moore	990L
Obama, Barack	Dreams from My Father: A Story of Race and Inheritance	N/A
Rose, Chris	1 Dead in Attic	N/A
Sloan, Wm. David and Jenn Burleson Mackay (editors)	Media Bias: Finding It, Fixing It	N/A
Thompson, Neal	Hurricane Season: A Coach, His Team, and Their Triumph in the Time of Katrina	1120L

Instructional Pathways

Teachers can build customized pathways through this unit by making purposeful choices about which resources to use based on students' learning needs. The charts below outline a few possible pathways to show how teachers might integrate digital assessments, Language Workshops, Close Reading Workshops, and Writing Workshops into instruction. Additional planning resources—including detailed standards correlations—are available on SpringBoard Digital.

English Language Arts Unit 4: Creating Perspectives

Activity	SBD Digital Assessments	Pacing	
Activity 4.1: Previewing the Unit	N/A	1	
Activity 4.2: The Evolution of Media	Activity Quiz 4.2	2	
Activity 4.3: Constructing Public Opinion	Activity Quiz 4.3	2	
Activity 4.4: Bias in News Reports	Activity Quiz 4.4	2	
Activity 4.5: Framing the Investigation	Activity Quiz 4.5	2	
Activity 4.6: Exploring Media Sources	Activity Quiz 4.6	3	
Activity 4.7: Throwing Light on the Situation	Activity Quiz 4.7	4	
LC 4.7: Language Checkpoint: Writing Logical Comparisons (optional)	Activity Quiz LC 4.7	1	
Activity 4.8: Creating a Research Plan	Activity Quiz 4.8	3	
Activity 4.9: Evaluating Sources	Activity Quiz 4.9	2	
Embedded Assessment 1: Examining How an Issue Is Presented in Media Texts	**Unit Assessment Part 1**	**3**	**1**
Activity 4.10: Unpacking Embedded Assessment 2	Activity Quiz 4.10	1	
Activity 4.11: Preparing to Persuade	Activity Quiz 4.11	1	
Activity 4.12: That Sounds Just Right	Activity Quiz 4.12	2	
Activity 4.13: Turning Research into Persuasion	Activity Quiz 4.13	2	
Activity 4.14: *Voir Dire*: Facing a Jury of Your Peers	Activity Quiz 4.14	1	
Embedded Assessment 2: Presenting an Argument	**Unit Assessment Part 2**	**4**	**1**

Total 50-minute Class Periods: 35–38

Language Development Pathway

Consider using some or all of the Language Workshop and Foundational Skills Workshop activities with English Language Learners or with any student who would benefit from extra support with academic English. More detailed guidance about the timing of Language Workshop and Foundational Skills Workshop activities in relation to the ELA unit and about the purpose of each activity can be found in the Language Workshop teacher edition.

Language Workshop 4A and 4B

Activity or Workshop		Pacing
Activity 4.1: Previewing the Unit		1
Activity 4.2: The Evolution of Media		2
Language Workshop 4A.7: Language Checkpoint		1
Activity 4.3: Constructing Public Opinion		2
Activity 4.4: Bias in News Reports		2
Language Workshop 4B.1: Genre Focus		1
Language Workshop 4B.2: Building Knowledge		1
Language Workshop 4B.3: Academic Vocabulary		1
Language Workshop 4B.4: Vocabulary Preview and Practice		1
Activity 4.5: Framing the Investigation **OR** Language Workshop 4B.5: Close Reading of an Anchor Text*	2	1
	Language Workshop 4B.6: Academic Collaboration*		1
Activity 4.6: Exploring Media Sources		3
Language Workshop 4A.1: Genre Focus		1
Language Workshop 4A.2: Building Knowledge		1
Language Workshop 4A.3: Academic Vocabulary		1
Language Workshop 4A.4: Vocabulary Preview and Practice		1
Activity 4.7: Throwing Light on the Situation **OR** Language Workshop 4A.5: Close Reading of an Anchor Text*	4	1
	Language Workshop 4A.6: Academic Collaboration*		1

Activity or Workshop		Pacing	
LC 4.7: Language Checkpoint: Writing Logical Comparisons (optional)		1	
Activity 4.8: Creating a Research Plan		3	
Activity 4.9: Evaluating Sources		2	
Embedded Assessment 1: Examining How an Issue Is Presented in Media Texts	OR **Collaborative Embedded Assessment: Writing an Editorial**	3	4
Activity 4.10: Unpacking Embedded Assessment 2		1	
Activity 4.11: Preparing to Persuade		1	
Language Workshop 4B.7: Language Checkpoint		1	
Activity 4.12: That Sounds Just Right		2	
Activity 4.13: Turning Research into Persuasion		2	
Activity 4.14: *Voir Dire*: Facing a Jury of Your Peers		1	
Embedded Assessment 2: Presenting an Argument	OR **Collaborative Embedded Assessment: Writing and Presenting a Persuasive Speech**	4	7
Total 50-minute Class Periods:		35–50	

* These activities are available in Spanish.

Foundational Skills Workshop

The Foundational Skills Workshop offers instructional and practice materials for providing small-group instruction to students who are still developing foundational reading skills.

Activity	Pacing
Activity 1: Practicing Letter-Sound Relationships	15 min.
Activity 2: Recognizing Words by Sight	10 min.
Activity 3: Words with Inconsistent but Common Spellings	
Activity 4: Irregularly Spelled Words	
Activity 5: Common Prefixes	
Activity 6: Common Suffixes	35–40 min. per activity
Activity 7: Using Roots and Affixes to Read Multisyllabic Words	
Activity 8: Reading Multisyllabic Words	
Activity 9: Reading Informational Text with Purpose and Understanding	
Activity 10: Reading Poetry with Fluency	

Flexible Pathways

Teachers may build a flexible pathway that focuses on developing students' close reading and writing skills with the Close Reading and Writing Workshops. Each workshop addresses a specific set of standards and includes multiple assessment opportunities to allow students to demonstrate the knowledge and skills that are the focus of that workshop.

Close Reading Workshops

Workshop	Genre Focus	Assessment Opportunities	Pacing
Close Reading Workshop 2: Argumentative Nonfiction Texts	Legal Documents Cartoons Editorials	Writing Prompt Debate/Discussion Multimedia Presentation	8
Close Reading Workshop 6: Informational Texts in STEM	Informational Texts Tables	Writing Prompt Debate/Discussion Multimedia Presentation	8

Writing Workshops

Workshop	Genre Focus	Assessment Opportunities	Pacing
Writing Workshop 3: Explanatory Writing: Synthesis	Informational Texts	Writing as a Class Independent Writing	6
Writing Workshop 6: Research Writing	Research	Class Research Presentation Group Research Presentation Independent Research	9

UNIT 4

VISUAL PROMPT
Think about the individuals who lived in the homes flooded during a hurricane. What different experiences, stories, and perspectives might they have? How does the media distill a multitude of stories into a single narrative?

CREATING PERSPECTIVES

In the online environment where information comes as a steady linear stream, where it's not divided up with a front page, an opinion page, and different specialized news sections (that prioritize news information according to prominence, urgency, civic importance, or local, national, and international orientation), it's all just mixed together.

—from "How News Has Changed," by Michael Griffin

Leveled Differentiated Instruction Directory

For guidance on differentiating tasks for English language learners at various levels of language proficiency, refer to the Leveled Differentiated Instruction suggestions in these activities:

4.1: Help students plan their independent reading strategies by giving them the option to read an article in their home language.

4.2: Use the **Conclusion Builder** graphic organizer to support students' analysis of news sources.

4.3: Use the **Idea and Argument Evaluator** graphic organizer to help students analyze the author's claims and reasons.

4.4: Use the **Paragraph Frame for Conclusions** graphic organizer to support writing an argumentative essay about bias in news stories.

UNIT 4

Read aloud the quote under "Creating Perspectives," and ask students to think about how they get news and information in today's online environment. Ask students to share responses in partner, small-group, or whole-class discussion. It may be helpful to distribute copies of print newspaper sections to students to activate prior knowledge about the structure of a traditional newspaper compared with the online environment described in the quote.

Read aloud the visual prompt. Have students look at the image and respond to the visual prompt. Have students write short responses for each question and **think-pair-share** with a partner to discuss their responses.

⭐ TEACHER TO TEACHER

Prompt students to think about the media sources they use. Ask them how they think social media has affected the way they share and consume news. Have students think about media sources by posing the unit's Essential Questions: How do media sources influence our understanding of the truth and significance of an issue? How are media texts constructed to support an agenda or interpretation?

CONTENTS

Have the students skim/scan the activities and texts in this unit. Have them note any texts they have heard about but never read, and any activities that sound particularly interesting.

GOALS

Have students read the goals for the unit and mark any words that are unfamiliar. Have students add these words to the classroom Word Wall, along with definitions.

You may also want to post these goals in a visible place in the classroom for the duration of this unit, allowing you and your students to revisit the goals easily and gauge progress throughout the unit.

UNIT 4

VOCABULARY DEVELOPMENT

Adding to vocabulary knowledge is essential for reading fluency. Students will encounter new vocabulary in this course in multiple ways:

- Academic Vocabulary
- Literary Terms
- Vocabulary in Context (unfamiliar terms glossed in text selections)
- Word Connections
- Oral discussions

Encourage students to use new vocabulary expressively in class discussions and in writing. Have them keep a **Reader/Writer Notebook** in which they record new words, their meanings, and their pronunciations.

See the Resources section for examples of graphic organizers suitable for word study. Having students use word-study graphic organizers will greatly enhance their understanding of new words and their connection to unit concepts and to the broader use of advanced and discipline-based terms.

Have students review the list of academic and literary terms and sort them in a **QHT** chart. Revisit the chart periodically to see how students' understanding progresses throughout the unit.

LANGUAGE DEVELOPMENT

Several recurring SpringBoard features focus on building students' knowledge of grammar and usage concepts. Language & Writer's Craft features guide students to examine a writer's use of a language concept in context before incorporating the concept into their own writing. Grammar & Usage features briefly highlight and explain an interesting grammar or usage concept that appears in a text, both to improve students' reading comprehension and to increase their understanding of the concept. Periodic Language Checkpoints offer in-depth practice with standard English conventions and usage and guide students to revise sample sentences as well as their own work.

UNIT 4 — Creating Perspectives

GOALS

- To develop and support inferences and analyses by synthesizing information from a variety of informational texts
- To work collaboratively with a team, offering ideas, judgments and insightful questions, while working toward common research goals
- To critique and evaluate how authors present information and organize ideas based on purpose
- To write an argumentative text that cites credible academic sources to support claims
- To formulate and present a persuasive argument using elements of classical speeches
- To analyze how different critical perspectives shape the reporting and interpreting of events

VOCABULARY

ACADEMIC
agenda
archival footage
annotated bibliography
conventions
documentary
media
media channel
primary footage
rhetorical context

LITERARY
logical fallacy
rhetorical slanters

Leveled Differentiated Instruction Directory (continued)

4.5: Provide students with the **Conversation for Quickwrite** graphic organizer to help them respond to the Quickwrite.

4.6: Support students' prewriting by providing a translation of a film trailer or infographic.

4.7: To support reading comprehension, have small groups complete the **Paraphrasing Map** graphic organizer as they read an article.

4.11: Challenge students by having pairs informally debate the speaker's claim.

4.14: Have students do a **quickwrite** to describe their ideas through their chosen critical lens.

CONTENTS

Texts not included in these materials.

📖 My Independent Reading List

UNIT 4

INDEPENDENT READING

In this unit, students will explore the influence of media and other informational sources and how they offer interpretation and opinion. Their independent reading selections should complement the unit's focus on media, journalism, and news events. The Planning the Unit section of the Teacher's Edition and the Resources section of the Student Edition contain reading lists to help you and your students find the right books.

Independent Reading Links in the unit periodically prompt students to reflect on the reading they are doing outside of class and to make connections to the texts, themes, and ideas addressed in the unit.

KNOWLEDGE QUEST

Within the unit, students will engage in two Knowledge Quests. They will read collections of texts about the role of the media and the process of recovery following natural disasters, building their understanding of the topics and related vocabulary. Each Knowledge Quest begins with a knowledge question and supporting questions that focus student learning. After students read the final text in a set, they will have the opportunity to return to the Knowledge Question and express their growing understanding of the topic by responding to a writing-to-sources prompt or engaging in an academic discussion.

▶ TEACHER TO TEACHER

The SpringBoard program is designed so that students interact with texts in meaningful ways, such as notetaking and annotating, to facilitate comprehension and analysis. Have students use Reader/Writer Notebooks actively for vocabulary study, answers to text-dependent questions, predictions and questions about texts, reflections, responses to Independent Reading Links, and so on. The Reader/Writer Notebooks are not listed as part of the materials for each activity, but the expectation is that students will access them frequently.

PLAN

Materials: chart paper; markers; print examples of media texts
Suggested Pacing: 1 50-minute class period

TEACH

1 Briefly review the Learning Targets and Preview with students.

2 Direct students to read the About the Unit section. Activate prior knowledge by leading a class discussion in which students share information on what types of news events interest them and tell how and where they gather news. Work with students to create an anticipation guide showing what they might learn in this unit. Post the completed anticipation guide in the classroom.

3 Consider reviewing the various critical lenses with students, using manipulatives if necessary.

4 Vocabulary Development: Review the meaning of the term *agenda* with students. Have them work in pairs to define the term in their own words and think of both examples and non-examples.

5 Ask students to respond to the two Essential Questions and share their responses in a discussion group. Provide each group with some print examples of media texts and a list of different media sources that may be familiar to them.

6 After groups share their responses to the Essential Questions, ask students to work with their discussion group to compare some of the different interests, experiences, assumptions, and biases held by various group members, explaining how those differences might impact the way they interpret news. Monitor groups to ensure students are interacting in a meaningful and respectful way.

TEACHER TO TEACHER

Students may have a difficult time identifying their own interests, experiences, assumptions, and biases. Develop a list of possible filters as part of a whole-class discussion.

Previewing the Unit

Learning Strategies

Close Reading
Graphic Organizer
Marking the Text
Summarizing

VOCABULARY

ACADEMIC

The word agenda may refer to a list of items to be discussed during a meeting. As used here, however, it refers to an underlying, often ideological, plan or program that guides behavior and opinion.

Learning Targets

- Preview the big ideas for the unit.
- Identify and analyze the skills and knowledge needed to complete Embedded Assessment 1 successfully.
- Create a plan for reading independently.

Preview

In this activity, you will explore the big ideas and tasks of the unit, identify the skills and knowledge you will need to be successful on the first Embedded Assessment, and make plans for your independent reading.

About the Unit

We are not passive consumers of media; rather, as active participants we bring our own sets of interests, experiences, assumptions, and biases to what we read, see, and hear, as do those who produce what we read, see, and hear. When we care about an event, we want to know how to determine what is true about the event and how to get close to that truth. However, it is important to recognize our own filters—those personal interests, experiences, assumptions, and biases—and how they influence our ability to discern the truth. Media and government reports, like literary texts, need to be read or "decoded" carefully. In this unit, you will use critical perspectives to analyze informational texts.

Essential Questions

Based on your current knowledge, write answers to these questions in the My Notes space.

1. How do media sources influence our understanding of the truth and significance of an issue?

2. How are media texts constructed to cater to media consumers' interests, experiences, assumptions, and biases or to promote a particular agenda?

Unpacking Embedded Assessment 1

Read the following assignment for Embedded Assessment 1 and summarize the major elements in your Reader/Writer Notebook.

Your assignment is to write an argumentative essay that argues for the use of a particular critical lens to interpret an event. Your essay must include an annotated bibliography and evidence from at least five texts gathered alone or with your group members.

Summarize in your own words what you will need to know for this assessment. With your class, create a graphic organizer that represents the skills and knowledge you will need to accomplish this task, and strategize how you will complete the assignment. As you complete your graphic organizer, be sure to review the criteria in the Scoring Guide.

My Notes

College and Career Readiness Standards

Focus Standards:

RI.11–12.10 By the end of grade 12, read and comprehend literary nonfiction at the high end of the grades 11–CCR text complexity band independently and proficiently.

W.11–12.4 Produce clear and coherent writing in which the development, organization, and style are appropriate to task, purpose, and audience.

W.11–12.10 Write routinely over extended time frames (time for research, reflection, and revision) and shorter time frames (a single sitting or a day or two) for a range of tasks, purposes, and audiences.

4.1

ⓣ Planning Independent Reading

During this unit, you will read a variety of information texts, including a series of texts on the topic of Hurricane Katrina. For your independent reading during the first part of this unit, consider choosing nonfiction relating to the media, such as a biography about a prominent journalist or books about the experiences of journalists reporting from the front lines. Later in the unit, find independent reading texts that will deepen your understanding about Hurricane Katrina and its long-term effects. Discuss your selections with a small group. Explain why you would or would not recommend your choices to your classmates.

My Notes

ACTIVITY 4.1 continued

7 Lead students through a **close reading** of the prompt, steps, and Scoring Guide criteria for Embedded Assessment 1.

8 Ask partners to **summarize/ paraphrase** the prompt. Guide the class in creating a **web graphic organizer** that lists the knowledge and skills. Revisit the graphic organizer during the unit.

9 Have students complete the Planning Independent Reading. Offer specific examples of appropriate nonfiction, such as the titles found in the Planning the Unit section.

LEVELED DIFFERENTIATED INSTRUCTION

Students may benefit from further guidance as they choose texts for their independent reading.

Beginning Consider giving students who are at an early stage of English language development the option of reading a text in their home language. These students can build on native language literacy as they begin to develop academic English.

Bridging Encourage students who are at an advanced level of proficiency to select an option that exhibits a deeper level of news analysis than the selections in the unit.

ASSESS

Use students' marked text, summaries, and graphic organizers to assess their understanding of the Embedded Assessment assignment and the knowledge and skills for writing an argumentative essay.

ADAPT

Model the process in one section of the graphic organizer, and then allow students to work in pairs.

PLAN

Materials: chart paper
Suggested Pacing: 2 50-minute class periods

TEACH

1 Read aloud the Learning Targets and Preview.

2 Direct students' attention to the Academic Vocabulary box. You may want to activate prior knowledge by pointing out that the definition names traditional, not social, media channels.

3 Instruct students to employ the definitions and also consider how they use social media channels as they complete the **graphic organizer**.

The Evolution of Media

Learning Strategies

Discussion Groups
Graphic Organizer
Note-taking

VOCABULARY

ACADEMIC

Media, collectively, refers to the organizations that communicate information to the public. A media channel is one method an organization uses to communicate, such as radio, television, website, newspaper, or magazine.

Learning Targets

- Explain how informational texts reflect or reveal critical perspectives.
- In collaborative groups, develop criteria and strategies for selecting supporting evidence from texts.
- Write an argument citing evidence from an informational text.

Preview

In this activity, you will read an article that traces the history of the media industry since the advent of television news. Through discussion and writing, you will analyze some of the article's key ideas through various critical perspectives.

What Is the Media?

1. Take a minute to consider how you gather information about events that take place in the world around you, using **media**. Complete the following graphic organizer with information about current events and the **media channels** that you use.

School/Local Event	Details/Facts I Know About Event	Media Channel

State/National Event	Details/Facts I Know About Event	Media Channel

International Event	Details/Facts I Know About Event	Media Channel

---

College and Career Readiness Standards

Focus Standards:

RI.11–12.2 Determine two or more central ideas of a text and analyze their development over the course of the text, including how they interact and build on one another to provide a complex analysis; provide an objective summary of the text.

RI.11–12.3 Analyze a complex set of ideas or sequence of events and explain how specific individuals, ideas, or events interact and develop over the course of the text.

4.2

As You Read

- Underline any specific references to time periods or years, and highlight phrases that help answer the question posed in each heading.
- Circle unknown words and phrases. Try to determine the meaning of the words by using context clues, word parts, or a dictionary.

My Notes

About the Author

Michael Griffin, an associate professor of media and cultural studies at Macalester College, is a researcher, writer, and public speaker with more than 30 years of college-level teaching experience. Griffin, who earned his doctorate in visual communications and media studies from the Annenberg School for Communication at the University of Pennsylvania, has worked as a documentary filmmaker and nonfiction editor. He's also written extensively on topics including the functions of media in society.

Article

How News Has Changed

by **Michael Griffin**

What should we know about media history?

1   Many current concerns about the news can be traced back to long-term changes that began as early as the 1960s and accelerated in the 1980s, when media companies were bought by large conglomerates and chains, and increasing media concentration became a progressively larger problem.

2   In the middle of the 20th century, television network leadership believed that providing news was a public service. News wasn't expected to make money for national broadcasters. During that time CBS, for example, built up a high-quality news division, with distinguished journalists such as Edward R. Murrow opposing McCarthyism and Walter Cronkite, who became "the most trusted man in America," anchoring a highly respected nightly news broadcast watched by tens of millions. CBS also created foreign news bureaus around the world to inform the American public about international issues. It was referred to as the "Tiffany Network," alluding to the perceived high quality of CBS programming during the tenure of CEO William S. Paley. Network news was something that great numbers of Americans relied upon and could share; it gave them a common set of facts upon which they could have discussions and debates.

3   In 1986 CBS was bought by Loews Corp., then mainly a hotel and movie theater company headed by Larry Tisch. By the 1980s and 1990s these types of acquisitions were happening across the media industry, CBS and Tisch being just one example. Whenever a big entertainment company or conglomerate

College and Career Readiness Standards

SL.11–12.1c Propel conversations by posing and responding to questions that probe reasoning and evidence; ensure a hearing for a full range of positions on a topic or issue; clarify, verify, or challenge ideas and conclusions; and promote divergent and creative perspectives.

W.11–12.1 Write arguments to support claims in an analysis of substantive topics or texts, using valid reasoning and relevant and sufficient evidence.

Additional Standards Addressed:

RI.11–12.1, RI.11–12.5, RI.11–12.6, W.11–12.1a, W.11–12.1c, W.11–12.1d, W.11–12.1e W.11–12.5, W.11–12.10, L.11–12.5b

4 Review the As You Read instructions with students.

5 **FIRST READ:** Chunk the text according to its headings for a paced independent read. At the end of each section, ask individual students to share their answer to the question posed in the heading.

TEXT COMPLEXITY

Overall: Complex
Lexile: 1190L
Qualitative: Moderate Difficulty
Task: Challenging (Evaluate)

TEACHER TO TEACHER

Students may not be familiar with Walter Cronkite or Edward R. Murrow. To give them context for the first few sections of the article, consider showing historic news clips that feature Cronkite and Murrow.

4.2

My Notes

came in, the news divisions had to answer to shareholders and improve the bottom line. For the first time, there was an expectation that the news divisions had to make money, just like the entertainment divisions. And a major way to improve the profitability of the news was to cut costs. At CBS, cuts included the foreign bureaus, documentary division, and enormous numbers of people in the newsroom. This was an erosion of the concept and standards of quality news, and it happened precipitously in the 1980s and 1990s.

Then what happened?

4 At the same time, market segmentation was increasing. As advertisers began to analyze large amounts of demographic data, they were able to target their products and advertising more precisely than ever before. Everything shifted to target marketing, and that means the national audience got sliced and diced. That happened first with magazines: the demise of the national general interest magazines—Collier's, Life, Saturday Evening Post—and the proliferation of thousands of little special interest magazines hyper-targeted to specific audiences.

5 Right after that came cable television. Instead of three channels (ABC, CBS, and NBC) dividing up a big, diversified national audience, cable TV came along and targeted narrow niche audiences. Instead of spending big money to reach a mass audience, advertisers could spend less money and reach the narrow demographics they were really seeking. The ad money moved away from the big networks, and the emphasis for news companies changed. News became just another commodity.

How did cable TV change news?

6 Cable television's new 24-hour news cycle brought major changes. It meant newsrooms didn't have longer periods of time to prepare content, check it, edit it, vet it, and then present it to audiences. Reporters were pressured to go straight to air with current events and any new information that was presented to them. That began to result in rushed and incomplete reports, inaccuracy, distortion, and misleading material.

7 If you believe the polls, there's now a real lack of trust in the media among the public. Some polls show that more than half of Americans don't trust the media to tell them the truth. But this distrust isn't something that only began in the last election cycle. This trust has been eroding slowly and steadily for 30 or 40 years. And it is going to take a long time to build up again.

How does target marketing change what we see online?

8 As a product of these targeted audiences, silos emerged. Silos create echo chambers, which characterized developments on television even before the web began to have a big impact. As the web opened access to the internet for a large number of people beginning in the late 1990s, it accelerated these echo chambers.

9 Everything about the way the web works—and the algorithms that track the patterns of your internet activity—reinforces the idea that there's a feedback loop that constantly redirects us toward what we're already interested in. It's a natural human quality to want your already-held opinions and perceptions

precipitously: dramatically

Scaffolding the Text-Dependent Questions

2. According to the article, what were some of the factors that contributed to the quality of network news in the middle of the 20th century? Use the headings and the transitions between paragraphs as a guide to how the author has organized information in this article. RI.11–12.2, RI.11–12.3

3. How does the author characterize the quality of television news in the 1980s and 1990s? Use details from the text to paraphrase the description of news media during this period. Use the text marking clues you used for the As You Read step to help find relevant details from the text to help you respond. RI.11–12.1, RI.11–12.6

about the world reinforced. The web specifically caters to that tendency. It creates patterns in which we only tend to look at—or even get access to—information that confirms our already-held positions.

10   And all of that matches up beautifully with the niche marketing and target marketing that's been going on for 50 years. What better information could advertisers get about your tendencies, tastes, interests, hobbies, and consumption patterns than what you're doing on the web? This tells advertisers almost perfectly what they want to know about you, and it solidifies the silos that are already in place. This has gotten worse as more and more people are on the web, more and more of the time. And it means that the traditional media continue to lose ad dollars...

What has that meant for newspapers?

11   In the early 2000s, newspapers weren't experiencing a significant readership dropoff yet, but they were starting to lose advertising money. Before the rise of the web, if you lived in Minneapolis and you were looking for a used car, you'd go to the Star Tribune classifieds section, the paper's single biggest revenue source prior to the 2000s. When the web became more accessible, sites like Craigslist or Cars.com were more efficient resources. Who would still pore over the classifieds when you could just do a quick search online?

12   That was the first really serious blow to the traditional news media. When their ad and classified revenues dropped, the only **recourse** in their view at the time was to cut costs. By 2005–06, this was leading to massive layoffs in the newsroom. The newspapers became smaller, with fewer printed pages and less content. And then, not surprisingly, people weren't as interested in subscribing. A death spiral for newspapers began to develop.

Did moving news online work?

13   When people tried to move newspapers to the web, they found out immediately that the print advertising mostly did not follow them online. As the newspapers were spiraling down, there simply was not the same number of reporters and editors doing serious journalism. There were blogs on the web, where lots of people were writing opinionated commentary, and aggregation sites that were recycling existing stories from other publications. But the amount of original reporting nationwide began to diminish tremendously. Reliable quality news reporting, as opposed to content re-purposing and commentary, was no longer being supported in the same way by commercial, ad-supported news media institutions.

14   Because of this, there's no longer a model that most citizens in our country share for standards that news should meet. We're getting more and more of our news online, and more and more of that news—in Facebook feeds and web browsing—is suspect in terms of its status as news. When someone on Facebook sends me a story, the first thing I do is see where it's from. If it's from someplace I've never heard of, then red flags go up for me right away, and I check to see what that organization is. But most people do not have a working frame of reference for distinguishing different types of news sources.

GRAMMAR & USAGE

Notice the following sentence from the section "Did moving news online work?":

> "As the newspapers were spiraling down, there simply was not the same number of reporters and editors doing serious journalism."

On first reading, it may seem like Griffin's use of the verb "was" does not agree with the subject of the sentence. But the sentence's subject is "number," not "reporters and editors," so the subject and verb actually agree because they are both singular. It's also helpful to remember when reading and writing that a prepositional phrase such as "of reporters and editors" will never contain the subject of a sentence, nor does it affect whether the actual subject is singular or plural.

As you write, be sure to reread your drafts with an eye toward subject/verb agreement—and don't be thrown off by prepositional phrases that come in between the subject and the verb. If a sentence sounds odd, try rewriting it to make the relationship between the subject and verb more evident.

---

recourse: option.

---

6 **Vocabulary Development:** Pause after paragraph 12 to read the Word Connections box. Select a few compelling terms from the text, such as *death spiral*, and ask students about the author's possible intent for using them. Elicit other words that the author could have used.

7 Direct students to read the Grammar & Usage box. Answer any questions they have about subject-verb agreement. Make sure students understand that the object of a preposition is never the subject.

Scaffolding the Text-Dependent Questions

4. What effects did the changes to television news and the move toward online news have on newspapers? Considering the decline in newspaper classified advertising, what inferences can you make about the changes in the quality of newspapers from the early 2000s to today? RI.11–12.2, RI.11–12.3

5. What is the effect of the organizational method used in Griffin's article? Taking a close look at the headings and other transitional devices, how would you summarize the progression of events in this article? RI.11–12.5

6. What is the effect of the author's use of rhetorical questions in his article? What do all the headings in this article have in common? Why do you think the author chose to write the headings in this way? Where else does he use sentences of this type? RI.11–12.6

8 After students finish reading the article, address the Making Observations questions in a whole-class discussion.

9 To formatively assess student comprehension, introduce the Focus on the Sentence task. If needed, review the definition of subordinating conjunctions and model the task using another sentence starter.

4.2

WORD CONNECTIONS

Etymology

Michael Griffin says that newspapers experienced a "**death spiral**" when online classified ads became a threat to print newspaper profits. The term *death spiral* originated in the early 20th century in aeronautical literature to describe the habit of early airplanes to slip into dangerous, downward spins that were difficult to recover from. Figure skaters named a challenging pairs maneuver "the death spiral" in the late 1920s before the term eventually made its way into business parlance to describe a swift and financially destructive sequence of events.

My Notes

prominence: importance

How is online news different from traditional news?

15 There's not very much new original reporting on the web anymore, unless you go to the traditional news sites that are still run by traditional, respectable newspapers. We have fewer paid reporters than we did 15 years ago, and you're not going to get the same kind of coverage if you have vastly fewer people doing the work. But websites still have to fill up their spaces with content—so what do they fill it up with if they don't have verifiable original reporting? You see a decrease in actual news and an increase in opinion, commentary, and blogging, not to mention the vast quantities of frivolous entertainment-oriented content and click-bait.

16 In the online environment where information comes as a steady linear stream, where it's not divided up with a front page, an opinion page, and different specialized news sections (that prioritize news information according to **prominence**, urgency, civic importance, or local, national, and international orientation), it's all just mixed together. It's a relatively undifferentiated wash of stories and information. As a result, more and more young people don't have a clear notion of the distinction between something that's a news article and something that's just an opinion piece. It's all just "the next thing on the page" because they've grown up being online.

Making Observations
- What reactions do you have to this article?
- What ideas from the article stand out to you?
- What questions do you have after reading the article for the first time?

☑ Focus on the Sentence

Use information from the article to write two sentences starting with subordinating conjunctions.

Before the rise of the web, newspapers could depend on advertising money to support the development of content.

After the shift online, the amount of original reporting diminished and content re-purposing, commentary, and blogging increased.

Scaffolding the Text-Dependent Questions

7. What is the author's purpose? What is he trying to achieve by writing this article? What are some details you learned about the early days of television news from this article? How does the history and background provided by the author help you understand the points he makes in the article's final section? RI.11–12.6

Returning to the Text

- Return to the article as you respond to the following questions. Use textual evidence to support your responses.
- Write any additional questions you have about the article in your Reader/Writer Notebook.

2. According to the article, what were some of the factors that contributed to the quality of network news in the middle of the 20th century?

At the time, providing news was considered a public service, so network news divisions

were not expected to turn a profit. In fact, networks invested in hiring high-quality reporters,

such as Edward Murrow, and opened and operated foreign news bureaus to keep Americans

informed about events around the world.

3. How does the author characterize the quality of television news in the 1980s and 1990s? Use details from the text to paraphrase the description of news media during this period.

The quality of the news was in decline. The companies that bought up networks expected

news divisions to be profitable. To achieve this, networks cut costs in areas like "foreign

bureaus, documentary division, and enormous numbers of people in the newsroom." As a

result, the standards for quality news declined.

4. What effects did the changes to television news and the move toward online news in the middle of the 20th century have on newspapers?

At first, there was not a major impact on newspaper readership. But advertising began to move

online. For instance, classified ads for cars moved to easily accessible sites like Cars.com. As

newspapers lost ad dollars, they had to cut costs. This reduced the amount and the quality of

reporting they could provide.

10 **RETURNING TO THE TEXT:** Guide students to respond to the text-dependent questions in small groups. Encourage them to use some quotations from the article to support their responses.

11 Move from group to group and listen in as students answer the text-dependent questions. If they have difficulty, scaffold the questions by rephrasing them or breaking them down into smaller parts. See the Scaffolding the Text-Dependent Questions for suggestions.

12 Direct students to complete the Working from the Text tasks. Instruct them that their answers and observations will help them complete the writing prompt.

LEVELED DIFFERENTIATED INSTRUCTION

In this activity, students might need support with prewriting before they respond to the writing prompt.

Developing Group students, and have them focus on the historical critical perspective. Have them complete the **Conclusion Builder** graphic organizer as prewriting support, discussing and recording how important historical events transformed the news industry. Provide transition words, such as *and*, *but*, *so*, and *or*, to help with cohesion.

Expanding Group students and have them use the **Conclusion Builder** graphic organizer to record evidence that shows how the development they have chosen affected the news industry. Provide transitions, such as *because*, *moreover*, *however*, and *therefore*, to help create cohesion.

Bridging Allow students to work collaboratively to complete the **Conclusion Builder** graphic organizer as prewriting support. Encourage them to first record evidence for their chosen development and then allow that evidence to inform their thesis statements.

4.2

5. **What is the effect of the organizational structure used in Griffin's article?**

Griffin uses chronological order to logically outline the shifts in media consumption. He also uses headings to structure each section of the article. The questions at the beginning of each section emphasize the message the author is trying to send to the reader.

6. **What is the effect of the author's use of rhetorical questions in his article?**

Griffin poses a rhetorical question in paragraph 10 to remind readers of the serious impact of advertising agencies knowing about them. In paragraph 15, the author emphasizes the overall effect of the changes in the media by asking his readers how websites will fill up empty space.

7. **What is the author's purpose? What is he trying to achieve by writing this article?**

Griffin wants to illustrate the history of the media industry from the middle of the 20th century to today and how changes in media have affected the way people consume information. He provides this history to give his audience the background to compare the news industry of then and now.

Working from the Text

8. Consider this sentence from the last paragraph of the article:

> "As a result, more and more young people don't have a clear notion of the distinction between something that's a news article and something that's just an opinion piece."

Do you agree or disagree with the author's claim? With a partner, share your opinion, making sure to support it with examples from your personal experience that either refute or back up the ideas in the article.

9. Use the guiding questions to analyze Griffin's article through three different critical lenses (cultural, historical, and Marxist). Skim the article again and focus on gathering claims and evidence that fit each lens.

Guiding Question 1: What do changes in media coverage reveal about changing cultural perspectives of the news?

Guiding Question 2: How have historical developments influenced the role of news in America?

Guiding Question 3: How have economic or market factors affected news coverage in America?

10. In a group, share your observations based on one of the three lenses you used to analyze the text. Then write a concise thesis statement in your Reader/Writer Notebook that explains the change in how news is delivered and consumed, interpreted through one specific lens.

11. Read the following quotations. Use three colors to highlight the quotations by type: cultural, historical, Marxist. Then, in the second column on the left, rank the quotes within each color category based on their potential usefulness as evidence. Which would best serve as evidence to support your interpretive take on "How the Media Has Changed"? Why?

Quotes	Lens	Reasoning
In the middle of the 20th century, television network leadership believed that providing news was a public service. News wasn't expected to make money for national broadcasters.	H and M	
Whenever a big entertainment company or conglomerate came in, the news divisions had to answer to shareholders and improve the bottom line. For the first time, there was an expectation that the news divisions had to make money, just like the entertainment divisions.	H and M	
Right after that came cable television. Instead of three channels (ABC, CBS, and NBC) dividing up a big, diversified national audience, cable TV came along and targeted narrow niche audiences.	H and C	
If you believe the polls, there's now a real lack of trust in the media among the public. Some polls show that more than half of Americans don't trust the media to tell them the truth.	C	
Everything about the way the web works—and the algorithms that track the patterns of your internet activity—reinforces the idea that there's a feedback loop that constantly redirects us toward what we're already interested in.	C	
In the early 2000s, newspapers weren't experiencing a significant readership dropoff yet, but they were starting to lose advertising money.	C and H	
When their ad and classified revenues dropped, the only recourse in their view at the time was to cut costs. By 2005–06, this was leading to massive layoffs in the newsroom.	M, C and H	
… there's no longer a model that most citizens in our country share for standards that news should meet.	C	
As a result, more and more young people don't have a clear notion of the distinction between something that's a news article and something that's just an opinion piece.	C	

13 Have some students share their responses to the graphic organizer. Remind students that they can also use other quotations from the article to support ideas in their responses to the writing prompt.

4.2

14 Read the Language & Writer's Craft with the class. Consider displaying two or three additional quotes and asking students to paraphrase each. Have students share their practice responses with the class.

15 Lead the class in a brief discussion of the Check Your Understanding prompt, recording answers on chart paper. Display these answers during the remainder of the unit as a reference for the established criteria.

16 Give students an opportunity to demonstrate what they have learned about the transformation of the news industry by having them complete the writing prompt.

TEACHER TO TEACHER

For homework, students might complete their response to the writing prompt or revise it to use stronger supporting evidence. To encourage students to cite evidence from the text, you might provide copies of the article for them to take home.

ASSESS

Review the criteria students listed in response to the Check Your Understanding. Students should identify criteria for selecting textual evidence.

Review students' responses to the writing prompt. Responses should clearly employ one of the critical perspectives and identify a single development as the most significant driver of changes in the news industry. Students should support their ideas with cited evidence and interpretive statements. Some of that cited evidence should be in the form of relevant and properly cited quotations.

ADAPT

If students need additional help identifying how to paraphrase or use quotations from a source, model doing so with an example.

If students need additional help supporting their ideas with properly cited evidence and interpretive statements, select one quote from the previous page with which to model the process.

My Notes

LANGUAGE & WRITER'S CRAFT: Citing Quotations

Documentaries, research papers, and other kinds of nonfiction often incorporate direct quotations to provide specifics about the topic. Direct quotations use a speaker's or writer's exact words, enclosed in quotation marks:

Example: The author explains, "[The 24-hour news cycle] meant newsrooms didn't have longer periods of time to prepare content, check it, edit it, vet it, and then present it to audiences."

Notice the term in brackets. When quoting a sentence with a pronoun that would be unclear to readers without context, you may replace the pronoun with its antecedent, and use brackets to indicate this small change to the original text. While this approach is acceptable, it should not be used very often.

Writers can also paraphrase speakers, citing sources while making the words their own:

Example: The author explains that newsrooms needed to produce content much more quickly, and with looser editorial standards, to keep up with the pace of the 24-hour news cycle.

Adding quotations to your writing is a great way to add color and alternate voices to make your writing more compelling and persuasive. They also help make nonfiction writing seem more authentic and less filtered through an author's voice.

PRACTICE Add support to your thesis statement from the previous page by citing one quotation and one paraphrase from the article.

☑ Check Your Understanding

What are some criteria for selecting quotations to support an interpretive claim?

📝 Writing Prompt: Argumentative

Use one of the critical perspectives to argue which of the following developments was most instrumental in catalyzing the changes in the news industry since the middle of the 20th century: conglomerates buying out media companies, the rise of cable news, the increase of target marketing, the decline of newspapers, or the rise of the internet as a news source. Develop the topic thoroughly by selecting the most significant and relevant examples from the text and citing them properly. Be sure to:

- Include a clear arguable thesis statement.
- Smoothly incorporate quotations and paraphrased details from the article to support your ideas.
- Create cohesion by using an appropriate organizational structure and transitions.
- Write a conclusion that follows from your arguments and evidence.

📝 WRITING PROMPT: ARGUMENTATIVE

The following standards are addressed in the writing prompt:

- RI.11–12.1
- W.11–12.1a
- W.11–12.1c
- W.11–12.1d
- W.11–12.1e

Constructing Public Opinion

Learning Targets

- Evaluate and critique two texts that present competing arguments.
- Form an argument and communicate your claim and supporting evidence effectively in a debate.
- Address a counterclaim in your argumentative writing.
- Integrate ideas from multiple texts to build knowledge and vocabulary about perspective and media.

Preview

In this activity, you will read and analyze two texts that present different perspectives on the root cause of media bias. Then you will present your own perspective in classroom debate and complete a written response.

Learning Strategies

Debate
Graphic Organizer
Marking the Text
Quickwrite
Think-Pair-Share

Media Study

1. Working with a partner, write definitions for the following terms in relation to media study in your Reader/Writer Notebook. Leave space to add to or revise your definitions later. Consult references—either print or online—to clarify and validate your understanding, and then find or write a sentence that uses the term in what you believe to be the proper context.

Term	Definition
Target Audience	
Objectivity	
Perspective	
Agenda	
Bias	

Quickwrite: Keeping your definitions in mind, to what extent do you think media coverage shapes and influences our perception of issues and events?

My Notes

ACTIVITY 4.3

PLAN

Materials: four-corners signs ("Strongly Agree," "Agree," "Disagree," "Strongly Disagree")
Suggested Pacing: 2 50-minute class periods

TEACH

1 Read aloud the Learning Targets and Preview. You may want to lead a whole-class discussion in which students discuss their experience with **debates**.

2 Ask students to complete the **graphic organizer**, using their background knowledge or reference materials readily available in your classroom to generate initial definitions of the terms in the chart. You might discuss these terms to assess students' familiarity with them.

3 Have students complete the **Quickwrite** individually before discussing their answers in a small group.

College and Career Readiness Standards

Focus Standards:

RI.11–12.3 Analyze a complex set of ideas or sequence of events and explain how specific individuals, ideas, or events interact and develop over the course of the text.

SL.11–12.4 Present information, findings, and supporting evidence, conveying a clear

and distinct perspective, such that listeners can follow the line of reasoning, alternative or opposing perspectives are addressed, and the organization, development, substance, and style are appropriate to purpose, audience, and a range of formal and informal tasks.

4 Introduce the Opening Writing Prompt by reading it aloud to students. Before students respond to the question, ask them how the article's introduction is different from other nonfiction articles they have read, including the one from the previous activity.

5 Read the As You Read section with your students. Help them understand the instructions for annotation. Explain that they will complete the first reading of both texts before rereading them to answer text-dependent questions.

TEACHER TO TEACHER

It will be important for students to ably summarize each article and identify the perspective of the author. If you think students would benefit from it, consider using SOAPSTone as a strategy to analyze each article.

6 Read the About the Author section with students. Ask students to consider how an advanced degree in psychology might influence the writing of a journalist such as Konnikova.

4.3

My Notes

Opening Writing Prompt

Read the first few sentences of the article "How Headlines Change the Way We Think," and answer the following question in a quickwrite.

How Headlines Change the Way We Think

"Why Headlines Matter." "Misleading Headlines Can Lead You Astray." "How What You Read Affects What You See." "How Bad Headlines Make Bad Memories." "Eleven Reasons Headlines Are Important." "You'll Never Believe How Important an Accurate Headline Is."

Those are all possible titles for this piece that I discussed with my editor. And, actually, the one that we picked may be the most important part of this article.

Why do you think the Konnikova suggests that the headline might be the most important part of her article? What purpose do headlines serve in an informational text?

As You Read

- Put a star next to each specific example of a headline used to support the author's thesis.
- Circle unknown words and phrases. Try to determine the meaning of the words by using context clues, word parts, or a dictionary.

About the Author

Maria Konnikova (b. 1984) is an author and journalist whose work has appeared in publications including *The Smithsonian*, *The Atlantic*, and *The New Yorker*, where she is a contributing writer. Following graduation from Harvard University, she went on to Columbia University to earn her Ph.D. in psychology in 2013. Konnikova's first book, *Mastermind: How to Think Like Sherlock Holmes*, is a New York Times bestseller and has been translated into 17 languages.

College and Career Readiness Standards

W.11–12.1b Develop claim(s) and counterclaims fairly and thoroughly, supplying the most relevant evidence for each while pointing out the strengths and limitations of both in a manner that anticipates the audience's knowledge level, concerns, values, and possible biases.

W.11–12.9 Draw evidence from literary or informational texts to support analysis, reflection, and research.

Additional Standards Addressed:

RI.11–12.1, RI.11–12.2, RI.11–12.4, RI.11–12.5, RI.11–12.6, L.11–12.1b, L.11–12.2, L.11–12.3a, L.11–12.4d, L.11–12.5a, W.11–12.1a, W.11–12.1e

Article

How Headlines Change the Way We Think

by **Maria Konnikova**
December 17, 2014

1 "Why Headlines Matter." "Misleading Headlines Can Lead You Astray." "How What You Read Affects What You See." "How Bad Headlines Make Bad Memories." "Eleven Reasons Headlines Are Important." "You'll Never Believe How Important an Accurate Headline Is."

2 Those are all possible titles for this piece that I discussed with my editor. And, actually, the one that we picked may be the most important part of this article. By now, everyone knows that a headline determines how many people will read a piece, particularly in this era of social media. But, more interesting, a headline changes the way people read an article and the way they remember it. The headline frames the rest of the experience. A headline can tell you what kind of article you're about to read—news, opinion, research, LOLcats—and it sets the tone for what follows.

3 Psychologists have long known that first impressions really do matter—what we see, hear, feel, or experience in our first encounter with something colors how we process the rest of it. Articles are no exception. And just as people can manage the impression that they make through their choice of attire, so, too, can the crafting of the headline subtly shift the perception of the text that follows. By drawing attention to certain details or facts, a headline can affect what existing knowledge is activated in your head. By its choice of phrasing, a headline can influence your mindset as you read so that you later recall details that coincide with what you were expecting. For instance, the headline of this article I wrote—"A Gene That Makes You Need Less Sleep?"—is not inaccurate in any way. But it does likely prompt a focus on one specific part of the piece. If I had instead called it "Why We Need Eight Hours of Sleep," people would remember it differently.

4 As a result of these shifts in perception, problems arise when a headline is ever so slightly misleading. "Air pollution now leading cause of lung cancer," ran a headline last year in the U.K. paper Daily Express. The article, however, said no such thing, or, rather, not exactly. Instead, it reported that pollution was a leading "environmental" cause; other causes, like smoking, are still the main culprits. It is easy to understand a decision to run that sort of opening. Caveats don't fit in single columns, and, once people are intrigued enough to read the story, they'll get to the nuances just the same. But, as it turns out, reading the piece may not be enough to correct the headline's misdirection.

KNOWLEDGE QUEST

Knowledge Question:

How does the media shape our view of the world, or how does our view shape our perception of the media?

In Activity 4.3 you will read two articles about how we frame the media and how the media frames us. As you read and build knowledge about the topic, think about your answer to the Knowledge Question.

Headlines quickly grab readers' attention and help steer them from story to story.

ACTIVITY 4.3 continued

7 Direct students to the Knowledge Question. Ask students if they think personal experience or the media itself has more influence on how we interpret the news. Lead the class in a brief discussion about bias and how it can exist in both readers and journalists. Then have small groups discuss responses to the Knowledge Question.

8 **FIRST READ:** You may want to lead the class in guided reading of the first few paragraphs of this article. Model strategies for **marking the text** and finding information to guide a SOAPSTone analysis. After modeling through guided reading, select the reading strategy that is the best fit for students in your class.

⚠ TEXT COMPLEXITY

Overall: Complex
Lexile: 1000L
Qualitative: Moderate Difficulty
Task: Challenging (Evaluate)

9 Monitor students' progress as they read. Be sure they are engaged with the text. Students should be marking the headlines the author uses to support her thesis as well as circling unknown words and phrases. Evaluate whether the selected reading mode is effective.

10 Point out that the author relies heavily on an academic study for evidence. Ask students to explain how the author's reliance on study results impacts her persuasiveness.

Scaffolding the Text-Dependent Questions

2. Is the use of short sentences, in the form of a list of rejected titles for the article, effective in the opening paragraph? Why might the author have opened her article this way? Reread the first two paragraphs of this article after reading the Grammar & Usage sidebar about sentence variety. What can you conclude about why the author opens the article in this way? RI.11–12.5

3. According to Konnikova's arguments, how does the headline frame the rest of the reader's experience? Cite details from the text to support your answer. Reread paragraphs 2–3. Why does the author relate headlines to first impressions? How does she support that analogy? RI.11–12.1, RI.11–12.5

11 Remind students to attend to the Grammar & Usage box on sentence variety when they return to the text for the second reading. Consider extending this lesson by having students adopt this approach in their writing prompt response. Ask them to include an introductory paragraph with a series of short sentences before introducing their thesis formally in the second paragraph. Explain that the two paragraphs together would actually serve as an introduction to a longer paper/article/essay. Organize students in small groups to share their paragraphs and sentences. Lead a whole-class discussion about the effectiveness of this writing strategy. Make sure students understand that such a strategy is only effective when used infrequently.

4.3

GRAMMAR & USAGE

Sentence Variety

Varying the length and syntax of your sentences helps maintain the interest of your readers. Too many long sentences can wear your reader out, and too many short sentences can feel dull.

However, you can use a series of short sentences to grab the readers' attention. Notice how short the eighth paragraph of this article is compared to all the other paragraphs. It contains only two sentences that slow the reader down and help focus attention on the information that the writer is presenting.

As you write, think about how you can vary the length of your sentences to create variety, power, and emphasis.

My Notes

_____

_____

_____

_____

_____

_____

_____

_____

_____

_____

anomalous: unusual

5 It's these sorts of misleading maneuvers that Ullrich Ecker, a psychologist and cognitive neuroscientist at the University of Western Australia, was pondering when he decided to test how slight—and slightly misleading—shifts in headlines can affect reading. In Ecker's prior work, he had looked at explicit misinformation: when information that's biased influences you, no matter what you're subsequently told. This time around, he wanted to see how nuance and slight misdirection would work.

6 In a series of studies, out this month in the Journal of Experimental Psychology: Applied, Ecker had people in Australia read either factual or opinion pieces, where the only shifting variable was the headline. (He had his subjects read a total of four articles—two factual, two opinion.) One factual article, for instance, talked about a change in burglary rates over the last year—a rise of 0.2 percent—that ran counter to a ten percent decline over the past decade. The slight rise, the article pointed out, was an anomalous side note; the longer trend was what was important. The accompanying headline highlighted either the smaller or the larger of the two trends: "Number of burglaries going up" and "Downward trend in burglary rate," respectively. The opinion pieces pitted the thoughts of an expert against those of a layperson—for instance, one piece contrasted a citizen's concerns about the safety of genetically modified food with the opinion of a scientist from the fictional company Organic Food Science Australia. The headline focused on one of the two sides. In this case, it read either "GM foods may pose long-term health risks" or "GM foods are safe." Each participant read all four articles.

7 Ecker's goal was to test whether the degree of the slant would matter. With the factual piece, the misdirection was obvious—the entire piece was about a broader trend, with one tiny deviation. In the opinion piece, it was much more subtle. The article was, first of all, opinion, and each voice was given its own space; it was up to the reader to judge how the opinions should be considered.

8 After reading each article, the University of Western Australia students rated it on five different scales, to gauge things like interest and ease of reading. Once a student had read the complete set of pieces, she was given a surprise six-question quiz, with questions concerning both recollection and inference.

9 The headline, it turns out, had done more than simply reframe the article. In the case of the factual articles, a misleading headline hurt a reader's ability to recall the article's details. That is, the parts that were in line with the headline, such as a declining burglary rate, were easier to remember than the opposing, non-headlined trend. Inferences, however, remained sound: the misdirection was blatant enough that readers were aware of it and proceeded to correct their impressions accordingly. According to the study, "No matter which headline they saw, they predicted that, next year, the crime rate would go down."

10 In the case of opinion articles, however, a misleading headline, like the one suggesting that genetically modified foods are dangerous, impaired a reader's ability to make accurate inferences. For instance, when asked to predict

Scaffolding the Text-Dependent Questions

4. What does Konnikova mean by the phrase "Caveats don't fit in single columns"? Consult a dictionary to find the definition for *caveat*. In this article, how do you think the word applies to headlines and headline writing? RI.11–12.4

5. According to the article, why was the misdirection in the headline easier to detect for the factual pieces used in the Ullrich Ecker study than in the opinion pieces? How would you summarize the differences between most fact-based articles and opinion-based articles? Skim paragraphs 9–10. What characteristics of an opinion-based article might impair readers' ability to make accurate inferences about it? RI.11–12.2

the future public-health costs of genetically modified foods, people who had read the misleading headline predicted a far greater cost than the evidence had warranted.

11 Ecker and his colleagues then replicated the results in a second study—this time, the discrepancies were between the headline and the image, rather than between the headline and the text. ...

12 For conscientious readers and editors, Ecker's findings across the two studies give cause for concern. First, misinformation appears to cause more damage when it's subtle than when it's blatant. We see through the latter and correct for it as we go. The former is much more insidious and persistent. It is also, unfortunately, much more likely to be the result of sloppiness or inconsideration rather than a deliberate effort to lead readers astray. Take this article from the Times in May. "Selling a Fake Painting Takes More Than a Good Artist," reads the headline. Alongside it: a photograph of a gallery owner who is not actually one of the culprits. A criminal implication is paired with a photograph, and the photograph may **inadvertently** be tainted as well.

13 Here's the other thing: almost every journalist has experienced the aggravation of having readers give aggrieved, enraged, dismissive, or, really, any other type of negative reaction to an article based solely on a headline. "Read the article!" the writer often wants to scream...What Ecker's work shows, though, is that with the right—or, rather, wrong—headline, reading the article may not be enough. Even well-intentioned readers who do go on to read the entire piece may still be reacting in part to that initial formulation.

14 If I had titled this column "Why Headlines Matter," I would be picking the broadest possible option. Next week, you might be able to remember that headlines are important but not be able to tell your friend exactly why. If I had called it "Misleading Headlines Can Lead You Astray," you might have forgotten the details of the study showing that we can actually overcome factually misleading headlines. "Eleven Reasons Headlines Matter"? More people might have clicked, but they might not have retained the information. It's not always easy to be both interesting and accurate, but, as Ecker's study shows, it's better than being exciting and wrong.

⌀ Knowledge Quest

- What is the author's main idea in this article?
- Which details from Ullrich Ecker's study stand out to you the most?
- What is your immediate impression about whether or not headlines can affect how you think?

GRAMMAR & USAGE

Integrating Quotations
Notice how Konnikova integrates quoted headlines and other quoted material in a variety of ways by varying the placement of the quoted portion in sentences:

For instance, the headline of this article I wrote—"A Gene That Makes You Need Less Sleep?"—is not inaccurate in any way. But it does likely prompt a focus on one specific part of the piece. If I had instead called it "Why We Need Eight Hours of Sleep," people would remember it differently.

"Read the article!" the writer often wants to scream...

According to the study, "No matter which headline they saw, they predicted that, next year, the crime rate would go down."

Varying the ways quotations are integrated keeps the writing from being dull or repetitive. Highlight each integrated quote on this page, and discuss how this variety in syntax affects the flow of the writing.

---

inadvertently: accidentally

ACTIVITY 4.3 continued

12 As students prepare to reread the text, point out the Grammar & Usage feature on integrating quotations. Prompt students to find additional examples of varied syntax in sentences with quotations.

13 Have students answer the Knowledge Quest questions for the Konnikova article.

Scaffolding the Text-Dependent Questions

6. What is the author's purpose for including the Ecker study in this article? Reread paragraphs 3–4. How does the information on Ullrich Ecker's study connect to the examples the author provides in the third and fourth paragraph of the article? RI.11–12.5, RI.11–12.6

7. What is Konnikova's purpose for repeating the rejected titles for her article that she used at the beginning of the article in her conclusion? Reread the first two paragraphs. Based on the article's final paragraph, do you think the author and her editor chose the right headline for the piece? Taken together, what effect do the article's first few paragraphs and final paragraph have on you as a reader? RI.11–12.5, RI.11–12.6

14 Read aloud the About the Author section on Matthew C. Nisbet and remind students to continue using the SOAPSTone strategy as they read the second article.

15 Review the Knowledge Question with students. Remind them to think about their answer to the Knowledge Question as they read and build knowledge about the topic.

16 **FIRST READ:** As students begin the second text, remind them to continue annotating unknown words and phrases. Based on observations you made during the reading of the first text, you may decide to change the reading mode for the second text.

 TEXT COMPLEXITY

Overall: Very Complex
Lexile: 1660L
Qualitative: High Difficulty
Task: Challenging (Evaluate)

17 Remind students to read the footnote and the definitions of glossed vocabulary to support their comprehension.

18 Review the concept of paradox — a statement that appears to contain two contradictory or incompatible points, but upon closer examination can reveal a hidden truth.

 TEACHER TO TEACHER

If your class includes English learners, consider using a cognate bridge. Add to the class word wall cognates that relate to *paradox* to create a bridge between English vocabulary terms and their cognates in other languages. Spanish cognates include *paradoja* and *paradójico*.

4.3

My Notes

KNOWLEDGE QUEST

Knowledge Question:
How does the media shape our view of the world, or how does our view shape our perception of the media?

emanated: originated

As You Read

- Underline the claim and star examples that the writer uses throughout the article.
- Circle unknown words and phrases. Try to determine the meaning of the words by using context clues, word parts, or a dictionary.

About the Author

Matthew C. Nisbet is a professor of communication studies at Northeastern University and serves as editor-in-chief of the journal *Environmental Communication* and senior editor of *ORE Climate Science*. Nisbet studies and writes about the role of communication, journalism, and advocacy in shaping discourse and debates over meaningful policy issues including climate change and income inequity.

Article

Why Partisans View Mainstream Media as Biased and Ideological Media as Objective

by **Matthew C. Nisbet**
July 21, 2011

1   We've reached a unique paradox in American political culture today: Both liberals and conservatives view the mainstream media as biased, yet tend to believe that their own ideologically-like minded outlets and commentators provide objective coverage. Claims of media bias have long been the lingua franca[1] of the conservative movement with the creation of rival outlets first in the form of magazines such as the *National Review*, then political talk radio, and culminating with Fox News and right-wing blogs.

2   Yet over the past decade, harsh criticism of the mainstream media has also increasingly emanated from the left with claims of biased coverage a fundamental core belief of progressive advocates working on issues ranging from climate change to social policy. In turn these same progressives tend to prefer the "objective" coverage at magazines like the *Nation*, blogging platforms

---

[1] A *lingua franca* is a common language used between people who speak different native languages.

Scaffolding the Text-Dependent Questions

8. Konnikova writes, "It's not always easy to be both interesting and accurate, but, as Ecker's study shows, it's better than being exciting and wrong." Apply this to what the article is trying to say about headlines. Consider what types of headlines grab your attention, especially online. Do you agree with the author's final sentence? Why or why not? RI.11–12.3

9. What is the difference between "mainstream" and "ideological" media? Why is their difference a paradox? Reread the first two paragraphs. Use the information in the article to write a working definition for mainstream media and ideological media. According to Nisbet, what are the defining differences between them? L.11–12.5a, RI.11–12.2, RI.11–12.4

like the *Huffington Post*, and most prominently MSNBC which has positioned itself as the liberal counter-weight to Fox News.

3   Research in the field of communication has tracked the psychological under-pinning of this societal trend, explaining why partisans view mainstream coverage as biased but perceive their preferred ideological outlets as fair and balanced. In a recently published book chapter on the social psychology of political communication, my colleague Lauren Feldman and I review and explain this research, drawing in part on Feldman's own work in the area.

4   Here is an excerpt on media bias, from that chapter.

5   Across national settings, there is an ever **pervasive** belief in various forms of media bias. In the U.S., over the past two decades, the dominant belief regarding media bias is that the mainstream news media favor liberal causes and political candidates. Yet, when researchers conduct content analyses to search for systematic patterns of partisan bias in coverage of elections, across studies they are unable to find definitive evidence (D'Alessio D. & Allen, 2000). If social scientists using the best tools available to them find it difficult to observe hard evidence of liberal bias, why are beliefs among the public so widespread? Moreover, across country settings and issues, what explains the difference between subjective perceptions of media bias and objective indicators relative to coverage?

6   In research on perceptions of the news media, credibility is understood as a subjective assessment, influenced by the partisan or ideological background of the audience and the claims about bias that might emanate from trusted sources such as political commentators or like-minded friends. In the U.S. context, these claims are typically focused on a liberal bias charged by conservative elites and reinforce a widespread belief among conservative-leaning audiences (Watts, Domke, Shah, & Fan, 1999). Audiences, then, do not typically assess story content on its own merits but rather on the basis of preconceived notions about the news media—often stemming from journalists' tendency in many stories to cover and reflect on their own potential liberal bias. A number of other studies have also suggested that individuals' expectations for bias in a news source or in the media, more generally, are likely to influence their perceptions of bias in news coverage (Arpan & Raney, 2003; Baum & Gussin, 2007).

7   Perhaps the most crucial determinant of perceptions of bias in the news, however, is the extent to which news coverage is seen as disagreeing with one's own views. Individuals who feel most strongly about an issue tend to see their own side's views as being more a product of objective analysis and **normative** concerns, and less influenced by ideology, than the other side's views (Robinson, Keltner, Ward, & Ross, 1995). This human tendency translates directly to judgments about the media. In a range of studies, when news

My Notes

_____

_____

_____

_____

_____

_____

_____

_____

_____

_____

_____

_____

_____

_____

_____

_____

_____

_____

_____

_____

_____

_____

_____

_____

_____

pervasive: widespread
normative: standard-setting

LEVELED DIFFERENTIATED INSTRUCTION

In this activity, students might need support developing their understanding of the authors' claims and reasons.

Developing   After the first reading, group students and assign them one of the two articles. Have them complete the **Idea and Argument Evaluator** graphic organizer to record their understanding of the author's claim and evidence. Regroup students and have them share their findings. Students can then collaborate on answering the text-dependent questions.

Expanding   After the first reading, pair students and assign each pair one article. Have partners work together to complete the **Idea and Argument Evaluator** graphic organizer. Then group pairs together to share their organizers and allow them to collaborate on answering the text-dependent questions.

Bridging   Provide student partners with the **Idea and Argument Evaluator** graphic organizer to complete for each article after the first reading. Circulate to provide guidance and feedback as partners solidify their understanding of the author's claim and evidence. Then have students answer the text-dependent questions individually.

Extend   Have students work with their partners to write three or four alternate headlines for Nisbet's article. Encourage them to apply what they may have learned about headline writing from "How Headlines Change the Way We Think." You may also want to provide students some basic instructions on headline writing from a source such as NPR's training website.

Scaffolding the Text-Dependent Questions

10. What is the meaning of progressive as it is used in paragraph 2? Use an online or print dictionary and thesaurus to confirm your understanding. How have you heard the word progressive or progressives used in a political context? In what other ways can the word progressive be used? L.11–12.1b

11. According to the text, what is the "hostile media effect"? What does it mean when a person is hostile toward a person? Reread paragraph 7. How might someone be hostile toward an idea or organization? RI.11–12.4

4.3

My Notes

audiences who **hew** to opposing sides on an issue are given the same news coverage of the topic to evaluate, both view this identical coverage as biased in favor of the other side (Gunther & Schmitt, 2004; Vallone et al., 1985). The phenomenon is commonly referred to as the "hostile media effect." Researchers believe that the explanation for this hostile media effect is selective categorization: opposing partisans attend to, process, and recall identical content from a news presentation but mentally categorize and label the same aspects of a story differently—as hostile to their own position (Schmitt, Gunther, & Liebhart, 2004).

8   The original hostile media effect assumes that news coverage is inherently balanced. The relative hostile media perception (Gunther, Christen, Liebhart, & Chia, 2001) relaxes this assumption, making it applicable to news that is slanted in favor of or against a particular issue. In the presence of the relative hostile media effect, supporters and opponents of a given issue perceive bias in a consistent direction (i.e., leaning toward one side), but each group perceives coverage as significantly more unfavorable to their own position relative to those in the other group. In other words, partisans perceive less bias in news coverage slanted to support their view than their opponents on the other side of the issue.

9   Interestingly, then, whereas the implication of the original hostile media effect is a partisan public perceiving media bias where none was present and thus potentially rejecting useful information, the implications of the relative hostile media effect are somewhat different. Of consequence here is that partisans will fail to recognize bias in news that is in fact biased, in instances when that bias is **congruent** with their pre-existing views. This bias against news bias is troubling. Americans' trust in news sources has become deeply **polarized** in recent years— with Republicans, for example, attributing more credibility to the conservative Fox News and less to most other news organizations than Democrats (Pew Research Center, 2008). In other countries, similar perceptions of a left or right bias to news or alternatively a bias relative to national or ethnic identity exist.

10 In each context, as news—particularly on cable TV and online—is infused with increasing amounts of opinion and ideology, this may make it even easier for partisans to validate their personal political beliefs—by accepting at face value information that comports with their views while rejecting information that advocates for the other side. Thus, the relative hostile media effect may not only reflect partisan divides in news perceptions but may also contribute to the further polarization of political attitudes and knowledge across political systems.

hew: adhere
congruent: in agreement
polarized: divided into sharply opposing sides

Scaffolding the Text-Dependent Questions

12. Compare the opinions of Konnikova and Nisbet toward the news media. Do they view journalists as generally responsible? According to Konnikova, how do headlines affect readers? What does she suggest journalists are trying to accomplish with their headlines? Reread paragraph 10 of Nisbet's article. What evidence of media bias does he believe exists? RI.11–12.1, RI.11–12.3, RI.11–12.6

My Notes

After reading the articles in this activity, respond to the Essential Question: How are media texts constructed to cater to an audience or to promote a particular agenda?

Knowledge Quest

- What ideas from the author's introduction stand out to you?
- What questions do you have after reading the excerpt the first time?
- What are your first thoughts about partisan bias versus media bias?

ACTIVITY 4.3 continued

19 Have students answer the Knowledge Quest questions for the Nisbet article.

20 RETURNING TO THE TEXT: Have students answer the text-dependent questions. If you used pairing during Leveled Differentiated Instruction, consider having students work with their partners to answer the questions.

21 If students have difficulty, scaffold the text-dependent questions by rephrasing them or breaking them down into smaller parts. See the Scaffolding the Text-Dependent Questions boxes for suggestions.

4.3

Returning to the Text
- Reread the articles to answer these text-dependent questions.
- Write any additional questions you have about the texts in your Reader/Writer Notebook.

"How Headlines Change the Way We Think"

2. Is the use of short sentences, in the form of a list of rejected titles for the article, effective in the opening paragraph? Why might the author have opened her article this way?

   The first paragraph is effective because the unusual format immediately hooks the reader, which might be why the author starts the article in this way. Some of the rejected headlines also hint at the ideas that will be covered in the article.

3. **KQ** According to Konnikova's arguments, how does the headline frame the rest of the reader's experience? Cite details from the text to support your answer.

   The headline can tell the reader the subject. It also activates the reader's prior knowledge about media and headlines. In paragraph 9, the author writes that headlines shift the reader's mindset in a way that could change which details the reader remembers later, especially when it comes to factual articles.

4. What does Konnikova mean by the phrase "Caveats don't fit in single columns"?

   She is making the point that headlines have to be brief, which doesn't leave much room for words or phrases that could work to clarify a misleading headline.

5. According to the article, why was the misdirection in the headline easier to detect for the factual pieces used in the Ullrich Ecker study than in the opinion pieces?

   The participants of the study were able to use the facts of the article to clear up any misconceptions created by the headline. On the other hand, the content of the opinion pieces does not provide the factual information necessary to allow readers to correct assumptions in the headlines.

6. **KQ** What is the author's purpose for including the Ecker study in this article?

   The study offers strong support and specific examples to back up her thesis that headlines change the way people think. It also shows that even when readers can use the facts in the article to lessen the impact of a misleading headline, the headline still changes how they process and remember what they read.

7. What is Konnikova's purpose for repeating the rejected titles for her article that she used at the beginning of the article in her conclusion?

Repetition is an effective rhetorical device, and, in this case, the author uses it to illustrate how each of the different titles might have changed readers' perception of the article. This conclusion sums up the piece and bolsters support for her thesis without introducing any new information.

8. Konnikova writes, "It's not always easy to be both interesting and accurate, but, as Ecker's study shows, it's better than being exciting and wrong." Apply this to what the article is trying to say about headlines.

She's making the point that it is often difficult to write headlines that catch readers' attention. It is also challenging to write headlines that accurately reflect the content of articles given limits such as the time and space constraints headline writers face. However, accuracy should outweigh all other factors because of the importance of headlines.

"Why Partisans View Mainstream Media as Biased and Ideological Media as Objective"

9. **KQ** What is the difference between "mainstream" and "ideological" media? Why is their difference a paradox?

"Mainstream" media are the conventional news outlets. "Ideological" media are news outlets that present either liberal or conservative viewpoints. The paradox is that liberals and conservatives both see the mainstream media as biased, so they seek news from like-minded ideological media, which they see as objective.

10. What is the meaning of *progressive* as it is used in paragraph 2? Use an online or print dictionary and thesaurus to confirm your understanding.

In this paragraph, *progressive* has a similar meaning to *liberal*: politically left-leaning. It is used neutrally in showing that both the left and right criticize the mainstream media and gravitate toward like-minded news sources."

11. **KQ** According to the text, what is the "hostile media effect"?

It is a phenomenon described by Gunther & Schmitt as the way people perceive the same media as hostile toward their beliefs, regardless of which way their ideologies slant.

22 Return to the Knowledge Question. Have students work with a partner to reflect on the readings' impact on their understanding of media influence. Ask volunteers to share their answers with the class.

23 Encourage students to continue building knowledge on this topic as suggested in the Independent Reading Link.

4.3

12. **KQ** Compare the opinions of Konnikova and Nisbet toward the news media. Do they view journalists as generally responsible?

Konnikova identifies as a journalist and acknowledges that headlines are

sometimes misleading. Nisbet, who studies media, acknowledges that some

media outlets reflect partisan bias but suggests media bias is overstated.

INDEPENDENT READING LINK

You can continue to build your knowledge about the media by reading other articles at ZINC Reading Labs. Search for keywords such as *media bias*, *confirmation bias*, and *hostile media effect*.

ZINC

Knowledge Quest

Think about how both authors explore media bias: the way media can shape a reader's perception and the way the reader's perception can shape how media is interpreted. Which do you think is more influential? Write an argumentative paragraph about whether the media or the reader's interpretation is more powerful. Be sure to:

• Provide a well-reasoned claim that is clearly stated.

• Use significant and relevant examples, details, or quotations from one or both articles that thoroughly develop and support your claim.

• Provide an engaging conclusion that supports the claim and examines its implications.

Working from the Text

13. Use a two-column graphic organizer to evaluate and critique the arguments made in each article. For the purposes of framing your thinking, it is worth noting that Konnikova's article focuses more on journalists' role in the news process while Nisbet focuses more on the readers' role.

"How Headlines Change the Way We Think"	"Why Partisans View Mainstream Media as Biased and Ideological Media as Objective"
Claim:	Claim:
Reasons/Evidence:	Reasons/Evidence:
Structure:	Structure:
Evaluation and Critique:	Evaluation and Critique:

24 Direct students to the Working from the Text questions. Advise students that they will respond to these questions to prepare for a classroom debate. First, review debate elements by asking students how to construct a clear claim. Ask volunteers to describe how to recognize reasons and evidence as relevant and sufficient. Remind students to anticipate and address counterclaims and to structure their arguments using a clear line of reasoning.

25 On the board, write the claim "Konnikova is more persuasive than Nisbet." Mark four corners of the room with the signs "Strongly Agree," "Strongly Disagree," "Agree," and "Disagree." Have students move to the corner that represents their response to the claim.

26 Stage a 15- to 20-minute four-corners debate of the claim. Explain to students that only one speaker may speak at a time. Then, ask a student from each corner to attempt to persuade the class to adopt the same position. Ask students to provide reasoning. In preparation for the task, guide student discussion about what makes for compelling reasoning. Ask students to cite specific examples of compelling reasoning from one of the articles. After one representative from each corner has had an opportunity to speak, students who have been persuaded may change corners. Repeat, giving different students a chance to explain their reasoning and persuade their classmates.

27 After the debate, have students respond to the discussion questions on the student page. Lead students in a debrief of how the debate and the discussion have affected their perspective on news media and their own biases as viewers. Then have them complete the Check Your Understanding task.

ASSESS

Review student responses to the Check Your Understanding task. They should include reasoning and examples to support their assertions. Use student participation in the class debate to assess their ability to evaluate conflicting perspectives, to support their ideas with evidence, and to participate in group discussions.

When reviewing student responses to the writing prompt, look for a clear opinion on who holds responsibility for media bias. Students should use—or refute—at least one relevant argument and counterargument from the classroom debate while supporting their argument. Responses should end with a call to action related to media bias, summing up the student's opinion.

ADAPT

If students need additional support to apply arguments and counterarguments from the debate, consider assigning a class secretary to record key ideas during the debate. Alternatively, provide students with any notes you created during the debate. If students need additional help citing evidence in a debate, model doing so with one point from the text.

4.3

My Notes

14. Review your response to the Opening Writing Prompt about the importance of headlines as well as your answer to the final "Returning to the Text" question about Nisbet's article. Based on those responses and the information from your graphic organizer, respond to the following questions: Who holds responsibility for avoiding media bias in the news: the creators of the news or the consumers of the news?

15. Outline your position to prepare for a classroom debate on the question. Your outline should include:
    - A concise statement of your claim
    - Three points of evidence, taken from the text, to support your claim
    - A concluding statement that includes a call to action

16. Share your opinion in a class debate. Be sure to:
    - Listen and respond to your classmates' points before adding a new point to the discussion.
    - Cite textual evidence to support your claim. (Refer to your graphic organizer when responding to other students' points.)

17. After discussing the two articles, reflect on the following questions.
    - How much did your existing personal opinions influence your perspective on which author was more persuasive regarding media bias?
    - How much did your existing personal opinions influence your perspective on which author was more correct regarding media bias?
    - What's the difference between being persuasive and being correct?
    - In general, to what extent does our perspective on what is correct influence our perspective on what is persuasive and vice versa?

☑ Check Your Understanding

Write one sentence in which you agree with another student's argument or present a counterargument in response to another student's claim.

✍ Writing Prompt: Argumentative

Who holds more responsibility for media bias, the journalist or the reader? Write a brief argument defending your position. Weave in at least one counterargument made by your peers in the class debate. Be sure to:
- Include a clear claim, supporting evidence from the text, and a conclusion.
- Address counterarguments and use evidence from the texts to support your point of view.
- Include a conclusion with a call to action.

WRITING PROMPT: ARGUMENTATIVE

The following standards are addressed in the writing prompt:
- W.11–12.1a
- W.11–12.1b
- W.11–12.1e
- RI.11–12.1

Bias in News Reports

PLAN

Materials: two online news segments on the same subject or event but with different perspectives, such as segments from Fox News and MSNBC, or two blogs/online articles that discuss the same political issue from different perspectives, from websites such as thenation.com and townhall.com

Suggested Pacing: 2 50-minute class periods.

TEACH

1 Read the Learning Targets and Preview with the class.

2 Tell students that they will be analyzing the reporting of an event, including the *who, what, when, where, why,* and *how* of the event. They will also report how differing news sources create different representations of that same event.

3 To encourage students to make connections with the material, lead a whole-class discussion in which students share any personal experience with reporting and writing news—perhaps for the school newspaper or for a blog.

4 Vocabulary Development: Review the meaning of the Literary Vocabulary *logical fallacy* and *rhetorical slanters* with students. Have them work in pairs to define these terms in their own words and think of both examples and non-examples.

5 To increase students' awareness of how language itself influences our perspective on a subject, review the various rhetorical slanters and examples. Ask students to offer their own original examples.

Learning Targets
- Evaluate media texts for credibility, bias, accuracy, and faulty reasoning.
- Craft a written argument that fairly and accurately identifies an example of biased reporting.

Preview
In this activity, you will watch two reports of a news event, noting any reporting and filming techniques that indicate bias. Then you will write an argument exposing the bias and logical fallacies evident in one of the news reports.

Learning Strategies
Discussion Groups
Graphic Organizer
Visual Prompt

LITERARY
A **logical fallacy** is an error in reasoning that weakens an argument.
Rhetorical slanters are words that put a negative or positive spin on what the speaker or writer is saying.

VOCABULARY

Slanting the News

Writers and directors can influence our perspective on a subject through the use of selection and omission, source control, and other manipulations of content, but rhetoric itself may be the most powerful tool through which our perceptions can be influenced. The following rhetorical slanters (adapted from Brooke Noel Moore and Richard Parker's *Critical Thinking*, 8th ed., 2007) identify key techniques often used to influence readers and viewers:

Rhetorical Slanter	Example
Rhetorical Analogy: the use of a figurative comparison (sometimes a simile or a metaphor) to convey a positive or negative feeling toward the subject	"The environment needs this candidate like farmers need a drought."
Rhetorical Definition: the use of emotionally charged language to express or elicit an attitude about something	"Capital punishment is government-sanctioned murder."
Rhetorical Explanation: expressing an opinion as if it were fact, and doing so in biased language	"Joe didn't have the guts to fight back," as compared to "Joe did not take a swing."
Innuendo: the use of language to imply that a particular inference is justified, as if saying "go ahead and read between the lines"	"Think carefully about whom you choose; you want a mayor who will be ready to do the job on day one."
Downplayers: the use of qualifier words, phrases, or punctuation to make someone or something look less important or significant	"She's a 'reporter' for a blog that hardly anyone reads."
Hyperbole: the use of extravagant overstatement	"The building quivered from the audience's momentous applause."
Truth Surrogates: hinting that proof exists to support a claim without actually citing that proof	"There's every reason to believe that …"
Ridicule/Sarcasm: the use of language that suggests the subject is worthy of scorn	"The news media themselves are oh-so-clearly impervious to the predispositions and prejudice that afflict their audience."

TEACHER TO TEACHER

The news clips you choose should be no more than 2 to 3 minutes long to allow for repeated viewings if necessary. One or more of the clips should lend itself to a thoughtful discussion about the use of logical fallacies in media reporting.

College and Career Readiness Standards

Focus Standards:

RI.11–12.7 Integrate and evaluate multiple sources of information presented in different media or formats (e.g., visually, quantitatively) as well as in words in order to address a question or solve a problem.

SL.11–12.3 Evaluate a speaker's point of view, reasoning, and use of evidence and rhetoric, assessing the stance, premises, links among ideas, word choice, points of emphasis, and tone used.

W.11–12.1 Write arguments to support claims in an analysis of substantive topics or texts, using valid reasoning and relevant and sufficient evidence.

Additional Standards Addressed:

RI.11–12.1, RI.11–12.2, RI.11–12.3, RI.11–12.4, RI.11–12.5, RI.11–12.6, W.11–12.5, L.11–12.1b, L.11–12.5a

ACTIVITY 4.4 continued

6 Have students work with partners to complete the **graphic organizer** for News Source 1 as they watch the first source twice. During the first viewing, students should complete the left-hand column concerning the facts of the event. During the second, they should complete the right-hand column, noting indications of bias in how the event is reported. Explain that the bottom row ("labels/titles/word choice") refers to rhetorical slanters. Have students share answers, and monitor student understanding.

 TEACHER TO TEACHER

You might lead a review of ways to detect bias in a text. For each type listed, have students draft a framing question that will help them look for evidence of bias. Record these categories and questions, and post them in your classroom.

- Bias by headlines—Example: Does the headline express approval or disapproval?
- Bias by photos, captions, or angles—Example: Is the subject shown in a flattering or unflattering way?
- Bias through omission—Example: What facts has the author left out?
- Bias by source selection— Example: Who gets to speak? Who is silenced or paraphrased?
- Bias through statistics— Example: Are any numbers used in a way that gives an unfair representation of the subject?
- Bias through labels, titles, word choice—Example: Does the reporter use loaded language to discuss the subject?

7 Repeat the process for News Source 2. After students have completed the second graphic organizer, organize **discussion groups** of three to five students, and have each group develop a Venn diagram comparing the way the two clips covered the event.

8 Call for volunteers to share their group's findings with the class. Ask students to discuss what the news reports have in common and how they differ. Then, discuss how the differences between the clips reveal their biases.

4.4

News anchors earn credibility by having a record of presenting factual and objective information.

My Notes

_____
_____
_____
_____
_____
_____
_____
_____
_____
_____
_____
_____
_____
_____
_____
_____
_____
_____
_____
_____
_____

1. As you watch the two video clips, complete the graphic organizers. Closely evaluate the information presented for bias and credibility.

News Source 1

Facts	Example of Bias
Bias by headline?	
Bias by photos, captions, camera angles?	
Bias through omission?	
Bias by source selection? Who is the information supplied by?	
Bias through statistics/ number inflation?	
Bias through labels/titles/ word choice?	

News Source 2

Facts	Example of Bias
Bias by headline?	
Bias by photos, captions, camera angles?	
Bias through omission?	
Bias by source selection? Who is the information supplied by?	
Bias through statistics/ number inflation?	
Bias through labels/titles/ word choice?	

✅ **Check Your Understanding**

How does bias affect the credibility of a source?

Finding the Logical Fallacy

2. A logical fallacy is an error in reasoning. Some authors use such faulty reasoning intentionally in an effort to convince readers without adequate evidence. Other writers might use it unintentionally. Whether used purposefully or accidentally, logical fallacies negatively impact the accuracy and credibility of the information or ideas being presented. Here are three common types of flawed reasoning and an example of each:

Faulty Analogy

Assuming that if two things are alike in one or more ways, they are automatically alike in other respects.

Example: Buying a stock is just like betting on a horse race. You can never be sure of picking a winner.

Slippery Slope

Assuming that one event will lead to another or to a chain of events that lead to an undesirable result.

Example: If a high school student doesn't study for one test, they are sure to fail it and eventually drop out of school.

Straw Man

Distorting or oversimplifying your opponent's argument, and then building your counterargument against the distorted argument.

Example: Opponents of capital punishment think the lives of victims are less valuable than the lives of criminals.

✅ **Focus on the Sentence**

Write two sentences about logical fallacies, one in the form of a statement and one in the form a question. Be sure to use correct capitalization and punctuation.

Statement (.) Arguments that use the logical fallacy slippery slope are formed by using extreme hypothetical situations.

Question (?) If readers are ill informed on a topic, can they still discern if an author is using a straw man?

ACTIVITY 4.4 continued

9 Invite students to discuss the relationship between bias and credibility in the Check Your Understanding task.

10 Read the Finding the Logical Fallacy section with students. If the clips you selected contain logical fallacies, replay or review them, instructing students to look for any fallacies.

11 If the selected clips do not include examples of logical fallacies, collect examples from other media channels that do. Have students work with a partner to identify the fallacy before working together to complete the Focus on the Sentence task. Review the pairs' work in a whole-class discussion.

12 Have students respond to the writing prompt either in class or for homework. Remind them to refer to their graphic organizers and the "Bias by" chart posted in the classroom to frame their responses.

LEVELED DIFFERENTIATED INSTRUCTION

In this activity, students might need support writing an argumentative essay about bias in news stories.

Developing Arrange students into groups of four, and then assign pairs to read or view one of the media sources. Have pairs use the **Paragraph Frame for Conclusions** graphic organizer as a note-taking tool to record details and quotes that support their claim. Then have the group of four share their findings in a jigsaw fashion and collaborate to complete their essays.

Expanding Pair students and provide the **Paragraph Frame for Conclusions** graphic organizer to help each partner focus on one article or news clip. Have them use the organizer to record details and quotes that support their claim. Then have partners discuss their findings and work together to complete their essays.

Extend Help expand students' understanding of how rhetorical slanting works by choosing a pertinent issue affecting your school. Have students choose one or more of the rhetorical techniques to use in a short description of the issue. Have them juxtapose this approach with a more "legitimate" description and share the two versions with the class.

ASSESS

Review student responses to the Check Your Understanding question and the Focus on the Sentence exercise through whole-class discussion. Students should note the role perception plays in media bias and how this in turn affects notions of credibility. If you sense students' understanding of key concepts might be limited, ask them to turn in their Check Your Understanding as a quickwrite so you can review students' work individually.

ADAPT

If students need additional help identifying bias and rhetorical slanters, review a text that shows clear evidence of bias, looking for these elements and co-constructing a response to the writing prompt.

4.4

Writing Prompt: Argumentative

Write an argument exposing the bias evident in the way one of the news stories reports the event. In addition to using the information from your graphic organizer, identify any use of logical fallacies in the story. Be sure to:

- Develop a precise and arguable claim.
- Cite details and quotes from the news story to support your claim.
- Acknowledge and refute counterclaims fairly and thoroughly.
- Conclude by evaluating how the bias affects the credibility and accuracy of the text.
- Check for correct spelling, punctuation, grammar, and usage.

WRITING PROMPT: ARGUMENTATIVE

The following standards are addressed in the writing prompt:
- RI.11–12.6
- SL.11–12.3
- W.11–12.1

Framing the Investigation

Learning Targets

- Investigate how critical lenses can both shape and reveal perspectives about real-world events and issues.
- Use different critical lenses to frame research questions.
- Ask questions to evaluate the effectiveness of structural characteristics in nonfiction texts related to the same topic.

Preview

In this activity, you will begin exploring the ways the media, public figures, and government organizations shape or construct the meaning of a historical event: Hurricane Katrina. You will start by reading several texts that help frame and contextualize the event.

As You Read

- Put a star next to actions Congress will take and put a dash next to actions Congress expects individuals, state governments, and local governments to take.
- Circle unknown words and phrases, including legal language used in the document. Try to determine the meaning of the words by using context clues, word parts, or a dictionary.

Law

The Robert T. Stafford Disaster Relief and Emergency Assistance Act, Section 101

Sec. 101. Congressional Findings and Declarations (42 U.S.C. 5121)

a. The Congress hereby finds and declares that

1. because disasters often cause loss of life, human suffering, loss of income, and property loss and damage; and

2. because disasters often disrupt the normal functioning of governments and communities, and adversely affect individuals and families with great severity; special measures, designed to assist the efforts of the affected States in expediting the rendering of aid, assistance, and emergency services, and the reconstruction and rehabilitation of devastated areas, are necessary.

Learning Strategies

Discussion Groups
Marking the Text
Note-taking
Quickwrite
Think-Pair-Share

My Notes

INDEPENDENT READING LINK

Read and Connect

Much has been written about Hurricane Katrina and its massive effects on the people, environment, government, and history of the Gulf Region. Find and read an informational or fiction text about Hurricane Katrina that interests you. Take notes as you read it to help you develop contextual understandings about the event. Record your notes in your Reader/Writer Notebook.

College and Career Readiness Standards

Focus Standards:

RI.11–12.2 Determine two or more central ideas of a text and analyze their development over the course of the text, including how they interact and build on one another to provide a complex analysis; provide an objective summary of the text.

RI.11–12.5 Analyze and evaluate the effectiveness of the structure an author uses in his or her exposition or argument, including whether the structure makes points clear, convincing, and engaging.

ACTIVITY 4.5

PLAN

Suggested Pacing: 2 50-minute class periods

TEACH

1 Read aloud the Learning Targets and Preview. You may want to discuss with the class how you define *public figure* for the purposes of this unit.

2 Write the following quote from Willa Cather on the board: "There are some things you learn best in calm, and some in storm." In a **quickwrite**, ask students to respond to this quote. Then discuss their responses.

3 Remind students to complete the Independent Reading Link. Help them find texts about Hurricane Katrina online or in your school's media center. Several titles included in this unit's Planning the Unit section relate to Hurricane Katrina. You may want to extend it to include reading about other recent natural disasters that have impacted the U.S.

4 Explain to students that in the next few activities, which are designed to help prepare them for Embedded Assessment 1, they will be investigating the various issues surrounding Hurricane Katrina, the 2005 storm that devastated much of the Gulf Coast. The first text they will read is one part of a longer legal document that formally established the government's responsibilities in addressing natural disasters like hurricanes.

5 Read the As You Read section with your students. Help them understand the instructions for annotation and preview the structure of the text.

6 FIRST READ: This is a brief passage that is already chunked, so it may be a good opportunity for students to practice reading independently.

 TEXT COMPLEXITY

Overall: Moderate
Lexile: 1440L
Qualitative: Moderate Difficulty
Task: Accessible (Understand)

7 As students are reading, monitor their progress. Be sure they are engaged with the text and are marking actions Congress will take and actions Congress expects others to take. Check to see that students are marking unknown words, such as legal terms. Evaluate whether the selected reading mode is effective.

TEACHER TO TEACHER

The full text of the Stafford Act is available on fema.gov, the website of the Federal Emergency Management Agency (FEMA). Consider using a longer portion of this text to support students' understanding of the way legal documents use a specific organizational structure and text features.

8 Lead a whole-class discussion and ask student volunteers to share their responses to the Making Observation questions.

4.5

My Notes

b. It is the intent of the Congress, by this Act, to provide an orderly and continuing means of assistance by the Federal Government to State and local governments in carrying out their responsibilities to alleviate the suffering and damage which result from such disasters by

3. revising and broadening the scope of existing disaster relief programs;

4. encouraging the development of comprehensive disaster preparedness and assistance plans, programs, capabilities, and organizations by the States and by local governments;

5. achieving greater coordination and responsiveness of disaster preparedness and relief programs;

6. encouraging individuals, States, and local governments to protect themselves by obtaining insurance coverage to supplement or replace governmental assistance;

7. encouraging hazard mitigation measures to reduce losses from disasters, including development of land use and construction regulations; and (6) providing Federal assistance programs for both public and private losses sustained in disasters.

Making Observations
- What stands out about the document's structure?
- What are your initial thoughts on Congress's plan?

alleviate: relieve
mitigation: lessening

College and Career Readiness Standards

W.11–12.8 Gather relevant information from multiple authoritative print and digital sources, using advanced searches effectively; assess the strengths and limitations of each source in terms of the task, purpose, and audience; integrate information into the text selectively to maintain the flow of ideas, avoiding plagiarism and overreliance on any one source and following a standard format for citation.

Additional Standards Addressed:
RI.11–12.1, RI.11–12.3, RI.11–12.4, RI.11–12.6, RI.11–12.8, L.11–12.4c, W.11–12.10

4.5

Returning to the Text

- Reread the legal document to answer these text-dependent questions.
- Write any additional questions you have about the text in your Reader/Writer Notebook.

1. According to this document, why and how does the federal government step in to assist state and local governments in the event of a disaster?

   Disasters cause hardships to individuals and families and disrupt normal state and local

   government functions. The federal government steps in to help provide "aid, assistance,

   and emergency services, and the reconstruction and rehabilitation of devastated areas" in a

   timely way.

2. What is the primary purpose of this document? Who is the intended audience?

   This document offers state and local governments an overview of the role the federal

   government will play in helping deal with a disaster and the type of aid the federal government

   will provide during a disaster. Given this context, it can be inferred that the most likely

   audience would be federal, state, and local government officials.

3. According to subsection (b), what is the government's responsibility in times of disaster?

   The government's responsibility is to "alleviate the suffering and damage" caused by

   disasters.

4. How do subsections (a) and (b) differ in purpose? What is the overall effect of using these text features?

   Subsection (a) states that special measures are necessary in times of disaster, while

   subsection (b) states the Congress's intent to provide federal aid to state and local

   governments in times of disaster and how it will do so. Clearly defined sections show that this

   text has a functional and legal purpose.

As You Read

- As you read "Day Long Efforts to Repair Levee Fail," underline words and phrases that help you visualize the scene.
- Circle unknown words and phrases. Try to determine the meaning of the words by using context clues, word parts, or a dictionary.

ACTIVITY 4.5 continued

9 **RETURNING TO THE TEXT:** Have students answer the text-dependent questions in small groups. If they have difficulty, scaffold the questions by rephrasing them or breaking them down into smaller parts. See the Scaffolding the Text-Dependent Questions boxes for suggestions.

10 As students move to the next text, explain that it is a front-page news article from *The Times-Picayune*, a prominent newspaper in New Orleans. It was published two days after Hurricane Katrina came ashore in Plaquemines Parish, Louisiana, approximately 70 miles from New Orleans.

 TEACHER TO TEACHER

You may want to display *The Times-Picayune*'s website and share some information about the publication.

Scaffolding the Text-Dependent Questions

1. According to this document, why and how does the federal government step in to assist state and local governments in the event of a disaster? Look for the words "governments and communities." Why is federal assistance "necessary"? RI.11–12.2

2. What is the primary purpose of this document? Who is its intended audience? What does the document's title tell you about its purpose? Who or what receives "assistance" under the document's provisions? RI.11–12.6

3. According to subsection (b), what is the government's responsibility in times of disaster? Look for the word "responsibilities" in subsection (b). RI.11–12.2

4. How do subsections (a) and (b) differ in purpose? What is the overall effect of using these text features? Reread the introductions for each subsection and use what you know about outlining to address this question. RI.11–12.5

11 Read the As You Read and About the Author sections with your students. Help them understand the instructions for annotation for the next text they will read. You may want to share the website for *The Advocate* and explain that although that newspaper is based in Baton Rouge it is a competitor of *The Times-Picayune*.

12 **Vocabulary Development:** Discuss the Word Connections with students. Ask students how the words are similar in the meaning, based on the word *lever*.

13 **FIRST READ:** Have students read the article in pairs and **think-pair-share** to discuss their responses to the Making Observation questions and point out details their partner may have missed.

 TEXT COMPLEXITY

Overall: Accessible
Lexile: 1130L
Qualitative: Moderate Difficulty
Task: Moderate (Analyze)

14 As students are reading, monitor their progress. Be sure they are engaged with the text and underlining phrases that help them visualize the scene.

4.5

WORD CONNECTIONS

Etymology
Levee is a noun derived from the French word *lever*, "to raise." A levee is a wall or raised ridge of soil alongside a river, built to prevent flooding. Other words derived from the word *lever* include alleviate, elevate, elevator, leverage, levity, and relieve.

My Notes

About the Author

Dan Shea (b. 1963) is the publisher of *The Advocate*. Prior to this role, Shea served as the managing editor of *The Times-Picayune* for 19-years. At *The Times-Picayune*, Shea supervised newsroom operations, presentations, photography, and copyediting. He also played a pivotal role in the continued print and online coverage of the harrowing days after Hurricane Katrina. The reporting under Shea's leadership led *The Times-Picayune* to win the Breaking News Pulitzer Prize in 2006.

Article

Daylong Efforts to Repair Levee Fail

by **Dan Shea**
The Times-Picayune, **August 31, 2005**

1   New Orleans became an unimaginable scene of water, fear and suffering Tuesday after a levee breach in the 17th Street Canal sent billions of gallons of Lake Pontchartrain coursing through the city.

2   As the day wore on, the only dry land was a narrow band from the French Quarter[1] and parts of Uptown, the same small strip that was settled by Bienville[2] amid the swamps.

3   On Tuesday night, it appeared the city was returning to swamp when a daylong effort to shore the levee near the Hammond Highway failed. Mayor Ray Nagin said pumps were being overwhelmed and warned that a new deluge would bury the city in up to 15 feet of water.

4   With solid water from the lake to the French Quarter, the inundation and depopulation of an entire American city was at hand.

5   "Truth to tell, we're not too far from filling in the bowl," said Terry Ebbert, the city's director of homeland security. The waters were still rising at 3 inches per hour, and eventually could move close to the French Quarter levee.

6   Although the breach occurred on the Orleans side of the canal, it did not spare the Jefferson side. Water found its way into much of the east bank, meeting the flow that came in from the west from Hurricane Katrina's storm surge Monday.

---

[1] The French Quarter is New Orleans's oldest neighborhood.
[2] Jean-Baptiste Le Moyne de Bienville was governor of Louisiana and founder of New Orleans.

Scaffolding the Text-Dependent Questions

5. **Which major levee breach is the focus of this article? At the time of printing, what were the plans for repairing it? How will this help rescue efforts?** Reread paragraph 1. Which levee is named? Reread paragraphs 26 and 27. What does Ebbert say is to be done after rescue efforts? RI.11–12.2

7 An accurate tally of death was hard to determine. Five deaths related to Katrina have been confirmed in Jefferson Parish[3], officials said. There also are seven people missing who decided to ride out Katrina on Grand Isle.

…

My Notes

8 As to the living, with the absence of cars and electric motors in the powerless city, a sad tableau played itself out in an eerie quiet.

9 All day, a weary army of storm victims trudged through waist-deep muddy water toward the Superdome, where more than 20,000 people took refuge. The next problem is what to do with them. Late Tuesday Gov. Blanco ordered them out, saying the facility was too damaged to house people and the atmosphere too dangerous. Officials said the National Guard soon would begin driving them out to dry ground, then airlift them out of southeast Louisiana.

10 In other areas, lawlessness took hold.

11 The giant new Wal-Mart in the Lower Garden District was looted, after a limited distribution of supplies broke down in chaos. The entire gun collection was taken.

12 "There are gangs of armed men in the city moving around the city," Ebbert said.

13 One looter shot a New Orleans police officer, who was in critical condition with a head wound.

14 Although local police focused solely on rescue, a call for help was answered by swarms of deputies from western Louisiana parishes.

15 But cops on the street, cut off from their superiors by a failure of the communications system, complained of chaos.

16 "Put this in your paper," one officer on Canal Street said. "They told us nothing. We were unprepared. We are completely on our own."

17 If it wasn't coordinated, the rescue was heroic.

18 Firefighters, police and Coast Guardsmen waded through water and climbed to roofs.

19 "We've got boats everywhere," said Capt. Tim Bayard of the New Orleans Police Department. "We're going to try and get who we can get and take them to higher ground. We may have to come back for some."

20 They were joined by an armada of Louisiana sportsmen in flat-bottomed boats, who responded to an appeal for help.

21 Ferdinand Emory rescued about 100 people, ten at a time in his boat.

22 Ebbert estimated 1,500 to 2,000 people were saved in Lakeview and Mid-City.

A woman is carried out of floodwaters after being trapped in her home after Hurricane Katrina.

[3] Jefferson Parish is one of 64 parishes (rather than counties) into which Louisiana is divided.

Scaffolding the Text-Dependent Questions

6. What is the implied connection between the events in paragraphs 11 and 12? Reread both paragraphs. What happened at the new Wal-Mart? What was happening in the city? What connection is unspoken between the two occurrences? RI.11–12.1

7. Summarize paragraphs 10–16. Whom does the officer blame for the chaotic rescue effort? Use details to support your inference. Reread paragraphs 15 and 16. Who are the "they" to whom the officer refers? Why does he feel that he and fellow officers are on their own? RI.11–12.1, RI.11–12.2

15 Have students jot down responses to the Making Observations so that they will be prepared to share them during class discussion.

4.5

My Notes

23 But rescue from the water didn't mean an end to misery. They were simply dropped off at the few stretches of dry ground, overpasses and parking lots along Metairie Ridge.

24 Aleck Scallan, 63, a paraplegic, was ferried in a boat from his Lakeview home. But he had been sitting for more than six hours on an overpass, with no clear indication when he and scores of others would be picked up.

25 Along the Metairie Road railroad embankment, the only passage through two parishes, people wandered aimlessly, along with dogs and cats that headed for high ground.

26 After the rescue effort, the next priority is trying to heal the breach. Ebbert said plans called for giant panels to be dropped in place by helicopter, accompanied by 50, 3,000-pound sandbags. Next the Interstate 10 underpass under the railroad trestle would have to be drained, after the giant new pumping station utterly failed its first test. That would give disaster recovery teams open access to the city from the west.

27 The failure of the Industrial Canal levee created massive flooding in St. Bernard and the 9th Ward[4] on Monday.

28 Estimates on when the city would become habitable again ranged from two weeks to months.

People wade through high water in front of the Superdome August 30, 2005 in New Orleans, Louisiana, days after Hurricane Katrina.

Making Observations
- What images come to mind while reading this article?
- What emotions do you feel after reading this article?

---

[4] The 9th Ward is the largest of 17 wards, or areas, into which New Orleans is divided.

Scaffolding the Text-Dependent Questions

8. Why do Aleck Scallan and others have no idea when they will be picked up from the overpass? What is the first priority of local police? Are Scallan and those with him safe on the overpass? RI.11–12.1, RI.11–12.3

Returning to the Text

- Reread the article to answer these text-dependent questions.
- Write any additional questions you have about the text in your Reader/Writer Notebook.

5. Which major levee breach is the focus of this article? At the time of printing, what were the plans for repairing it? How will this help rescue efforts?

The article focuses on the levee breach in the 17th Street Canal. Officials plan to drop giant

panels and sandbags and to drain the Interstate 10 underpass. Repairing the breach will allow

recovery teams into the area, but only after rescue efforts are over.

6. What is the implied connection between the events in paragraphs 11 and 12?

The writer implies that the armed men of paragraph 11 are the looters who stole the guns

from the Wal-Mart in paragraph 12 or that looters in general were stealing guns to arm

themselves.

7. Summarize paragraphs 10–16. Whom does the officer blame for the chaotic rescue effort? Use details to support your inference.

Paragraphs 10–16 describe the lack of organization in New Orleans after the hurricane. In

paragraph 16, the officer says, "They told us nothing... We are completely on our own." We can

infer that he is referring to his superiors, since paragraph 15 states that "cops on the streets"

were "cut off from their superiors."

8. Why do Aleck Scallan and others have no idea when they will be picked up from the overpass?

Earlier paragraphs say that local police are focused solely on rescuing people stuck in the

flood by dropping them on dry land. Since Scallan and others are now on dry land, they are

less of a priority than people in immediate need of rescue, despite being stranded. Also, the

article states breach repair will be another key focus of first responders.

As You Read

- Underline the priorities that President Bush mentions in his speech.
- Circle unknown words and phrases. Try to determine the meaning of the words by using context clues, word parts, or a dictionary.

16 **RETURNING TO THE TEXT:** Have students answer the text-dependent questions with their reading partners. If they have difficulty, scaffold the questions by rephrasing them or breaking them down into smaller parts. See the Scaffolding the Text-Dependent Questions boxes for suggestions.

17 After students have analyzed the news story, engage in a brief discussion about how the article connects to any of the critical lenses they have studied. Are economic, cultural, gender, or historical elements evident in the text?

18 Introduce the next selection by going over the As You Read, About the Author, and Academic Vocabulary box with students. Help them understand the instructions for annotation.

19 Have students preview the photos that accompany President Bush's speech. Point out that in the second photo, President Bush is likely viewing a scene very similar to the one shown in the first photo. Ask students to tell what Bush is likely thinking and feeling, based on his expression in the photo.

20 **FIRST READ:** Because this selection is the text of a speech, you might want to read it aloud to students for the first read. Remind students that this speech was delivered by President George W. Bush on August 31, 2005, after his flight over the affected Gulf Coast area. Encourage students to pay attention to ways the text links to the critical lenses.

 TEXT COMPLEXITY

Overall: Moderate
Lexile: 1120L
Qualitative: Moderate Difficulty
Task: Moderate (Analyze)

21 During the read-aloud, monitor student progress. Be sure students are engaged with the text and are annotating the numbers President Bush gives and the priorities he mentions.

VOCABULARY

ACADEMIC
Rhetorical context refers to the subject, purpose, audience, occasion, or situation in which writing or speaking occurs.

My Notes

About the Author

George W. Bush (b. 1946) was the 43rd president of the United States. Before becoming president, Bush served as Governor of Texas from 1995–2000. His presidency was shaped by the terrorist attacks on September 11, 2001, which occurred eight months into his presidency. After his presidency, Bush founded the George W. Bush Presidential Center in Dallas, Texas and created a collection of paintings, *Portraits of Courage: A Commander in Chief's Tribute to America's Warriors*, to honor American veterans.

Speech

President Outlines Hurricane Katrina Relief Efforts

by **President George W. Bush**
August 31, 2005

1 I've just received an update from Secretary Chertoff and other Cabinet Secretaries involved on the latest developments in Louisiana, Mississippi, and Alabama. As we flew here today, I also asked the pilot to fly over the Gulf Coast region so I could see firsthand the scope and magnitude of the devastation.

2 The vast majority of New Orleans, Louisiana, is under water. Tens of thousands of homes and businesses are beyond repair. A lot of the Mississippi Gulf Coast has been completely destroyed. Mobile is flooded. We are dealing with one of the worst natural disasters in our nation's history.

3 And that's why I've called the Cabinet together. The people in the affected regions expect the federal government to work with the state government and local government with an effective response. I have directed Secretary of Homeland Security Mike Chertoff to chair a Cabinet-level task force to coordinate all our assistance from Washington. FEMA[5] Director Mike Brown is in charge of all federal response and recovery efforts in the field. I've instructed them to work closely with state and local officials, as well as with the private sector, to ensure that we're helping, not hindering, recovery efforts. This recovery will take a long time. This recovery will take years.

4 Our efforts are now focused on three priorities: Our first priority is to save lives. We're assisting local officials in New Orleans in evacuating any remaining citizens from the affected area. I want to thank the state of Texas, and particularly Harris County and the city of Houston and officials with the Houston Astrodome, for providing shelter to those citizens who found refuge

---

[5] The acronym FEMA stands for Federal Emergency Management Agency.

Scaffolding the Text-Dependent Questions

9. **Based on details in the text, infer the rhetorical context of this speech.** Reread paragraphs 1–3. Where is President Bush? To whom is he speaking? What does he want to tell them? RI.11–12.1, RI.11–12.6

10. **According to President Bush, what are the federal government's three priorities? How would you categorize them?** Review paragraphs 4, 8, and 10. Which priorities does he list? What examples does he give? Who or what does each priority help? RI.11–12.1, RI.11–12.2

in the Super Dome in Louisiana. Buses are on the way to take those people from New Orleans to Houston.

5 FEMA has deployed more than 50 disaster medical assistance teams from all across the country to help the affected—to help those in the affected areas. FEMA has deployed more than 25 urban search and rescue teams with more than a thousand personnel to help save as many lives as possible. The United States Coast Guard is conducting search and rescue missions. They're working alongside local officials, local assets. The Coast Guard has rescued nearly 2,000 people to date.

A U.S. Coast Guard Petty Officer and a rescue crew sent from Clearwater, Florida, look for survivors near the Louisiana bayou town of Buras.

6 The Department of Defense is deploying major assets to the region. These include the USS *Bataan* to conduct search and rescue missions; eight swift water rescue teams; the Iwo Jima Amphibious Readiness Group to help with disaster response equipment; and the hospital ship USNS *Comfort* to help provide medical care.

7 The National Guard has nearly 11,000 Guardsmen on state active duty to assist governors and local officials with security and disaster response efforts. FEMA and the Army Corps of Engineers are working around the clock with Louisiana officials to repair the breaches in the levees so we can stop the flooding in New Orleans.

8 Our second priority is to sustain lives by ensuring adequate food, water, shelter and medical supplies for survivors and dedicated citizens—dislocated citizens. FEMA is moving supplies and equipment into the hardest hit areas. The Department of Transportation has provided more than 400 trucks to move 1,000 truckloads containing 5.4 million Meals Ready to Eat—or MREs, 13.4 million liters of water, 10,400 tarps, 3.4 million pounds of ice, 144 generators, 20 containers of pre-positioned disaster supplies, 135,000 blankets and 11,000 cots. And we're just starting.

9 There are more than 78,000 people now in shelters. HHS and CDC are working with local officials to identify operating hospital facilities so we can help them, help the nurses and doctors provide necessary medical care. They're distributing medical supplies, and they're executing a public health plan to control disease and other health-related issues that might arise.

10 Our third priority is executing a comprehensive recovery effort. We're focusing on restoring power and lines of communication that have been knocked out during the storm. We'll be repairing major roads and bridges and other essential means of transportation as quickly as possible.

My Notes

_____

Scaffolding the Text-Dependent Questions

11. What does President Bush mean by 'major assets' in paragraph 6? What examples does he provide? What are assets? What types of assets would the Department of Defense have? Look at the examples. RI.11–12.4, RI.11–12.5

---

22 After the reading, have students refer back to their annotations to help them answer the Making Observation questions.

⭐ TEACHER TO TEACHER

If any of your students need support with English language development, consider differentiating instruction with the corresponding Language Workshop 4B activities available on SpringBoard Digital. Built around President Bush's speech, these activities offer a scaffolded approach to developing academic language through vocabulary study (Activity 3), guided close reading (Activity 5), and collaborative academic discussion (Activity 6). When planning differentiation, make sure to have students return to portions of the ELA activity that provide essential practice for the Embedded Assessment.

23 After the reading, have students refer back to their annotations to help them answer the Making Observation questions.

4.5

My Notes

11 There's a lot of work we're going to have to do. In my flyover, I saw a lot of destruction on major infrastructure. Repairing the infrastructure, of course, is going to be a key priority.

12 The Department of Energy is approving loans from the Strategic Petroleum Reserve to limit disruptions in crude supplies for refineries. A lot of crude production has been shut down because of the storm. I instructed Secretary Bodman to work with refiners, people who need crude oil, to alleviate any shortage through loans. The Environmental Protection Agency has granted a nationwide waiver for fuel blends to make more gasoline and diesel fuel available throughout the country. This will help take some pressure off of gas price. But our citizens must understand this storm has disrupted the capacity to make gasoline and distribute gasoline.

13 We're also developing a comprehensive plan to immediately help displaced citizens. This will include housing and education and health care and other essential needs. I've directed the folks in my Cabinet to work with local folks, local officials, to develop a comprehensive strategy to rebuild the communities affected. And there's going to be a lot of rebuilding done. I can't tell you how devastating the sights were.

14 I want to thank the communities in surrounding states that have welcomed their neighbors during an hour of need. A lot of folks left the affected areas and found refuge with a relative or a friend, and I appreciate you doing that. I also want to thank the American Red Cross and the Salvation Army and the Catholic Charities, and all other members of the armies of compassion. I think the folks in the affected areas are going to be overwhelmed when they realize how many Americans want to help them.

. . .

15 The folks on the Gulf Coast are going to need the help of this country for a long time. This is going to be a difficult road. The challenges that we face on the ground are unprecedented. But there's no doubt in my mind we're going to succeed. Right now the days seem awfully dark for those affected—I understand that. But I'm confident that, with time, you can get your life back in order, new communities will flourish, the great city of New Orleans will be back on its feet, and America will be a stronger place for it.

President George W. Bush looks out the window of Air Force One as he flies over New Orleans, Louisiana, surveying the damage left by Hurricane Katrina.

infrastructure: buildings, roads, and utility systems

Making Observations
- What details from this speech stand out to you?
- What are your thoughts on the priorities that the President lays out in his speech?

Scaffolding the Text-Dependent Questions

12. What does President Bush compare charitable relief agencies to in paragraph 14? How might this comparison appeal to his audience? What are the "armies of compassion"? What positive connotations might the words *armies* and *compassion* have for listeners? RI.11–12.4, RI.11–12.5, RI.11–12.6

13. How does President Bush structure paragraph 15 to appeal to his audience? Reread paragraph 15. Look closely at each sentence. Notice the sentences that begin with the transition word *but*. How do these sentences contrast the sentences that come before them? What effect does this create? RI.11–12.5, RI.11–12.6

Returning to the Text

- Reread the speech to answer these text-dependent questions.
- Write any additional questions you have about the text in your Reader/Writer Notebook.

9. Based on details in the text, infer the rhetorical context of this speech.

   The president seems to be addressing the public relatively soon after Hurricane Katrina,

   based on the fact that he says he recently flew over the affected area. His purpose is to

   inform the public of the government's planned response to the disaster and to reassure the

   public.

10. According to President Bush, what are the federal government's three priorities? How would you categorize them?

    The three priorities are "to save lives" through search and rescue, "to sustain lives" by

    providing necessities, and "executing a comprehensive recovery effort" to restore and rebuild

    the area. The first two priorities deal with helping people, while the third deals primarily with

    logistics.

11. What does President Bush mean by "major assets" in paragraph 6? What examples does he provide?

    He means military equipment and personnel, including "the USS *Bataan* ...; eight swift water

    rescue teams; the Iwo Jima Amphibious Readiness Group ...; and the hospital ship USNS

    Comfort."

12. What does President Bush compare charitable relief agencies to in paragraph 14? How might this comparison appeal to his audience?

    Bush calls relief agencies "the armies of compassion." This draws a figurative comparison to

    actual armies. This might appeal to his target audience since armies connote strength and

    large numbers of well-organized soldiers working toward a goal.

13. How does President Bush structure paragraph 15 to appeal to his audience?

    Bush first acknowledges the audience's fears, then offers hope. For example, the first three

    sentences are somber, stressing the difficult recovery ahead. The fourth sentence starts with

    "But," to counter negative opinions. Next, he says that "the days seem awfully dark," then

    follows it with another *but* sentence—stressing his confidence in the future.

24 **RETURNING TO THE TEXT:** Have students answer the text-dependent questions independently. If they have difficulty, scaffold the questions by rephrasing them or breaking them down into smaller parts. See the Scaffolding the Text-Dependent Questions boxes for suggestions.

25 After students have read all three texts and answered the text-dependent questions, lead a brief discussion about the connections apparent among the three texts. Guide students to consider the function of each text. Ask students to evaluate how each text's purpose may affect the choice of language and structure.

26 Have students complete the Gaining Perspectives activity with a partner. Ask students to share their responses. Have students reference their notes and organize the class into two groups for a brief debate on the benefits and drawbacks of government involvement.

27 Turn to the Working from the Text section. Begin by having students write a brief response to the Essential Question, as described in student step 14. Next, divide the class into numbered groups and instruct even-numbered groups to revisit the news article, while odd-numbered groups revisit President Bush's speech. Have them work through their assigned texts using the questions in student step 15. Then combine even- and odd-numbered groups to report on their analyses.

28 Students should begin developing guiding questions for their research. Remind them to use the three bulleted points to help them structure effective guiding questions.

29 Read aloud the description of guiding questions. Assign partners to **think-pair-share** as they work through the questions and brainstorming exercise in student step 16. Then have pairs report their observations to the rest of the class.

30 Using the observations of the pairs of students, lead the class through the process of generating guiding questions for further investigation of Hurricane Katrina's media coverage.

4.5

My Notes

 Gaining Perspectives

When a natural disaster happens, local, state, and federal governments provide disaster relief to the community; however, these events don't happen every day. With a partner, pick one topic that affects the daily lives of the people living in your community, such as education, transportation, or crime prevention. How does the government provide for your community at the local, state, and federal levels? Are there problems that are related to your topic where you think the government could be taking a more active or proactive role? What would happen if the government, at any level, wasn't involved? Summarize your discussion in your Reader/Writer Notebook.

Working from the Text

14. Based on the texts that you've read, respond to the Essential Question: How do media sources influence our understanding of the truth and significance of an issue? Write a one-paragraph response in your Reader/Writer Notebook.

15. Revisit either the news article, "Daylong Efforts to Repair Levee Fail," or President Bush's Rose Garden address, and briefly annotate evidence that links to any of the critical lenses you have studied. Then use the following questions to analyze how the lenses might connect to bias in the text.

   • What is being reported (the who, what, where, when, why, and how of the event)?

   • How is it being reported? How objective is the coverage? Identify textual details (slanters, titles, labeling, omission, and so forth) that reveal bias.

   • Who is the target audience for the publication/broadcast? How does the text's rhetorical context affect what it talks about and its language and tone? What inferences can you draw about the writer's or speaker's expectations about the audience's perspective?

   • If you read only this article or heard only this speech, what would you think is the key issue? In other words, how does the article frame the truth and significance of the event?

   • What critical lens or lenses can be seen in how the text approaches the issue? What specific language reveals the lens(es)?

Guiding Questions

Guiding questions are questions about a specific aspect of a topic that you can research in order to learn more about that facet of the topic and the topic as a whole. If you are writing a research paper, good guiding questions should be:

• Focused enough that it is possible for you to search for, gather, and analyze information that will give you new knowledge about a topic

• Significant enough to have been addressed in reputable research materials

• Complex enough to require in-depth research and analysis

16. In preparation for further investigation of Hurricane Katrina, use guiding questions to develop focus questions to guide your research. Use the following steps and questions to narrow your thinking down to guiding questions that are more specific to what you have read about Hurricane Katrina:

My Notes

- Review your understanding of the critical perspectives (archetypal, cultural, feminist, historical, Marxist, reader response). Which ones seem relevant to this topic? Why? Which ones do not? Why not?

  Cultural and Historical Criticism seem central to the issue because the hurricane had major, lasting effects on the people of the region and the United States more broadly. An individual's experience of the event may have been affected by his or her status within the broader culture.

  Archetypal Criticism might be relevant if the event is reported with typical story patterns (e.g., humans versus nature) or character types (e.g., the hero).

  Marxist Criticism may be relevant because the event had an economic impact on people in the region and on gas prices across the country. Issues of class and economic power might play a role.

  Feminist Criticism doesn't seem to be as relevant because the issue doesn't seem to involve gender issues specifically.

- Based on background knowledge and your preliminary investigation of the topic, brainstorm connections between each relevant lens and the topic.

  Cultural: dominant groups and marginalized groups had different experiences of the storm; people's views on the responsibilities of local and federal government vary depending on their political ideologies; international vs. American perspectives on the event may differ

  Historical: Katrina was one of the most devastating natural disasters to occur in U.S. history; lessons learned (or not learned) from previous hurricanes; conflicts taking place outside of the country at the same time; evolving perspective on Bush and criticism of his responses to national crises

  Marxist: gas prices shot up in the days immediately after the storm; emergency loans kept refineries running despite disruption to crude oil supplies; economic impact of recovery; connection between residents' class status and their experience before, during, and after storm

  Archetypal: humans versus nature; the hero; mass exodus

LEVELED DIFFERENTIATED INSTRUCTION

In this activity, students might need support completing a quickwrite prompt that confirms their understanding of critical lenses.

Developing Have small groups complete the **Conversation for Quickwrite** graphic organizer to identify key words to help them explain which elements from the event can be described using Historical Criticism.

Expanding Have student partners restate the prompt in their own words, and then choose a critical lens to focus on. Provide the **Conversation for Quickwrite** graphic organizer to help them generate and explain their ideas about what parts of the event are most relevant to that lens.

Bridging Have students work independently to respond to the quickwrite. Encourage them to include specific evidence from more than one of the texts in the activity.

Support If students have difficulty, model interpreting the first story element through one of the lenses. Then break the class into small groups and provide the **Conversation for Quickwrite** graphic organizer. Give groups time to complete part of the graphic organizer and invite volunteers to share their ideas. Use student responses to evaluate understanding and use questions to prompt clarification before having groups complete the graphic organizer.

Extend Ask students who need an extra challenge to lead a small group and complete the **Conversation for Quickwrite** graphic organizer. Have leaders first summarize and review the various critical lenses with their group before leading the group in completing the graphic organizer.

31 Ask students to respond to the Check Your Understanding task individually.

ASSESS

Review student responses to the Check Your Understanding. Assess students' ability to cite specific elements of the story and offer a convincing rationale for why these elements are relevant to the lens they have chosen.

ADAPT

If students need additional help choosing a critical lens that relates to the event, review the types of lenses. Model relating one lens to the event, and then prompt student thinking with another lens before having them continue.

4.5

My Notes

17. Draft an initial closed (yes/no) question linking the lens to the subject.

    Was the response so slow because so many of the affected residents were poor? Was the economic impact on the country's oil supply prioritized over the human impact? Were the people who looted stores after the storm villains?

18. Modify the question to make it open-ended by using one of the following stems:

    • To what extent did X influence Y?

      To what extent did residents' economic status influence their experience of the hurricane?

    • In what ways did ...?

      In what ways did race play a role in the media coverage of the event?

    • What does the controversy surrounding (this topic) reveal about attitudes toward the (underlying issue)?

      What does the controversy surrounding the response to Hurricane Katrina reveal about attitudes toward the role of government?

    • What recurring story patterns are evoked by ...?

      What recurring story patterns, characters, or images are evoked by the events that followed the storm?

☑ **Check Your Understanding**

Quickwrite: Choose a lens you think applies to the event, and briefly explain what elements of the story may be most relevant through this lens.

Exploring Media Sources

Learning Targets
- Analyze ideas and details in informational material to gain an understanding of the aftermath of Hurricane Katrina.
- Closely examine and evaluate a film trailer, infographic, and podcast for credibility and bias.
- Use details in a series of visual and audio texts to make inferences about the creators' perspective.

Preview
In this activity, you will examine a variety of media. You will evaluate the texts to determine their value as research sources, considering credibility and bias in forming your judgments.

Learning Strategies
Graphic Organizer
Note-taking
Visual/Audio Prompts

My Notes

Viewing the Photographs

1. With your group, analyze the images from Hurricane Katrina by discussing your observations and making inferences. Evaluate the captions by using the critical perspective questions that follow:

Cultural Criticism: How might issues of race, age, or power be at play?

Feminist Criticism: What are some ways in which gender and gender roles represented in the photos?

Historical Criticism: What contemporary trends, conflicts, or developments might provide important context for understanding the images today?

Marxist Criticism: To what extent might questions of class be relevant for the viewer to consider?

A mother feeds her 9-day-old baby as she awaits evacuation from the Superdome in New Orleans, Louisiana. A riot erupted, and shots were fired outside of the arena as thousands fought to board buses heading to Houston, Texas.

Dillion Chancey, seven years old, is amongst those who have lost everything that they had in the wake of Hurricane Katrina. He and his parents endured the hurricane in Biloxi, Mississippi.

College and Career Readiness Standards

Focus Standards:

RI.11–12.7 Integrate and evaluate multiple sources of information presented in different media or formats (e.g., visually, quantitatively) as well as in words in order to address a question or solve a problem.

SL.11–12.2 Integrate multiple sources of information presented in diverse formats and media (e.g., visually, quantitatively, orally)

in order to make informed decisions and solve problems, evaluating the credibility and accuracy of each source and noting any discrepancies among the data.

SL.11–12.3 Evaluate a speaker's point of view, reasoning, and use of evidence and rhetoric, assessing the stance, premises, links among ideas, word choice, points of emphasis, and tone used.

ACTIVITY 4.6

PLAN

Materials: Trailer: *Trouble the Water* (2008), available online, and a podcast reporting on the aftermath of Hurricane Katrina
Suggested Pacing: 3 50-minute class periods

TEACH

1 Read aloud the Learning Targets and Preview.

2 Inform students that they will be closely evaluating sources for credibility. Note that the goal of this activity is for each student to gain experience in evaluating texts that present information in different media or formats to prepare them for conducting their own research for Embedded Assessment 1.

3 You may want to provide a **graphic organizer** to help students organize the notes they take while analyzing the photos as a group in student step 1.

★ TEACHER TO TEACHER

Consider modeling how to analyze an image and caption using a critical perspective with another editorial image related to Hurricane Katrina. Students may benefit from first using the SMELL strategy to analyze language used in a caption.

4 Ask groups to evaluate the infographic, the film trailer, and a podcast you have selected. Students might benefit from creating a double-entry journal in their Reader/Writer Notebook in which they answer the bulleted questions on one side and list supporting evidence from the text on the other.

TEACHER TO TEACHER

Many excellent podcasts have been produced on the topic of Hurricane Katrina. As with any media, be sure to preview the podcast to assess its appropriateness for your specific students and school setting before assigning it to students. A few podcasts to consider include:

- the series from New Orleans Public Radio called "Katrina: The Debris"
- the "Radiolab" episode "Playing God"
- "Diving Deeper: Hurricane Katrina Ten Years Later" from the National Ocean Service
- the 2005 series from *This American Life* called "After the Flood"

5 Encourage students to consider the source of each of the texts. Provide information about the sources or allow students to research the sources online.

LEVELED DIFFERENTIATED INSTRUCTION

In this activity, students might need support prewriting before they respond to the writing prompt.

Beginning For students who are at the beginning stages of English-language acquisition, a closed-caption version of the film trailer in their native language allows them to access the materials in their home language. Obtain a Spanish translation of the infographic from the CDC website.

Support If students are having difficulty organizing their notes, consider providing each group with questions that go along with their assigned media source.

4.6

President George W. Bush boards Air Force One after delivering a speech to the nation about Hurricane Katrina's damage from Jackson Square in New Orleans, September 15, 2005. In his speech Bush calls for the nation to prepare for a long-term effort to rebuild New Orleans.

A firefighter helps evacuate a man out of toxic flood waters as homes burn in the 7th Ward of New Orleans during the aftermath of Hurricane Katrina. The mixture of toxic chemicals and human waste in the New Orleans floodwaters increased the environmental toll of this natural disaster.

My Notes

Evaluating Multimedia Sources

2. Analyze and discuss initial impressions of the multimedia texts with your group. Evaluate the infographic, podcast, and video for any initial signs of bias or other flaws that could compromise their credibility as research sources.

Viewing the Infographic

3. Analyze the details in the infographic that follows, taking note of the data and sources presented in your Reader/Writer Notebook.

- Based on the information presented, what might be the creator's main purpose?
- How does the use of print and graphic features impact the data presented?
- What critical perspectives can you use to analyze this infographic?
- In your view, are the sources credible? How can you determine their validity?
- In your opinion, were the authors successful in achieving their goals? How did you arrive at that point of view?
- Does this infographic appear to be a credible source of information? Are there rhetorical slanters or biases present in the infographic?

College and Career Readiness Standards

W.11–12.8 Gather relevant information from multiple authoritative print and digital sources, using advanced searches effectively; assess the strengths and limitations of each source in terms of the task, purpose, and audience; integrate information into the text selectively to maintain the flow of ideas, avoiding plagiarism and overreliance on any one source and following a standard format for citation.

Additional Standards Addressed:
W.11–12.2a, W.11–12.2b, W.11–12.10

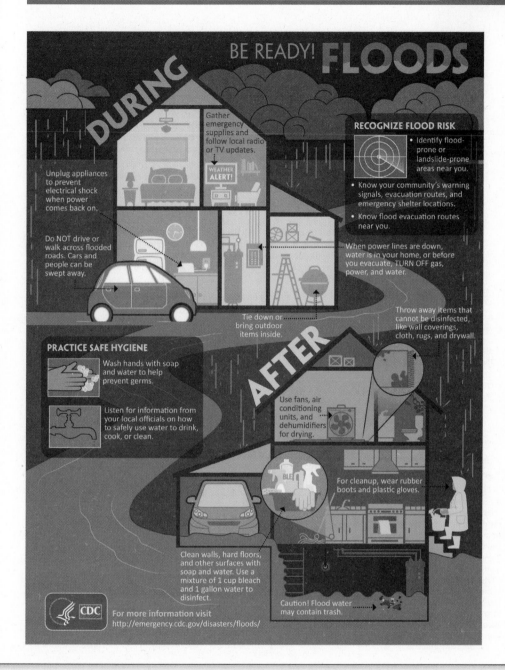

BE READY! FLOODS

DURING

Gather emergency supplies and follow local radio or TV updates.

WEATHER ALERT!

Unplug appliances to prevent electrical shock when power comes back on.

Do NOT drive or walk across flooded roads. Cars and people can be swept away.

RECOGNIZE FLOOD RISK
- Identify flood-prone or landslide-prone areas near you.
- Know your community's warning signals, evacuation routes, and emergency shelter locations.
- Know flood evacuation routes near you.

When power lines are down, water is in your home, or before you evacuate, TURN OFF gas, power, and water.

Tie down or bring outdoor items inside.

Throw away items that cannot be disinfected, like wall coverings, cloth, rugs, and drywall.

PRACTICE SAFE HYGIENE

Wash hands with soap and water to help prevent germs.

Listen for information from your local officials on how to safely use water to drink, cook, or clean.

AFTER

Use fans, air conditioning units, and dehumidifiers for drying.

For cleanup, wear rubber boots and plastic gloves.

Clean walls, hard floors, and other surfaces with soap and water. Use a mixture of 1 cup bleach and 1 gallon water to disinfect.

Caution! Flood water may contain trash.

CDC
For more information visit
http://emergency.cdc.gov/disasters/floods/

LEVELED DIFFERENTIATED INSTRUCTION

Extend For students with a high level of interest in the material, provide links to some of the other podcasts suggested for this activity. Ask them to use their Reader/Writer Notebook to reflect on how each podcast reflects different aspects of the broad story/history of Hurricane Katrina.

6 Note that the podcast should be teacher-selected. Pause frequently to allow students to take notes to help them answer the questions in the Listening to the Podcast section.

7 Before playing the film trailer, help students create a graphic organizer to take notes while they watch. Consider making a three-column chart for students to record what they hear, read, and see.

8 Remind students to be attentive for signs of bias or other flaws that could compromise the texts' credibility.

9 Consider distributing the **News Source** graphic organizer in Activity 4.4 to help students take notes on the conclusions they reach as a group.

10 After students have completed their analysis of the three texts, conduct a large group discussion. First, have small groups share their analysis of the infographic. Guide a class discussion to refine ideas and elicit deeper analysis of any points of disagreement. Encourage students to reference specific textual details in support of their points.

11 Vocabulary Development: Review the Academic Vocabulary with students. Ask them to work with their groups to describe how the terms *documentary*, *primary,* and *archival footage* are related.

12 Repeat this process for the film trailer and the podcast. To wrap up the discussion, encourage students to make connections between and among texts. Strongly emphasize the importance of citing supporting textual details.

13 Direct students to complete the Independent Reading Link. If students need assistance, consider using one of the nonfiction pieces from earlier in the unit to model a Reader/Writer Notebook entry that addresses the Read and Respond questions.

ASSESS

Review students' writing prompt responses to determine their ability to evaluate a multimedia source. Students' critiques should include a reasonable statement regarding the effectiveness of the piece and should support the evaluation with details from the piece, including textual details, producing techniques, use of images, and so on. Make sure students also include well-founded commentary on the credibility of the piece as a source for research.

ADAPT

If student responses are lacking, model the writing process using two photos that appeared earlier in the unit.

4.6

My Notes

_____

_____

_____

_____

_____

_____

_____

_____

_____

_____

VOCABULARY

ACADEMIC

A documentary film is based on factual events. Primary footage refers to footage shot by the filmmaker for the text at hand. Archival footage is footage taken from another, previously recorded source.

📖 INDEPENDENT READING LINK

Read and Respond

If you are reading nonfiction, think about the choices that the author has made about what information to include and what to omit. Do you sense the ways in which the author's opinions and preference create a filter through which you take in the information? What do you observe about the author's take on his or her subject? Record your observations in your Reader/Writer Notebook.

Listening to the Podcast

4. As you listen to the podcast, jot down notes in preparation for your group discussion in your Reader/Writer Notebook.

- How would you summarize the theme or message of this podcast?
- How do the additional sounds (music, etc.) contribute to the theme?
- In your opinion, were the podcast creators successful in expressing their theme? How did you arrive at that point of view?
- Does this podcast appear to be a credible source of information? Why or why not? Try to be as specific as possible when citing details to support your answer.
- What critical perspectives can you use to analyze this infographic?

Watching the Film Trailer

5. Documentary filmmakers use both primary and archival footage to present their case. As you watch the trailer for *Trouble the Water*, remember that directors of nonfiction films make choices similar to those made by fiction film directors. Such choices reveal bias, whether in subtle or blatant ways. Be prepared to support a claim regarding the level and nature of bias in the text after viewing the clip.

- What do we hear (dialogue, narration)?
- What do we read (subtitles, graphics, labels, and so on)?
- What do we see (primary or archival footage, interviews, still images, the filmmaker, cinematic techniques, narrative elements)?
- In your opinion, were the directors successful in expressing their theme? Provide textual details to support your answer.
- Does this trailer appear to be a credible source of information? Why or why not? Provide textual details to support your answer.
- What is the theme/message of the film? What "truth" does it convey about the subject? What lenses are most helpful?

☑ Check Your Understanding

What are some key choices photographers, directors, and graphic designers can make in order to influence viewers' understanding of the truth and significance of an event?

📝 Writing Prompt: Informational

After discussing the infographic, podcast, and video in groups, write a brief essay explaining how producers of media can select information–interviews, statistics, images, or sounds–to frame the information they present through a particular critical lens. Cite a specific critical lens and examples from your analysis and discussion to support your argument. Be sure to:

- Use the guiding questions to inform your thesis and analysis.
- Support your claims by using vivid descriptions of elements of one or more of the media sources discussed.

✍ WRITING PROMPT: ARGUMENTATIVE

The following standards are addressed in the writing prompt:

- RI.11–12.1
- W.11–12.2a
- W.11–12.2b
- W.11–12.8

Throwing Light on the Situation

Learning Targets

- Closely read and analyze an informational text in order to present key information to peers.
- Evaluate different organizational options to choose the clearest structure for information you plan to present.
- Integrate ideas from multiple texts to build knowledge and vocabulary about the effects of Hurricane Katrina.

Preview

In this activity, you will closely read and analyze a text, and then you will work together with your peers to synthesize evidence from multiple texts in a presentation and a written analysis.

As You Read

- Use metacognitive markers to annotate important, surprising, confusing, or key details in the text.
- Circle unknown words and phrases. Try to determine the meaning of the words by using context clues, word parts, or a dictionary.

Editorial

An Editorial: It's Time for a Nation to Return the Favor

The Times-Picayune
November 20, 2005

1   The federal government wrapped levees around greater New Orleans so that the rest of the country could share in our bounty.

2   Americans wanted the oil and gas that flow freely off our shores. They longed for the oysters and shrimp and flaky Gulf fish that live in abundance in our waters. They wanted to ship corn and soybeans and beets down the Mississippi and through our ports. They wanted coffee and steel to flow north through the mouth of the river and into the heartland.

3   They wanted more than that, though. They wanted to share in our spirit. They wanted to sample the joyous beauty of our jazz and our food. And we were happy to **oblige** them.

4   So the federal government-built levees and convinced us that we were safe.

5   We weren't.

6   The levees, we were told, could stand up to a Category 3 hurricane.

7   They couldn't.

Learning Strategies

Close Reading
Marking the Text
Think-Pair-Share

My Notes

KNOWLEDGE QUEST

Knowledge Question:

What are the major challenges in responding to natural disasters, both immediately and in the long term?

In Activity 4.7 you will read articles and reports that each interpret the impact and aftermath of Hurricane Katrina differently. As you read and build knowledge about the topic, think about your answer to the Knowledge Question.

oblige: allow

College and Career Readiness Standards

Focus Standards:

RI.11–12.3 Analyze a complex set of ideas or sequence of events and explain how specific individuals, ideas, or events interact and develop over the course of the text.

RI.11–12.7 Integrate and evaluate multiple sources of information presented in different media or formats (e.g., visually, quantitatively) as well as in words in order to address a question or solve a problem.

PLAN

Materials: projector for modeling text annotation
Suggested Pacing: 4 50-minute class periods

TEACH

1 Read the Learning Targets and Preview with the class.

2 Inform students that they will be studying how media texts from a variety of sources and time frames present different interpretations of the meaning and significance of a news event. Note that the goal of this activity is for each student to gain experience in the **close reading**, analysis, and synthesis of sources in preparation for their work on Embedded Assessment 1.

3 Create groups of three to four students, and assign each group one of the articles. When grouping students and assigning texts, take into consideration student reading proficiency and text complexity. Note that the texts in this activity vary in length and complexity, so some students may need greater support when reading and analyzing certain texts.

4 Consider grouping students by Embedded Assessment groups in order to give them practice working together.

LEVELED DIFFERENTIATED INSTRUCTION

Students will closely read and analyze a text in order to present it to peers. They will work with peers to synthesize information from different texts in a presentation and in writing.

Developing Consider the "Attitude of Resilience" article for students at this proficiency level and for reluctant readers because of its length and readability.

Expanding The "Who's a Looter?" article, "The Press, Race, and Katrina" article, or the "A Failure of Initiative" report would be good choices for students who exhibit a high level of language proficiency. These pieces also take a deeper dive into societal issues.

Support The "Looters Leave Nothing" article may be the best choice for students who need extra support because it is fact-based and uses short paragraphs.

Extend Consider using the "Need for Science" report as the basis for an extension assignment.

5 Read the As You Read section with the class. Help students understand the process for this activity: The whole class will read the editorial, and then student groups will read one of the remaining texts in preparation for a jigsaw. Later, they will present an analysis of their text to the class. Explain that they will use evidence from all of the sources in the written analysis for this activity.

6 Direct students to the Knowledge Question. Engage students by asking them to share what details most stood out to them about Hurricane Katrina. Then have small groups discuss their responses to the Knowledge Question.

 TEXT COMPLEXITY

Overall: Moderate
Lexile: 780L
Qualitative: Moderate Difficulty
Task: Moderate (Analyze)

7 FIRST READ: Model the close reading process for this activity using the first text.

8 To model what will be expected as students read and analyze the various articles, walk the class through a close reading of the *Times-Picayune* editorial. Project the text and demonstrate how to annotate for the first read.

9 Be sure students attend to the Grammar & Usage features alongside the various readings in this activity.

10 Have student volunteers respond verbally to the Knowledge Quest questions.

Notes for Close Reading of "An Editorial: It's Time for a Nation to Return the Favor"

(paragraph 1) Historical Criticism: The article starts by providing

GRAMMAR & USAGE

Rhetorical Devices
Writers use a number of rhetorical devices to make their writing more persuasive. In this editorial, the authors use anaphora, or repetition, to emphasize a point. Notice how the authors repeat the phrase "they wanted" to emphasize how much the rest of the nation demanded from New Orleans.

Find one more example of a rhetorical device in this text, and compare your findings with a partner.

My Notes

_____
_____
_____
_____
_____
_____
_____
_____
_____
_____
_____
_____
_____
_____
_____
_____
_____
_____
_____

8 By the time Katrina surged into New Orleans, it had weakened to Category 3. Yet our levee system wasn't as strong as the Army Corps of Engineers said it was. Barely anchored in mushy soil, the floodwalls gave way.

9 Our homes and businesses were swamped. Hundreds of our neighbors died.

10 Now, this metro area is drying off and digging out. Life is going forward. Our heart is beating.

11 But we need the federal government—we need our Congress—to fulfill the promises made to us in the past. We need to be safe. We need to be able to go about our business feeding and fueling the rest of the nation. We need better protection next hurricane season than we had this year. Going forward, we need protection from the fiercest storms, the Category 5 storms that are out there waiting to strike.

12 Some voices in Washington are arguing against us. We were foolish, they say. We settled in a place that is lower than the sea. We should have expected to drown.

13 As if choosing to live in one of the nation's great cities amounted to a death wish. As if living in San Francisco or Miami or Boston is any more logical.

14 Great cities are made by their place and their people, their beauty and their risk. Water flows around and through most of them. And one of the greatest bodies of water in the land flows through this one: the Mississippi.

15 The federal government decided long ago to try to tame the river and the swampy land spreading out from it. The country needed this waterlogged land of ours to prosper, so that the nation could prosper even more.

16 Some people in Washington don't seem to remember that. They act as if we are a burden. They act as if we wore our skirts too short and invited trouble.

17 We can't put up with that. We have to stand up for ourselves. Whether you are back at home or still in exile waiting to return, let Congress know that this metro area must be made safe from future storms. Call and write the leaders who are deciding our fate. Get your family and friends in other states to do the same. Start with members of the Environment and Public Works and Appropriations[1] committees in the Senate, and Transportation and Appropriations in the House. Flood them with mail the way we were flooded by Katrina.

18 Remind them that this is a singular American city and that this nation still needs what we can give it.

⌀ Knowledge Quest
- Which of the authors' claims stand out to you the most?
- What captures your attention as the worst outcome of Katrina?

[1] *Appropriations:* House and Senate Appropriations Committees pass bills that set aside money for specific federal agencies and programs.

College and Career Readiness Standards

SL.11–12.4 Present information, findings, and supporting evidence, conveying a clear and distinct perspective, such that listeners can follow the line of reasoning, alternative or opposing perspectives are addressed, and the organization, development, substance, and style are appropriate to purpose, audience, and a range of formal and informal tasks.

Additional Standards Addressed:

RI.11–12.1, RI.11–12.2, RI.11–12.4, RI.11–12.5, RI.11–12.6, RI.11–12.8, SL.11–12.1a, SL.11–12.1c, SL.11–12.1d, W.11–12.2a, W.11–12.2b, W.11–12.2c, W.11–12.2d, W.11–12.2e

Returning to the Text

- Reread the editorial to answer these text-dependent questions.
- Write any additional questions you have about the text in your Reader/Writer Notebook.

1. What is the "favor" in the editorial's title?

   New Orleans did the rest of the United States a favor by sharing its natural resources, its ports,

   and its cultural spirit.

2. According to the text, how has the federal government failed to uphold its promises? What does it need to do to make up for that failure? Cite evidence to support your answer.

   In the past, the federal government "built levees and convinced us that we were safe" and said

   that "the levees … could stand up to a Category 3 hurricane." The government failed because

   New Orleans wasn't safe, and the levees did not hold up to a Category 3 hurricane. The writers

   want the government to "fulfill the promises made to us in the past."

3. **KQ** What does describing displaced New Orleanians as "in exile" suggest about how they view themselves?

   Living "in exile" typically means being forced to live outside your native country, often due to

   political reasons. Using this phrase to refer to displaced New Orleanians suggests that they

   view themselves as being forced from their homes and barred from returning. The phrase also

   suggests that their reason for being unable to return may be a political one.

4. What counterarguments do the writers present? How do they respond to them?

   They acknowledge that "(s)ome voices in Washington are arguing against us. We were foolish,

   they say. We settled in a place that is lower than the sea." They respond by saying that other

   great cities, such as San Francisco, Miami, and Boston, are also located in areas susceptible to

   natural disasters, places where water is all around.

Scaffolding the Text-Dependent Questions

1. What is the "favor" in the editorial's title? Reread paragraphs 1–3. What has New Orleans given the rest of the country? RI.11–12.4, RI.11–12.5

2. According to the text, how has the federal government failed to uphold its promises? What does it need to do to make up for that failure? Cite evidence to support your answer. Reread paragraphs 4–11. What did the government do and say in the past? What was the result of the failures? What do the writers say needs to be done for New Orleans to be safe? RI.11–12.1, RI.11–12.2

3. What does describing displaced New Orleanians as "in exile" suggest about how they view themselves? What is exile? Are New Orleanians truly exiles? Why might they feel like exiles? RI.11–12.4

ACTIVITY 4.7 continued

context for the failure of the levee system, which led to the majority of damage caused by Hurricane Katrina. Whom does the article blame?

(paragraphs 2 & 3) Marxist Criticism: The writer presents a snapshot of the resources Americans took from New Orleans. Is the interaction described positively or negatively? Does this shift within the text?

(paragraph 8) Cultural Criticism: Saying "our levee system wasn't as strong as the Army Corps of Engineers said it was" implies that the government was ignorant or dishonest. Where else is the writer's bias regarding government revealed?

(paragraph 12) Cultural Criticism: The article doesn't name names but instead points fingers at "some voices in Washington." It also doesn't give specific quotes but paraphrases what "they say." What political impact does this rhetoric have?

(about the writer) *The Times-Picayune*, New Orleans's primary newspaper, published continuously online during the Katrina disaster and returned to print four days later. It was a lifeline to the community, relaying vital information, such as where to get food and water. This editorial is part of the coverage that earned the paper the 2006 Pulitzer Prize for Breaking News Reporting and Public Service Journalism. What weight does the paper's community standing give to this editorial?

 TEACHER TO TEACHER

If your students need support with English language development, consider differentiating instruction with the Language Workshop 4A activities available on SpringBoard Digital. Built around the *Times-Picayune* editorial, these activities offer a scaffolded approach to vocabulary study (Activity 3), guided close reading (Activity 4), and collaborative academic discussion (Activity 5). When planning differentiation, make sure to have students return to portions of the ELA activity that provide essential practice for the Embedded Assessments.

11 As you read the first text as a class, monitor students' progress. Be sure they are engaged with the text, recording ideas about rhetorical context, noting critical lenses, and circling unknown words and phrases.

12 **RETURNING TO THE TEXT:** During the second reading, students will answer the text-dependent questions. You may choose to have students reread and work on the questions in small groups.

13 If students have difficulty, scaffold the questions by rephrasing them or breaking them down into smaller parts. See the Scaffolding the Text-Dependent Questions boxes for suggestions.

TEACHER TO TEACHER

To help manage this jigsaw reading activity, consider assigning one student in each group the role of "spokesperson," and asking that student to communicate with you if the group needs additional support reading the text or answering the text-dependent questions.

5. What comparison is implied by the sentence, "They act as if we wore our skirts too short and invited trouble." Is this an effective analogy?

The analogy compares attitudes toward New Orleans to some people's attitude about women who wear short skirts—both should be blamed for "inviting trouble." In the case of New Orleans, the city is seen as "inviting trouble" because its location makes it prone to flooding. The analogy might appeal to some readers' sense of justice, but it could offend others.

6. **KQ** What was the purpose of this editorial? Cite details to support your answer.

The editorial's purpose is to outline the "favor" New Orleans has done for the nation throughout the city's history in order to convince readers that the nation owes New Orleans something in return. The editorial's headline and the last sentence are specific calls to action.

Scaffolding the Text-Dependent Questions

4. What counterarguments do the writers present? How do they respond to them? Reread paragraphs 12–14. Who does not agree with the writers' argument? What do they say? Why do the writers point to other U.S. cities in their response? RI.11–12.5

5. What comparison is implied by the sentence, "They act as if we wore our skirts too short and invited trouble." Is this an effective analogy? Reread paragraph 16. Where have you heard the argument that short skirts invite trouble? How would this argument apply to New Orleans? Why might people like or dislike this analogy? RI.11–12.1, RI.11–12.6

Article

Looters Leave Nothing Behind in Storm's Wake:

Police officers seen joining in on free-for-all

by **Mike Perlstein and Brian Thevenot**

The Times-Picayune, **August 31, 2005**

1   Law enforcement efforts to contain the emergency left by Katrina slipped into chaos in parts of New Orleans Tuesday—with some police officers and firefighters even joining looters in picking stores clean.

2   At the Wal-Mart on Tchoupitoulas Street, an initial effort to hand out provisions to stranded citizens quickly disintegrated into mass looting. Authorities at the scene said bedlam erupted after the giveaway was announced over the radio.

3   While many people carried out food and essential supplies, others cleared out jewelry racks and carted out computers, TVs and appliances on handtrucks.

4   Some officers joined in taking whatever they could, including one New Orleans cop who loaded a shopping cart with a compact computer and a 27-inch flat screen television.

5   Officers claimed there was nothing they could do to contain the anarchy, saying their radio communications had broken down and they had no direction from commanders.

6   "We don't have enough cops to stop it," an officer said. "A mass riot would break out if you tried."

7   Inside the store, the scene alternated between celebration and frightening bedlam. A shirtless man straddled a broken jewelry case, yelling, "Free samples, free samples over here."

8   Another man rolled a mechanized pallet, stacked six feet high ... Perched atop the stack was a bewildered toddler.

9   Throughout the store and parking lot, looters pushed carts and loaded trucks and vans alongside officers. One man said police directed him to Wal-Mart from Robert's Grocery, where a similar scene was taking place.

10   A crowd in the electronics section said one officer broke the glass DVD case so people wouldn't cut themselves.

KNOWLEDGE QUEST

Knowledge Question:

What are the major challenges in responding to natural disasters, both immediately and in the long term?

WORD CONNECTIONS

Etymology

Bedlam is a noun used for a scene of noise and confusion. The word can be traced back to the Hospital of Saint Mary of Bethlehem in London, which became an institution for people with mental illnesses in 1402. It soon became known as *Bedlam*, a Middle English corruption of *Bethlehem*. Later the word came to be used for any chaotic scene similar to conditions found in early hospitals for people with mental illnesses.

My Notes

_____

_____

_____

_____

_____

_____

_____

_____

_____

_____

_____

_____

Scaffolding the Text-Dependent Questions

6. What was the purpose of this editorial? Cite details to support your answer. Reread the headline and final paragraph of the article and identify the call to action. RI.11–12.1, RI.11–12.6

7. What is the writers' purpose for this article and who is their likely audience? Reread the headline and first paragraph to cull ideas about purpose. Also think about the general purpose for all news articles and broadcasts. When thinking about audience, ask yourself, "Who would have wanted to read this story in the days immediately following the hurricane?" RI.11–12.6

14 Review the Knowledge Question with students. Remind them to think about their answer to the Knowledge Question as they read and build knowledge about the topic.

15 **FIRST READ:** After completing the whole-class reading of the editorial, give student groups time to read their assigned text and annotate it. Monitor the groups' progress and provide support as needed. Encourage students to take notes alongside the text to support their discussions when they arrive at the Working from the Text section.

 TEXT COMPLEXITY

Overall: Moderate
Lexile: 1180L
Qualitative: Moderate Difficulty
Task: Moderate (Analyze)

16 **Vocabulary Development:** Remind students to discuss the Word Connections box after reading paragraph 2. Have students look up synonyms for the word *bedlam* in a print or digital thesaurus. Then have them discuss the connotation of each word with a partner.

Notes for Close Reading

(paragraph 3) Marxist Criticism: The article distinguishes between people who "carried out food and essential supplies" and "others who cleared out jewelry racks and carted out computers, TVs, and appliances on handtrucks." What does the article imply about the effect of class in this situation?

(paragraph 4) Cultural Criticism: The writers describe a scene with "one New Orleans cop" stealing a computer and television; however, they do not state the source of this information. Other reports of police misbehavior are attributed to unnamed sources, some of whom are looters. Also note the instances where police officers are referred to as "officers" and "cops." How might these differences in word choice reflect bias?

(about the writer)

Perlstein and Thevenot were staff writers for the New Orleans *Times-Picayune*. This article was part of the paper's Pulitzer Prize–winning coverage of Hurricane Katrina.

17 When the article has been read, pose the Knowledge Quest questions. Ask students to think about their initial reaction to the article.

4.7

GRAMMAR & USAGE

Appositives

An appositive is a word, phrase, or clause that is in apposition to, or side by side with, a noun or pronoun. The purpose of an appositive is to identify or describe the noun or pronoun.

Appositives are either essential or nonessential. If an appositive is nonessential, containing supplemental rather than essential information, it should be set off by commas. Find a nonessential appositive in this example from the article:

Toni Williams, 25, packed her trunk with essential supplies, such as food and water, but said mass looting disgusted and frightened her.

My Notes

11 "The police got all the best stuff. They're crookeder than us," one man said.

12 Most officers, though, simply stood by powerless against the tide of law breakers. One veteran officer said, "It's like this everywhere in the city. This tiny number of cops can't do anything about this. It's wide open."

13 At least one officer tried futilely to control a looter through shame.

14 "When they say take what you need, that doesn't mean an f-ing TV," the officer shouted to a looter. "This is a hurricane, not a free-for-all."

15 Sandra Smith of Baton Rouge walked through the parking lot with a 12-pack ... under each arm.

16 "I came down here to get my daughters," she said, "but I can't find them."

17 The scene turned so chaotic at times that entrances were blocked by the press of people, shopping carts and traffic jams that sprouted on surrounding streets.

18 Some groups organized themselves into assembly lines to more efficiently cart off goods.

19 Toni Williams, 25, packed her trunk with essential supplies, such as food and water, but said mass looting disgusted and frightened her.

20 "I didn't feel safe. Some people are going overboard," she said.

21 Inside the store, one woman was stocking up on make-up. She said she took comfort in watching police load up their own carts.

22 "It must be legal," she said. "The police are here taking stuff, too."

An unidentified official takes part in looting a K-Mart on August 30, 2005 after Hurricane Katrina devastated Louisiana.

✒ Knowledge Quest

- Which details in the article help you envision the scene?
- Which quotes are particularly striking?

Scaffolding the Text-Dependent Questions

8. How were police responding to the emergency? Cite details from the article to support your answer. Reread paragraphs 5 and 6. How did the storm disrupt communication? What would happen if police tried to stop the looting? RI.11–12.1

9. What effect does describing the looters as "a tide of law breakers" have on readers? Reread paragraph 12. What connotations does the word *tide* have? How might the metaphor bear special meaning to survivors of Katrina? RI.11–12.4

Returning to the Text
- Reread the article to answer these text-dependent questions.
- Write any additional questions you have about the text in your Reader/Writer Notebook.

7. What is the writers' purpose for this article and who is their likely audience?

    The purpose of the article is to inform readers about the atmosphere in New Orleans after the

    hurricane. The likely audience is readers who are not in New Orleans. They may be residents

    who have evacuated, or people who live elsewhere and are looking for credible reports from

    the major local newspaper.

8. How were police responding to the emergency? Cite details from the article to support your answer.

    Officers said that broken-down radio communication left them with "no direction from

    commanders" and that their small numbers meant that trying to stop looters would lead to "a

    mass riot," so many stood by watching looters rather than trying to actively stop them. The

    article also cites examples of officers joining in the looting.

9. **KQ** What effect does describing the looters as "a tide of law breakers" have on readers?

    "A tide of lawbreakers" compares the people to a natural force, one which officers are

    "powerless against." This image is likely to call to mind the tide of flood waters that washed

    over the city when Katrina struck. The metaphor reinforces negative feelings towards the

    looters and links them to the hurricane that destroyed the city.

10. **KQ** What is the key idea of the text? How does this text complement the message in the editorial "It's Time for a Nation to Return the Favor"?

    The central idea of the text is that New Orleans after Katrina is so chaotic that even police

    are breaking the law. The text complements the message of the editorial by conveying the

    desperation people feel in the aftermath of Hurricane Katrina.

Scaffolding the Text-Dependent Questions

10. What is the key idea of the text? How does this text complement the message in the editorial "It's Time for a Nation to Return the Favor"? What is the central idea of the text? What does the woman say in the last paragraph? How does this build on the message of the editorial? RI.11–12.1, RI.11–12.2, RI.11–12.5

TEXT COMPLEXITY

Overall: Moderate
Lexile: 1180L
Qualitative: Moderate Difficulty
Task: Moderate (Analyze)

18 Review the Knowledge Question with students. Remind them to think about their answer to the Knowledge Question as they read and build knowledge about the topic.

Notes for Close Reading

(paragraph 1) Cultural Criticism: The article's topic is race and the media. Encourage students not only to look at the photos at the center of the controversy (easily found online by doing an image search for "Katrina looter race") but also at the types of news media stirring the controversy (e.g., Flickr, Daily Kos, BoingBoing). Are these sources credible?

4.7

KNOWLEDGE QUEST

Knowledge Question:
What are the major challenges in responding to natural disasters, both immediately and in the long term?

My Notes

Article

Who's a Looter? In Storm's Aftermath, Pictures Kick up a Different Kind of Tempest

by **Tania Ralli**

New York Times, **September 5, 2005**

1 Two news photographs ricocheted through the Internet last week and set off a debate about race and the news media in the aftermath of Hurricane Katrina.

2 The first photo, taken by Dave Martin, an Associated Press photographer in New Orleans, shows a young black man wading through water that has risen to his chest. He is clutching a case of soda and pulling a floating bag. The caption provided by the A.P.[2] says he has just been "looting a grocery store."

"A young man walks through chest deep flood water after looting a grocery store in New Orleans on Tuesday, Aug. 30, 2005. Flood waters continue to rise in New Orleans after Hurricane Katrina did extensive damage when it made landfall on Monday." (AP Photo/Dave Martin)

3 The second photo, also from New Orleans, was taken by Chris Graythen for Getty Images and distributed by Agence France-Presse. It shows a white couple up to their chests in the same murky water. The woman is holding some bags of food. This caption says they are shown "after finding bread and soda from a local grocery store."

---

[2] *A.P. stands for Associated Press.*

Scaffolding the Text-Dependent Questions

11. Based on this article, what made the two photos controversial? Review the photos and reread paragraphs 2–5. What do the photos' captions imply about some people's perceptions and how small variations in language can impact meaning? RI.11–12.2

12. Who do you think would be the most likely audience for this article? Support your answer with evidence from the text. Reread the headline first for ideas about the article's purpose. Then review paragraph 4. When thinking about audience, ask yourself, "Who would have wanted to read this story in the days immediately following the hurricane and who would have access to the sources of information outlined in paragraph 4?" RI.11–12.1, RI.11–12.6

4 Both photos turned up Tuesday on Yahoo News, which posts automatic feeds of articles and photos from wire services. Soon after, a user of the photo-sharing site Flickr juxtaposed the images and captions on a single page, which attracted links from many blogs. The left-leaning blog Daily Kos linked to the page with the comment "It's not looting if you're white."

5 The contrast of the two photo captions, which to many indicated a double standard at work, generated widespread anger toward the news media that quickly spread beyond the Web.

6 On Friday night, the rapper Kanye West ignored the teleprompter during NBC's live broadcast of "A Concert for Hurricane Relief," using the opportunity to **lambaste** President Bush and criticize the press. "I hate the way they portray us in the media," he said. "You see a black family, it says they're looting. You see a white family, it says they're looking for food."

7 Many bloggers were quick to point out that the photos came from two different agencies, and so could not reflect the prejudice of a single media outlet. A writer on the blog BoingBoing wrote: "Perhaps there's more factual substantiation behind each copywriter's choice of words than we know. But to some, the difference in tone suggests racial bias, implicit or otherwise."

8 According to the agencies, each photographer captioned his own photograph. Jack Stokes, a spokesman for the A.P., said that photographers are told to describe what they have seen when they write a caption.

9 Mr. Stokes said the A.P. had guidelines in place before Hurricane Katrina struck to distinguish between "looting" and "carrying." If a photographer sees a person enter a business and emerge with goods, it is described as looting. Otherwise the A.P. calls it carrying.

10 Mr. Stokes said that Mr. Martin had seen the man in his photograph wade into a grocery store and come out with the sodas and bag, so by A.P.'s definition, the man had looted.

11 The photographer for Getty Images, Mr. Graythen, said in an e-mail message that he had also stuck to what he had seen to write his caption, and had actually given the wording a great deal of thought. Mr. Graythen described seeing the couple near a corner store from an elevated expressway. The door to the shop was open, and things had floated out to the street. He was not able to talk to the couple, "so I had to draw my own conclusions," he said.

"Two residents wade through chest-deep water after finding bread and soda from a local grocery store after Hurricane Katrina came through the area on August 29, 2005, in New Orleans, Louisiana. Katrina was downgraded to a Category 4 storm as it approached New Orleans." (Photo by Chris Graythen/Getty Images)

lambaste: harshly criticize

(paragraph 9) Marxist Criticism: The AP clearly distinguished between *looting* and *carrying*. What do these definitions suggest about the economic disparity of post-natural-disaster impulses?

(paragraph 11) Cultural Criticism: Mr. Graythen states that he "had to draw [his] own conclusions" about whether the white couple had stolen food from the corner store. Does this absolve the photo caption from the criticism that it is racist?

Scaffolding the Text-Dependent Questions

13. **What different perspectives on the photographs are introduced in the first three paragraphs? How does the author frame the issue?** What does the use of the word *ricocheted* tell you about the impact of these photographs? How does the author describe the first photograph? Why does he emphasize the photo's caption? How does the author describe the second photograph? How is "finding" something better or worse than "looting"? What do the differences imply? RI.11–12.1, RI.11–12.5

(paragraph 17) Cultural Criticism: Calas says that the caption "was a consequence of a series of negligences, not ill intent." What role does intent play in determining whether an action is racist or not?

19 After students have read the article the first time, remind them to discuss the Knowledge Quest questions. Have students discuss their responses with their small group.

My Notes

12 In the extreme conditions of New Orleans, Mr. Graythen said, taking necessities like food and water to survive could not be considered stealing. He said that had he seen people coming out of stores with computers and DVD players, he would have considered that looting.

13 "If you're taking something that runs solely from a wall outlet that requires power from the electric company—when we are not going to have power for weeks, even months—that's inexcusable," he said.

14 Since the photo was published last Tuesday Mr. Graythen has received more than 500 e-mail messages, most of them supportive, he said.

15 Within three hours of the photo's publication online, editors at Agence France-Presse rewrote Mr. Graythen's caption. But the original caption remained online as part of a Yahoo News slide show. Under pressure to keep up with the news, and lacking the time for a discussion about word choice, Olivier Calas, the agency's director of multimedia, asked Yahoo to remove the photo last Thursday.

16 Now, in its place, when readers seek the picture of the couple, a statement from Neil Budde, the general manager of Yahoo News, appears in its place. The statement emphasizes that Yahoo News did not write the photo captions and that it did not edit the captions, so that the photos can be made available as quickly as possible.

17 Mr. Calas said Agence France-Presse was bombarded with e-mail messages complaining about the caption. He said the caption was unclear and should have been reworded earlier. "This was a consequence of a series of negligences, not ill intent," he said.

18 For Mr. Graythen, whose parents and grandparents lost their homes in the disaster, the fate of the survivors was the most important thing. In his e-mail message he wrote: "Now is no time to pass judgment on those trying to stay alive. Now is no time to argue semantics about finding versus looting. Now is no time to argue if this is a white versus black issue."

⊘ Knowledge Quest
- What is your initial reaction to the captions to the article?
- What are your first thoughts about how the people in both photos were affected by Katrina?

Scaffolding the Text-Dependent Questions

14. Define *objective coverage* in your own words and apply your definition to the article. Does it provide objective coverage? What evidence supports your conclusion? Are all parties involved in the captioning of the photographs quoted? Does the author seem to give time and weight to both parties' decisions about the captions? Does the author include her own opinion on the issue? RI.11–12.5, RI.11–12.6

Returning to the Text

- Reread the article to answer these text-dependent questions.
- Write any additional questions you have about the text in your Reader/Writer Notebook.

11. **KQ** Based on this article, what made the two photos controversial?

The content of the two photos was very similar; the key difference is one featured a black man

and the other featured a white couple. The photos were controversial because the caption of

the photo of the black man indicated he was "looting" while the caption of the other people

indicated they were pictured after "finding" the goods they were carrying.

12. Who do you think would be the most likely audience for this article? Support your answer with evidence from the text.

The likely audience was comprised of people not devastated by Hurricane Katrina. Since

much of the article focuses on how media outlets gather information, rather than on matters

essential to rescue and recovery operations, people generally unaffected by the storm would

be most interested in this article.

13. What different perspectives on the photographs are introduced in the first three paragraphs? How does the author frame the issue?

The difference in perspectives lies in the way the photographs are captioned—one caption

says that a black man is "looting" while a white couple is depicted as "finding" food. The

author is framing the issue through the lens of race and how different connotative language is

used for each caption.

14. **KQ** Define *objective coverage* in your own words and apply your definition to the article. Does it provide objective coverage? What evidence supports your conclusion?

Although the article describes a sensitive topic, the author attempts to give information from

all sides of the debate, and therefore the article comes across as objective. This can be seen in

the way the author uses quotes from all parties and attempts to leave a personal opinion out

of the reporting.

TEXT COMPLEXITY

Overall: Moderate
Lexile: 1500L
Qualitative: Moderate Difficulty
Task: Moderate (Analyze)

20 Review the Knowledge Question with students. Remind them to think about their answer to the Knowledge Question as they read and build knowledge about the topic.

Notes for Close Reading

(paragraph 1) Historical Criticism: This article was published one year after Hurricane Katrina devastated the Gulf Coast. Students should note how time benefits the writer, who can gather information from multiple sources. The writer begins with sympathy toward the news managers who had to make "on-the-spot editorial decisions," which may not have been accurate.

21 Remind students to pause to discuss the Word Connections box after they read paragraph 4.

4.7

My Notes

KNOWLEDGE QUEST

Knowledge Question:
What are the major challenges in responding to natural disasters, both immediately and in the long term?

WORD CONNECTIONS

Cognates
The word palpable is a cognate in Spanish and English. In both languages, the word is an adjective meaning "able to be touched or felt" or "easy to perceive."

About the Author

Madison Gray is a seasoned editor and writer who has contributed to online publications such as Ebony.com, CBSNews.com, Time.com, and TheRoot.com over the past decade. Gray served as chief producer for *Time Magazine* from 2006–2014, where he created quality content for the website's homepage and recorded podcasts for TIME's Assignment Detroit project. Currently, his reporting is focused on urban issues affecting the New York area.

Article

The Press, Race, and Katrina

by **Madison Gray**

Time Magazine, **August 30, 2006**

1   If you watched any television, listened to any radio, picked up a newspaper or visited a news website in the days that followed Hurricane Katrina last year, you probably were witness to the result of dozens of on-the-spot editorial decisions made by news managers around the country.

2   As much as we may have wanted to avoid the issue in those first confusing days, because New Orleans was 67% African American prior to the storm, race played a significant role in criticisms of government, both local and federal, humanitarian aid and not surprisingly, the media. Fortunately, the fourth estate3 has its own self-policing mechanisms and is much faster than government and other industries at evaluating and scrutinizing itself. But it is only in recent years that the media has taken a look at how it relates to the country's racial divisions, and Katrina provided an opportunity to do just that.

3   Keith Woods, faculty dean of the Poynter Institute, a St. Petersburg, Fla.-based journalism training organization, said many mistakes were made by the media, but in bringing attention to the crisis, the press got it right.

4   "The media brought a palpable sense of outrage with the coverage from the very beginning," said Woods. "If you looked at NPR, CNN and scattered sightings of the networks and newspapers, where they did well was to recognize the size of the story and the need to stay with it."

---

3 The fourth estate refers to the press.

Scaffolding the Text-Dependent Questions

15. How does the article frame the issue in the first two paragraphs? What does the author mean by "self-policing mechanisms"? How does the author's use of "you" in the opening sentence make you think of your own experience reading about Hurricane Katrina? Does the author imply that race played a small or large part in the media's portrayal? How can media "self-police" when it comes to portraying racial issues? RI.11–12.4, RI.11–12.5

My Notes

5   But where race comes in is more difficult, he told me. Where journalism failed is not in any lack of emphasis on how disproportionately blacks were affected, but in how "too many people were making the surface observation that there were lots of blacks affected without spending the time parsing the facts that would make it meaningful or informative."

6   In fact, many journalists who monitored the coverage felt in hindsight that African Americans caught in Katrina's wake were misrepresented in the press.

7   "I don't think African Americans were portrayed in the best light," said Camille Jackson, a staff writer for the Southern Poverty Law Center's Tolerance. org website. "It came out just how uncomfortable the media is when it comes to race, with the exception of a few."

8   Jackson authored a series of articles for the website that spoke to media outlets referring to victims as "hoodlums," "animals" and "thugs." But she said it comes from cultural insensitivity in the media, which led to false news reports and eventually to a curtailing of emergency response.

9   She warned that the important lesson to be learned is "to be an honest journalist, to tell the whole story, and be aware of your own personal biases. I know it's scary, but we're going to have to start talking about race so that we can get at the fear."

10   Buttressing criticisms of the press response to Katrina was a bipartisan Congressional report released in February that outright accuses the media of making a bad situation worse. It does not specify race in its pages, but its accusations implicate press reports that it says contributed to the confusion. The report from the bipartisan House committee investigated preparations for and responses to Katrina and found that media reports of gunshots fired at rescue helicopters, rapes and murders in the Superdome, and mass rioting in the streets were unsubstantiated at best, and many were simply false. "It's clear accurate reporting was among Katrina's many victims," the report says. "If anyone rioted, it was the media."

11   But Margaret Engel, managing editor of the Newseum, an Arlington, Va.-based interactive news museum said there are more important things to consider, like images that seemingly cast a divide between black and white survivors. Two in particular were now-infamous captions placed with Agence France-Presse and Associated Press photos. The AFP photo caption described two whites as "finding" food, while the AP caption described a black youth as "looting" a store.

12   "That to me is much more troubling than reporters quoting cops who didn't really know," said Engel. "I think you'll find that some of the stories on that day of looting were wildly overstated. It's not good that the press reported that, but it is a footnote to the overall coverage which riveted the nation over the lack of response." She added: "I think for Congress to cast the media response as rumor-mongering is to miss the forest for the trees."

Scaffolding the Text-Dependent Questions

16. What impact does the author's use of words like *hoodlums*, *animals*, *thugs*, and *looting* have on the tone of the article? What are the connotations of these words? How is the purpose of the article reflected in these choices? RI.11–12.1, RI.11–12.4

17. Apply Gray's critique to the editorial, "It's Time for a Nation to Return the Favor." How would you evaluate the editorial in its treatment of the aftermath of Hurricane Katrina and issues of racial division? What does Gray say in his article? Does the editorial present a fair argument? RI.11–12.5

(paragraph 8) Cultural Criticism: Media outlets referred to victims as *hoodlums*, *animals*, and *thugs*. How do these words show the media's subtext? Students should note the use of the word *victims* in contrast to the negative *hoodlums*, *animals*, and *thugs*.

(paragraph 10) Historical Criticism: This paragraph explains how a bipartisan House committee admonished the media. Was its criticism fair?

★ TEACHER TO TEACHER

Several texts in this activity have interconnections that the students might not realize if they do not read the entire set. You might want to guide students to observe these connection points:

- Paragraph 10 of "The Press, Race, and Katrina" mentions the Congressional report, *A Failure of Initiative*, excerpted in this activity. The excerpt does not contain the precise sentence mentioned in the article, but the full report is accessible online.

- Paragraph 11 of "The Press, Race, and Katrina" mentions the "now-infamous captions" of the photographs discussed in the previous article, "Who's a Looter? In Storm's Aftermath, Pictures Kick Up a Different Kind of Tempest."

- Paragraph 22 of the excerpt from the Congressional report, *A Failure of Initiative*, refers to the Stafford Act, from which students read an excerpt in Activity 4.5.

- Paragraphs 3 and 4 of the report, "The Need for Science in Restoring Resilience to the Northern Gulf of Mexico," provide data connected to statements in paragraph 2 of the editorial, "It's Time for a Nation to Return the Favor."

22 When the article has been read, the small group reading this text should discuss the Knowledge Quest questions.

4.7

My Notes

_____
_____
_____
_____
_____
_____
_____
_____
_____
_____
_____
_____
_____
_____
_____
_____
_____
_____
_____
_____
_____
_____
_____
_____
_____
_____
_____
_____
_____
_____
_____
_____
_____
_____
_____
_____

13 Despite the varied points of view, two things are clear. First, mistakes were made. As Woods pointed out, there has never been a how-to book on covering a disaster that nearly wipes out a whole city. Secondly, and most importantly, if African Americans in New Orleans are to be fairly served, the story must be told. "Now that the initial event has passed, the problem is maintaining people's attention," said Richard Prince, chairman of the National Association of Black Journalists' Media Monitoring Committee. "People are desperate for media attention because they fear the country will forget them. While a lot of reporters have covered the follow-up, it has not been compelling enough."

14 Prince said that the way to learn from what happened is for journalists to continually go to the Gulf Coast Region and find new stories, which are abundant. "They call it one of the worst natural disasters in the history of the country. So many people have a story to tell; somehow those stories have to be told."

Knowledge Quest
- Whose perspective does this article present?
- What aspect of Hurricane Katrina's aftermath stands out to you the most after reading this article?

Returning to the Text

- Reread the article to answer these text-dependent questions.
- Write any additional questions you have about the text in your Reader/Writer Notebook.

15. How does the article frame the issue in the first two paragraphs? What does the author mean by "self-policing mechanisms"?

The article frames the issue of the press, race, and Hurricane Katrina through an examination

of media portrayals of racial division in the immediate aftermath of the hurricane. The author

uses the phrase "self-policing" to describe the ways in which the media reacts to its own

portrayal of the role that media outlets play in describing racial divisions.

16. **KQ** What impact does the author's use of words like *hoodlums*, *animals*, *thugs*, and *looting* have on the tone of the article?

The author includes quotes that use these words to show how the media was at times careless

and inflammatory in the way it described people in the aftermath of the hurricane, particularly

African Americans. These words are connotative and highly charged, and the author includes

them to show the effect they can have on readers looking for unbiased information.

17. **KQ** Apply Gray's critique to the editorial, "It's Time for a Nation to Return the Favor." How would you evaluate the editorial in its treatment of the aftermath of Hurricane Katrina and issues of racial division?

The editorial has a unifying quality, advocating for the needs of all New Orleans residents.

It does not discuss racial division, but it does observe that the people of New Orleans are in

some ways "blamed" for choosing to live there, even though other cities are also vulnerable to

severe weather.

TEXT COMPLEXITY

Overall: Moderate
Lexile: 1180L
Qualitative: Moderate Difficulty
Task: Moderate (Analyze)

23 Review the Knowledge Question with students. Circulate among the small groups as they work on their assigned essays, and remind them to think about their answer to the Knowledge Question as they read and build knowledge about the topic.

Notes for Close Reading

(paragraph 1) Historical Criticism: The report begins with the history behind the forming of the committee. What was the political climate at the time? How do other major historical events of the decade—like the attacks of 9/11—influence the authors' agenda or the ways they frame their arguments?

4.7

KNOWLEDGE QUEST

Knowledge Question:
What are the major challenges in responding to natural disasters, both immediately and in the long term?

My Notes

Report

A Failure of Initiative: Report by the Select Bipartisan Committee to Investigate the Preparation for and Response to Hurricane Katrina

Union Calendar No. 205
109th Congress
2nd Session
Report 109–377

1   On September 15, 2005, the House of Representatives approved H. Res. 437, which created the Select Bipartisan Committee to Investigate the Preparation for and Response to Hurricane Katrina ("the Select Committee").

2   According to the resolution, the Committee was charged with conducting "a full and complete investigation and study and to report its findings to the House not later than February 15, 2006, regarding—(1) the development, coordination, and execution by local, State, and Federal authorities of emergency response plans and other activities in preparation for Hurricane Katrina; and (2) the local, State, and Federal government response to Hurricane Katrina."

3   The Committee presents the report narrative and the findings that stem from it to the U.S. House of Representatives and the American people for their consideration. Members of the Select Committee agree unanimously with the report and its findings. Other members of Congress who participated in the Select Committee's hearings and investigation but were not official members of the Select Committee, while concurring with a majority of the report's findings, have presented additional views as well, which we offer herein on their behalf.

4   First and foremost, this report is issued with our continued thoughts and prayers for Katrina's victims. Their families. Their friends. The loss of life, of property, of livelihoods and dreams has been enormous. And we salute all Americans who have stepped up to the plate to help in any way they can.

5   It has been said civilization is a race between education and catastrophe. With Katrina, we have had the catastrophe, and we are racing inexorably toward the next. Americans want to know: what have we learned?

6   Two months before the Committee was established, former Speaker of the House Newt Gingrich testified before a Government Reform subcommittee

My Notes

about the need to move the government to an "entrepreneurial" model and away from its current "bureaucratic" model, so that we can get government to move with Information Age speed and effectiveness.

7   "*Implementing* policy effectively," Speaker Gingrich said, "is ultimately as important as *making* the right policy."

8   The Select Committee first convened on September 22, 2005, understanding, like Speaker Gingrich, that a policy that cannot be implemented effectively is no policy at all.

9   The Select Committee was created because, in the tragic aftermath of Katrina, America was again confronted with the vast divide between policy creation and policy implementation. With the life-and-death difference between theory and practice.

10   The Select Committee has spent much of the past five months examining the aftermath of this catastrophic disaster. It has become increasingly clear that local, state, and federal government agencies failed to meet the needs of the residents of Louisiana, Mississippi, and Alabama. It has been our job to figure out why, and to make sure we are better prepared for the future.

11   Our mandate was clear: gather facts about the preparation for and response to Katrina, at all levels of government.

12   Investigate aggressively, follow the facts wherever they may lead, and find out what went right and what went wrong. Ask why coordination and information sharing between local, state, and federal governments was so dismal.

- Why situational awareness was so foggy, for so long.
- Why *all* residents, especially the most helpless, were not evacuated more quickly.
- Why supplies and equipment and support were so slow in arriving.
- Why so much taxpayer money aimed at better preparing and protecting the Gulf coast was left on the table, unspent or, in some cases, misspent.
- Why the adequacy of preparation and response seemed to vary significantly from state to state, county to county, town to town.
- Why unsubstantiated rumors and uncritically repeated press reports—at times fueled by top officials—were able to delay, disrupt, and diminish the response.
- And why government at all levels failed to react more effectively to a storm that was predicted with unprecedented timeliness and accuracy.

13   We agreed early on that the task before us was too important for carping. This was not about politics. Katrina did not distinguish between Republicans and Democrats.

14   This was about getting the information we need to chart a new and better course for emergency preparation and response. The American people want the

> carping: petty complaining

(paragraph 6) Marxist Criticism: former Speaker Gingrich called for the government to follow an "entrepreneurial" model rather than a "bureaucratic" model. What connotations do those two words have? Would an entrepreneurial model favor a particular group in an economic power struggle?

Scaffolding the Text-Dependent Questions

18. How does the use of bulleted lists and questions enhance the main argument of the report? What issue is the report aiming to undertake? What are some questions you might have about how they will go about it? Reread the two sets of bullet points. Do they address the same questions you have? Are the questions they ask important and balanced? RI.11–12.5

(paragraph 16) Historical Criticism: Hurricane Pam was a weeklong mock hurricane exercise conducted by federal and state agencies that took place in 2004, one year before the Hurricane Katrina disaster. Plans developed as a result of the exercise were never put into action. What responsibility does the government have for conducting a lengthy and costly exercise but failing to act upon its findings?

(paragraph 21) Marxist Criticism: This paragraph describes the "bad luck" that "aggravated the inadequate response" to Katrina. How might the disproportionate effect on people with fixed income be a reflection on the economic conditions, rather than "bad luck"?

My Notes

sovereign: independent
sanctify: redeem or save
litany: long list

facts, and they've been watching. They alone will judge whether our review has been thorough and fair. Our final exam is this report.

…

15 Our investigation revealed that Katrina was a national failure, an abdication of the most solemn obligation to provide for the common welfare. At every level—individual, corporate, philanthropic, and governmental—we failed to meet the challenge that was Katrina. In this cautionary tale, all the little pigs built houses of straw.

16 Of all we found along the timeline running from the fictional Hurricane Pam to the tragically real devastation along the Gulf coast, this conclusion stands out: A National Response Plan is not enough.

17 What's needed is a National Action Plan. Not a plan that says Washington will do everything, but one that says, when all else fails, the federal government must do something, whether it's formally requested or not. Not even the perfect bureaucratic storm of flaws and failures can wash away the fundamental governmental responsibility to protect public health and safety.

18 Still, no political storm surge from Katrina should be allowed to breach the sovereign boundaries between localities, states, and the federal government. Our system of federalism wisely relies on those closest to the people to meet immediate needs. But faith in federalism alone cannot sanctify a dysfunctional system in which DHS and FEMA simply wait for requests for aid that state and local officials may be unable or unwilling to convey. In this instance, blinding lack of situational awareness and disjointed decision making needlessly compounded and prolonged Katrina's horror.

19 In many respects, our report is a litany of mistakes, misjudgments, lapses, and absurdities all cascading together, blinding us to what was coming and hobbling any collective effort to respond.

20 This is not to say there were not many, many heroes, or that some aspects of the preparation and response were not, by any standard, successful. We found many examples of astounding individual initiative that saved lives and stand in stark contrast to the larger institutional failures. Nor do we mean to focus on assigning individual blame. Obtaining a full accounting and identifying lessons learned does not require finger pointing, instinctively tempting as that may be.

21 There was also an element of simple bad luck with Katrina that aggravated the inadequate response. The hurricane arrived over a weekend, at the end of the month. People on fixed incomes had little money for gas or food or lodging, making them more likely to remain in place and wait for their next check. Communicating via television or radio with families enmeshed in their weekend routines was difficult at best, as was finding drivers and other needed volunteers.

22 Over the past several months, we have become more than familiar with the disaster declaration process outlined in the Stafford Act. We understand

Scaffolding the Text-Dependent Questions

19. What is the point of view of the authors of this report on the preparation and response to Hurricane Katrina? Use evidence in the text to support your answer. Compare their view to that expressed in the editorial, "It's Time for a Nation to Return the Favor." Would these writers agree? What do their opinions seem to be? What language conveys their opinions? RI.11–12.1, RI.11–12.6

20. Based on the context, what is the meaning of the word *dismal* in paragraph 12? Reread the first bullet point list of the report. How can this list be considered "dismal" in regard to the government's response? What other examples does the report list to back this up? RI.11–12.3, RI.11–12.4

4.7

the goals, structure and mechanisms of the National Response Plan. We've digested the alphabet soup of "coordinating elements" established by the Plan: the HSOC (Homeland Security Operations Center) and RRCC (Regional Response Coordination Center); JFOs (Joint Field Offices) and PFOs (Principal Federal Officials); the IIMG (Interagency Incident Management Group); and much more.

23 But the American people don't care about acronyms or organizational charts. They want to know who was supposed to do what, when, and whether the job got done. And if it didn't get done, they want to know how we are going to make sure it does the next time.

…

24 What this Select Committee has done is not rocket science.

25 We've gathered facts and established timelines based on some fairly rudimentary but important questions posed to the right people in both the public and private sectors.

- What did you need and what did you get?
- Where were you in the days and hours right before, during, and after the storm?
- Who were you talking to?
- What were you doing?
- Does that match what you were *supposed* to be doing? Why or why not?

26 In other words, the Select Committee has matched what was *supposed* to happen under federal, state, and local plans against what *actually* happened.

27 Our findings emerged from this process of matching.

28 Too often there were too many cooks in the kitchen, and because of that the response to Katrina was at times overdone, at times underdone. Too often, because everybody was in charge, nobody was in charge.

29 Many government officials continue to stubbornly resist recognizing that fundamental changes in disaster management are needed. This report illustrates that we have to stop waiting for the disaster that fits our response plan and instead design a scalable capacity to meet whatever Mother Nature throws at us. It's not enough to say, "We wouldn't be here if the levees had not failed." The levees *did* fail, and government and other organizations failed in turn—in many, many ways.

30 It remains difficult to understand how government could respond so ineffectively to a disaster that was anticipated for years, and for which specific dire warnings had been issued for days. This crisis was not only predictable, it was predicted.

31 If this is what happens when we have advance warning, we shudder to imagine the consequences when we do not. Four and a half years after 9/11, America is still not ready for prime time.

My Notes

(paragraph 31) Historical Criticism: The committee draws a parallel between the terrorist attacks on September 11, 2001, and the Katrina disaster, "four and a half years later." Is this comparison appropriate? Why or why not?

(about the writers) Cultural Criticism: The committee members' names are included at the end of the report's preface. Encourage students to research the committee members' backgrounds, including which geographic areas they represent and their party affiliations. How might these factors influence the perspectives of the individuals on the committee?

24 Ask students to answer the Knowledge Quest questions individually, before giving them time to discuss their answers in small groups. Circulate as students discuss to ensure comprehension of each group's assigned reading.

4.7

My Notes

...

32 With Katrina, there was no shortage of plans. There were plans, but there was not enough plan-*ning*.

33 Government failed because it did not learn from past experiences, or because lessons thought to be learned were somehow not implemented. If 9/11 was a failure of imagination, then Katrina was a failure of initiative. It was a failure of leadership.

Tom Davis

Harold Rogers

Christopher Shays

Henry Bonilla

Steve Buyer

Sue Myrick

Mac Thornberry

Kay Granger

Charles W. "Chip" Pickering

Bill Shuster

Jeff Miller

Ⓩ Knowledge Quest
- What stands out about Congress's grasp of the aftermath of Hurricane Katrina?
- Which of Congress's claims is the most striking to you?

Returning to the Text

- Reread the report excerpt to answer these text-dependent questions.
- Write any additional questions you have about the text in your Reader/Writer Notebook.

18. How does the use of bulleted lists and questions enhance the main argument of the report?

The report includes a list of points that the committee would like to investigate. It implies

that the issues surrounding the response to the hurricane were so complex that each issue

requires investigation. A bulleted list of questions the committee worked to answer helps the

reader understand the measures that were taken in the investigation to get a full account.

19. KQ What is the point of view of the authors of this report on the preparation and response to Hurricane Katrina? Use evidence in the text to support your answer. Compare their view to that expressed in the editorial, "It's Time for a Nation to Return the Favor." Would these writers agree?

The authors mention a "vast divide between policy creation and policy implementation"

and see this as a "life-and-death difference." This conveys that the authors take this issue

seriously and that there is no room for politics. The authors of both texts agree that many

mistakes were made, and they agree that the federal government needs to help.

20. KQ Based on the context, what is the meaning of the word *dismal* in paragraph 12?

The word *dismal* means terrible or disgraceful, as evidenced by the bulleted points that

follow its use. The report considers why residents were not evacuated quickly. The findings

demonstrate that the aftermath of Katrina could have been better mitigated had the

government's involvement been carried out differently.

TEXT COMPLEXITY

Overall: Accessible
Lexile: 590L
Qualitative: Low Difficulty
Task: Moderate (Analyze)

25 Review the Knowledge Question with students. Remind them to think about their answer to the Knowledge Question as they read and build knowledge about the topic.

Notes for Close Reading

(paragraph 5) Feminist Criticism: The writer's initial reaction to the post-Katrina world, despite having been a successful professional, reflects a mindset that single women need to be protected by others. She equates her feelings after the disaster to "divorce … and loss of relationships." How do her feelings change as time passes? Could she have achieved this change on her own, without the influence of the two brothers?

(paragraph 6) Cultural Criticism: The writer comes from a world where she "sold parties, petals and pretties" and includes plantations as "all the best of New Orleans." How do her perceptions change when all that is lost? What factor do the two Brazilian brothers play in her transformation? Is it true that all Americans "have every right to own your own business"?

4.7

KNOWLEDGE QUEST

Knowledge Question:
What are the major challenges in responding to natural disasters, both immediately and in the long term?

My Notes

About the Author

Simone Bruni is a Louisiana native and founder of Demo Diva. After losing her home and career during Hurricane Katrina, Bruni began a demolition business on the campus of Xavier University in 2005. With no prior experience in demolition, Bruni has created a highly successful business that is based in New Orleans.

Article

'Attitude of Resilience' Helped Create Demo Diva

by **Simone Bruni**

Chicago Tribune, **September 3, 2015**

1   How many times in life do we have to start over? How many times do we have to reinvent ourselves just to survive?

2   Hurricane Katrina washed through my house, my city and my life. In the blink of an eye, the comfortable routine I had known was over. The high-heeled world of a party planner came crashing down. My home was flooded. I lost my job. No neighbors. No friends nearby. Everyone had evacuated elsewhere. My city was devastated. Everything was turned upside down.

3   I fell to my knees in grief.

4   As a corporate event planner, I sold parties, petals and pretties. I showcased and show-boated all the best of New Orleans: restaurants, hotels, musicians, plantations and bayous. The sounds of clinking china and crystal, the laughter and revelry were now drowned out by the National Guard and heavy machinery rolling through our streets. Blanketed in a film of mud and toxicity, the city was grey and lifeless.

5   Oh my gosh, I'm single. Who is going to protect me? Who is going to put my shelter back together? How am I going to survive? What other type of work can I do? Do I have any other skills? These are the most basic questions we ask ourselves in the middle of any type of disaster: divorce, death, unemployment, and loss of relationships. This is when our survival instincts give us options: morph or die!

6   My answer came from the most unlikely source one afternoon. Two Brazilian brothers were gutting the mildewed walls of my little house. I was sitting on a 5-gallon paint can watching them and holding my head in despair. I seemed to be in my own trance, mumbling to myself, "What am I going to do? What am I going to do?" They spoke an epiphany, "You are an American. You have every right to own your own business. You have

Scaffolding the Text-Dependent Questions

21. The author opens her essay with questions. What effect does this have on readers? How does she begin to answer those questions in the next three paragraphs? What do these questions make you think about? How would you answer them? Why do you think the author wants you to consider them? Reread the second paragraph. Is this a subjective or objective account? How does the author answer her own questions? How does her answer frame the rest of her piece?   RI.11–12.5, RI.11–12.6

opportunities that we do not have in our country. You don't know how lucky you are. Go start a business."

7   In that moment, I received the greatest lesson of my life. Two simple, down-to-earth boys showed me the way. When catastrophe hit, it didn't matter that I was a doctor's daughter; that I had private-school education; or that I knew the best concierges, restaurant owners and all those other meaningless things. I had a choice of how I was going to react to my circumstances. I had to choose my attitude. I chose to be hopeful. I chose to humble myself. I chose to be positive and it paid off: The Demo Diva Co. was born.

8   Equipped with hot pink business cards and yard signs, I sold my demolition services across the city. Door to door. Flyers on windshields. At first, I knew nothing about the demolition equipment but I assured my customers that they could trust me to help them. I would solve their problem. It worked.

9   Six years later, I own a fleet of hot pink dumpsters, dump trucks and excavators. Our equipment is all over the city. I can't go into a grocery store or gas station around town without a young or old person singing the jingle from my commercial. "Who fights the Blight, Demo Diva fights the Blight!" Demo Diva isn't just a demolition company. It's an attitude of resilience. It's the personification of us—the people of New Orleans and we, Americans!

10   It took immigrants to show me the light. It took my passion to help my community. But I have influenced a male-dominated industry with a little pink flair and emerged with a successful small business.

Simone Bruni's demotion company has gained recognition for using a fleet of hot pink dumpsters and dump trucks.

⊘ Knowledge Quest
- What are your initial thoughts about Bruni's perspective on the aftermath of Katrina?
- What is the emotional effect of this article on the reader?

WORD CONNECTIONS

Cognates
The English word **catastrophe** and the Spanish word *catástrofe* are cognates. Both words mean a sudden, unexpected disaster. Many English words spelled with the letters *ph* are spelled with the letter *f* in Spanish: *metamorfosis*, *teléfono*, and *foto* are a few examples.

My Notes

_____
_____
_____
_____
_____
_____
_____
_____
_____
_____
_____
_____
_____
_____
_____
_____
_____
_____
_____
_____
_____
_____
_____
_____

ACTIVITY 4.7 continued

(paragraph 8) Marxist Criticism: The writer claims that her privileged upbringing no longer mattered when the catastrophe hit. How might less-fortunate survivors of the disaster respond to this idea?

(paragraph 9) Feminist Criticism: The writer uses hot pink business cards and dumpsters in her business. How might these gender signals help or hinder her business?

26 Remind students to pause after paragraph 7 to discuss the Word Connections box.

27 Have the small group analyzing this article discuss the Knowledge Quest questions when they complete their first read.

Scaffolding the Text-Dependent Questions

22.   What is the author's point of view regarding how the aftermath of the hurricane affected her life? How would her account be different if it were told objectively rather than subjectively? Is the author's experience ultimately positive or negative? What is the outcome of her loss and ordeal? What does she learn? What impact does it have on her and her community? Do you think she feels good or bad about it? If this story was told with only facts and descriptions, would it have the same emotional quality? How might that change the way you felt after reading the article? RI.11–12.5, RI.11–12.6

23.   Compare Bruni's actions to the ideas expressed in the editorial, "It's Time for a Nation to Return the Favor." In what ways would she agree with the editorial? In what ways might she disagree? How are the texts similar? How do they differ in tone? RI.11–12.5

4.7

Returning to the Text

- Reread the article to answer the text-dependent questions.
- Write any additional questions you have about the text in your Reader/Writer Notebook.

21. The author opens her essay with questions. What effect does this have on readers? How does she begin to answer those questions in the next three paragraphs?

Beginning the essay with questions forces the reader to consider how they would answer the

questions. It also sets up the structure of the essay in which responses to those questions are

discussed. In the next three paragraphs, the author shares her own experience with Hurricane

Katrina and the impact the devastation has on her life.

22. KQ What is the author's point of view regarding how the aftermath of the hurricane affected her life? How would her account be different if it were told objectively rather than subjectively?

The author's point of view is losing so much in the hurricane led her to begin her own

business, which helped connect her to the community. If her story were told objectively, it

would be reduced to mostly facts and descriptions, and it likely wouldn't have as substantial a

personal and emotional impact as it currently does.

23. KQ Compare Bruni's actions to the ideas expressed in the editorial, "It's Time for a Nation to Return the Favor." In what ways would she agree with the editorial? In what ways might she disagree?

Bruni describes the devastation she felt initially in the aftermath of Hurricane Katrina, echoing

the needs stated in the editorial. She adapted to the new circumstances, creating a new

business that responded to the needs of the community—a business that would compete for

federal disaster relief funds among other sources of income.

Report

The Need for Science in Restoring Resilience to the Northern Gulf of Mexico

from *Science and the Storms: the USGS Response to the Hurricanes of 2005*

by Gregory J. Smith

> …thousands of people had to chop their way through rooftops or cling to trees waiting for rescue…thousands are camped upon broken levees…this is a pitiable plight of a lost battle…

Description of the human tragedy following the 1927 Mississippi River flood in *Rising Tide* by John M. Barry

> …thousands of people being rescued from their rooftops and attics…there's a lot more people who need assistance…

Description of the human tragedy following the 2005 Hurricane Katrina landfall broadcast by WWL-AM New Orleans radio following the post hurricane levee breaches

Unprecedented Events

1   No recent events in the history of the United States have so highlighted the discord between the human landscapes (development patterns) and natural landscapes of coastal America as did the hurricanes of 2005. Hearing the news of stranded citizens after Hurricane Katrina made many recall the plight of those stranded by the 1927 Mississippi River flood. In the nearly 80 years following the great Mississippi River flood of 1927, the U.S. population, indeed the world's population, has migrated to coastal areas. During Hurricane Katrina, the Mississippi River and delta, the coastal habitats, the urban environments, and the massive storm came together on August 29, 2005, in coastal Louisiana. This storm produced a massive loss of life and property as well as an economic impact along the Gulf Coast that was unprecedented in U.S. history. Hurricanes Dennis, Rita, and Wilma were also powerful hurricanes that affected the Gulf Coast in 2005 and were among the record 27 named storms of that year. The most intense storms took people's lives, homes, property, livelihoods, and futures as the world witnessed in disbelief, via sophisticated satellite technology, the raw, massive forces of nature. Of the record number of cyclonic storms in 2005, Katrina and its aftermath stand as perhaps the best example of the critically urgent need to harmonize and integrate scientific, social, and economic coastal planning on a scale that has never before been attempted.

KNOWLEDGE QUEST

Knowledge Question:
What are the major challenges in responding to natural disasters, both immediately and in the long term?

My Notes

⚠ TEXT COMPLEXITY

Overall: Complex
Lexile: 1540L
Qualitative: High Difficulty
Task: Moderate (Analyze)

28 Inform students that the United States Geological Survey (USGS) is a federal agency whose mission includes "providing reliable scientific information to describe and understand the Earth [and] minimize loss of life and property from natural disasters." Ask them to consider the likely intended audience of this report.

29 Review the Knowledge Question with students. Remind them to think about their answer to the Knowledge Question as they read and build knowledge about the topic.

Notes for Close Reading

(paragraph 1) Historical Criticism: The report begins by providing historical context for the Hurricane Katrina disaster. How did human migration patterns in the 20th century contribute to the problem? How did the 2005 hurricane compare to other years?

Scaffolding the Text-Dependent Questions

24. What clues does the title of this report give about its overall purpose? Reread the title and identify four key words. Review the report's subheadings to confirm inferences about the author's purpose and central message. RI.11–12.1

25. Why did the author begin the report with descriptions of two disasters? How are the two descriptions similar? What words are repeated? What images do the two descriptions call to your mind? Are they similar or different? What impact do they have on you emotionally? Why might the author have put them together? RI.11–12.5

(paragraph 3) Marxist Criticism: This paragraph lays out the economic benefits New Orleans brings to the United States. How have those benefits led to people living and working in a potential disaster zone?

(paragraph 6) Historical Criticism: This paragraph describes differences between pre-Katrina and post-Katrina coastal restoration efforts. What is the major difference? What is the greatest challenge moving forward?

4.7

My Notes

USGS Response to the Storms

2 The geological and geographic setting, the hydrologic[4] regime, and the biological landscapes of the northern Gulf of Mexico coast have intersected with human coastal development, creating a vulnerable coast. In many ways science, engineering, and technology played a role in the development of this situation; it is these same enterprises that offer the greatest opportunity for transforming our coasts from ones that are vulnerable, like those impacted in 2005, to ones that are resilient…

A Valuable Coast

3 The benefits of the Gulf Coast to the Nation's economy are numerous. For example, in Louisiana alone, the Port of South Louisiana handles more tonnage than any other port in the Nation; nearly 34 percent of the U.S. natural gas supply and over 29 percent of the Nation's crude oil supply moves through the State (U.S. Army Corps of Engineers, 2004). Additionally, the Mississippi River Delta is the gateway to the Nation's lifeline for moving goods and materials to and from the heart of the United States and the rest of the world. The Gulf Coast region accounted for the largest U.S. commercial fish and shellfish landings, by weight, in the lower 48 States, in 200304 (National Oceanic and Atmospheric Administration, 2004).

4 Beyond the stark economic figures, the Gulf Coast provides important natural benefits, such as the critical coastal habitat for wintering waterfowl and birds migrating from North America to South and Central America. Additionally, these valuable habitats of marshlands and barrier islands are critical to buffering human populations and property from the winds and flood waters of storms.

5 The economic and ecological benefits of the coast are considerable and are critical to America. Harmonizing economic and ecological processes and recovering the human landscape while restoring the natural landscapes are formidable tasks. Scientists, engineers, and resource managers, working together and using an adaptive management approach, offer the greatest promise of transforming a vulnerable coast to a resilient coast for the future. Adaptive management is a type of natural resource management in which decisions are made as part of an ongoing science-based process. It involves testing, monitoring, and evaluating applied strategies and incorporating new knowledge based on scientific findings and the needs of society. Results are used to modify management policy, strategies, and practices (Unified Federal Policy for Watershed Approach to Federal Land and Resource Management, 2000).

…

Science and a Resilient Coast

6 In the aftermath of the storms of 2005, there was an increase in the already active efforts for coastal restoration and planning that have involved biologists, hydrologists, geologists, engineers, planners, and the public. Previously, virtually all of the coastal restoration efforts and programs had cited hurricane protection

---

[4] *Hydrologic* relates to the study of water, its properties, and its movements on earth.

Scaffolding the Text-Dependent Questions

26. What effect does the author hope to achieve by including such specific figures in the report's third paragraph? How effective is it? Reread paragraph three. What are some of the purposes Gulf Coast ports serve? How does port activity there impact the rest of the country? RI.11–12.5, RI.11–12.6

27. Through which lens does the author approach the issue of Hurricane Katrina? Is it an objective or subjective article? How do you know? Reread the title of the article. What does *resilience* mean? How can people be resilient? How can places be resilient? Does the author seem to be referring mainly to people or to places in his article? What issues does the author seem to be concerned with? Does he offer any emotional responses, or does he mostly convey facts? RI.11–12.1, RI.11–12.6

as a key benefit to restoring coastal Louisiana (Coastal Wetlands Planning, Protection and Restoration Act, 1990; Louisiana Coastal Wetlands Conservation and Restoration Task Force, 1998; U.S. Army Corps of Engineers, 2004). Following the 2005 storm season, it has become obvious not only that coastal restoration efforts are urgently needed but also that these efforts must be completely harmonized with hurricane protection, flood control, navigation, river and hydrological management, and ultimately with human development and activities. Restoration of the coast affords the opportunity to integrate and harmonize the diverse activities and ecological benefits provided by a resilient coast ecosystem. Integrating these massive enterprises will require that goals transcend each of these independent endeavors beyond the interests of any single stakeholder group. Maintaining navigation of the Mississippi and Atchafalaya Rivers, flood control structures, hurricane levees, and storm protection—while simultaneously restoring land lost to the northern Gulf of Mexico to an ecologically functional system—will be a massive and complex challenge for the future. The hurricanes of 2005, with their dramatic impact on lives and property, have clearly brought a new sense of urgency to this challenge in which the entire Nation holds a stake.

7 Two major efforts that pointed to the need for integrated, harmonized planning across human and natural landscapes were focused on a new planning framework and a new vision for the future of the Gulf Coast (Working Group for Post-hurricane Planning for the Louisiana Coast, 2006; Technical Group, 2006). These efforts have built consensus and recommendations for approaches to building a resilient coast.

8 One such recommendation focuses on retaining Mississippi River sediments in coastal wetlands instead of allowing them to bypass the Continental Shelf. This retention of sediments would emulate the historical geological and hydrological processes on the coast that once built land and sustained the wetlands that are now critically needed to protect coastal communities. Such recommendations focus on restoring the coast as opposed to simply armoring the coast (with levees, barriers, and other hard structures). The diversity of factors that drive recovery and restoration will certainly include hard structures and will deal with both flood control and hurricane protection. Scientific studies, however, have made it clear that the restoration of natural coastal wetlands and ecosystem function must be a part of this equation if we are to achieve a sustainable coastal landscape.

USGS Science and the Storms

9 This volume contains a **synoptic** overview of the immediate scientific assessments that were conducted by USGS throughout the Gulf Coast region. The science addressed issues as they arose, since establishing a research design and specific study area prior to the occurrence of a hurricane is unrealistic. While post-storm science tends to focus on impacts and rely less on experimental methods, there is a great deal to be learned through assessing the changes caused by these storms in relation to the human landscape. These studies provide important understandings and point to additional scientific work that is needed to produce further knowledge critical in transforming our coast from a state of vulnerability to one that is resilient and sustainable.

My Notes

synoptic: general

LEVELED DIFFERENTIATED INSTRUCTION

In this activity, students might need support paraphrasing and sharing information from an article during the jigsaw reading activity.

Developing To support students' comprehension of the articles, have small groups complete the **Paraphrasing Map** graphic organizer for their assigned article. Then have them share in a group discussion and add any additional ideas or paraphrases that emerge from the discussion.

Expanding Provide partners with the **Paraphrasing Map** graphic organizer to help them paraphrase their assigned article before beginning the second reading. Encourage them to review the text-dependent questions after each article and to expand on their organizers as needed during the second read.

Support Remind students that an objective summary is free of personal opinion and bias. Provide students with the **Paraphrasing Map** graphic organizer as a way of solidifying their understanding of their assigned article. Guide them to be objective, and not to state whether they personally agree or disagree with the article.

Extend Pair students who need an additional challenge. Ask them to paraphrase two different articles, including a subtle bias in one of their paraphrases. Have students share their paraphrases with one another and attempt to identify which one reflects a bias. Ask pairs to discuss how the bias can be remedied.

30 Remind the small group analyzing this reading to discuss the Knowledge Quest questions when they complete their first read. Check students' general comprehension of the text based on their responses, asking follow-up questions as needed.

31 RETURNING TO THE TEXT: During the second reading, students will answer the text-dependent questions for their assigned texts. You may choose to have students reread and work on the questions in the same small groups in which they read the text. Model the process with the first text that you are reading as a class.

32 If students have difficulty, scaffold the questions by rephrasing them or breaking them down into smaller parts. See the Scaffolding the Text-Dependent Questions boxes for suggestions.

4.7

Knowledge Quest
- What is your initial reaction to the aftermath of natural disasters discussed in this report?
- What fact in the report is particularly surprising or striking?

Returning to the Text
- Reread the report to answer these text-dependent questions.
- Write any additional questions you have about the text in your Reader/Writer Notebook.

24. **KQ** What clues does the title of this report give about its overall purpose?

The title indicates that the report will focus on scientific research and that scientific research should be an important component in planning and implementing the recovery efforts on the Gulf Coast. Readers can also infer from the title that the damage to the coast was significant and that it should be repaired in a way that reduces risk in future.

25. Why did the author begin the report with descriptions of two disasters?

The author begins with these striking quotations to draw parallels between the two events and draw the reader in. Pairing quotations from different time periods emphasizes the recurrence of natural disasters, and it creates a sense of alarm.

26. What effect does the author hope to achieve by including such specific figures in the report's third paragraph? How effective is it?

The author cites specific statistics in the paragraph in an effort to emphasize the region's economic importance to the nation as a whole. While it is effective in achieving that goal, the lack of the same level of specifics in the paragraph focusing on the region's environmental importance might downplay that part of the report for some readers.

27. **KQ** Through which lens does the author approach the issue of Hurricane Katrina? Is it an objective or subjective article? How do you know?

The author discusses Hurricane Katrina through a historical and a geographical lens, discussing the "discord between human landscapes and natural landscapes" and then the geographical impact of the hurricane on residents. The article is objective because it relies on facts and statistics, not the author's personal emotions about the event.

4.7

 Knowledge Quest

Think about how the articles and reports explore all elements of Hurricane Katrina, including the aftermath. Within your small group, discuss which article or report makes the most compelling claim about what needs to change in the aftermath of future, similar disasters. Be sure to:

- Prepare by analyzing and evaluating what you have learned about how New Orleanians and other people and organizations view Hurricane Katrina's initial impact and aftermath.

- Ask and respond to questions to clarify details, evidence, and ideas.

- Acknowledge perspectives and reasoning that are different from your own.

 INDEPENDENT READING LINK

You can continue to build your knowledge about how different people and organizations respond to natural disasters by reading other articles at ZINC Reading Labs. Search for keywords such as *natural disaster* and *natural disaster relief*.

🍁 | ZINC

ACTIVITY 4.7 continued

33 Return to the Knowledge Question. Have students work in small groups to collaboratively discuss and evaluate the Knowledge Quest Closing. Review discussion expectations with students using the "be sure to" points. Invite volunteers to share their ideas. Then lead the class in a discussion about how their response to the Knowledge Question has changed after reading the articles and reports.

34 Encourage students to continue building knowledge on this topic by reading other articles as suggested in the Independent Reading Link.

35 Once groups have had time to complete a first and second reading of their assigned texts, allow them to move on to the Working from the Text section. Students should be familiar with these questions after using them in Activity 4.5. Have them answer the bulleted questions in their Reader/Writer Notebooks and discuss their answers in their small groups.

36 After their analysis of their assigned reading is complete, student groups should begin planning how to present the information from their assigned text to the rest of the class.

37 Draw students' attention to the sentence stem in student step 34. Review these guiding sentences, providing examples of ways in which students might complete the stems for the analyses of lens(es). This may support English-language learners and other students.

38 Have students brainstorm and complete the graphic organizer to decide on an organizational structure for their presentations.

39 Give student groups time to develop a plan for presenting their article to their classmates.

4.7

Working from the Text

28. Based on the text you have read, respond to your assigned Essential Question. Once you have listened to each group's presentation, respond to the other Essential Question based on the information you learned about one of the other informational texts.

Article Read	Essential Question
"Looters Leave Nothing Behind in Storm's Wake," by Mike Perlstein and Brian Thevenot "Who's a Looter? In Storm's Aftermath, Pictures Kick Up a Different Kind of Tempest," by Tania Ralli "'Attitude of Resilience' Helped Create Demo Diva," by Simone Bruni "The Need for Science in Restoring Resilience to the Northern Gulf of Mexico," by Gregory J. Smith	How do media sources influence our understanding of the truth and significance of an issue?
"An Editorial: It's Time for a Nation to Return the Favor," from The Times-Picayune "The Press, Race, and Katrina," by Madison Gray "A Failure of Initiative," by the Select Bipartisan Committee to Investigate the Preparation for and Response to Hurricane Katrina	How are media texts constructed to cater to media consumers' interests, experiences, assumptions, and biases or to promote a particular agenda?

29. **Revisit the Text:** With your reading group, reread the text to locate evidence as you answer the following questions in a small group discussion. Record notes from your discussion in your Reader/Writer Notebook.

30. Summarize the information covered in the text and connect it to the original news event.

31. How objective is the coverage? Identify and list (or highlight in the article) specific textual details (titles, labeling, omissions, and so on) that reveal any bias in the text.

32. What is the target audience for the publication/broadcast? How does the text's rhetorical context affect the language and tone used?

33. What is the writer's point of view? How do the evidence and the rhetoric support that point of view?

34. If you read only this article or report, what would you think is the key issue? In other words, how does the text frame the truth and/or significance of the event?

35. Which critical lenses are evident in how the text approaches the issue? Provide examples to support your answer.

Planning Your Presentation: Now that you have completed your analysis, come up with a plan for preparing and presenting the article or report to the class. Your group's presentation to your peers should include the following:

- **The most significant information from your text:** Be sure that your presentation summarizes the text in a way that allows classmates to understand its main ideas.

- **A discussion of how the text frames the event and its aftermath:** What issue(s) does it focus on? How slanted is the language? Does it include obvious examples of faulty reasoning? Be ready to cite specific examples to support your evaluation of the text.

- **An analysis of what lens(es) connect to the text:** Which quotations from the text support your claims about its perspective? If needed, use the following stem:

  When we read this text through a _____ lens, we notice that _____.

36. Consider the information from your presentation plan. Brainstorm different organizational strategies your group could use to present your article to your classmates. Once you've identified the strengths and weaknesses of each approach, it might be helpful to try to outline the presentation using a few of the approaches that seem to fit best. Evaluate the results as a group to choose the approach you plan to take in the final draft.

Organizational Approach	Strengths and Weaknesses of This Approach
Topically, using the questions for analysis on the previous page	
Topically, using areas described in the bulleted list	
Topically, focusing on the lenses explored in the text	
Chronologically, following the timeline of event and the aftermath	
Structurally, based on the article's organization	
As a critical argument: hook, claim, support, counterclaim, concession/refutation, call to action	

37. Based on your evaluation of your options, which approach will you use to present your article and why?

ACTIVITY 4.7 continued

40 Before beginning presentations, have students write a guiding question at the center of the concept map on this student page. As they watch the other student presentations, they should use the space around the question to chart connections to articles and pieces of evidence that link to their question.

TEACHER TO TEACHER

Distribute copies of the Presenting Scoring Guide and/or Audience Notes and Feedback graphic organizer from the Resources section. For each presentation, assign one member of each group in the audience to take notes on the delivery of the presentation. Rotate this responsibility among the students so that each student has a chance to focus on presentation content as well as delivery.

41 After groups have finished presenting key information and findings from the articles, give students an opportunity to ask clarifying questions as needed to help them synthesize what they have learned.

42 Have students discuss the Check Your Understanding task and respond to the prompt, using their concept maps and the articles.

ASSESS

Use student responses to the writing prompt to synthesize ideas from multiple texts. Students' essays should present a clear answer to their guiding question and should use evidence from several of the texts. Look for effective integration of textual evidence.

ADAPT

If students need additional help synthesizing the information from the texts, have them use their concept maps as a prewriting tool.

4.7

My Notes

Analyzing Presentations

38. As you listen to the presentations of the other groups, use the space to create a concept map. Record titles, ideas, and page numbers as you make connections between your guiding question and the information presented in the other groups' presentations.

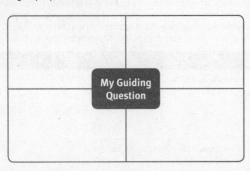

39. In addition to listening for the ideas each group shares, observe and evaluate each group's presentation techniques. Use your Reader/Writer Notebook to record observations and questions you might like to ask after each presentation, as well as any relevant insights you think the class might find interesting or helpful. When listening, be sure to evaluate the following:

- Is the speaker's reasoning sound and well supported by evidence?
- What specific rhetorical strategies are used in the presentation? Are they effective?
- How does the speaker link ideas and make connections to the premise of the piece?
- What points does the speaker emphasize, and how do they support the overall premise?

☑ Check Your Understanding

When writing or presenting a critical interpretation, what key questions should guide your decision about what to include and how to organize it?

> ### ✍ Writing Prompt: Informational
>
> Write a brief essay using evidence from the various articles you have discussed to answer your guiding question. Be sure to:
>
> - Choose an organizational approach that will engage your audience.
> - Integrate quotations in different ways to create syntactic variety in your writing.
> - Tailor your rhetoric to your target audience.
> - Punctuate your paper correctly and check for spelling errors.

✍ WRITING PROMPT: INFORMATIONAL

The following standards are addressed in the writing prompt:

- RI.11–12.1
- W.11–12.2a
- W.11–12.2b
- W.11–12.2c
- W.11–12.2d
- W.11–12.2e

Language Checkpoint: Writing Logical Comparisons

PLAN

Suggested Pacing: 1 50-minute class period

TEACH

1 Read the Learning Targets and Preview with the class. Then read Understanding Logical Comparisons.

2 Post the example sentences from the table without posting the name and explanation of the error. Lead a class discussion gauging prior knowledge to see if students can explain and correct the error in each sentence.

3 Have students work individually to complete the first quickwrite. Ask student volunteers to share responses. If students have a difficult time putting their thoughts into words, lead a class discussion on why the sentences from the table were understandable despite their comparison errors.

SAT® CONNECTIONS

This activity provides practice with this important SAT skill: recognizing and correcting cases in which unlike terms are compared.

Learning Targets

- Recognize the structure of a logical comparison.
- Understand what makes a comparison illogical.
- Revise in order to maintain logical comparisons in writing.

Preview

In this activity you will learn and practice using logical comparisons. After reading some examples and completing some exercises, you will demonstrate your new knowledge in a paragraph about how illogical comparisons can weaken your writing.

Understanding Logical Comparisons

Writers frequently use comparisons to help their audience understand their ideas. Comparisons are usually made between two nouns. For example:

> Hurricane Katrina caused more financial damage than Hurricane Sandy.

Two similar things are being compared—the financial damage caused by two storms. This comparison is logical, and a reader will clearly understand what the writer is trying to say.

A couple of different mistakes are common when making comparisons:

Error	Example	Why It Is an Error
Illogical Comparison	I like the restaurants in New Orleans better than Houston.	The things being compared are not actually similar. Because of the way this sentence is written, restaurants are being compared with a city.
Comparing one specific thing to all things of that type	Hurricane Katrina was worse than any natural disaster.	The comparison doesn't acknowledge that Hurricane Katrina is a natural disaster and can't, logically, be worse than itself.

1. **Quickwrite:** Why might a writer accidentally make an illogical comparison? Why might a reader be able to understand the comparison even though it is illogical?

College and Career Readiness Standards

Focus Standards:

RI.11–12.5 Analyze and evaluate the effectiveness of the structure an author uses in his or her exposition or argument, including whether the structure makes points clear, convincing, and engaging.

W.11–12.5 Develop and strengthen writing as needed by planning, revising, editing, rewriting, or trying a new approach, focusing on addressing what is most significant for a specific purpose and audience. (Editing for conventions should demonstrate command of Language standards 1–3 up to and including grades 11–12 here.)

Additional Standards Addressed:

W.11–12.8, W.11–12.10

4 Direct students to complete student steps 2–5 independently before discussing their answers with a partner. As students work, circulate around the room to gauge understanding.

5 Read Fixing Illogical Comparisons with the class. Have students work with their partners to write one additional error-and-correction sentence pair to demonstrate each way of fixing an illogical comparison: one pair using parallel noun phrases, one using possessives, and one using a determiner. Have volunteers share their responses.

LC 4.7

2. What is the illogical comparison in the following sentence?

The music scene in New Orleans in more robust than Houston.

A city's music scene is being compared to a city.

3. Revise the sentence to make the comparison logical.

The music scene in New Orleans is more robust than Houston's.

4. What is the illogical comparison in the following sentence?

New Orleans is the most fascinating city.

New Orleans is not really being compared with anything else in this sentence, so the reader does not have enough content or context to make a logical comparison.

5. Revise the sentence to make the comparison logical.

New Orleans is the most fascinating city in the American South.

Fixing Illogical Comparisons

Revising illogical comparisons is important for ensuring that the meaning of the writing is clear to readers. There are a few ways that illogical comparisons can be revised and made logical.

Rewrite a sentence's noun phrases so that each is parallel with the other.

> I found **Maria Konnikova's arguments** about the effect of headlines more convincing than **Matthew C. Nisbet's arguments** about partisan readers' biases.

> **Konnikova's writing style** was more conversational than **Nisbet's writing style**.

6 Ask students to continue working with their partners to complete student step 6. Move around the room as students work to monitor comprehension.

When two phrases are parallel, they have a similar construction that makes clear which things are being compared. For example, in the sentences provided, the noun phrases—in bold—are parallel. So it is clear that the authors' writing styles and techniques are what are being compared.

Rewrite the noun phrases so that each uses a possessive noun, or a noun that shows ownership.

> **Government report writers'** word choice is more complex than **newspaper reporters'** word choice.

> **Academics'** writing style is also more complicated than most **news reporters'** style.

In the first sentence, both *government report writers* and *newspaper reporters* are possessive, so the sentence implies that both groups have a writing style and that is what is being compared. In the second sentence, both *academics* and *reporters* are possessive, so the sentence implies that the groups are being compared.

Add a determiner to the sentence.

> The damage caused by Hurricane Katrina was more widespread than <u>that</u> of Hurricane Sandy.

> Hurricane Katrina's highest wind speeds were faster than <u>those</u> measured during Hurricane Sandy.

A determiner is a kind of pronoun that shows ownership. The determiner *that* agrees with a singular antecedent and the determiner *those* agrees with a plural antecedent. In the first sentence, the antecedent of *that* is *damage*, which is singular. In the second sentence, the antecedent of *those* is *speeds*, which is a plural.

---

6. Work with a partner to make each of the following comparisons logical.

a. The audiences in New York were larger than San Francisco.

> The audiences in New York were larger than the audiences in San Francisco. / The audiences in New York were larger than those in San Francisco.

b. The president's approval ratings were lower than her opponent.

> The president's approval ratings were lower than her opponent's. / The president's approval ratings were lower than those of her opponent.

c. The United States swim relay team was faster than the Italians.

> The United States swim relay team was faster than the Italian team.

7 Project the paragraph from the Revising section. Work as a class to mark the illogical comparisons and then rewrite the paragraph to correct them.

8 Have students complete the Practice activity independently.

9 Have students work independently to complete the Check Your Understanding in class or for homework.

ASSESS

Check the paragraph students wrote for the Practice prompt to assess their understanding of illogical comparisons. Make sure students have attended to all parts of the prompt: They should explain why illogical comparisons are confusing, include an example of each type, and give advice about avoiding them.

ADAPT

If students are using illogical comparisons in their writing, consider adding an item addressing the issue to a Writer's Checklist that is displayed in the classroom. Alternatively, assist students in adding such an item to their Editor's Checklist.

LC 4.7

Revising

Read the following paragraph. It includes some illogical comparisons. Mark each illogical comparison, and then rewrite it.

[1] Edward R. Murrow was the best journalist. [2] He reported many stories that were better than Walter Cronkite. [3] His reporting was more thorough than Cronkite. [4] However, they were both excellent and well-respected journalists. [5] And Cronkite's stories had impact, as did Murrow. [6] Today's journalists could learn from them both.

[1] Edward R. Murrow was one of the best television journalists in history. [2] He reported many stories that are better remembered than those of Walter Cronkite, his CBS colleague. [4] Murrow's reporting was more extensive than Cronkite's. [5] And Cronkite's stories had impact, as did Murrow's.

Practice

Write a short paragraph explaining why illogical comparisons can be confusing to readers. In your paragraph, be sure to include one original example of each type of faulty comparison explained in the table. In your paragraph, include advice and information on how writers can avoid faulty comparisons.

☑ Check Your Understanding

Take a few minutes to think about why illogical comparisons creep up in writing and how you can keep your eye out for them in the future. Are there any words that often occur in comparisons that you can look out for?

Creating a Research Plan

Learning Targets
- Work collaboratively to generate a list of potential research topics.
- Use your preliminary topic as a starting point for developing a guiding research question, investigating it, and synthesizing relevant information from multiple sources.

Preview

In this activity, you will collaborate to select a topic and generate a research question to explore for the remainder of the unit. Your group research will inform your argumentative essay.

Learning Strategies

Activating Prior Knowledge
Brainstorming
Discussion Groups

My Notes

Preparing for Research

Before selecting a preliminary topic for your individual and group assessments, work with your group members to complete the following steps.

1. Based on the different ways in which you have been thinking about Hurricane Katrina in this unit, work with your classmates to generate a list of potential issues and topics. Consider topics that will:
   - provide opportunities to analyze the subject through various critical perspectives
   - change over time as cultural perspectives change
   - appear in a range of print and nonprint media texts
   - reveal contrasting values and beliefs
   - reveal differing representations of the truth of what happened

2. Brainstorm a list of potential topics or issues. Write your ideas in your Reader/Writer Notebook.

3. With your group members, explore the possible topics and issues you generated. When a specific topic seems interesting to the group, brainstorm about what a research plan and report might include. Use this graphic organizer to take notes.

Topic	Key Research Points	Advantages/Disadvantage of Topic	Group members' views on topic
Response to Katrina vs. other hurricanes	Compare federal responses across time. Look at changes in federal policy	Broad topic that would require lots of background research. Hard to compare hurricanes that caused different amounts of damage	

College and Career Readiness Standards

Focus Standards:

SL.11–12.1b Work with peers to promote civil, democratic discussions and decision-making, set clear goals and deadlines, and establish individual roles as needed.

W.11–12.7 Conduct short as well as more sustained research projects to answer a question (including a self-generated question) or solve a problem; narrow or broaden the inquiry when appropriate; synthesize multiple sources on the subject, demonstrating understanding of the subject under investigation.

ACTIVITY 4.8

PLAN

Materials: computer access to conduct online research if possible
Suggested Pacing: 3 50-minute class periods

TEACH

1 Read the Learning Targets and Preview. You may want to review some collaborative writing strategies to **activate students' prior knowledge.**

2 Tell students that in this activity they will work with their group to select a topic to explore during the remainder of this unit. They will then draft a research proposal and discuss their plan to study this issue. Their research proposal will begin with guiding questions that explore a subject by applying multiple critical perspectives. The ways in which students engage with, examine, and investigate this issue will serve as the centerpiece for an individual argumentative essay (Embedded Assessment 1) and will culminate in a presentation (Embedded Assessment 2).

3 Direct students' attention to step 1 on the student page and to the task of generating ideas. Briefly discuss why the response to the Hurricane Katrina disaster was a rich topic for exploration.

4 Have each student list four or five topics that interest him or her. Then have students form **discussion groups** to refine ideas in student step 3. Since each group member will need to focus through a different lens, groups of three to four are ideal.

5 Have each group select a tentative topic. Then model for students the process of narrowing a topic and selecting an issue by providing the following examples.

The topic might be Hurricane Katrina; the event might be post-Katrina looting. Issues might be (1) race factors in media coverage, (2) the impact of gender on media reactions, and/or (3) the conflict between the "haves" and "have nots" in crisis situations.

6 Have groups narrow their own topics by **brainstorming** potential events (moments of controversy connected to the topic) and identifying potential issues to explore.

 TEACHER TO TEACHER

You may want to suggest students use the RAFT (Role, Audience, Format, Text) strategy to help the group generate and agree on a manageable topic.

7 Have students conduct a preliminary investigation to determine whether sufficient resources (print and nonprint) are available to explore their issues. Model using the three column chart by choosing a generic natural disaster-related topic and using some of the articles, reports, and other pieces from this unit to begin building a resource list.

8 Review the process for generating guiding questions (Activity 4.5), and have students define guiding questions (student step 7). Each student could answer the same general question through his or her lens, but it will work best if each comes up with a question specific to his or her lens.

4.8

4. When you narrow down your group's ideas to a few potential topics, brainstorm resources you might be able to use to conduct your research. Draw on your knowledge of the different sources you've already read in this unit to generate ideas in the graphic organizer. Assign each member a potential topic to brainstorm.

Topic	Resource	Contribution to Research
		(Sum up how the resource relates to the topic.)

5. Work to come to an agreement on your group's issue and event. Offer ideas to help the group develop a strong research topic. For example, is it possible to include relevant aspects of more than one topic to address the interest areas of everyone in the group? Review the information gathered in the first two steps to decide on a topic.

6. How did your group select an issue and event? For instance, did the group vote on an issue and choose the one favored by the majority? Write your issue in the space that follows and provide a brief rationale for how the group chose it.

    Issue and Rationale:

7. Apply your knowledge about guiding questions and formulate a strong guiding question that stems from the issue your group selected and reflects your specific critical lens. Then, work as a group to collect information from the texts you've read that could help answer the question. Make notes in your Reader/Writer Notebook.

8. Use the chart that follows to consider what approaches each of you might take to complete your individual essay for Embedded Assessment 1. How will you support each other in crafting guiding questions?

College and Career Readiness Standards

W.11–12.8 Gather relevant information from multiple authoritative print and digital sources, using advanced searches effectively; assess the strengths and limitations of each source in terms of the task, purpose, and audience; integrate information into the text selectively to maintain the flow of ideas, avoiding plagiarism and overreliance on any one source and following a standard format for citation.

Additional Standards Addressed:

W.11–12.2a, W.11–12.2b, W.11–12.2e, W.11–12.5

Criticism	Can you analyze the issue through this lens?	What elements of the issue does the critical perspective link to?	What could be the guiding question?
Archetypal			
Cultural			
Feminist			
Historical			
Marxist			

9 If the issue and research question seem feasible, each group member should draft a proposal for research, using the graphic organizer provided.

10 Review information for selecting credible sources from previous activities from this unit. You may want to model evaluating an online source for the class.

11 You may want to ask each group to turn in their proposed guiding question including a quickwrite that briefly explains the group's thoughts, so you can review questions for suitability.

Refining Your Research Question

9. Using the insights from the chart, how might you revise your guiding question to make it a stronger foundation for a research paper?

10. Is the question focused enough that it is possible for you to search for, gather, and analyze information that will give you new knowledge about a topic? Add to the graphic organizer created by the group by individually conducting on-the-spot research using online sources to locate one additional resource that could be used to gather information on your group's chosen topic. Be sure to include a sentence on the resource's possible contribution to knowledge.

11. Collect all the charts and other notes from the group and use the information to craft a single guiding question that will be the backbone of your group research paper.

12 Following your review, have groups complete the research proposal chart.

13 Encourage students to make a clear plan for using technology as they develop their Embedded Assessment essays. If students are unfamiliar with document-sharing sites or with using a word processor to add and track footnotes and endnotes, try to connect them with a librarian or teacher who can offer support.

14 Have students respond to the writing prompt.

ASSESS

Use student responses to the writing prompt to assess their ability to write a research proposal. Check student work for the following:

- a clear guiding question
- significant details that support the critical perspective
- explicit description of additional research needed

ADAPT

To provide additional support to students in writing research proposals, guide them through Writing Workshop 6: Research Writing. After reviewing some of the fundamentals of research writing, pair groups that need additional help with groups who have clear proposals and have them share ideas for improving the weaker proposals.

4.8

12. A research proposal informs the reader about your research question and how you intend to answer it. Organizing your thoughts before writing your research proposal will help you to synthesize your ideas in a logical way.

Research Proposal Notes
Issue/Event: What issue and event has the group chosen?
Review of the Issue: Write a summary of what you currently know about your chosen issue.
Critical Perspective: Which lens will you apply while exploring the issue? How will you apply the critical lens to your group's issue?
Research Question: What question will you use to guide your research?
Research Plan: How will you further explore the issue through your research?

Writing Prompt: Informational

Use your notes to write a one-page research proposal that explains your topic, briefly notes any information you have already learned, states which critical perspective you plan to use to examine the issue, and defines your guiding question. Mention any sources you have identified and plan to include in your final research report. Lastly, indicate where and how you will continue to conduct research to answer your guiding question. Be sure to:

- Identify your guiding question.
- Include significant details related to your critical perspective.
- Review your notes on what you already know about the issue and identify additional research needed to find supporting evidence for your group's ideas.
- Read and revise your research proposal draft to make sure your proposal demonstrates a command of standard English conventions.

 WRITING PROMPT: INFORMATIONAL

The following standards are addressed in the writing prompt:

- W.11–12.2a
- W.11–12.2b
- W.11–12.2e
- W.11–12.5
- W.11–12.7

Evaluating Sources

Learning Targets

- Locate and evaluate sources for credibility, bias, accuracy, and evidence of faulty reasoning or other issues that might make them unsuitable for research.
- Use sources accurately and cite them adequately to avoid plagiarism.

Preview

In this activity, you will use a checklist to determine whether specific sources are relevant to your research question and are suitable as references based on their accuracy and other factors critical to collecting high-quality information.

Researching Your Topic

Locating reliable sources is a central part of the research process. Remember that sources are generally classified as primary or secondary.

Primary Source: Provides direct evidence or testimony about an event and is created as the event is happening. Primary sources include articles written soon after an event takes place or reporting events as they happened, as well as video footage taken during an event.

Secondary Source: Analyzes and/or interprets an event, often through the use of primary sources, after it has occurred. As an example, a documentary about the Vietnam War could use wartime footage but, as a whole, would be considered a secondary source. Newspaper or magazine articles that offer opinions, historical perspective, or reflection on past events are also secondary sources.

1. Revisit the sources you have read in the unit. What kind of sources are they?

Criteria for Evaluating Sources

2. It is important to be able to identify if sources will help to strengthen your argument. Think about which search engines and terms you will use and how you will know that sources are credible and accurate. This task requires you to examine each source for credibility, accuracy, bias, and relevance. Use the following questions to evaluate sources for use for Embedded Assessment 1. Keep in mind that you should be able to analyze each source through one or multiple critical lenses.

Learning Strategies

Graphic Organizer
Note-taking

My Notes

PLAN

Materials: MLA style manuals
Suggested Pacing: 2 50-minute class periods

TEACH

1 Read the Learning Targets and Preview with the class. If necessary, review the terms *credibility*, *bias*, *accuracy*, and *relevance*.

2 Review the definitions of primary and secondary sources. Have students work in their groups to categorize the sources in one of the activities from this unit.

3 Each student should identify a minimum of five possible sources (three primary and two secondary) for his or her group's essay. Students should use the criteria for evaluation listed on this page to evaluate each possible source they identify.

4 Read aloud Criteria for Evaluating Sources and direct students to complete source evaluations for their proposed sources. Remind students to carefully evaluate and assess sources for reliability, accuracy, and credibility and to follow the standard format for citations. While students are completing source evaluations for each resource they select, remind them to read the text for quotations that support or challenge the interpretive claims they are developing.

College and Career Readiness Standards

Focus Standards:

RI.11–12.5 Analyze and evaluate the effectiveness of the structure an author uses in his or her exposition or argument, including whether the structure makes points clear, convincing, and engaging.

W.11–12.7 Conduct short as well as more sustained research projects to answer a question (including a self-generated question) or solve a problem; narrow or broaden the inquiry when appropriate; synthesize multiple sources on the subject, demonstrating understanding of the subject under investigation.

5 This source evaluation exercise calls for a sophisticated analysis. Use references to the work students did with the earlier Hurricane Katrina articles to indicate the level of sophistication you expect to see in students' evaluations. Consider revisiting the congressional report "A Failure of Initiative" or Simone Bruni's essay. Use both texts to emphasize that a slanted or personal text could still be a valid source. Ask students to analyze how the writer's language is linked to the text's context and purpose.

4.9

Credibility

3. Who is the identified author?

_____

4. What is the reputation of the author, publisher, or sponsor of the information?

_____

5. What is the author's research technique?

_____

6. Does the author cite sources that highlight different points of view?

_____

7. Does the author address counterarguments?

_____

8. How does the author's use of the following features impact his or her credibility?

   - Multiple sources
   - Headlines or captions
   - Photos or other visuals

_____

Bias

9. Are any of the following logical fallacies or rhetorical slanters evident in the source? How do these impact the reliability of the source?

   - Emotional language
   - Political leanings
   - Missing information or selective use of facts
   - Other (straw man, slippery slope, faulty analogy)

_____

10. What does the text's publication context reveal about the author's agenda?

_____

College and Career Readiness Standards

W.11–12.8 Gather relevant information from multiple authoritative print and digital sources, using advanced searches effectively; assess the strengths and limitations of each source in terms of the task, purpose, and audience; integrate information into the text selectively to maintain the flow of ideas, avoiding plagiarism and overreliance on any one source and following a standard format for citation.

W.11–12.9 Draw evidence from literary or informational texts to support analysis, reflection, and research.

Additional Standard Addressed

SL.11–12.4

6 Have students list their resources and answer the question in the Check Your Understanding. Review students' responses to ensure sources pass the credibility test before students move toward drafting an annotated bibliography.

7 Go over the information about ethical use of sources with students and answer any questions. Emphasize that proper use and citing of sources will lend credibility to students' academic writing.

11. What might be the effect of this bias?

_____

_____

Accuracy

12. How does this source cover the content?

- statistics and similar evidence that support the author's claims
- relevant examples to support claims (from a peer-reviewed scientific study, for example)
- experts cited or quoted to support the author's position
- relevant information taken directly from primary sources

13. What quotations might you cite as support for your claims?

_____

_____

Relevance

14. Is the information relevant to your research?

Is yes, then how?

If no, then why not?

_____

_____

15. Has the information on this subject changed since the publication date?

_____

_____

16. How can you analyze the text through a critical lens?

_____

_____

☑ Check Your Understanding

Make a list of the resources you plan to use for your research paper. Do they pass the test for relevancy, accuracy, credibility, and absence of bias?

Ethical Use of Sources

When you paraphrase, summarize, or quote other people's work in your own, it is important to cite that work using the appropriate academic style. Not only does citing your sources help you avoid plagiarism, but it also gives your work credibility because it adheres to ethical standards of academic writing. This shows you have consulted experts to join a scholarly conversation.

8 Vocabulary Development: Direct students' attention to the Academic Vocabulary box. Ask them to work with their groups to brainstorm words to define the concept of an *annotated bibliography*. You may wish to display an example of a complete annotated bibliography to give students a visual reference.

9 Explain that students will need to draft an annotated bibliography for their group's sources. If possible, have group members divide the entries for the annotated bibliography equally.

TEACHER TO TEACHER

To help groups write the annotated bibliography together, consider using an online collaborative word processor, such as Google Docs. Make multiple copies of the source evaluation form in the Student Edition so that each student can be responsible for finding two or more sources.

10 If possible, provide students with additional examples of how to cite sources in MLA style. If students are already familiar with MLA style, work as a class to create example references for a book or book chapter, a government publication, and an infographic.

11 Have students complete the Independent Reading Checkpoint. Prompt them to make connections between their independent reading and the Embedded Assessment.

ASSESS

Review student annotations to assess their ability to use correct bibliographic formats accurately and write thoughtful annotations about each source.

ADAPT

If students need additional help creating annotations, review the process and/or model writing an annotation. To extend learning, have students include in each annotation a description of how the source provides a point of view not otherwise represented in the research.

4.9

VOCABULARY

ACADEMIC
An annotated bibliography is a list of citations used in a work, in which each citation includes additional information about the quality and relevance of the source.

Creating an Annotated Bibliography

17. An annotated bibliography is a list of references used in a work in which each reference includes a paragraph, or annotation, in order to provide readers additional information about the sources used to produce a piece of research. Use the samples that follow as models for the annotations you write for your sources. The following models show the MLA standard format for citing bibliographic information. Note that the examples include a summary of the source, an assessment of the usefulness of the source in providing information about a topic, and a reflection on how the source might be used to address the research question.

Magazine or Newspaper Article

Author(s). "Title of Article." *Title of Periodical*, Day Month Year: pages. Medium of publication.

Smith, Gregory J. "Science and the storms—the USGS response to the hurricanes of 2005." *U.S. Geological Survey Circular 1306*, 1 October 2007: 1–4. Web.

Smith provides a comprehensive assessment of the impacts of the 2005 hurricanes in the Gulf of Mexico as well as the important role of science in landscape restoration and community recovery. This work is relevant because it provides extensive information about the effects of Hurricane Katrina and comes from a reputable government source.

Website Entry

Author(s). "Article Title." *Name of Site*. Name of institution/organization affiliated with the site, date of resource creation (if available). Medium of publication. Date of access.

Blumberg, Alex. "After the Flood: Social Studies Lesson." *ThisAmericanLife.org*. WBEZ Chicago, 9 September 2005. Web. 4 May 2016.

In the days after the storm, radio producer Alex Blumberg interviews Ashley Nelson, an 18-year-old resident of one of New Orleans' many flooded neighborhoods. After listening to a clip from a news program claiming that the aftermath of Hurricane Katrina had more to do with class than race, Ashley reflects on the effect of socioeconomic status on residents' actions before and during the storm and their ability to survive after.

Film or Video Recording

Title of Film. Director, Distributor, Release year. Medium.

Trouble the Water. Directed by Carl Deal, Zeitgeist Films, 2008. DVD.

New Orleans residents record their efforts to weather Hurricane Katrina and their struggles to rebuild their lives in the aftermath of its devastation. The film provides a unique insiders' look into the city after the storm and examines how one community banded together to survive.

🎯 Independent Reading Checkpoint

Review the independent reading you have completed so far. Read any notes you took about how the texts discuss or explain the role of the media. Reflect on how you might use the information from these selections as you begin working on the Embedded Assessment. Share your observations with a group of peers.

Examining How an Issue Is Presented in Media Texts

ASSIGNMENT

Your assignment is to write an argumentative essay that argues for the use of a particular critical lens to interpret an event. Your essay must include an annotated bibliography and evidence from at least five texts gathered alone or with your group members.

Planning and Prewriting: Take time to make a plan for your essay.	▪ Which insights gained from learning about this event from multiple viewpoints can help you form a critical interpretation? ▪ Which evidence from your sources will you need to support your interpretation and show the different ways the event is represented in the media?
Drafting: Determine the structure and how you will incorporate your evidence.	▪ How will you craft a thesis so that your audience will understand your critical perspective and see how that perspective influences your response to the texts you are analyzing? ▪ How can you use evidence to support your analysis of the event and how it is depicted? ▪ How can you weave together engaging analysis and support to make your ideas and writing flow in a logical order? ▪ How can you use varied and appropriate diction and syntax to enhance the rhetorical effectiveness of your claims?
Evaluating and Revising the Draft: Make your work the best it can be.	▪ How will you use the Scoring Guide and peer responses to help guide your revision? ▪ How can examining another writer's essay help you evaluate your own use of evidence and analysis?
Checking and Editing for Publication: Confirm that your final draft is ready.	▪ How will you check for grammatical and technical accuracy? ▪ What sort of outside resources can help you to check your citations and annotated bibliography? ▪ How can you complete an effective final read-through of your essay?

Reflection

After completing this Embedded Assessment, think about how you went about accomplishing this assignment, and respond to the following:

- How did your own perspective on your chosen issue affect your work on this essay? Consider how you responded to each of the sources and their varied interpretations of the event.

College and Career Readiness Standards

Focus Standards:

W.11–12.1 Write arguments to support claims in an analysis of substantive topics or texts, using valid reasoning and relevant and sufficient evidence.

W.11–12.5 Develop and strengthen writing as needed by planning, revising, editing, rewriting, or trying a new approach, focusing on addressing what is most significant for a specific purpose and audience. (Editing for conventions should demonstrate command of Language standards 1–3 up to and including grades 11–12 here.)

EMBEDDED ASSESSMENT 1

Materials: access to multiple media accounts of an event
Suggested Pacing: 3 50-minute class periods

★ TEACHER TO TEACHER

If you choose to modify this Embedded Assessment by changing the prompt for some or all of your students, be sure that you have properly scaffolded the necessary skills and knowledge.

To support learning, you might choose an event and multiple texts about the event and ask students to choose a critical lens from two options that you preselect.

1 **Planning and Prewriting:** Because this assignment has many pieces to organize, you may want to review useful organizational patterns with the class.

2 **Drafting:** Remind students to integrate quotations into their work, citing sources accurately. They will be creating an annotated bibliography, so they will need to pay special attention to their sources.

3 Urge students to check the Scoring Guide before they complete their essays. Clarify any questions on how essays will be assessed.

4 **Evaluating and Revising the Draft:** You may want to take the time to develop a student-generated Writer's Checklist based on the Scoring Guide for students to use in their writing groups.

5 Encourage students to make separate passes looking for ways to improve diction and to vary syntax for meaning and effect.

6 **Checking and Editing for Publication:** As students are editing their revised work, remind them of the resources available: dictionaries, handbooks, online spell-checkers and grammar checkers, as well as peers and parents.

7 Have students turn in all drafts of their work as well as their outlines.

8 **Reflection:** Be sure students address the reflection question as a separate part of the Embedded Assessment assignment.

9 **Portfolio:** All notes for and drafts of the essay should be collected and presented together to show the process students used to respond to this assessment. You may also want students to keep their research information as support for their argument.

SCORING GUIDE

When you score this Embedded Assessment, you may wish to make copies or download and print copies of the Scoring Guide from SpringBoard Digital. In this way you can have a copy to mark for each student's work.

SCORING GUIDE

Scoring Criteria	Exemplary	Proficient	Emerging	Incomplete
Ideas	The essay • effectively combines the sources and the writer's position to argue for using a particular lens to interpret a single event discussed in multiple texts • contextualizes the event and presents the critical lens in a clear thesis • includes a conclusion that suggests the larger significance of the writer's position on the event.	The essay • adequately combines the sources and the writer's position to argue for using a particular lens to interpret a single event discussed in multiple texts • briefly contextualizes the issue and identifies the critical lens in a straightforward thesis • concludes logically but repeats the thesis somewhat.	The essay • inadequately argues how a particular lens can be used to interpret a single event discussed in multiple texts • presents a weak thesis or one that is lost in a summary of sources • concludes by returning directly to the attempted thesis, or offers no conclusion.	The essay • provides a confusing argument on how a particular lens can be used to interpret a single event discussed in multiple texts • presents an incomplete thesis that summarizes rather than describes a position • offers no conclusion.
Structure	The essay • sequences material to reinforce the ideas of the argument • paraphrases and summarizes information from sources in a way that provides strong support for its claims. • uses transitions that enhance the essay's coherence • includes an extensive annotated bibliography.	The essay • sequences material to support the ideas of the argument • paraphrases and summarizes information from sources in a way that provides adequate support for its claims • uses transitions to move between ideas • includes a complete annotated bibliography.	The essay • organizes ideas ineffectively or jumps too rapidly between ideas • paraphrases and summarizes information from sources in a way that provides inadequate support for its claims • lacks effective transitions • includes an incomplete or inaccurate annotated bibliography.	The essay • organizes ideas ineffectively or jumps too rapidly between ideas • does not paraphrase or summarize information from sources to support its claims • does not use transitions • does not include an annotated bibliography.
Use of Language	The essay • demonstrates a mature style that advances the writer's ideas • employs precise diction and a skillful use of syntax and punctuation to create an authoritative and engaging voice • follows standard writing conventions, including accurate citation of sources.	The essay • demonstrates a style that adequately supports the writer's ideas • employs logical diction, clear syntax, and effective punctuation to create a suitable voice • largely follows standard writing conventions, including accurate citation of sources; minor errors do not interfere with meaning.	The essay • demonstrates a limited style that ineffectively supports the writer's ideas • includes lapses in diction, syntax, or punctuation which may make the writer's voice inconsistent • is affected by errors in standard writing conventions, which interfere with meaning.	The essay • demonstrates a limited style that ineffectively supports the writer's ideas • includes significant lapses in diction, syntax, or punctuation that reflect a confused writer's voice • contains numerous errors in standard writing conventions, which seriously interfere with meaning.

College and Career Readiness Standards

W.11–12.7 Conduct short as well as more sustained research projects to answer a question (including a self-generated question) or solve a problem; narrow or broaden the inquiry when appropriate; synthesize multiple sources on the subject, demonstrating understanding of the subject under investigation.

Additional Standards Addressed:
RI.11–12.2, L.11–12.6, W.11–12.6

Unpacking Embedded Assessment 2

Learning Targets
- Reflect on concepts, essential questions, and vocabulary relating to the unit.
- Analyze the skills and knowledge needed to complete Embedded Assessment 2 successfully.

Preview
In this activity, you will revisit this unit's Essential Questions, closely examine the Embedded Assessment 2 assignment, and plan your independent reading.

Making Connections
In the first part of this unit, you examined how various speakers and writers, including reporters, government officials, scientists, and ordinary citizens, contributed to an unfolding narrative about a single event: Hurricane Katrina. You studied the ways that ideological and critical perspectives may surface in the coverage of an event, and you evaluated how a particular critical perspective can help illuminate truths about an event of historical significance. In this part of the unit, you will shift from examining and researching others' texts to creating your own media text. You will collaborate with peers to create an engaging presentation that employs elements of classical speeches to persuade your audience.

Essential Questions
Based on your study of the first part of this unit, how would you answer these questions now?

1. How do media sources influence our understanding of the truth and significance of an issue?

2. How are media texts constructed to cater to media consumers' interests, experiences, assumptions, and biases or to promote a particular agenda?

Unpacking Embedded Assessment 2
Closely read the assignment for Embedded Assessment 2: Presenting an Argument.

🔊 Your assignment is to present an argument in a medium of your choice (persuasive speech, short documentary film, video news broadcast, podcast) in which you transform the information you gathered from your research in the first part of the unit into an argument concerning the topic/issue you have chosen. Your presentation should last five to seven minutes. It may be recorded or presented live.

With your classmates, identify the skills and knowledge you will need to complete this assessment successfully. Create a graphic organizer listing all the specific skills and knowledge.

📦 Planning Independent Reading
For your independent reading during this part of the unit, consider reading additional informational texts related to the topic you will be addressing for the Embedded Assessment. Discuss with your group what information you should seek out in your independent reading in order to support the successful completion of a presentation for the Embedded Assessment.

Learning Strategies
Close Reading
Graphic Organizer
Marking the Text

My Notes

College and Career Readiness Standards

Focus Standards:

RI.11–12.4 Determine the meaning of words and phrases as they are used in a text, including figurative, connotative, and technical meanings; analyze how an author uses and refines the meaning of a key term or terms over the course of a text (e.g., how Madison defines faction in Federalist No. 10).

SL.11–12.1b Work with peers to promote civil, democratic discussions and decision-making, set clear goals and deadlines, and establish individual roles as needed.

SL.11–12.1d Respond thoughtfully to diverse perspectives; synthesize comments, claims, and evidence made on all sides of an issue; resolve contradictions when possible; and determine what additional information or research is required to deepen the investigation or complete the task.

ACTIVITY 4.10

PLAN

Suggested Pacing: 1 50-minute class period

TEACH

1 Ask students to think-pair-share as they review responses to the two Essential Questions. Ask students to note how their responses since Activity 4.1 have changed.

2 Lead students through a **close reading** of the Embedded Assessment 2 assignment and Scoring Guide. Instruct students to highlight the places in the text that mention a skill or knowledge necessary to succeed on the assessment.

3 Help students locate the Presenting Scoring Guide in the Resources section of the Student Edition. Clarify any expectations specific to the presentation component of the Embedded Assessment.

4 Instruct students to paraphrase in small groups the skills and knowledge they have highlighted. As you conduct a group discussion, revise or add to the web **graphic organizer** that lists the knowledge and skills they will need in Embedded Assessment 2.

5 Direct students' attention to the Independent Reading Link. Help them select appropriate informational texts online or in print that will help them complete Embedded Assessment 2.

ASSESS

Check students' summaries and monitor discussion to ensure understanding of the skills and knowledge needed for the next assessment.

ADAPT

Revisit the web graphic organizer throughout the rest of the unit. Doing so will reinforce the purpose of each activity and highlight how it allows students to practice the skills and knowledge needed for success on the Embedded Assessment.

PLAN

Suggested Pacing: 1 50-minute class period

TEACH

1 Read aloud the Learning Targets and Preview. Explain to students that in this activity they will conduct a close read of a persuasive speech in order to prepare them to persuade others.

2 Direct students to read About the Speech. Then, ask students to consider the setting and timing of the speech. Discuss why President Bush might have chosen to give a persuasive speech at a school in New Orleans.

3 **FIRST READ:** Have students take turns reading paragraphs of the speech aloud. Direct them to use the My Notes space to record questions about the text and what the audience's reaction to the text might be. Ask students to note any words in the speech unfamiliar to them so that they can be reviewed and discussed in class.

TEXT COMPLEXITY

Overall: Moderate
Lexile: 1440L
Qualitative: Moderate Difficulty
Task: Accessible (Understand)

Learning Strategies

Graphic Organizer
Quickwrite
SOAPSTone

My Notes

Learning Targets

- Closely read and analyze a persuasive speech by considering the speaker's purpose, audience, and message.
- Critique and evaluate the characteristics and structural elements of a speech in a written review.

Preview

In this activity, you will read and closely analyze a persuasive speech by President George W. Bush to understand its structure, ideas, and persuasive elements. Then you will work with classmates to write a review of the speech.

About the Speech

President George W. Bush (b. 1946) delivered the following remarks to an audience at Warren Easton Charter High School in New Orleans, Louisiana on August 28, 2015. The former president, along with First Lady Laura Bush, first visited the school in 2006. They returned in 2015 as part of a series of events to mark the tenth anniversary of Hurricane Katrina. The school was the first public high school in the state of Louisiana and became a charter school during the reconstruction period after Hurricane Katrina.

As You Read

- Imagine the audience's reactions to the speech. Jot down notes in the margin to indicate where the audience might laugh or applaud.
- Circle unknown words or phrases. Try to determine the meaning of the words by using context clues, word parts, or a dictionary.

Speech

Remarks by **President George W. Bush at Warren Easton Charter High School on the 10th Anniversary of Hurricane Katrina**

by **President George W. Bush**

August 28, 2015

1   Thank you all. As has been mentioned, in 2006 Laura and I came here to Warren Easton Charter High School a year after Katrina hit, and we are honored and pleased to be back on the tenth anniversary of that devastating storm. I can't think of a better place to come here in New Orleans, except for

College and Career Readiness Standards

Focus Standards:

RI.11–12.1 Cite strong and thorough textual evidence to support analysis of what the text says explicitly as well as inferences drawn from the text, including determining where the text leaves matters uncertain.

RI.11–12.5 Analyze and evaluate the effectiveness of the structure an author uses

in his or her exposition or argument, including whether the structure makes points clear, convincing, and engaging.

RI.11–12.6 Determine an author's point of view or purpose in a text in which the rhetoric is particularly effective, analyzing how style and content contribute to the power, persuasiveness, or beauty of the text.

some of the restaurants. The slogan that guided the school when we first visited is true today: "We believe in success." And because of the success that schools like this have achieved, you have given all Americans reason to believe that New Orleans is back and better than ever.

...

2   In a cruel twist, Hurricane Katrina brought despair during what should have been a season of hope—the start of a new school year. Students who had recently gone back to school suddenly had no school to go back to. Many had nowhere to live. The floodwaters, as you all know better than most, claimed schools and homes alike. As Laura mentioned, the ground we're on today was underwater. All of us who are old enough to remember will never forget the images of our fellow Americans amid a sea of misery and ruin. We will always remember the lives lost across the Gulf Coast. Their memories are in our hearts—and I hope you pray for their families.

3   Hurricane Katrina is a story of loss beyond measure; it is also a story of commitment and compassion. I hope you remember what I remember, and that is 30,000 people were saved in the immediate aftermath of the storm by U.S. military personnel, by Louisiana law enforcement, and by citizens who volunteered. I hope you remember what I remember, and that is the thousands who came here on a volunteer basis to provide food for the hungry and to help find shelter for those who had no home to live in. There are people all around our country who prayed for you, many of whom showed up so they could say they helped a fellow citizen who was hurting.

4   One of the groups that stepped forward to serve were the educators of New Orleans. At a time when it would have been easy to walk away from the wreckage, the educators here today thought of the children who would be left behind. You understood that bringing New Orleans back to life required getting students back to school. And even though some of the educators had lost almost everything you owned, you let nothing stand in your way. Today, we celebrate the resurgence of New Orleans schools—and we honor the resilience of a great American city whose levees gave out but whose people never gave up.

5   Out of the devastation of Katrina, you vowed to do more than just open the schools. You vowed to challenge the status quo. Long before the great flood, too many students in this city drifted from grade to grade without ever learning the skills needed for success. Parents lacked choices and the power to intervene. Principals and teachers lacked the authority to chart a more hopeful course. It was a system that stranded more than sixty percent of students failing in schools. It was what I called the "soft bigotry of low expectations."

6   The decisions you made in the dark hours after Katrina sparked a decade of reform. Rather than just reopen the schools, you reorganized many into charter schools[1] that are independently operated but publicly accountable for achieving high standards. More than nine in ten public school students in this city now call a charter school home. Administrators at these schools have the

[1] A charter school is an independently operated, publicly funded school.

My Notes

---

4 Vocabulary Development: After paragraph 5, pause to discuss the Word Connection box. Select a few compelling words from the text, such as status quo, and ask students about the author's possible intent for using them. Elicit other words that the author could have used.

WORD CONNECTIONS

Etymology

The term status quo comes from Latin and literally means "the state in which." In English, the term refers to the existing state of something, and it is often used negatively in political discourse to criticize acceptance of current conditions and the slow pace of social or political change. Reread paragraph 5 of the speech and look for Bush's use of the term status quo. What does he mean by it in this context?

College and Career Readiness Standards

SL.11–12.1d Respond thoughtfully to diverse perspectives; synthesize comments, claims, and evidence made on all sides of an issue; resolve contradictions when possible; and determine what additional information or research is required to deepen the investigation or complete the task.

Additional Standards Addressed:

L.11–12.6, SL.11–12.6, W.11–12.2a, W.11–12.2b, W.11–12.2d, W.11–12.2e, W.11–12.10

My Notes

freedom to slice through red tape and the freedom to innovate. Parents at these schools have choices if dissatisfied. And the results at these schools have been extraordinary. The reason we know is because we measure, and any attempt to undermine accountability in our school system does a huge disservice to the students who go to the schools in New Orleans.

7   According to a new report by the Cowen Institute, the percentage of New Orleans' students graduating on time has soared since Katrina. The percentage of students who attend schools that score better than the state average almost doubled, and so has the percentage of students meeting basic standards. And you've got to ask, "Why?" It just didn't happen. A lot of it was structural, and a lot of it requires strong leadership—people who stared into the eye of a storm and who refused to back down. And so Laura and I are here in New Orleans to remind our country about what strong leadership means, and we're here to salute the leaders.

8   I think of Jenny Rious here at Warren Easton. After Katrina, Jenny left New Orleans, was forced to leave New Orleans. She started a website called Warren Easton in Exile. The site reunited students scattered across the country around a vision for returning to New Orleans, and reopening this school. When Jenny returned to New Orleans, the first place she went was not her house. It was this school. And as she put it, "I would rather see my own house burn down than this school." Jenny would give anything for Easton and today, we give teachers like her our sincere thanks.

9   It's amazing what happened in this city after the storm wiped out the school system. Educational entrepreneurs decided to do something about the devastation, and the failure. I met a lot of them when I was President, and subsequent to my presidency. Neerav Kingsland is one such person. He took a leadership role at an organization called New Schools for New Orleans, where he worked with others to help launch dozens of new schools and to turn ideas into reform into reality. In other words, this isn't just a theoretical exercise. It's important for our country to look at New Orleans and realize this is an exercise of implementing a plan which works.

10   He—Neerav was so encouraged by what he sees here that he—he's talking up the reforms that worked to other cities across the country. Isn't it amazing—the storm that nearly destroys New Orleans, and yet now New Orleans is the beacon for school reform. Neerav represents the virtues that Bill Clinton and I had in mind when we announced the new Presidential Leadership Scholars program—and we're honored that Neerav was among the first class of scholars.

11   Achieving these results took librarians who salvaged their collections from the watery wreckage. Listen, I know something about librarians. I married one. I'm really proud of the Laura Bush Foundation. She talked about the grants; she talked about Pam and Marshall. These are citizens who supported this Foundation who, if they'd been in New Orleans, they didn't stay very long. And yet, like many around the country, they care deeply about the

future of this city. I hope the students here—I'm really thrilled you're here by the way and thank you for staying awake. I hope you realize the compassion of others in helping you realize a good education.

12 It turns out that every good school that's succeeding—a school that's succeeding—a school that's succeeding—and we know it's succeeding, because we measure against other standards—requires strong principals. And there's no doubt that Lexi Medley is a strong leader. I love when she says—when she says, "If you fail, we fail. The student's our product. We don't believe in putting out anything but the best." In order to succeed, in order to lead properly, you've got to set high goals and high expectations. And that's what Lexi and this school have done. As you heard, this school has graduated 100 percent of its seniors for the past five years. Lexi, you've earned our admiration and our gratitude, along with our best wishes for a happy birthday tomorrow.

13 It's the stories of schools like this one and others that we see a determination to rebuild better than before. And it—it's a spirit much stronger than any storm. It's a spirit that's lifted communities laid low by tornadoes or terrorist attacks. It's a spirit that I saw in New Orleans ten years ago, and that is very evident today.

14 We see that spirit in the population that has ticked back up as families settle back down. We see it in the tourists who are drawn here not only by this city's rich heritage but the new hotel rooms and restaurants. We see it in the spirit in Lauren LeDuff. As Laura mentioned—Lauren mentioned—Laura and I first met her in 2006 when she was a senior at Easton. She's happy to be back at the school she loved—she was happy to be back at the school she loved at the time. And you know what she told me? She said, "I want to be a teacher." And here she is as a member of this faculty, teaching English. I probably needed her when I was in high school. When asked how students have overcome adversity, Lauren says, "We teach our kids to be resilient. That's in the culture of this city."

15 Lauren's right. The resilience you teach at Warren Easton is the same resilience that this city showed the world in the wake of Hurricane Katrina. On this anniversary, the work of making a stronger and more hopeful New Orleans goes on. You've achieved a lot over the last ten years. And with belief in success, and a faith in God, New Orleans will achieve even more. The darkness from a decade ago has lifted. The Crescent City has risen again. And its best days lie ahead.

Former President Bush and Laura Bush visit Warren Easton Charter School in New Orleans, 2015.

My Notes

Making Observations
- What emotions does the speech evoke?
- Which statements in the speech are the most thought-provoking?

5 Guide students in pairs or small groups through Making Observations and Working from the Text. Ask students to note how and in what way they have improved their understanding of the ideas in the speech.

6 Arrange students into two groups and direct each group to consider elements of the **SOAPSTone** chart. Group One students could be directed to collaborate on the answers to the first three questions (Speaker, Occasion, and Audience) with their analysis and textual support, while Group Two students answer the subsequent three (Purpose, Subject, and Tone). An alternative might be to assign the SOAPTone tasks so that the kinds of considerations are mixed (i.e., Group One tackles analysis and textual support for Speaker, Audience, and Subject, while Group Two takes on Occasion, Purpose, and Tone).

7 Monitor the progress of each group as they develop their responses.

4.11

Working from the Text

1. Choose one or two of the questions you wrote during the first reading of this speech and pose them to your classmates in a small group discussion. Listen and respond as your classmates do the same with their questions. Jot down notes in the space to capture any new understanding or information gained from the questions.

2. With your group, use the **SOAPSTone** strategy to examine the speech "Remarks by President George W. Bush at Warren Easton Charter High School" more closely. Conduct on-the-spot research as needed to find additional details about the speech. Record your analysis and supporting textual evidence in the graphic organizer.

SOAPSTone	Analysis	Textual Support
Speaker What do you know about the speaker?	The speaker is former President George W. Bush, who was still serving as president when Hurricane Katrina hit New Orleans in 2005. He supports school reform efforts including school choice and charter schools.	In paragraph 5, Bush describes the situation in New Orleans schools before Hurricane Katrina as "the soft bigotry of low expectations." In paragraph 6, he states that reforms like charter schools, increased school autonomy, and parental choice have resulted in better student outcomes.
Occasion What are the circumstances surrounding the speech?	The speech was delivered on the 10th anniversary of Hurricane Katrina during an event at a charter school.	The title and opening sentence of the text indicate that it was delivered on the 10th anniversary of Hurricane Katrina.

SOAPSTone	Analysis	Textual Support
Audience Who is the audience?	First Lady Laura Bush, the school's principal, teachers, and students are in the audience. It is also likely that members of the community, elected officials, and members of the press are in the audience.	In paragraphs 2, Bush says, "As Laura mentioned," which implies that she spoke before him. In paragraph 12, he wishes the principal, Lexi Medley, a happy birthday, indicating that she is in the audience. He also addresses students (paragraph 11) and several teachers (paragraphs 8, 9, and 14).
Purpose What is the purpose of this speech?	The speech serves several purposes. First, it serves as an opportunity for the president to lead the audience in reflecting on the loss, tragedy, and hardship brought by Hurricane Katrina. The president also uses the speech to recognize and honor the resilience, humanity, and determination of the people who helped respond to the storm and rebuild the city. Last, the speech serves as an opportunity for Bush to persuade his audience that school reform policies he favors have, in his estimation, proved effective.	In paragraph 2, Bush focuses mainly on remembering the tragedy of the hurricane. In paragraph 3, he switches the focus to praising "thousands who came here" to help after the storm. In paragraph 4, he praises educators specifically, and then in paragraph 5 and throughout the remainder of the speech he makes the argument that New Orleans schools were not performing well before the storm but have improved as a result of reforms that were implemented as the schools were rebuilt.
Subject What topic(s) is the speech about?	The speech is mainly about the improvements in education in New Orleans since Hurricane Katrina, and the reasons for those improvements.	Starting in paragraph 4 and continuing through the rest of the speech, President Bush speaks about educators and the work they have done to improve schools in New Orleans. In paragraph 6, he says, "The decisions you made in the dark hours after Katrina sparked a decade of reform." He then provides numerous examples of reforms and reformers, and he cites evidence (paragraph 7 especially) in support of his argument.
Tone What is the speaker's tone?	The tone is one of reflection, gratitude, and pride. At times, the president uses a playful and familiar tone. The speech ends with a hopeful tone.	The tone in paragraphs 1–4 is largely reflective, with the president repeating lines like "I hope you remember what I remember…" Starting in paragraph 4, the tone becomes one of appreciation but also pride that certain school reforms were enacted and seem to have worked. The tone is occasionally playful and funny, as in the second sentence when he says, "I can't think of a better place to come here in New Orleans except for some of the restaurants," and the speech ends with Bush saying hopefully, "The Crescent City has risen again. And its best days lie ahead."

ACTIVITY 4.11 continued

8 Have both groups share their analyses so that students in both groups have an opportunity to examine all major ideas presented in the speech.

9 As students share their responses with each other, check for comprehension. Monitor whether responses are well supported by textual evidence. If necessary, reread key passages with students to aid in comprehension.

10 With a partner or in small groups, have students work through the Focus on the Sentence section. Check that students form their ideas directly from the text by asking them to point out specific paragraphs that support their ideas.

11 Have students read Evaluating Characteristics and Structural Elements of a Speech.

12 Review the characteristics and elements of a persuasive argument: thesis, evidence, appeals, treatment of counterarguments, and structure of the argument.

13 Provide an example of each element, making reference to another text from the unit.

LEVELED DIFFERENTIATED INSTRUCTION

Students may benefit from additional modeling of the characteristics and structural elements of a persuasive speech as they develop their plans to construct their own speeches.

Developing Help students understand the parts of an argumentative speech by focusing closely on a few paragraphs. Have students work independently or in pairs to identify one characteristic or element of argument in a paragraph. Ask students to first paraphrase the paragraph, and then to explain why it exemplifies a characteristic or element of argument.

Expanding Ask students to examine the speech for instances of primary sources and secondary sources (Activity 4.9) kinds of information and identify them, offering evidence to support their choices. They might also conduct an independent research to investigate why the school was changed to a charter.

Bridging Pair students. Ask pairs to identify one claim in the speech. Then, have one partner argue the supporting position and the other partner argue the opposing position. Direct students to gather information from the speech and other Unit 4 texts to support their positions.

14 Have students break out in small groups to collaboratively reread the speech. Ask students to annotate and underline details that express each characteristic or element of the argument.

15 Direct students to answer the Guiding Questions as they critique the speech. Prompt students to explain how they scored each category. Have small groups share their critiques with the class. Generate discussion on how groups may agree or disagree.

☑ Focus on the Sentence

Summarize the central thesis of President Bush's speech by expanding the short sentence.

Kernel: They improved schools.

Who? educators and educational entrepreneurs

When? after Hurricane Katrina

Where? New Orleans

How? by introducing reforms like charter schools and school choice

Expanded Sentence:

Possible response: After Hurricane Katrina, educators and educational entrepreneurs improved

schools in New Orleans by introducing reforms like charter schools and school choice.

Evaluating Characteristics and Structural Elements of a Speech

Now that you have examined the rhetorical context and central message of the speech, you will look more closely at its persuasive elements.

With your group, reread the speech to identify and evaluate the characteristics and structural elements listed in the chart. Use the guiding questions to drive your discussion and to help you assign a score to each characteristic or element. Be prepared to justify the score with evidence from the text and thoughtful analysis.

Characteristic or Element of Argument	Guiding Questions	Score 1 – not effective at all 5 – highly effective
Thesis	What is the thesis of the speech? Is the thesis clearly stated? Is it arguable?	
Evidence	What evidence is presented? Is the evidence credible? Is the evidence convincing?	
Appeals	What appeals to the audience's sense of logic, emotions, or ethics does the president use? How likely is it that each appeal would persuade the audience?	
Treatment of Counterarguments	To what extent does the president acknowledge and respond to counterarguments? How effective is the response to counterarguments?	
Structure of the Argument	How is the argument structured? Is the introduction clear and convincing? Does the argument unfold in a logical manner? Is there a convincing conclusion and call to action?	

3. Based on your group's evaluation of the characteristics and structural elements of the speech, come to consensus about an overall critique. How effective is President Bush's argument? What makes it effective and/or what would make it more effective?

4. Now that your group has evaluated the argumentative characteristics and elements of the speech, share your critique with the rest of the class. To what extent do other groups agree? Do any of the other groups present valid evidence that would convince you to modify your response?

☑ Check Your Understanding

Quickwrite: How can you apply your evaluation and critique of President Bush's speech to the development of your own argumentative speech for Embedded Assessment 2? What elements and characteristics of President Bush's speech might you use as a model? What will you try to do differently?

🖉 Writing Prompt: Informational

Write a short review of the speech, "Remarks by President George W. Bush at Warren Easton Charter High School on the 10th Anniversary of Hurricane Katrina." The review should express a thoughtful, critical examination of the speech's argumentative characteristics and structural elements. Be sure to:

- Clearly state your overall critique of the speech.
- Use text evidence and thoughtful commentary to justify your evaluation.
- Write with well-chosen vocabulary and an appropriate level of formality.

My Notes

---

16 Monitor students as they write a short review of the speech in response to the Writing Prompt. Check that students write a well-considered commentary supported by evidence from the text.

17 Call students' attention to the Check Your Understanding feature. After they have written their responses, give them time to share their answers in pairs or small groups.

ASSESS

Check students' review responses in the Writing Prompt and monitor discussion to assess students' understanding of the skills and knowledge needed for the next assessment. Ensure that students demonstrate an understanding of how each section of the Scoring Guide works.

ADAPT

Encourage students to revisit their evaluations, reviews and critiques of the speech as they prepare to construct their own speeches. As they work, this review allows them to examine how their perceptions about argumentative speeches may change or deepen so that they can practice the skills and knowledge needed for success on the Embedded Assessment.

🖉 WRITING PROMPT: INFORMATIONAL

The following standards are addressed in the writing prompt:

- W.11–12.2a
- W.11–12.2b
- W.11–12.2d
- W.11–12.2e
- W.11–12.5

PLAN

Materials: Teacher-selected videoclip
Suggested Pacing: 2 50-minute class periods

TEACH

1 Bring students' attention to the Learning Targets and the Preview for this activity. Discuss how participation in a collaborative discussion can help them choose a medium for their presentations.

2 Review with students the elements of a presentation that enable a speaker to effectively convey ideas to an audience, including eye contact, speaking rate, enunciation and appropriate gestures. You may wish to model both effective and ineffective presentation methods of addressing an audience.

3 Divide the class into presentation groups so students can discuss and record their responses to the Planning to Present questions.

4 Have students remain in their groups and read student step 2. Guide students to understand that they should make use of media elements, including digital media, that will emphasize their key points, increase understanding, and engage the audience.

ACTIVITY 4.12

That Sounds Just Right

Learning Strategies

Brainstorming
Discussion Groups
Graphic Organizer

My Notes

Learning Targets

- Participate in a collaborative discussion to plan the creation of an argumentative presentation.
- Analyze and evaluate the ways that presentation elements such as eye contact, speaking rate, enunciation, and gestures contribute to the effective delivery of a speech.

Preview

In this activity, you will work collaboratively to choose a medium through which to present your argument for Embedded Assessment 2. Then you will watch a video of a persuasive speech and evaluate the speaker's delivery.

Planning to Present

Before you actually develop your presentation—whether it takes the form of a documentary, a speech, or another medium—you should begin thinking about some of the basic components of a good plan. Carefully consider the rhetorical context of your presentation: your topic/issue, your audience, why you are writing/creating a work on this particular topic or issue.

1. Discuss the following questions with your group before you go further in planning your presentation.

   Topic/Issue: What is your topic/issue? What event, person, text, or conflict are you focusing on? What critical lens(es) are you using to illuminate that subject for your audience? What messages or interpretation do you wish to convey?

   Purpose: What is your purpose? What do you want your audience to think/feel/know/do as a result of viewing your text?

   Audience: Decide on an audience to whom you will address your argument. Settle on an identifiable audience that you expect will have some interest in your topic. Your target audience should extend beyond your teacher and the other students in your class.

   Speaker: Who are you as the speaker? What is your stake in the topic?

   Occasion: What is the occasion for the presentation of your argument? Are you developing it in response to an incident or event, or to celebrate or acknowledge a situation? Would this be shown in a theater, on television, or online?

   Tone: What tone will best help you achieve your desired purpose? What specific music, visuals, sound effects, language choices, and elements of speech could you use to establish your tone? What tone will evoke the desired response in your audience?

2. Taking into consideration your responses to the questions listed, what presentation format or medium will your group use to present your argument? Help move the group toward the goal of consensus by offering thoughtful and purposeful ideas and judgments as you discuss your options. Make sure you decide on the following:

College and Career Readiness Standards

Focus Standards:

SL.11–12.1 Initiate and participate effectively in a range of collaborative discussions (one-on-one, in groups, and teacher-led) with diverse partners on grades 11–12 topics, texts, and issues, building on others' ideas and expressing their own clearly and persuasively.

SL.11–12.3 Evaluate a speaker's point of view, reasoning, and use of evidence and rhetoric, assessing the stance, premises, links among ideas, word choice, points of emphasis, and tone used.

- Brainstorm a list of media channels that you might use to present your various points of view. Which option would best allow your group to explore your subject?
- Will you present live or use a recorded format for your presentation?
- How will your chosen mode of delivery enable you to communicate your research findings effectively?
- What equipment or materials will your group need to create the presentation?
- How will each group member contribute?

☑ Check Your Understanding

Write down at least five steps you and your group will need to take to create your presentation. Then put a star next to the step you will take first.

Viewing a Speech

In the previous activity, you analyzed and evaluated the text of a speech by President George W. Bush. Now you will view a video of the same speech, or another speech selected by your teacher, paying close attention to the speaker's delivery.

3. When viewing the speech, record your observations and evaluation of the speaker's delivery.

Element of Delivery	Observations	Evaluation
Eye contact		
Speaking rate and pauses		
Volume		
Enunciation		
Gestures		

College and Career Readiness Standards

SL.11–12.5 Make strategic use of digital media (e.g., textual, graphical, audio, visual, and interactive elements) in presentations to enhance understanding of findings, reasoning, and evidence and to add interest.

Additional Standards Addressed:

W.11–12.5, SL.11–12.1b

ACTIVITY 4.12 continued

5 Direct groups to read the Check Your Understanding prompt. Give students time to discuss group actions and roles before writing their responses to the prompt.

6 Ask a volunteer to read aloud the prompt in the Viewing a Speech section.

7 Show the selected video to the class. Pause occasionally to give students time to take notes.

 TEACHER TO TEACHER

"Former President George W. Bush Remarks on the 10th Anniversary of Hurricane Katrina" can be found on c-span.org. The speech as it appears in SpringBoard is an excerpt of the complete presentation. You may wish to select the viewing to start at 00:22:00, which is where the text on the student page begins.

8 After showing the video, give students time to individually complete the Evaluation column of the graphic organizer. Then, arrange students into their Embedded Assessment 2 presentation groups. Ask them to discuss their reactions to the speech.

9 Direct groups to complete student steps 4 and 5. Ask groups to discuss their responses to the prompt in each step, and then to record their answers individually.

10 Have students complete the Check Your Understanding.

ASSESS

Circulate among the groups to evaluate progress and determine if students are using the five elements of effective delivery as they read their chosen paragraph.

ADAPT

To support students who need help comprehending the text, pair students and have them paraphrase a paragraph together. Having students return to the notes they made while reading and viewing examples of a persuasive presentation or speech supports their ability to plan their group presentations. In addition, this supports students in preparing to evaluate their peers' presentations.

4.12

My Notes

4. With your presentation group, choose one paragraph from the speech and practice delivering it to your group, experimenting with the delivery elements listed in the graphic organizer. What is the effect when you vary the delivery? What makes for the most effective delivery?

5. Write statements summarizing your group's goals for the effective use of each delivery element.

Eye contact:

Speaking rate and pauses:

Volume:

Enunciation:

Gestures:

☑ **Check Your Understanding**

How will you apply the observations you made of President Bush's delivery to your own presentation?

Turning Research into Persuasion

PLAN

Materials: clip from a television news magazine show to model how to identify key stylistic conventions (optional)
Suggested Pacing: 2 50-minute class periods

TEACH

1 Call attention to the Learning Targets of the activity so that students can plan how they will synthesize research findings and determine which organizational structure will best support their presentation.

2 Have students assemble into their presentation groups and revisit their group's guiding questions from Activity 4.8. Review these questions with the various groups.

3 If students need an example of a common guiding question, ask them to view the guiding questions in Activity 4.11. Have each group review its common guiding question to ensure that it is broad enough to apply to each group member's individual question.

4 Review students' responses to student step 3 before they begin work on student step 4. If necessary, model how to change a guiding question from a previous activity into a thesis statement.

Learning Targets
- Generate a clear plan for synthesizing information from research to create a coherent presentation that reflects depth of thought.
- Select an organizational structure strategically based on the purpose, audience, topic, and context of a presentation.
- Identify characteristics of your chosen presentation format and plan how to use those genre characteristics in the presentation.

Preview

In this activity, you will work collaboratively to plan elements of your presentation.

Learning Strategies
Brainstorming
Discussion Groups
Graphic Organizer

My Notes

Developing Your Media Text

1. **Revisiting Your Guiding Questions:** Review the guiding questions you previously generated as a group, and write the questions in the following space.

   Responses will vary.

   To what extent did public opinion of President Bush influence the backlash against the director of FEMA, Michael Brown?

   In what ways did residents' socioeconomic status contribute to their decision to evacuate or stay during the storm?

   What does the backlash surrounding FEMA and other government agencies and officials reveal about attitudes toward government and individual responsibility?

   What recurring story patterns, characters, or images are evoked by what happened as a result of Hurricane Katrina?

2. **Defining a Common Question:** Work together to define a common guiding question. The goal is to identify a question that is broad enough to be an umbrella under which each of your individual questions falls.

3. **Writing a Thesis Statement:** Once you have your central question, write a strong thesis statement that answers the question.

College and Career Readiness Standards

Focus Standards:

SL.11–12.5 Make strategic use of digital media (e.g., textual, graphical, audio, visual, and interactive elements) in presentations to enhance understanding of findings, reasoning, and evidence and to add interest.

W.11–12.7 Conduct short as well as more sustained research projects to answer a question (including a self-generated question) or solve a problem; narrow or broaden the inquiry when appropriate; synthesize multiple sources on the subject, demonstrating understanding of the subject under investigation.

5 Give students time to review their work in Activity 4.11 to help them generate responses to the step 4 prompt.

6 Ask students to review their work in Activity 4.7 and complete student step 5 individually before discussing as a group. If students within a group disagree on organizational approaches, encourage them to look at the Embedded Assessment 2 scoring guide. Ask groups which approaches are most effective for clearly presenting a thesis and supporting ideas.

7 Consider allowing groups to revise their responses to student step 5 after they define their group roles in student step 6.

8 Remind students to complete the Independent Reading Link.

LEVELED DIFFERENTIATED INSTRUCTION

Groups may be in need of specific parameters within which to plan and execute a feasible presentation.

Developing Lead a discussion about group roles with each group. Make a list of tasks, and help students divide them amongst themselves. Guide students to choose tasks that showcase their strengths. For instance, a student at the beginning stages of English acquisition can be in charge of finding photographs and other graphics.

Expanding If groups show signs of devoting too much time to planning their presentation, remind them that enough time will also have to be spent rehearsing each step so that it flows smoothly from one idea to the next supported by appropriate audio/visual enhancements.

4.13

My Notes

4. **Synthesizing Research:** How will your group thoughtfully synthesize information from your research in order to create an effective argumentative presentation? What information is most useful for each part of the presentation? Are there any gaps in research that you could fill to strengthen your argument or your treatment of counterarguments?

5. **Evaluating Organizational Options:** Revisit the presentation you and other groups delivered for Activity 4.7. What organizational approaches worked best? Why? Which approaches might work best for your current text? What other options might work?

6. **Defining Roles:** Using your collective research on your issue, and considering the medium you have selected, decide what roles each group member will play. If you are creating a documentary, for example, who are your subjects or characters? If your presentation will take the form of a speech, who are the speakers? These may be actual people who were involved in or influenced by the event, or they may be composite characters that represent particular points of view. Decide in your group who will play each role.

INDEPENDENT READING LINK

Read and Connect

Choose one or more of your independent reading texts. Consider what elements from your independent reading text could serve as a model to influence the development of presentation. Select a passage that demonstrates a particularly strong use of structure, language, rhetorical choices, or organization, and share it with your group.

College and Career Readiness Standards

W.11–12.8 Gather relevant information from multiple authoritative print and digital sources, using advanced searches effectively; assess the strengths and limitations of each source in terms of the task, purpose, and audience; integrate information into the text selectively to maintain the flow of ideas, avoiding plagiarism and overreliance on any one source and following a standard format for citation.

Additional Standards Addressed:
SL.11–12.3, SL.11–12.4, SL.11–12.6, L.11–12.6, W.11–12.6

4.13

7. **Identifying Conventions:** Make a list of typical structural and stylistic conventions of the medium you have selected for your presentation. You might dissect a professional model to help you identify key features to emulate.

ACADEMIC

Conventions are the standard features, practices, and forms associated with the way something is usually done. Different media channels and types of media texts have different genre conventions.

VOCABULARY

As your group considers the structural and stylistic conventions of your medium, offer ideas or judgments that will move the group toward its goal.

Using Digital Media: To evaluate how best to apply digital media to your presentation, discuss the following questions within your group.

- What advantage does the use of digital media have over the use of print media in your presentation?
- How does the use of media impact the audience and their view of your reasoning and evidence?

8. **Revising the Presentation:** How can the Internet serve as a tool for production, publication, and collaboration? Brainstorm and list ideas and make decisions with your group.

9. **Complete the Presentation Plan:** Preview the Presentation Plan graphic organizer and then complete it with your group.

My Notes

_____
_____
_____
_____
_____
_____
_____
_____
_____
_____
_____
_____
_____
_____
_____
_____
_____
_____
_____
_____
_____
_____

ACTIVITY 4.13 continued

9 **Vocabulary Development:** Before students begin student step 7, have them work in pairs to define *conventions* in their own words and think of both examples and non-examples.

10 Note that Embedded Assessment 2 allows students to present a live performance or a media text, but either choice should be guided by an effort to model the product on a particular media channel or show.

11 Have each group identify the common structural and stylistic conventions of the specific medium they will be using. Explain, for example, that a journalistic interview might use close-ups, archival footage as a prompt for discussion, opening credits, a title graphic during the interview, theme music, an attention-getter that links to the subject of the interview, and so on.

12 Encourage students to watch a professional example of the medium as a model for their own presentation. Consider doing this with the whole class using a clip from a television news magazine show.

13 Help students consider how to strategically use digital media to strengthen their presentations. Model how to decide the best places to use multimedia to increase audience interest and understanding. Have groups discuss and note their ideas.

14 Guide students to understand the value of using technology to write, publish, and collaborate on their presentation. Invite volunteers to share and describe tools they are familiar with. Then have groups brainstorm and list their own ideas.

15 With these conventions and the selected mode(s) in mind, have the groups develop presentation plans using the graphic organizer in the student book. Note that a presentation plan such as this is not as detailed as a storyboard. Encourage students to consider their plans in greater detail by writing scripts or creating storyboards.

16 When evaluating student presentation plans and organization, give feedback on the feasibility of their ideas and suggest conventional elements the group could add to their presentation to make it appear more professional.

ASSESS

Review students' graphic organizers to ascertain each detail of what the group expects their audience will experience and how the group envisions this will contribute to a persuasive result.

ADAPT

If student groups need additional help creating a realizable plan, prompt their thinking with examples of sensory detail that the audience may experience according to available resources, such as music or sound effects, the incorporation of a short video into a live debate between presenters, poster displays, or other visual/audio elements.

Consider limiting students to particular media channels and products rather than having them choose from among a wide variety. Providing a selected number of choices will allow students to focus on the substance of their presentations and the goal of presenting a specific concept supported by logical reasoning.

4.13

Presentation Plan
Our thesis:
Our chosen medium/format:
Conventions of this medium/format:

What will the audience see? What images will be shown? If filming a video, what angles, framing, and composition will be used?	**What will the audience hear?** What tone are we striving for? How will we use voice, music, or sound effects to achieve our purpose?	**What will the audience think/feel?** What rhetorical devices and appeals will we incorporate to persuade our audience? What will the audience learn? What will they believe/know after the presentation?

Voir Dire: Facing a Jury of Your Peers

Learning Targets

- Use a juror ballot to critically examine and provide feedback about a presentation.
- Reflect on feedback from peers in order to improve the effectiveness of a planned presentation.

Preview

In this activity, you will practice evaluating an argumentative presentation in preparation for serving as a peer jury during your classmates' presentations for Embedded Assessment 2.

Juror Ballot

As other groups present their arguments to the class, you will use a juror ballot to take notes and ultimately evaluate their presentations. Becoming familiar with the ballot will not only help you use it effectively during others' presentations but will also help you in your own presentation planning.

1. As you watch a video that presents an argument, complete the following juror ballot. Assess the quality of the argumentative text and the degree to which you think it successfully engages and persuades the intended audience. Read through each section of the ballot before viewing.

Section 1: Make a Double-Entry Journal	
As you view the presentation, record observations you make, evidence you encounter, questions that come to mind, and your interpretations or responses. Be sure to note evidence of the critical perspective(s) that you see expressed through the presentation. Use the same close observation and analysis skills that you would bring to bear on a written text.	
Observations / Evidence / Questions	**Your Interpretation / Response**

Learning Strategies

Discussion Groups
Double-Entry Journal
Paraphrasing

WORD CONNECTIONS

Etymology

Voir dire is a legal term referring to the practice of questioning jurors to evaluate their suitability to serve on a jury. It is derived from an Old French term meaning "to speak the truth."

ACTIVITY 4.14

PLAN

Materials: video clip of a speech, documentary, or news story on the topic of charter schools.
Suggested Pacing: 1 50-minute class period

TEACH

1 Read aloud the Learning Targets and Preview with your students. Make sure students understand that this activity is designed to model the process they will use as peer jurors for the presentations given in Embedded Assessment 2.

2 **Vocabulary Development:** Discuss the Word Connections with students. Have them work in pairs to define *voir dire* in their own words.

 TEACHER TO TEACHER

Select a video of a speech, short documentary, or news story that presents an argument about charter schools or another topic that has been introduced in this unit. Consider the following options:

- PBS News Hour segment "In reforming New Orleans, have charter schools left some students out?" (8 minutes)
- PBS News Hour segment "New Orleans rebuilds education system with charter schools" (10 minutes)
- One of the videos from the series "A Perfect Storm," from the Southern Education Foundation (5–15 minutes)

3 Before beginning the activity, discuss the Juror Ballot with students and review what will be required of them to complete each section.

4 Provide students with the **Activity Listening Notes** graphic organizer to use as a note-taking tool to record what they hear and see during the video clip.

5 Following the viewing, have students fill out each section of the Juror Ballot. Monitor their progress.

College and Career Readiness Standards

Focus Standards:

SL.11–12.1 Initiate and participate effectively in a range of collaborative discussions (one-on-one, in groups, and teacher-led) with diverse partners on grades 11–12 topics, texts, and issues, building on others' ideas and expressing their own clearly and persuasively.

SL.11–12.3 Evaluate a speaker's point of view, reasoning, and use of evidence and rhetoric, assessing the stance, premises, links among ideas, word choice, points of emphasis, and tone used.

Additional Standards Addressed:

SL.11–12.1c, SL.11–12.1d

4.14

Section 2: Identify the Argument

Paraphrase the group's thesis statement, record the main reasons and evidence they provide, and note any treatment of counterarguments.

Paraphrased Thesis:

Reasons and Evidence:

Treatment of Counterargument(s):

Section 3: Respond in a Quickwrite

After viewing the presentation, quickwrite your overall impressions. Be sure to praise the parts of the presentation that are done well.

Section 4: Evaluate the Presentation

For each of the areas listed, discuss the choices made by the group. How effective are these choices at supporting their argument with their target audience?

Structure of the Argument

4.14

Chosen Medium

Style and Conventions

Delivery / Production

Section 5: Write a Review

Write a review of the group's final product that shows a thoughtful critique and evaluation of the content and presentation of the argument. Address how effective you think the presentation would be at persuading the audience and illuminating the critical significance of their subject.

2. Partner with a classmate who is not in your presentation group. Compare notes from the juror ballot and briefly share your overall reviews of the video you viewed.

ACTIVITY 4.14 continued

6 • Have students choose a partner who is not in their presentation group to compare notes made in the juror ballot and exchange ideas about the plans their respective groups have formed so far. If indicated, refer student pairs to the Scoring Guide they will be using for Embedded Assessment 2.

LEVELED DIFFERENTIATED INSTRUCTION

In this activity, students might need support taking and assessing notes they took on the documentary clip or in making appropriate entries on the ballots.

Developing Field specific questions students have noted as they viewed the clip. Guide students in identifying examples from the clip and analyzing one critical feature for each.

Expanding Prompt students to refer to their Independent Reading Checkpoint. Ask them to do a quickwrite that describes the main ideas of the presentation through their chosen critical lens.

Bridging Have students speculate on the changes they might make to their presentations if they were to target a different audience, such as scientists or news professionals.

7 Have students rejoin their presentation groups. Allow them time to complete the Check Your Understanding.

8 Remind students to complete the Independent Reading Checkpoint.

ASSESS

The Check Your Understanding responses should demonstrate that students are able to effectively engage the ballot sections and the scoring guide and engage a clear application of an appropriate critical lens from the unit.

ADAPT

If students need additional help using the juror ballot appropriately, review the key terms and help them internalize the structure of the ballot. If time allows, show the clip a second time, pausing frequently to offer observations and evaluations that could be entered into the ballot and to point out which sections they would go in.

4.14

My Notes

3. Next, discuss questions or comments you have about using the ballot. How prepared do you feel to use the ballot while viewing classmates' presentations?

4. Continue working with your partner by exchanging the plans your groups have made so far for your argumentative presentations. Review your partner's plan, evaluating the likely effectiveness of the proposed plan and providing suggestions for how to make it more effective. You might reference the Scoring Guide for Embedded Assessment 2 as you evaluate their proposal.

☑ **Check Your Understanding**

Based on the feedback you received about your group's presentation plan, decide what changes or additions will make your planned presentation more effective. Write your ideas down and then share them with your presentation group.

⊕ **Independent Reading Checkpoint**

Review your independent reading selections. What questions can you ask about each text using the critical lenses you have studied? What new understanding or information emerges when you question the texts from these perspectives? Write a short reflection about which critical lenses have been the most revealing over the course of your reading in this unit and beyond. How will you continue using the lenses in your future readings?

Presenting an Argument

 ASSIGNMENT

Your assignment is to present an argument in a medium of your choice (persuasive speech, short documentary film, video news broadcast, podcast) in which you transform the information you gathered from your research in the first part of the unit into an argument concerning the topic/issue you have chosen. Your presentation should last five to seven minutes. It may be recorded or presented live.

Planning and Prewriting: Take time to plan for your research and the structure of your presentation.	▪ What roles are necessary for the presentation, and who will take on each role? ▪ How will you divide up the writing tasks so that everyone has an equal share of work to do? ▪ How can you ensure that the group works purposefully to maintain focus and move toward goals?
Drafting: Write a script and a plan for supporting information (visuals, media, etc.).	▪ What genre conventions, including elements of classical speeches, will you follow as you create your presentation? ▪ What other steps will you need to plan and complete besides writing the script (creating visuals, rehearsing, filming and editing if recording the performance)? ▪ How will you appropriately display academic citations and use source materials ethically?
Evaluating and Revising: Create opportunities to review and revise your work.	▪ What changes or additions do you need to make in order to ensure that the work of the different group members becomes one coherent presentation? ▪ How can you use the feedback of others to improve your work? ▪ How can you use the Scoring Guide as a resource to evaluate your draft?
Checking and Editing for Publication: Confirm that your final draft is ready for publication (or delivery).	▪ How will you check for adherences to standard English conventions? ▪ What sort of outside resources can help you to check your work? ▪ How will you ensure that elements of delivery, such as eye contact, volume, and gestures, are used effectively?

Reflection

After completing this Embedded Assessment, think about how you went about accomplishing this assignment, and respond to the following:

• This assessment involved working as a team and combining the ideas of several people. How did the presence of multiple perspectives provide advantages for your group? How did it make the process more difficult?

College and Career Readiness Standards

Focus Standards:

SL.11–12.2 Integrate multiple sources of information presented in diverse formats and media (e.g., visually, quantitatively, orally) in order to make informed decisions and solve problems, evaluating the credibility and accuracy of each source and noting any discrepancies among the data.

SL.11–12.4 Present information, findings, and supporting evidence, conveying a clear and distinct perspective, such that listeners can follow the line of reasoning, alternative or opposing perspectives are addressed, and the organization, development, substance, and style are appropriate to purpose, audience, and a range of formal and informal tasks.

EMBEDDED ASSESSMENT 2

Materials: the technology necessary for various media options; multiple copies of juror ballots; copies of Presenting Scoring Guide and Audience Notes and Feedback graphic organizer (optional)
Suggested Pacing: 4 50-minute class periods

⭐ TEACHER TO TEACHER

If you choose to modify this Embedded Assessment by changing the assignment for some or all of your students, be sure that you have properly scaffolded the necessary skills and knowledge.

1 To support learning, you might preselect which type(s) of media students will work in, such as podcast or news broadcast. Keeping the technology simple will allow students to focus on the content they are presenting.

2 **Planning and Prewriting:** You might encourage students to submit drafts of storyboards, scripts, or other planning documents so you can make sure they are on the right track with planning.

3 **Drafting:** Have students decide in advance how they will track their sources and credit them appropriately.

4 **Evaluating and Revising:** Remind students to use the Scoring Guide criteria to ensure that they will meet the expectations for this assessment.

5 **Checking and Editing for Publication:** If students are speaking live or being recorded, suggest that they consult dictionaries with pronunciation guides to check difficult or unfamiliar pronunciations. Most online dictionaries (e.g., dictionary.com) provide audio of pronunciations for most entries.

6 **Reflection:** Be sure students address the Reflection question as a separate part of the Embedded Assessment assignment so they can include it separately.

★ TEACHER TO TEACHER

You may want to make multiple copies of the Juror Ballot to be used by you and the class when viewing presentations. Or consider having students respond and collaborate electronically using a cloud-based, document-sharing site.

7 All notes for and drafts of the plan for the documentary (including a script) should be collected and presented together to show the process teams completed in successfully accomplishing the task.

Juror Ballot

As you view a group's presentation, you will complete this juror ballot. Your task is to assess the quality of the presentation you're viewing and the degree to which you believe it will successfully persuade the intended audience.

Section 1: Make a Double-Entry Journal

As you view the presentation, record observations you make, evidence you encounter, questions that come to mind, and your interpretations or responses. Be sure to note evidence of the critical perspective(s) that you see expressed through the presentation. Use the same close observation and analysis skills that you would bring to bear on a written text.

Observations / Evidence / Questions	Your Interpretation / Response

Section 2: Identify the Argument

Paraphrase the group's thesis statement, record the main reasons and evidence they provide, and note any treatment of counterarguments.

Paraphrased Thesis:

Reasons and Evidence:

Treatment of Counterargument(s):

College and Career Readiness Standards

SL.11–12.5 Make strategic use of digital media (e.g., textual, graphical, audio, visual, and interactive elements) in presentations to enhance understanding of findings, reasoning, and evidence and to add interest.

SL.11–12.6 Adapt speech to a variety of contexts and tasks, demonstrating a command of formal English when indicated or appropriate.

Additional Standards Addressed:

RI.11–12.1, SL.11–12.1b, SL.11–12.1d, SL.11–12.3, SL.11–12.5

TEACHER TO TEACHER

You may choose to manage student presentations in a variety of ways depending on the length and style of the presentations, the number of students per class, and the amount of class time you want to devote to live presenting. There are a number of media resources available online that can facilitate digital video or audio submissions. Video- and audio-sharing websites can also provide a platform for students to view each other's presentations and leave peer feedback.

Section 3: Respond in a Quickwrite

After viewing the presentation, quickwrite your overall impressions. Be sure to praise the parts of the presentation that are done well.

Section 4: Evaluate the Presentation

For each of the areas listed, discuss the choices made by the group. How effective are these choices at supporting their argument with their target audience?

Structure of the Argument

Chosen Medium

Style and Conventions

Delivery / Production

Section 5: Write a Review

Write a review of the group's final product that shows a thoughtful critique and evaluation of the content and presentation of the argument. Address how effective you think the presentation would be at persuading the audience and illuminating the critical significance of their subject.

SCORING GUIDE

Scoring Criteria	Exemplary	Proficient	Emerging	Incomplete
Ideas	The presentation • reveals an insightful analysis and mature understanding of the topic through a script and an annotated bibliography • demonstrates thorough investigation, insightful application of the lenses, and thoughtful understanding of the topic • includes a reflective text that demonstrates a thorough and detailed analysis of the entire process.	The presentation • demonstrates careful analysis and clear understanding of the topic • demonstrates adequate investigation, application of the lenses, and clear understanding of the topic • includes a reflective text that demonstrates adequate analysis of the process.	The presentation • reveals a limited analysis and understanding of the topic • demonstrates inadequate investigation and/or misunderstanding of the lenses or how they apply • includes a reflective text that demonstrates inadequate analysis of the complete process.	The presentation • reveals little or no analysis and/or understanding of the topic • demonstrates inadequate investigation and/or misunderstanding of the lenses or how they apply • does not include a reflective text.
Structure	The presentation • is organized in a precisely appropriate way that enhances the intended message for the target audience • features a polished presentation that creates focus and maintains energy • demonstrates equal sharing of responsibility.	The presentation • is organized appropriately for the selected presentation format and makes clear the intended message • features an organized, coherent presentation • demonstrates sharing of responsibility that is mostly balanced.	The presentation • is organized inappropriately for the selected presentation format and may convey an unclear message • includes a disorganized presentation • demonstrates an unequal division of responsibilities.	The presentation • does not use the selected presentation format appropriately • includes a confusing and disorganized presentation • demonstrates an unequal division of responsibilities.
Use of Language	The presentation • demonstrates a mature style that advances the group's ideas • crafts language that is precisely appropriate to the media channel.	The presentation • demonstrates a style that adequately supports the group's ideas • crafts language that is appropriate to the media channel.	The presentation • demonstrates a limited style that ineffectively supports the group's ideas • includes language that is inappropriate to the media channel.	The presentation • demonstrates confusing language that does not support the group's ideas • includes language that is inappropriate for the media channel and presents the topic inaccurately.

EMBEDDED ASSESSMENT 2

SCORING GUIDE

When you score this Embedded Assessment, you may wish to download and print copies of the Scoring Guide from SpringBoard Digital. In this way, you can have a copy to mark for each student's work. The Presenting Scoring Guide and **Audience Notes and Feedback** graphic organizer are available in the Resources section of the Student and Teacher Editions.

Resources

Independent Reading

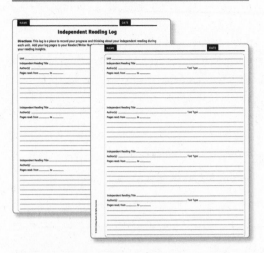

Learning Strategies

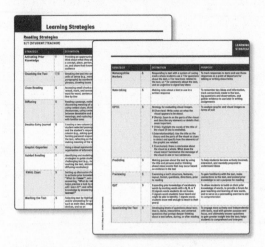

Graphic Organizers

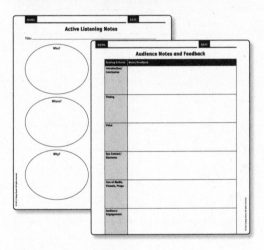

English-Spanish Glossary

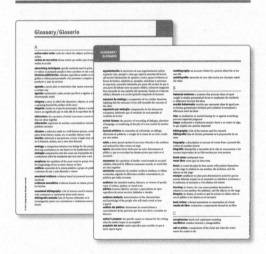

Index of Skills

Index of Authors and Titles

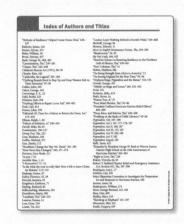

Independent Reading Log

Directions: This log is a place to record your progress and thinking about your independent reading during each unit. Add your log pages to your Reader/Writer Notebook or keep them as a separate place to record your reading insights.

Unit _____

Independent Reading Title _____

Author(s) _____ Text Type _____

Pages read: from _____ to _____

_____

_____

_____

_____

_____

Independent Reading Title _____

Author(s) _____ Text Type _____

Pages read: from _____ to _____

_____

_____

_____

_____

_____

_____

Independent Reading Title _____

Author(s) _____ Text Type _____

Pages read: from _____ to _____

_____

_____

_____

_____

_____

_____

Unit _____

Independent Reading Title _____

Author(s) _____ Text Type _____

Pages read: from _____ to _____

_____

_____

_____

_____

_____

_____

Independent Reading Title _____

Author(s) _____ Text Type _____

Pages read: from _____ to _____

_____

_____

_____

_____

_____

_____

Independent Reading Title _____

Author(s) _____ Text Type _____

Pages read: from _____ to _____

_____

_____

_____

_____

_____

_____

Independent Reading Title _____

Author(s) _____ Text Type _____

Pages read: from _____ to _____

_____

_____

_____

_____

_____

_____

Learning Strategies

Reading Strategies

S/T (STUDENT/TEACHER)

STRATEGY		DEFINITION	PURPOSE
Activating Prior Knowledge	T	Providing an opportunity for students to think about what they already know about a concept, place, person, culture, and so on, and share their knowledge with a wider audience	To prepare students to encounter new concepts, places, persons, cultures, and so on, prior to reading a text; an Anticipation Guide and a Quickwrite can be used to activate and assess prior knowledge
Chunking the Text	T/S	Breaking the text into smaller, manageable units of sense (e.g., words, sentences, paragraphs) by numbering, separating phrases, drawing boxes	To reduce the intimidation factor when encountering long words, sentences, or whole texts; to increase comprehension of difficult or challenging text
Close Reading	S	Accessing small chunks of text to read, reread, mark, and annotate key passages, word-for-word, sentence-by-sentence, and line-by-line	To develop comprehensive understanding by engaging in one or more focused readings of a text
Diffusing	S	Reading a passage, noting unfamiliar words, discovering meaning of unfamiliar words using context clues, dictionaries, and/or thesauruses, using context to distinguish between denotative and connotative meanings, and replacing unfamiliar words with familiar ones	To facilitate a close reading of text, the use of resources, an understanding of synonyms, and increased comprehension of text
Double-Entry Journal	S	Creating a two-column journal with a student-selected passage in one column and the student's response in the second column (e.g., asking questions of the text, forming personal responses, interpreting the text, reflecting on the process of making meaning of the text)	To assist in note-taking and organizing key textual elements and responses noted during reading in order to generate textual support that can be incorporated into a piece of writing at a later time
Graphic Organizer	S	Using a visual representation for the organization of information from the text	To facilitate increased comprehension and discussion
Guided Reading	T	Identifying and modeling a series of strategies to guide students through challenging text (e.g., making predictions, marking the text, skimming the text, diffusing vocabulary)	To model for students the use of multiple strategies to make meaning of challenging texts and help them learn to apply the strategies independently
KWHL Chart	S	Setting up discussion that allows students to activate prior knowledge by answering, "What do I **know**?"; sets a purpose by answering, "What do I **want** to know?"; helps preview a task by answering, "**How** will I learn it?"; and reflects on new knowledge by answering, "What have I **learned**?"	To organize thinking, access prior knowledge, and reflect on learning to increase comprehension and engagement
Marking the Text	S	Selecting text by highlighting, underlining, and/or annotating for specific components, such as main idea, imagery, literary devices, and so on	To focus reading for specific purposes, such as author's craft, and to organize information from selections; to facilitate reexamination of a text

STRATEGY		DEFINITION	PURPOSE
Metacognitive Markers	S	Responding to text with a system of cueing marks where students use a ? for questions about the text; a ! for reactions related to the text; an * for comments about the text; and an underline to signal key ideas	To track responses to texts and use those responses as a point of departure for talking or writing about texts
Note-taking	S	Making notes about a text to use in a written response	To remember key ideas and information, track connections made to the text, log questions and observations, and gather evidence to use later in writing assignments
OPTIC	S	Strategy for evaluating visual images. **O** (Overview): Write notes on what the visual appears to be about. **P** (Parts): Zoom in on the parts of the visual and describe any elements or details that seem important. **T** (Title): Highlight the words of the title of the visual (if one is available). **I** (Interrelationships): Use the title as the theory and the parts of the visual as clues to detect and specify how the elements of the graphic are related. **C** (Conclusion): Draw a conclusion about the visual as a whole. What does the visual mean? Summarize the message of the visual in one or two sentences.	To analyze graphic and visual images as forms of text
Predicting	S	Making guesses about the text by using the title and pictures and/or thinking ahead about events that may occur based on evidence in the text	To help students become actively involved, interested, and mentally prepared to understand ideas
Previewing	S	Examining a text's structure, features, layout, format, questions, directions, prior to reading	To gain familiarity with the text, make connections to the text, and extend prior knowledge to set a purpose for reading
QHT	S	Expanding prior knowledge of vocabulary words by marking words with a **Q**, **H**, or **T** (Q signals words students do not know; H signals words students have heard and might be able to identify; T signals words students know well enough to teach to their peers)	To allow students to build on their prior knowledge of words, to provide a forum for peer teaching and learning of new words, and to serve as a prereading exercise to aid in comprehension
Questioning the Text	S	Developing levels of questions about text; that is, literal, interpretive, and universal questions that prompt deeper thinking about a text before, during, or after reading	To engage more actively and independently with texts, read with greater purpose and focus, and ultimately answer questions to gain greater insight into the text; helps students to comprehend and interpret

STRATEGY		DEFINITION	PURPOSE
Paraphrasing	S	Restating in one's own words the essential information expressed in a text, whether it be narration, dialogue, or informational text, while maintaining the original text's meaning	To encourage and facilitate comprehension of challenging text
RAFT	S	Primarily used to generate new text, this strategy can also be used to analyze a text by examining the role of the speaker (R), the intended audience (A), the format of the text (F), and the topic of the text (T)	To initiate reader response; to facilitate an analysis of a text to gain focus prior to creating a new text
Rereading	S	Encountering the same text with more than one reading	To identify additional details; to clarify meaning and/or reinforce comprehension of texts
SIFT	S	Analyzing a fictional text by examining stylistic elements, especially symbol, imagery, and figures of speech, in order to show how all work together to reveal tone and theme	To focus and facilitate an analysis of a fictional text by examining the title and text for symbolism, identifying images and sensory details, analyzing figurative language, and identifying how all these elements reveal tone and theme
Skimming/Scanning	S	Skimming by rapid or superficial reading of a text to form an overall impression or to obtain a general understanding of the material; scanning focuses on key words, phrases, or specific details and provides speedy recognition of information	To quickly form an overall impression prior to an in-depth study of a text; to answer specific questions or quickly locate targeted information or detail in a text
SMELL	S	Analyzing a persuasive speech or essay by asking five essential questions: • **S**ender-receiver relationship—What is the sender-receiver relationship? Who are the images and language meant to attract? Describe the speaker of the text. • **M**essage—What is the message? Summarize the statement made in the text. • **E**motional Strategies—What is the desired effect? • **L**ogical Strategies—What logic is operating? How does it (or its absence) affect the message? Consider the logic of the images as well as the words. • **L**anguage—What does the language of the text describe? How does it affect the meaning and effectiveness of the writing? Consider the language of the images as well as the words.	To analyze a persuasive speech or essay by focusing on five essential characteristics of the genre; analysis is related to rhetorical devices, logical fallacies, and how an author's use of language achieves specific purposes
SOAPSTone	S	Analyzing text by discussing and identifying **S**peaker, **O**ccasion, **A**udience, **P**urpose, **S**ubject, and **T**one	To facilitate the analysis of specific elements of nonfiction, literary, and informational texts, and show the relationship among the elements to an understanding of the whole

STRATEGY		DEFINITION	PURPOSE
Summarizing	S	Giving a brief statement of the main points or essential information expressed in a text, whether it be narration, dialogue, or informational text	To facilitate comprehension and recall of a text
Think Aloud	S/T	Talking through a difficult passage or task by using a form of metacognition whereby the reader expresses how he/she has made sense of the text	To reflect on how readers make meaning of challenging texts and to facilitate discussion
TP-CASTT	S	Analyzing a poetic text by identifying and discussing **T**itle, **P**araphrase, **C**onnotation, **A**ttitude, **S**hift, **T**heme, and **T**itle again	To facilitate the analysis of specific elements of a literary text, especially poetry. To show how the elements work together to create meaning
Visualizing	S	Forming a picture (mentally and/or literally) while reading a text to deepen understanding	To increase reading comprehension, deepen understanding, and promote active engagement with text
Word Maps	S	Using a clearly defined graphic organizer such as concept circles or word webs to identify and reinforce word meanings	To provide a visual tool for identifying and remembering multiple aspects of words and word meanings
Word Sort	T	Organizing and sorting words into categories designated by the teacher or selected by the student and providing a written or oral justification for the classifications	To solidify understanding of word meanings by considering the multiple uses, meanings, and relationships of word parts, words, and groups of words

Writing Strategies

S/T (STUDENT/TEACHER)

STRATEGY		DEFINITION	PURPOSE
Adding	S	Enhancing a text by finding areas to add facts, details, examples, and commentary; smoothing out transitions; and clarifying and strengthening ideas and assertions	To improve, refine, and clarify the writer's thoughts during drafting and/or revision
Brainstorming	S	Using a flexible but deliberate process of listing multiple ideas in a short period of time without excluding any idea from the preliminary list	To generate ideas, concepts, or key words that provide a focus and/or establish organization as part of the prewriting or revision process
Deleting	S	Enhancing a text by eliminating words, phrases, sentences, or ideas that inhibit clarity and cohesiveness	To improve, refine, and clarify the writer's thoughts during drafting and/or revision
Drafting	S	Composing a text in its initial form before developing it	To incorporate brainstormed or initial ideas into a written format
Freewriting	S	Writing freely without constraints in order to generate ideas and capture thinking	To generate ideas when planning a piece of writing, or to refine and clarify thoughts, spark new ideas, and/or generate content during drafting and/or revision
Generating Questions	S	Clarifying and developing ideas by asking questions of the draft. May be part of self-editing or peer editing	To clarify and develop ideas in a draft; used during drafting and as part of writer response
Graphic Organizer	S	Organizing ideas and information visually (e.g., Venn diagrams, flowcharts, cluster maps)	To provide a visual system for organizing multiple ideas, details, and/or textual support to be included in a piece of writing
Guided Writing	T	Modeling the writing that students are expected to produce by guiding students through the planning, generation of ideas, organization, drafting, revision, editing, and publication of texts before students are asked to perform the same process; co-constructing texts with students as part of guided writing	To demonstrate the writing process
Looping	S	Selecting one section of a draft to elaborate on by generating new ideas, and then repeating the process with the newly-written section	To generate new content during drafting and revision
Manipulatives	T	Providing tactile and kinesthetic experiences to engage students in the process of writing by physically maneuvering words, phrases, or sentences to reconstruct text in as many different ways as possible and note how meaning changes with each rearrangement	To appeal to kinesthetic learners and help students visualize the form and function of various parts of speech, stylistic concerns, sentence structure, and so on

STRATEGY		DEFINITION	PURPOSE
Mapping	S	Creating a graphic organizer that serves as a visual representation of the organizational plan for a written text	To plan the structure and organization of a text
Marking the Draft	S	Interacting with a draft by highlighting, underlining, color-coding, and annotating to indicate edits and suggestions for revision	To encourage focused, reflective thinking about revising and editing drafts
Note-taking	S	Making notes about a discussion to use in a written response	To record relevant evidence and information shared in discussion to use later in writing assignments
Outlining	S	Using a system of numerals and letters in order to identify topics and supporting details and ensure an appropriate balance of ideas	To plan the structure and organization of a text
Quickwrite	S	Writing for a short, specific amount of time in response to a prompt provided	To generate multiple ideas in a quick fashion that could be turned into longer pieces of writing at a later time
RAFT	S	Generating a new text and/or transforming a text by identifying and manipulating its Role, Audience, Format, and Topic	To generate a text by identifying the Role, Audience, Format, and/or Topic that will be most appropriate for the intended purpose
Rearranging	S	Selecting components of a text and moving them to another place within the text and/or modifying the order in which the author's ideas are presented	To refine and clarify the writer's thoughts during drafting and/or revision
Self-Editing/Peer Editing	S	Working individually or with a partner to examine a text closely in order to identify areas that might need to be corrected for grammar, punctuation, spelling	To provide a systematic process for editing a written text to ensure correctness of identified components such as conventions of standard English
Sharing and Responding	S	Communicating with another person or a small group of peers who respond to a piece of writing as focused readers (not necessarily as evaluators)	To make suggestions for improvement to the work of others and/or to receive appropriate and relevant feedback on the writer's own work, used during the drafting and revision process
Sketching	S	Drawing or sketching ideas or ordering of ideas (includes storyboarding, visualizing)	To generate and/or clarify ideas by visualizing them (may be part of prewriting)
Substituting/Replacing	S	Replacing original words or phrases in a text with new words or phrases that achieve the desired effect	To refine and clarify the writer's thoughts during drafting and/or revision; to develop the writer's diction
TWIST	S	Arriving at a thesis statement that incorporates the following literary elements: Tone, Word choice (diction), Imagery, Style, and Theme	To craft an interpretive thesis in response to a prompt about a text

STRATEGY		DEFINITION	PURPOSE
Visual/Auditory Prompts	T	Providing visual stimuli (e.g., a piece of art, film clip, visual media) or auditory stimuli (e.g., music, sound effects, radio broadcast, etc.) prior to writing	To encourage response to varied stimuli; to provide an opportunity for students of various learning styles to create a written text
Webbing	S	Developing a graphic organizer that consists of a series of circles connected with lines to indicate relationships among ideas	To generate ideas, concepts, or key words that provide a focus and/or establish organization prior to writing an initial draft and/or during the revision process
Writer's Checklist	T/S	Using a co-constructed checklist (that could be written on a bookmark and/or displayed on the wall) in order to look for specific features of a writing text and check for accuracy	To focus on key areas of the writing process so that the writer can effectively revise a draft and correct mistakes
Writing Groups	S	A type of discussion group devoted to sharing and responding to student work	To facilitate a collaborative approach to generating ideas for and revising writing

Speaking and Listening Strategies

S/T (STUDENT/TEACHER)

STRATEGY		DEFINITION	PURPOSE
Choral Reading	T/S	Reading text lines aloud in student groups and/or individually to present an interpretation	To develop fluency; differentiate between the reading of statements and questions; practice phrasing, pacing, and reading dialogue; show how a character's emotions are captured through vocal stress and intonation
Debate	T	Engaging in a structured argument to examine both sides of an issue	To provide students with an opportunity to collect and orally present evidence supporting the affirmative and negative arguments of a proposition or issue
Drama Games	T	Participating in creative dramatics (e.g., pantomime, tableau, role-playing) to reinforce an oral literacy skill or develop a deeper understanding of a concept	To engage students in the reading and presenting of text and to create meaning through a kinesthetic approach
Fishbowl (Inner/outer circles)	T	Discussing specific topics within groups; some students will form the inner circle and model appropriate discussion techniques while an outer circle of students listens to and evaluates the discussion process of the inner circle in order to respond effectively	To provide students with an opportunity to engage in a formal discussion and to experience roles both as participant and active listener; students also have the responsibility of supporting their opinions and responses using specific textual evidence
Note-taking	S	Creating a record of information while listening to a speaker or reading a text	To facilitate active listening or close reading; to record and organize ideas that assist in processing information
Oral Reading	S	Reading aloud one's own text or the texts of others (e.g., echo reading, choral reading, paired readings)	To share one's own work or the work of others; build fluency and increase confidence in presenting to a group
Rehearsal	T/S	Encouraging multiple practices of a piece of text prior to a performance	To provide students with an opportunity to clarify the meaning of a text prior to a performance as they refine the use of dramatic conventions (e.g., gestures, vocal interpretations, facial expressions)
Role-Playing	S	Assuming the role or persona of a character	To develop the voice, emotions, and mannerisms of a character to facilitate improved comprehension of a text
Socratic Seminar	T	Tying a focused discussion to an essential question, topic, or selected text in which students ask questions of each other; questions initiate a conversation that continues with a series of responses and additional questions	To help students formulate questions that address issues (in lieu of simply stating their opinions) to facilitate their own discussion and arrive at a new understanding; students also have the responsibility of supporting their opinions and responses using specific textual evidence

Collaborative Strategies

S/T (STUDENT/TEACHER)

STRATEGY		DEFINITION	PURPOSE
Discussion Groups	T/S	Engaging in an interactive, small-group discussion, often with an assigned role; to consider a topic, text, or question	To gain new understanding of or insight into a text from multiple perspectives
Jigsaw	T	In groups, students read different texts or passages from a single text, then share and exchange information from their reading with another group. They then return to their original groups to share their new knowledge.	To summarize and present information to others in a way that facilitates an understanding of a text (or multiple texts) without having each student read the text in its entirety
Literature Circles	T	Groups of students read the same text to participate in a mutual reading experience; based on the objective(s) of the lesson, students take on a variety of roles throughout the reading experience; texts may be selected based on individual preferences or on the demands of the text.	To provide opportunities for students to interact with one another as they read, respond to, and interpret a common text
Think-Pair-Share	T/S	Pairing with a peer to share ideas before sharing ideas and discussion with a larger group	To construct meaning about a topic or question; to test thinking in relation to the ideas of others; to prepare for a discussion with a larger group

English Language Development Strategies

S/T (STUDENT/TEACHER)

STRATEGY		DEFINITION	PURPOSE
Choral Reading	S/T	Reading a text or part of a text aloud in pairs, groups, or as a whole class	To build students' fluency, expression, and self-confidence when reading short texts and to provide a model for fluent reading as students follow along
Cloze Reading	T	Reading aloud a text in which certain key words—such as target vocabulary terms or words with strong context clues—have been omitted and replaced with blanks; when reading the text aloud, the teacher pauses to allow students to fill in the blanks, sometimes with the support of a word bank. Teachers may differentiate by omitting more words for students with higher language proficiency.	To support students in processing and constructing meaning from texts rather than just reading words without comprehension; cloze reading can be used to encourage struggling readers to consider context as they read a passage, and it can also be used with more proficient students as a way to study word choice, shades of meaning, and register (or formality) of words

STRATEGY		DEFINITION	PURPOSE
Cognate Bridge	S/T	Adding cognates to the class Word Wall to create a bridge between English vocabulary terms and their cognates; cognates are words in different languages that sound alike and have a similar meaning because they have a common origin. For example, the words *analogy* and *analogía* in English and Spanish both derive from the Greek word *analogos*.	To facilitate the development of academic language in English by leveraging students' native language resources; highlighting cognates can also help students build vocabulary by recognizing patterns in word roots, prefixes, and suffixes
Conferencing	S/T	Students collaborate with peers to eliminate gaps in understanding or confusion about a text or task. Students first work in pairs to generate questions. Then they join another pair to try to answer their questions. The class debriefs as needed.	To build learner autonomy by encouraging students to identify gaps in understanding and to fill those gaps through meaningful interaction with peers
Discourse Starters	S/T	Students use sentence starters with key academic language to engage in academic conversations. (See the **Discourse Starters** available in the Resources section of the student and teacher editions.)	To promote academic conversations by providing patterned expressions often used in academic discourse; this can alleviate some of the challenge of impromptu class discussions, allowing students to focus their thinking on ideas rather than on the formulation of a response
Echo Reading	S/T	Modeling the pronunciation and intonation of a word, phrase, sentence, paragraph, or other segment of text and then having students imitate, or echo, the teacher's reading	To model pronunciation, phrasing, and intonation of new or challenging language; to boost reading fluency and expression in struggling students
Four Corners	T	Labeling the four corners of the classroom with opinion statements (e.g., Strongly Agree, Agree, Disagree, Strongly Disagree) and having students move into the corner that corresponds to their opinion about a claim; students then discuss their reasoning with their corner group before reporting to the class. Four Corners can by modified in numerous ways. For example, corners can be labeled with words with shades of meaning (e.g., *capable, proficient, skillful, talented*) so that students can discuss the best word choice in a given context.	To provide students with a low-stakes opportunity to state an opinion and discuss ideas or reasoning before speaking in front of a larger group; to allow for additional processing time before asking students to share their ideas; to formatively assess students' ability to support ideas with reasoning and/or evidence

STRATEGY		DEFINITION	PURPOSE
Visual Response	S/T	Using visuals—like pictures, sketches, flow charts, pantomime, or graphic organizers—to demonstrate thinking, analysis, or interpretation of a text or other stimulus; for example, students could use sketches to depict the emotional or physical changes a character experiences over the course of a story.	To foster critical thinking and processing of information without depending on language as the primary medium for communicating one's thinking; to enable students to engage in the cognitive demands of a lesson even when they are still developing English language proficiency
Reading Roles	S/T	Students are divided into groups and assigned defined roles (see below) as they read and discuss a text. After reading a predetermined portion of the text, students pause to engage in a discussion as follows: • **Summarizer**: briefly restates the main points of the text selection • **Questioner**: poses questions about the text • **Clarifier**: tries to address the questions posed in the previous step • **Predictor**: offers a prediction of what will come next in the text	To support reading, analysis, and discussion of a text with a structured, student-centered protocol; roles can be assigned based on students' language proficiency (e.g., stronger students serve as clarifiers), and additional roles may be used for broader differentiation. For example: • **Cognate finder**: looks for any words that seem similar to words in another, known language • **Visualizer**: sketches visuals to accompany the passage
Visual Prompts	T	Using visuals to introduce new vocabulary, build background knowledge, clarify information, provide instructions, or otherwise support understanding with visual aids	To support comprehension and learning with nonlinguistic input
Round Table Writing	S/T	Students engage in the writing, editing, and revising process in a group by writing a brief response to a prompt, such as a quickwrite, and then shifting papers to the next person in the group. That person writes feedback before shifting papers again to the next group member. The process repeats until all members of the group have provided feedback. Students then discuss the feedback and revise their writing. Teachers have the option of instructing students to read for different elements at each rotation; for example, the first reader could check for spelling, the second for word choice, the third for ideas, and so on.	To scaffold the peer editing process and to provide a way for students to support each other's language development

Graphic Organizer Directory

Contents

Active Listening Feedback

Presenter's name: _____

Content

What is the presenter's purpose? _____

What is the presenter's main point? _____

Do you agree with the presenter? Why or why not? _____

_____

_____

Form

Did the presenter use a clear, loud voice? ☐ yes ☐ no

Did the presenter make eye contact? ☐ yes ☐ no

One thing I really liked about the presentation:

_____

_____

_____

One question I still have:

_____

_____

_____

Other comments or notes:

Active Listening Notes

Title: _____

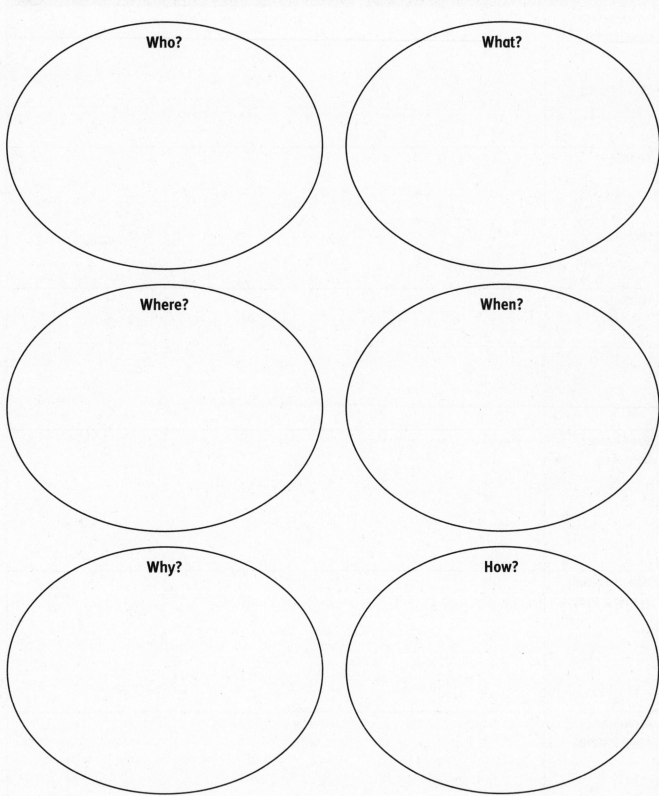

Who?

What?

Where?

When?

Why?

How?

Audience Notes and Feedback

Scoring Criteria	Notes/Feedback
Introduction/ Conclusion	
Timing	
Voice	
Eye Contact/ Gestures	
Use of Media, Visuals, Props	
Audience Engagement	

Cause and Effect

Title: _____

Cause: What happened?		Effect: An effect of this is
	→	

Cause: What happened?		Effect: An effect of this is
	→	

Cause: What happened?		Effect: An effect of this is
	→	

Cause: What happened?		Effect: An effect of this is
	→	

Character Map

Character name: _____

What does the character look like?

How does the character act and feel?

What do other characters say or think about the character?

Collaborative Dialogue

Topic: _____

Use the space below to record ideas.

"Wh-" Prompts
Who?   What?   Where?   When?   Why?

Speaker 1

Speaker 2

Conclusion Builder

Evidence

Evidence

Evidence

Based on this evidence, I can conclude

Conflict Map

Title: _____

What is the main conflict in this story?

What causes this conflict?

How is the conflict resolved?

What are some other ways the conflict could have been resolved?

Conversation for Quickwrite

1. Turn to a partner and restate the prompt in your own words.

2. Brainstorm key words to use in your quickwrite response.

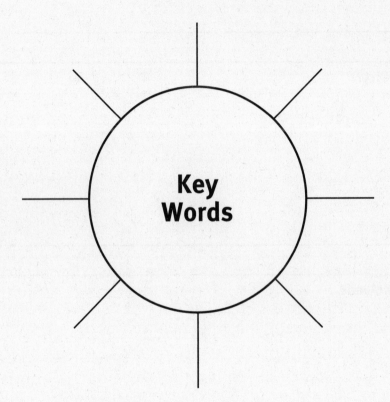

Key Words

3. Take turns explaining your ideas to your partner. Try using some of the key words you brainstormed.

4. On your own, write a response to the quickwrite.

Definition and Reflection

Academic Vocabulary Word
Definition in own words
Illustration (literal or symbolic)

My experiences with this concept:

- I haven't really thought about this concept.

  _____

- I have only thought about this concept in English Language Arts class.

  _____

- I have applied this concept in other classes.

  _____

- I have applied this concept outside of school.

  _____

My level of understanding:

- I am still trying to understand this concept.

  _____

- I am familiar with this concept, but I am not comfortable applying it.

  _____

- I am very comfortable with this concept and I know how to apply it.

  _____

- I could teach this concept to another classmate.

  _____

Discourse Starters

Questioning and Discussing a Text

One question I have is _____.

Could this mean _____?

Why do you think the author _____?

I understand _____, but I wonder _____.

I notice that _____.

I think this (word/sentence/paragraph) means _____.

I think _____ because the text says _____.

In paragraph _____, the author says _____.

According to the text, _____.

One way to interpret _____ is _____.

Summarizing

The main events that take place are _____.

The major points of the text are _____.

The main idea of _____ is _____.

One central idea of this text is _____.

Another central idea is _____.

All in all, the message is _____.

The author's main purpose is to _____.

Basically, the author is saying that _____.

Comparing and Contrasting

_____ and _____ are similar because _____.

_____ and _____ are similar in that they both _____.

_____ is _____. Similarly, _____ is _____.

One thing _____ and _____ have in common is _____.

_____ and _____ are different because _____.

_____ and _____ are different in that _____.

_____ is _____. On the other hand, _____ is _____.

One difference between _____ and _____ is _____.

Clarifying

I'm not sure I understand the instructions.

Could you repeat that please?

I have a question about _____.

I am having trouble with _____.

Will you explain that again?

Could you clarify _____?

Would you mind helping me with _____?

Which (page/paragraph/section) are we reading?

How do you spell/pronounce _____?

Discourse Starters

Agreeing and Disagreeing

I agree with the idea that _____ because _____.

I share your point of view because _____.

You made a good point when you said _____.

I agree with (a person) that _____.

Although I agree that _____, I also think _____.

I understand where you're coming from, but _____.

I disagree with the idea that _____ because _____.

I see it a different way because _____.

You have a point, but the evidence suggests _____.

Arguing and Persuading with Evidence

I believe that _____ because _____.

It is clear that _____ because _____.

One reason I think _____ is _____.

Based on evidence in the text, I think _____.

Evidence such as _____ suggests that _____.

An example to support my position is _____.

This is evident because _____.

What evidence supports the idea that _____?

Can you explain why you think _____?

Evaluating

This is effective because _____.

The evidence _____ is strong because _____.

This is convincing because _____.

I see why the author _____, but I think _____.

This is not very effective because _____.

The evidence _____ is weak because _____.

This would have been better if _____.

What do you think about the writer's choice to _____?

Why do you think _____ (is/isn't) effective?

Giving Feedback and Suggesting

The part where you _____ is strong because _____.

What impressed me the most is how you _____.

This is a good start. Maybe you should add _____.

I like how you _____, but I would try _____.

You might consider changing _____.

I would suggest revising _____ so that _____.

One suggestion would be to _____.

Why did you choose _____?

A better choice might be _____.

This would be clearer if _____.

Editor's Checklist

Over the course of the year with SpringBoard, customize this Editor's Checklist as your knowledge of language conventions grows. The three examples below show you how to write a good checklist item.

	Are all the sentences complete?
	Do the subject and verb of each sentence agree?
	Do all the sentences have correct punctuation?

Writer's Checklist

Ideas	
	Does your first paragraph hook the reader?
	Is the purpose of your writing clear (to inform, to make an argument, etc.)?
	Is the genre of writing appropriate for your purpose?
	Is your main idea clear and easy to summarize?
	Does your text contain details and information that support your main idea?
	Are the ideas in the text well organized?
	Do you connect your ideas by using transitions?
	Do you use parallel structure to keep your ideas clear?
	Does each paragraph have a conclusion that transitions to the next paragraph?
	Does your writing end with a strong conclusion that restates the original purpose of the text?

Language	
	Do you keep a consistent point of view throughout?
	Do you use the present tense when writing about a text?
	Are any shifts in verb tense easy to follow and necessary?
	Have you removed unnecessary or confusing words?
	Do you use vivid verbs and descriptive adjectives when appropriate?
	Do you use different styles of language (like figurative or sensory) when appropriate?
	Do you use a variety of sentence types?
	Do you vary the way you begin your sentences?
	Did you split up run-on sentences?
	Are your pronoun references clear?

Evaluating Online Sources

The URL
• What is its domain?
    • .com = a for-profit organization
    • .gov, .mil, .us (or other country code) = a government site
    • .edu = affiliated with an educational institution
    • .org = a nonprofit organization
• Is this URL someone's personal page?
• Do you recognize who is publishing this page?	

Sponsor: • Does the website give information about the organization or group that sponsors it? • Does it have a link (often called "About Us") that leads you to that information? • What do you learn?	
Timeliness: • When was the page last updated (usually this is posted at the top or bottom of the page)? • Is the topic something that changes frequently, like current events or technology?	
Purpose: • What is the purpose of the page? • What is its target audience? • Does it present information, opinion, or both? • Is it primarily objective or subjective? • How do you know?	
Author: • What credentials does the author have? • Is this person or group considered an authority on the topic?	
Links • Does the page provide links? • Do they work? • Are they helpful? • Are they objective or subjective?	

Fallacies 101

Ad Baculum (Scare Tactics)	If you don't support the party's tax plan, you and your family will be reduced to poverty. Chairman of the Board: "All those opposed to my arguments for the opening of a new department, signify by saying, 'I resign.'"
Ad hoc	Person 1: I should have gotten an A on that test. Person 2: You didn't study for that test at all. Person 1: That class is useless!
Ad Hominem (Against the Man)/ Genetic Fallacy	"My opponent, a vicious and evil person, should absolutely never be elected to office." The Volkswagen Beetle is an evil car because it was originally designed by Hitler's army.
Ad Populum	You should turn to channel 6. It's the most watched channel this year. There is always a long line at that restaurant, so the food must be really good.
Appeal To Pity	"Jonathan couldn't have cheated! He's such a nice boy and he tries so hard."
Argument from Outrage	The airline cancelled my flight an hour before takeoff and wouldn't tell me why. This is an outrage! We should all boycott the company.
Circular Reasoning	Emotional support animals should be allowed on airplanes, so the airline should change its policy. The policy should be changed because emotional support animals should be allowed on planes!
Either/Or (False Dilemma)	We can either stop using cars or destroy Earth. We must drill now or we'll remain dependent on foreign oil suppliers.
Faulty Analogies	Buying into the stock market is the same as betting on a horse race.
Hasty Generalization	They hit two home runs in the first inning of the season. This team is going all the way to the World Series!
Non-sequitur	I always see her with a book in her hands. She must hate watching TV.
Post Hoc	I ate a turkey sandwich and now I feel tired, so the turkey must have made me tired.
Red Herring	The new dress code banning t-shirts isn't fair. Students have the right to free speech just like anyone else.
Slippery Slope Fallacy	"If I don't study for the test, then I'm going to get a bad grade. If I get a bad grade on the test, I'll get a bad grade in the class, and I won't get into a good college. Getting into a good college is the most important part of getting a good job; so if I don't study for the test, I won't get a good job!"
Straw Man	People say that Mark Twain was a good author, but I disagree. If he was such a good author, why didn't he write using his own name?

Idea and Argument Evaluator

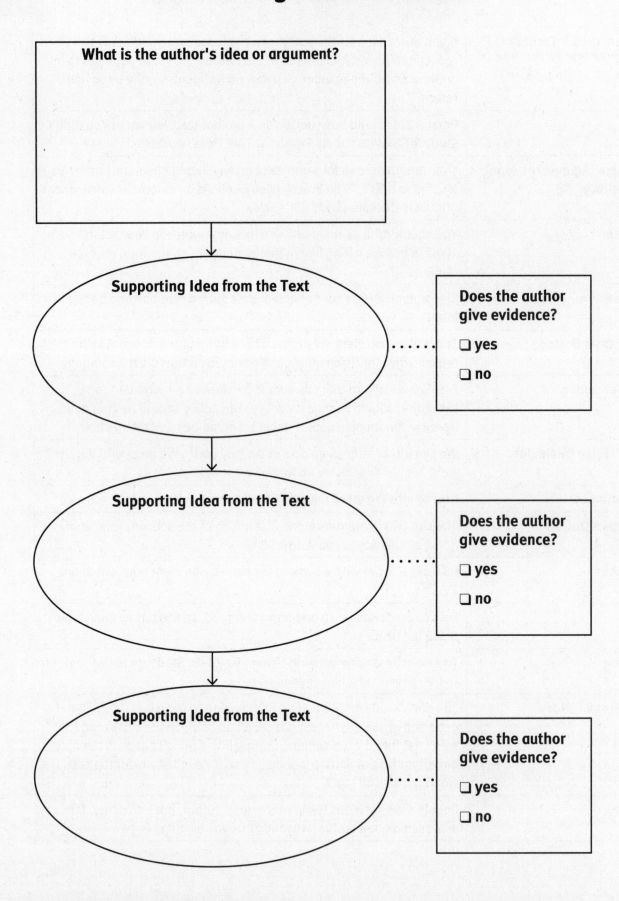

What is the author's idea or argument?

Supporting Idea from the Text

Does the author give evidence?

❏ yes

❏ no

Supporting Idea from the Text

Does the author give evidence?

❏ yes

❏ no

Supporting Idea from the Text

Does the author give evidence?

❏ yes

❏ no

Idea Connector

Directions: Write two simple sentences about the same topic. Next, write transition words around the Idea Connector. Then, choose an appropriate word to connect ideas in the two sentences. Write your combined sentence in the space below.

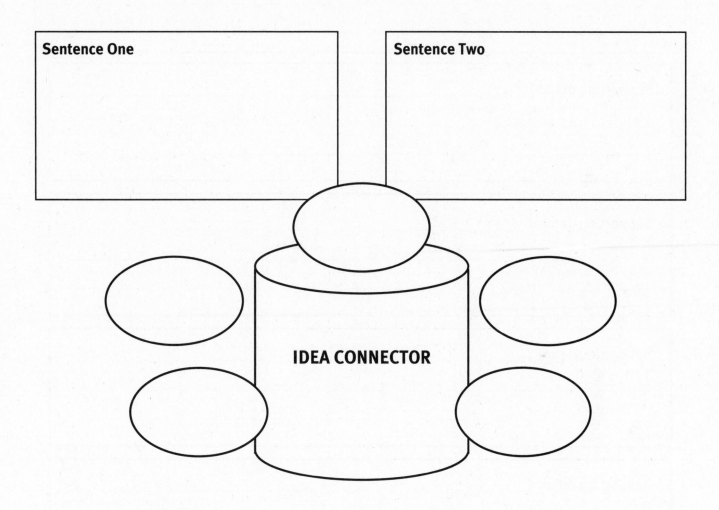

Sentence One

Sentence Two

IDEA CONNECTOR

Combined Sentence

Key Idea and Details Chart

Title/Topic _____

Key Idea _____

_____

_____

Supporting detail 1 _____

_____

_____

Supporting detail 2 _____

_____

_____

Supporting detail 3 _____

_____

_____

Supporting detail 4 _____

_____

_____

Restate topic sentence: _____

_____

Concluding sentence: _____

_____

Narrative Analysis and Writing

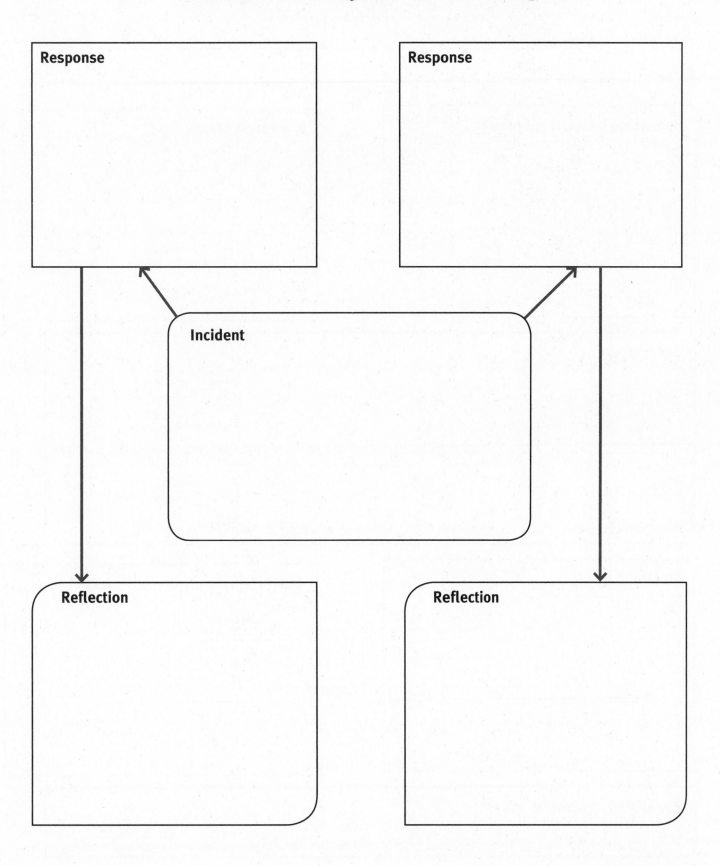

Response

Response

Incident

Reflection

Reflection

Notes for Reading Independently
Fiction

Title: _____

Author: _____

Something interesting I noticed:	A question I have:

Summary:

Illustration:

Connections to my life/other texts I've read:

How challenging this text was:
Easy   1   2   3   4   5   6   7   8   9   10   *Challenging*

Notes for Reading Independently
Nonfiction

Title: _____

Author: _____

Main idea:

Facts I learned:

Summary:

Questions I still have:

Connections to my life/other texts I've read:

How challenging this text was:

Easy   1   2   3   4   5   6   7   8   9   10   *Challenging*

Opinion Builder

Reason

Reason

Based on these reasons, my opinion is

Reason

Reason

OPTIC

Title of Piece:

Artist: _____   **Type of artwork:** _____

Overview	Look at the artwork for at least 10 seconds. Generate questions; e.g., What is the subject? What strikes you as interesting, odd, etc.? What is happening?
Parts	Look closely at the artwork, making note of important elements and details. Ask additional questions, such as: Who are the figures? What is the setting and time period? What symbols are present? What historical information would aid understanding of this piece?
Title	Consider what the title and any written elements of the text suggest about meaning. How does the title relate to what is portrayed?
Interrelationships	Look for connections between and among the title, caption, and the parts of the art. How are the different elements related?
Conclusion	Form a conclusion about the meaning/theme of the text. Remember the questions you asked when you first examined it. Be prepared to support your conclusions with evidence.

Paragraph Frame for Conclusions

Conclusion Words and Phrases

shows that

based on

suggests that

leads to

indicates that

influences

The _____ (story, poem, play, passage, etc.)

shows that (helps us to conclude that) _____

_____

_____

There are several reasons why. First, _____

_____

_____

_____

_____

A second reason is _____

_____

_____

_____

_____

Finally, _____

_____

_____

_____

In conclusion, _____

_____

_____

_____

_____

Paragraph Frame for Sequencing

Sequence Words and Phrases

at the beginning

in the first place

as a result

later

eventually

in the end

lastly

In the _____ *(story, poem, play, passage, etc.)*

there are three important _____

(events, steps, directions, etc.)

First, _____

_____

_____

_____

_____

Second, _____

_____

_____

_____

_____

Third, _____

_____

_____

_____

_____

Finally, _____

_____

_____

_____

_____

Paraphrasing and Summarizing Map

What does the text say?	How can I say it in my own words?

How can I use my own words to summarize the text?

Peer Editing

Writer's name: _____

Did the writer answer the prompt? ☐ yes ☐ no

Did the writer use appropriate details or evidence to develop their writing? ☐ yes ☐ no

Is the writing organized in a way that makes sense? ☐ yes ☐ no

Did the writer use a variety of sentence types to make the writing more interesting? ☐ yes ☐ no

Are there any spelling or punctuation mistakes? ☐ yes ☐ no

Are there any grammar errors? ☐ yes ☐ no

Two things I really liked about the writer's story:

1. _____
   _____
   _____

2. _____
   _____
   _____

One thing I think the writer could do to improve the writing:

1. _____
   _____
   _____

Other comments or notes:

Persuasive/Argument Writing Map

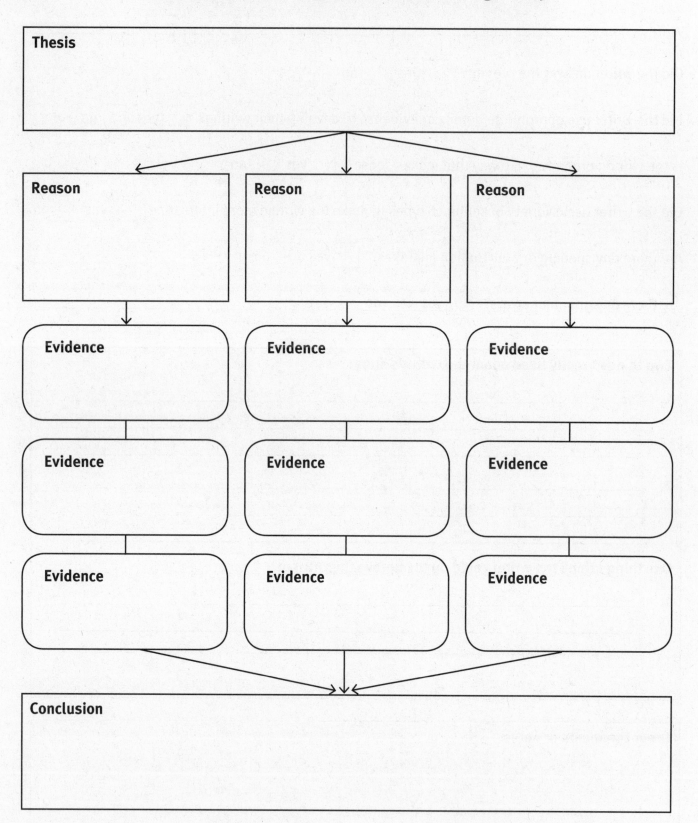

Thesis

Reason

Reason

Reason

Evidence

Evidence

Evidence

Evidence

Evidence

Evidence

Evidence

Evidence

Evidence

Conclusion

Presenting Scoring Guide

Scoring Criteria	Exemplary	Proficient	Emerging	Incomplete
Introduction / Conclusion	The presentation • provides a clear, engaging, and appropriate introduction to the topic or performance • provides a clear, engaging, and appropriate conclusion that closes, summarizes, draws connections to broader themes, or supports the ideas presented.	The presentation • provides a clear and appropriate introduction to the topic or performance • provides a clear and appropriate conclusion that closes, summarizes, draws connections to broader themes, or supports the ideas presented.	The presentation • provides an adequate introduction to the topic or performance • provides an adequate conclusion that closes, summarizes, draws connections to broader themes, or supports the ideas presented.	The presentation • does not provide an introduction to the topic or performance • does not provide a conclusion that closes, summarizes, draws connections to broader themes, or supports the ideas presented.
Timing	The presentation • thoroughly delivers its intended message within the allotted time • is thoughtfully and appropriately paced throughout.	The presentation • mostly delivers its intended message within the allotted time • is appropriately paced most of the time.	The presentation • delivers some of its intended message within the allotted time • is sometimes not paced appropriately.	The presentation • does not deliver its intended message within the allotted time • is not paced appropriately.
Voice (Volume, Enunciation, Rate)	The presentation • is delivered with adequate volume enabling audience members to fully comprehend what is said • is delivered with clear enunciation.	The presentation • is delivered with adequate volume enabling audience members to mostly comprehend what is said • is delivered with mostly clear enunciation.	The presentation • is delivered with somewhat adequate volume enabling audience members to comprehend some of what is said • is delivered with somewhat clear enunciation.	The presentation • is not delivered with adequate volume, so that audience members are unable to comprehend what is said • is delivered with unclear enunciation.
Eye Contact / Gestures	The presentation • is delivered with appropriate eye contact that helps engage audience members • makes use of natural gestures and/or body language to convey meaning.	The presentation • is delivered with some appropriate eye contact that helps engage audience members • makes use of gestures and/or body language to convey meaning.	The presentation • is delivered with occasional eye contact that sometimes engages audience members • makes some use of gestures and/or body language to convey meaning.	The presentation • is not delivered with eye contact to engage audience members • makes little or no use of gestures and/or body language to convey meaning.
Use of Media, Visuals, Props	The presentation • makes use of highly engaging visuals, multimedia, and/or props that enhance delivery.	The presentation • makes use of visuals, multimedia, and/or props that enhance delivery.	The presentation • makes use of some visuals, multimedia, and/or props that somewhat enhance delivery.	The presentation • makes use of few or no visuals, multimedia, and/or props that enhance delivery.
Audience Engagement	The presentation • includes thoughtful and appropriate interactions with and responses to audience members.	The presentation • includes appropriate interactions with and responses to audience members.	The presentation • includes a few interactions with and responses to audience members.	The presentation • does not include interactions with and responses to audience members.

RAFT

Role	Who or what are you as a writer?
Audience	As a writer, to whom are you writing?
Format	As a writer, what format would be appropriate for your audience (essay, letter, speech, poem, etc.)?
Topic	As a writer, what is the subject of your writing? What points do you want to make?

Roots and Affixes Brainstorm

Directions: Write the root or affix in the circle. Brainstorm or use a dictionary to find the meaning of the root or affix and add it to the circle. Then, find words that use that root or affix. Write one word in each box. Write a sentence for each word.

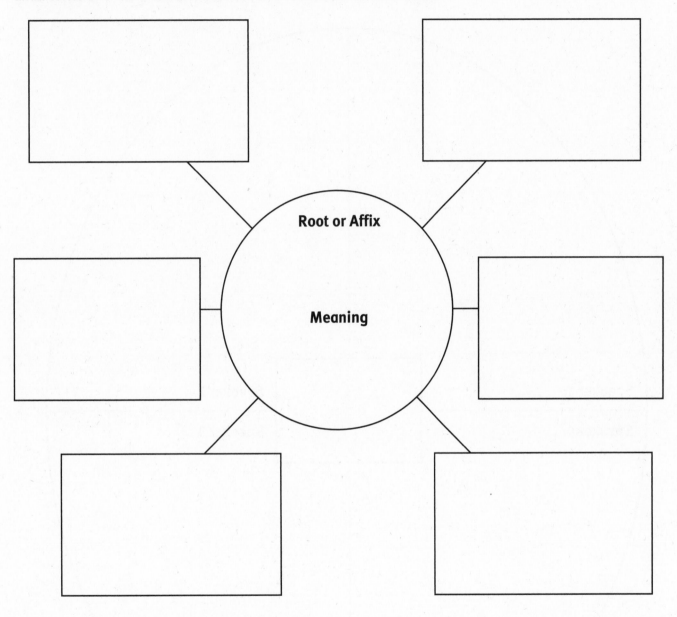

Root or Affix

Meaning

Round Table Discussion

Directions: Write the topic in the center box. One student begins by stating his or her ideas while the student to the left takes notes. Then the next student speaks while the student to his or her left takes notes, and so on.

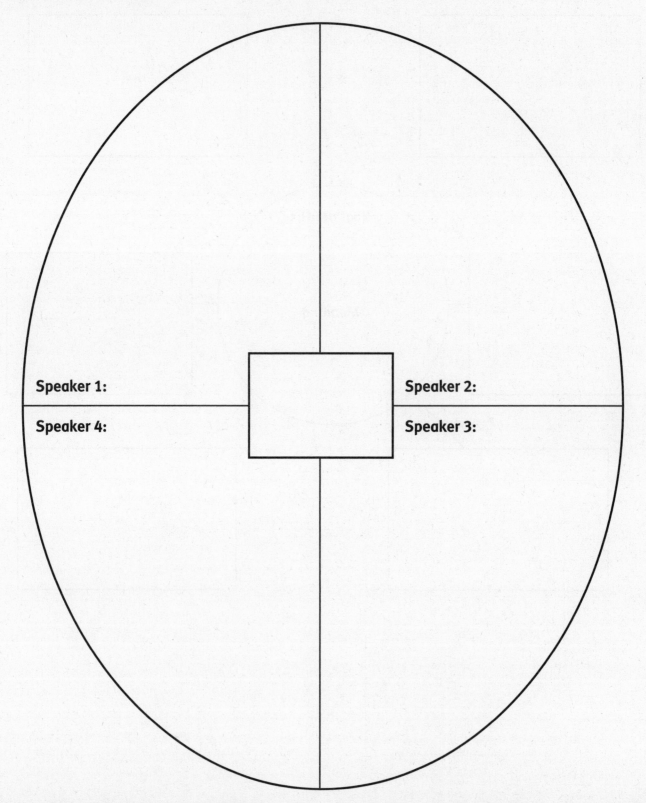

Speaker 1:

Speaker 2:

Speaker 4:

Speaker 3:

Sequence of Events Time Line

Title: _____

What happened first?	Next?

Beginning   **Middle**   **End**

Then?	Finally?

SMELL

Sender-Receiver Relationship—Who are the senders and receivers of the message, and what is their relationship (consider what different audiences the text may be addressing)?

Message—What is a literal summary of the content? What is the meaning/significance of this information?

Emotional Strategies—What emotional appeals (*pathos*) are included? What seems to be their desired effect?

Logical Strategies—What logical arguments/appeals (*logos*) are included? What is their effect?

Language—What specific language is used to support the message? How does it affect the text's effectiveness? Consider both images and actual words.

SOAPSTone

SOAPSTone	Analysis	Textual Support
Subject What does the reader know about the writer?		
Occasion What are the circumstances surrounding this text?		
Audience Who is the target audience?		
Purpose Why did the author write this text?		
Subject What is the topic?		
Tone What is the author's tone, or attitude?		

Text Structure Stairs

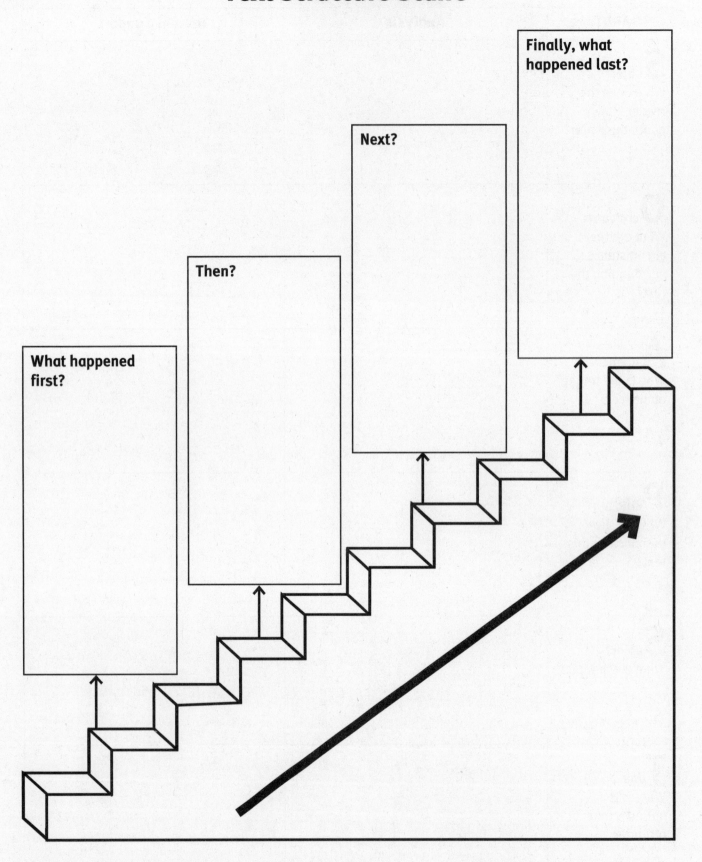

Finally, what happened last?

Next?

Then?

What happened first?

TP-CASTT Analysis

Poem Title:

Author:

Title: Make a Prediction. What do you think the title means before you read the poem?

Paraphrase: Translate the poem in your own words. What is the poem about? Rephrase difficult sections word for word.

Connotation: Look beyond the literal meaning of key words and images to their associations.

Attitude: What is the speaker's attitude? What is the author's attitude? How does the author feel about the speaker, about other characters, about the subject?

Shifts: Where do the shifts in tone, setting, voice, etc., occur? Look for time and place, keywords, punctuation, stanza divisions, changes in length or rhyme, and sentence structure. What is the purpose of each shift? How do they contribute to effect and meaning?

Title: Reexamine the title. What do you think it means now in the context of the poem?

Theme: Think of the literal and metaphorical layers of the poem. Then determine the overall theme. The theme must be written in a complete sentence.

TP-CASTT

Poem Title:

Author:

Title		
Paraphrase		
Connotation		
Attitude		
Shifts		
Title		
Theme		

Unknown Word Solver

Can you find any context clues? List them.

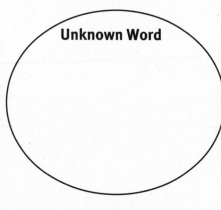

Unknown Word

Do you recognize any word parts?

Prefix:

Root Word:

Suffix:

Do you know another meaning of this word that does not make sense in this context?

Does it look or sound like a word in another language?

What is the dictionary definition?

How can you define the word in your own words?

Venn Diagram for Writing a Comparison

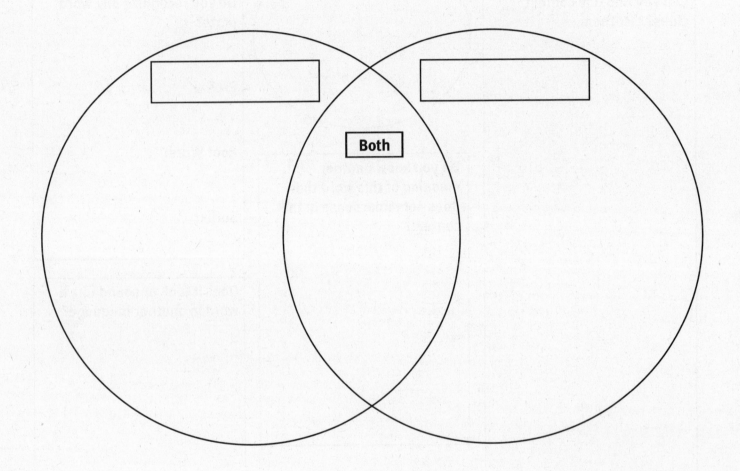

Both

They are similar in that _____
_____
_____
_____
_____
_____

They are different in that _____
_____
_____
_____
_____
_____

Verbal & Visual Word Association

Definition in Your Own Words	Important Elements

Academic Vocabulary Word

Visual Representation	Personal Association

Web Organizer

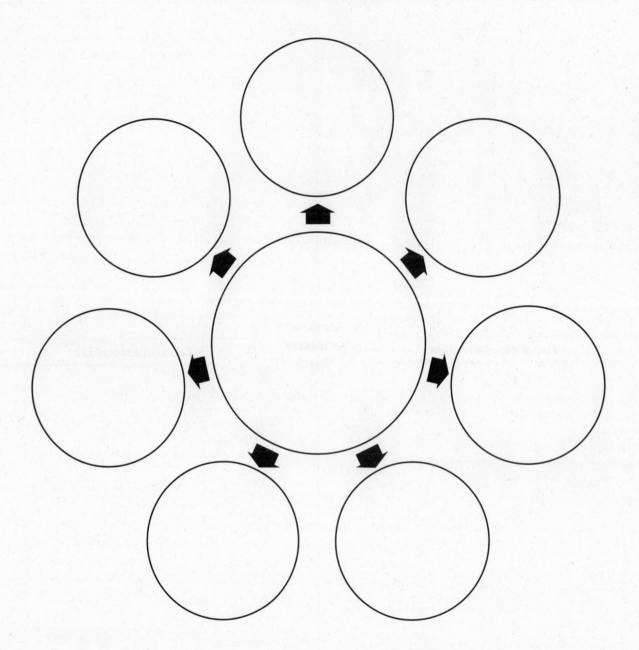

Word Choice Analyzer

Word or phrase from the text	Definition of word or phrase	How can I restate the definition in my own words?	What effect did the author produce by choosing these words?

Explain Your Analysis

The author uses the word or phrase _____ , which means

_____

Another way to say this is _____

_____

I think the author chose these words to _____

_____

_____

One way I can modify this sentence to add detail is to _____

_____

Word Map

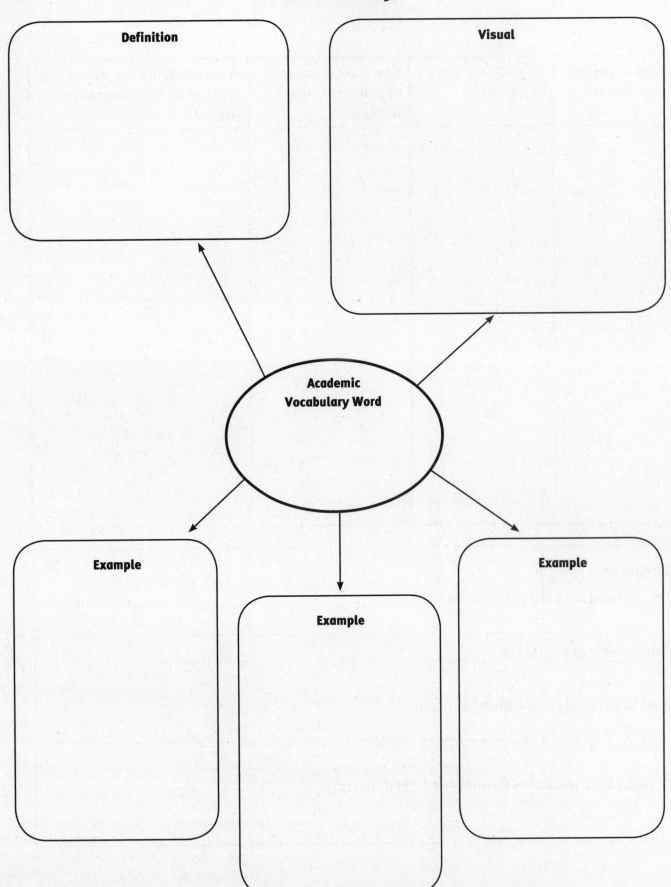

Definition

Visual

Academic Vocabulary Word

Example

Example

Example

Glossary/Glosario

A

active-voice verbs: verbs for which the subject performs the action

verbos en voz activa: forma verbal que indica que el sujeto realiza la acción

advertising techniques: specific methods used in print, graphics, or videos to persuade people to buy a product or use a service

técnicas publicitarias: métodos específicos usados en impresos, gráfica o videos para persuadir a las personas a comprar un producto o usar un servicio

agenda: a secret plan or motivation that causes someone to act in a certain way

agenda: motivación o plan secreto que lleva a alguien a actuar de determinado modo

allegory: a story in which the characters, objects, or actions have a meaning beyond the surface of the story

alegoría: cuento en el que los personajes, objetos o acciones tienen un significado que va más allá de la superficie de la historia

alliteration: the repetition of initial consonant sounds in words that are close together

aliteración: repetición de sonidos consonánticos iniciales en palabras cercanas

allusion: a reference made to a well-known person, event, or place from history, music, art, or another literary work

alusión: referencia a una persona, evento o lugar muy conocidos de la historia, música, arte u otra obra literaria

analogy: a comparison between two things for the purpose of drawing conclusions on one based on its similarities to the other

analogía: comparación entre dos cosas con el propósito de sacar conclusiones sobre las semejanzas que una cosa tiene a otra

anaphora: the repetition of the same word or group of words at the beginnings of two or more clauses or lines

anáfora: repetición de la misma palabra o grupo de palabras al comienzo de una o más cláusulas o versos

anecdotal evidence: evidence based on personal accounts of incidents

evidencia anecdótica: evidencia basada en relatos personales de los hechos

annotated bibliography: a list of sources used in research along with comments or summaries about each source

bibliografía anotada: lista de fuentes utilizadas en la investigación, junto con comentarios o resúmenes acerca de cada fuente

antagonist: the character who opposes or struggles against the main character

antagonista: personaje que se opone o lucha contra el personaje principal

aphorism: a short statement expressing an opinion or general truth

aforismo: afirmación corta que expresa una opinión o verdad general

appeals: the efforts to persuade an audience that a certain concept is true by directing statements toward reasoning or logic, character, or senses and emotions

llamados: serie de esfuerzos que alguien realiza con el fin de convencer a una audiencia de que determinado concepto es verdadero, persuadiéndola de ello mediante el uso del razonamiento o la lógica o bien apelando a su carácter, sentidos o emociones

Archetypal Criticism: criticism that deals with symbols and patterns that recur in the literature of widely diverse cultures

crítica de arquetipos: examinación de la literatura basada en símbolos y diseño

archetypes: universal symbols—images, characters, motifs, or patterns—that recur in the myths, dreams, oral traditions, songs, literature, and other texts of peoples widely separated by time and place

arquetipos: símbolos universales—imágenes, personajes, motivos o patrones—reiterativos en los mitos, el arte y la literatura alrededor del mundo

archival footage: film footage taken from another, previously recorded, source

cortometraje de archivo: fragmento de película tomada de otra fuente grabada previamente

argument: a form of writing that presents a particular claim or idea and supports it with evidence

argumento: forma de redacción que presenta una opinión o idea particular y la apoya con evidencia

argumentation: the act or process of arguing that includes the *hook* (quotation, example, or idea that catches readers' attention), *claim* (the opinion or thesis statement), *support* (evidence in the form of facts, statistics, examples, anecdotes, or expert opinions), *concession* (the writer's admission that the other side of the argument has a valid point), *refutation* (a well-reasoned denial of an opponent's point, based on solid evidence), and *call to action* (a request of readers)

argumentación: la estructura de una argumentación incluye el *gancho* (cita, ejemplo o idea que capta la atención del lector), *afirmación* (declaración de opinión o tesis), *apoyo* (evidencia en forma de hechos, estadísticas, ejemplos, anécdotas u opiniones de expertos), *concesión* (admisión por parte del escritor de que la otra parte del debate tiene un punto válido), *refutación* (negación bien razonada de una opinión del oponente, basada en evidencia sólida) y *llamado a la acción* (petición inspirada de lectores)

argument by analogy: a comparison of two similar situations, implying that the outcome of one will resemble the outcome of the other

argumento por analogía: comparación de dos situaciones semejantes, infiriendo que el resultado de será parecido al resultado de la otra

artistic license: the practice of rewording of dialogue, alteration of language, or reordering of the plot of a text created by another artist

licencia artística: la costumbre de reformular un diálogo, aliteración de palabras, o arreglo de la trama de un texto creado por otro artista

aside: a short speech spoken by an actor directly to the audience and unheard by other actors on stage

aparte: alocución breve dicha por un actor directamente al público y que no escuchan los demás actores que están en el escenario

assonance: the repetition of similar vowel sounds in accented syllables, followed by different consonant sounds, in words that are close together

asonancia: repetición de sonidos vocálicos similares en sílabas acentuadas, seguida de diferentes sonidos consonánticos, en palabras que están cercanas

audience: the intended readers, listeners, or viewers of specific types of written, spoken, or visual texts

público: lectores objetivo, oyentes o espectadores de tipos específicos de textos escritos, hablados o visuales

audience analysis: determination of the characteristics and knowledge of the people who will read a work or hear a speech

análisis del público: determinar las características y conocimiento de las personas que leen una obra o escuchan un discurso

author's purpose: the specific reason or reasons for the writing; what the author hopes to accomplish

propósito del autor: razón específica para escribir; lo que el autor espera lograr

autobiography: an account written by a person about his or her own life

autobiografía: narración de una vida escrita por el propio sujeto del relato

B

balanced sentence: a sentence that presents ideas of equal weight in similar grammatical forms to emphasize the similarity or difference between the ideas

oración balanceada: oración que representa ideas de igual peso en formas gramaticales similares para enfatizar la semejanza o diferencia entre las ideas

bias: an inclination or mental leaning for or against something; prevents impartial judgment

sesgo: inclinación o tendencia mental a favor o en contra de algo, lo que impide una opinión imparcial

bibliography: a list of the sources used for research

bibliografía: lista de fuentes primarias en la preparación de un texto

biography: a description or account of events from a person's life, written by another person

biografía: descripción o narración de la vida de una persona o los sucesos importantes de su vida escritos por otra persona

blank verse: unrhymed verse

verso libre: verso que no tiene rima

block: to create the plan for how actors will position themselves on the stage in relation to one another, the audience, and the objects on the stage

ensayar: establecer un plan para determinar la posición que los actores deberán ocupar en un escenario en relación a sí mismos, a la audiencia, al escenario y a los objetos del mismo

blocking: in drama, the way actors position themselves in relation to one another, the audience, and the objects on the stage

bloqueo: en drama, el modo en que los actores se sitúan entre sí, con el público y los objetos en el escenario

book review: a formal assessment or examination of a book

reseña de libro: evaluación o examinación formal de un libro

C

cacophonous: harsh and unpleasant sounding

cacofónico: sonidos molestos y desagradables

call to action: a restatement of the claim and what the writer wants the reader to do

llamado a la acción: repetición de la afirmación y lo que el escritor quiere que el lector responda

caricature: a visual or verbal representation in which characteristics or traits are exaggerated or distorted for emphasis
caricatura: representación visual o verbal en la que las características o rasgos se exageran o se distorsionan para dar énfasis

catalog poem: a poem that uses repetition and variation in the creation of a list, or catalog, of objects or desires, plans, or memories
lista en poema: poema que usa repetición y variación en la creación de una lista o catálogo, de objetos o deseos o planes o memorias

cause: an action, event, or situation that brings about a particular result
causa: acción, suceso o situación que produce un resultado particular

caveat: a cautionary detail to be thought through carefully when analyzing something
exhortación: advertencia o consejo a tener muy en cuenta a la hora de interpretar o analizar algo

censor: to examine materials for objectionable content
censurar: examinar materiales por contenido desagradable

censorship: the act of suppressing public speech or publication of materials deemed to be offensive by the censor
censura: acto de suprimir un discurso público o publicación de materiales considerados ofensivos por un censor

challenge: to oppose or refute a statement that has been made
poner en duda: oponerse a algo o refutar una declaración que alguien ha hecho

characterization: the methods a writer uses to develop characters
caracterización: métodos que usa un escritor para desarrollar personajes

characters: people, animals, or imaginary creatures that take part in the action of a story. A short story usually centers on a *main character* but may also contain one or more *minor characters*, who are not as complex, but whose thoughts, words, or actions move the plot along. A character who is *dynamic* changes in response to the events of the narrative; a character who is *static* remains the same throughout the narrative. A *round* character is fully developed—he or she shows a variety of traits; a *flat* character is one-dimensional, usually showing only one trait.

personajes: personas, animales o criaturas imaginarias que participan en la acción de un cuento. Un cuento corto normalmente se centra en un *personaje principal*, pero puede también contener uno o más *personajes secundarios*, que no son tan complejos, pero cuyos pensamientos, palabras o acciones hacen avanzar la trama. Un personaje que es *dinámico* cambia según los eventos del relato; un personaje que es *estático* permanece igual a lo largo del relato. Un personaje *complejo* está completamente desarrollado: muestra una diversidad de rasgos; un personaje *simple* es unidimensional, mostrando normalmente sólo un rasgo.

character foil: a character whose actions or thoughts are juxtaposed against those of a major character in order to highlight key attributes of the major character
antagonista: personaje cuyas acciones o pensamientos se yuxtaponen a los de un personaje principal con el fin de destacar atributos clave del personaje principal

character sketch: a brief description of a literary character
reseña del personaje: breve descripción de un personaje literario

chorus: in traditional or classic drama, a group of performers who speak as one and comment on the action of the play
coro: en el drama tradicional o clásico, grupo de actores que hablan al unísono y comentan la acción de la obra teatral

cinematic elements: the features of cinema—movies, film, video—that contribute to its form and structure: *angle* (the view from which the image is shot), *framing* (how a scene is structured), *lighting* (the type of lighting used to light a scene), *mise en scène* (the composition, setting, or staging of an image, or a scene in a film), and *sound* (the sound effects and music accompanying each scene)
elementos cinematográficos: las características del cine—películas, filmaciones, video—que contribuyen a darle forma y estructura: *angulación* (vista desde la cual se toma la imagen), *encuadre* (cómo se estructura una escena), iluminación (tipo de *iluminación* que se usa para una escena), y *montaje* (composición, ambiente o escenificación de una imagen o escena en una película), y *sonido* (efectos sonoros y música que acompañan cada escena)

cinematic techniques: the methods a director uses to communicate meaning and to evoke particular emotional responses from viewers
técnicas cinematográficas: métodos que emplea un director para comunicar un significado y evocar cierta respuesta emocional de los videntes

claim: a thesis statement describing the position the writer is taking on an issue
afirmación: declaración de opinión (o tesis) que asevera una idea o establece un debate hacia una posición específica

cliché: an overused expression or idea
cliché: expresión o idea que se usa en exceso

climax: the point at which the action reaches its peak; the point of greatest interest or suspense in a story; the turning point at which the outcome of a conflict is decided
clímax: punto en el que la acción alcanza su punto culminante; punto de mayor interés en un cuento; punto de inflexión en el que se decide el resultado del conflicto

coherence: the quality of unity or logical connection among ideas; the clear and orderly presentation of ideas in a paragraph or essay
coherencia: calidad de unidad o relación lógica entre las ideas; presentación clara y ordenada de las ideas en un párrafo o ensayo

commentary: the expression of opinions or explanations about an event or situation
comentario: expresión oral o escrita de opiniones o explicaciones sobre una situación, tema o suceso

commentary: explanations about the significance or importance of supporting details or examples in an analysis
comentario: explicaciones acerca de la importancia de los detalles que tienen apoyo o ejemplos en un análisis

complementary: combined in a way that enhances all elements combined
complementario: combinar dos o más elementos de una manera que mejora los dos

complex character: a character that has multiple or conflicting motivations
personaje complejo: personaje que tiene motivaciones multiples o conflictivas

complex sentence: a sentence containing one independent clause and one or more subordinate clauses
oración compleja: oración que contiene una cláusula independiente y una o más cláusulas subordinadas

complications: the events in a plot that develop a conflict; the complications move the plot forward in its rising action
complicaciones: sucesos de una trama que desarrollan el conflicto; las complicaciones hacen avanzar la trama en su acción ascendente

components: the parts or elements of a whole
componentes: partes o elementos que conforman un todo

compound sentence: a sentence containing two independent clauses
oración compuesta: oración que contiene dos cláusulas independientes

concession: an admission in an argument that the opposing side has valid points
concesión: admitir en un debate que el lado opositor tiene opiniones válidas

concluding statement: a statement that follows from and supports the claim made in an argument
declaración concluyente: declaración que sigue de la afirmación, o la apoya, en un argumento

conflict: a struggle or problem in a story. An *internal conflict* occurs when a character struggles between opposing needs or desires or emotions within his or her own mind. An *external conflict* occurs when a character struggles against an outside force. This force may be another character, a societal expectation, or something in the physical world.
conflicto: lucha o problema en un cuento. Un *conflicto interno* ocurre cuando un personaje lucha entre necesidades o deseos o emociones que se contraponen dentro de su mente. Un *conflicto externo* ocurre cuando un personaje lucha contra una fuerza externa. Esta fuerza puede ser otro personaje, una expectativa social o algo del mundo físico.

connotation: the associations and emotional overtones attached to a word beyond its literal definition, or denotation; a connotation may be positive, negative, or neutral
connotación: asociaciones y alusiones emocionales unidas a una palabra más allá de su definición literal o denotación; una connotación puede ser positiva, negativa, o neutra

consonance: the repetition of final consonant sounds in stressed syllables with different vowel sounds
consonancia: repetición de sonidos consonánticos finales en sílabas acentuadas con diferentes sonidos vocálicos

context: the circumstances or conditions in which something exists or takes place
contexto: circunstancias o condiciones en las que algo ocurre

conventions: standard features, practices, and forms associated with the way something is usually done
convenciones: prácticas y formas usuales asociadas con las costumbres de hacer algo

counterarguments: the arguments that can be made to oppose a viewpoint
contraargumentos: argumentos que se presentan para rebatir un punto de vista

counterclaim: a position taken by someone with an opposing viewpoint

contrareclamación: posición que toma una persona con un punto de vista contrario

couplet: two consecutive lines of verse with end rhyme; a couplet usually expresses a complete unit of thought

copla: dos líneas de versos consecutivos con rima final; una copla normalmente expresa una unidad de pensamiento completa

credibility: the quality of being trusted or believed

credibilidad: calidad de ser confiable o creíble

critical lens: a particular identifiable perspective as in Reader Response Criticism, Cultural Criticism, etc., through which a text can be analyzed and interpreted

ojo crítico: punto de vista particular identificable como por ejemplo Teoría de la recepción, Crítica sociocultural, etc., por medio del que se puede analizar e interpretar un texto

cultural conflict: a struggle that occurs when people with different cultural expectations or attitudes interact

conflicto cultural: lucha que ocurre cuando interactúan personas con diferentes expectativas o actitudes culturales

Cultural Criticism: criticism that focuses on the elements of culture and how they affect one's perceptions and understanding of texts

crítica cultural: analizar un texto basándose en elementos culturales y como ellos afectan la percepción y lacomprensión de textos

culture: the shared set of arts, ideals, skills, institutions, customs, attitude, values, and achievements that characterize a group of people, and that are passed on or taught to succeeding generations

cultura: conjunto de artes, ideas, destrezas, instituciones, costumbres, actitud, valores y logros compartidos que caracterizan a un grupo de personas, y que se transfieren o enseñan a las generaciones siguientes

cumulative (or loose) sentence: a sentence in which the main clause comes first, followed by subordinate structures or clauses

oración acumulativa (o frases sueltas): oración cuya cláusula principal viene primero, seguida de estructuras o cláusulas subordinadas

D

deductive reasoning: a process of drawing a specific conclusion from general information

razonamiento deductivo: proceso en que se usa información general para sacar una conclusión específica

defend: to support a statement that has been made

defender: dar apoyo a una declaración que alguien ha hecho

denotation: the precise meaning of a word

denotación: significado literal de una palabra

detail: a specific fact, observation, or incident; any of the small pieces or parts that make up something else

detalle: hecho, observación o incidente específico; cualquiera de las pequeñas piezas o partes que constituyen otra cosa

dialect: the distinctive language—including the sounds, spelling, grammar, and diction—of a specific group or class of people

dialecto: lenguaje distintivo, incluyendo sonidos, ortografía, gramática y dicción, de un grupo o clase específico de personas

dialogue: the words spoken by characters in a narrative or film

diálogo: palabras que dicen los personajes en un relato o película

dialogue tags: the phrases that attribute a quotation to the speaker, for example, *she said* or *he bellowed*

marcas del diálogo: frases que atribuyen la cita de un hablante, por ejemplo, *dijo ella* o *bramó él.*

diction: a writer's word choices, which often convey voice and tone

dicción: selección de palabras por parte del escritor; elemento estilístico que ayuda a transmitir voz y tono

diegetic sound: any sound that can logically be heard by characters on screen

sonido diegético: sonidos lógicos que los personajes pueden oír en una escena en la pantalla

direct characterization: specific information about a character provided by the narrator or author

caracterización directa: información específica sobre un personaje creada por un narrador o autor

discourse: the language or speech used in a particular context or subject

discurso: lenguaje o habla usada en un contexto o tema en particular

documentary or nonfiction film: a genre of filmmaking that provides a visual record of actual events using photographs, video footage, and interviews

documental o película de no-ficción: género cinematográfico que realiza un registro visual de sucesos basados en hechos por medio del uso de fotografías, registro en videos y entrevistas

dominant group: a more powerful group that may perceive another group as marginalized or subordinate

grupo dominante: un grupo más poderoso que puede percibir a otro grupo como maginado o subordinado

drama: a play written for stage, radio, film, or television, usually about a serious topic or situation

drama: obra teatral escrita para representar en un escenario, radio, cine o televisión, normalmente sobre un tema o situación seria

dramatic irony: a form of irony in which the reader or audience knows more about the circumstances or future events than the characters within the scene

ironía dramática: una forma de la ironía en que los lectores o el público sabe más sobre las circunstancias o sucesos futuros que los personajes en la escena

dramaturge: a member of an acting company who helps the director and actors make informed decisions about the performance by researching information relevant to the play and its context

dramaturgo: socio de una compañía teatral que ayuda al director y a los actores tomar decisiones informadas sobre la interpretación investigando información relevante a la obra teatral y su contexto

dynamic (or round) character: a character who evolves and grows in the story and has a complex personality

personaje dinámico: personaje complejo que evoluciona a lo largo de la trama literaria

E

editorial: an article in a newspaper or magazine expressing the opinion of its editor or publisher

editorial: artículo de periódico o revista, que expresa la opinión de su editor

effect: the result or influence of using a specific literary or cinematic device; a result produced by a cause

efecto: resultado o influencia de usar un recurso literario o cinematográfico específico; resultado o producto de una causa

elaborate: to expand on or add information or detail about a point and thus to develop the point more fully

elaborar: extender o agregar información o detalles sobre un asunto, y así desarrollar el asunto de manera más completa

empirical evidence: evidence based on experiences and direct observation through research

evidencia empírica: evidencia basada en experiencias y en la observación directa por medio de la investigación

emulate: to imitate an original work or person

emular: imitar una obra original

enfranchisement: having the rights of citizenship, such as the right to vote

emancipación: tener los derechos de la ciudananía, tales como el derecho al voto

epigram: a short, witty saying

epigrama: dicho corto e ingenioso

epigraph: a phrase, quotation, or poem that is set at the beginning of a document or component

epígrafe: frase, cita, o poema que aparece al comienzo de un documento o componente

epithet: a descriptive word or phrase used in place of or along with a name

epíteto: palabra o frase descriptiva usada en lugar de o junto con un nombre

ethos: (ethical appeal) a rhetorical appeal that focuses on the character or qualifications of the speaker

ethos: (recurso ético) recurso retórico centrado en la ética o en el carácter o capacidades del orador

euphonious: a harmonious or pleasing sound

eufónico: un sonido armonioso y agradable

evaluate: to make a judgment based on an analysis about the value or worth of the information, idea, or object

evaluar: dar una opinión basándose en un análisis sobre el valor o mérito de la información, idea, u objeto

evidence: the information that supports a position in an argument; forms of evidence include facts, statistics (numerical facts), expert opinions, examples, and anecdotes; *see also* anecdotal, empirical, and logical evidence

evidencia: información que apoya o prueba una idea o afirmación; formas de evidencia incluyen hechos, estadística (datos numéricos), opiniones de expertos, ejemplos y anécdotas; *ver también* evidencia anecdótica, empírica y lógica

exaggeration: a statement that represents something as larger, better, or worse than it really is

exageración: representar algo como más grande, mejor o peor que lo que realmente es

exemplification: the act of defining by example by showing specific, relevant examples that fit a writer's definition of a topic or concept

ejemplificación: definir por ejemplo mostrando ejempos específicos y relevantes que se ajustan a la definición de un tema o concepto del escritor

explanatory writing: a form of writing whose purpose is to explain, describe, or give information about a topic in order to inform a reader

escrito explicativo: forma de la escritura cuyo propósito es explicar, describir o dar información sobre un tema para informar al lector

explicit theme: a theme that is clearly stated by the writer
tema explícito: tema que está claramente establecido por el escritor

exposition: events that give a reader background information needed to understand a story (characters are introduced, the setting is described, and the conflict begins to unfold)
exposición: sucesos que dan al lector los antecedentes necesarios para comprender un cuento. Durante la exposición, se presentan los personajes, se describe el ambiente y se comienza a revelar el conflicto.

extended metaphor: a comparison between two unlike things that continues throughout a series of sentences in a paragraph or lines in a poem
metáfora extendida: metáfora que se extiende por varios versos o a través de un poema completo

external coherence: unity or logical connection between paragraphs with effective transitions and transitional devices
coherencia externa: unidad o conexión lógica entre párrafos con transiciones efectivas y recursos transitionales

eye rhymes: words that appear to rhyme because of identical spelling patterns but do not actually rhyme, for example, *cough* and *through*
falsas rimas: palabras, en inglés, que poseen una terminación idéntica y, por tanto, nos llevan erróneamente a pensar que riman, tales como *cough* y *through*

F

fallacy: a false or misleading argument
falacia: argumento o poema falso o engañoso

falling action: the events in a play, story, or novel that follow the climax, or moment of greatest suspense, and lead to the resolution
acción descendente: sucesos de una obra teatral, cuento o novela posteriores al clímax, o momento de mayor suspenso, y que conllevan a la resolución

faux pas: an embarrassing act or remark in a social situation (borrowed from French)
metedura de pata: comportamiento o comentario embarazoso en el marco de una situación social

Feminist Criticism: criticism that focuses on relationships between genders and examines a text based on the patterns of thought, behavior, values, enfranchisement, and power in relations between and within the sexes

crítica feminista: se enfoca en la relación entre los sexos y examina un texto basándose en el diseño de pensamiento, comportamiento, valores, emancipación, y poder en las relaciones entre los sexos

figurative: symbolic or emblematic; not literal
figurativo: simbólico o emblemático, no literal

figurative language: the use of words to describe one thing in terms of another
lenguaje figurativo: lenguaje imaginativo o figuras retóricas que no pretenden ser tomados literalmente; el lenguaje figurativo usa figuras literarias

film techniques: the methods a director uses to communicate meaning and to evoke particular emotional responses in viewers
técnicas cinematográficas: metodos que usa un director en la comunicación del significado y evocar una respuesta emocional específica en los videntes

fixed form: a form of poetry in which the length and pattern are determined by established usage of tradition, such as a sonnet
forma fija: forma de poesía en la que la longitud y el patrón están determinados por el uso de la tradición, como un soneto

flashback: an interruption or transition to a time before the current events in a narrative
flashback: interrupción en la secuencia de los sucesos para relatar sucesos ocurridos en el pasado

flat (or static) character: a character who is uncomplicated and stays the same without changing or growing during the story
personaje estático: personaje no complicado que permanece del mismo caracter y que no cambia a lo largo de una historia

folktale: a story without a known author that has been preserved through oral retellings
cuento folclórico: cuento sin autor conocido que se ha conservado por medio de relatos orales

footage: literally, a length of film; the expression is still used to refer to digital video clips
metraje: literalmente, la longitud de una película; la expresión aún se usa para referirse a video clips digitales

foreshadowing: the use of hints or clues in a narrative to suggest future action
presagio: uso de claves o pistas en un relato para sugerir una acción futura

form: the particular structure or organization of a work
forma: estructura o organización particular de una obra

found poem: a poem consisting of words, phrases, and/or lines that come directly from another text
poema encontrado: poema compuesto de palabras, frases o pasajes sacados directamente de otros textos

free verse: poetry without a fixed pattern of meter and rhyme
verso libre: poesía que no sigue ningún patrón, ritmo o rima regular

G

genre: a kind or style of literature or art, each with its own specific characteristics. For example, poetry, short story, and novel are literary genres. Painting and sculpture are artistic genres.
género: tipo o estilo de literatura o arte, cada uno con sus propias características específicas. Por ejemplo, la poesía, el cuento corto y la novela son géneros literarios. La pintura y la escultura son géneros artísticos.

genre conventions: the essential features and format that characterize a particular genre, or style of literature or art
convenciones genéricas: características básicas y el formato que caracterizan un género específico

graphic novel: a book-length narrative, or story, in the form of a comic strip rather than words
novela gráfica: narrativa o cuento del largo de un libro, en forma de tira cómica más que palabras

graphics: images or text used to provide information on screen
gráfica: imágenes o texto que se usa para dar información en pantalla

H

hamartia: a tragic hero's fatal flaw; an ingrained character trait that causes a hero to make decisions leading to his or her death or downfall
hamartia: error fatal de un héroe trágico; característica propia de un personaje que causa que un héroe tome decisiones que finalmente llevan a su muerte o caída

hero: the main character or protagonist of a play, with whom audiences become emotionally invested
héroe: personaje principal o protagonista de una obra teatral, con el que el público se involucra emocionalmente

historical context: the circumstances or conditions in which something takes place

contexto historico: circuntancias o condiciones en las cuales algo sucede o pasa

Historical Criticism: criticism used to uncover meaning in a literary text by examining the text in the context of the time period in which it was created
historicismo: método crítico que se usa para revelar el significado de un texto literario mediante el examen de dicho texto en el contexto de la época en que fue escrito

hook: an opening in an argument or a piece of writing that grabs the reader's attention
gancho: cita, anécdota o ejemplo interesante al comienzo de un escrito, que capta la atención del lector

Horatian satire: satire that pokes fun at human foibles and folly with a witty, gentle, even indulgent tone
sátira de Horacio: sátira en que se burla de las debilidades y locuras con un tono suave, ingenioso, hasta indulgente

humor: the quality of being amusing
humor: calidad de ser divertido

hyperbole: exaggeration used to suggest strong emotion or create a comic effect
hipérbole: exageración que se usa para sugerir una emoción fuerte o crear un efecto cómico

I

iamb: a metrical foot that consists of an unstressed syllable followed by a stressed syllable
yambo: pie métrico que consta de una sílaba átona seguida de una sílaba acentuada

iambic pentameter: a rhythmic pattern of five feet (or units), each consisting of one unstressed syllable followed by a stressed syllable
pentámetro yámbico: patrón rítmico de cinco pies (o unidades) de una sílaba átona seguida de una sílaba acentuada

image: a word or phrase that appeals to one of more of the five senses and creates a picture
imagen: palabra o frase que apela a uno o más de los cinco sentido y crea un cuadro

imagery: the verbal expression of sensory experience; descriptive or figurative language used to create word pictures; imagery is created by details that appeal to one or more of the five senses
imaginería: lenguaje descriptivo o figurativo utilizado para crear imágenes verbales; la imaginería es creada por detalles que apelan a uno o más de los cinco sentidos

imperialism: a policy of extending the rule or influence of a country over other countries or colonies; the political, military, or economic domination of one country by another

imperialismo: política de extender el dominio o la influencia de un país sobre otros países o colonias; dominio político; militar o económico de un país sobre otro(s)

implied theme: a theme that is understood through the writer's diction, language construction, and use of literary devices

tema implícito: tema que se entiende a través de la dicción del escritor, construcción lingüística y uso de recursos literarios

indirect characterization: a narrator's or author's development of a character through the character's interactions with others, thoughts about circumstances, or speaking his or her thoughts aloud

caracterización indirecta: el desarrollo de un personaje según un narrador o autor por las interacciones del personaje con otros, pensamientos sobre las circunstancias, o su habilidad de enunciar sus pensamientos en voz alta

inductive reasoning: a process of looking at individual facts to draw a general conclusion

razonamiento inductivo: proceso de observación de hechos individuales para sacar una conclusión general

inference: a conclusion about ideas or information not directly stated

inferencia: conclusión sobre las ideas o información no presentadas directamente

interior monologue: a literary device in which a character's internal emotions and thoughts are presented

monólogo interior: recurso literario en el que se presentan las emociones internas y pensamientos de un personaje

interpretation: the act of making meaning from something, such as a text

interpretación: acto de interpretar un significado de algo, tal como un texto

internal coherence: unity or logical connection within paragraphs

coherencia interna: unidad o conexión lógica entre párrafos

irony: a literary device that exploits readers' expectations; irony occurs when what happens turns out to be quite different from what was expected. *Dramatic irony* is a form of irony in which the reader or audience knows more about the circumstances or future events in a story than the characters within it; *verbal irony* occurs when a speaker or narrator says one thing while meaning the opposite; *situational irony* occurs when an event contradicts the expectations of the characters or the reader.

ironía: recurso literario que explota las expectativas de los lectores; la ironía ocurre cuando lo que se espera resulta ser bastante diferente de lo que realmente ocurre. La *ironía dramática* es una forma de ironía en la que el lector o la audiencia saben más acerca de las circunstancias o sucesos futuros de un cuento que los personajes del mismo; la *ironía verbal* ocurre cuando un orador o narrador dice una cosa queriendo decir lo contrario; la *ironía situacional* ocurre cuando un suceso contradice las expectativas de los personajes o del lector.

J

justice: the quality of being reasonable and fair in the administration of the law; the ideal of rightness or fairness

justicia: calidad de ser razonable e imparcial en la administración de la ley; ideal de rectitud o equidad

Juvenalian satire: satire that denounces, sometimes harshly, human vice and error in dignified and solemn tones

sátira de Juvenal: sátira de denuncia, a veces con aspereza, los vicios y errores humanos con tonos dignos y solemnes

juxtaposition: the arrangement of two or more things for the purpose of comparison

yuxtaposición: ordenamiento de dos o más cosas con el objeto de compararlas

L

lede: an alternative spelling of lead; the opening of a news article or a single sentence that describes the main point of the article

entradilla: comienzo de una información periodística que resume lo más importante de ella

lining out: the process of creating line breaks to add shape and meaning in free verse poetry

llamada y respuesta: proceso de crear rupturas de lineas para dar forma y significado en la poesía del verso libre

literal: explicitly stated in a text; exact

literal: algo expresado de modo explícito y exacto en un texto

literal language: the exact meanings, or denotations, of words

lenguaje literal: los signficados y denotaciones exactos de las palabras

Literary Criticism: the formal practice of interpreting, evaluating, and explaining the meaning and significance of literary works

crítica literaria: práctica formal de interpretar, evaluar y explicar el significado y el valor de obras literarias

literary theory: a systematic study of literature using various methods to analyze texts

teoría literaria: intento de establecer principios para interpretar y evaluar textos literarios

logical evidence: evidence based on facts and a clear rationale
evidencia lógica: evidencia basada en hechos y una clara fundamentación

logical fallacy: a statement that is false because it is based on an error in reasoning
argumento falaz: afirmación de carácter falso por el hecho de estar basada en un error de razonamiento

logos: (logical appeal) a rhetorical appeal to reason or logic
logos: (apelación lógica) apelación retórica que usa la evidencia factual y la lógica para apelar al sentido de la razón

M

main idea: a statement (often one sentence) that summarizes the key details of a text
idea principal: declaración (con frecuencia una oración) que resume los detalles claves de un texto

marginalize: to relegate or confine a person to a lower or outer limit
marginar: relegar o confinar a una persona a un límite bajo o ajeno

Marxist Criticism: criticism that asserts that economics provides the foundation for all social, political, and ideological reality
crítica marxista: ver un text a través de la perspectiva en que la economía proporciona la fundación de toda realidad social, política, e ideológica

media: collectively refers to the organizations that communicate information to the public
medios de comunicación: colectivamente refiere a las organizaciones que comunican información al público

media channel: a method an organization uses to communicate, such as radio, television, website, newspaper, or magazine
canales mediaticos: método que usa una organización en la comunicación como radio, televisión, sitios de web, periódico, o revista

metacognition: the ability to know and be aware of one's own thought processes; self-reflection
metacognición: capacidad de conocer y estar consciente de los propios procesos del pensamiento; introspección

metaphor: a comparison between two unlike things in which one thing is spoken of as if it were another, for example, the moon was a crisp white cracker

metáfora: comparación entre dos cosas diferentes en la que se habla de una cosa como si fuera otra, por ejemplo, la luna era una galletita blanca crujiente

meter: a pattern of stressed and unstressed syllables in poetry
métrica: patrón de sílabas acentuadas y átonas en poesía

mise en scène: the composition, or setting, of a stage
puesta en escena: la composición o el lugar de un escenario

monologue: a dramatic speech delivered by a single character in a play
monólogo: discurso dramático que hace un solo personaje en una obra teatral

montage: a composite picture that is created by bringing together a number of images and arranging them to create a connected whole
montaje: cuadro compuesto que se crea al reunir un número de imágenes y que al organizarlas se crea un todo relacionado

mood: the atmosphere or predominant emotion in a literary work, the effect of the words on the audience
carácter: atmósfera o sentimiento general en una obra literaria

motif: a recurrent image, symbol, theme, character type, subject, or narrative detail that becomes a unifying element in an artistic work or text
motivo: imagen, símbolo, tema, tipo de personaje, tema o detalle narrativo recurrente que se convierte en un elemento unificador en una obra artística

motive: a character's reason for behaving in a certain way
motivación: razón esgrimida por un personaje para obrar de determinado modo

musical (or sound) device: the use of sound to convey and reinforce the meaning or experience of poetry
aparatos musicales: uso del sonido para transmitir y reforzar el significado o experiencia de la poesía

myth: a traditional story that explains the actions of gods or heroes or the origins of the elements of nature
mito: cuento tradicional que explica las acciones de dioses o héroes, o los orígenes de los elementos de la naturaleza

N

narration: the act of telling a story
narración: acto de contar un cuento

narrative: a story about a series of events that includes character development, plot structure, and theme; can be a work of fiction or nonfiction

narrativa: narración sobre una serie de sucesos que incluye el desarrollo de personajes, estructora del argumento, y el tema; puede ser una obra de ficción o no ficción

narrative arc: the story line of a text, including a beginning (*exposition*), a middle (the *rising action*), a high point (*climax*), and an end (the *falling action* and *resolution*)

arco narrativo: línea argumental de un texto, que consta de un comienzo (*exposición*), una parte media (*acción creciente*), un punto culminante (*clímax*) y un final (*acción decreciente* y *resolución*)

narrative pacing: the speed at which a narrative moves

compás de la narrativa: la rapidez en que una narrativa pasa

narrator: the person telling the story

narrador: persona que cuenta una historia

non-diegetic sound: sound that cannot logically be heard by the characters on screen; examples include mood music and voice-overs

sonido no diegético: voces y comentarios superpuestos; sonidos que no provienen de la acción en pantalla.

nut graf: an abbreviation of the expression *nutshell paragraph*; a statement that tells readers of a news article why they should care about what happened

epítome: texto introductorio que hace entender a los lectores por qué debería importarles la noticia que se relata a continuación

O

objective: based on factual information

objetivo: basado en información de hechos

objective tone: a tone that is more clinical and that is not influenced by emotion

tono objetivo: tono que es mas aséptico y que no se deja influir por la emoción

objectivity: the representation of facts or ideas without injecting personal feelings or biases

objetividad: representación de los hechos o ideas sin agregar sentimientos o prejuicios personales

ode: a lyric poem expressing feelings or thoughts of a speaker, often celebrating a person, event, or thing

oda: poema lírico que expresa sentimientos o pensamientos de un orador, que frecuentemente celebra a una persona, suceso o cosa

omniscient narrator: a narrator who knows all and tells a story from the perspective of multiple characters

narrador omnisciente: narrador que conoce todo lo sucedido sobre un determinado acontecimiento y relata la historia desde la perspectiva de varios personajes

onomatopoeia: the occurrence of a word whose sound suggests its meaning

onomatopeya: palabras cuyo sonido sugiere su significado

oral interpretation: a planned oral reading that expresses the meaning of a written text

interpretación oral: lectura oral planeada que interpreta el signficado de un text escrito

oral tradition: the passing down of stories, tales, proverbs, and other culturally important ideas through oral retellings

tradición oral: traspaso de historias, cuentos, proverbios y otras historias de importancia cultural por medio de relatos orales

oxymoron: words that appear to contradict each other; for example, cold fire

oxímoron: palabras que parecen contradecirse mutuamente; por ejemplo, fuego frío

P

paradox: a statement that contains two seemingly incompatible points

paradoja: declaración que contiene dos asuntos aparentemente incompatibles

parallel structure (parallelism): refers to a grammatical or structural similarity between sentences or parts of a sentence, so that elements of equal importance are equally developed and similarly phrased for emphasis

estructura paralela (paralelismo): se refiere a una similitud gramatical o estructural entre oraciones o partes de una oración, de modo que los elementos de igual importancia se desarrollen por igual y se expresen de manera similar para dar énfasis

paraphrase: to briefly restate ideas from another source in one's own words

parafrasear: volver a presentar las ideas de otra fuente en nuestras propias palabras

parenthetical citations: used for citing sources directly in an essay

citas parentéticas: usadas en citas de fuentes primarias en un ensayo

parody: a literary or artistic work that imitates the characteristic style of an author or a work for comic effect or ridicule

parodia: obra literaria o artística que imita el estilo característico de un autor o una obra para dar un efecto cómico o ridículo

passive-voice verbs: verb form in which the subject receives the action; the passive voice consists of a form of the verb *be* plus a past participle of the verb

verbos en voz pasiva: forma verbal en la que el sujeto recibe la acción; la voz pasiva se forma con el verbo *ser* más el participio pasado de un verbo

pathos: (emotional appeal) a rhetorical appeal to the reader's or listener's senses or emotions

pathos: (apelación emocional) apelación retórica a los sentidos o emociones de los lectores u oyentes

patriarchal: having the male as head of the household and with authority over women and children

patriarcal: sociedad en que el varón es jefe del hogar en el cual mantiene autoridad sobre las mujeres y niños

perception: one person's interpretation of sensory or conceptual information

percepción: interpretación de una persona en cuanto a información sensorial o conceptual

periodic sentence: a sentence that makes sense only when the end of the sentence is reached, that is, when the main clause comes last

oración periódica: oración que tiene sentido sólo cuando se llega al final de la oración, es decir, cuando la cláusula principal viene al final

persona: the voice assumed by a writer to express ideas or beliefs that may not be his or her own

personaje: voz que asume un escritor para expresar ideas o creencias que pueden no ser las propias

personification: a figure of speech that gives human qualities to an animal, object, or idea

personificación: figura literaria que da características humanas a un animal, objeto o idea

perspective: a way of looking at the world or a mental concept about things or events, one that judges relationships within or among things or events

perspectiva: manera de visualizar el mundo o concepto mental de las cosas o sucesos, que juzga las relaciones dentro o entre cosas o sucesos

persuasive argument: an argument that convinces readers to accept or believe a writer's perspective on a topic

argumento persuasivo: argumento que convence a los lectores a aceptar o creer en la perspectiva de un escritor acerca de un tema

photo essay: a collection of photographic images that reveal the author's perspective on a subject

ensayo fotográfico: recolección de imágenes fotográficas que revelan la perspectiva del autor acerca de un tema

plagiarism: the unattributed use of another writer's words or ideas

plagio: usar como propias las palabras o ideas de otro escritor

plot: the sequence of related events that make up a story

trama: secuencia de sucesos relacionados que conforman un cuento o novela

poetic structure: the organization of words, lines, and images as well as ideas

estructura poética: organización de las palabras, versos e imágenes, así como también de las ideas

poetry: language written in lines and stanzas

poesía: género literario que se concreta en un poema y está sujeto a medida o cadencia

point of view: the perspective from which a narrative is told, that is, first person, third-person limited, or third-person omniscient

punto de vista: perspectiva desde la cual se cuenta un relato, es decir, primera persona, tercera persona limitada o tercera persona omnisciente

precept: a rule, instruction, or principle that guides a person's actions and/or moral behavior

precepto: regla, instrucción o principio que guía las acciones de una persona y/o conducta moral de alguien

primary footage: film footage shot by the filmmaker for the text at hand

metraje principal: filmación hecha por el cineasta para el texto que tiene a mano

primary source: an original document or image created by someone who experiences an event first hand

fuente primaria: documento original que contiene información de primera mano acerca de un tema

prologue: the introduction or preface to a literary work

prólogo: introducción o prefacio de una obra literaria

prose: ordinary written or spoken language, using sentences and paragraphs, without deliberate or regular meter or rhyme; not poetry or song

prosa: forma común del lenguaje escrito o hablado, usando oraciones y párrafos, sin métrica o rima deliberada o regular; ni poesía ni canción

prosody: the pattern and rhythm of sounds in poetry, including stress and intonation

prosodia: rasgos fónicos de la métrica de la poesía, incluidos el énfasis y la entonación

protagonist: the central character in a work of literature, the one who is involved in the main conflict in the plot

protagonista: personaje central de una obra literaria, el que participa en el conflicto principal de la trama

proverb: a short saying about a general truth

proverbio: dicho corto sobre una verdad general

Q

qualify: to consider to what extent a statement is true or untrue (to what extent you agree or disagree)
calificar: consider hasta qué punto una declaración es verdadera o falsa

quatrain: a four-line stanza in a poem
cuarteta: en un poema, estrofa de cuatro versos

R

rationale: an explanation for a belief, statement, or behavior
fundamento: cimientos o bases en los que se apoya una creencia, afirmación o comportamiento

Reader Response Criticism: criticism that focuses on a reader's active engagement with a piece of print or nonprint text; shaped by the reader's own experiences, social ethics, moral values, and general views of the world
crítica de reacción del lector: análisis de un texto basado en las experiencias, ética social, valores, y percepciones generales del mundo

reasoning: the thinking or logic used to make a claim in an argument
razonamiento: pensamiento o lógica que se usa para hacer una afirmación en un argumento

rebuttal: a reason why a counterargument is wrong
refutación: razón por la cual un contraargumento es erróneo

refrain: a regularly repeated line or group of lines in a poem or song, usually at the end of a stanza
estribillo: verso o grupo de versos que se repiten con regularidad en un poema o canción, normalmente al final de una estrofa

refutation: the reasoning used to disprove an opposing point
refutación: razonamiento que se usa para rechazar una opinión contraria

reliability: the extent to which a source provides quality and trustworthy information
confiabilidad: grado en el que una fuente da información confiable y de buena calidad

renaissance: a rebirth or revival
renacimiento: un volver a nacer o una reanimación

repetition: the use of any element of language—a sound, a word, a phrase, a line, or a stanza—more than once
repetición: uso de cualquier elemento del lenguaje—un sonido, una palabra, una frase, un verso o una estrofa—más de una vez

resolution (denouement): the end of a text, in which the main conflict is finally resolved

resolución (desenlace): final de una obra teatral, cuento o novela, en el que el conflicto principal finalmente se resuelve

résumé: a document that outlines a person's skills, education, and work history
currículum vitae: documento que resume las destrezas, educación y experiencia laboral de una persona

retrospective: looking back to analyze the events in one's past
retrospectiva: mirar atrás en el tiempo para analizar los acontecimientos del pasado de una persona

revise: to rework or reorganize a piece of writing to improve its logic and flow after completing a first draft
revisar: rehacer o reorganizar un escrito para mejorar su lógica y fluidez tras haber terminado un primer borrador

rhetoric: the art of using words to persuade in writing or speaking
retórica: arte de usar las palabras para persuadir por escrito o de manera hablada

rhetorical appeals: emotional, ethical, and logical arguments used to persuade an audience to agree with the writer or speaker
recursos retóricos: uso de argumentos emocionales, éticos y lógicos para persuadir por escrito o de manera hablada

rhetorical context: the subject, purpose, audience, occasion, or situation in which writing or speaking occurs
contexto retórico: sujeto, propósito, audiencia, ocasión o situación en que ocurre el escrito

rhetorical devices: specific techniques used in writing or speaking to create a literary effect or enhance effectiveness
dispositivos retóricos: técnicas específicas que se usan al escribir o al hablar para crear un efecto literario o mejorar la efectividad

rhetorical question: a question that is asked for effect or one for which the answer is obvious
pregunta retórica: pregunta hecha para producir un efecto o cuya respuesta es obvia

rhetorical slanters: rhetorical devices used to present a subject in a biased way
sesgos retóricos: recursos retóricos que se usan para presentar un determinado asunto de un modo tendencioso

rhyme: the repetition of sounds at the ends of words
rima: repetición de sonidos al final de las palabras

rhyme scheme: a consistent pattern of rhyme throughout a poem
esquema de la rima: patrón consistente de una rima a lo largo de un poema

rhythm: the pattern of stressed and unstressed syllables in spoken or written language, especially in poetry

ritmo: patrón de sílabas acentuadas y no acentuadas en lenguaje hablado o escrito, especialmente en poesía

rising action: the movement of a plot toward a climax or moment of greatest excitement; the rising action is fueled by the characters' responses to the conflict

acción ascendente: movimiento de una trama hacia el clímax o momento de mayor emoción; la acción ascendente es impulsada por las reacciones de los personajes ante el conflicto

dynamic (or round) character: a character who evolves and grows in the story and has a complex personality

personaje dinámico: personaje que evoluciona y crece en la historia y que tiene una personalidad compleja

S

sarcasm: deliberate, often ironic ridicule

sarcasmo: burla deliberada, de carácter generalmente irónico

satire: a manner of writing that mocks social conventions, actions, or attitudes with wit and humor

sátira: manera de escribir en que se burla de convenciones sociales, acciones, o actitudes con ingenio y humor

scenario: an outline, a brief account, a script, or a synopsis of a proposed series of events

escenario: bosquejo, relato breve, libreto o sinopsis de una serie de sucesos propuestos

secondary audience: a group that may receive a message intended for a target audience

audiencia secundaria: grupo que puede recibir un mensaje orientado a una audiencia específica

secondary source: a discussion about or commentary on a primary source; the key feature of a secondary source is that it offers an interpretation of information gathered from primary sources

fuente secundaria: discusión o comentario acerca de una fuente primaria; la característica clave de una fuente secundaria es que ofrece una interpretación de la información recopilada en las fuentes primarias

sensory details: details that appeal to or evoke one or more of the five senses—sight, sound, smell, taste, and touch

detalles sensoriales: detalles que apelan o evocan uno o más de los cinco sentidos—vista, oído, gusto, olfato, y tacto

sensory images: images that appeal to the reader's senses—sight, sound, smell, taste, and touch

imágenes sensoriales: imágenes que apelan a los sentidos del lector—vista, oído, olfato, gusto, y tacto

sequence of events: the order in which things happen in a story

secuencia de eventos: orden en que los sucesos de una historia pasan:

setting: the time and place in which a story happens

ambiente: tiempo y lugar en el que ocurre un relato

simile: a comparison of two different things or ideas using the words *like* or *as*, for example, the moon was as white as milk

símil: comparación entre dos o más cosas o ideas diferentes usando las palabras *como* o *tan*, por ejemplo, la luna estaba tan blanca como la leche

situational irony: a form of irony that occurs when an event contradicts the expectations of the characters or the reader

ironía situacional: ocurre cuando un evento contradice las espectativas de los personajes o el lector

slanters: rhetorical devices used to present the subject in a biased way

soslayo: recursos retóricos para presentar el tema de modo sesgado

slogan: a short, catchy phrase used for advertising by a business, club, or political party

eslogan: frase corta y tendenciosa que usa como publicidad para un negocio, club o partido político

social commentary: an expression of an opinion with the goal of promoting change by appealing to a sense of justice

comentario social: expresión de una opinión con el objeto de promover el cambio al apelar a un sentido de justicia

soliloquy: a long speech delivered by an actor alone on the stage; represents the character's internal thoughts

soliloquio: discurso largo realizado por un actor sobre el escenario que representa sus pensamientos internos

sonnet: a 14-line lyric poem, usually written in iambic pentameter and following a strict pattern of rhyme

soneto: poema lírico de catorce versos, normalmente escrito en un pentámetro yámbico y que sigue un patrón de rima estricto

sound bite: a short excerpt from the recording of a speech or piece of music which captures the essence of the longer recording

cuña: corto fragmento de una grabación o de una pieza musical que capta la esencia de la grabación completa

speaker: the imaginary voice or persona of the writer or author

orador: voz o persona imaginaria del escritor o autor

stage directions: instructions written into the script of a play that indicate stage actions, movements of performers, or production requirements

direcciones escénicas: instrucciones escritas en un guión o drama que indican acción, movimiento de actors, o requisitos de la producción

stakeholder: a person motivated or affected by a course of action
participante: persona motivada o afectada por el curso de una acción

stanza: a group of lines, usually similar in length and pattern, that form a unit within a poem
estrofa: grupo de versos, normalmente similares en longitud y patrón, que forman una unidad dentro de un poema

static (or flat) character: a character who is uncomplicated and remains the same without changing or growing throughout a narrative
personaje estático: personaje que no cambia a lo largo de una narrativa

stereotype: an oversimplified, generalized conception, opinion, and/or image about particular groups of people
estereotipo: concepto generalizado, opinión y/o imagen demasiado simplificada acerca de grupos específicos de personas

stichomythia: in drama, the delivery of dialogue in a rapid, fast-paced manner, with actors speaking emotionally and leaving very little time between speakers
esticomitia: en el drama, es la rendición del diálogo de una manera rápida con actores que hablan con emoción, dejando espacio muy breve entre los hablantes

storyboard: a tool to show images and sequencing for the purpose of visualizing a film or a story
guión gráfico: método de mostrar imágenes y secuencias con el propósito de visualizar una película o historia

strategize: to plan the actions one will take to complete a task
estrategizar: planear las acciones de uno para complir una tarea

structure: the way a literary work is organized; the arrangement of the parts in a literary work
estructura: manera en que la obra literaria está organizada; disposición de las partes en una obra literaria

style: the distinctive way a writer uses language, characterized by elements of diction, syntax, imagery, organization, and so on
estilo: manera distintiva en que un escritor usa el lenguaje, caracterizada por elementos de dicción, sintaxis, lenguaje figurado, etc.

subculture: a smaller subsection of a culture, for example, within the culture of a high school may be many subcultures
subcultura: subsección más pequeña de una cultura, por ejemplo, dentro de la cultura de una escuela secundaria puede haber muchas subculturas

subjective: based on a person's point of view, opinions, values, or emotions

subjetivo: basado en el punto de vista, las opiniones, los valores o las emociones de alguien

subjective tone: a tone that is obviously influenced by the author's feelings or emotions
tono subjetivo: tono obviamente influído por los sentimientos o emociones del autor

subjectivity: judgment based on one's personal point of view, opinion, or values
subjetividad: en base en nuestro punto de vista, opinión o valores personales

subordinate: a person or group that is perceived as having a lower social or economic status
subordinado: persona o grupo percibido de ser de rango social o estado económico bajo

subplot: a secondary or side story that develops from and supports the main plot and usually involves minor characters
argumento secundario: una historia secundaria o periférica que apoya el argumento principal y que suele involucrar a personajes secundarios o menores

subtext: the underlying or implicit meaning in dialogue or the implied relationship between characters in a book, movie, play, or film; the subtext of a work is not explicitly stated
subtexto: significado subyacente o implícito en el diálogo o la relación implícita entre los personajes de un libro, película, u obra teatral. El subtexto de una obra no se establece de manera explícita.

survey: a method of collecting data from a group of people; it can be written, such as a print or online questionnaire, or oral, such as an in-person interview
encuesta: método para recolectar datos de un grupo de personas; puede ser escrita, como un impreso o cuestionario en línea, u oral, como en una entrevista personal

symbol: anything (object, animal, event, person, or place) that represents itself but also stands for something else on a figurative level
símbolo: cualquier cosa (objeto, animal, evento, persona o lugar) que se representa a sí misma, pero también representa otra cosa a nivel figurativo

symbolic: serving as a symbol; involving the use of symbols or symbolism
simbólico: que sirve como símbolo; que implica el uso de símbolos o simbolismo

synecdoche: a figure of speech in which a part is used to represent the whole or vice versa
sinécdoque: figura retórica en que una parte se usa para representar el todo, o vice-versa

syntax: the arrangement of words and the order of grammatical elements in a sentence; the way in which words are put together to make meaningful elements, such as phrases, clauses, and sentences

sintaxis: disposición de las palabras y orden de los elementos gramaticales en una oración; manera en que las palabras se juntan para formar elementos significativos como frases, cláusulas y oraciones

synthesis: the act of combining ideas from different sources to create, express, or support a new idea

síntesis: acto de combinar ideas de diferentes fuentes para crear, expresar o apoyar una nueva idea

synthesize: to combine ideas from different sources to create, express, or support a new idea or claim

sintetizar: combinar ideas procedentes de distintas fuentes para crear, expresar o sustentar una nueva idea o afirmación

T

target audience: the intended group for which a work is designed to appeal or reach

público objetivo: grupo al que se pretende apelar o llegar con una obra

tenor: the intent, tone, or attitude conveyed by the words in a text

tenor: intención, tono o actitud transmitida por las palabras de un texto

textual evidence: the details, quotations, and examples from a text that support the analysis or argument presented

evidencia textual: detalles, citas, y ejemplos de un texto que apoyan el análisis o la argumentación presentada

theatrical elements: elements used by dramatists and directors to tell a story on stage. Elements include *costumes* (the clothing worn by actors to express their characters), *makeup* (cosmetics used to change actors' appearances and express their characters), *props* (objects used to help set the scene, advance a plot, and make a story realistic), *set* (the place where the action takes place, as suggested by objects, such as furniture, placed on a stage), and *acting choices* (gestures, movements, staging, and vocal techniques actors use to convey their characters and tell a story).

elementos teatrales: elementos utilizados por los dramaturgos y directores para contar una historia en el escenario. Los elementos incluyen *vestuario* (ropa que usan los actores para expresar sus personajes), *maquillaje* (cosméticos que se usan para cambiar la apariencia de los actores y expresar sus personajes), *elementos* (objetos que se usan para ayudar a montar la escena, avanzar la trama y crear una historia realista), *plató* (lugar donde tiene lugar la acción, según lo sugieren los objetos, como muebles, colocados sobre un escenario), y *opciones de actuación* (gestos, movimientos, representación y técnicas vocales que se usan para transmitir sus personajes y narrar una historia).

thematic statement: an interpretive statement articulating the central meaning or message of a text

oración temática: afirmación interpretativa que articula el significado o mensaje central de un texto

theme: a writer's central idea or main message; *see also* explicit theme, implied theme

tema: idea central o mensaje principal acerca de la vida de un escritor; *véase también* tema explícito, tema implícito

thesis: the main idea or point of an essay or article; in an argumentative essay the thesis is the writer's position on an issue

tesis: idea o punto principal de un ensayo o artículo; en un ensayo argumentativo, la tesis es la opinión del autor acerca de un tema

thumbnail sketch: a small drawing made to plan the composition of a more detailed or finished image that will be created later

boceto en miniatura: pequeño dibujo realizado para planificar la composición de una imagen más amplia o detallada que será posteriormente creada

tone: a writer's (or speaker's) attitude toward a subject, character, or audience

tono: actitud de un escritor u orador acerca de un tema

topic sentence: a sentence that states the main idea of a paragraph; in an essay, the topic sentence also makes a point that supports the thesis statement

oración principal: oración que establece la idea principal de un párrafo; en un ensayo, la oración principal también establece una proposición que apoya el enunciado de la tesis

tragedy: a dramatic play that tells the story of a character, usually of a noble class, who meets an untimely and unhappy death or downfall, often because of a specific character flaw or twist of fate

tragedia: obra teatral dramática que cuenta la historia de un personaje, normalmente de origen noble, que encuentra una muerte o caída imprevista o infeliz, con frecuencia debido a un defecto específico del personaje o una vuelta del destino

tragic hero: an archetypal hero based on the Greek concept of tragedy; the tragic hero has a flaw that makes him or her vulnerable to downfall or death

héroe trágico: héroe arquetípico basado en el concepto griego de la tragedia; el héroe trágico tiene un defecto que lo hace vulnerable a la caída o a la muerte

transcript: a written copy or record of a conversation that takes place between two or more people

transcripción: copia escrita de una conversación que sucede entre dos o más personas

U

unconventional: eccentric; unusual; original
no convencional: excéntrico; inusual; original

understatement: the representation of something as smaller or less significant than it really is; the opposite of exaggeration or hyperbole

subestimación: representación de algo como más pequeño o menos importante de lo que realmente es; lo opuesto a la exageración o hipérbole

V

valid: believable or truthful
válido: creíble o verídico

validity: the quality of truth or accuracy in a source
validez: calidad de verdad o precisión en una fuente

verbal irony: a form of irony that occurs when a speaker or narrator says one thing while meaning the opposite

ironía verbal: ocurre cuando un hablante o narrador dice una cosa mientras quiere decir lo opuesto

verbatim: in the exact words of a source
textualmente: palabras citadas exactamente como fueron expresadas

verify: to prove or confirm that something is true
verificar: probar o confirmar que algo es verdadero

vignette: a picture or visual or a brief descriptive literary piece
viñeta: ilustración o representación visual o pieza literaria descriptiva breve

visual delivery: the way a performer on stage interprets plot, character, and conflict through movement, gestures, and facial expressions

presentación visual: manera en que un actor en un escenario interpreta trama, carácter, y conflicto a través de movimiento, gestos, y expresiones de la cara

visual rhetoric: an argument or points made by visuals such as photographs or by other visual features of a text

retórica visual: argumentos o asuntos representados en visuales como fotos u otros rasgos visuales de un texto

visualize: to form a mental picture of something
visualizar: formarse una imagen mental de algo

vocal delivery: the way a performer on stage expresses the meaning of a text through volume, pitch, rate or speed of speech, pauses, pronunciation, and articulation

presentación vocal: manera en que se expresan las palabras en el escenario, por medio del volumen, tono, rapidez o velocidad del discurso, pausas, pronunciación y articulación

voice: a writer's (or speaker's) distinctive use of language to express ideas as well as his or her persona

voz: manera en que el escritor u orador usa las palabras y el tono para expresar ideas, así como también su personaje o personalidad

Index of Skills

Literary Skills

Adaptations, 284, 288, 290, 318, 319, 331, 332, 361

Allegory, 36, 37, 43, 140

Alliteration, 21, 338

Allusion, 40, 202, 205, 206

Analogy, 418

Archetypal Criticism, 7, 147–152, 183
    characters, 147, 166, 167, 187
    hero's journey, 147
    images, 147
    motifs, 147
    perspectives, 207, 252, 308, 409, 453
    symbols, 167

Archetype, 7, 147, 148, 152, 153, 161, 162, 163, 166, 167, 168, 173, 187, 189, 192, 194, 197, 222

Argument, 43, 46, 49, 58, 60, 61, 62, 64, 69
    appeals, 43, 54, 60, 61, 62, 64, 71
    characteristics, 54
    counterclaim, 51, 54, 181, 206, 395, 417
    evidence, 54
    graphic organizer, 62, 391
    structure, 54

Argumentative essay, 47–47

Argumentative text, 65–66

Article, 205, 301, 371–374, 381–383, 384–386, 400–402, 419–420, 422–424, 426–428, 436–437

Artistic license, 186

Aside, 304, 305

Assonance, 21

Attitude (*See also* Tone (attitude))
    of author/speaker, 15, 16, 17, 46, 87, 88, 89, 92, 95, 109, 135, 174, 282, 288, 349
    of characters, 136, 137, 180, 182, 191
    of reader, 17, 18, 30, 136, 183
    satire as, 174
    of society, 9, 192, 198, 238, 281, 344, 410

Audience, 4, 28, 30, 40, 43, 45, 46, 47, 51, 52–53, 55, 58, 62, 88, 90, 96, 148, 173, 174, 185, 190, 191, 205, 252, 262, 263, 267, 280, 288, 291, 304, 346, 379, 399, 406, 407, 408, 415, 421, 425, 444, 462, 467, 468, 476, 479

Author background, 12, 14, 22, 24, 26, 36, 40, 47, 55, 71, 77, 82, 84, 92, 101, 112, 124, 153, 155, 166, 190, 201, 211, 225, 243, 245, 259, 274, 292, 332, 371, 380, 384, 400, 404, 426, 436, 462

Author's choices, 4, 21, 23, 25, 26, 30, 31, 35, 39, 40, 43, 45, 46, 52–53, 60, 61, 62, 64, 74, 136, 185, 187, 195, 198, 218, 414

Author's purpose, 40, 45, 46, 47, 49, 52–53, 68, 121, 160, 205, 263, 344, 376, 388, 389, 390, 418, 421

Bias, 4, 147, 199, 368, 379, 395, 425, 444, 455, 456–457

Big ideas, 4, 74, 146, 197, 252, 331, 368

Bulleted lists, 435

Call to action, 55, 58, 62, 392, 468

Characterization, 137, 140, 146, 153, 159, 160, 164, 167, 168, 174, 179, 180, 182, 187, 189, 193, 197, 201, 217, 218, 221, 222, 235, 267, 273, 282, 287, 301, 332
    external factors, 194
    graphic organizer, 321
    internal factors, 194
    motivation, 183

Character(s), 5, 68, 124, 147, 174, 281, 291, 323, 327, 328
    analyzing, 274, 280, 283
    archetypes, 7
    character sketch, 281
    dynamics, 182, 269
    graphic organizer, 182, 270, 271, 307–308
    minor, 307
    motivation, 169, 304, 305, 320, 322, 329
    point of view, 309
    secondary, 353
    social class, 270
    traits, 306

Claims, 58, 60, 61, 62, 64, 71, 291, 348, 376, 416

Climax, 164, 174, 185, 317

Comedy, 172

Comparison, 160, 407, 418

Concept map, 446

Conclusion, 9, 10, 36, 60, 61, 62, 64, 80, 140, 147, 184, 185, 189, 194, 236, 316, 319, 326, 327, 328, 348, 378, 389, 390, 392, 416, 421, 425, 468

Conflict, 9, 68, 110, 113, 135, 137, 164, 167, 174, 175, 182, 183, 186, 218, 238, 270, 273, 280, 298, 309, 317, 320, 411, 470

Connotation, 15, 16, 17, 96

Consonance, 21

Creating meaning, 35, 397

Critical lenses (perspectives), 7, 76, 80, 89, 91, 100, 147, 190, 193, 194, 195, 197, 252, 258, 269, 274, 279, 280, 291, 301, 303, 307, 308, 309, 311, 314, 315, 316, 317, 318, 323, 328, 329, 331, 332, 345, 353, 354, 357, 358, 359, 361, 362, 368, 370, 376, 377, 378, 397, 408, 409, 411, 412, 414, 442, 444, 445, 451, 459, 480
    graphic organizer, 324, 325, 453

Cultural Criticism, 8, 74, 76, 80, 81, 139, 258–249, 279, 280, 281–267, 300, 302, 348, 411, 453
    colonialism, 88
    cultural backgrounds, 80, 136, 258
    cultural context, 96, 263, 281, 346, 451
    cultural perspectives, 89, 281
    dominant culture, 81, 263
    imperialism, 81, 82, 88, 89, 91, 92, 96, 100
    marginalization, 76, 81, 258, 263
    outsider, 298

Defining, 41

Description, 137, 281, 442

Details, 107, 108, 119, 120, 136, 137, 201, 204, 233, 276, 277, 283, 286, 383, 420, 442, 444
    graphic organizer, 34

Dialect, 212

Dialogue, 146, 168, 177, 187, 215, 217, 280

Diction (word choice), 15, 28, 30, 33, 39, 40, 42, 43, 46, 51, 60, 61, 62, 64, 71, 87, 89, 120, 121, 135, 136, 137, 217, 429

Drama, 146, 252
    blocking, 311
    dramatic arc, 164
    dramatic elements, 306, 317, 362
    dramatic structure, 354
    monologue, 284–286
    stereotypes, 297, 298, 299
    structure, 185, 353

Editorial, 415–416

Effect, 42, 91, 399, 421, 437, 442

Epithet, 281

Essay, 93–94, 113–119, 125–134, 332–343

Essential questions, 4, 35, 74, 146, 197, 252, 331, 368, 408, 444, 461

Evaluating, 15

Evidence, 60, 61, 62, 64, 71, 348

Exposition, 146

Extended metaphor, 22, 36, 38

Fairy tale, 201, 204, 207

Reading Skills

Media Skills

Speaking and Listening Skills

Acting company, 254, 279, 280, 288, 301, 303, 304, 310, 315, 348, 355, 362
 actors, 254
 blocking, 311, 315, 356
 contract, 257
 director, 254, 257, 316, 357
 dramaturge, 254, 257
 gesture, 357
 graphic organizer, 355–356
 letter writing, 361
 lighting, 356
 mood, 356
 music, 356
 naming, 254
 playbill, 358, 359
 plot mapping, 353
 props, 356
 scene selection, 254
 staging, 311, 315, 331, 348, 353, 357
 timing, 356
 vocal delivery, 315, 316, 356, 357
Acting styles, 344, 345
Adaptation, 280
Analyzing, 268
Argument, 181, 481
 counterclaims, 181
 drafting, 481
 editing, 481
 evaluation, 477–479
 planning, 481
 prewriting, 481
 revision, 481
Audience, 140, 261, 267, 280, 290, 304, 306, 311, 319, 355, 470, 477, 482–484
Blocking, 306, 310
Body language, 176, 267, 303
Collaboration, 89, 147, 179, 200, 237, 254, 326, 358, 359, 362, 451
Costume, 147
Debate, 179, 181, 379, 392
Delivery, 176, 290, 471, 472
 enunciation, 471
 eye contact, 471
 gesture, 471
 practicing, 472
 rate, 471
 volume, 471

Dialect, 167
Dialogue, 176, 179, 180
Director, 348
Emphasizing, 178, 446
Enunciation, 288
Eye contact, 200, 267, 279
Facial expression, 176
Feedback, 67–68, 99, 112, 123, 140, 184, 185, 200, 210, 253, 288, 306, 326, 328, 329, 362, 377, 477, 480
Fluency, 288
Gesture, 176, 267, 288
Group discussion, 5, 10–11, 30, 31, 62, 80, 81, 123, 124, 152, 166, 169, 174, 176, 178, 179, 190, 193, 200, 201, 205, 206, 211, 219, 220, 237, 240, 253, 263, 266, 270, 283, 288, 291, 300, 306, 308, 310, 313, 320, 322, 323, 325, 331, 332, 361, 369, 377, 411, 412, 414, 415, 443, 444, 451, 452, 458, 461, 466, 469, 470, 473, 474
Group writing, 268
Inference, 176
Inflection, 288
Jury ballot, 477–479, 482–484
Listening, 122, 237, 253, 259, 300, 322
Matching activity, 323
Meaning, 176
Media text
 common question, 473
 defining roles, 474
 guiding questions, 473
 organization, 474
 synthesizing research, 474
 thesis statement, 473
Monologue, 284
Movement, 278
Music, 122, 259, 263
Note taking, 254, 288, 289, 310, 322
Oral interpretation, 288
Oral reading, 176
Organization, 268, 445
Pacing, 176, 279
Partner discussion, 22, 30, 35, 39, 45, 52–53, 96, 99, 122, 161, 166, 178, 182, 183, 189, 192, 195, 208, 210, 280, 281, 290, 291, 303, 308, 311, 350, 351, 357, 376, 379, 449, 479–480
Pauses, 288

Peer editing, 67–68, 112, 123, 184, 189, 195, 241, 327–328
 checklist, 189
Peer review, 123, 189, 477
Performance, 254, 268, 279, 306, 314, 331
 graphic organizer, 267
Persuasion, 461, 468
 appeals, 468
 audience, 461, 470, 477, 482–484
 counterargument, 468
 critique, 469
 effectiveness, 469
 elements of, 468
 evidence, 468, 469
 occasion, 470
 planning, 470–472
 presentation medium, 470–472
 purpose, 470
 rhetorical context, 468
 speaker, 470
 structure, 468
 theme (universal truth), 468
 thesis, 468
 tone, 470
 topic/issue, 470
Planning, 353, 444, 473
Presentation, 68, 140, 198, 267, 323, 324, 415, 444, 461
 assigning roles, 324
 graphic organizer, 445, 476
 planning, 480
 revision, 480
 techniques, 446
Presentation medium, 470
Pronunciation, 200
Purpose, 288
Questioning, 169, 322
Rate, 288
Rationale, 280
Reflection, 89
Register, 200
Rehearsing, 267, 279, 288, 314, 316, 353, 357, 362
Research questions, 199
Research report, 481
Rhetorical strategies, 446
Scenario, 310
Scene interpretation, 254
Set design, 147
Setting, 303

Index of Authors and Titles

Credits

Unit 1

"In Just-" Copyright 1923, 1951, © 1991 by the Trustees for the E. E. Cummings Trust. Copyright © 1976 by George James Firmage, from *Complete Poems: 1904-1962* by E. E. Cummings, edited by George J. Firmage. Used by permission of Liveright Publishing Corporation.

"Mushrooms" from *The Colossus and Other Poems* by Sylvia Plath, copyright © 1957, 1958, 1959, 1960, 1961, 1962 by Sylvia Plath. Used by permission of Alfred A. Knopf, a division of Random House, Inc.

"Water" by Anne Sexton, from *Poetry*, August 1962.

"I Remember" by Edward Montez, California Poetry Project.

"Prologue," from *Invisible Man* by Ralph Ellison, copyright 1952 by Ralph Ellison. Used by permission of Random House, Inc.

"Clothing Brands Need to Step Up and Keep Women Safe in Their Factories" by Aruna Kashyap, from the Human Rights Watch, July 5, 2018, copyright © 2018 Human Rights Watch.

"Profiting on the Backs of Child Laborers" by Victoria Riskin and Mike Farrell. Copyright © 2000, Human Rights Watch.

"Tipping System Exacerbates Unfair Pay at Restaurants" by Kathleen Kingsbury, from *The Boston Globe*, February 17, 2014, copyright © 2014 The Boston Globe.

Unit 2

"Speaking With Hands" from *The Concrete River*, copyright 1993 by Luis J. Rodriguez. Reprinted with permission of Curbstone Press.

"On Seeing England for the First Time," originally published in Harper's. Copyright © 1991 by Jamaica Kincaid, reprinted with permission of the Wylie Agency, LLC.

"Shooting an Elephant" from *Shooting an Elephant and Other Stories* by George Orwell, copyright © 1950 by Sonia Brownell Orwell and renewed 1978 by Sonia Pitt-Rivers, reprinted by permission of Houghton Mifflin Harcourt Publishing Company.

"'Is this what the west is really like?' How it felt to leave China for Britain" by Xiaolu Guo, from *The Guardian*, January 10, 2017, copyright © 2017 The Guardian.

"Stranger in the Village" from *Notes of a Native Son* by James Baldwin. Copyright © 1955, renewed 1983 by James Baldwin. Reprinted by permission of Beacon Press, Boston.

"Orpheus Sings: Pygmalion and the Statue" from *The Metamorphoses of Ovid* translated with an introduction by Mary M. Innes (Penguin Classics, 1955). Copyright © Mary M. Innes, 1955. Used by permission of Penguin Group (UK) Ltd.

"Cinderella, the Legend," from *Kiss Sleeping Beauty Good-Bye* by Madonna Kolbenschlag. Used by permission of Women & Leadership Archives, Loyola University Chicago.

From "Why Women Always Take Advantage of Men," from *Mules and Men* by Zora Neale Hurston. Copyright © 1935 by Zora Neale Hurston; renewed © 1963 by John C. Hurston and Joel Hurston. Reprinted by permission of HarperCollins Publishers.

"The Landlady," from *Kiss Kiss*, by Roald Dahl, text copyright © 2011 by Roald Dahl Nominee Limited. Used by permission of Michael Joseph, a non-fiction imprint of Random House, a division of Random House LLC and David Higham Associates. All rights reserved. Any third party use of this material, outside of this publication, is prohibited. Interested parties must apply directly to Random House LLC for permission.

"The Chaser" by John Henry Noyes Collier from *The New Yorker* by permission of Harold Matson, Agent. Copyright 1940 by John Collier.

Unit 3

The Moor in English Renaissance Drama by Jack D'Amico. Copyright 1991 by University of South Florida Press. Reproduced by permission of the University Press of Florida.

"*Othello* on Stage and Screen" by Sylvan Barnet, copyright © 1963, 1986, 1998 by Sylvan Barnet, from *The Tragedy of Othello* by William Shakespeare, edited by Alvin Kernan. Used by permission of Phyllis Fogelman Books, a division of Penguin Group (USA) Inc.

Unit 4

"How News Has Changed" by Michael Griffin, from *Macalester News*, April 10, 2017, copyright © 2017 Macalester College.

"How Headlines Change the Way We Think" by Maria Konnikova, from *The New Yorker*, December 17, 2014, copyright © 2014 The New Yorker.

"Why Partisans View Mainstream Media as Biased and Ideological Media as Objective" by Matthew C. Nisbet from bigthink.com, copyright © 2011 by Matthew C. Nisbet.

"Daylong Efforts to Repair Levee Fail" by Dan Shea, from the *Times-Picayune*, August 31, 2005.

"An Editorial: It's Time for a Nation to Return the Favor" from the *Times-Picayune*, November 20, 2005.

"Looters Leave Nothing Behind in Storm's Wake" by Mike Perlstein and Brian Thevenot, from *The Times-Picayune*, August 31, 2005.

"Who's a Looter? In Storm's Aftermath, Pictures Kick Up a Different Kind of Tempest" by Tania Ralli, from *The New York Times*, September 5, 2005, copyright © 2005 The New York Times.

"The Press, Race, and Katrina" by Madison Gray, *Time Magazine*, August 30, 2006. Copyright © 2006 Time, Inc.

"'Attitude of Resilience' Helped Create Demo Diva" by Simone Bruni, from *The Chicago Tribune*, September 3, 2015. Copyright © 2015 The Chicago Tribune.

Image Credits

n/a olaser/iStock; 1 Jasper James/Stone/Getty Images; 9 Soldiers without guns/Adolph Treidler/Library of Congress/ Prints and Photographs Division; 9 Give the world the once over in the United States Navy Apply at Navy Recruiting Station / / James H. Daugherty ; Press Navy Recruiting Bureau N.Y./Library of Congress/ Prints and Photographs Division; 10 The Miriam and Ira D. Wallach Division of Art, Prints and Photographs: Art & Architecture Collection, The New York Public Library. "Vicereine. A shoe of high degree for women of quality." The New York Public Library Digital Collections. 1895 - 1917. http://digitalcollections.nypl.org/items/510d47e2-90ed-a3d9-e040-e00a18064a99; 10 Give to the needy Join the mayor's welfare milk fund : Monster vaudeville show at the Laurel Theatre/ Library of Congress/ Prints and Photographs Division; 12 Education Images / Contributor/Getty Images; 14 Sarin Images / GRANGER — All rights reserved; 22 StampCollection / Alamy Stock Photo; 24 Science History Images / Alamy Stock Photo; 26 Everett Collection Historical / Alamy Stock Photo; 36 IanDagnall Computing / Alamy Stock Photo; 37 Pobytov/iStockphoto; 40 Everett Collection Historical / Alamy Stock Photo; 41 David David Gallery / SuperStock; 48 Sony Ramany/NurPhoto/Getty Images; 55 Library of Congress/Corbis Historical/Getty; 57 488 Macon, Ga. Lewis W. Hine 1-19-1909. Bibb Mill No. 1 Many youngsters here. Some boys were so small they had to climb up on the spinning frame to mend the broken threads and put back the empty bobbins. Location: Macon, Georgia/National Child Labor Committee collection/ Library of Congress/ Prints and Photographs Division; 71 © Kathleen Kingsbury; 77 Damian Dovarganes/AP Photo; 82 By [Elliott & Fry] [Public domain], via Wikimedia Commons; 90 The first step toward lightening the White man's burden in through teacing the virtues of cleanliness/Library of Congress/ Prints and Photographs Division; 92 Sueddeutsche Zeitung Photo / Alamy Stock Photo; 93 FrankRamspott/iStock; 101 George Orwell (gouache on paper), Baraldi, Severino (b.1930) / Private Collection / © Look and Learn / Bridgeman Images; 105 DaddyBit/iStock; 107 Popperfoto/Getty Images; 112 David Levenson/Getty Images; 119 johnkellerman/iStock; 124 Peter Turnley/Corbis/VCG/Getty Images; 126 ValeStock/Shutterstock; 143 AF archive / Alamy Stock Photo; 148 Emma Kim/Cultura/Getty Images; 149 Aliyev Alexei Sergeevich/Cultura/Getty Images; 150 Elli Thor Magnusson/Cultura/Getty Images; 151 Mike Agliolo/Corbis/Getty Images; 153 Ovid (engraving), English School, (19th century) / Private Collection / Bridgeman Images; 154 "Pygmalion and Galatea No. 1" by Elisabeth Caren 155 GL Archive / Alamy Stock Photo; 158 Frankenstein, English School, (20th century) / Private Collection / © Look and Learn / Bridgeman Images; 165 United Archives GmbH / Alamy Stock Photo; 165 Moviestore collection Ltd / Alamy Stock Photo; 165 CBS Photo Archive / Contributor/ Getty Images; 165 CBS Photo Archive / Contributor/ Getty Images; 166 George Bernard Shaw - / Lebrecht Authors / Bridgeman Images; 173 Geraint Lewis / Alamy Stock Photo; 176 Hill Street Studios/Getty Images; 180 CBS Photo Archive/Getty Images; 186 Everett Collection; 203 Everett Collection; 211 Everett Collection Historical / Alamy Stock Photo; 214 Mimomy/123rf; 222 Andrey Kryuchkov/123rf; 225 Ronald Dumont/Daily Express/Hulton Archive/Getty Images; 227 Natalia Mikhalchuk / Shutterstock; 232 Yulia Avgustinovich/123rf; 243 GRANGER / GRANGER — All rights reserved.; 249 Othello and Desdemona, 1859 (oil on panel), Maclise, Daniel (Croquis, Alfred) (1806-70) / Private Collection / Photo © Christie's Images / Bridgeman Images; 259 Classic Image / Alamy Stock Photo; 274 Science History Images / Alamy Stock Photo; 276 Iago convinces Roderigo to wake Brabantio, Desdemona's father, and tell him about his daughter's elopement. / British Library, London, UK / © British Library Board. All Rights Reserved / Bridgeman Images; 281 Othello and Desdemona before the Venetian Senate, from Shakespeare's Othello (colour litho), European School, (20th century) / Private Collection / © Look and Learn / Bridgeman Images; 286 Mounet-Sully in the title role in Othello (coloured photo), French Photographer, (20th century) / Private Collection / © Look and Learn / Bridgeman Images; 301 Othello and Desdemona in Venice, 1850 (oil on panel), Chasseriau, Theodore (1819-56) / Louvre, Paris, France / Bridgeman Images; 305 Shakespeare Othello Act 3 Sc.3: Iago leads Othello to believe that Desdemona is unfaithful. 19th century engraving. / Universal History Archive/UIG / Bridgeman Images; 319 Album / Alamy Stock Photo; 320 Othello. Act V, Scene I (gravure), Darley, Felix Octavius Carr (1822-88) (after) / Private Collection / © Look and Learn / Bridgeman Images; 339 Everett Collection Historical / Alamy Stock Photo; 343 Everett Collection; 360 GRANGER / GRANGER — All rights reserved.; 365 Phil Coale/AP Photo; 371 © Michael Griffin; 374 Pixellover RM 3 / Alamy Stock Photo; 380 © Elyse Cheney Literary Associates, LLC; 381 Hadrian/Shutterstock; 387 Vm/iStockphoto; 394 Simonkr/E+/Getty Images; 400 © The Advocate; 401 Mario Tama/Getty Images; 402 Mark Wilson/Getty Images; 404 IanDagnall Computing / Alamy Stock Photo; 405 U.S. Coast Guard photo by Petty Officer 2nd Class NyxoLyno Cangemi [Public domain], via Wikimedia Commons; 406 Paul Morse/White House/Getty Images; 411 Michael Appleton/NY Daily News Archive/Getty Images; 411 Carolyn Cole/Los Angeles Times/Getty Images; 412 Shannon Stapleton/Reuters; 412 Larry Downing/Reuters; 420 Marko Georgiev/Getty Images; 422 AP Photo/Dave Martin; 423 Chris Graythen/Getty Images; 436 © The Demo Diva LLC; 437 © The Demo Diva LLC; 462 Joe Raedle/Getty Images; 465 Joe Raedle/Getty Images; 475 Asiseeit/iStockphoto